Eat, Drink & Sleep Smoke-free

HEADWAY BOOKS

First published in 1991 by Catherine Mooney and Headway Books
Birch Hagg House, Low Mill, York, YO6 6XJ

This 4th edition published 1995

Catherine Mooney, 1995

ISBN 1 899583 00 9

Printed by Redwood Books, Trowbridge, Wiltshire.

For dad

Perfectos, finos.....

Introduction

Do you mind if I smoke? That is becoming an increasingly rare question. Non-smokers - and even many smokers - certainly do mind if anyone smokes around them. This is what the *Eat, Drink and Sleep Smoke-Free* guide is about. Here we provide you with nearly 2000 hotels, guest houses, restaurants and even pubs, where you can find smoke-free air. Some of these establishments have gone as far as to ban smoking completely, while others at least provide a no-smoking area. It is for you to choose which best suits your needs.

Of course, although we have made a great deal of progress in achieving smoke-free air over the past few years, ASH is not complacent. We will not consider our work finished until non-smoking is the norm in society, with designated areas provided for smoking only where necessary and possible. Just as public health campaigners in the latter half of the last century considered their goal to be a clean water supply and the elimination of cholera, so we have a goal of clean air and the elimination of diseases induced by passive smoking.

Ultimately, we believe that we will see legislation introduced in the United Kingdom that will guarantee non-smokers the right to breathe smoke-free air. We believe that the pressure from non-smokers, who form the majority of the population will be too great for the Government to resist. The Government is already showing signs of weakening. In 1991 they brought out a Code of Practice and in their Health White Paper in 1991 they said that if satisfactory progress was not made by voluntary means then "if necessary . . . . legislation will be introduced."

In the meantime, we will look carefully at legislation protecting non-smokers in other nations. In the autumn of 1992 French non-smokers welcomed the introduction of a law to protect them from passive smoking. One often quoted survey showed 84% approval for the law. We shall look very carefully at the enforcement of that law and learn the lessons for the time when the UK follows suit. But there are many other examples which are already long established and working well. For example, New York City has had minimum standards applying to the provision of smoke-free air for some years - and it is working well.

Before any law is introduced in the United Kingdom, however, we will need to campaign for change. ASH has already made a good start, by producing reliable information to help employers, restaurateurs, bus operators, banks and others to go smoke-free. Our work was given a boost by the courageous and vigourous campaign mounted by the late Roy Castle, who had lung cancer caused by passive smoking. Roy's highly public fight against his illness and against its cause - passive smoking - earned him the admiration of many. He also showed how vital it is to protect non-smokers from passive smoking. He was a prime example of the dreadful consequences of being forced to breathe in other people's tobacco smoke. That is why we undertook our *Breathing Space* campaign - a consumer driven campaign for smoke-free air which we hope will enlist the vast army of non-smokers to press for change. Contact us for further news of this unique venture.

By buying this guide you have stated your preference for smoke-free air. We hope that you enjoy visiting the places listed here. We also hope that you will work with us towards a smoke-free society.

David Pollock

Director ASH

About ASH

Action on Smoking and Health (ASH) was founded in 1971 by the Royal College of Physicians. It strives by education and by advocacy of effective controls to reduce the toll of diseases, disability and death caused by smoking. It is a charity and draws on the suppport of many eminent persons, particularly in the medical profession.

ASH maintains a comprehensive database of information on all aspects of smoking - medical, social, commercial, industrial - and of tobacco control measures and smoking cessation methods, both at home and worldwide. It publishes a special bulletin twice a month intended primarily for health professionals.

ASH campaigns for better control of tobacco. The main steps required are:

* to ban all tobacco advertising and promotion, including tobacco sponsorship of the arts and sport
* Regular tax increases to produce a constant rise in the real price of cigarettes
* Laws to make public indoor places smoke-free as a protection against the dangers of passive smoking
* a major campaign of health and education

ASH Workplace Services is a consultancy offering advice to employers on how to introduce smoking policies at work. It offers professional consultancy, seminars and a detailed manual.

ASH supporters receive in return for their subscription a quarterly newsletter and briefings on **ASH**'s campaigns plus special offers on **ASH** books and merchandise.

For further information write to:

Action on Smoking and Health
109 Gloucester Place
London W1H 3PH
Tel: (0171) 935 3519
Fax: (0171) 935 3463

ASH Scotland	ASH Wales	ASH Northern Ireland
8 Frederick Street	372a Cowbridge Road	Ulster Cancer Foundation
Edinburgh	Canton	40 Eglantine Avenue
EH2 2HB	Cardiff CF5 1HF	Belfast BT9 6DX
Tel: (0131) 225 4725	Tel: (01222) 641101	Tel: (01232) 663281
Fax: (0131) 220 6604	Fax: (01222) 641045	Fax: (01232) 660081

Passive Smoking Basics

The Health Risk:

Passive smoking - breathing other people's smoke

- *Can cause lung cancer in non-smokers*. The Government's Independent Scientific Committee on Smoking and Health concluded in March 1988 that passive smoking leads to several hundred lung cancer deaths in the United Kingdom each year. The lung cancer risk from passive smoking is more than 100 times greater than that from exposure to asbestos in buildings.

- *May cause heart disease*: the evidence is mounting of this suspected link.

- *Can seriously affect the health of young children*. Wheezing, coughs, bronchitis, asthma, middle ear and upper respiratory tract infections are all more common among the children of smokers. Recent estimates suggest that 17,000 under-fives are admitted to hospital every year because their parents smoke. Up to 25% of cot deaths could also be attributable to parental smoking.

- *Can harm unborn babies*. Babies born to non-smoking mothers who have been exposed to environmental tobacco smoke tend to weigh less than babies born to unexposed mothers. Their average weight lies between that of the babies of non-smoking women reportedly unexposed to passive smoking and that of the babies of women who smoke.

- *Exacerbates respiratory problems in adults*. Non-smokers exposed to passive smoking can suffer from a range of non-fatal but unpleasant respiratory ailments, and can have existing breathing problems, such as asthma, made much worse.

- *Passive smoking exposes the non-smoker to a large number of toxic chemicals and substances*. Examples include formaldehyde (used for preserving dead bodies), arsenic (a deadly poison), benzene (used for dry-cleaning), ammonia (strong disinfectant), nicotine (insecticide) and nickel (widely used in industry for metalwork and plating). All these substances end up in non-smokers' lungs - some of them in greater concentrations even than smokers receive.

Times are changing:

Non-smokers are in the majority - 7 out of 10 of the population do not smoke.

Most people would welcome smoke-free air. Opinion polls show that:

- 82% of the population agree that passive smoking is a health hazard (*NOP 1990*)

- 87% of the general population and 77% of smokers agree that people who do not smoke should have the right to work in air free of tobacco smoke (*EOS Gallup 1992*)

- 97% of non-smokers and 70% of smokers think that all restaurants should provide no-smoking areas (*NOP 1989*)

- 66% agree that there should be no smoking on public transport (NOP 1987)

- When asked which change in pubs people would most like to see, no-smoking rooms came top of the list - above longer and more flexible opening hours! (*Which? Magazine, 1988*)

Other countries, for example Belgium, Australia, Canada, France, Italy and almost all states in the USA, have actually passed laws that ensure public place of various sorts - restaurants, schools, offices etc. - are smoke-free. More and more countries are introducing such legislation.

No-smoking rules are almost always readily observed and welcomed by the overwhelming majority of people, wherever such rules are introduced.

CONTENTS

ENGLAND

NORTHERN IRELAND

SCOTLAND

WALES

HOW WE COLLECTED OUR INFORMATION

This edition of Eat, Drink & Sleep Smoke-free was compiled from information received on detailed questionnaires which were completed by participating establishments in 1993/4. It has not been possible to verify the information that has been given by visiting each place and accordingly the information provided in this book is presented in the good faith that it is correct but with the recommendation that customers check with a particular establishment before booking to ensure that the provision meets their requirements and has not altered since the information was compiled.

HOW TO USE THIS BOOK

This guide is divided into five sections: *England, The Channel Islands, Northern Ireland, Scotland* and *Wales*. The *England* section of the book is divided into 11 principal areas in which the English counties within these areas are listed alphabetically; hotels and guest houses are listed within each county section under an alphabetical list of cities, towns and, if they are especially significant, villages. Establishments themselves are listed alphabetically by name under their city, town or village heading.

Scotland, Wales, Northern Ireland and *The Channel Islands* are smaller sections so it was not thought necessary to divide them into area by area sections. Instead the regions within *Scotland, Wales* and *N. Ireland* (and the islands for *The Channel Islands*) are listed alphabetically and within that format the listing is exactly the same as for the English entries.

The information given about each establishment is largely self-explanatory but the following should be noted:

The prices for B. & B. are per person per night and represent the cheapest high season price offered by each establishment - this is usually based on the price of a couple sharing a room; single rooms may cost significantly more than the B. & B. price given. Although prices were correct at the time of collecting our information, it is advisable to check the price before booking.

The reference to access for the disabled is based on the information we have been supplied with by the establishments. It has not been possible to verify the extent of the provision for those with varying degrees of physical disability. It is advisable to check before booking.

We have tried to keep abbreviations to a minimum, however the following have been used throughout the book:

   = Totally smoke-free establishment

N/S = No smoking
V   = Vegetarian
VE   = Vegan
S.D. = Special diets
B/A = By arrangement

W.Isles

Highlands

Gramps.

Tayside

Cent.

Fife

Loth.

Strath.

Borders

Dumf. & Gall.

The
N. East.

Cumbria
&
the
N. West

Yorks. & Humb.

East Midlands

Gwynedd

Clwyd

Powys

Central
England

East Anglia

Dyfed

Gwent

Glamorgan

Thames
& Chilts.

Lond.
& M'sex

South East

The South West

The South

Orkneys and Shetlands

The South West
Avon

ACCOMMODATION

BATH

Ⓧ *Aaron House*

NUMBER NINETY THREE, 93 WELLS ROAD, BATH, AVON, BA2 3AN   TEL: (01225) 317977
ETB commended. Within easy walking distance of city centre, B.R. & coach stations.
OPEN ALL YEAR. NO SMOKING. S.D. B/A. CHILDREN WELCOME. EN SUITE, TV & BEVERAGES IN ROOMS.
CREDIT CARDS. B. & B. FROM £19

Ⓧ *Bathhurst Guest House*

11 WALCOT PARADE, LONDON ST, BATH, AVON, BA1 5NF   TEL: (01225) 421884
Beautiful terraced Georgian house with 6 spacious guest rooms, just a short stroll from the
Roman Baths & antique shops in the city centre.
OPEN ALL YEAR Ex. Xmas & New Year. NO SMOKING. VE, S.D. B/A. CHILDREN & PETS WELCOME. 2 EN SUITE
ROOMS. TV & BEVERAGES IN ROOMS. B. & B. £16-18.50.

Ⓧ *Bloomfield House*

146 BLOOMFIELD RD, BATH, AVON, BA2 2AS   TEL: (01225) 420105   FAX: (01225) 481955

Bloomfield House is an imposing Grade II listed building which stands close to the centre of the Georgian city of Bath. Commissioned by the Henshaws (later to become the Lord Mayor and Lady Mayoress of the city), the house was built to the specifications of Bath's chief architect and shares the characteristics of the city's finest buildings, including the mellow honey-coloured stone. The house has been very sympathetically restored (original features have been retained) and offers accommodation of an exceptionally high standard: several of the guest rooms have wonderful views of the city and are furnished with canopied beds and antique furniture; the en suite bathrooms are mahogany panelled and have polished brass fittings. A silver service English breakfast is served with great style in an elegant dining room. Along with the Vatican City and Florence, Bath is one of only three World Heritage Cities: in addition to the architecture, Roman Baths, Abbey and Pump Rooms, which have deservedly earned it its place, visitors will be charmed by the city's quaint streets, pubs, restaurants and shops.
OPEN ALL YEAR. NO SMOKING. S.D. B/A. OLDER CHILDREN WELCOME. EN SUITE, TV, DD PHONE & BEVERAGES IN ROOMS. B. & B. £25 - £42.50. Single £40 - £55.

Ⓧ *Cairngorm Guest House*

3 GLOUCESTER RD, LOWER SWAINSWICK, BATH, AVON   TEL: (01225) 429004
A charming detached property; superb views & lovely gardens. Good food, pleasant walks.
OPEN ALL YEAR. NO SMOKING. S.D. CHILDREN WELCOME. EN SUITE, TV & BEVERAGES IN ROOMS. B. &
B. FROM £15.

Ⓧ *Cedar Lodge*

13 LAMBRIDGE, LONDON RD, BATH, AVON, BA1 6EJ. TEL: (01225) 423468

Cedar Lodge is a unique detached Georgian house which was built during the reign of George III. and is listed as being of both architectural historical importance. It stands in its own grounds with a private car park at the rear. The front of the house overlooks the Avon valley and the hills which surround the city. Your hosts, Mr and Mrs Beckett, offer excellent bed and breakfast accommodation in beautifully furnished and individually designed bedrooms, such as The Pine Room, with its half testerbed, the twin-bedded Mahogany Room and the Walnut Room with four-poster bed. Tea, coffee or soft drinks are there to greet you on

arrival and evening meals can be prepared by arrangement. You are within easy reach of the city centre (there are frequent bus services which pass the door) and the Kennet an Avon Canal and numerous countryside walks. Self-catering accommodation is also available.
OPEN ALL YEAR. NO SMOKING. S.D. B/A. CHILDREN WELCOME. NO PETS. TV, EN SUITE & PRIVATE BATH AVAILABLE. B. & B. FROM £19

Clearbrook Farm

MIDFORD, BATH, AVON, BA2 7DE   TEL: (01225) 723227

Clearbrook is a charming Grade II listed farmhouse which stands in a large garden surrounded by wooded countryside just 10 minutes' drive from the centre of Bath. Accommodation is in prettily decorated bedrooms with firm beds sharing two bathrooms one of which has a shower; there is also a conservatory for cooler sunny days together with a sitting room with a log fire for chilly evenings. A full English breakfast is served to guests but there is also a fridge for the storage of food. You are within easy reach of a number of interesting places including Wells, Cheddar, Longleat and Stourhead. Singles, couples and families can all be accommodated.
OPEN ALL YEAR. NO SMOKING. V, S.D. B/A. CHILDREN & PETS. BEVERAGES & TV IN ROOMS. B. & B. £16.

Devonshire House

143 WELLSWAY, BATH, AVON, BA2 4RZ   TEL: (01225) 312495
19th C. house incorporating antiques shop, with all the comforts of home. Well-appointed, spacious bedrooms. B'fast of your choice in Victorian dining room. Secure car parking.
OPEN ALL YEAR. NO SMOKING. V, S.D. B/A. EN SUITE, BEVERAGES & TV IN ROOMS. B. & B. FROM £19.

Grove Lodge Guest House

11 LAMBRIDGE, LONDON RD, BATH, AVON, BA1 6BJ   TEL: (01225) 310860.
An elegant Georgian House built in 1788, set in beautiful gardens, offering well-proportioned single, double and family rooms.
OPEN ALL YEAR. NO SMOKING. VE, COEL. B/A. CHILDREN WELCOME. BEVERAGES ON REQUEST. T.V. IN BEDROOMS. B. & B. FROM £20

Haydon House

9 BLOOMFIELD PARK, BATH, AVON, BA2 2BY   TEL & FAX: (01225) 427351 / 444919

From the outside Haydon House looks like many another unassuming Edwardian detached house so typical of the residential streets of Bath. Inside, however, 'an oasis of tranquillity and elegance' prevails; certainly the proprietor, Magdalene Ashman, has done everything possible to make your stay, so near and yet so far from the tourist throng of Bath, a truly happy and welcome one: rooms are tastefully decorated (lots of Laura Ashley and soft furnishings) and though breakfast is the only available meal, this too has a little special something added (porridge is served with whisky or rum and muscavado sugar, for instance, and a fresh fruit platter is available for less staunch appetites).
OPEN ALL YEAR. NO SMOKING. V BFAST. CHILDREN B/A. CREDIT CARDS. EN SUITE, TV & BEVERAGES IN ROOMS. B. & B. FROM £26 (3 For Price Of 2 mid-Nov. - mid-Mar.).

Holly Lodge

8 UPPER OLDFIELD PARK, BATH, AVON, BA2 3JZ   TEL: (01225) 424042 FAX: (01225) 481138
Holly Lodge is a large Victorian house set in its own grounds and enjoying magnificent views over the city of Bath. The house has been extensively renovated and beautifully decorated in recent years but with an eye to retaining all the period features of the original building (marble fireplaces, ceiling cornices, *etc*) so that the original architectural elegance is maintained. Breakfast is the only meal available at Holly Lodge but guests dine in a charming room which has views of the city and gives diners a chance to contemplate which of Bath's 80 fine restaurants they will choose for their evening meal. Facilities are also available for small conference parties.
OPEN ALL YEAR. NO SMOKING. V, S.D., B/A. CHILDREN B/A. EN SUITE, BEVERAGES, T.V. & PHONE IN ALL BEDROOMS. CREDIT CARDS. B. & B. FROM £37.50.

Kinlet Villa Guest House

99 WELLSWAY, BATH, AVON, BA2 4RX   TEL: (01225) 420268
ETB 1 Crown. Attractive guest house within easy walking distance of Bath city centre.
OPEN ALL YEAR.   NO SMOKING.   S.D.   CHILDREN WELCOME.   BEVERAGEs & T.V. IN ROOMS.   B. & B. FROM £16

Meadowland

36 BLOOMFIELD PARK, BATH, AVON, BA2 2BX   TEL: (01225) 311079

 Meadowland is a large family residence standing in about ½ acre of secluded grounds, including lovely gardens and private parking, in the beautiful Georgian city of Bath. Entirely non-smoking, it has been elegantly furnished and decorated throughout (Meadowland has been awarded a Highly Commended status by the ETB and has been 5 Qs Premier Selected by the AA), and the spacious, colour-coordinated en suite bedrooms offer accommodation of the highest standard including remote control TV, a hair dryer and trouser press; there is a large comfortable lounge, with a selection of books and magazines, for guests' use. Breakfast is the only meal to be offered at Meadowland, but there are several imaginative choices and special diets can be accommodated by arrangement; there are a number of good restaurants within easy reach to which your host will gladly direct you for your evening meal. Sporting and other leisure activities can also be arranged for you should you so wish. Non-smokers only.
OPEN ALL YEAR.   NO SMOKING.   V, S.D., B/A.   CHILDREN WELCOME.   EN SUITE, TV & BEVERAGES IN ROOMS. WHEELCHAIR ACCESS "YES, WITH HELP."   B. & B. FROM £25.

The Old Red House

37 NEWBRIDGE RD, BATH, AVON   TEL: (01225) 330464
Romantic Victorian guest house with stained glass windows and canopied beds. B'fast is served in a sunny conservatory - hearty or healthy, the choice is yours. Private parking.
OPEN ALL YEAR.   NO SMOKING.   V STD. S.D. B/A.   1 GROUND FLOOR ROOM.   CHILDREN WELCOME.   PETS B/A.   EN SUITE, TV & BEVERAGES IN ROOMS.   ACCESS, VISA.   B. & B. £19.

The Old School House

CHURCH ST, BATHFORD, BATH, AVON, BA1 7RR   TEL: (01225) 859593   FAX: (01225) 859590

 ***ETB Highly Commended. AA Premier Selected 5Qs.*** The Old School House, is situated within the conservation area of the village of Bathford, overlooking the beautiful Avon valley and Browne Folly Nature Reserve. It was the villaeg school between 1839 and 1970, then becoming a private house, only recently converted to use as a private hotel. Accommodation is in most pleasantly appointed rooms of which 2 are on the ground floor suitable for the less mobile. Guests dine by candlelight (24 hrs notice for dinner) on superb cuisine typically featuring home-made soup or feta cheese salad followed by Salmon Steak with Asparagus Sauce and a selection of tempting desserts. Bath is just 3 m away and the energetic may choose to visit it via the towpath walk along the canal.
OPEN ALL YEAR.   NO SMOKING.   S.D. (within reason).   LICENSED.   EN SUITE, BEVERAGES, PHONE & T.V. IN BEDROOMS.   DISABLED ACCESS: 2 GROUND FLOOR, LEVEL-ENTRY BEDROOMS AVAILABLE.   CREDIT CARDS. B. & B. FROM £30.   Special breaks Nov. - Mar.

*Parkside Guest House*

11 MARLBOROUGH LANE, BATH, AVON, BA1 2NQ   TEL: (01225) 429444
NO SMOKING.   V, VE, S.D. B/A.   OVER 5S.   PETS B/A.   EN SUITE.   BEVERAGES & T.V.   B. & B. FROM £9.

Serendipity

19F BRADFORD RD, WINSLEY, NR BATH, AVON, BA15 2HW   TEL: (01225) 722380
Bungalow with beautiful gardens in quiet area 5m from Bath. Good wheelchair access.
OPEN ALL YEAR.   NO SMOKING.   S.D. B/A.   CHILDREN.   BEVERAGES & TV IN ROOMS.   B. & B. FROM £14.

Ⓝ *Sheridan Guest House*

95 WELLSWAY, BEAR FLAT, BATH, BA2 4RU　TEL: (01225) 429562
Edwardian villa within walking distance of city centre. Warm, friendly welcome.
OPEN ALL YEAR.　NO SMOKING.　OVER 3s WELCOME.　TV & BEVERAGES IN BEDROOMS.

Ⓝ *Somerset House*

35 BATHWICK HILL, BATH, BA2 6LD　　TEL: (01225) 466451
Fine Regency house 1m from city centre; excellent food from home-grown produce.
OPEN ALL YEAR.　NO SMOKING.　VE, VEG, WH, ORG.　LICENSED.　OVER 10s.　EN SUITE & BEVERAGES IN
BEDROOMS.　T.V. LOUNGE.　CREDIT CARDS.　B. & B. 25 - 34.

Ⓝ *Sydney Gardens Hotel (B. & B.)*

SYDNEY ROAD, BATH, AVON, BA2 6NT　TEL: (01225) 464818/445362
Spacious Italianate, Victorian house in a unique parkland setting on the fringe of Bath's
city centre; carefully refurbished in keeping with its period and now offers a very high
standard of accommodation to guests. Each of bedrooms have beautiful views. Breakfast
is served in an elegant dining room and there are numerous excellent restaurants in Bath.
OPEN ALL YEAR Ex. Xmas & Jan.　NO SMOKING.　OVER 4S ONLY.　PETS B/A.　EN SUITE, BEVERAGES, T.V. &
PHONE IN ROOMS.　CREDIT CARDS.　B. & B. ONLY FROM £34.

Ⓝ *21 Newbridge Road*

BATH, AVON, AVON, BA1 3HE　TEL: (01225) 314694
Attractive Victorian family house with spacious rooms and views. 1m from Bath centre on
the A4 road to Bristol. Jan & John Shepherd, for health reasons, follow special diets.
Though not vegetarian, they have a good knowledge of various dietary requirements.
OPEN Feb. - Nov.　NO SMOKING.　V, VE, D & G-FREE, WH, BA.　CHILDREN WELCOME.　T.V. IN LOUNGE.
BEVERAGES AVAIL.　B. & B. FROM £15.

BRISTOL

Ⓝ *Arches Hotel*

132 COTHAM BROW, COTHAM, BRISTOL, AVON, BS6 6AE　　TEL: (0117) 924 7398
OPEN ALL YEAR Ex. xmas.　NO SMOKING.　V, S.D. B/A.　CHILDREN WELCOME. PETS B/A　BEVERAGES & TV IN
ALL BEDROOMS.　CREDIT CARDS.　B. & B. AROUND £17.

Ⓝ *Basca House*

19 BROADWAY RD, BRISTOL, AVON, BS7 8ES　TEL: (0117) 924 2182
Elegant Victorian house in a quiet residential area close to A38. Beautifully restored.
Home-cooking. Vegetarians can be accommodated by arrangement.
OPEN ALL YEAR ex. Xmas.　NO SMOKING.　V, VE, S.D. B/A.　CHILDREN WELCOME. TV & BEVERAGES IN
ROOMS.　B. & B. £18, Sgle. £19, D. £9.

Ⓝ *Moorledge Farm*

MOORLEDGE LANE, CHEW MAGNA, NR BRISTOL, AVON, BS18 8TL　TEL: (0117) 933 2383
OPEN Mar. - Oct.　NO SMOKING.　V.　CHILDREN WELCOME.　B. & B. FROM £15.

Ⓝ *Vicarage Lawns*

BRISTOL RD, WEST HARPTREE, BRISTOL, AVON, BS18 6HF　TEL: (01761) 221668
Vicarage Lawns is is a comfortable country home which stands amidst an acre of lovely
walled gardens in the pretty village of West Harptree at the foot of the Mendip Hills.
Accommodation is in exceptionally well-appointed and tastefully decorated bedrooms (all
with garden views), one of which has a spa bath and most of which have en suite facilities;
a wholesome breakfast is offered to guests (evening meals can be provided by prior
arrangement). The tranquil rural setting of Vicarage Lawns, with its proximity to Chew
Valley Lake with its fishing, wildlife and lovely walks, makes it a perfect choice for a
relaxing away-from-it-all break; additionally you will find yourself within easy reach of
Bath, Bristol, Wells, Cheddar and Weston-Super-Mare.
OPEN ALL YEAR.　NO SMOKING.　V B/A.　CHILDREN WELCOME.　SOME ROOMS EN SUITE.　T.V. IN LOUNGE.
BEVERAGES & T.V. IN BEDROOMS.　B. & B. FROM £14.

WESTON-SUPER-MARE

PURN HOUSE FARM BLEADON, WESTON, AVON, BS24 0QE　　TEL: (01934) 812324
OPEN Mar. - Nov.　N/S ex. public lounge. V, S.D. B/A.　WHEELCHAIR ACCESS.　CHILDREN.　B. & B. AROUND £19.

RESTAURANTS

BATH

BATH SPORTS & LEISURE CENTRE, NORTH PARADE, BATH, AVON
TEL: 50% NO SMOKING

CANARY, 3 QUEEN ST, BATH, AVON
TEL: (01225) 424846   50% NO SMOKING.

CIRCLES RESTAURANT, JOLLYS, MILSOM ST, BATH, BA1 1DD
TEL: (01225) 462811   SOME NO-SMOKING SEATS.

CLARETS, 7A KINGSMEAD SQUARE, BATH, AVON, BA1 2AB
TEL: (01225) 466688 1 N/S ROOM.

The Crown Inn

2 BATHFORD HILL, BATHFORD, BATH, AVON, BA1 7SL   TEL: (01272) 852297
Situated at the bottom of Bathford Hill, this charming pub is known to have been on this
site since 1757. Excellent food prepared to order. Serving food 12 - 2, 7 - 9.30
N/S GARDEN ROOM.   V STD.   CHILDREN WELCOME.   PETS B/A.   CREDIT CARDS.   WHEELCHAIR ACCESS.

Demuth's Restaurant & Coffee Shop

2 NORTH PARADE PASSAGE, ABBEY GREEN, BATH.   TEL: (01225) 446059
OPEN MON. TO SAT. 9.30 - 6, SUN. 10 - 5. L. & D. AROUND £5.   NO SMOKING.   V. STD.   LICENSED.

Hands Dining and Tearoom

9 YORK STREET, BATH, AVON, BA1 1NG   TEL: (10225) 463928
Charming small restaurant situated in a Georgian House (with most of the Georgian features
intact) serving a wide variety of freshly prepared meals throughout the day.
OPEN 9.30 - 5.30.   NO SMOKING.   L. FROM AROUND £4.   LICENSED. DISABLED ACCESS.

HUCKLEBERRY'S, 34 BROAD ST, BATH, AVON
TEL: (01225) 464876   N/S 1 OF 2 DINING ROOMS

OLD ORLEANS, 1 ST ANDREWS TERR., BARTLETT ST, BATH, AVON
TEL: (01225) 333233   N/S 55%

THE PUMP ROOMS, STALL ST, BATH, AVON
TEL: (01225) 444477/88   50% N/S.

Sally Lunn's House

4 NORTH PARADE PASSAGE, BATH, AVON, BA1 1NX   TEL: (01225) 461634

Sally Lunn's is the oldest house in Bath - and indeed housed within the
premises'cellar is a museum bearing testament to the interesting history
of this reputedly 15th C. building. Sally Lunn herself, who was said to
have arrived in Bath in 1680, was the creator of one of the city's
delicacies - the Sally Lunn bun (which is still baked on the premises).
Indeed the eponymous bun - and many other wonderful delicacies - may
be sampled in the 'refreshment house.' Open throughout the day and
serving a wide range of snacks and light meals, Sally Lunn's would
serve 250 customers on a typical day, and is also open for evening
meals. The varied menu would typically feature such imaginative dishes
as Chestnut Paté, followed by Breast of Chicken stuffed with Leek and
Stilton in a cream and wine sauce, or a vegetarian alternative such as
Cashew Nut Casserole with Carrot and Green Pepper in a white wine
and herb sauce, and Orange filled with Sorbet.
OPEN 10 - 6 DAYTIME MENU, 6 - 10.30 DINNER MENU. CLOSED MON. EVE.   D. AROUND
£11. NO SMOKING. V, VE STD.   LICENSED.   CHILDREN.   CREDIT CARDS. Booking Essential Sat. & Sun. Eves.

BRISTOL

CHERRIES, 122 ST MICHAELS HILL, BRISTOL, AVON, BS2 8BU
TEL: (0117) 929 3675 50% N/S.

CHINA PALACE RESTAURANT, 18A BALDWIN ST, BRISTOL, BS1 1SE
TEL: (0117) 926 2719 SEPARATE AREA FOR SMOKERS.

 THE COFFEE SHOP, JOHN LEWIS PARTNERSHIP, THE HORSEFAIR.
TEL: (0117) 927 9100 NO SMOKING.

DEBENHAMS, 1-5 ST JAMES BARTON, BRISTOL, BS99 7JX   TEL: (0117) 929 1021
Intermission: self-service family restaurant serving popular snacks & lunches.
OPEN STORE HOURS. NO SMOKING. V STD. DISABLED ACCESS. CHILDREN WELCOME. CREDIT CARDS.

THE MENDIP GATE GUEST HOUSE, BRISTOL RD, CHURCHILL, BRISTOL
TEL: (01934) 852333 NO SMOKING.

MICHAEL'S, 129 HOTWELL ROAD, BRISTOL
TEL: (0117) 927 6190 NO SMOKING.

MILLWARD'S VEGETARIAN REST, 40 ALFRED PL, KINGSDOWN
TEL: (0117) 924 5026 NO SMOKING.

WESTON-SUPER-MARE

THE CORN DOLLY, 134 HIGH ST, WORLE, WESTON-SUPER-MARE
TEL: (01934) 510041 NO SMOKING

PUBS & WINE BARS
BATH

The Crown Inn

2 BATHFORD HILL, BATHFORD, BATH, BA1 7SL   TEL: (01272) 852297
N/S Garden Room.

THE OLD GREEN TREE, GREEN ST, BATH, AVON. TEL: (01225) 448259
N/S PART OF PUB. V, GLUTEN-FREE STD. LICENSED. DISABLED ACCESS.

Cornwall

ACCOMMODATION
BODMIN

Mount Pleasant Moorland Hotel

MOUNT VILLAGE, NR BODMIN, CORNWALL, PL30 4EX   TEL: (01208) 82342
Peaceful country village hotel in an area of Outstanding Natural Beauty. Excellent food including free-range eggs for breakfast. 1 hr's drive from north & south Cornish coasts.
OPEN Easter - Sept. inc. N/S DINING R, BEDRS & LOUNGE. V, S.D. B/A. LICENSED. CHILDREN WELCOME. EN SUITE, TV & BEVERAGES IN ROOMS. D., B. & B. FROM £25.

BOSCASTLE

The Old Coach House

TINTAGEL RD, BOSCASTLE, NORTH CORNWALL, PL35 0AS   TEL: (01840) 250398
Relax in beautiful 300 year-old former coach house. Friendly & helpful owners.+
OPEN mid. Mar. - mid. Oct. N/S DINING R & LOUNGE. S.D. OVERS 6s WELCOME. WHEELCHAIR ACCESS. EN SUITE, TV & BEVERAGES IN BEDROOMS. B. & B. £15 - 22.50.

CRACKINGTON HAVEN

CRACKINGTON MANOR, CRACKINGTON HAVEN, CORNWALL, EX23 0JG
Peaceful hotel splendidly situated amongst spectacular cliff scenery.
OPEN ALL YEAR. NO SMOKING. V STD, S.D. B/A. LICENSED. CHILDREN WELCOME. EN SUITE & TV.

FALMOUTH

Kentina Hotel

3 EMSLIE RD, FALMOUTH, CORNWALL, TR11 4BG TEL: (01326) 313232
Smoke-free guest house in harbour town close to sea front.
OPEN ALL YEAR ex. Xmas. NO SMOKING. CHILDREN WELCOME. SOME EN SUITE ROOMS. BEVERAGES & TV IN ROOMS. B. & B. FROM £14.50.

Penmorvah Manor Hotel

BUDOCK, NR FALMOUTH, CORNWALL, TR11 5ED   TEL: (01326) 250277

Penmorvah Manor Hotel is a fine Victorian manor house which stands amidst 6 acres of private woodland and mature gardens with giant rhododendrons, camellias and magnolias. It has been beautifully furnished and appointed: most of the 27 en suite bedrooms have garden and woodland views, and each has a direct dial phone and baby listening service. Meals are prepared from fresh, local produce and are served in a candle-lit dining room; there is an excellent choice of wines, and guest may enjoy a drink in one of the hotel's two licensed bars. The hotel is just 2 miles away from the hustle and bustle of Falmouth (with its excellent facilities for yachtsmen) and just 15 miles from the cathedral town of Truro which can be reached by river or road.

OPEN ALL YEAR.   N/S DINING R.   S.D. B/A.   CHILDREN WELCOME.   LICENSED.   EN SUITE, TV & BEVERAGES IN ROOMS.   WHEELCHAIR ACCESS.   B. & B. FROM £27.50.

Tresillian House Hotel

3 STRACEY ROAD, FALMOUTH, CORNWALL, TR11 4DW   TEL: (01326) 312425/311139

ETB 3 Crowns Commended. Tresillian House is a small, friendly, family-run hotel which is situated in a quiet road near the main sea front and close to the beach and coastal walks. The 12 comfortable, en suite bedrooms have each been tastefully decorated and furnished with a good range of amenities including colour TV, hair dryer, radio intercom and baby listening service. The cooking is excellent: traditional food is served in generous portions, in an attractive dining room with lovely garden views, and after-dinner coffee is served in the comfortable lounge. Falmouth is a perfect fishing town with one of the world's deepest natural harbours. For those wanting to spend a day lazing on its lovely beaches, or exploring further afield, the proprietors will prepare picnic lunches on request.

OPEN MAR. TO OCT.   N/S DINING R & 1 LOUNGE.   V, DIAB,S.D B/A.   LICENSED.   CHILDREN WELCOME. EN SUITE, BEVERAGES & T.V. IN BEDROOMS.   CREDIT CARDS.   D., B. & B. FROM £25.

HELSTON

 ## Caerthillian Farmhouse

THE LIZARD, HELSTON, CORNWALL, TR12 7NX   TEL: (01326) 290596

330 yr old farmhouse with sea views and beautiful walks. Excellent food.

OPEN Mar.-Nov. inc. NO SMOKING. S.D. CHILDREN WELCOME. BEVERAGES IN ROOMS.   B. & B. FROM £13.50.

Tregildry Hotel

GILLAN, MANACCAN, HELSTON, CORNW., TR12 6HG TEL: (01326) 231378 FAX: (01326) 231561

Tregildry Hotel is beautifully situated on the Cornish coastal path and enjoys panoramic sea views over Falmouth Bay. You are very close to Helford River (Frenchman's Creek) and a private path leads down to the secluded beach where there is safe bathing. The area is excellent for birdwatching and fishing, and boat hire is available nearby. Enthusiastic walkers will enjoy the opportunities afforded by the coastal path and inland walks.

OPEN Mar. - Oct.   N/S DINING R. & BEDROOMS.   V, S.D. B/A.   LICENSED.   CHILDREN & DOGS WELCOME.   EN SUITE, BEVERAGES & TV IN ROOMS.   B. & B. £25-31. ·

ISLES OF SCILLY

Star Castle Hotel

THE GARRISON, ST MARY'S, ISLES OF SCILLY. TEL: (01720) 22317 FAX: (0720) 22343

Star-shaped castle garrison built in 1590s. Now an attractive hotel overlooking the sea.

OPEN MAR. - OCT. N/S DINING R. S.D. CHILDREN & PETS WELCOME. LICENSED. EN SUITE, TV & BEVERAGES IN BEDROOMS. CREDIT CARDS. D. B. & B. FROM £40.

Carnwethers Country Guesthouse

PELISTRY BAY, ST MARYS, ISLES OF SCILLY, CORNWALL, TR21 0NX   TEL: (01720) 422415

 Carnwethers Guest House, at one time the farmhouse for Pelistry farm, stands in an acre of lovely grounds (complete with croquet lawn and heated swimming pool) amidst the most natural and unspoilt part of St Mary's, high above beautiful and secluded Pelistry Bay. Carnwethers is situated away from the hustle and bustle of St Mary's - and as such enjoys the peace and tranquillity of the off islands - but the little town is close enough for guests to enjoy its many amenities. The original farmhouse has been tastefully

modernised and extended over the years and now boasts eight very comfortable guest rooms - all with excellent facilities. There is also a very pleasant lounge which is divided into two parts - one for reading and for conversation, and the other housing a general library, including Scillonian subjects, (there is also a VCR with videos about the island). A traditional English Breakfast and 4-course dinner are offered - the latter accompanied by a selection of 60 or so modestly priced wines. Please phone for brochure.
OPEN 8th APR. - 7TH OCT.   N/S PUBLIC ROOMS & BEDRMS.   LICENSED.   CHILDREN: OVER 6S ONLY.   EN SUITE, TV & BEVERAGES IN ROOMS.   HALF BOARD £30 - 46.

LAUNCESTON

 ## The Old Vicarage

TRENEGLOS, LAUNCESTON, CORNWALL, PL15 8UQ   TEL: (01566) 781351

ETB Highly Commended 2 Crowns. The Old Vicarage is an elegant Grade II listed Georgian vicarage which stands in its own grounds in peaceful seclusion near the spectacular North Cornwall coast. It has been furnished and decorated in a style which complements the 18th C. vicarage, and there are fresh flowers in each of the guest bedrooms (also equipped with a hairdryer, radio alarm clock and electric blanket). The delicious food is prepared from organically home-grown vegetables, fruit and herbs, and locally supplied meat and free-range eggs. All jams, marmalades, biscuits, cakes and even ice creams are home-maade, and a Cornish cream tea served in the tranquil gardens is a special treat!
OPEN Easter - Oct.   NO SMOKING.   V, S.D. B/A.   CHILDREN WELCOME.   EN SUITE, TV & BEVERAGES IN BEDROOMS.   B. & B. £16 - 19, d. £10.

LOOE

 ## Coombe Farm

WIDEGATES, NR LOOE, CORNWALL, PL13 1QN   TEL: (01503) 240223

ETB 2 Crown Highly Commended. AA QQQQ RAC Highly Acclaimed. Coombe Farm is a delightful 8-bedroomed country house which stands amidst 10 acres of lawns, meadows, woods, streams and ponds with magnificent views down an unspoilt wooded valley to the sea. The house itself has been carefully furnished with antiques, paintings and bric-a-brac, and in cooler weather there are open log fires in the dining room and lounge; each of the comfortable bedrooms has lovely country views. Meals are served in a candlelit dining room with views down the valley to the sea, and the food matches the setting: everything is home-cooked and a typical evening meal would feature home-made soup with crusty rolls, followed by honey roast duck with apple sauce and fresh seasonal vegetables, and a refreshing dessert such as fresh fruit salad and clotted cream; coffee or tea is served in the dining room or lounge. There are 3 acres of lawns in which guests can play croquet, lounge in the sun with a cool drink, or perhaps take a dip in the outdoor heated pool; additionally there is a snug, stone outhouse which has been converted to a games room with snooker, table tennis or a variety of board games.
OPEN MAR. TO OCT. INC.   NO SMOKING.   VE, S.D. B.A. LICENSED.   OVER 5s.   GUIDE DOGS ONLY.   EN SUITE, TV, PHONES & BEVERAGES IN ALL BEDROOMS.   WHEELCHAIR ACCESS TO DINING R, LOUNGE & 5 GROUND FLOOR BEDROOMS. .   B. & B. from £18. D. from £12. (Bargain breaks available).

The Gulls

HANNAFORE, WEST LOOE, CORNWALL   TEL: (01503) 262531

The Gulls is aptly named: it stands high up in a fabulous position directly opposite the main bathing beach with uninterrupted, panoramic views of East and West Looe, the harbour, river, sea and the spectacular Cornish coastline sweeping round to Rames Head. It is a small, family-run hotel - and as such offers friendly, personal service and has a warm, informal atmosphere: the care extends to the food, which is home-cooked from fresh local ingredients and served to you in a lovely dining room which, again, has panoramic sea views. The Gull s has many regular guest who return year after year - lured very probably by the prospect of being able to relax on the patio and the lounge and just watch the yachts and boats in the harbour and the changing moods of the river. They have chosen a lovely town in which to holiday: Looe has a fascinating history from 1154 - when it first appeared on records - through the smuggling era of 1760 and right up to the present day.
OPEN ALL YEAR.   NO SMOKING.   V, S.D. B/A.   LICENSED.   CHILDREN & PETS WELCOME.
EN SUITE IN SOME ROOMS.   TV & BEVERAGES IN BEDROOMS.   B. & B. FROM £19.50.

MARAZION

CASTLE GAYER, LEYS LANE, MARAZION, CORNWALL, TR17 0AQ TEL: (01736) 711548
NO SMOKING. V, S.D. B/A. EN SUITE, TV & BEVERAGES IN ROOMS. B. & B. AROUND £25.

 The Chymorvah Private Hotel

MARAZION, CORNWALL, TR17 0DQ TEL: (01736) 710497

The Chymorvah is an elegant Victorian family home which was built by a wealthy mine-owner in in the mid-1800s in order to house his increasing family. The solidly built granite house stands on a cliff top above Mount's Bay and has superb views from The Lizard to Penzance and across to St Michael's Mount. Although much of the atmosphere and architectural features of the original house are retained, guests are made to feel very much at home; the atmosphere is undeniably special, however, and yourhosts pay attention to the tiny details that make a place memorable (bed linen is laundered at the hotel and dried on the cliff top - the fresh smell is exhilirating). The food freshly cooked on the Aga - any special diets can be accommodated - and there is a tea garden serving snacks and beverages throughout the day. There is a good choice of individually furnished rooms (one has a four-poster and several have sea views), and families can be accommodated in the larger rooms.
OPEN ALL YEAR ex. Xmas. NO SMOKING. S.D. LICENSED. CHILDREN & PETS WELCOME.
EN SUITE, TV & BEVERAGES IN BEDROOMS. WHEELCHAIR ACCESS & TO 2 BEDROOMS. B. & B. £24.50-29.

NEWQUAY

 Crawtock Plains Farmhouse

CUBERT, NR NEWQUAY, CORNWALL, TR8 5PH   TEL: (01637) 830253

Charming 250 yr-old farmhouse with beams & a log fire. Elec. blankets, home-cooking.
OPEN ALL YEAR ex. Xmas. NO SMOKING. S.D. CHILDREN WELCOME. SOME EN SUITE ROOMS. BEVERAGES
IN BEDROOMS. B. & B. £14-18, D. £8 (en suite extra).

 The Michelle Guest House

3 MANEWAS WAY, NEWQUAY, CORNWALL, TR7 3AH   TEL: (01637) 874521

The Michelle Guest House is a lovely detached property which stands in a quiet, level residential area just a few yards from Lusty Glaze Beach and the National Coast Path. It has been furnished and equipped to a very high standard and each of the en suite bedrooms has a range of helpful amenities; some have sea views and two are on the ground floor. Good home-cooked food is served, and there is a pleasant lounge for guests' use.
OPEN ALL YEAR. NO SMOKING. S.D. B/A. OVER 9s WELCOME. WHEELCHAIR ACCESS. EN SUITE, TV &
BEVERAGES IN ROOMS. B. & B. FROM £16, D £7.

 SHELDON, NON-SMOKERS HAVEN, 198 HENVER RD, TR7 3EH TEL: (01637) 874552
OPEN June - Aug. inc. NO SMOKING. OVER 10S ONLY. TV LOUNGE. B. & B. AROUND £120 p.w.

 ## PADSTOW

TREVONE BAY HOTEL, TREVONE, PADSTOW, PL28 8QS   TEL: (01841) 520243

Small, friendly family-run hotel overlooking the beach 2m from picturesque fishing port with panoramic views. Excellent home-baked food - including the bread rolls - and fresh local produce and home-grown vegetables are used where possible in cooking.
OPEN easter - Oct. NO SMOKING. V, S.D. B/A. LICENSED. CHILDREN & PETS WELCOME. EN SUITE & BEVER-
AGES IN ROOMS. TV IN LOUNGE. D. B. & B. AROUND £150 p.w.

PENZANCE

Keigwin Hotel

ALEXANDRA RD, PENZANCE, CORNWALL, TR18 4LZ TEL: (01736) 63930

Quiet, comfortable, small, family-run hotel. Excellent cooking. On street parking.
OPEN ALL YEAR (ex. Xmas) N/S DINING R. & BEDRS. CHILDREN WELCOME. EN SUITE, TV & BEVERAGES IN
BEDROOMS. B. & B. £12 - 16.

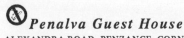**Penalva Guest House**

ALEXANDRA ROAD, PENZANCE, CORNWALL, TR18 4LZ   TEL: (01736) 69060
Small, private hotel in pleasant tree-lined avenue.
OPEN ALL YEAR; NO EVENING MEALS JUL. & AUG.   NO SMOKING.   VE, S.D. B/A.   CHILDREN WELCOME.   EN
SUITE IN 5 ROOMS.   COLOUR TV & BEVERAGES IN BEDROOMS.   B. & B. FROM £11. D. £8.

PERRANPORTH

Beach Dunes Hotel

RAMOTH WAY, REEN SANDS, PERRANPORTH, CORNWALL, TR6 0BY   TEL: (01872) 572263
FAX: (0872) 573824

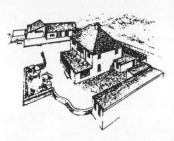

ETB 3 Crowns Beach Dune Hotel is a small, friendly, family-run establishment which, as its name suggests, is situated in sand dunes with panoramic views of the sea, beach and beautiful surrounding countryside. The hotel has been comfortably furnished and a wide variety of well-equipped en suite bedrooms are available - some on the ground floor; additionally there is a hotel annexe with 3 purpose-built holiday suites - each with their own entrance - which are suitable for holidaying families or honeymooners. The hotel has several other excellent leisure amenities for guests - including an indoor swimming pool and squash court - and it has the further advantage of adjoining an 18-hole golf course (there is a 30% fee reduction for guests staying at the hotel).The food is good - and reasonably priced - and there is a well-stocked residents'bar. With its easy access to the 3 miles of Perrans sandy beach and the hotel's own spacious lawns and patios, the Beach Dunes Hotel is an ideal holiday base, and is an excellent centre for touring. Private parking.
OPEN Easter - Oct.   N/S DINING R & LOUNGE BAR. S.D. B/A.   LICENSED.   OVER 4s.   GROUND FLOOR ROOMS. EN
SUITE, TV, PHONE & BEVERAGES IN ROOMS. ACCESS, VISA.   B. & B. FROM £23.50, D. B. & B. FROM £28.50.

REDRUTH

SYCAMORE LODGE, PRIMROSE TERR., PORTREATH, TR16 4JS TEL: (01209) 842784
OPEN ALL YEAR.   NO SMOKING.   OVER 7s ONLY.   BEVERAGES & TV.   B. & B. AROUND £18.

ST BLAZEY

NANSCAWEN HSE, PRIDEAUX RD, ST BLAZEY, NR PAR, PL24 2SR TEL: (01726) 814488
Nanscawen House stands in five acres of beautiful grounds and gardens with outdoor heated swimming pool. Beautifully furnished and appointed: each bedrooms has views. Excellent food prepared from fresh ingredients - some home-grown.
OPEN ALL YEAR ex. Xmas.   NO SMOKING.   V B/A.   RESIDENTIAL LICENSE.   OVER 12S ONLY.   EN
SUITE, TV & BEVERAGES IN ROOMS. ACCESS, VISA.   B. & B. AROUND £30.

ST COLUMB

BRENTONS FARM, GOSS MOOR, ST COLUMB, CORN., TR9 6WR TEL: (01726) 860632
OPEN Feb. - Nov. inc.   NO SMOKING.   V, S.D. B/A.   CHILDREN WELCOME.   BEVERAGES.   B. & B. AROUND £14.

ST IVES

Boswednack Manor

ZENNOR, ST IVES, CORNWALL, TR26 3DD   TEL: (01736) 794183
Peaceful granite-built farmhouse in wildest part of Cornwall with magnificent views of moor & sea. Meditation room, conservatory. Natural history courses. S/C cottage available.
OPEN ALL YEAR.   NO SMOKING.   VE. STD; VE, BA.   CHILDREN WELCOME.   NO PETS OR TV.   2 EN SUITE ROOMS.
BEVERAGES IN BEDROOMS.   B. & B. FROM £14.50, D. £7.

Woodcote Vegetarian HoteL

THE SALTINGS, LELANT, ST IVES, CORNWALL, TR26 3DL   TEL: (01736) 753147
OPEN MAR. - OCT.   N/S DINING R, BEDROOMS & LOUNGE.   D. B. & B. FROM £24.

ST NEWLYN EAST

TREWERRY MILL, TRERICE, ST NEWLYN EAST, CORN, TR8 5HS TEL; (01872) 510345
OPEN Easter - OCt inc.   NO SMOKING.   V, S.D. B/A.   LICENSED.   OVER 7s ONLY.   B. & B. AROUND £17.

TORPOINT

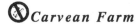 **THE COPSE, ST WINNOLLS, POLBATHIC, TORPOINT, PL11 3DX TEL: (01503) 30205**
Attractive farmhouse forming part of a mixed farm in the rural hamlet of St Winnolls.
1m A374 and 2m to beaches. Full English Breakfast features home-produced milk.
OPEN Mar. - Sept. NO SMOKING. CHILDREN: OVER 10S ONLY. SOME EN SUITE ROOMS. BEVERAGES & TV IN
ROOMS. B. & B. AROUND £18.

TRURO

Carvean Farm

PROBUS, TRURO, CORNWALL, TR2 4HY   TEL: (01872) 520243

 Carvean is an ancient, secluded farmhouse set in 20 acres
of pasture and woodland about 5 miles east of Truro and
close to the Roseland peninsula. A settlement at Carvean
was mentioned in the Domesday Book, although facilities have improved considerably since then! The
house is about 500 yards off the road, and you are more
likely to be woken by the birds than the traffic. The
delicious home-cooking is prepared from fresh, local
produce and Carvean's Table Licence enables you to
enjoy an aperitif or glass of wine with your meal. Friend-
ly and informal in ambience, Carvean is an ideal base for touring Cornwall.
OPEN ALL YEAR. NO SMOKING. V, VE,S.D. B/A. CHILDREN WELCOME. PETS B/A. EN SUITE & BEVERAGES
IN ROOMS. B. & B. £16, D. £12.

Marcorrie Hotel

20 FALMOUTH RD, TRURO, CORNWALL, TR1 2AX   TEL: (01872) 77374
ETB 3 Crown Commended. Privately owned, family-run Victorian hotel pleasantly
situated in conservation area few mins' walk from town centre. Ideal base for touring
Cornwall. Car parking.
OPEN ALL YEAR. N/S DINING R. & SOME BEDROOMS. VEG, SD BA. CHILDREN & PETS. LICENSED. EN SUITE,
BEVERAGES & TV IN ALL BEDROOMS. CREDIT CARDS. B. & B. FROM £19.

Trenerry Farmhouse

TRENERRY, ST ALLEN, TRURO, CORNWALL, TR4 9QX   TEL: (01872) 540479
Trenerry is a family-run dairy farm which stands amidst beautiful countryside with easy
access to both the North and South Cornish coasts, and the cathedral city of Truro. Your
hostess, Jackie Prowse, offers a full English breakfast to guests (non-smokers are
preferred), and accommodation is in comfortably appointed bedrooms. Those seeking a
peaceful country holiday - with the choice of excursions to the sea-side - would be
excellently placed at Trenerry Farm.
OPEN Apr. - Oct. NO SMOKING. S.D. B/A. CHILDREN & PETS. TV, BEVERAGES & H.C. B. & B. FROM £15.

RESTAURANTS

LAUNCESTON

THE GREENHOUSE VEGETARIAN WHOLEFOOD REST, MADFORD LN, LAUNCESTON.
TEL: (01566) 773670 NO SMOKING. V EXC. LICENSED. DISABLED ACCESS 'GOOD'. CHILDREN.

PENZANCE

ENZO RESTAURANT, NEWBRIDGE, PENZANCE, CORNWALL, TR20 8QU
SEPARATE ROOM FOR SMOKERS. V STD. LICENSED. CHILDREN WELCOME.

THE OLIVE BRANCH RESTAURANT, 3A THE TERRACE, MARKET JEW ST, PENZANCE
TEL: (01736) 62438 N/S SEPARATE DINING ROOM.

PIZZA WORLD, 96 MARKET JEW STREET, PENZANCE, CORNWALL
TEL: (01736) 60678   SEPARATE SMOKE-FREE SECTION. V STD. LICENSED. CHILDREN WELCOME.

POLPERRO

THE OLD BARKHOUSE COFFEE SHOP AND EATING HOUSE, THE QUAY,

PORTH LEVEN

CRITCHARD'S SEAFOOD RESTAURANT, HARBOUR HEAD, PORTH LEVEN

PUBS & WINE BARS

PENDOGGETT

THE CORNISH ARMS, PENDOGGETT, PORT ISAAC, PL30 3HH TEL: (01208) 880263
Delightful 16th C. coaching inn 1m inland from the historic fishing village of Port Isaac.
Accommodation is in comfortable, spacious bedrooms, and delicious freshly prepared
meals are served in both the bar and the inn's excellent restaurant.
OPEN ALL YEAR.   N/S 50% OF RESTAURANT, THE FRONT BAR AND SOME BEDROOMS. V STD, OTHER S.D.
ON REQUEST. LICENSED.   WHEELCHAIR ACCESS.   CHILDREN & PETS WELCOME.   EN SUITE. BEVER-
AGES, PHONE, SATELLITE AND T.V. IN ROOMS.

SCORRIER

FOX & HOUNDS, SCORRIER, NR REDRUTH, CORNWALL, TR16 5BS
TEL: (01209) 820205   NO SMOKING IN SMALL LOUNGE EXTENSION.

Devon

ACCOMMODATION

ASHBURTON

⊘ *Cuddyford*

REW RD, ASHBURTON, DEVON, TQ13 7EN   TEL: (01364) 53325
OPEN ALL YEAR Ex. Xmas.   NO SMOKING.   V, VE, GLUTEN-FREE & MACROB. STD. CHILDREN WELCOME.
PETS B/A. BEVERAGES. T.V. ON REQUEST.   B. & B. FROM £12.50. D. £10.

⊘ **MIDDLE LEAT, HOLNE, ASHBURTON, DEVON, TQ13 7SJ   TEL: (013643) 413**
NO SMOKING. V STD. CHILDREN WELCOME. DISABLED ACCESS.   B. & B. AROUND D £18.

The Old Coffee House

27-29 WEST ST, ASHBURTON, DEVON, TQ13 7DT   TEL: (01364) 52539
Charming 16th century Grade II listed building offering comfortable accommodation on
the southern edge of Dartmoor National Park. Open as a restaurant throughout the day.
OPEN ALL YEAR.   NO SMOKING.   V B/A.   BEVERAGES & TV IN ROOMS.   B. & B. AROUND £15.

BARNSTAPLE

⊘ **NORWOOD FARM, HISCOTT, BARNSTAPLE, DEVON TEL: (01271) 858260**
OPEN ALL YEAR.   NO SMOKING.   V STD. EN SUITE, TV & BEVERAGES IN ROOMS.

BIGBURY-ON-SEA

HENLEY HOTEL, FOLLY HILL, BIGBURY-ON-SEA, TQ7 4AR TEL; (01548) 810240/810331
OPEN ALL YEAR.   NO SMOKING.   V, DIAB STD. S.D. B/A. LICENSED. CHILDREN & PETS WELCOME.

BOVEY TRACEY

Tamara

20 PARKELANDS, BOVEY TRACEY, DEVON, TQ13 9BJ   TEL: (01626) 832913
Comfortable B. & B. close to A38 Exeter/Plymouth. Family room. Riding, golf.
OPEN ALL YEAR.   NO SMOKING.   CHILDREN WELCOME.   EN SUITE & BEVERAGES IN BEDROOMS.   GUEST
LOUNGE CTV. B. & B. £26 - 30 Dbl.

⊘ *Willmead Farm*

BOVEY TRACEY, NR NEWTON ABBOT, DEVON, TQ13 9NP   TEL: (01647) 277214
Willmead Farm is a superb 15th C. thatched farmhouse which stands amidst 31 acres of
woodland duckpond and streams in the midst of the beautiful Dartmoor National Park. The
house itself dates from 1437: the hall still has a minstrel's gallery and the attractive beamed
dining room has a stone fireplace bedecked with gleaming copper and brass. Guests are
accommodated in 3 attractive bedrooms, all with ample facilities, and the full English
breakfast features a delicious range of home-made preserves. A holiday at Willmead Farm
is totally peaceful and you are within easy reach of all the attractions of South Devon.
OPEN ALL YEAR ex. Xmas & New Year. NO SMOKING.   VE., S.D. B/A.   OVER 10S ONLY.   1 ROOM EN SUITE.
BEVERAGES ON REQUEST.   T.V. IN DRAWING ROOM.   B. & B. FROM £21.

BRIXHAM

 WOODLANDS GUEST HOUSE, PARKHAM RD, BRIXHAM, DEVON, TQ5 9BU
TEL: (01803) 852040   NO SMOKING

CHAGFORD

 St Johns West

MURCHINGTON, CHAGFORD, TQ13 8HJ   TEL: (01647) 432468
Fine 19th C. granite-built house which stands against Dartmoor, some 800 feet above
sea-level, overlooking the beautiful Teign Valley; beautiful views. Comfortable rooms and
an excellent Aga-cooked breakfast.
OPEN ALL YEAR. NO SMOKING. S.D. B/A.   CHILDREN WELCOME. PETS B/A. 1 EN SUITE ROOM. BEVERAGES
IN ROOMS.   B. & B. AROUND £19.

COLYTON

 The Cobblers

DOLPHIN ST, COLYTON, EAST DEVON, EX13 6NA   TEL: (01297) 552825
The Cobblers is a licensed restaurant and cosy guest house which stands in the historic
town of Colyton. Although one of the country's oldest towns, Colyton regularly wins the
Best Kept Village in Devon Award, and its streets are lined with ancient buildings.
Accommodation at the Cobblers is in centrally heated twin and double rooms, all with a
charming village outlook, and the delicious food served in the Carvery restaurant is very
good value. Your hosts are exceptionally helpful and accommodating: breakfast is served
at a time to suit yourself, and a morning paper is delivered to your door. The Colyton staff
are also happy to advise on outings, car hire and any thing else that would enhance the
pleasure of your stay.
OPEN ALL YEAR. NO SMOKING. S.D. B/A. LICENSED. CHILDREN B/A. EN SUITE & BEVERAGES IN BEDROOMS.
TV IN LOUNGE. B. & B. FROM £20.25.

DARTMOOR

 *Slate Cottage*

THE GREEN, NORTH BOVEY, NR MORETONHAMPSTEAD, TQ13 8RB   TEL: (01647) 40060
18th C. cottage offering peace and comfort, overlooking thatched houses, 13th C. church,
oak-tree'd green and undulating moorland, all in a picturesque Dartmoor village.
OPEN ALL YEAR.   NO SMOKING.   VE, S.D., B/A.   OVER 12S ONLY.   BEVERAGES IN BEDROOMS. B. & B. FROM
£20, Sgle £25.

Two Bridges Hotel

TWO BRIDGES, DARTMOOR, DEVON, PL20 6SW   TEL: (01822) 890581

This 18th century posting inn, set in the heart of
Dartmoor some 1,000 feet above sea-level, is situated
near to the junction of the two main roads over the
moor and has boundless views on each side of the
unspoilt beauty of this lovely National Park. In the
heart of a beautiful wilderness it is therefore reassuring
to discover that the atmosphere at Two Bridges is *cosy*:
log fires warm footsore travellers in the beautifully
furnished lounge and bar, and good home-cooked food
accompanied by sensibly priced wines is the order of
the day in the dining room (cream teas are also served
daily). With some 60 acres of hotel grounds alone,
holiday-makers could walk for days within the vicinity of Two Bridges and not retrace a
single path - but the proprietors organise guided National Park walks and there is riding
and fishing to be enjoyed nearby (the West Dart River flows through the grounds).
OPEN ALL YEAR.   N/S DINING R, LOUNGE, MOST BEDR.   V STD. S.D. B/A.   LICENSED.   DISABLED ACCESS.
CHILDREN WELCOME. PETS B/A.   EN SUITE MOST ROOMS.   BEVERAGES & T.V. (+ SATELLITE) IN ROOMS.   B.
& B. FROM £24.50 (2-DAY BREAKS FROM £75 FOR D.B. & B.).

EXETER

 CLAREMONT, 36 WONFORD RD, EXETER, EX2 4LD TEL: (01392) 74699
Regency style town house in quiet part of Exeter; very high standards.
OPEN ALL YEAR.   NO SMOKING.   V. S.D. B/A.   OVER 5s WELCOME.   EN SUITE, TV & BEVERAGES.

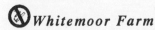The Royal Oak Inn

DUNSFORD, EXETER, DEVON, EX6 7DA   TEL: (01647) 52256
ETB Listed & Approved. Traditional village inn in Dartmoor National Park with all facilities. Six real ales & home-made food.
OPEN ALL YEAR.   N/S DINING R.   V STD, S.D., VE B/A.   ORG. WHERE POSS.   CHILDREN & PETS WELCOME.
WHEELCHAIR ACCESS.   EN SUITE & BEVERAGES IN ROOMS.   TV AVAIL.   B. & B. 17.50-25.

Whitemoor Farm

DODDISCOMBSLEIGH, NR EXETER, DEVON, EX6 7PU   TEL: (01647) 252423

Whitemoor Farm is an attractive 16th C. listed thatched farmhouse, with exposed beams, oak doors and staircase, set in the seclusion of its own mature garden and farmland within easy reach of Exeter, Dartmoor, the South Devon coast, Haldon Racecourse and many forestry walks. The farmhouse is warm and comfortable, with central heating and double glazing, and log fires in winter. Breakfast is a generous feast which includes home-made preserves and cordials; evening meals are available by arrangement and are also available at a nearby inn whose culinary reputation is well known. The area is excellent for birdwatching and there is a nearby golf course.
OPEN ALL YEAR.   NO SMOKING.   V STD.   CHILDREN & PETS WELCOME.   BEVERAGES IN ROOMS.   T.V. IN
GUESTS' LOUNGE.   B. & B. FROM £16.50. D. £8.

EXMOUTH

Stevenstone House

STEVENSTONE RD, EXMOUTH, DEVON.   TEL: (01395) 266106 FAX: (01395) 276816
Large, attractive Edwardian house with grounds in elegant area of Exmouth. Comfortably furnished throughout. home-cooked meals are prepared from fresh, local produce and home-grown herbs, and there is an aperitif on the house before dinner!).
OPEN ALL YEAR.   NO SMOKING. V, S.D. B/A.   BYO WINE.   CHILDREN WELCOME (EX. BABIES).   EN SUITE, TV
& BEVERAGES IN ROOMS.   B. & B. AROUND £20.

ILFRACOMBE

Elmfield Hotel

TORRS PARK, ILFRACOMBE, DEVON, EX34 8AZ   TEL: (01271) 863377

The Elmfield Hotel as built as a gentleman's residence in 1880 and stands on the side of a valley with the Wilder stream running through its lower grounds; its beautiful gardens are terraced with an abundance of shrubs and flowers. The house has been skilfully converted to a 14 bedroom hotel each of whose rooms has been beautifully appointed to a very high standard including the two de luxe rooms, which are particularly spacious. Meals are served in an attractive dining room, and the freshly prepared cuisine features an appetising choice of English and Continental dishes. The amenities of the Elmfield are exceptional: there is a 32'indoor heated swimming pool with a jacuzzi, sauna, solarium, mini-gym and games room; and for those venturing further afield there is much to explore in the beautiful countryside with its sea views, cliff walks and coastal drives.
OPEN APR.-NOV., Xmas.   N/S DINING R.   V, S.D.   LICENSED.   OVER 8s ONLY.   EN SUITE, TV & BEVERAGES IN
ROOMS.   CREDIT CARDS.   B. & B. £240 P.W

Two Ways

ST BRANNOCKS RD, ILFRACOMBE, DEVON, EX34 8EP   TEL: (01271) 864017
Two Ways is a lovely, large Victorian house situated 100 yards from Bicclescombe Park on the main A361 Barnstaple Ilfracombe Road (there is easy parking). It has been very comfortably furnished and appointed and there is an emphasis on 'good old-fashioned service' - with every modern comfort; each of the bedrooms has been equipped with radio clocks, individual heating and electric blankets. Two Ways offers just bed and breakfast, but this generous morning feast is a bumper-full English break-

fast, cooked to order. For the faint-hearted, there are lighter, and healthier, alternatives such as fresh fruit, yoghurt, wholemeal toast and rolls with a choice of preseves. You are just 10 minutes walk from both the shops and seafront at Two Ways and your hosts will happily collect you from the station if you do not wish to bring your car.

OPEN ALL YEAR ex. Xmas.   NO SMOKING.   SOME S.D. B/A. LICENSED. SORRY, NO PETS. 3 EN SUITE ROOMS. BEVERAGES IN ALL BEDROOMS.   T.V. IN LOUNGE & SOME BEDROOMS.

KINGSBRIDGE

Helliers Farm

ASHFORD, AVETON GIFFORD, KINGSBRIDGE, DEVON, TQ7 4ND   TEL: (01548) 550689

ETB 2 Crowns. Dating from 1749, this small working sheep farm is set on a hillside in the heart of Devon's unspoiled South Hams countryside. Recently modernised, the farm has been converted to a most comfortable family guest house whose accommodation includes, in addition to four pleasantly furnished bedrooms, a spacious dining room, a comfortable lounge and a games room. Outside a charming little paved courtyard leads onto a water garden and, a little further down the hill, an extensive trout pool. Evening meals are not usually available but your hosts will be happy to advise you of good local eateries. The area is excellent for walking - and a number of National Trust walks begin nearby.

OPEN ALL YEAR.   NO SMOKING.   CHILDREN.   BEVERAGES.   T.V. LOUNGE.   B. & B. from £16 (1 double, en suite : from £18)

Burton Farm

GALMPTON, KINGSBRIDGE, DEVON, TQ7 3EY   TEL: (01548) 561210

OPEN ALL YEAR ex Xmas & New Year.   NO SMOKING. V, VE, S.D., B/A. LICENSED.   CHILDREN WELCOME. SOME ROOMS EN SUITE.   BEVERAGES IN ROOMS.   T.V.   B. & B. FROM £17.

Old Walls

SLAPTON, KINGSBRIDGE, DEVON, TQ7 2QN   TEL: (01548) 580516

South-facing Georgian house with lovely gardens in the centre of Slapton village.

OPEN ALL YEAR.   N/S D/R, BEDS, LOUNGE.   VE, S.D., B/A.   CHILDREN WELCOME.   PETS B/A.   BEVERAGE-MAKING.   T.V. IN LOUNGE.   B. & B. FROM £13.50. D. £7.

 START HOUSE, START, SLAPTON, NR KINGSBRIDGE, DEVON, TQ7 2QD
    TEL: (01548) 580254 NO SMOKING. V, S.D. B/A. CHILDREN. BYO WINE. B. & B. AROUND £18.

LAPFORD

NYMET BRIDGE COUNTRY HOUSE, LAPFORD, DEVON, EX17 6QX

Peaceful 14th C. country house surrounded by beautiful gardens. Good home cooking.

TEL: (01363) 83334 NO SMOKING. V STD. LICENSED. EN SUITE BEDROOMS.

LYDFORD

Moor View Hotel

VALE DOWN, LYDFORD, DEVON, EX20 4BB   TEL: (01822) 82220

Moor View was originally a farmhouse built in 1869 and it was not until the early 1980s that it became a small hotel and restaurant; it has been very comfortably appointed - there are open fires in cooler weather - and the drawing room, bar and guest rooms have each been furnished in traditional style. The house enjoys Dartmoor as its garden to the front and magnificent views for some 30 miles of Devonshire countryside and into Cornwall at its rear; there are spectacular views of the setting sun each evening. The hotel is run by the Sharples family who do everything they can to make your stay a happy and memorable one, including providing excellent home-cooked English food, a four course evening meal featuring home-made soup or plaice stuffed with spinach, a choice of main dishes such as braised steak with mustard sauce, and a choice of desserts; cheese, biscuits and coffee complete the meal.

OPEN ALL YEAR.   N/S ex. BAR.   VE, S.D., B/A.   LICENSED.   PETS WELCOME. EN SUITE, BEVERAGES & T.V. IN ROOMS.   CREDIT CARDS.   B. & B. FROM £35.

LYNTON

Alford House Hotel

3 ALFORD TERRACE, LYNTON, DEVON, EX35 6AT   TEL: (01598) 52359

ETB 3 Crowns. RAC Acclaimed. Alford House is an elegant, Georgian-style hotel nestling on the slopes of Sinai Hill which has spectacular views out over Lynton town and the beautiful Exmoor coast. Built around 1840, the hotel has been carefully restored and refurbished and retains the charm and peaceful ambience of its original period without forsaking modern comforts and conveniences (the bedrooms - some with mahogany 4-poster beds - all have en suite facilities and have each been well-equipped with a range of amenities including colour TV and tea/coffee-making facilities). Your hosts, June and David Ronson, offer good, old-fashioned hospitality and imaginative home-cooking: fresh, local produce is used wherever possible - including Devon lamb and Exmoor trout - and meals are served in a lovely dining room with garden views. Lynton is a charming town with much to commend it (including the unique carriage lift to its sister town, Lynmouth, and its harbour); it stands on the North Devon Coastal path from which it is possible to walk to Watersmeet, the Valley of the Rocks or Lee Bay.
OPEN ALL YEAR.   N/S DINING ROOM & BEDRS.   V, S.D. B/A.   LICENSED.   OVER 9S ONLY.   7 EN SUITE ROOMS.
TV & BEVERAGES IN ROOMS.   CREDIT CARDS.

Longmead House Hotel

9 LONGMEAD, LYNTON, DEVON, EX35 6DQ   TEL; (01598) 52523

This delightful old Lynton house is quietly situated amongst lovely level gardens near the Valley of the Rocks and is overlooked by the wooded Hollerday Hill. Accommodation is in comfortable and attractively decorated bedrooms. The evening menu is imaginative, with all home-cooked dishes prepared from fresh produce whenever possible. Dinner is served in an oak-panelled dining room with a majestic fireplace. Lynton is perched 500 feet above the Bristol Channel and is a perfect centre for exploring the natural beauties of Exmoor National Park. Not to be missed is the famous Victorian Cliff Railway to Lynmouth and the beautiful walks along the East Lynn River. Car park.
OPEN Mar. - Nov.   NO SMOKING.   V, S.D. B/A.   LICENSED.   CHILDREN WELCOME.   PETS B/A.   EN SUITE &
BEVERAGES IN ROOMS.   B. & B. FROM £16, D. FROM £10

SYLVIA HOUSE HOTEL, LYDIATE LANE, LYNTON, EX35 6HE (0598) 52391
Delightful Georgian hotel combining elegance and old fashioned hospitality, at moderate terms. Exceptionally pretty with drapes, cameos and beautiful pictures. Some of the bedrooms have four-posters. The food is exceptionally scrumptious and has been prepared from fresh ingredients which have been bought daily.
OPEN ALL YEAR.   N/S ALL PUBLIC ROOMS & MOST BEDRS.   V, S.D. B/A.   LICENSED.   CHILDREN WELCOME. PETS
B/A.   MOST ROOMS EN SUITE.   BEVERAGES & TV IN ROOMS.   B. & B. AROUND £17.

NEWTON ABBOT

RUTHERFORD HOUSE, WIDECOMBE IN THE MOOR, NR NEWTON ABBOT, TQ13 7TB
Large detached house amidst pretty gardens in a beautiful valley.
TEL: (01364) 2264   NO SMOKING.   V, VE, DIAB ON REQUETS.   OVER 9s ONLY.   B. & B. AROUND £16.

NEWTON POPPLEFORD

JOLLY'S, THE BANK, NEWTON POPPLEFORD, DEVON, EX10 0XD TEL: (01395) 68100
NO SMOKING.   V STD, S.D. B/A.   LICENSED.   CHILDREN BEVERAGES & TV.   B. & B. AROUND £15.

OKEHAMPTON

HOWARD'S GORHUISH, NORTHLEW, OKEHAMPTON, EX20 3BT TEL: (01837) 53301
OPEN 1-12.   NO SMOKING.   V, VE B/A.   OVER 10s.   EN SUITE, BEVERAGES & TV.   B. & B. AROUND £20.

Stowford House

STOWFORD, LEWDOWN, OKEHAMPTON, DEVON, EX20 4BZ   TEL: (01568) 83415
Charming former rectory in peaceful gardens near Okehampton. Beautifully appointed guest rooms. Outstandingly good food: everything is home-cooked from fresh ingredients.
OPEN Mar. - Nov. N/S DINING R. V, S.D. B/A. LICENSED. CHILDREN B/A. EN SUITE, TV & BEVERAGES IN ROOMS.
CREDIT CARDS.   B. & B. AROUND £22.

OTTERY ST MARY

Coach House Hotel

SOUTHERTON, OTTERY ST MARY, DEVON, EX11 1SE.   TEL: (01395) 568577

This original coach house, in 2 ½ acres of grounds, has been extended to provide 6 en suite bedrooms, each with clock radio & DD phone. Fresh produce is used to provide tasty meals. OPEN ALL YEAR. NO SMOKING. S.D. B/A. LICENSED. EN SUITE, TV & BEVERAGES IN BEDROOMS. CREDIT CARDS. B. & B. FROM £24, D.B. & B. £30.

Fluxton Farm Hotel

OTTERY ST MARY, DEVON, EX11 1RJ   TEL: (01404) 812818

Fluxton Farm is a cat lovers'paradise. The owners keep lots of cats - most of them rescues - so cat lovers only! The farm itself was once a 16th C. long house, and is now a charming white-washed hotel, pleasantly situated in lovely farming country amidst pretty sheltered gardens complete with stream and trout pond; almost all the bedrooms enjoy splendid views over the Otter Valley. There is a healthy emphasis in the preparation of the excellent cuisine on the use of fresh, locally purchased or home-produced ingredients: free-range eggs come from the house hens. Meals are served in a bright airy dining room (log fires in cooler weather) with candlelight in spring and autumn. You are just 4 miles from the sea and a stone's throw from the pretty country town of Ottery St Mary.

OPEN ALL YEAR. N/S DINING R & 1 LOUNGE. V, S.D. B/A. LICENSED. CHILDREN & PETS WELCOME. EN SUITE, TV & BEVERAGES IN ROOMS. B. & B. FROM £22.50 D., B. & B. FROM £28.50.

PLYMOUTH

Churston Hotel

APSLEY ROAD, PLYMOUTH, DEVON, PL4 6PJ   TEL: (01752) 664850

ETB 2 Crowns. Hotel close to city centre & B.R. "Arrive as guests, depart as friends!". OPEN ALL YEAR.   N/S DINING ROOM & SOME BEDROOMS.   V S.D. B/A.   LICENSED.   CHILDREN B/A. BEVERAGES & TV IN ROOMS. CREDIT CARDS.   B. & B. FROM £13.50, en suite from £16.

The Trillium Guest House

4 ALFRED ST, THE HOE, PLYMOUTH, PL1 2RP   TEL & FAX: (01752) 670452

Comfortable family guest house; homely, friendly atmosphere near city centre & seafront. Home-cooking. Quiet area. English language courses. Reservation for car park needed. OPEN ALL YEAR.   N/S DINING R. ON REQUEST.   CHILDREN WELCOME.   V, S.D. B/A. EN SUITE, TV & BEVERAGES IN ROOMS.   B. & B. £15 - 23, D. £11.

 WINDWHISTLE FARM, HEMERDEN, PLYMOUTH, PL7 5BU TEL: (01752) 340600 NO SMOKING. V, S.D. B/A. LICENSED. CHILDREN. BEVERAGES & TV. B. & B. AROUND £19

SALCOMBE

Lyndhurst Hotel

BONAVENTURE ROAD, SALCOMBE, DEVON, TQ8 8BG   TEL: (01548) 842481

Winner of the South Hams Tourist Award 1993 for Excellence, Service, Quality and Value. The Lyndhurst is a small, private hotel - formerly the harbour master's residence - which stands on the side of a hill overlooking the town and harbour and with glorious views of the estuary. All bedrooms are comfortable and very well-appointed, and the hotel has a spacious lounge (with log fire in cooler weather) and a well-stocked bar. The dining room has panoramic views over the harbour and surrounding countryside, and the excellent home-cooked meals feature a range of dishes prepared from fresh, local produce. Salcombe is renowned as a yachtsman's paradise, while the miles of safe, sandy beaches make it an excellent choice for a family holiday.

OPEN Feb. - Nov.   NO SMOKING.   VE, DIAB, LOW-FAT B/A.   LICENSED.   OVER 7s.   EN SUITE, TV & BEVERAGES IN BEDROOMS.   B. & B. FROM £18.50. D., B. & B. FROM £30.

Trennels Hotel

HERBERT ROAD, SALCOMBE, DEVON, TQ8 8HR   TEL: (01548) 842500

ETB 3 Crowns, AA QQQ. Trennels Hotel is built of local stone and was at one time a Victorian sea captain's house; these days it has been carefully converted into a charming small hotel but still has the wonderful views of Salcombe Estuary that its former occupant doubtless enjoyed. The house has been very comfortably furnished and appointed and there

are double, single or family rooms available: most bedrooms have en suite facilities and many have glorious harbour views. Your hosts take care to ensure that there is a very friendly and relaxed atmosphere at the Trennels Hotel and a generous breakfast is served to guests in the pleasant, airy dining room. Salcombe is the most southerly resort in Devon and stands at the mouth of a magnificent estuary: there are miles of golden sandy beaches and, as much of the coast is owned and protected by the National Trust, there are some splendid unspoilt coastal footpaths.
OPEN EASTER - OCT *(inc)*   NO SMOKING. OVER 4s ONLY.   LICENSED. EN SUITE MOST ROOMS. BEVERAGES IN ROOMS.   T.V. IN EN SUITE ROOMS.   B. & B. FROM £19.

ROCARNO, GRENVILLE RD, SALCOMBE, DEVON   TEL; (01548) 842732
OPEN ALL YEAR. NO SMOKING. V B/A. PETS B/A. CHILDREN WELCOME. BEVERAGES & TV.

SEATON

THE BULSTONE, HIGHER BULSTONE, BRANSCOMBE, NR SEATON, EX12 3BL
TEL: (01297) 80446 N/S ex 1 LOUNGE. V, S.D. B/A. LICENSED. CHILDREN WELCOME. EN SUITE & TV.

SIDMOUTH

Broad Oak

SID RD, SIDMOUTH, DEVON, EX10 8QP   TEL: (01395) 513713

Broad Oak was built in 1830 as a gentleman's residence, but has been lovingly restored by its present owners to provide every modern comfort while retaining its Victorian charm. It stands in a peaceful location amidst delightful gardens overlooking The Byes and the River Sid, yet is just a five minute stroll from both the Esplanade and Sidmouth's town centre. The house has full central heating and accommodation is in comfortable rooms (one king-size, one twin and a single) each of which has been equipped with a range of halpful amenities including a hairdryer and shaver point. A generous English breakfast is served to guests.
OPEN Feb. - Nov.   NO SMOKING. V, S.D. B/A. GUIDE DOGS ONLY.   EN SUITE, TV & BEVERAGES IN ROOMS.
B. & B. £20 - 25.

TEIGNMOUTH

Fonthill

TORQUAY RD, SHALDON, TEIGNMOUTH, DEVON, TQ14 0AX   TEL: (01626) 872344
Beautiful Georgian house in 25 acres of private grounds on the edge of Shaldon, a delightful village on the South Devon coast. Visitors come to enjoy the peace and quiet afforded by its tranquil situation. Shaldon overlooks the lovely Teign Estuary where birdwatching, fishing and sailing may all be enjoyed; there is a tennis court in the Fonthill grounds and a golf course nearby. Several nearby pubs and restaurants serve evening meals.
OPEN MAR. TO DEC.   NO SMOKING.   V, S.D. B/A.   CHILDREN WELCOME.   EN SUITE OR PRIVATE BATH AVAILABLE.   BEVERAGES IN BEDROOMS.   B. & B. FROM £21-24.

Leicester House

2 WINTERBOURNE ROAD, TEIGNMOUTH, DEVON, TQ14 8JT   TEL: (01626) 773043
NO SMOKING.   CHILDREN. PETS B/A.   EN SUITE. BEVERAGES & T.V. IN ROOMS.   B. & B. FROM £11.

TORQUAY

Bampfylde House Hotel

42 BAMPFYLDE RD, TORQUAY, DEVON, TQ2 5AY   TEL: (01803) 292697

The Bampfylde House Hotel is a very small privately run hotel which stands conveniently close to all the amenities of Torquay. Accommodation is in comfortable well-equipped bedrooms each of which has been individually styled with colour co-ordinating fabrics. Guests dine on superb home-cooked food (the chef prepares meals with vegetables which have been culled fresh from the garden) and the full licence enables you to enjoy a glass of wine with your meal. The oriental style garden provides a relax-

ing sun-trap for those wishing to stay within the confines of the hotel. Your hosts, Mr and Mrs Hodgson, will gladly collect you from rail or coach station although they have excellent parking facilities for those arriving by car.
OPEN Easter - Oct.   NO SMOKING.   LICENSED.   EN SUITE, BEVERAGES & TV IN ROOMS.   B. & B. FROM £12.

THE BEEHIVE, STEEP HILL, MAIDENCOMBE, NR TORQUAY   TEL: (01803) 314647
The Beehive is situated in the peaceful conservation area of Maidencombe. All room have magnificent views of the sea, coastline and valley. Thatched tavern just 2 minutes' walk away (with bar snacks and a restaurant). 4 mins cove, 30 mins Dartmoor.
OPEN ALL YEAR.   NO SMOKING.   TV & BEVERAGES IN ROOMS.   B. & B. £15 - 16.

Hotel Sydore

MEADFOOT ROAD, TORQUAY, DEVON, TQ1 2JP   TEL: (01803) 294758 FAX: (01803) 294489

Hotel Sydore, a Grade II listed building, is a Georgian villa set in two acres of wooded and award-winning grounds. The hotel has a sun terrace, ample parking and is just a short walk from the Harbour and award-winning Meadfoot beach. Accommodation is in comfortable, centrally heated and well-appointed rooms, which have been equipped with a tea maker, colour TV, hair dryer, trouser press and radio. The restaurant offers a wide selection of meals, including an extensive snack menu, and there is always a good choice of vegetarian meals on the vegetarian à la carte menu.
OPEN ALL YEAR.   N/S RESTAURANT.   V STD, S.D. B/A.   LICENSED.   DISABLED ACCESS.   PETS B/A.   CHILDREN WELCOME.   EN SUITE, TV & BEVERAGES IN ROOMS.   CREDIT CARDS.   B. & B. FROM £17.

Millbrook House Hotel

OLD MILL ROAD, CHELSTON, TORQUAY, DEVON, TQ2 6AP   TEL: (01803) 297394

Millbrook House is a small, elegantly furnished hotel situated close to Tor Abbey Sands and Cockington Village in the Chelston area of Torquay. The charming bedrooms are all equipped to a very high standard, and there are a number of more spacious deluxe rooms available, including a four-poster. The leisure amenities are impressive too: there is a lovely secluded garden and patio, and a mini-gym for guests' use. The dining room offers superb cuisine, prepared from fresh local ingredients and beautifully served on tables laid with linen and cut glass. A typical evening meal would feature Sherried Chicken Livers followed by Monkfish in Brandy and Cream Sauce and a selection of sweets, including home-made ice-cream; there is a helpful wine recommendation to accompany each menu.
OPEN ALL YEAR.   N/S ex. basement bar.   VE, S.D., B/A.   LICENSED.   CHILDREN B/A.   EN SUITE, TV & BEVERAGES IN BEDROOMS.   B. & B. FROM £20, D. £9.

SUNNYBRAE, 38 BAMFYLDE ROAD, TORQUAY, TQ2 5AR TEL: (01803) 296073
OPEN Jun. To Sep.   NO SMOKING.   CHILDREN B/A.   BEVERAGES T.V. LOUNGE. B. & B. AROUND £18.

TREES HOTEL, BRONSHILL RD, BABBACOMBE, TORQUAY TEL: (01803) 326073
OPEN ALL YEAR.   NO SMOKING.   LICENSED.   WHEELCHAIR ACCESS.   CHILDREN: OVER 7S ONLY.   EN SUITE, BEVERAGES & TV IN ROOMS.   VISA.   B. & B. around £18.

Walnut House Holiday Residence

7 WALNUT RD, CHELSTON, TORQUAY, SOUTH DEVON.   TEL: (01803) 606854
Small, select guest house. Spacious rooms & a warm welcome. 5 mins sea, 3 mins station. Highly recommended and patronised by locals with visiting friends & relatives.
OPEN ALL YEAR.   NO SMOKING.   CHILDREN B/A.   1 GROUND FLOOR ROOM. EN SUITE SHOWER, BEVERAGES & TV IN ROOMS.   B. & B. £13 - 14., D. (Easter - Sept) £5 - 6.

TOTNES

Dorsley Park Farmhouse

HIGHER PLYMOUTH ROAD, TOTNES, DEVON, TQ9 6DN   TEL; (01803) 863680
18th C. farmhouse which has been pleasingly converted to provide excellent accommodation just 500 yards from Totnes.
OPEN ALL YEAR.   N/S AT BFAST & BEDROOMS.   V, S.D. B/A.   CHILDREN WELCOME.   PETS B/A. TEA/COFFEE. T.V. IN LOUNGE.   B. & B. FROM £13.

🚭 *Great Court Farm*

WESTON LANE, TOTNES, DEVON, TQ9 6LB   TEL: (01803) 862326
Large Victorian farmhouse 1m Totnes. Comfortable rooms & good food. Central heating.
OPEN ALL YEAR.   NO SMOKING.   S.D. B/A.   CHILDREN WELCOME.   BEVERAGES IN ROOMS.   TV IN LOUNGE.   B. & B. £13.50 - 15.

🚭 *The Old Forge at Totnes*

SEYMOUR PLACE, TOTNES, DEVON, TQ9 5AY   TEL: (01803) 862174

No church bells

ETB Highly Commended. Holder of AA Merit Award. This charming stone-built hotel was converted recently from a 600 year-old smithy; it has a lovely walled garden which makes it a rural retreat in the heart of Totnes; the property has had an interesting history and has partly reverted back to its primary use - Peter Allnutt now runs a busy wrought iron business while his wife, Jeannie, runs the hotel. The highest standard of accommodation is offered to guests: the cottage-style bedrooms are prettily and tastefully furnished, and the food (served in very plentiful quantities) is prepared from the best of healthy ingredients. A typical breakfast menu features a variety of fish and vegetarian options and, in addition to four different types of bread, *two* different sorts of decaffeinated coffee are also offered. Healthily conscientious indeed. Traditional breakfasts are also available as well as fruit, yoghurts, waffles and pancakes.
OPEN ALL YEAR.   NO SMOKING.   V, S.D. B/A.   LICENSED.   CHILDREN WELCOME.   PETS IN CARS ONLY. DISABLED ACCESS TO SOME GROUND FLOOR ROOMS.   EN SUITE IN MOST ROOMS.   BEVERAGES & T.V. IN ALL BEDROOMS.   CREDIT CARDS.   B. & B. FROM £20.

RESTAURANTS

ASHBURTON

🚭 THE OLD COFFEE HOUSE, 27-29 WEST ST, ASHBURTON, TQ13 7DT TEL: (01364) 52539
For further details please see under entry in accommodation section.

BARNSTABLE

🚭 HEAVENS ABOVE, 4 BEAR ST, BARNSTABLE, DEVON. TEL: (01271) 77960
NO SMOKING.   V, VE, EXC. WH. STD.   LICENSED.   CHILDREN WELCOME.

BIDEFORD

🚭 BANKS COFFEE SHOP, 16 HIGH ST, BIDEFORD, DEVON. TEL: (01237) 476813
NO SMOKING.   V STD.   DISABLED ACCESS.   CHILDREN WELCOME.

SLOOPS, BRIDGE STREET, BIDEFORD, DEVON   TEL: (01237) 471796
NO SMOKING AFTER 12 NOON.   V STD.   ACCESS, VISA. .

THYMES RESTAURANT, THE BAKEHOUSE, QUEEN ST, BIDEFORD. TEL: (01237) 473399
ONLY 3 SMOKING TABLES.   LICENSED.   CHILDREN WELCOME.

BOVEY TRACEY

🚭 *Devon Guild of Craftsmen*

RIVERSIDE MILL, BOVEY TRACEY, DEVON   TEL: (01626) 832223
Granary cafe serving teas, coffees, light lunches annexed to specialist exhibition centre & retail shop selling work of 200 craftsmen & women; outside seating in walled courtyard.
OPEN 10 - 5. L. FROM £3.25.   NO SMOKING.   V STD.   LICENSED.   DISABLED ACCESS.   CHILDREN WELCOME (TOYS AVAILABLE).   CREDIT CARDS.

CREDITON

🚭 WILD THYMES, 100 HIGH ST, CREDITON, DEVON. TEL: (01363) 77 2274
Friendly little restaurant serving a variety of wholesome meat-free dishes.
NO SMOKING.   V, WH EXC.   BYO   CHILDREN WELCOME.

DARTINGTON

Ⓝ **CRANKS, CIDER PRESS CENT., SHINNERS BRIDGE, DARTINGTON TEL: (01803) 862388**
NO SMOKING. V EXC. LICENSED. DISABLED ACCESS.

EAST BUDLEIGH

Ⓝ **GRASSHOPPERS, 16 HIGH ST, EAST BUDLEIGH, BUDLEIGH SALTERTON, EX9 7DY**
TEL: (013954) 2774 NO SMOKING. V STD. DISABLED ACCESS.

EXETER

BRAMBLES, 3L NEW BRIDGE STREET, EXETER, DEVON. TEL: (01392) 74168
50% N/S. S.D. ON REQUEST. BYO WINE. CHILDREN WELCOME.

THE CAFÉ, 38 SOUTH STREET, EXETER, DEVON. TEL: (01392) 410855
Light, airy 'conservatory' restaurant, with pleasant *al fresco* dining area, in converted
chapel; excellent food. 'Thai nights'are a special feature Wednesdays & Thursdays eves.
OPEN 10.30 - 6 MON. TO SAT. N/S 80% OF RESTAURANT & IN LARGE GARDEN. LICENSED. DISABLED ACCESS.
CHILDREN WELCOME. CREDIT CARDS.

HERBIES, 15 NORTH STREET, EXETER, DEVON. TEL: (01392) 58473
60% N/S. V EXC, VE STD. LICENSED. CHILDREN WELCOME

Ⓝ **KILLERTON HOUSE (NAT. TRUST), BROADCLYST, NR EXETER. TEL: (01392) 881691**
NO SMOKING. V STD, S.D. B/A LICENSED. CHILDREN WELCOME.

MILL ON THE EXE, BONHAY ROAD, EXETER, DEVON. TEL: (01392) 214464
SEPARATE N/S SECTION. V STD. DISABLED ACCESS.

EXMOUTH

Ⓝ **WILLOWS, 53 THE STRAND, EXMOUTH, DEVON TEL: (01395) 264398**
NO SMOKING. VEGETARIAN. LICENSED. CHILDREN WELCOME.

HONITON

HONEY BEES, 160 HIGH ST, HONITON, DEVON TEL: (01404) 43392
50% N/S. V STD. DISABLED ACCESS. CHILDREN WELCOME.

ILFRACOMBE

THE RED PETTICOAT RESTAURANT, 7 THE QUAY, ILFRACOMBE TEL: (01271) 863273
SEPARATE N/S AREA. DISABLED ACCESS. CHILDREN WELCOME.

KINGS KERSWELL

Ⓝ **PITT HOUSE RESTAUR'T, 2 CHURCH END RD, KINGS KERSWELL TEL: (01803) 873374**
NO SMOKING. LICENSED. DISABLED ACCESS.

NEWTON ABBOT

Ⓝ **DEVON GUILD OF CRAFTSMEN, RIVERSIDE MILL, NEWTON ABBOT, TQ13 9AF**
TEL: (01626) 832223 NO SMOKING. V STD. LICENSED. DISABLED ACCESS.

NEWTON POPPPLEFORD

JOLLY'S VEGETARIAN RESTAURANT, THE BANK, NEWTON POPPLEFORD, EX10 0XD
For further details please see under the entry in the accommodation section.

PLYMOUTH

Ⓝ *Debenhams*
ROYAL PARADE, PLYMOUTH, DEVON, PL1 1SA   TEL: (01752) 266666
A self-service restaurant with cheerful staff; serving popular food throughout the day.
OPEN STORE HOURS. NO SMOKING. V STD. DISABLED ACCESS. CHILDREN WELCOME. CERDIT CARDS.

TIVERTON

Ⓝ *Angel Gallery*
1 ANGEL TERRACE, TIVERTON, DEVON, EX16 6PD   TEL: (01884) 254778
Art gallery with café & takeaway serving vegetarian food with Mediterranean and world
cuisine influences. Historic castle and award-winning museum nearby.
OPEN 10 - 5, Mon-Sat. NO SMOKING. L. FROM £1.50, TAKEAWAY. V STD. CHILDREN WELCOME

TORQUAY

Debenhams

13 - 15 THE STRAND, TORQUAY, DEVON   TEL: (01803) 295921
A self-service restaurant with cheerful staff serving popular food throughout the day.
OPEN STORE HOURS.   NO SMOKING.   V STD. DISABLED ACCESS. CHILDREN WELCOME. CREDIT CARDS.

TOTNES

Willow Vegetarian Restaurant

87 HIGH ST, TOTNES, DEVON.   TEL: (01803) 862605
The Willow wholefood vegetarian restaurant is situated in The Narrows at the top of the
charming town of Totnes. A café by day and a restaurant by night, the Willows has a lovely
garden and is exceptionally customer-friendly (there is a room with toys and a childrens'
table). The food is first-rate too: everything is prepared from fresh, wholefood ingredients
- most of the vegetables are organic - and a typical lunch menu would feature French Onion
Soup followed by Homity Pie and a range of healthy desserts, such as soya icecream or
amazing Rocombe Farm Icecream made with organic milk and natural ingredients. Every
week there is a special feature night and a delicious choice of reasonably priced and healthy
dishes such as Indian patties in spiced yoghurt with fresh coconut chutney followed by
Mushroom Stroganoff and 10 or so desserts (crunchy topped peach, cinnamon and banana
pie or carob chop and mocha cake).
N/S except in garden.   V, S.D. STD.   LICENSED.   DISABLED ACCESS.   CHILDREN WELCOME.

Dorset

ACCOMMODATION

BLANDFORD FORUM

La Belle Alliance

WHITE CLIFF MILL STREET, BLANDFORD FORUM, DORSET, DS11 7BP   TEL: (01258) 452842
Elegant country house style restaurant and hotel offering first-rate accommodation and
food just a short walk from the centre of Blandford Forum. Individually decorated bedrooms with a wide range of helpful extras (bottled Dorset water, toileteries, magazines and
books). An aperitif is served in the lounge before dining in the pretty dining room (flowers
and linen on the table); all dishes have been prepared from fresh ingredients (local wherever
possible), and the imaginative menu changes seasonally.
OPEN Feb. - Dec.   N/S DINING R.   V, S.D. B/A.   LICENSED.   CHILDREN WELCOME.   BABIES B/A.   PETS B/A.
EN SUITE, TV & BEVERAGES IN BEDROOMS. ACCESS, VISA, AMEX. B. & B. FROM £29.

BOURNEMOUTH

The Cottage

12 SOUTHERN RD, SOUTHBOURNE, BOURNEMOUTH, DORSET, BH6 3SR   TEL: (01202) 422764

*ETB 3 Crowns Commended.*The Cottage is a delightful small
hotel, pleasantly located in a quiet select area of Southbourne
mid-way between Bournemouth and Christchurch. The zig-zag
paths to the clean, sandy beach and the shops are only a short
level stroll away. For nature lovers The New Forest and Dorset
countryside can both be reached by a quick car journey. The
resident proprietors Ronald and Valarie Halliwell offer a
friendly personal service and are proud of their spotlessly
clean, tastefully furnished accommodation to which guests
return year after year. The Cottage is noted for home-prepared
fresh cooking; a typical evening meal consisting of Sea Food Salad, Chicken Breasts in
Mushroom and White Wine Sauce (with a selection of vegetables), followed by home-made
Lemon Meringue Pie; cheese, biscuits, coffee & mints. Ample forecourt parking.
OPEN ALL YEAR.   NO SMOKING.   S.D. B/A.   LICENSED.   GROUND FLOOR & EN SUITE BEDROOMS.   OVER 4
YRS ONLY.   BEVERAGES IN ROOMS.   T.V. LOUNGE.   B. & B. FROM £16, D.B. & B. FROM £23.

ⓝ *Cransley Hotel*

11 KNYVETON RD, EAST CLIFF, BOURNEMOUTH, BH1 3QG   TEL: (01202) 290067

12-bedroomed establishment in attractive gardens in a quiet tree-lined road 0.5 miles from East Cliff with its lovely sandy beach. Comfortable bedrooms and a lovely lounge with large French windows which lead out onto a patio and southfacing garden. The food is wholesome and satisfying: home-prepared from fresh ingredients. Packed lunches, flask filling and other light refreshments are also available at a reasonable cost.

OPEN Easter - Oct. NO SMOKING. V, S.D. B/A.   GROUND FLOOR ROOMS.   CHILDREN & PETS WELCOME. EN SUITE, TV & BEVERAGES IN ROOMS.   B. & B. AROUND £19.

Durley Grange Hotel

6 DURLEY ROAD, WEST CLIFF, BOURNEMOUTH, BH2 5JL TEL: (01202) 554473/290743

Large, white-washed and pantiled building, in a quiet corner of the West Cliff and just 5 mins walk from the sea and town centre. Bedrooms are well-appointed and the dining room is a charming place in which to dine on dishes chosen from a traditional British menu,Ozone treated indoor pool, sauna, solarium and whirlpool.

OPEN ALL YEAR.   N/S DINING R, PART OF BAR AREA, POOL AREA AND SOLARIUM.   V, DIAB B/A. LICENSED. WHEELCHAIR ACCESS. OVER 5S ONLY. PETS B/A. EN SUITE, BEVERAGES, T.V. AND PHONE IN ALL ROOMS. ACCESS, VISA. CAR PARKING. B. & B. AROUND £32.

ⓝ *Kingsley Hotel*

20 GLEN RD, BOSCOMBE, BOURNEMOUTH, DORSET, BH5 1HR   TEL: (01202) 398683

The Kingsley is a small, 10-bedroomed hotel which, under the supervision of the resident proprietors, Janet and Martin Smith, offers personal service and a warm, friendly atmosphere. It is situated on a quiet road, away from passing traffic, yet is only 5 minutes from the cliff top gardens, glorious sandy beaches, shopping centre and coach pick up points; all the attractions of Bournemouth are just a short distance away. The bedrooms are bright and well-furnished and have en suite facilities and a hairdryer; there is a comfortable lounge and a separate lounge bar in which you can also enjoy snacks and bedtime drinks. Out of season visitors in Spring and Autumn can enjoy special bargain breaks and senior citizens staying for a week or more qualify for special discounts in all seasons. Boscombe is an ideal touring centre for visiting many other places of interest including the New Forest, Poole Harbour, Christchurch and Beaulieu.

OPEN MAR. - OCT.   NO SMOKING.   LICENSED.   CHILDREN WELCOME.   EN SUITE , TV & BEVERAGES IN ROOMS.   CREDIT CARDS. D., B. & B. FROM £27 £150 - 180 p.w.

ⓝ**MARVEN HOTEL, 5 WATKIN RD, BOSCOMBE, BOURNEMOUTH, BH5 1HP**
TEL: (01202) 397099 NO SMOKING. V, S.D. B/A. LICENSED. CHILDREN WELCOME.

ⓝ *Shelley Villa Hotel*

22 WILFRED RD, BOSCOMBE MANOR, DORSET, BH5 1ND TEL: (01202) 302400

Shelley Villa is a charming 9-bedroomed detached hotel with an ETB 3 Crown Classification. It stands in a quiet tree-lined avenue in a select residential part of Bournemouth close to a park (which has tennis, bowls and a childrens' playground), promenade and seven miles of sandy beaches. Your hosts, Sandra and Laurie Andrews, provide every home comfort, and serve pleasantly varied, home-cooked fresh food, catering for most special diets on request. Each en suite bathroom has a double-glazed window, full-size bath and separate thermostatic high-flow shower-head. Water temperature and pressure are constant even if all guests use their bath or shower at the same time. There is guaranteed parking in the hotel grounds and, it is just a short, level walk to the centre of Boscombe where there is a pedestrianised shopping centre and buses every few minutes. Weekly terms for dinner, bed and breakfast are £108 to £169 depending on the season and whether or not en suite facilities are required.

OPEN ALL YEAR.   NO SMOKING.   S.D. B/A.   LICENSED.   CHILDREN.   EN SUITE, TV & BEVERAGES IN BEDROOMS.   WHEELCHAIR ACCESS.   D. B. & B. £108 - 169 P.W.

 *St. Antoine Guest House*

2 GUILDHILL RD, SOUTHBOURNE, BOURNEMOUTH, DORSET, BH6 3EY   TEL: (01202) 433043

The St Antoine Guest House is a friendly family-run establishment in Bournemouth. It has the best of several worlds, being close to the river, sea and forest, in addition, of course, to the amenities of Bournemouth. Your hostess, Kathrin Mackie, offers a very warm welcome to guests: bedrooms are comfortable and inviting and there are two en suite family rooms. The food is particularly delicious: everything is home-cooked from fresh ingredients - including home-grown vegetables when in season - and vegetarians are also very welcome as Kathrin is able to create some imaginative meat-free options.

OPEN Mar. - Nov.   NO SMOKING.   V, S.D. B/A.   CHILDREN WELCOME.   EN SUITE & BEVERAGES IN BEDROOMS.   TV LOUNGE.   B. & B. £15 - 17, D.B.& B. £21 - 23.

BRIDPORT

Britmead House

WEST BAY ROAD, BRIDPORT, DORSET, DT6 4EG   TEL: (01308) 422941

ETB 3 Crown Commended. At Britmead the proprietors, Ann and Dan Walker, put your comfort first. The house is just a short, level walk from both the historic town of Bridport, Chesil Beach, the Dorset Coastal Path and the harbour of West Bay, with its beaches, golf course and walks. The seven well-appointed and individually decorated bedrooms (one of which is on the ground floor) have many thoughtful little extras. There is an airy, comfortable south-facing lounge and dining room overlooking the garden and beyond to the open countryside. The food is excellent; whenever possible, meals are prepared from fresh produce & locally caught fish. The dinner menu changes daily. Car parking.

OPEN ALL YEAR.   N/S DINING R.   V, S.D. B/A.   LICENSED.   CHILDREN WELCOME.   PETS B/A. EN SUITE, TV & BEVERAGES IN ROOMS.   CREDIT CARDS.   B. & B. FROM £19 - 26, D. £12. Bargain breaks avail.

Chimneys Guest House

MAIN ST, CHIDEOCK, BRIDPORT, DORSET, DT6 6JH   TEL: (01297) 89368

 This charming 17th C. thatched cottage with its beamed ceilings, log fires and delightful gardens is pleasantly situated in the unspoilt village of Chideock where many other similarly thatched and interesting buildings nestle together just 5 minutes from the sea in a fold of the West Dorset hills. The proud owners of Chimneys, Ann and Brian Hardy, take especial pride in offering generous and home-cooked meals to guests - a typical evening menu featuring home-made Tomato and Basil Soup followed by home-made Chicken Pie and a delicious dessert, such as (home-made again)   liquer ice-cream. There is lots to see and do within the vicinity of this BTA Commended guest house including paying a visit to Dorchester (where Judge Jeffreys lived), and taking an outing at Lyme Regis with its charming cobbled streets and sandy beaches.

OPEN ALL YEAR (ex. Xmas)   NO SMOKING.   V, S.D. B/A.   LICENSED.   OVER 5S WELCOME. EN SUITE MOST ROOMS.   TV 1 ROOM.   BEVERAGES ALL ROOMS.   B. & B. £16.50 - 26.

THE MILL HOUSE, EAST RD, BRIDPORT, DORSET, DT6 4AG   TEL: (01308) 25147
NO SMOKING.   V, S.D. B/A.   OVER 8S ONLY.   1 EN SUITE ROOMS.

CHARMOUTH

Newlands House

STONEBARROW LANE, CHARMOUTH, WEST DORSET, DT6 6RA   TEL: (01297) 60212

 This former 16th C. farmhouse is set in 2 acres of gardens and orchard on the fringe of the pretty village of Charmouth. It is comfortably furnished and in the dining room, with its exposed stone walls, excellent food is served. A typical dinner menu features Oriental Style Mushrooms, Salmon Steaks with Watercress Sauce and a home-produced dessert such as Raspberry Streudl with cream.   Charmouth is an ideal

centre for walking and touring and is situated in an area of outstanding natural beauty. It is also famous for the fossil cliffs and beaches of Lyme Bay. Special breaks.
OPEN MAR. TO OCT.   N/S ex. BAR LOUNGE.   V B/A.   LICENSED.   OVER 6S ONLY.   EN SUITE, TV & BEVERAGES IN ROOMS.   B. & B. FROM £22.50, D, B. & B. FROM £36.

DORCHESTER

"Badgers Sett"
CROSS LANES, MELCOMBE BINGHAM, NR DORCHESTER, DORSET, DT2 7NY   TEL & FAX: (01258) 880697
Mellow 17th C. flint and brick cottage carefully modernised to retain such original features as oak beams and inglenook fireplaces; all bedrooms are en suite with TV, radio and kettle.
OPEN ALL YEAR.   NO SMOKING.   V, S.D. B/A.   CHILDREN WELCOME.   PETS B/A).   EN SUITE, TV & BEVERAGES IN ROOMS.   B. & B. FROM £17.50.

The Creek
RINGSTEAD, DORCHESTER, DORSET, DT2 8NG   TEL: (01305) 852251
Lovely white-washed house on Dorset coast with the sea at the bottom of the garden. Fabulous views across Weymouth Bay
OPEN ALL YEAR.   NO SMOKING.   V, VE, S.D. B/A.   CHILDREN WELCOME.   BEVERAGES IN ROOMS.   T.V. IN LOUNGE.   B. & B. FROM £17.50, D. FROM £9.50.

East Knighton Farm
EAST KNIGHTON, DORCHESTER, DORSET, DT2 8LG   TEL: (01305) 852933
Period farmhouse renovated to a high standard.
OPEN Easter - end Sept.   NO SMOKING.   V, S.D. B/A.   EN SUITE, TV & BEVERAGES IN ROOMS.   B. & B. £21.

FORGE COTTAGE, DUCK ST, CERNE ABBAS, DORCHESTER, DT2 7LA
NO SMOKING.   V, S.D. B/A.   CHILDREN WELCOME.   EN SUITE, TV & BEVERAGES IN ROOMS.

The Manor Hotel
WEST BEXINGTON, DORCHESTER, DORSET, DT2 9DF TEL: (01308) 897616 FAX: (01308) 897035

The Manor Hotel, the ancient Manor House of West Bexington, snuggles in a pocket of tree and garden on a gentle slope just a saunter from the sea at Chesil Bank; an old stone building, mellowed by nine centuries of sea and sun, the Manor Hotel has, nonetheless, every modern comfort you could wish for together with a few welcome traditional values of hospitality and service (crisp bed linen, warming log fires, real ales served in the stone-lined cellar bar); most bedrooms have uninterrupted sea views. The food is prepared with integrity and flair from fresh, local and seasonal ingredients (lobster, game, seafood, etc.), and there is a good childrens'menu (younger guests will also enjoy playing on the swings and slides in the garden). Its a wonderful place to come for those in search of safe sandy beaches (Weymouth, Charmouth & Lyme Regis are within easy reach), & historic towns, houses & gardens abound.
OPEN ALL YEAR.   N/S CONSERVATORY.   V, S.D. B/A.   LICENSED.   WHEELCHAIR ACCESS TO RESTAURANT. CHILDREN.   EN SUITE, TV & BEVERAGES IN ROOMS.   B. & B. FROM £38, D. B. & B. FROM £56.

LYME REGIS

Coverdale Guest House
WOODMEAD RD, LYME REGIS, DORSET, DT7 3AB   TEL: (01297) 442882
Coverdale is situated in a quiet residential area of Lyme Regis overlooking Woodland Trustland and sea views; the town centre town is a short walk away. The accommodation is comfortable and the food is served in an attractive dining room (organically home-grown vegetables and herbs are used in cooking when tavailable).
OPEN MAR. - OCT. INC.   NO SMOKING.   S.D. B/A.   CHILDREN WELCOME.   PETS B/A.   EN SUITE AVAILABLE. BEVERAGES IN ROOMS.   TV LOUNGE.   B. & B. FROM £10.

KERSBROOK HOTEL, POUND ROAD, LYME REGIS, DORSET.   TEL: (01297) 442596
N/S DINING R & BEDS.   V, S.D. B/A.   LICENSED.   PETS B/A. EN SUITE & BEVERAGES.

Pitt White

MILL LANE, UPLYME, LYME REGIS, DORSET. TEL: (01297) 442094

Large Victorian house in superb countryside just a mile from the sea at Lyme Regis. It is surrounded by an acre and a half of garden, with (believe it or not), the most comprehensive selection of bamboos in Europe; the River Lym winds its way through the garden. The food is wholesome and delicious: everything is home-cooked from fresh ingredients (including locally produced meats and free-range eggs) and there is a strong wholefood emphasis - vegetarian food is a speciality.

OPEN ALL YEAR.   NO SMOKING. VSTD. S.D. B/A. CHILDREN & PETS WELCOME.   EN SUITE, TV & BEVERAGES IN ROOMS. B. & B. £18 - 23.

POOLE

GULL COTTAGE, 50 TWEMLOW AVE, LOWER PARKSTONE, POOLE. TEL: (01202) 721277
NO SMOKING. V B/A.   CHILDREN WELCOME. EN SUITE ROOMS.

SHAFTESBURY

Sunridge Hotel

BLEKE ST, SHAFTESBURY, DORSET   TEL: (01747) 53130

Listed 19th C. building in the centre of Shaftesbury. Comfortably furnished and tastefully decorated throughout, the hotel has a sauna and a heated indoor swimming pool. The food is imaginative and delicious and feature fresh, locally grown vegetables.

OPEN ALL YEAR.   N/S DINING R & 50% OF BEDRS.   V, S.D. B/A.   CHILDREN WELCOME.   LICENSED. EN SUITE, TV & BEVERAGES IN ROOMS.   CREDIT CARDS.   B. & B. AROUND £29.

SHERBORNE

Frampton Farm

CHETNOLE RD, LEIGH, SHERBORNE, DORSET, DT9 6HJ   TEL: (01935) 872269

Listed 17th C. farmhouse in quiet village 6½ miles from abbey town of Sherborne.

OPEN Apr. - Sept. NO SMOKING.   S.D. B/A.   TV IN LOUNGE.   BEVERAGES IN BEDROOMS.   B. & B. FROM £15, d. FROM £10 B/A.

MIDDLE PICCADILY NATURAL HEALING CENTRE, HOLWELL, SHERBORNE, DORSET.
TEL: (0196) 323468   NO SMOKING.   V STD. S.D. B/A.   BEVERAGES.   FULL BOARD FROM £46.

SWANAGE

Crowthorne Hotel

CLUNY CRESCENT, SWANAGE, DORSET, BH19 2BT   TEL: (01929) 422108

The Crowthorne Hotel is a Victorian villa-style residence that its owners describe as being a Country House by the sea. Quite exceptional standards of hospitality are offered, from a welcoming pot of tea on arrival and the provision of home-made biscuits in all the bedrooms, to the preparation of packed lunches and the seemingly endless supplies of coffee and toast at breakfast. The hotel has been very comfortably appointed: each of the bedrooms has been individually designed and decorated, and there are several en suite rooms. The food is first-rate: menus offer a tempting choice of deliciously imaginative home-cooked fare, and guests can choose from a wide variety of good quality and good value wines. A holiday at the Crowthorne Hotel offers the best of several worlds: the beautiful seascape on the Dorset Heritage Coast Path, or the unspoilt beauty of Durlston Country Park.

OPEN Feb. - Nov.   NO SMOKING.   S.D. B/A. V STD.   LICENSED.   CHILDREN.   50% EN SUITE.   BEVERAGES IN ROOMS.   B. & B. FROM £15, d £10.

Seashells Vegetarian Hotel

7 BURLINGTON RD, SWANAGE, DORSET, BH19 1LR TEL: (01929) 422794

Family hotel oppos. safe, sandy beach. Light, airy en suite rooms. Excellent walking.

OPEN ALL YEAR.   NO SMOKING.   V STD.   CHILDREN WELCOME.   LICENSED.   EN SUITE, TV & BEVERAGES
IN ROOMS.   B. & B. £16 - 20.

Skelmorlie House
50 QUEENS RD, SWANAGE, DORSET, BH19 2EU   TEL: (01929) 424643
ETB 2 Crowns Commended. Beautiful sea views and delicious home-cooking prepared
from fresh ingredients, at this small guest house in a quiet part of Swanage. Relaxed and
friendly atmosphere.
OPEN Apr. - Sept.   NO SMOKING.   V, S.D. B/A.   OVER 5s WELCOME.   SOME EN SUITE.   BEVERAGES & TV IN
ROOMS.   B. & B. £15 - 17, D. £8.

WAREHAM

Highfield
COOMBE KEYNES, WAREHAM, DORSET, BH20 5PS   TEL & FAX: (01929) 463208
Highfield is a lovely family home which backs onto open fields and stands amidst thatched
cottages in the peaceful hamlet of Coombe Keynes. Accommodation is in comfortable
rooms with wash basins - one of which has an en suite shower, WC and wash basin - and
a full English breakfast is served to guests. You are just 5 minutes drive from Lulworth
Cove and the coastal walks are magnificent; additionally horse-riding, golf and watersports
can all be enjoyed nearby.
OPEN EASTER - SEPT inc.   NO SMOKING.   S.D. B/A.   CHILDREN WELCOME.   1 EN SUITE.   BEVERAGES IN
BEDROOMS.   B. & B. £17.50 - 20.

WEYMOUTH

THE BEEHIVE, OSMINGTON, NR WEYMOUTH, DORSET, DT3 6EL   TEL: (01305) 834095
NO SMOKING.   V, S.D. B/A.   OVER 5S ONLY.   PETS B/A   1 EN SUITE ROOM.

FAIRLIGHT, 50 LITTLEMOOR RD, PRESTON, WEYMOUTH.   TEL: (01305) 832293
NO SMOKING.   V B/A.   OVER 4S ONLY.   TV & BEVERAGES IN BEDROOMS.

RESTAURANTS

BOURNEMOUTH

DEBENHAMS, THE SQUARE, BOURNEMOUTH, BH2 5LY   TEL: (01202) 22177
Intermission is a friendly self-service family restaurant serving popular snacks, hot lunches
and a wide range of hot and cold drinks.
OPEN STORE HOURS.   NO SMOKING.   V STD.   DISABLED ACCESS.   CHILDREN.   CREDIT CARDS.

THE SALAD CENTRE, 22 POST OFFICE RD, BOURNEMOUTH.   TEL: (01202) 21720
NO SMOKING.   V, VE, WH EXC.

CERNE ABBAS

OLD MARKET HOUSE, 25 LONG ST, CERNE ABBAS, DORSET.   TEL: (01300) 3680
OPEN Mar. - OCt.   NO SMOKING.   V STD.

LYME REGIS

PILOT BOAT INN, BRIDGE ST, LYME REGIS, DORSET, DT7 3QA   TEL: (012974) 43157
NO SMOKING.   V A SPECIALITY.   LICENSED.   DISABLED ACCESS.   CHILDREN.

LYTCHETT MINSTER

SLEPE COTTAGE TEA ROOMS, DORCHESTER RD, LYTCHETT MINSTER
NO SMOKING.   LICENSED.   CHILDREN WELCOME.

POOLE

The Clipper Restaurant
100 DOLPHIN CENTRE, POOLE, DORSET, BH15 1SS   TEL: (01202) 683334
Restaurant in shopping centre specialising in home-made dishes & cakes.

OPEN 9.30 TO 5.   N/S 75% OF RESTAURANT.   SEPARATE VEGETARIAN COUNTER.   LICENSED.   DISABLED
ACCESS.   CHILDREN WELCOME.

PUBS & WINE BARS

ABBOTSBURY

ILCHESTER ARMS HOTEL, 9 MARKET STREET, ABBOTSBURY, DT3 4JR
TEL: (01305) 871243   N/S CONSERVATORY.   V STD.   CHILDREN WELCOME IN CONSERVATORY.

DORCHESTER

THE BRACE OF PHEASANTS, PLUSH, DORCHESTER, DT2 7RQ   TEL: (013004) 357
N/S 1 ROOM.   V STD.   SOME WHEELCHAIR ACCESS.   CHILDREN WELCOME.

Somerset

ACCOMMODATION

BRIDGWATER

Ⓝ *Parsonage Farm*
OVER STOWEY, BRIDGWATER, SOMERSET, TA5 1HA   TEL: (01278) 733237

Parsonage Farm is a traditional 17th C. farmhouse which is located in a quiet Quantock Hill village directly adjacent to the parish church. It has spacious rooms, quarry tile floors and log fires, and is surrounded by an organic smallholding with large, walled kitchen garden from which are gathered the delicious vegetables, fruit and free range eggs used in cooking. Dining at Parsonage Farm is a real treat: breakfast features porridge cooked overnight in the Aga, home-made breads and jams, and house specialities of waffles or blackcurrant pancakes with maple syrup. Evening meals are predominantly vegetarian and include seasonal fruits and vegetables. Your hosts are keen ramblers and enjoy helping guests choose their walks which begin at the doorstep; additionally the garden is a peaceful place in which to relax.
OPEN ALL YEAR.   NO SMOKING.   ORG, WH, V, VE STD, S.D. B/A.   CHILDREN WELCOME.   PETS B/A.   TV IN
SITTING ROOM.   B. & B. £16 - 18.

Ⓝ *Waterpitts Farm*

BROOMFIELD, QUANTOCK HILLS, NR BRIDGWATER, TA5 1AT   TEL: (01823) 451679
A 5 acre small-holding with sheep, chickens, geese, ducks, cats & dogs in a secluded part of the Quantock Hills. Ideal for walking, cycling, fishing, riding & golf. Stables avail. for guests' horses. Pub with excellent food nearby. 6 m M5, Taunton & Bridgwater. B. & B.
OPEN ALL YEAR.   NO SMOKING.   V, S.D. B/A.   CHILDREN WELCOME.   PETS B/A.   TV IN 1 BEDROOM.
BEVERAGES ON ARRIVAL & IN ROOM B/A. B. & B. £14-20.

CHARD

Ⓝ *Watermead Guest House*
83 HIGH ST, CHARD, SOMERSET, TA20 1QT   TEL: (01460) 62834
Charming Victorian detached guest house; comfortable accommodation; full English b'fast.
OPEN ALL YEAR.   N/S/ DINING ROOM.   SOME S.D.   CHILDREN WELCOME.   PETS B/A.   EN SUITE, TV &
BEVERAGE-MAKING IN BEDROOMS.   B. & B. £15 - 22.

Ⓝ *Yew Tree Cottage*
HORNSBURY HILL, CHARD, SOMERSET, TA20 3DB TEL: (01460) 64735 FAX: (01460) 68029
Yew Tree is a modernised cottage which stands in an acre of lovely garden. Guests are accommodated in individually furnished rooms and there is a ground floor apartment which would suit a part-disabled guest and which can be used on a B. & B. or S/C basis; evening meals may be taken by arrangement. Within easy reach of the coast, Dartmoor and Exmoor,

Yew Tree Cottage is an ideal base for touring Devon, Dorset, and Somerset. There are many gardens and historic houses to be visited, and numerous inland and coastal walks.
NO SMOKING. S.D. B/A. WELL-BEHAVED CHILDREN & SMALL PETS WELCOME. EN SUITE & BEVERAGES IN ROOMS. 1 ROOM WITH TV. B. & B. £15 - 19.

DUNSTER

⊗BURNELLS FARM, KNOWLE LN, DUNSTER, TA24 6UU   TEL: (01643) 821841
NO SMOKING. V, S.D. B/A. OVER 8S ONLY. PETS B/A. TV IN LOUNGE.

⊗*Dollons House*

10 CHURCH ST, DUNSTER, SOMERSET, TA24 6SH   TEL: (01643) 821880.

Dollons House is a Grade II listed building, believed to be much older than its early 19th C. facade. The house is situated in the heart of mediaeval Dunster beneath the castle which is now owned by the National Trust. Dunster is probably the prettiest village in the Exmoor National Park and is ideally situated for exploring Exmoor, the Lorna Doone Country and the Devon and Somerset coastline. Over 100 years ago Dollons House owned the local pharmacy which, as well as potions, produced a marmalade of such high quality that they supplied the Houses of Parliament. These days home-made marmalade is still served at breakfast, and vegetarian options are available on request. The en suite bedrooms are all attractively decorated. There is a Tulip Room and one dubbed 'T'Bear Esquire for full-grown teddy bear fans. Dunster is an interesting village with cobbled pavements, a Yarn Market, village gardens, working water mill and castle.
OPEN ALL YEAR (ex Xmas day & Boxing Day). NO SMOKING. S.D. EN SUITE, TV & BEVERAGES IN ROOMS. B. & B. FROM £20.50

⊗*Exmoor House Hotel*

12 WEST ST. DUNSTER, SOMERSET, TA24 6SN   TEL: (01643) 821268
Grade II Georgian listed building. Farm-fresh produce is used where possible in cooking.
OPEN FEB. TO NOV. NO SMOKING. V B/A. LICENSED. 1 GROUND FLOOR BEDROOM. DOGS B/A. EN SUITE, BEVERAGES & T.V. IN ALL ROOMS. B. & B. FROM £25.50

⊗SPEARS CROSS HOTEL, WEST ST, DUNSTER, TA24 6SN   TEL: (01643) 821439
NO SMOKING. V B/A. LICENSED. OVER 12S. EN SUITE, TV & BEVERAGES.

EAST BRENT

⊗KNOLL LODGE, CHURCH RD, EAST BRENT, SOMERSET, TA9 4HZ   TEL: (01278) 760294
NO SMOKING. V, S.D. B/A. CHILDREN WELCOME. EN SUITE, TV, BEVERAGES.

FROME

⊗*Old Ford House*

OLD FORD, FROME, SOMERSET, BA11 2NF   TEL: (01373) 462142
Lovely period building with a Regency front and a 16th C. back; beautiful large garden
OPEN ALL YEAR. NO SMOKING. S.D. B/A. BRING YOUR OWN WINE. CHILDREN B/A. EN SUITE/PRIVATE BATH & BEVERAGES IN BEDROOM. TV IN DRAWING ROOM. B. & B. £17.

GLASTONBURY

⊗*Greinton House*

GREINTON, NR GLASTONBURY, SOMERSET, TA7 9BW   TEL: (01458) 210307
Lovely house standing on the southern slopes of the Polden Hills amidst delightful gardens, with tennis court and croquet lawn. Near Quaker burial ground.
OPEN ALL YEAR. NO SMOKING. CHILDREN B/A. EN SUITE IN SOME BEDROOMS. BEVERAGES IN ALL ROOMS. B. & B. FROM £15.

⊗*Waterfall Cottage*

20 OLD WELLS RD, GLASTONBURY, SOMERSET, BA6 8ED TEL; (01458) 831702
OPEN ALL YEAR. NO SMOKING. V, S.D. B/A. CHILDREN B/A. BEVERAGES & TV. B. & B. £14 - 16.

KEINTON MANDEVILLE

Mathias House

HIGH ST, KEINTON MANDEVILLE, SOMERTON,
SOMERSET, TA11 6DZ   TEL & FAX: (01458) 223921
Mathias House is a large detached house which
stands on the edge of the quiet village of Keinton
Mandeville. Accommodation is in comfortable en
suite rooms each of which has a TV and a welcoming
tray of beverages; there is a separate lounge for
guests'use. Guests dine on good home-cooked foood
prepared by your hostess, Mrs Jenny Ruddle. Mathias House is ideally situated for touring Somerset:
Glastonbury, Wells, the New Clarks village and
many National Trust Houses and gardens are within easy reach, and the Dorset Coast is
just one hour's drive away.
OPEN ALL YEAR. NO SMOKING. EN SUITE, TV & BEVERAGES IN ROOMS. D, B. & B. £28.

MINEHEAD

Hillside

HIGHER ALLERFORD, NR MINEHEAD, TA24 8HS   TEL & FAX: (01643) 862831
Lovely West Country thatched cottage in peaceful sunny garden in the foothills of Exmoor;
the location is outstanding (the cottage is owned by the National Trust) and there are
wonderful views of vale, moor and sea; the sunsets are breathtaking. Free-range eggs,
home-made bread, preserves and garden produce for breakfast.
OPEN ALL YEAR. N/S DINING R. V, S.D. B/A CHILDREN & PETS WELCOME. BEVERAGES. TV IN
LOUNGE & BEDRS ON REQUEST. B. & B. AROUND £16.

Kildare Lodge

TOWNSEND RD, MINEHEAD, SOMERSET, TA24 5RQ.   TEL (01643) 702009 FAX (01643) 706516
Beautiful historic inn with 9 de luxe en suite guest rooms. Kildare Lodge has a friendly
pub with outstanding pub food and real ales. There is an extensive choice of vegetarian
meals on both the pub food and dining room menus. There is a dry, smoke-free TV lounge
and a 50 seat restaurant. Wedddings, birthdays, anniversary and private parties a speciality.
OPEN ALL YEAR.   N/S 95% DINING ROOM.   V, S.D. LICENSED. CHILDREN & PETS. CREDIT CARDS.
EN SUITE, TV & BEVERAGES IN BEDROOMS. B. & B. FROM £24.50, D.B & B. FROM £29.

Montrose

14 TREGONWELL RD, MINEHEAD, SOMERSET, TA24 5DW   TEL: (01643) 705136
ETB Two Crowns. Friendly family-run hotel 2 mins walk from sea front and shopping
centre of Minehead. Central heating. Pleasantly furnished T.V. lounge; refreshments may
be requested between 9 and 10 p.m. each evening. Out of season bargain breaks.
OPEN Mar. - Oct.   NO SMOKING. V, S.D. B/A.   OVER 3S ONLY.   2 EN SUITE ROOMS, 1 GROUND FLOOR.
BEVERAGES IN ROOMS. T.V. LOUNGE.   B. & B. AROUND £18.

MONTACUTE

Mad Hatters Tea Shop

1 SOUTH ST, MONTACUTE, SOMERSET   TEL: (01935) 823024
Listed Georgian property; picturesque conservation village. Walking, cycling, touring.
OPEN: Easter - Dec. For tea shop see restarant section.   NO SMOKING.   V., LOW-FAT, LOW-CAL STD. CHILDREN.
WHEELCHAIR ACCESS: tea garden only.   EN SUITE, TV & BEVERAGES IN ROOMS. B. & B. FROM £15.

Milk House Restaurant (with accommodation)

THE BOROUGH, MONTACUTE, SOMERSET, TA15 6XB   TEL: (01935) 823823
OPEN ALL YEAR Ex Xmas. N/S DINING R, LOUNGE, BEDROOMS; SEP. SMOKING ROOM. V, VE STD.   LICENSED.
OVER 12S ONLY. 2 EN SUITE ROOMS. T.V. D. FROM £19.80

PORLOCK

Bales Mead

WEST PORLOCK, SOMERSET, TA24 8NX   TEL: (01643) 862565
Small, elegant country house offering superb luxurious bed and breakfast in an outstanding
& peaceful setting. Magnificent panoramic views towards both sea & rolling countryside.
Ideally situated for walking/touring Exmoor and the North Devon Coast.
OPEN ALL YEAR (ex. Dec/Jan).   NO SMOKING.   V, S.D. B/A. BEVERAGES & TV IN ROOMS. B. & B.£22.

 *Fern Cottage*

ALLERFORD, NR PORLOCK, EXMOOR, SOMERSET   TEL: (01643) 862215
16th C Exmoor cottage in wooded National Trust vale. Classic/Bistro cooking. Fine cellar.
OPEN ALL YEAR.   NO SMOKING.   PETS WELCOME.   LICENSED. EN SUITE & BEVERAGES IN ROOMS. B. & B.
FROM £26.25, D, B. & B. £33.

SHAFTESBURY

QUIET CORNER FARM, HENSTRIDGE, TEMPLECOMBE, BA8 0RA   TEL: (01963) 63045
N/S DINING R, BEDRS & SITTING R.   V STD. S.D. B/A.   CHILDREN WELCOME.   1 EN SUITE.   BEVERAGES.   T.V.
LOUNGE.

SHEPTON MALLET

THE LONG HOUSE HOTEL, PILTON, SHEPTON MALLET, BA4 4BP
TEL: (01749) 890701   N/S DINING R & SOME BEDRS.   V, WH STD.   LICENSED.   CHILDREN WELCOME.   EN SUITE
ALL ROOMS.   BEVERAGES & T.V.

TAUNTON

RoadChef Taunton Deane

MOTORWAY SERVICE AREA M5 SOUTH & NORTHBOUND, TRULL, TAUNTON, SOMERSET,
BS26 2US   TEL: (01823) 271111

Conveniently located on the Somerset/Devon border, RoadChef Taunton Deane was the site for the first 39 bedroom motorway lodge in England, and is an ideal place for holiday-makers to break a journey to the South West. Each of the 39 bedrooms in its Lodge have been comfortably furnished and well-appointed with a trouser press, hairdryer and tea and coffee making facilities. The self-service Orchards restaurants have excellent smoke-free areas and serve a wide selection of popular meals. There is always a vegetarian option on the menu and baby foods are also available (there is a changing room). Additionally travellers will be pleased to find a helpful range of facilities including modern well-stocked shops and an auto-bank.
OPEN ALL YEAR ex Xmas day.   N/S MOST OF RESTAURANT & SOME BEDRS.   DISABLED ACCESS.   CHILDREN
WELCOME.   EN SUITE, TV (PLUS SKY) & BEVERAGES IN ROOMS.   CREDIT CARDS.   B. & B. AROUND £32.

 *Slimbridge Station Farm*

BISHOPS LYDEARD, TAUNTON, SOMERSET, TA4 3BX   TEL: (01823) 432223
Village farm of 140 acres offering accommodation in an attractive Victorian farmhouse.
OPEN ALL YEAR ex Xmas.   NO SMOKING.   V, S.D. B/A.   CHILDREN WELCOME.   PETS B/A. BEVERAGES & T.V.
IN ROOMS.   B. & B. FROM £15.

WEDMORE

 **NUT TREE FARM, SOUGHTON CROSS, WEDMORE, BS28 4QP   TEL: (01934) 712404**
NO SMOKING.   V, S.D. B/A.   2 EN SUITE ROOMS.   BEVERAGES IN ROOMS.   T.V. LOUNGE.

WELLS

Glencot House

GLENCOT LN, WOOKEY HOLE, NR WELLS, SOMERSET, BA5 1BH   TEL: (01749) 677160 FAX:
(01749) 670210

Tucked away in Glencot Lane in Wookey Hole is Glencot House, a late Victorian Mansion built in grand Jacobean style for the local Paper Mill owner. It stands amidst 18 acres of gardens and parkland with its own river frontage and cricket pitch. The original owner oversaw the design of the house and thus a wealth of beautiful features have been incorporated including carved ceilings and walnut panelling. When the house was purchased as a hotel in 1985 it was restored to its former splendour yet still retains its period elegance and the atmosphere of a family home. Each of the 12 en suite guest rooms enjoy views of the garden and countryside, (some have four-poster or half-tester beds). Guests may dine in the oak-panelled restaurant and enjoy a meal prepared from fresh local produce; afterwards they may relax in the library and drawing room (with log fires). There is also a small indoor pool, sauna, table tennis and snooker facilities. Glencot is an ideal venue for weddings, private parties, seminars or conferences.

OPEN ALL YEAR. N/S DINING R. S.D. B/A. LICENSED. CHILDREN & PETS WELCOME. EN SUITE, D.D. PHONE, TV & BEVERAGES IN BEDROOMS. B. & B. £27.50 - 35. Sgl £42.50 - 45, D. £15.50 & 19.50.

Ⓝ *Infield House*

36 PORTWAY, WELLS, SOMERSET, BA5 2BN TEL: (01749) 670989 FAX: (01749) 679093

AA QQQQ Selected. Infield House is a beautifully restored Victorian town house which stands just a few minutes' walk from Wells city centre, backing onto a wooded conservation area, thriving with birds and wildlife (reminding one of the proximity of the countryside).Each of the three spacious guest rooms has an original Victorian fireplace and has been furnished in keeping with the period (one has an antique brass bedstead), and there are views across the garden to the countryside beyond; there is also an elegant and comfortable lounge for guests' use. Breakfast is served in the lovely dining room with its Adam style fireplace and, after choosing from a cold buffet of juice, cereals and yoghurt, guests are offered a plate of fresh fruit prior to the cooked breakfast.Unlimited tea and coffee is also served. Having only 3 guest rooms enables your hosts, Julie and Maurice Ingerfield, to offer a degree of personal service not usually available in a larger establishment: they will do all they can to help make your stay a happy and memorable one.

OPEN ALL YEAR. NO SMOKING. V, S.D., B/A. RESIDENT'S LOUNGE. PRIVATE PARKING. EN SUITE, TV & BEVERAGES IN BEDROOMS. B. & B. £16 - 21. SEASONAL W/E BREAKS AVAILABLE. ACCESS, VISA, MASTERCARD, EUROCARD.

Ⓝ *Tor Guest House*

20 TOR ST, WELLS, SOMERSET, BA5 21LS TEL: (01749) 672322

The Tor Guest House is a delightful 17th C. listed building which is a family-run establishment, set in attractive grounds bordering National Trust woodland, overlooking Wells Cathedral and the Bishop's Palace. There is a choice of several comfortable, centrally heated and tastefully furnished bedrooms - some of which are en suite - and all of which enjoy fine views, and your hostess, Letitia Horne, offers excellent wholefood and vegetarian breakfasts. It is just a 3 minute walk alongside the Palace moat to the town centre (there is a large car park at Tor Guest House so there are no worries about town parking and you are perfectly placed for touring Somerset; Bath and Bristol are each 30 minutes away by car.

OPEN JAN - DEC. NO SMOKING. VE, WH, S.D. CHILDREN B/A. EN SUITE 5 ROOMS. TV, RADIO & BEVERAGES ALL ROOMS. B. & B. FROM £18

WINSFORD (EXMOOR)

Ⓝ *Karslake House Hotel*

WINSFORD, MINEHEAD, SOMERSET, TA24 7JE TEL: (01643) 851242

Karslake House Hotel is a 500-year-old Grade II listed building which was originally a brewer's malt house and stands in a secluded garden in the very pretty village of Winsford (there is a charming thatched inn nearby). The building has been extensively renovated and, although many of the original features have been retained, the alterations have made of Karslake House a most comfortable hotel with all modern amenities. The imaginative menu features some unusual international - as well as more traditional English - dishes, and a typical evening meal selection would feature Quail's Egg in Paté followed by Steak and Kidney Pie (with fresh vegetables) and a tempting dessert, such as Raspberry and Almond Flan. Winsford is

situated right in the heart of Exmoor and horse-riding, birdwatching, walking and fishing
may all be enjoyed.
OPEN EASTER TO OCT. INC.   NO SMOKING.   V, S.D., B/A.   LICENSED.   CHILDREN WELCOME.   PETS B/A.
EN SUITE 4 ROOMS.   BEVERAGES & T.V. IN BEDROOMS.   B. & B. FROM £24.50.

RESTAURANTS

BRIDGWATER

THE HOOD ARMS, KILVE, BRIDGWATER, SOMERSET, TA5 7EA   TEL: (01278) 74210
N/S RESTAURANT.   V STD

CASTLE CARY

THE OLD BAKEHOUSE, HIGH ST, CASTLE CARY, BA9 7AW   TEL: (01963) 50067
NO SMOKING.   V EXC.   LICENSED.   DISABLED ACCESS.   CHILDREN WELCOME.

DULVERTON

ROCK HOUSE INN, JURY RD, DULVERTON, TA22 9DU   TEL: (01398) 23558
NO SMOKING .   V STD.   LICENSED.   DISABLED ACCESS.   CHILDREN WELCOME.

DUNSTER

THE TEA SHOPPE, DUNSTER, SOMERSET, TA24 6SF   TEL: (01643) 821304
NO SMOKING.   V. STD.   LICENSED.   CHILDREN WELCOME.

GLASTONBURY

RAINBOWS END CAFÉ 17 HIGH ST, GLASTONBURY, SOMERSET.   TEL: (01458) 33896
NO SMOKING.   V STD. VE, GLUTEN-FREE SOMETIMES ON MENU.   LICENSED.   CHILDREN WELCOME.

MONTACUTE

Mad Hatters Tea Shop
1 SOUTH ST, MONTACUTE, SOMERSET.   TEL: (01935) 823024
OPEN: TEA SHOP Easter - Sept. Weekdays & Sats. (ex. Tues) 10 -5; Sundays 2 - 6.

Milk House
THE BOROUGH, MONTACUTE, SOMERSET, TA15 6XB   TEL: (01935) 823823
See entry in accommodation section.

KING'S ARMS INN, MONTACUTE, SOMERSET, TA15 GUU   TEL: (01935) 822513
N/S REQUESTED AT LUNCH TIME WHEN FOOD IS SERVED.

TAUNTON

**PAVILION COFFEE SHOP, DEBENHAMS, 19-26 NORTH ST, TAUNTON, TA1 1LL TEL:
(0823) 272626**

Pavilion is a friendly self-service coffee shop serving poular light lunches, snacks and a
wide range of hot and cold drinks.
OPEN STORE HOURS.   NO SMOKING.   V STD.   DISABLED ACCESS.   CHILDREN WELCOME.   CREDIT CARDS.

THE FALCON HOTEL, HENLADE, TAUNTON, TA3 5DH   TEL: (01823) 442502
N/S RESTAURANT.   V.   LICENSED.   DISABLED ACCESS.   CHILDREN WELCOME.

WELLS

THE GOOD EARTH RESTAURANT, 4 PRIORY RD, WELLS, SOMERSET, BA5 1SY
TEL: (01749) 678600   NO SMOKING.   LICENSED.   DISABLED ACCESS.   CHILDREN WELCOME.

THE WORTH HOUSE HOTEL AND TYLERS RESTAURANT, WORTH, WELLS, BA5 1LW
TEL: (01749) 72041 N/S RESTAURANT. LICENSED.

PUBS & WINE BARS

MONTACUTE

KING'S ARMS INN, MONTACUTE, SOMERSET, TA15 GUU   TEL: (01935) 822513
N/S requested in bar area where food is served at lunchtime.   LICENSED.   CHILDREN WELCOME.   CREDIT CARDS.

Wiltshire

ACCOMMODATION

AVEBURY

Windmill House

WINTERBOURNE MONKTON, NR AVEBURY, WILTS., SN4 9NN   TEL: (01672) 539446

Beautifully renovated miller's house set amidst stunning scenery; 1m from Avebury stone circle; comfortably furnished; excellent cuisine with home-baked bread & home-grown veg. Well water.

OPEN ALL YEAR.   NO SMOKING.   V, S.D., B/A.   ORG, WH.   OVER 5s WELCOME.   B. & B. FROM £16.

BRADFORD ON AVON

Barton Farm

POUND LANE, BRADFORD-ON-AVON, WILTS, BA15 1LF   TEL: (01225) 865383

Beautiful Grade I Listed 14th C. farmhouse in a country park adjacent to the historic Tithe Barn (the second biggest in Britain) where Robin Hood was filmed in 1984. Two spacious guest rooms. Families very welcome. Vegetarian hostess.

OPEN ALL YEAR.   NO SMOKING.   V EXC. S.D. B/A.   CHILDREN WELCOME.   BEVERAGES & TV IN ROOMS. B. & B. FROM £17.50.

Bradford Old Windmill

4 MASONS LANE, BRADFORD ON AVON, WILTS, BA15 1QN   TEL: (01225) 866842

Standing high above the ancient wool town of Bradford-on-Avon, the stump of its former windmill, which was used commercially as such for just 11 years of its life, has now been beautifully restored by its current owners, Priscilla and Peter Roberts, who have reinstated the timber sail gallery, renovated the whole of the 4 storey Cotswold stone tower (and added a new 2 storey extension) and have charmingly decorated and furnished all the new rooms (which naturally enough come in all sorts of shapes and sizes) with lots of stripped pine and 'the flotsam and jetsam of beachcombing trips around the world'. A holiday destination of a highly unusual - yet thoroughly charming - variety. The food is as imaginatively prepared and eclectic in style as the building: menus vary from provincial French (Cruditées followed by Duck Egg Quiche and real Creme Caramel) to Indian Thali.

OPEN ALL YEAR.   NO SMOKING.   V STD. VE & S.D. B/A.   OVER 6S ONLY.   EN SUITE IN SOME ROOMS. BEVERAGES & TV BEDROOMS. B. & B. FROM £24.50.

EAST KNOYLE

MILTON HOUSE, EAST KNOYLE, SALISBURY, SP3 6BG   TEL: (01747) 830397
NO SMOKING.   V, S.D. B/A.   CHILDREN WELCOME.   PETS B/A.   PRIVATE BATHROOM, T.V. & BEVERAGES FACILITIES.   B. & B. FROM £22.

MALMESBURY

Southfields Cottage

MILBOURNE, MALMESBURY, WILTS, SN16 9JB   TEL: (01666) 823168

Friendly welcome in charming, comfortable 17th C. stone cottage on Wiltshire Cycleway. Pretty garden with country views.

Full central heating. Lovely town and river walks.

OPEN ALL YEAR.   NO SMOKING.   V B/A.   OVER 12S WELCOME.   PETS WELCOME.   BEVERAGES & TV IN ROOMS.   B. & B. FROM £16.50.

MARLBOROUGH

 Laurel Cottage

SOUTHEND, OGBOURNE ST GEORGE, MARLBORO', WILTS, SN8 1SG   TEL: (01672) 841288
Exquisite 16th C. thatched cottage with gardens; oak-beams, inglenook fireplace, etc.
OPEN MAR. - OCT.   NO SMOKING.   V STD., S.D. B/A.   CHILDREN WELCOME.   SOME ROOMS EN SUITE.
BEVERAGES & T.V. IN ALL ROOMS.   B. & B. FROM £16.

 Silbury Hill Cottage

WEST KENNETT, MARLBOROUGH, WILTS, SN8 1QH   TEL: (01672) 539416
Charming thatched cottage located next to Silbury Hill and the West Kennett Long Barrow,
offering relaxed and friendly hospitality.
OPEN ALL YEAR.   NO SMOKING.   S.D.   CHILDREN WELCOME.   B. & B. £18 Sgle., £30 Dble.

 'WESTERLY', MILDENHALL, MARLBOROUGH, SN8 2LR   TEL: (01672) 514254
NO SMOKING.   V, S.D. B/A.   CHILDREN: OVER 8S.

MELKSHAM

 'Josel'

117 SEMINGTON RD, MELKSHAM, WILTS, SN12 6DP   TEL: (01225) 709490
Small, modern, detached private house conveniently situated near the M4 between Melk-
sham and Trowbridge. A very friendly welcome. Close to tourist attractions: the stone
circles at Avebury & Stonehenge, the National Trust village, Lacock, Bath & Salisbury.
OPEN ALL YEAR.   NO SMOKING.   LOW-CAL. & LOW-FAT STD. V, S.D. B/A.   CHILDREN WELCOME.   BEVER-
AGES & T.V. IN ALL ROOMS.   B. & B. FROM £12-£13.

SALISBURY

The Coach and Horses

WINCHESTER ST, SALISBURY, WILTSHIRE, SP1 1HG   TEL: (01722) 336254 FAX: (01722) 414319

 The Coach and Horses is Salisbury's oldest Inn and there are records showing it to be trading as early as 1482! Some five centuries later Martin and Angie Cooper, its present owners, completely renovated the building - gutting the bar, restaurant and kitchen - till now, beautifully refurbished (and still retaining some period features, such as timbered walls), the Coach and Horses has become one of the city's most popular eating and drinking establishments and has a well-deserved reputation for food and wine. Its menu is based around the inn's history as being one of the staging posts on the old A30 London to Pen-
zance route: appetiser, main course, fish course and dessert are each named after other staging posts (Bagshot...Andover...Exeter, etc.) until the Penzance section entitles you, appropriately enough, at the end of your meal to enjoy a 'Smugglers'(coffee with liqueur). OPEN ALL YEAR.   N/S RESTAURANT & BEDRS.   V STD, S.D. B/A.   LICENSED.   CHILDREN WELCOME.   EN SUITE, TV & BEVERAGES IN ROOMS.   CREDIT CARDS.   B. & B. FROM £49.50 PER DOUBLE ROOM.

The Gallery

36 WYNDHAM RD, SALISBURY, WILTS, SP1 3AB   TEL: (01722) 324586
The Gallery is a small family-run bed and breakfast situated just 10 minutes'walk from the
city centre and its cathedral, museums, leisure centre and swimming pool. Your hosts,
David and Rina Musselwhite aim to give real 'home from home'service and do everything
they can to make your stay a happy and memorable one. Each of the bedrooms has private
facilities and after a comfortable night's sleep you can look forward to a delicious home-
cooked breakfast with lots of choices including smoked mackerel and creamed mushrooms
as alternatives to the usual English breakfast platter; fruit and herb teas are also available
as well as the usual beverages. Salisbury has so much to commend it as a destination in
itself: the city and cathedral draw visitors from all over the world; you are also ideally
placed for visiting Avebury and Stonehenge stone circles.
OPEN ALL YEAR.   NO SMOKING.   V, S.D., B/A.   OVER 12S ONLY.   EN SUITE, TV & BEVERAGES IN BEDROOMS.   B.
& B. FROM £14

GLEN LYN GUEST HOUSE, 6 BELLAMY LN, MILFORD HILL, SP1 2SP TEL: (01722) 327880
NO SMOKING.   OVER 12S ONLY.   SOME EN SUITE ROOMS.   BEVERAGES & T.V.   B. & B. FROM £21

THE NEW INN, 41-43 NEW ST, SALISBURY, SP1 2PH TEL: (01722) 327679
NO SMOKING.   V STD.   LICENSED.   DISABLED ACCESS.   CHILDREN WELCOME.   EN SUITE, BEVERAGES & T.V. IN ALL ROOMS.   CREDIT CARDS.   B. & B. FROM £39-£55.

SCOTLAND LODGE, WINTERBOURNE STOKE, SP3 4TF TEL: (01980) 620943
NO SMOKING.   V STD.   CHILDREN WELCOME.   EN SUITE, BEVERAGES & T.V.   B. & B. FROM £17.50-£25.

Stratford Lodge

4 PARK LANE CASTLE RD, WILTSHIRE, SP1 3NP   TEL: (01722) 325177   FAX: (01722) 412699

Stratford Lodge is an elegant Victorian house which stands in a quiet lane overlooking Victoria Park. Your host, Jill Bayly, offers a special brand of gracious hospitality: the complementary sherry before dinner speaks volumes - and is a welcome herald to a first-rate meal prepared by Jill from fresh ingredients, some organically home-grown. It is always advisable to book for dinner lest you miss such delights as Baked Roquefort Pears followed by Salmon Steak with Herb Butter and a selection of home-made desserts, all served by candlelight on beautiful china. Each of the bedrooms has en suite facilities and has been decorated and furnished with flair - one room has a brass Victorian bed; the house has been furnished throughout with antiques and there is a lovely garden with flowering shrubs. Salisbury is a beautiful city - not the less appealing because of its proximity to so much unspoilt countryside and historically interesting towns and villages.
OPEN 2 JAN - 23 DEC.   NO SMOKING.   V STD, VE, S.D. B/A.   LICENSED.   OVER 8S WELCOME.   EN SUITE, TV & BEVERAGES IN BEDROOMS.   CREDIT CARDS.

YEW TREE COTTAGE, GROVE LN, REDLYNCH, SALISBURY TEL: (01725) 511730
NO SMOKING.   V, VE STD, S.D. B/A.   CHILDREN WELCOME.   TEA/COFFEE ON REQUEST. T.V. IN LOUNGE.

TROWBRIDGE

Ashton Hill Farm

83 YARNBROOK RD, WEST ASHTON, TROWBRIDGE, WILTS, BA14 6AR   TEL: (01225) 760359
A working farm on the banks of the River Biss. Central for touring historic Wiltshire and nearby Bath. Relaxed family atmosphere.
OPEN ALL YEAR (ex. Xmas)   NO SMOKING.   S.D. B/A.   CHILDREN WELCOME.   1 FAMILY/TWIN/DOUBLE EN SUITE.   BEVERAGES IN BEDROOMS.   B. & B. FROM £16.50.

WARMINSTER

Belmont B. & B.

9 BOREHAM RD, WARMINSTER, WILTS, BA12 9JP   TEL: (01985) 212799
Built in 1870, the Belmont B. & B. is a large, Victorian town house which has spacious bedrooms all with their own sinks, and a very friendly atmosphere.
OPEN ALL YEAR.   NO SMOKING.   S.D. on request.   CHILDREN WELCOME.   BEVERAGES & TV IN ROOMS.   B. & B. FROM £15

ZEALS

CORNERWAYS COTTAGE, LONGCROSS, ZEALS, BA12 6LL TEL: (01747) 840477
NO SMOKING.   V, S.D. B/A.   CHILDREN WELCOME.   PETS (SMALL DOGS) B/A.   EN SUITE IN 2 ROOMS. BEVERAGES.   T.V. IN LOUNGE.   B. & B. FROM £14 - 16.

STAG COTTAGE, FANTLEY LANE, ZEALS, BA12 6NA TEL: (01747) 840458
NO SMOKING.   V, S.D. B/A.   CHILDREN WELCOME - BABY SITTING AVAIL. BEVERAGES IN ROOMS.

RESTAURANTS

AVEBURY

STONES RESTAURANT, AVEBURY, MARLBOROUGH, SN8 1RE   TEL: (016723) 514
70% N/S.   V EXC.   LICENSED.   DISABLED ACCESS: GOOD.   CHILDREN WELCOME.

BRADFORD ON AVON

THE BRIDGE TEA ROOMS, 24A BRIDGE ST, BRADFORD ON AVON. TEL: (012216) 5537
NO SMOKING.   V AVAIL.   WHEELCHAIR ACCESS.

SALISBURY

HOB NOB COFFEE SHOP, THE KING'S HOUSE, 65 THE CLOSE, SALISBURY
NO SMOKING.   V.   DISABLED ACCESS.   CHILDREN WELCOME.

SWINDON

OASIS LEISURE CENTRE, NORTH STAR AVE, SWINDON, SN2 1EP TEL: (01793) 533404/5
NO SMOKING.   DISABLED ACCESS.   CHILDREN WELCOME.

WARMINSTER

JENNERS, 45 MARKET PLACE, WARMINSTER, BA12 9AZ   TEL: (01985) 213385
NO SMOKING.   LICENSED.   DISABLED: '1 SMALL STEP - DOUBLE DOORS & WIDE TOILET DOORS.'

PUBS & WINE BARS

SALISBURY

THE NEW INN AT SALISBURY, 41-43 NEW ST, SALISBURY, SP1 2PH TEL: (01722) 327679
For further details please see the entry in the accommodation section.

The South of England

Hampshire

ACCOMMODATION

ALTON

8 GOSLINGS CROFT, SELBOURNE, NR ALTON, GU34 3HZ   TEL: (01420) 50285
NO SMOKING.   V B/A.   CHILDREN WELCOME (FACILITIES FOR BABIES).   1 EN SUITE. TV & BEVERAGES
IN BEDROOMS.   CREDIT CARDS.   B. & B. FROM £14.75, SINGLE £19.50.

ANDOVER

ABBOTTS LAW, ABBOTTS ANN, ANDOVER, SP11 7DW   TEL: (01264) 710350
NO SMOKING.   V, S.D. B/A.   OVER 10S.   EN SUITE, BEVERAGES & T.V. IN ROOMS.   B. & B. FROM £21.

The Old Barn
AMPORT, ANDOVER, HANTS, SP11 8AE   TEL & FAX: (01264) 710410
Converted old barn in small village approx. 3m S.W. of Andover. Secluded but nr. A303.
OPEN ALL YEAR.   NO SMOKING.   S.D. B/A.   OVER 10S WELCOME.   EN SUITE, TV & BEVERAGES IN ROOMS.
B. & B. £15.50. Sgle £20.

BASINGSTOKE

Oaklea Guest House

LONDON RD, HOOK, NR BASINGSTOKE, HANTSM RG27 9LA   TEL: (01256) 762673
Fine Victorian house in an acre of walled gardens 1m from junction 5 of the M3. Beautifully
furnished throughout offering first-class accommodation. Breakfast is a hearty feast.
OPEN ALL YEAR.   N/S DINING R & SOME BEDRS.   V, S.D. B/A.   LICENSED.   CHILDREN WELCOME.   EN
SUITE, BEVERAGES & TV IN SOME ROOMS.   T.V. LOUNGE.   B. & B. FROM £19.

BEAULIEU

Coolderry Cottage

MASSEYS LANE, EAST BOLDRE, BEAULIEU, HANTS, SO42 7WE   TEL: (01590) 612428
Small, recently extended cottage in a quiet lane on the edge of East Boldre. Accommodation
is in comfortable rooms each overlooking fields at the back of the cottage. Traditional or
Continental breakfasts are served in a charming dining room.
OPEN ALL YEAR Ex. Xmas.   NO SMOKING.   V B/A.   CHILDREN WELCOME.   WELL-BEHAVED DOGS ACCEPTED.
BEVERAGES IN ROOMS.   T.V. AVAILABLE.   B. & B. £14-16.

BURLEY (NEW FOREST)

The Vicarage

MRS CLARKSON, CHURCH LN, BURLEY, HANTS, BH24 4AP   TEL: (01425) 402303 FAX: (01425)
403753
The Vicarage is a peaceful house set in its own well-kept grounds just three minutes'
pleasant walk from the centre of the village of Burley. It is a comfortable family home set
in the heart of the New Forest - in fact the forest ponies graze right up to the front gate!
Although the village is surrounded by the New Forest countryside, Burley has a range of
amenities, including a 9-hole golf course, pony-riding, Wagonette rides and a good
selection of shops. In addition to the charms of its location, The Vicarage is easily accessible
from the A31 or A35 and is within easy reach of the sea, the cathedrals of Salisbury and
Winchester, and the houses at Broadlands and Beaulieu.
OPEN ALL YEAR.   NO SMOKING.   V B'fast B/A.   CHILDREN WELCOME.   DOGS B/A.   TV & BEVERAGES IN
ALL BEDROOMS.   B. & B. FROM £15.

FOREST TEA HOUSE & B. & B., POUND LN, BURLEY, HANTS, BH24 4ED
OPEN ALL YEAR.   NO SMOKING IN HOUSE & RESTAURANT.   DISABLED ACCESS TO TEAROOM. CHILD-
REN IN TEAROOM (NOT B. & B.).   EN SUITE, TEA/COFFEE-MAKING, COLOUR T.V. IN ALL BEDROOMS.

CHANDLERS FORD

St Lucia

68 SHAFTESBURY AVE, CHANDLERS FORD, EASTLEIGH, HANTS, SO5 3BP   TEL: (01703) 262995
1920's detached home in a third of an acre of mature and well-maintained gardens in a
quiet residential area of Chandlers Ford. Comfortable, centrally heated bedrooms. Traditional or Continental breakfast option is served to guests. Home-made evening meals.
OPEN ALL YEAR.   NO SMOKING.   V, S.D. B/A.   CHILDREN: OVER 10S ONLY.   H & C, BEVERAGES & T.V. IN
ALL BEDROOMS.   PARKING FOR 5.   B. & B. FROM £14.

FORDINGBRIDGE

HILLBURY, 2 FIR TREE HILL, ALDERHOLT, FORDINGBRIDGE, HANTS, SP6 3AY
TEL: (01425) 652582   NO SMOKING.   V, S.D. B/A.   CHILDREN WELCOME.   1 ROOM EN SUITE.   TV &
BEVERAGES IN BEDROOMS.   B. & B. FROM £17. (CHILDREN *OVER 3 YRS* ½ *PRICE*)

HAVANT

High Towers

14 PORTSDOWN HILL RD, BEDHAMPTON, HAVANT, HANTS.   TEL: (01705) 471748
Large detached residence located on Portsdown Hill with magnificent views overlooking
Portsmouth, the sea and surrounding countryside. Close to ferries.
OPEN ALL YEAR.   NO SMOKING.   OVER 5s WELCOME.   EN SUITE, TV & BEVERAGES IN ROOMS.   B. & B. FROM
£18, £34 Double.

KILMESTON

Dean Farm

KILMESTON, NR ALRESFORD, HANTS, SO24 0NL   TEL: (01962) 771 286
*ETB Listed.*Welcoming 18th C. farmhouse in the picturesque village of Kilmeston forms part of a working mixed farm on the edge of the Hampshire Downs. Comfortable accommodation in rooms with lovely views; the large sitting room and dining room have log fires.
OPEN JAN. TO DEC.   NO SMOKING.   V STD. DIAB & LOW-FAT B/A.   OVER 5S WELCOME.   TEA/COFFEE ON REQUEST AT ANY TIME.   T.V. IN SITTING ROOM.   B. & B. FROM £15.

LYMINGTON

CANDLEFORD HOUSE, MIDDLE RD, TIPTOE, LYMINGTON.   TEL: (01590) 682069
NO SMOKING.   TV & BEVERAGES IN ROOMS.   B. & B. FROM £16.

REDWING FARM, PITMORE LN, SWAY, LYMINGTON, SO41 6BW   TEL: (01590) 683319
NO SMOKING.   V. STD.   2 BEDROOMS GROUND FLOOR.   B. & B. FROM £20

WHEATSHEAF HOUSE, GOSPORT ST, LYMINGTON, SO41 9BG   TEL: (01590) 679208
NO SMOKING.   CHILDREN WELCOME.   PETS B/A.   EN SUITE IN SOME ROOMS. T.V. IN SITTING ROOM. B. & B. FROM £18.

LYNDHURST, NEW FOREST

Little Hayes

ROMSEY RD, LYNDHURST, NEW FOREST, HANTS, SO43 7AR   TEL: (01703) 283000
Lovely, late-Victorian house standing in Lyndhurst village in the New Forest. Recently restored, it has been comfortably furnished and appointed with elegance and style. Breakfast is sumptuous, with many traditional and continental choices.
OPEN SPRING - AUTUMN INC.   NO SMOKING.   V, S.D. B/A.   OVER 5S ONLY.   1 PRIVATE BATHROOM. TV & BEVERAGES IN BEDROOMS.   B. & B. FROM £16.

NEW MILTON

St Ursula

30 HOBART RD, NEW MILTON, HANTS, BH25 6EG   TEL: (01425) 6135115
Large family home offering a high standard of accomodation and care. Pretty ground floor suite designed for disabled guests. Pick-up from station. 5 mins walk to town & restaurants.
OPEN ALL YEAR.   N/S ex. Garden Room.   S.D. B/A.   CHILDREN & PETS WELCOME.   WHEELCHAIR ACCESS.   EN SUITE, TV & BEVERAGES IN ROOMS.   B. & B. £16 - 20.

PETERSFIELD

Mizzards Farm

ROGATE, PETERSFIELD, HANTS, GU31 5HS   TEL: (01730) 821656
Lovely 17th C. farmhouse in peaceful setting & 13 acre gardens & fields; swimming pool.
OPEN ALL YEAR Ex. Xmas.   NO SMOKING.   V B/A.   LICENSED.   OVER 6S ONLY.   EN SUITE, TV & BEVERAGES IN ROOMS.   B. & B. FROM £22.

Trotton Farm

ROGATE, PETERSFIELD, HANTS, GU31 5EN   TEL: (01730) 813618
Lovely farmhouse situated in area of outstanding natural beauty with many attractions within 1 hr's drive; walks & fishing may be enjoyed within the environs of the farm.
OPEN ALL YEAR.   NO SMOKING.   V STD.   CHILDREN WELCOME.   EN SUITE & BEVERAGES IN ROOMS.   T.V. IN SITTING/GAMES ROOM.

PORTSMOUTH

HOLIDAY INN, NORTH HARBOUR, PORTSMOUTH, HANTS, PO6 4SH   TEL: (01705) 383151
N/S 40% DINING R & SOME BEDRS.   V, S.D. B/A.   LICENSED.   DISABLED ACCESS. CHILDREN & PETS WELCOME.   EN SUITE, TV & BEVERAGES IN ROOMS.

RINGWOOD

MOORTOWN LODGE, 244 CHRISTCHURCH RD, RINGWOOD, BH24 3AS TEL: (01425) 471404
N/S DINING R.   V, S.D. B/A.   LICENSED.   CHILDREN WELCOME.   EN SUITE IN DOUBLE/TWIN ROOMS.
BEVERAGES & T.V. ALL ROOMS.   CREDIT CARDS.   B. & B. FROM £26.

ROMSEY

Spursholt House

SALISBURY RD, ROMSEY, HANTS, SO51 6DJ   TEL: (01794) 512229   FAX: (01794) 523142

Spursholt House was originally built for one of Crom-
wells' generals; it later came into the hands of the
Palmerston family who lived at Broadlands and, in
the 1830s, was extended for occupation by Lord and
Lady Cowper. The result of these additions is the
charming country house you see today; surrounded
by a magnificent garden in which paved terraces with
urns of geraniums overlook a lawn, impressive topi-
ary and a view of Romsey Abbey, and beyond the
flowerbeds. Yew hedges enclose a succession of further pleasures - one garden leading into another, a
parterre followed by apple trees, a lily pool and a
dovecote with fan tails! The interior of the house has been furnished in keeping with its
character: one bedroom is oak-panelled and all contain antiques, extra large beds, elegant
sofas and have garden views. Downstairs the dining room has been handsomely furnished
in Victorian style, and there is a spectacular sitting room with a Knole sofa, a love seat and
carved fireplace.Breakfast and light suppers (advance order for the latter, please!) are the
only meals to be served at Spursholt House but there are a number of good local inns.
OPEN ALL YEAR.   NO SMOKING.   V, S.D. B/A.   CHILDREN & PETS WELCOME.   EN SUITE 1 ROOM. BEVER-
AGES IN BEDROOMS.   TV IN LOUNGE.   B. & B. £17.

SOUTHAMPTON

Novotel

1 WEST QUAY RD, SOUTHAMPTON, HANTS, SO1 0RA TEL: (01703) 330550   FAX: (01703) 222158
Modern well-equipped hotel with swimming pool & leisure facilities. Close to town centre.
OPEN ALL YEAR.   N/S PART DINING R., COFFEE LOUNGE & 2 FLOORS OF BEDRS.   S.D. STD.   CHILDREN & PETS
LICENSED.   EN SUITE, TV & BEVERAGES IN ROOMS.   WHEELCHAIR ACCESS.   B. & B. FROM £35.

RoadChef Rownhams Motorway Service Area

M27 SOUTH & NORTHBOUND   TEL: (01703) 734480

Tourists and business travellers heading for the Southern
ferries or the New Forest will find RoadChef Rownhams
near Southampton an ideal stop. Each of the 39 bedrooms in its Lodge have been comfortably furnished and
well-appointed with a trouser press, hairdryer and tea
and coffee making facilities. The self-service Orchards
restaurants have excellent smoke-free areas (200 of 350
seats are smoke-free), and serve a wide selection of
popular meals such as Golden Scampi Platter or Horse-
shoe Gammon Steak, served with chips and peas; there
is always a vegetarian option on the menu and baby
foods are also available (there is a changing room). Rownhams won the coveted Best Cup
of Tea Award for 1991: the only service area in the country to win it twice.
OPEN ALL YEAR ex. Xmas Day.   N/S MOST OF RESTAURANT & SOME BEDRS.   V STD.   DISABLED FACILITIES.
CHILDREN WELCOME.   EN SUITE, BEVERAGES & T.V. PLUS SKY IN ROOMS.   CREDIT CARDS. B. & B. FROM £32.

SOUTH WARNBOROUGH

Street Farmhouse

ALTON RD, SOUTH WARNBOROUGH, HANTS, RG25 1RS   TEL: (01256) 862225
Street Farmhouse dates from Jacobean times; listed building with beamed ceilings, large
inglenook fireplace and vaulted kitchen ceiling. Comfortable centrally heated bedrooms
and outdoor heated swimming pool; easy access to Guildford and London.
OPEN ALL YEAR.   N/S DINING R & BEDRS.   V B/A.   CHILDREN WELCOME.   PETS B/A.   EN SUITE IN 2 ROOMS.
TV & BEVERAGES IN BEDROOMS.   AMEX.   B. & B. £30 (PER TWIN ROOM).

SUTTON SCOTNEY

'Dever View'

17 UPPER BULLINGTON, SUTTON SCOTNEY, HANTS, SO21 3RB   TEL: (01962) 760566
OPEN ALL YEAR.   NO SMOKING.   V, DIAB. B/A.   CHILDREN WELCOME.   PETS B/A.   BEVERAGES IN ROOMS.
T.V. LOUNGE.   B. & B. FROM £15-18.

SWAY (NEW FOREST)

ARNEWOOD CORNER, LINNIES LN, SWAY, HANTS, SO41 6ES   TEL: (01590) 683690
NO SMOKING.   CHILDREN WELCOME.   T.V. IN ALL BEDROOMS.   B. & B. FROM £18.

The Nurse's Cottage

STATION RD, SWAY, LYMINGTON, HANTS. SO41 6BA TEL & FAX: (01590) 683402
ETB 2 Crown Commended. AA QQQQQ Premier Selected. Advance booking is advised at this charming cottage, formerly home to the District Nurse, with every possible comfort in the cosy en suite bedrooms. Visitors from around the world have praised the menu (specialities include Scottish Salmon in Cointreau; Bananas Flambées) and extensive wine list (an amazing selection of over 60 wines). Half-board packages recommended.
OPEN ALL YEAR.   NO SMOKING.   V, S.D. STD.   OVER 5s & PETS WELCOME.   LICENSED.   EN SUITE, TV & BEVERAGES
IN ROOMS.   MASTERCARD, VISA, ACCESS.   B. & B. FROM £22.50 (1995), £25 (1996); D. £12.50 (1995), £15 (1996).

WINCHESTER

Brambles

NORTHBROOK AVENUE, WINCHESTER, HANTS, SO23 8JW   TEL: (01962) 856387
OPEN ALL YEAR.   NO SMOKING.   V B/A. CHILDREN WELCOME.   B. & B. FROM £18.

The Wykeham Arms

75 KINGSGATE ST, WINCHESTER, HANTS, SO23 9PE   TEL: (01962) 853834 FAX: (01692) 854411

Town Pub of the Year. Tucked away in the back streets of the oldest part of the city, the 250-year old Wykeham Arms is one of the more established institutions in Winchester. Anthony Trollope considered it a very "third-rate hostelry", but the subsequent 150 years have seen more improvements than he would have been able to imagine, and present day travellers can look forward to a night's comfortable repose in beautifully furnished bedrooms which have been luxuriously appointed in a manner which does not detract from their character. Observance of this priority prevails throughout the Wykeham Arms: log fires and candle light all add to the sense of history and the efficient service is likewise redolent of a different age. It is the food, however, of which the proprietors are, perhaps the most proud - and with justification: the wine list alone has earned them the accolade of "Wine Pub of the Year 1991" (all items are available by the glass, incidentally); the food, prepared entirely from fresh, local produce, is outstanding, and the daily changing menu has earned them another award: Pub Caterer of the Year.
OPEN ALL YEAR.   N/S IN 3 OF 4 Eating Areas & B'fast Room.   V STD.   LICENSED.   DISABLED ACCESS.   OVER 14s
PETS WELCOME.   EN SUITE , TV & BEVERAGES IN ROOMS.   VISA, AMEX, MC.   B. & B. FROM £37.50, Sgle £65.

RESTAURANTS

ALRESFORD

THE OLD SCHOOL HOUSE RESTAURANT, 60 WEST STREET, ALRESFORD, SO24 9AU
TEL: (01962) 732134   NO SMOKING.   V, S.D.   LICENSED.

CHAWTON

Cassandra's Cup

THE HOLLIES, CHAWTON, NR ALTON, HANTS, GU34 1SB   TEL: (01420) 83144
Charming restaurant opposite Jane Austen's house at Chawton; cosy atmosphere. Morning coffee, light lunches. Home-made scones, cakes & gateaux. Afternoon cream teas.
L. AROUND £3.   NO SMOKING.   V STD.   LICENSED.   CHILDREN WELCOME.

HAVANT

NUTMEG RESTAURANT, OLD TOWN HALL, EAST ST, HAVANT TEL: (01705) 472700
NO SMOKING.   V EXC.   LICENSED.   DISABLED ACCESS.   CHILDREN.

SOUTHAMPTON

Springles Restaurant

DEBENHAMS, QUEENS BUILDINGS, QUEENSWAY, SO9 7BJ   TEL: (01703) 223888
Self-service Restaurant serving snacks, hot lunches & a wide range of hot and cold drinks.
OPEN STORE HOURS.   NO SMOKING.   V.   DISABLED ACCESS.   CHILDREN WELCOME.   CREDIT CARDS.

The Town House Restaurant

59 OXFORD STREET, SOUTHAMPTON, HANTS, SO1 1DL   TEL: (01703) 220498
OPEN ALL YEAR.   NO SMOKING.   LICENSED.   DISABLED ACCESS.   CREDIT CARDS.

SOUTHSEA

Springles Restaurant

DEBENHAMS, 44-66 PALMERSTON RD, PO5 3QG TEL: (01705) 822401
Friendly self-service restaurant serving snacks, hot lunches & hot and cold drinks.
OPEN STORE HOURS.   N/S.   V STD.   DISABLED ACCESS.   CHILDREN WELCOME. CREDIT CARDS.

WINCHESTER

Pavilion Coffee Shop

C & H FABRICS, 8 HIGH ST, WINCHESTER, S23 9LA   TEL: (01962) 841696
Friendly self-service coffee shop serving snacks, lunches & a range of hot & cold drinks.
OPEN STORE HOURS.   N/S.   V STD.   DISABLED ACCESS.   CHILDREN WELCOME.   CREDIT CARDS.

PUBS & WINE BARS

ROMSEY

STAR INN, EAST TYTHERLEY, NR ROMSEY, SO51 0LW TEL: (01794) 40225
Attractive pub serving very good food.
N/S DINING R & 1 BAR.   V STD.   LICENSED.   DISABLED ACCESS.   CHILDREN WELCOME.

WINCHESTER

THE WYKEHAM ARMS, 75 KINGSGATE STREET, SO23 9PE TEL: (01962) 853834
N/S IN 'BISHOPS BAR' AND 'WATCHMAKERS' DINING AREA.

Isle of Wight

ACCOMMODATION

COWES

14 MILTON RD, COWES, I.O.W., PO31 7PX   TEL: (01983) 295723
NO SMOKING.   V, VE, DIAB B/A.   OVER 6S ONLY.   EN SUITE IN 1 TWIN ROOM. BEVERAGES.   T.V.
AVAILABLE IN ROOMS.   B. & B. FROM £15. ETB LISTED.

FRESHWATER

BROOKSIDE FORGE, BROOKSIDE RD, FRESHWATER, PO40 9ER TEL: (01983) 754644
N/S DINING R & BEDRS.   V, VE, DIAB, STD.   LICENSED.   CHILDREN WELCOME. MOST ROOM EN SUITE.
BEVERAGES.   T.V.   ACCESS, VISA.   B. & B. FROM £20.

RYDE

HOLMSDALE GUEST HOUSE, 13 DOVER ST, RYDE, PO33 2AQ   TEL: (01983) 614805
N/S DINING R & PUBLIC AREAS.   V B/A.   OVER 3S ONLY.   PETS B/A.   EN SUITE IN ALL ROOMS.   B. & B.
FROM £16.

Hotel Ryde Castle

THE ESPLANADE, RYDE, I.O.W., PO33 1JA   TEL: (01983) 63755 FAX: (01983) 68925

This imposing building is a magnificent, creeper-clad castle with unparalleled views of the Solent and Straight; this is where the Marie Rose, Henry VIII's flagship, was raised, and the castle was built on the orders of the king to defend the island and its surrounding waters from invasion. With such perils happily past, Ryde Castle's more peaceably-motivated guests may now enjoy magnificent views of the Solent from this beautiful hotel which, under the direction of its proprietors, has recently undergone careful restoration and retains many beautiful period features (open fires, moulded ceilings) while offering every modern facility to guests. Food is first-rate: freshly caught fish features highly on the menu and all dishes have been home-cooked from fresh island ingredients; a typical evening meal would feature Avocado Vinaigrette followed by Golden Apricot Chicken (breast of chicken poached in Rose Wine with Apricot and Cointreau), and a truly delectable dessert such as Chocolate Roulade.

OPEN ALL YEAR.   N/S PART DINING R, SOME BEDRS, & BAR AREAS.   V STD.   VE, DIAB, LOW-FAT, S.D. B/A. LICENSED.   CHILDREN WELCOME.   PETS B/A.   EN SUITE, T . & BEVERAGES IN ALL ROOMS.   ACCESS, VISA, AMEX, DINERS.   B. & B. FROM £39.50.

SEAVIEW

Seaview Hotel and Restaurant

HIGH ST, SEAVIEW, ISLE OF WIGHT, PO34 5EX   TEL: (01983) 612711

Exquisite hotel in the small Victorian seaside resort of Seaview; beautifully furnished with antiques and designer fabrics; excellent cuisine prepared from fresh local produce.

OPEN ALL YEAR.   SMOKING IN DINING R. ONLY AT OTHER GUEST'S DISCRETION.   V, S.D. B/A.   LICENSED. CHILDREN WELCOME.   EN SUITE & T.V.   CREDIT CARDS.   B. & B. FROM £30, Sgle £40, Mid-week breaks £46.

SHANKLIN

 EDGECLIFFE HOTEL, CLARENCE GDNS, SHANKLIN, PO37 6HA TEL: (01983) 866199 NO SMOKING.   V, S.D. B/A.   LICENSED.   CHILDREN: OVER 3S ONLY. MANY ROOMS PRIVATE BATH. BEVERAGES & T.V. IN ALL ROOMS.   CREDIT CARDS.   B. & B. FROM £17.

St Boniface Hotel

6 ST BONIFACE RD, VENTNOR, I.O.W.   TEL: (01983) 853109

ETB 3 Crowns. Small, friendly hotel backing onto downs & overlooking sea 150 yds away.

OPEN Mar.- Nov.   NO SMOKING.   S.D. B/A.   SORRY, NO CHILDREN OR PETS.   EN SUITE & BEVERAGES IN ROOMS. TV LOUNGE.   B. & B., £18.50, D. £6.50.

TOTLAND

Sandford Lodge Hotel

THE AVENUE, TOTLAND, ISLE OF WIGHT.   TEL: (01983) 753478

Situated within easy walking distance of beaches, walks and and shops, this fine Edwardian house is a small, family-run hotel which has been very comfortably furnished and appointed. Accommodation is in pretty, spacious, en suite bedrooms and there is also a coffee lounge and library for guests use; on sunny days you may enjoy relaxing in the lawned garden. Your hosts, Mr and Mrs Malt, are a most hospitable couple who enjoy welcoming guests to their home: they will gladly help you to plan your stay and make arrangements for golf, tennis, horse-riding, coach tours, or any other holiday activity you choose, in addition to collecting you from Yarmouth ferry terminal.

OPEN MAR. - OCT.   NO SMOKING.   S.D. B/A.   CHILDREN WELCOME.   EN SUITE & BEVERAGES IN ROOMS. TV ON REQUEST.   B. & B. FROM £15, D. £10.50

VENTNOR

Hotel Picardie

ESPLANADE, VENTNOR, ISLE OF WIGHT, PO38 1JX   TEL: (01983) 852647

Hotel Picardie is an attractive villa-type hotel situated on the Esplanade just across the road from the sandy beach at Ventnor. The bedrooms have all been very tastefully furnished and comfortably appointed, and some family rooms are available with bunk beds for children and cots for babies (one room can accommodate up to three youngsters); there is a stair-lift for those who find stairs a difficulty. The food is excellent: the generous breakfast - with its varied options - should keep you going till mid-afternoon, and the home-cooked evening meal, prepared wherever possible from fresh ingredients, features both imaginative and traditional dishes such as Mushrooms in Garlic Butter, followed by Honey-Orange Lamb Chops and a tempting dessert, such as Blackberry and Apple Meringue; the vegetarian options are imaginative and tasty. Ventnor is a resort of character and charm: situated on the south coast it has a sunny, warm climate, as is testified to by the sub-tropical plants which flourish in almost every garden.

OPEN MAR. - OCT.   NO SMOKING ex. bar area.   V, S.D. B/A.   LICENSED.   CHILDREN WELCOME.   EN SUITE, TV & BEVERAGES IN ROOMS.   CREDIT CARDS.   B. & B. FROM £17.25. B., B. & D. £25.

WOOTTON BRIDGE

Bridge House

KITE HILL, WOOTTON BRIDGE, ISLE OF WIGHT, PO33 4LA   TEL: (01983) 884163

Bridge House is a listed Georgian residence of tremendous character standing in a beautiful garden on the water's edge at Wootton Bridge. It was not always so appealing: when its present owners first took it under their wing it was in a very sorry state of repair and it took a whole year of very careful and sympathetic restoration to transform it into the elegant and comfortable house you see today. Breakfast is the only meal to be served at Bridge House - but what a treat it is! All preserves are home-made from fruit culled from garden bushes or trees (grape and apple jam is a house speciality), and the toast, butter and coffee are served 'as long as guests want them'! There is much to see and do in the area immediately around Bridge House: Wootton Creek feeds into the Solent (there is a slipway adjacent to the property) and there is an abundance of forest walks in nearby Firestone Copse. There are lots of good local eating places for those seeking an evening meal, and 3 very good pubs are just a short walk away.

OPEN ALL YEAR.   NO SMOKING.   V, DIAB, S.D., (NOT VE) B/A. ORG WHEN AVAIL. WH B/A.   CHILDREN B/A. BEVERAGES IN ROOMS.   T.V. ON REQUEST.   B. & B. FROM £15.

West Sussex

ACCOMMODATION

ARUNDEL

Burpham Country Hotel and Restaurant

BURPHAM, ARUNDEL, W. SUSSEX, BN18 9RJ   TEL: (01903) 882160

Charming country house with mature garden & views over the South Downs. *ETB 3 Crowns. AA***

OPEN ALL YEAR.   N/S DINING R.   V, S.D. B/A.   LICENSED.   EN SUITE, TV & BEVERAGES IN ROOMS. CREDIT CARDS.   B. & B. FROM £29.

BOGNOR REGIS

Merryvale

WESSEX AVENUE, BOGNOR REGIS, W. SUSSEX, PO21 2QW   TEL: (01243) 864896
OPEN ALL YEAR ex. Xmas.   NO SMOKING.   V, S.D. B/A.   CHILDREN WELCOME.
GROUND FLOOR BEDROOMS.   EN SUITE, TV & BEVERAGES IN ROOMS.   B. & B. FROM £17.

CHICHESTER

Chichester Lodge,

OAKWOOD, CHICHESTER, W. SUSSEX, PO18 9AL   TEL: (01243) 786560

 Built in 1840, Chichester Lodge is a delightful Gothic style gate cottage to a large manor house; it stands in and acre and a half of rambling old world gardens, the whole surrounded by beautiful Sussex countryside. Accommodation is in comfortable double en suite rooms, and there is a garden room with a cosy wood burning stove for chilly days. Leading on from the garden room is a spaciou conservatory full of interesting plants and shrubs. Although Chichester Lodge is in the heart of the countryside, Chichester city - with its theatre, cathedral and museum - is just five minutes drive away. Additionally visitors may enjoy the numerous lovely walks to be had in the locality.
OPEN ALL YEAR. NO SMOKING. S.D., V. STD.   EN SUITE, TV & BEVERAGES IN ROOMS. B. & B. £17.50 - 22.50.

CROUCHERS BOTTOM COUNTRY HOTEL, BIRDHAM RD, APULDRAM, PO20 7EH
TEL: (01243) 784 995 N/S DINING R & BEDRS. V B/A. LICENSED.   4 GROUND FLOOR ROOMS, 1 SPECIFICALLY FOR THE DISABLED. CHILDREN.   EN SUITE, BEVERAGES & T.V.   B. & B. FROM £29.

COPTHORNE

 BROAD OAK, WEST PARK, RD, COPTHORNE, W. SUSS, RH10 3EX   TEL: (01342) 714882
NO SMOKING.   V, S.D. B/A.   CHILDREN WELCOME.   PETS B/A. BEVERAGES AVAILABLE. TV IN LOUNGE. B. & B. £19.50 PER PERSON, SINGLE £23.

CRAWLEY

School Cottages Guest House

2 SCHOOL COTTAGES, RUSPER RD, IFIELD GREEN, CRAWLEY, RH11 0HL TEL: (01293) 518813
FAX: (01293) 565153
School Cottages was originally the teacher's house to the 11th C. village of Ifield and is now the home of Gareth and Joy Flemington who specialise in providing reasonably priced accommodation for the Gatwick-bound traveller. Your hosts will provide transport to and from the airport and can arrange long-term parking with a local company.
OPEN ALL YEAR.   NO SMOKING.   V, S.D. B/A.   CHILDREN WELCOME. BEVERAGES & TV IN BEDROOMS.
CREDIT CARDS. B. & B. AROUND £20, SINGLE £30.

White Lodge Guest House

10 LANGLEY LN., IFIELD, CRAWLEY, RH11 0NA   TEL: (01293) 546222 FAX: (01293) 518813
200 year-old house down a private lane just 10 mins'drive from Gatwick airport. Courtesy transport service to and from Gatwick from 8 a.m. to 10.30 p.m. Within walking distance of both stations. Beautifully equipped rooms.
OPEN ALL YEAR Ex. Xmas.   NO SMOKING.   V, S.D. B/A.   OVER 6S WELCOME.   TV & BEVERAGES IN ROOMS.
CREDIT CARDS. B. & B. FROM £17.50.

EAST GRINSTEAD

'TOADS CROAK HOUSE', 30 COPTHORNE ROAD, FELBRIDGE, W. SUSSEX, RH1 2NS
TEL: (01342) 328524   NO SMOKING.   V, S.D. B/A.   CHILDREN WELCOME.   EN SUITE, BEVERAGES & T.V. IN ALL BEDROOMS.   B. & B. FROM £15.

HAYWARDS HEATH

Mattagami

61 FRANKLYNN RD, HAYWARDS HEATH, W. SUSSEX, RH16 4DS   TEL: (01444) 453506
Family home with parking for guests near centre of the town on the A272. Full central heating.
OPEN ALL YEAR.   NO SMOKING.   V, S.D. B/A.   CHILDREN WELCOME.   BEVERAGES ON REQUEST.   T.V. IN BEDROOMS.   B. & B. FROM £17.

HENFIELD

Little Oreham Farm

NR WOODSMILL, HENFIELD, W. SUSSEX, BN5 9SB   TEL: (01273) 492931
Charming, listed farmhouse - complete with wisteria and dovecot! - in quiet rural area.
OPEN ALL YEAR.   NO SMOKING.   V, S.D. B/A.   EN SUITE, BEVERAGES & T.V. IN BEDRS.   B. & B. FROM £17.50.

THE TITHE BARN, BRIGHTON RD, WOODMANCOTE, HENFIELD, W. SUSS, BN5 9ST
TEL: (01273) 492267   N/S. V, S.D. B/A.   CHILDREN WELCOME.   TV & BEVERAGES IN ROOMS.   B. & B.
FROM £15.

LITTLEHAMPTON

Bracken Lodge Guest House

43 CHURCH ST, LITTLEHAMPTON, W. SUSSEX, BN17 5PU   TEL: (01903) 723174
ETB 3 Crown Highly Commended. Large detached house of great character amidst lovely
prize-winning gardens. Beautifully furnished throughout. Relaxed and friendly atmos-
phere. Excellent cooked breakfast (there is an English, Continental or Scots option).
OPEN ALL YEAR.   NO SMOKING.   V, S.D. B/A.   LICENSED.   1 GROUND FLOOR BEDROOM.   OVER 2S ONLY.
EN SUITE, T.V. & BEVERAGES IN ALL BEDROOMS. ACESS, VISA.   B. & B. FROM £24.

Pindars

LYMINSTER, LITTLEHAMPTON, W. SUSSEX, BN17 7QF   TEL: (01903) 882628
Country house standing amidst beautiful gardens in the small village of Lyminster.
OPEN APRIL - OCT.   N/S DINING & BEDRS.   V B'fast B/A.   OVER 10S ONLY.   BEVERAGES & T.V. IN BED-
ROOMS.   B. & B. FROM £30.

PULBOROUGH

THE BARN OWLS RESTAURANT & GUESTEL, LONDON RD, COLDWALTHAM, RH20 1LR
TEL: (017982) 2498 N/S DINING R.   V.   LICENSED.   PETS B/A.   EN SUITE & BEVERAGES IN BEDROOMS. T.V.
LOUNGE.   ACCESS, VISA.   B. & B. FROM £24. D. £17.

STEYNING

NASH HOTEL, HORSHAM RD, STEYNING, W. SUSSEX.   **TEL: (01903) 814988**
NO SMOKING.   V, S.D. B/A.   LICENSED.   CHILDREN WELCOME.   PETS B/A.   EN SUITE IN 2 ROOMS. BEVER-
AGES & T.V. IN ALL BEDROOMS. B. & B. FROM £21.

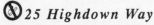
25 Highdown Way

FERRING, WORTHING, W. SUSSEX, BN12 6QQ   TEL: (01903) 507137
Warm and comfortable family bungalow with pleasant gardens in peaceful surroundings.
nestling betweeen sea and South Downs near golf course, racing and bowls at Worthing.
OPEN ALL YEAR.   NO SMOKING.   S.D. B/A.   EN SUITE, TV & BEVERAGES IN ROOMS.   B. & B. £17.50 (S.D. extra).

RESTAURANTS

CHICHESTER

DOLPHIN & ANCHOR HOTEL, WEST ST., CHICHESTER, W. SUSSEX, O19 1QE
TEL: (01243) 785121   N/S RESTAURANT.   V. STD.   LICENSED.   CHILDREN WELCOME.   CREDIT CARDS.

CRAWLEY

The George Hotel

HIGH ST, CRAWLEY, W. SUSSEX, RH10 1BS   TEL: (01293) 524215
N/S RESTAURANT.   LICENSED.   CHILDREN.

HOVE

WINDMILL ROOM, FORFARS BAKERS, 123 CHURCH RD, HOVE, W. SUSSEX
TEL: (01273) 727922   NO SMOKING.   CHILDREN WELCOME.

PLAISTOW

CLEMENTS VEGETARIAN RESTAURANT, RICKMAN'S LANE, PLAISTOW, RH14 0NT
TEL: (01403) 88246   OPEN Wed - Sat 12 - 2, 7 - 11 (last Orders 9.30, Sunday) 12 - 2. V, VE EXC. NO SMOKING.

RUDGWICK

QUEEN'S HEAD PUB, BUCKS GREEN, RUDGWICK, RH12 3JF
TEL: (01403) 2202   N/S RESTAURANT.   V ON REQUEST.   LICENSED.   CHILDREN WELCOME.

WORTHING

Pavilion Coffee Shop

DEBENHAMS, 14-20 SOUTH ST, WORTHING, W. SUSSEX, BN11 3AA   TEL: (01903) 34321
Friendly Self-service Coffee Shop serving popular light lunches, snacks, and a range of hot and cold drinks.
OPEN STORE HOURS.   NO SMOKING.   V AVAIL.   DISABLED ACCESS.   CHILDREN WELCOME. CREDIT CARDS.

East Sussex

ARLINGTON

Bates Green

ARLINGTON, POLEGATE, E. SUSSEX, BN26 6SH   TEL: (01323) 482039
Bates Green was originally an 18th C. game-keeper's cottage which has been restored and enlarged since 1922 and stands amidst a large tranquil garden, developed with enthusiasm since the 1970s: there is a rock garden, pond and a secluded area - in fact the garden is open under the National Garden Scheme and "garden chat is always welcomed" by your hostess, Carolyn McCutchan. Your host, John McCutchan, works the 130 acre sheep and turkey farm and was a past winner of the Country Life Farming and Wildlife Trophy. In addition to gardening and conservation farming, the McCutchans are warm and welcoming hosts: there is home-made cake and tea to greet you on arrival, and a log fire blazes in the sitting room grate in cooler weather; bedrooms are comfortable and well-equipped, and farmhouse cooking is the order of the day (there are also a number of good pubs and restaurants nearby). There is much to enjoy at Bates Green: in addition to the hard tennis court in the garden there are many lovely walks nearby and you are within easy reach of the South Downs, Eastbourne and Glyndebourne.
OPEN ALL YEAR ex. Xmas & New Year.   NO SMOKING.   V, S.D. B/A.   EN SUITE & BEVERAGES IN ROOMS.   TV IN 1 OF 2 LOUNGES.   B. & B. FROM £20.

BEXHILL-ON-SEA

'Helensholme'

HEATHERDUNE RD., BEXHILL-ON-SEA, TN39 4HB   TEL: (01424) 223545
Delightful chalet home peacefully situated on the outskirts of Bexhill overlooking the Downs. Lovingly furnished. Your host specialises in vegetarian cuisine and imaginative and tasty meals are prepared from fresh, local produce wherever possible.
OPEN ALL YEAR.   NO SMOKING.   V EXC. S.D WITH GOOD NOTICE.   CHILDREN: OVER 10S WELCOME. VANITY UNITS IN 2 ROOMS.   BEVERAGES.   T.V. LOUNGE.   B. & B. £17.

BRIGHTON

Dudley House

10 MADEIRA PLACE, BRIGHTON, E. SUSSEX, BN2 1TN   TEL: (01273) 676794
Spacious and charming Victorian guest house with many period features but every modern comfort near the sea front and the centre of Brighton. A very friendly welcome. Many bedrooms are en suite and have sea views.isit.
OPEN ALL YEAR.   NO SMOKING.   V, DIAB, S.D. B/A.   CHILDREN WELCOME.   SOME EN SUITE ROOMS.   T.V. IN ALL ROOMS.   B. & B. FROM £16.

Rozanne Mendick

14 CHATSWORTH RD., BRIGHTON, E. SUSSEX, BN1 5DB   TEL: (01273) 556584
Large, comfortable family home.
OPEN ALL YEAR.   NO SMOKING.   V, VE STD., S.D. B/A.   CHILDREN WELCOME.   BEVERAGES.   T.V. B. & B.
FROM £14.

COODEN

Beam Ends

175 COODEN DRIVE, COODEN BEACH, COODEN, E. SUSSEX, TN39 3AQ TEL: (014243) 3880
Comfortable family house 200 feet from the sea. Easy access to station and to London.
OPEN ALL YEAR.   NO SMOKING.   V, S.D. B/A.   CHILDREN: OVER 8S ONLY.   TV IN DRAWING ROOM.
BEVERAGES IN ROOMS.   B. & B. AROUND £22.

EASTBOURNE

Arden Hotel

17 BURLINGTON PLACE, EASTBOURNE, BN21 4AR TEL: (01323) 639639
Friendly, family run hotel, established for non-smokers only. Ideal for relaxing in Victorian
elegance or being active in the Sussex sea air. Some rooms have sea views. The hotel is
close to all amenities and is adjacent to Eastbourne's splendid Promenade.
OPEN Mid Jan. - end Nov.   NO SMOKING.   V, S.D., B/A.   LICENSED.   CHILDREN WELCOME.   9 EN SUITE
ROOMS.   BEVERAGES ON REQUEST.   T.V. IN LOUNGE & IN ROOMS.   CREDIT CARDS.   B. & B. FROM £20.

CUCKMERE HOUSE, 20 SOUTH CLIFF AVE, EASTBOURNE, BN20 7AH TEL: (01323) 20492
Pleasant well-furnished guest house in a peaceful tree-lined avenue one minute from the
sea front and close to theatres, etc. Centrally heated in all bedrooms.
OPEN ALL YEAR.   N/S ex. lounge.   V, S.D. B/A.   LICENSED.   CHILDREN: OVER 10S ONLY.   EN SUITE,
BEVERAGES, TV, RADIO IN ROOMS.   B. & B. AROUND £20, D. £7.

HARTFIELD

BOLEBROKE WATERMILL, EDENBRIDGE RD, HARTFIELD. TEL: (01892) 770425
Magical watermill in secluded woodland. Quaint, rustic rooms in miller's barn include
honeymooners' hayloft. '91 Winner *Best Breakfast in Britain & Int. Fairy Story Hotel*.
OPEN 1 March - 20 Dec.   NO SMOKING.   V B/A.   CHILDREN: OVER 7S ONLY.   EN SUITE, TV & BEVERAGES
IN ROOMS.   VISA, AMEX.   B. & B. AROUND £28. *ETB Highly Commended. RAC Highly Acclaimed.*

HASTINGS

NORTON VILLA, HILL ST., OLD TOWN, HASTINGS, E. SUSSEX. TEL: (01424) 428168
Delightful house built in 1847 set on cliffs overlooking the Channel, Old town and harbour.
4-poster room available in B. & B. Self-catering cottage available for summer let.
OPEN ALL YEAR.   N/S DINING R & MOST BEDRS.   CHILDREN: OVER 8S.   3 EN SUITE ROOMS.   BEVERAGES.
T.V.   OVERNIGHT CAR PARKING.   B. & B. AROUND £18.

HEATHFIELD

 ## 'Risingholme'

HIGH ST., HEATHFIELD, E. SUSSEX, TN21 8LS   TEL: (01435) 864645
OPEN ALL YEAR.   NO SMOKING.   V, S.D. B/.A.   OVER 10s WELCOME.   EN SUITE ROOMS.   BEVERAGES & T.V.
IN ROOMS.   B. & B. FROM £17.50.

LEWES

Crink House (B & B) & Trust Cottage (S/C)

BARCOMBE MILLS, LWEES, E. SUSSEX, BN8 5BJ TEL: (01273) 400625
Originally a Victorian farmhouse, surrounded on three sides by fields and breathtaking
views of the South Downs. Comfortable B. & B. (there is a 4-poster bed in one room and
twin beds in the other); breakfast features a choice of a traditional English or lighter
Continental option. S/C at Trust Cottage: heated by a wood-burning stove, and a twin and
a double room, plus microwave, a fridge-freezer, a dishwasher and washer/dryer.
OPEN ALL YEAR ex. Xmas.   NO SMOKING.   S.D. B/A.   CHILDREN WELCOME.   BOTH ROOMS EN SUITE.
BEVERAGES.   T.V. IN DINING R.   B. & B. AROUND £23.

Millers

134 HIGH ST, LEWES, E. SUSSEX, BN7 1XS   TEL: (01273) 475631

This 16th c. timber framed house has many historic associations including links with the Bloomsbury Group. Furnished and decorated in harmony with its unique character, all Millers' rooms have antique double beds. The architecture of the ancient county town of Lewes is well documented and its many interesting shops include those specialising in crafts and antiques. The town is an excellent centre for walking in the Downs, while Brighton, Newhaven and Glyndebourne are just a short drive away.
OPEN ALL YEAR ex. Xmas & New Year. NO SMOKING. V, B'fast B/A. 2 EN SUITE ROOMS. BEVERAGES & T.V. IN ROOMS. B. & B. FROM £23.

PEVENSEY

Montana B. & B.

THE PROMENADE, PEVENSEY BAY, PEVENSEY, E. SUSSEX, BN24 6HD   TEL: (01323) 764651

Quiet house in a convenient situation close to village shops, pubs and the beach.
OPEN ALL YEAR ex. Xmas & part April. NO SMOKING. S.D. B/A. CHILDREN WELCOME. BEVERAGES IN ROOMS. T.V. LOUNGE & IN 1 BEDROOM. B. & B. FROM £13.

RYE

Green Hedges

HILLYFIELDS, RYE HILL, RYE, E. SUSSEX, TN31 7NH   TEL: (01797) 222185

Large Edwardian country house superbly situated on rising ground, with wonderful views of Rye and the sea beyond. It is a comfortable family home and stands in a beautiful landscaped garden; heated outdoor swimming pool during summer. Breakfast is prepared from seasonal garden produce, home-made preserves and free range eggs.
OPEN ALL YEAR ex. Xmas. NO SMOKING. V STD. S.D. B/A. CHILDREN: OVER 12S ONLY. EN SUITE, BEVERAGES & TV IN ROOMS. B. & B. AROUND £24.

Jeake's House

MERMAID ST, RYE, E. SUSSEX, TN31 7ET TEL: (01797) 222828 FAX: (01797) 222623

Beautiful listed building, oak-beamed & wood-panelled, on a picturesque cobbled street.
OPEN ALL YEAR. N/S DINING R. V STD. LICENSED. CHILDREN WELCOME. PETS B/A. EN SUITE. BEVERAGES & TV IN ROOMS. B. & B. FROM £19.50.

The Old Vicarage Guest House

66 CHURCH SQUARE, RYE, E. SUSSEX, TN31 7HF   TEL & FAX: (01797) 225131

Listed 16th C. building delightfully situated in the quiet and picturesque Church Square.
OPEN ALL YEAR ex. Xmas. N/S DINING R & BEDRS. V STD, S.D. B/A. OVER 12S ONLY. EN SUITE. BEVERAGES & T.V. IN ROOMS. B. & B. FROM £17.50.

ST LEONARDS ON SEA

'Merryfield House'

3 ST MATTHEWS GARDENS, ST LEONARDS, TN38 OTS   TEL: (01424) 424953

Large Victorian house overlooking private gardens 1m from sea & Hastings town centre.
OPEN ALL YEAR ex. Xmas. NO SMOKING. V EXC. CHILDREN AND WELL BEHAVED DOGS WELCOME. BEVERAGES & TV IN ROOMS. B. & B. AROUND £16.

WADHURST

CHEVIOTS, COUSLEY WOOD, WADHURST, TN5 6HD TEL: (01892) 782952

Modern, centrally heated detached house in 2 acre garden.
OPEN mid-Mar. - mid-Nov. NO SMOKING. S.D. B/A. CHILDREN WELCOME. 2 EN SUITE ROOMS. BEVERAGES. T.V. IN ROOMS. B. & B. AROUND £20.

New Barn

WARDS LANE, WADHURST, E. SUSSEX, TN5 6HP   TEL: (01892) 782042

Beautiful 18th C. farmhouse overlooking Bewl Water and Trout Fishery. Beamed throughout; logs fires blaze in inglenook. B'fast features home-made jams, marmalades and preserves with local home-baked bread and free range eggs.
OPEN ALL YEAR. N/S ex. 1 lounge. V, S.D. B/A. CHILDREN. PETS B/A. EN SUITE & TV. B. & B. AROUND £24

RESTAURANTS

BRIGHTON

Debenhams

94-99 WESTERN RD, BRIGHTON, BN1 2LB   TEL: (01273) 26531
Friendly self service cafe serving snacks, hot lunches & a range of hot and cold drinks.
OPEN STORE HOURS.   NO SMOKING.   V STD.   DISABLED ACCESS.   CHILDREN.   CREDIT CARDS.

FLAVOUR OF LIFE, 17 REGENT ARCADE, EAST ST, BRIGHTON   TEL: (01273) 28236
Small sandwich shop with two tables and counter space.
NO SMOKING.   V STD.

Food for Friends

17A-18 PRINCE ALBERT ST., THE LANES, BRIGHTON BN1 1HF TEL: (01273) 202310
FAX: (01273) 202001
Licensed vegetarian wholefood restaurant in the heart of the Lanes area of Brighton.
Everything on the menu (which changes daily) has been prepared from additive-free
ingredients (some organic), and there is an excellent takeaway and home-delivery menu.
55 SEATS. OPEN 9 - 10. 50% NO SMOKING.   V EXC.   LICENSED. DISABLED ACCESS. CHILDREN.

Pavilion Coffee Shop

C & H FABRICS LTD, 180 WESTERN RD, BN1 2BA TEL: (01273) 28906
Friendly self service cafe serving snacks, hot lunches & a range of hot and cold drinks.
OPEN STORE HOURS.   NO SMOKING.   V STD.   DISABLED ACCESS.   CHILDREN. CREDIT CARDS.

**SLIMS HEALTHFOOD RESTAURANT, 92 CHURCHILL SQUARE, BRIGHTON, BN1 2EP
TEL: (01273) 24582**
Friendly health food restaurant established 16 years ago, offering a range of savoury
dishes, cakes, pastries & fresh salads. Vegetarian outside catering service.
OPEN 9.30 - 5.30. 50% NO SMOKING.   V EXC. VE, DIAB, GLUTEN FREE DIETS B/A.   LICENSED. DISABLED
ACCESS.   CHILDREN WELCOME.

EASTBOURNE

Pavilion Coffee Shop

C & H FABRICS LTD, 82-86 TERMINUS RD, BN21 3LX   TEL: (01323) 649301
Friendly self service café serving snacks, hot lunches & a range of hot and cold drinks.
OPEN STORE HOURS.   NO SMOKING.   VEGETARIAN.   DISABLED ACCESS.   CHILDREN WELCOME.
CREDIT CARDS.

HAILSHAM

The Homely Maid Restaurant and Pie Shop

2 HIGH ST, HAILSHAM, E. SUSSEX, BN27 1BJ   TEL: (01323) 841650
Cosy 13th century cottage with inglenook, oak beams, good home cooking & friendly
service. Traditional home-baked fare catering for most tastes including veg., low-fat, etc.
OPEN Mon-Fri. 9-5, Sat. 9-1.30.   NO SMOKING.   V. & LOW-FAT.   CHILDREN WELCOME.

HOVE

INGLENOOK RESTAURANT, 68 PORTLAND RD, HOVE, BN3 5DL TEL: (01273) 821335
Fine food, a friendly atmosphere, & crafts. Traditional English fare.
NO SMOKING.   LICENSED. DISABLED ACCESS.   CHILDREN WELCOME.

JEVINGTON

**THE HUNGRY MONK RESTAURANT, JEVINGTON, NR POLEGATE, E. SUSSEX.   TEL:
(01323) 482178**
D. 7-10, L (Sun only) 12-2.   N/S RESTAURANT (allowed in sitting room) V STD. LICENSED.

NEWHAVEN

HEALTHIBODY WHOLEFOOD & BODY CARE SPECIALISTS, 52 HIGH ST, BN9 9PD TEL: (01273) 512957
Cosy restaurant with varied menu of light and main meals.
OPEN MON - SAT., 9 - 5.   N/S 60% RESTAURANT.   V, VE STD.   CHILDREN WELCOME.

PUBS & WINE BARS

SEAFORD

The Golden Galleon

EXCEAT BRIDGE, SEAFORD, E. SUSSEX, BN25 4AB   TEL: (01323) 892247
Clean Catering Award. The Golden Galleon is a highly acclaimed free-hold pub (featured in many local and national guides) situated in an area of outstanding beauty, complete with landscaped gardens, patio and grass area. It has an attractive beamed room with coal fire and inglenook fireplace. There are always six cask conditioned beers in stock including many local and prize-winning ales and, as the proprietors are commited non-smokers, half the pub is smoke-free. The food is excellent: the blackboard choices include lasagne and other pasta dishes in addition to local pies and steaks and a range of snacks (ploughman's lunches, etc.). Excellent choice of ales notwithstanding, there are over 40 reasonably priced wines to choose from and - thumbs up for health awareness - decaffeinated coffee, fruit teas and freshly squeezed orange juice are also available as beverage choices.
N/S 50%.   V, LOW-CHOL STD.   DISABLED ACCESS: 'A FEW STEPS: HELP GIVEN.'

South East England

Kent

ASHFORD

Birchley

FOSTEN GREEN LANE, BIDDENDEN, ASHFORD, KENT, TN27 8DZ   TEL: (01580) 291413
'Highly Commended'in ETB's 1991 England for Excellence Awards as England's Bed & Breakfast of the Year 1991 Early 17th C. timber-framed listed house in a peacefully secluded 6 acre garden with covered heated swimming pool and miniature railway. Beautifully furnished and appointed: bedrooms are large and decorated in Laura Ashley style, while the oak-panelled sitting room has a welcoming log fire. Breakfast is served on an ancient refectory table in a large, oak-beamed dining room with a magnificent carved oak inglenook. A delicious 4-course evening meal can be served by arrangement.
OPEN ALL YEAR Ex. Xmas.   NO SMOKING.   V, S.D. B/A.   LICENSED.   CHILDREN: OVER 10S ONLY.   EN SUITE, T.V. & BEVERAGES IN ALL ROOMS.   CREDIT CARDS.   B. & B. FROM £25-£30.

AYLESFORD

Wickham Lodge

73 HIGH ST, AYLESFORD VILLAGE, ME20 7AY TEL: (01622) 717267 FAX: (01622) 718791
ETB 3 Crown Commended. Period house on river bank. Very comfortable rooms with views. Hearty breakfasts (with healthy options) & suppers B/A. Residents'drawing room.
OPEN ALL YEAR.   NO SMOKING.   V, S.D. B/A.   CHILDREN WELCOME.   1 EN SUITE ROOM.   TV & BEVERAGES IN ROOMS.   B. & B. £17.50 (£20 EN SUITE).   PRIVATE PARKING.

BECKENHAM

123 PARK RD, BECKENHAM, KENT, BR3 1QJ TEL: (0181) 650 1281
NO SMOKING.   EN SUITE & TV IN BEDROOMS.   CHILDREN & PETS.   B. & B. £15.

BENENDEN

CRIT HALL, CRANBROOK RD, BENENDEN, KENT, TN17 4EU   TEL: (0580) 240609 FAX: (0580) 241743
N/S DINING R & BEDRS.   V, S.D. B/A.   LICENSED.   CHILDREN: OVER 12S.   EN SUITE/PRIVATE BATH, TV & BEVERAGES IN ROOMS.   B. & B. FROM £22.50, D. £15.

CANTERBURY

Magnolia House

36 ST DUNSTAN'S TERR., CANTERBURY, KENT, CT2 8AX   TEL & FAX: (01227) 765121

ETB 2 Crown HIghly Commended. AA QQQQ Se-lected. Magnolia House is a charming detached late Georgian house situated in a quiet residential street near to the city centre and just 2 minutes' drive, or twenty minutes' walk, from the university. The house itself has much of architectural interest to commend it and has been decorated sympathetically with each bedroom being individually designed and coordinated in a light, bright decor (lots of Laura Ashley fabrics and wallcoverings, and one has a four-poster); there is a walled garden with fishpond, terraces and shrubberies (the perfect place to relax in after a day's sightseeing). Ann Davies, the proprietor, tells me, "because we only take 10 guests, each one is special", and guests are aware of this special treatment from the moment they arrive, when a welcome tray is offered. Breakfast is a generous meal with a wide range of options and special diets are treated sympathetically. Evening meals are available from November to February inclusive.

OPEN ALL YEAR.   NO SMOKING ex. lounge.   V, S.D. B/A.   CHILDREN WELCOME.   EN SUITE, TV, CLOCK RADIOS, HAIR DRYERS & BEVERAGES IN ROOMS.   CREDIT CARDS.   B. & B. FROM £24 - 40.

Walnut Tree Farm

LYNSORE BOTTOM, UPPER HARDRES, KENT, CT4 6EG   TEL: (01227) 87375

14th C. thatched farmhouse in 6 acres. Home-made bread, preserves & new laid eggs.
OPEN Feb.-Nov.   NO SMOKING.   V, S.D. B/A.   CHILDREN WELCOME.   EN SUITE, RADIO & BEVERAGES IN ALL ROOMS.   B. & B. FROM £16-£18.

Zan Stel Lodge

140 OLD DOVER RD, CANTERBURY, KENT, CT1 3NX   TEL: (01227) 453654

Zan Stel Lodge is an elegant Edwardian guest house which stands adjacent to the Kent County Cricket Ground just 10 minutes' walk from the city centre. Your hosts, Zandra and Ron Stedman, offer a particularly high standard of cleanliness and service, and each of the spacious, centrally heated bedrooms has a range of helpful facilities. A full English breakast may be enjoyed in the elegant dining room which overlooks the pretty walled garden, and vegetarians can be accommodated on request. There is also private parking - a particular attraction for visitors to the city.
NO SMOKING.   OPEN ALL YEAR.   V, S.D. B/A.   CHILDREN WELCOME.   BEVERAGES & TV IN BEDROOMS. SOME EN SUITE.   B. & B. FROM £17.

CRANBROOK

Hancocks Farmhouse

TILSDEN LANE, CRANBROOK, KENT, TN17 3PH   TEL: (01580) 714645

The earliest mention of Hancocks is in a will of 1520 in which the house was left by a clothier, Thomas Sheaffe, to his son Gervase. Today this fine well-preserved timber-framed building is a family home which also takes guests. Hancocks has been decorated and furnished with antiques, in keeping with its period origins and there is a large inglenook fireplace with log fires for cooler evenings. Set in a lovely garden and surrounded by farmland and beautiful views, Hancocks is the perfect place to come for those in search of peace and tranquillity. The food is first-rate: dinner is by prior arrangement and there is a complimentary afternoon tea in addition to a generous breakfast; organic and wholefood ingredients are used whenever availability permits. A typical evening menu would feature garlic stuffed mushrooms with home-made brown rolls, fresh white fish cooked with leeks and ginger, and a tempting dessert such as fresh lime tart.
OPEN ALL YEAR.   NO SMOKING.   V, S.D. B/A.   OVER 9s WELCOME.   EN SUITE & TV IN SOME ROOMS. BEVERAGES IN ALL ROOMS.   B. & B. FROM £18.

Hartley Mount Country House Hotel

HARTLEY RD, CRANBROOK, KENT, TN17 3QX   TEL: (01580) 712230

Hartley Mount Hotel is a fine old Edwardian country manor house set in 2 acres of gardens overlooking the glorious views of Cranbrook and the Weald of Kent. It has been sympathetically refurbished - all the grace and elegance of the Edwardian era have been retained in the decor and furnishings - yet has all the modern conveniences of a luxury hotel: breakfast is served in an Edwardian conservatory and the bedrooms are decorated in keeping with the period, with a heavily draped four-poster bed and 'old-time' bathroom en-suite. Meals are served in an elegant dining room and a typical evening meal would feature Scotch Woodcock followed by Blanquette of Lamb and a selection of home-made desserts. There is a good vegetarian menu and an extensive wine list and all food is prepared from fresh, local ingredients.

OPEN ALL YEAR.   N/S EX. IN CONSERVATORY.   V STD. S.D. B/A.   LICENSED.   CHILDREN WELCOME. EN SUITE, BEVERAGES & T.V. IN ROOMS.   ACCESS, VISA.   B. & B. FROM £35 (INC. VAT & SERVICE).

DOVER

CASTLE HOUSE, 10 CASTLE HILL RD, DOVER, CT16 1QW TEL: (01304) 201656 FAX: (01304) 210197
NO SMOKING.   OVER 12S ONLY.   EN SUITE, TV & TEA/COFFEE-MAKING.   B. & B. FROM £20.

East Lee Guest House

108 MAISON DIEU RD, DOVER, KENT, CT16 1RT   TEL & FAX: (01304) 210176

East Lee is a fine Victorian residence, formerly the home of the 19th C. artist William Henry East, which has been beautifully restored and tastefully decorated in period style throughout; it stands just 10 minutes walk down the famous White Cliffs from Dover Castle which historic fort has been continually garrisoned since Norman times. Your hosts, Patricia and Michael Knight, offer a very warm welcome to guests and the friendly atmosphere of this family house makes visitors feel very relaxed and at home. Bedrooms have been individually furnished in sympathetic style, and all rooms are well-appointed and have en suite facilities. East Lee is ideally suited for those seeking an early morning getaway to the continent via the nearby Hoverport and Ferry Services across the channel; accordingly your hosts will gladly serve a continental breakfast option in your room on request, while later risers can look forward to a generous English breakfast. Although most visitors to Dover tend to pass through it en route to other destinations, the town has much of interest to commend it: a crucial part of England's Maritime heritage, the town is near to Canterbury and Sandwich. RAC Highly Commended.

OPEN ALL YEAR. NO SMOKING. V, S.D., B/A.   CHILDREN.   EN SUITE, TV & BEVERAGES IN ROOMS. CREDIT CARDS.   B. & B. FROM £20

MAIDSTONE

HOMESTEAD, GREENHILL, OTHAM, NR MAIDSTONE, ME15 8RR   TEL: (01622) 862234
NO SMOKING.   CHILDREN WELCOME.   PETS B/A.   EN SUITE IN SOME ROOMS.   BEVERAGES IN ALL ROOMS. T.V. IN LOUNGE. B.& B. FROM £14.

SEVENOAKS

The Gables

36 DARTFORD RD, SEVENOAKS, KENT, TN13 3TQ   TEL: (01732) 456708

Built in 1870, The Gables is a friendly, comfortable and spacious Victorian house conveniently situated on the A225 just a short distance from Sevenoaks town and its railway station with frequent services to London and the coast. Bedrooms are comfortably furnished and decorated and each is equipped with a colour T.V. and beverage-making facilities. Sheila Castle offers a warm welome to guests - and a full English breakfast. There are many lovely walks in the locality and you are within easy reach of the many beautiful country houses

and castles of Kent, including Knole, Hever, Ightham Mote and Chartwell.
OPEN ALL YEAR ex. Xmas.   EXCLUSIVELY FOR NON-SMOKERS.   V, S.D. B/A (b'fast only).   PRIVATE BATH &
SHOWER ROOM. BEVERAGES & T.V. IN ROOMS.   B. & B. FROM £16.50.

TENTERDEN

 BRATTLE HOUSE, CRANBROOK RD, TENTERDEN, KENT, TN30 6UL TEL: (015806) 3565
NO SMOKING.   V, S.D. B/A.   OVER 12S ONLY.   EN SUITE & BEVERAGES.   B. & B. FROM £28.

TONBRIDGE

Goldhill Mill

GOLDEN GREEN, TONBRIDGE, KENT, TN11 0BA   TEL: (01232) 851626 FAX: (01232) 851881

 Picturesque Goldhill Mill was mentioned in the Domesday Book and was a working watermill for at least 850 years; peacefully standing in its own 20 acres, this beautiful old mill has been lovingly restored by its present owners and now offers accommodation of the very highest standard to guests. Three luxury double bedroom suites are available: two have jacuzzis and the third has a fourposter and gas/coal fire; additionally there is a cottage in the grounds offering the ultimate in luxury self-catering accommodation (crayfish and organic vegetables are available to guests staying therein). Breakfast is served in the splendid farmhouse kitchen with its Tudor beams (the mill machinery is on display behind glass) and anything from full English to Continental fare can be ordered. Goldhill Mill is an ideal touring base: Leeds Castle, Bodiam, Sissinghurst, Hever Castle and Chartwell are among the many places which may be comfortably visited in a day's drive and those wishing to spend a day *in situ* can enjoy the lovely garden & flood-lit tennis court.
OPEN 1 Jan.-15 July; 1 Sept.-31 Dec.   NO SMOKING.   V, S.D. B/A.   CHILDREN B/A.   EN SUITE, TV, D.D. PHONE
& BEVERAGES IN ROOMS. CREDIT CARDS. B. & B. £32.50.

TUNBRIDGE WELLS

Danehurst House Hotel

41 LOWER GREEN RD, RUSTHALL, KENT, TN4 8TW   TEL: (01892) 527739 FAX: (01892) 514804
Danehurst is a charming gabled guest house standing in a lovely rural setting in the heart of Kent; accommodation is in tastefully decorated rooms - all of which have private bathrooms and beverage-making facilities. The food is excellent: everything has been home-prepared from fresh, seasonal ingredients, and a typical evening menu would feature Carrot and Orange Soup followed by Chicken in Cream and Tarragon (with a selection of five seasonal vegetables and baby new potatoes), and a tempting dessert, such as Strawberry and Kiwi Fruit Shortcake with Cream; an English Cheeseboard, coffee and mints would complete the meal. You are just a short distance from Royal Tunbridge Wells and the gracious country houses of Kent are easily reached.
OPEN ALL YEAR.   N/S ex. in lounge.   V, S.D. B/A.   LICENSED.   CHILDREN WELCOME.   SOME EN SUITE
ROOMS.   BEVERAGES & T.V. IN ROOMS.   CREDIT CARDS.   B. & B. FROM £29.50.

WEST MALLING

Scott House

HIGH ST, WEST MALLING, KENT, ME19 6QH   TEL: (01732) 841380 / 870025
Scott House is a Grade II listed Georgian town house situated opposite the library in the lower part of West Malling High Street. It is a family home from which the owners, the Smiths, also run an antique business and is therefore, unsurprisingly enough, quite beautifully decorated in keeping with its period origins; all bedrooms are furnished with taste and style. Only breakfast is offered at Scott House but there are lots of healthy options on the menu including muesli, yoghurt and porridge as well as the usual 'Full English' fare. The Smiths assure me that there are several good restaurants in West Malling which has, in addition to this, several other features to commend it to the touring visitor including an 11th C. abbey, a craft centre and a lakeside country park with many delightful walks.
OPEN ALL YEAR Ex. Xmas.   NO SMOKING.   V, S.D. B/A.   EN SUITE, TV & BEVERAGES IN ALL ROOMS. ACCESS,
VISA, MASTERCARD, JCB.   B. & B. FROM £27.

RESTAURANTS, PUBS & WINE BARS

ASHFORD

 CORNERSTONE WHOLEFOOD RESTAURANT, 25A HIGH ST, ASHFORD, TN24 8TH
TEL: (01233) 642874   NO SMOKING.   V.   . DISABLED ACCESS: 'GOOD FOR WHEELCHAIRS'.   CHILDREN WELCOME.

BIDDENDEN

Claris's

1 - 3 HIGH ST, BIDDENDEN, NR ASHFORD, KENT, TN27 8AL TEL: (01580) 291025

 Claris's is a Grade I listed black and white timber framed building which forms part of a long row of houses in the High Street of the charming village of Biddenden. The proprietors have worked in harmony with the building to create an atmosphere of cosy intimacy: the inglenook fireplaces, oak beams and casement windows combine happily with the table settings of white lace and china. The fare is 'afternoon tea' and 'lunchtime snack' - but with a plus! Home-made creamed mushrooms on toast with fresh mushrooms and cream compete for attention with a plate of hand-made Smoked Salmon Paté served with toast and salad or home-made soup with thick buttered toast; the cakes are delectable (for example Claris's Cointreau Cake with pure orange juice, liqueur and fresh local cream).
OPEN 10.30 - 5.30 (closed Mon).   L. AROUND £4.   NO SMOKING.   V STD.   DISABLED ACCESS.   CHILDREN WELCOME.

BROMLEY

CHINWAGS COFFEE SHOP, DEBENHAMS, 44 HIGH ST, BROMLEY, KENT, BR1 1EJ TEL: (0181) 460 9977
Friendly self service coffee shop serving snacks, hot lunches & hot and cold drinks.
OPEN STORE HOURS.   NO SMOKING.   V STD.   CHILDREN VERY WELCOME.   CREDIT/DEBIT CARDS.

PAVILION COFFEE SHOP, DEBENHAMS, GLADES SHOPPING CENTRE, BROMLEY
Friendly self service coffee shop serving snacks, hot lunches & hot and cold drinks.
OPEN STORE HOURS.   NO SMOKING.   V STD.   CHILDREN VERY WELCOME.   CREDIT/DEBIT CARDS.

CANTERBURY

FOOD FOR LIVING EATS, 116 HIGH ST, CHATHAM, ME4 4BY TEL: (01634) 409291
V EXC. NO SMOKING.   DISABLED ACCESS.   CHILDREN WELCOME.   ACCESS, VISA.

FOLKESTONE

SPRINGLES RESTAURANT, DEBENHAMS, 48-66 SANDGATE RD, FOLKESTONE, KENT. TEL: (01303) 850171
Friendly self service coffee shop serving snacks, lunches & hot and cold drinks.
OPEN STORE HOURS.   NO SMOKING.   VSTD.   CHILDREN VERY WELCOME.   CREDIT/DEBIT CARDS.

HOLLAND & BARRETT REST., 80 SANDGATE RD, CT20 2AA   TEL: (01303) 243646
NO SMOKING.   V EXC. CHILDREN WELCOME.

MARDEN

BUTCHER'S MERE, COLLIER ST VILLAGE, MARDEN, KENT, TN12 9RR
12 SEATS.   OPEN 10 - 7.30.   L. AROUND £2.   NO SMOKING.   V.   DISABLED ACCESS.   CHILDREN.

SMARDEN

The Bell

BELL LANE, SMARDEN, KENT, TN26 3HH   TEL: (01233) 770283
Historic inn, built during the reign of Henry VIII, originally a farm which became a 'registered Ale House' in 1630. Oak beams & inglenooks. Good food, real ales, local wines.
OPEN 11.30 - 2.30, 6 - 11. SERVING FOOD 12 - 2, 6.30 - 10.   N/S 1 ROOM.   CHILDREN WELCOME IN FAMILY AREA

Surrey

ACCOMMODATION

CAMBERLEY

TEKELS PARK GUEST HOUSE, CAMBERLEY, SURREY, GU15 2LF TEL: (01276) 23159
OPEN ALL YEAR.   NO SMOKING.   V, VE EXC.

DORKING

DANESMORE, PILGRIMS WAY, WEST HUMBLE, DORKING, RH5 6AP TEL: (01306) 882734
NO SMOKING.   V, S.D. B/A.   PETS 'POSSIBLY, B/A'.   EN SUITE (SPA BATH), TV & BEVERAGES IN BEDROOMS.   B. & B. FROM £16.25, SINGLE £23.

GATWICK

The Lawn Guest House
30 MASSETTS ROAD, HORLEY, SURREY, RH6 7DE TEL: (01293) 775751 FAX (01293) 821803

 ***ETB 2 Crowns Highly Commended.***The Lawn Guest House, run by Ken and Janet Stocks, is a lovely Victorian house and stands in a pleasant rural location despite its being just over a mile from Gatwick airport! A cooked breakfast of bacon, egg and tomato is included in the price, with an optional light breakfast of fruit juice, fresh fruit, yoghurt, cereals and toast also being available. Horley town centre, with its excellent restaurants, shops and pubs, is just two minutes away and from its mainline railway station services run regularly to London and the South Coast. The Lawn is also ideal for those using Gatwick Airport. AA & RAC listed.
OPEN ALL YEAR ex. Xmas.   NO SMOKING.   PETS B/A.   EN SUITE MOST ROOMS.   BEVERAGES & T.V. ALL ROOMS.   ACCESS, VISA, AMEX, DINERS.   B. & B. FROM £21.

GUILDFORD

Beevers Farm
CHINTHURST LN, BRAMLEY, GUILDFORD, SURREY, GU5 0DR   TEL: (01483) 898764
Farmhouse in 5 acres of natural garden with wildlife; peaceful rural setting; free-range eggs.
OPEN Mar.-Oct. NO SMOKING.   CHILDREN WELCOME.   PETS B/A.   1 EN SUITE IN 1 ROOM.   BEVERAGES & T.V. IN ROOMS.   B. & B. FROM £13.

WEYBROOK HOUSE, 113 STOKE RD, GUILDFORD, SURREY, GU1 1ET TEL: (01483) 302394
N/S DINING R & ALL PUBLIC AREAS.   V.   CHILDREN WELCOME.   B. & B. FROM £18.

HORLEY

Woodlands Guest House
42 MASSETTS RD, HORLEY, SURREY, RH6 7DS   TEL: (01293) 782994   FAX: (01293) 776358

 The Woodlands Guest House is conveniently situated a mile from Gatwick airport - ideal for early morning departures or late night return flights. It is also close to the M25 and is just five minutes from Horley railway station with its fast London connections. The house has full central heating and double glazing throughout and all bedrooms are furnished and equipped to a high standard. You are assured of a friendly, personal service by the Moore family. Car parking facilities are available at £10 per week if you wish to leave your car whilst holidaying abroad; a courtesy car to the airport is available from 6 a.m. to 10 p.m.
OPEN ALL YEAR ex. Xmas.   NO SMOKING.   OVER 4s ONLY.   EN SUITE, BEVERAGES & T.V. IN ROOMS.
B. & B. FROM £27.50 (SINGLE), £38 (DOUBLE).

LEATHERHEAD

HAZELGROVE, EPSOM RD, WEST HORSLEY, NR LEATHERHEAD TEL: (014865) 4467
NO SMOKING.   OVER 6s.   BEVERAGES IN ROOMS. T.V. LOUNGE. B. & B. FROM £18.

OXTED

THE NEW BUNGALOW, OLD HALL FARM, TANDRIDGE LN, NR OXTED, SURREY, RH8 9NS
TEL: (01342) 892508   NO SMOKING .   WHEELCHAIR ACCESS.   CHILDREN WELCOME.   PETS B/A.   TV & BEVERAGES IN BEDROOMS.   B. & B. FROM £16.

ROSEHAVEN, 12 HOSKINS RD, OXTED, SURREY, RH8 9HT   TEL: (01883) 712700
NO SMOKING.   V, S.D. B/A.   CHILDREN WELCOME.   BEVERAGES & T.V.   B. & B. FROM £17.

RESTAURANTS

CROYDON

Intermission Restaurant

DEBENHAMS, 11-31 NORTH END, CROYDON, SURREY   TEL: (0181) 688 4455
Friendly family restaurant serving snacks, hot lunches & a range of hot and cold drinks.
OPEN STORE HOURS.   NO SMOKING.   V STD.   DISABLED ACCESS.   CHILDREN WELCOME. CREDIT CARDS.

HOCKNEYS VEGETARIAN RESTAURANT, 96/98 HIGH ST, CROYDON, CRO 1ND
NO SMOKING.   V EXC.   CHILDREN WELCOME.   ACCESS, VISA, AMEX, DINERS.

SELSDON PARK HOTEL, SANDERSTEAD, SOUTH CROYDON, CR2 8YA
TEL: (0181) 657 8811   N/S PHOENIX BRASSERIE.   V.   LICENSED.   DISABLED ACCESS WITH PRIOR NOTICE.
CHILDREN.

DORKING

CHAUCER'S RESTAURANT, THE WHITE HORSE, HIGH ST, DORKING, RH4 1BE
TEL: (01306) 881138   NO SMOKING.   V STD.   LICENSED.   CHILDREN WELCOME.   CREDIT CARDS.

PIZZA PIAZZA, 77 SOUTH ST, DORKING, RH4 2JU   TEL: (01306) 889790
40% N/S.   V STD.   LICENSED.   CHILDREN WELCOME.   ACCESS, VISA, AMEX, SWITCH.

GUILDFORD

Intermission Restaurant

DEBENHAMS, MILLBROOK, GUILDFORD, SURREY, GU1 3UU   TEL: (01483) 301300
Friendly self-service family restaurant serving snacks, hot lunches & range of hot & cold drinks.
OPEN STORE HOURS.   NO SMOKING.   V. STD.   DISABLED ACCESS.   CHILDREN WELCOME.   CREDIT/DEBIT CARDS.

SUTTON

Pavilion Coffee Shop

UNIT 21-22, TIMES 2, HIGH ST, SUTTON, SURREY, SM1 1LF   TEL: (0181) 643 9519
Friendly self-service coffee shop serving snacks, hot lunches & a range of hot & cold drinks.
OPEN STORE HOURS.   NO SMOKING.   V.   DISABLED ACCESS.   CHILDREN WELCOME.   CREDIT CARDS.

London & Middlesex

London

ACCOMMODATION

N19

Parkland Walk Guest House

12 HORNSEY RISE GARDENS, LONDON, N19 3PR   TEL: (0171) 263 3228 FAX: (0171) 831 9489
ETB Listed Commended. Certificate of Distinction in BTA's Best Small Hotel in London Competition. Small, friendly B. & B. in pretty, comfortable Victorian family house with easy access to M1, A1 and Central London, Kings Cross and Euston; also within easy reach of Hampstead, Alexandra Palace, Muswell Hill, Crouch End and Islington. There is a good choice of cooked breakfasts plus fresh fruits, yoghurt, home-made jams and wholemeal bread. You are within walking distance of over 40 restaurants. Brochure including map on request.
OPEN ALL YEAR.   NO SMOKING.   V, VE, WH STD.   ORG, S.D. B/A.   CHILDREN WELCOME.   SOME EN SUITE ROOMS.   TV & BEVERAGES IN ALL ROOMS.   AMEX.   B. & B. FROM £23.

NW3

HAMPSTEAD VILLAGE GUEST HOUSE, 2 KEMPLAY RD, NW3 1SY TEL: (0171) 435 8679
NO SMOKING.   V B/A.   CHILDREN WELCOME.   BEVERAGES & T.V. IN ROOMS.   B. & B. FROM £22.

NW4

18 GOLDERS RISE, HENDON, LONDON, NW4 2HR   TEL: (0181) 202 5321
NO SMOKING.   CHILDREN WELCOME.   T.V. LOUNGE.   B. & B. FROM £16.

Mount View

31 MOUNT VIEW RD, LONDON, N4 4SS   TEL: (0181) 340 9222   FAX: (081) 342 8494
Mount View is a smart 3-storey Victorian house which stands on a tree-lined street in a residential area. It has three tastefully decorated double bedrooms (each of which can be let as a single), one of which has en suite facilities. There is a choice of an English, Continental or health food breakfast served in a downstairs dining room opening on to the patio and garden. The nearest tube station is Finsbury Park, on the Piccadilly and Victoria lines with fast, direct access to central London.
OPEN ALL YEAR.   N/S DINING R.   S.D. B/A.   CHILDREN WELCOME.   EN SUITE, BEVERAGES AND TV IN BEDROOMS.   B. & B. FROM £15.

NW8

LONDON REGENTS PARK HILTON, 18 LODGE RD, ST JOHN'S WOOD, NW8 7JT
TEL: (0171) 722 7722   N/S PART OF DINING R.   V B/A.   LICENSED.   CREDIT CARDS.

W1

THE CUMBERLAND HOTEL, MARBLE ARCH, LONDON, W1A 4RF   TEL: (0171) 262 1234
50% N/S RESTAURANT & SOME BEDRS.   V STD.   LICENSED.   DISABLED ACCESS. CHILDREN WELCOME. PETS B/A.   EN SUITE , TV & BEVERAGES IN ROOMS.

THE HILTON ON PARK LANE, 22 PARK LANE, LONDON, W1A 2HH   TEL: (0171) 493 8000
N/S PART OF DINING R & SOME BEDRS.   V, S.D. STD.   LICENSED.   DISABLED ACCESS.   CHILDREN WELCOME. EN SUITE, BEVERAGES & T.V. IN ALL ROOMS. CREDIT CARDS.

THE MAYFAIR HOTEL, STRATTON ST, W1A 2AN   TEL: (0171) 629 1459
N/S PART OF DINING R.   V STD.   LICENSED.   DISABLED ACCESS.   CHILDREN WELCOME.   PETS B/A.   EN SUITE & T.V. IN ALL ROOMS.   CREDIT CARDS.

BERNERS PARK PLAZA HOTEL LONDON, 10 BERNERS ST, W1 TEL: (0171) 636 1629
N/S 50% DINING R & SOME BEDRS.   V STD.   LICENSED.   DISABLED: '10 ROOMS EQUIPPED FOR DISABLED GUESTS'.   CHILDREN WELCOME.   EN SUITE & T.V. IN ALL ROOMS.   CREDIT CARDS.

WC1

BLOOMSBURY CREST HOTEL, CORAM ST, WC1N 1HT   TEL: (0171) 837 1200
N/S 66% DINING R & SOME BEDRS.   V, DIAB, STD.   LICENSED.   DISABLED ACCESS.   CHILDREN WELCOME.
EN SUITE, BEVERAGES & T.V. IN ALL ROOMS.   CREDIT CARDS.

W4

Elliott Hotel

62 ELLIOTT RD, TURNHAM GREEN, LONDON, W4 1PE   TEL: (0181) 995 9794

2 lovely Victorian houses, joined & converted into very comfortable accommodation.
OPEN ALL YEAR.   N/S DINING R. & SOME BEDROOMS.   OVER 5S ONLY. B. & B. FROM £20.

W9

Colonnade Hotel

2 WARRINGTON CRESCENT, LONDON, W9 1ER   TEL: (0171) 286 1052

The Colonnade Hotel is an elegant, Grade II listed Victorian building which is situated in the fashionable residential area of Little Venice just 10 minutes' by bus or tube from London's West End. Beautifully refurbished in a manner in keeping with its original period features, the Colonnade Hotel offers an excellent choice of comfortably furnished en suite rooms to suit all tastes, including single, twin, double and four-poster bedded suites, each of which has been equipped with a helpful range of amenities including a hair dryer, trouser press and direct dial phone; foam pillows, featherless eiderdowns, cots and bed boards are all available on request. An excellent English breakfast is served daily and there is also the newly refurbished 'Cascades on the Crescent' restaurant and bar in which a full table d'hôte or light refreshment menu is served daily.

OPEN ALL YEAR.   N/S PART OF DINING R & SOME BEDROOMS.   V STD.   LICENSED.   DISABLED ACCESS.
CHILDREN WELCOME.   PETS B/A.   EN SUITE, BEVERAGES & T.V. IN ALL ROOMS.   B. & B. FROM £40.

SW1

Elizabeth Hotel & Apartments

37 ECCLESTON SQUARE, SW1V 1PB   TEL: (0171) 828 6812

The Elizabeth Hotel is a friendly, privately owned hotel in a quiet location, overlooking the magnificent gardens of a stately residential square (circa 1835) on the fringe of Belgravia, yet it is situated only 750 yards from the Victoria travel network. It offers thoroughly clean and comfortable accommodation and a good English breakfast at moderate prices. Every effort has been made to retain the atmosphere of a mid-19th C. London house where guests can enjoy a "home away from home" which is what a hotel, after all, is really supposed to be! The hotel - which has 40 bedrooms and a lift in which smoking is banned - was a 1986 winner of the BTA's London B. & B. Award. Single, double, twin and family rooms are available. There are also luxury studio and 2-bedroom apartments for minimum rental periods of 3 months. Special car parking arrangements.

OPEN ALL YEAR. N/S B'FAST ROOM. CHILDREN WELCOME. EN SUITE IN MANY ROOMS.   B. & B. FROM £30

SW7

ASTER HOUSE HOTEL, 3 SUMNER PLACE, SW7   TEL: (0171) 581 5888
N/S RESTAURANT & BEDRS.   EN SUITE & T.V. IN ROOMS.

SE10

TRADITIONAL B. & B, 34 DEVONSHIRE DR., GREENWICH, SE10 8JZ   TEL: (0181) 691 1918
N/S DINING R.   V STD. VE, DIAB, S.D.B/A.   CHILDREN.   T.V. & BEVERAGES IN ROOMS. B. & B. FROM £16.

RESTAURANTS

N1

PIZZA EXPRESS, 820 HIGH RD, NORTH FINCHLEY, N12 TEL: (0181) 445 7714
N/S PART OF RESTAURANT.   V.   LICENSED.   DISABLED. CHILDREN.

NW11

All' Italiana

8 PRINCES PARADE, GOLDERS GREEN RD, LONDON, NW11 9PS TEL: (0181) 458 9483

All' Italiana is a lively pasta bar which has an appeal for all age groups. In addition to a wide range of pastas and thin-based Italian style pizzas there is a choice of chicken or veal specialities and salads; over half the dishes are suitable for vegetarians and these are clearly marked on the menu. Sauces are freshly prepared and can be tailored to customers' requirements; prices are very reasonable. Three is also a take-away service.
OPEN ALL YEAR (7 eves & Sun. lunch, ex. for 3 summer wks)   NO SMOKING.   V STD.   CHILDREN WELCOME. LICENSED.   £12 -15.

W1

COUNTRY LIFE VEGETARIAN BUFFET, 1B HEDDON ST, W1 TEL: (0171) 434 2922
OPEN MOST LUNCHTIMES.   NO SMOKING.   V EXC.

Debenhams Intermission Coffee Shop

334-348 OXFORD ST, LONDON, W1A 1DF   TEL: (071) 580 3000

A Friendly Self-service Coffee Shop serving lunches, snacks & hot and cold drinks.
OPEN STORE HOURS.   NO SMOKING.   V STD. DISABLED ACCESS.   CHILDREN WELCOME. CREDIT CARDS.

Mildred's Wholefood Cafe and Take-Away

58 GREEK ST, LONDON, W1V 5LR   TEL: (0171) 494 1634

Acclaimed vegetarian and wholefood restaurant serving very reasonably priced meals.
OPEN 12 NOON - 11 P.M.   NO SMOKING.   V STD.   LICENSED.   CHILDREN WELCOME.

Ming

35-36 GREEK ST, LONDON, W1V 5LN   TEL: (0171) 437 0292

A peaceful, friendly Chinese restaurant in Soho.
OPEN 12 - 11.45.   N/S PART SEPARATE PART OF RESTAURANT.   V STD.   LICENSED.   CHILDREN WELCOME. CREDIT CARDS.

THE ROYAL ACADEMY RESTAURANT, BURLINGTON HOUSE, PICCADILLY,
TEL: (0171) 287 0752   OPEN 10 - 5.30 DAILY. SUNDAY BRUNCH A SPECIALITY 11.45 - 2.45.   NO SMOKING.
V.   LICENSED.   EXCELLENT DISABLED ACCESS.

WC1

GREENHOUSE VEG. RESTAURANT, 16 CHENIES ST, WC1E 7EX TEL: (0171) 637 8038
NO SMOKING.   V.   DISABLED: 'BY PRIOR ARRANGEMENT'.

Wagamama

4 STREATHAM ST, LONDON, WC1A 1JB   TEL: (0171) 323 9223   FAX: (0171) 323 9224

Highly acclaimed Japanese-style noodle bar.
OPEN ALL YEAR (ex. Xmas Day & New Year's Day).   NO SMOKING.   V STD.   CHILDREN WELCOME. LICENSED.

W2

SEASONS VEGETARIAN RESTAURANT, 22 HARCOURT ST, W2
TEL: (0171) 402 5925   N/S PART OF RESTAURANT, UPSTAIRS.   V, VE EXC.   LICENSED.

WC2

THE CANADIAN MUFFIN CO., 5 KING ST, COVENT GARDEN, LONDON, WC2E 8HN
TEL: (0171) 379 1525   NO SMOKING.   V.   CHILDREN WELCOME.

BRIXTONIAN BACKYARD, 4 NEAL'S YARD, COVENT GARDEN, WC2 9DP
TEL: (0171) 240 2769   NO SMOKING.   V STD.   LICENSED.

Food For Thought

31 NEAL ST, LONDON, WC2H 9PA   TEL: (0171) 836 0239   FAX: (0171) 379 1249

Food For Thought, situated in the heart of Covent Garden, is one of London's most popular vegetarian restaurants and has been serving excellent meat-free fare since 1974. It is a friendly family-run concern, serving delicious food at healthy prices (a 3-course meal costs under £10). The menu changes daily and offers a tempting variety of innovative dishes such as Tom Yam Soup, Kirsch and Dill Fondue, Chilli Gambo, and the irresistible Banoffi Pie - all freshly prepared on the premises. Ideal for pre-theatre dining. BYOs very welcome (no corkage charge). Wheat-free and vegan dishes always available.
OPEN 12 - 8.   NO SMOKING.   V, VE EXC.   CHILDREN WELCOME.

THE NATIONAL GALLERY RESTAURANT, TRAFALGAR SQUARE, WC2N 5DN
TEL: (0171) 389 1760   75% N/S (SEP. ROOM).   V STD.   LICENSED.   DISABLED ACCESS.   CHILDREN.

Smollensky's On The Strand

105 THE STRAND, LONDON, WC2R 0AA   TEL: (0171) 497 2101   FAX: (0171) 836 3270

Smollensky's on the Strand is a large, bustling 'fun' restaurant situated right in the heart of central London. It is patronised by many faithful clientele who come to enjoy its terrific atmosphere (Americabilia bedeks the walls), dancing on Thursdays, Fridays and Saturdays and its excellent food. The something-for-everyone menu includes a range of steak options (tender beef in French bread, Steak Tartare, a choice of six accompanying sauces), imaginative vegetarian dishes (Tricolour Pasta Gateau, Wild Rice and Vine Leaf Risotto), special food for children and a range of daily changing specialities. Desserts are scrumptious (Very, Very Chocolate Fudge Cake (sic.), New York Toffee Cheesecake) and the wine list competes for attention with the exotic range of house cocktails (there is the usual Bloody Mary and Pina Colada, but also some less familiar choices such as Long Island Iced Tea: 4 heavy duty spirits, a dash of Coke and a strong sense of adventure).
OPEN Mon.-Thurs. 12 Noon-Midnight; Thurs, Fri. & Sat. 12 Noon-12.30a.m.; Sun. 12 Noon-10.30 p.m.   50% N/S.   V STD.
LICENSED.   CHILDREN WELCOME.   CREDIT CARDS.

SW1

CAFÉ FIGARO, 6 LOWER REGENT ST, LONDON
NO SMOKING.

WILKINS NATURAL FOOD, 61 MARSHAM ST, SW1 P3DP   TEL: (0171) 222 4038
NO SMOKING.   V, VE EXC.   DISABLED ACCESS.   CHILDREN WELCOME.

THE WREN AT ST JAMES'S, 35 JERMYN ST, SW1Y 6JD   TEL: (0171) 437 9419
NO SMOKING.   V, VE EXC.   DISABLED ACCESS.

SW6

WINDMILL WHOLEFOODS, 486 FULHAM RD, SW6 5NH   TEL: (0171) 385 1570
NO SMOKING.   V, VE EXC.   LICENSED.   DISABLED ACCESS.   CHILDREN WELCOME.

SW7

NATURAL HISTORY MUSEUM REST., CROMWELL RD, SW7 5BD TEL: (0171) 938 8149
NO SMOKING.   V.   LICENSED.   DISABLED ACCESS.   CHILDREN WELCOME.

NEW RESTAURANT, THE VICTORIA AND ALBERT MUSEUM, CROMWELL RD, SW7 2RL
N/S 40%.   V.   LICENSED.   DISABLED ACCESS.   CHILDREN WELCOME.

TERRACE CAFE RESTAURANT, MUSEUM OF LONDON.
N/S 60%.   V STD.   LICENSED.   DISABLED ACCESS.   CHILDREN WELCOME.

SW9

Brixtonian

11 DORRELL PLACE, BRIXTON, LONDON, SW9 3PL   TEL: (0171) 978 8870
OPEN 7 - 11.30.   NO SMOKING. V STD.   LICENSED.   DISABLED ACCESS TO DOWNSTAIRS.   CHILDREN WELCOME.

E17

Gannets Vegetarian Café & Restaurant

458 HOE ST, WALTHAMSTOW, LONDON, E17 9AH   TEL: (0181) 558 6880
Wholefood & vegetarian restaurant using organic & unsprayed products wherever possible.
The café & restaurant menus have daily specials depending on seasonal availability of
products.
OPEN: Café: Tues.-Fri. 10-4; Sat. 9-5. Restaurant: Thurs.-Sat. 7 (last orders 10 p.m.).   NO SMOKING.   WHEELCHAIR
ACCESS.   CHILDREN WELCOME.   LICENCE PENDING (BYO)

E2

Cherry Orchard Vegetarian Restaurant

241 GLOBE RD, LONDON, E2   TEL: (0181) 980 6678
OPEN Mon, Thurs, Fri 11-4, Tues, Wed, 11-7.   NO SMOKING.   V, VE, S.D., WH STD.   DISABLED ACCESS.
CHILDREN WELCOME.

PUBS & WINE BARS

SE1

THE ANCHOR TAP, 20A HORSELEYDOWN LN, LONDON, SE1.   TEL: (0171) 403 4637
SEPARATE SMOKE-FREE ROOMS.   V STD.   CHILDREN WELCOME.

THE LAMB, 94 LAMBS CONDUIT ST, BLOOMSBURY, WC1
NO SMOKING PART OF PUB.

THREE LORDS, THE MINORIES, CITY, EC3
NO SMOKING PART OF PUB.

Crown & Greyhound

73 DULWICH VILAGE, LONDON, SE21   TEL: (0181) 693 2466
Situated in the heart of South London, Dulwich Village is a haven of rural peace and has
much of unique interest including the Dulwich Picture Gallery (the oldest in London) and
a toll-gate (which is the only one in the city). Most significantly for our purposes is the
tradition of hospitality which has prevailed at the Crown & Greyhound since the 18th C.
and whose 19th C. customers included Charles Dickens and John Ruskin. There have, of
course, been changes over the years but these have not included the addition of wall-to-wall
muzak and there is still a friendly, intimate atmosphere despite the pub's obvious popularity.
The food is good, generous, reasonably priced pub fare and the room which served as a
banqueting suite in the old building is now still a splendid venue for parties or conferences.
N/S FAMILY ROOM.   V STD.   CHILDREN WELCOME.   CREDIT CARDS.

Middlesex

ACCOMMODATION

HEATHROW AIRPORT/WEST DRAYTON

Holiday Inn Crowne Plaza London Heathrow

STOCKLEY RD, WEST DRAYTON, MIDD'X, UB7 9NA   TEL: (01895) 445555 FAX: (01895) 445122

The Holiday Inn Crowne Plaza London Heathrow is situated just 2 miles from Heathrow airport and offers a superb choice of 375 executive bedrooms and suites - 50% of which are non-smoking. The upgraded hotel - now one of Holiday Inns' 4 star de luxe properties - has two new restaurants: the informal Café Galleria (offering famous regional dishes, light snacks, breakfasts and superb hot and cold tables) has a light summery atmosphere, while the more formal Marlowe Restaurant offers superb food and wine in an elegant ambience. Thirty new meeting rooms with extensive conference facilities and a purpose-built training centre are available and guests may additionally take advantage of Reflexions Health and Leisure Centre with its indoor swimming pool, steam room, sauna, plunge pool, whirlpool spa, sunbed, gym and beauty therapy room.

OPEN ALL YEAR.   N/S 50% RESTAURANTS & BEDR.   V, S.D. B/A.   LICENSED.   DISABLED ACCESS. CHILDREN WELCOME.   PETS B/A.   EN SUITE, BEVERAGES & T.V. IN ROOMS.   CREDIT CARDS.   B. & B. FROM £130.

EXCELSIOR HOTEL, HEATHROW, BATH RD, WEST DRAYTON, UB7 0DU
TEL: (0181) 759 6611 N/S PART OF RESTAURANT & IN SOME BEDRS.   V STD.   LICENSED.   DISABLED ACCESS.
CHILDREN WELCOME.   EN SUITE, TV & BEVERAGES IN ALL ROOMS.   B. & B. FROM £110.

RESTAURANTS

HARROW

Debenhams

STATION RD, HARROW, HA1 1NA   TEL: (0181) 427 4300

Intermission, A Friendly Self-service Restaurant serving lunches, snacks, hot & cold drinks.
OPEN STORE HOURS.   NO SMOKING.   V.   DISABLED ACCESS.   CHILDREN WELCOME.   CREDIT CARDS.

NORTH HARROW

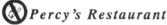

Percy's Restaurant

66-68 STATION RD, NORTH HARROW, HA2 7SJ   TEL: (0181) 427 2021

Percy's is an elegant, spacious restaurant with 1930s decor offering modern English cuisine in the form of an original and innovative menu. Many of the vegetables, herbs and salads are grown on Percy's own farm in Devon. Typical first courses would include Warm Pepper Salad on a bed of tender spinach leaves, with marinated Feta cheese, fresh marjoram, smoked garlic and Balsamic vinegar, or Home-Cured Gravad Lax with a dill, mustard and honey dressing. Main courses include Fillet of Skate encasing Swiss chard, shallots and Buffalo Mozzarella, cooked with fresh chives, crushed pink peppercorns, raspberries and a red onion vinaigrette; Fresh Pike poached wth baby leeks and white wine, with fresh asparagus and Sauce Mousseline; Tenderloin of Wild Venison, cooked pink, with forest mushrooms and juniper glaze, or Goat's Cheese, Avocado and Asparagus baked in a herbed puff pastry crust with wild sorrel sauce. Desserts include Lemon Tart with rosemary icecream; Lavender Crème Brulée, or Chocolate and Rum Pithivier with cardamom ice cream.

OPEN Tues. - Sat. Lunch & Eves   LAST ORDERS 10.30.   NO SMOKING.   L. FROM £13.   V STD. S.D. B/A.
LICENSED.   DISABLED ACCESS.   OVER 10s WELCOME.   ACCESS, VISA, AMEX, DINERS.

Thames and Chilterns

Berkshire & Bedfordshire

ACCOMMODATION

COOKHAM DEAN

🚭Primrose Hill

BRADCUTTS LN., COOKHAM DEAN, BERKS., SL6 9TL   TEL: (01628) 528179
Large turn of the century house in rural location close to Windsor, Heathrow, Henley &
Marlow. Easily accessible from M40 & M4.
OPEN ALL YEAR ex. Xmas.   NO SMOKING.   V B/A.   TV   B. & B. £15-17.50.

NEWBURY

🚭 **11 DONNINGTON SQUARE, NEWBURY, BERKS, RG13 1PJ TEL: (01672) 46771**
Late Georgian house in quiet residential square 10 mins walk from town centre.
NO SMOKING.   B. & B. AROUND £22.

THE BELL AT BOXFORD, LAMBOURN RD, NEWBURY, BERKS, RG16 8DD
N/S DINING R & SOME BEDRS.   V. LICENSED.   CHILDREN.

FISHERS FARM, SHEFFORD WOODLANDS, NEWBURY, RG16 7AB TEL: (048838) 466
N/S EX. SITTING ROOM.   V. STD.   NOT LICENSED, BUT WINE INCLUDED.   CHILDREN.   B. & B. FROM £24.

READING

🚭 **THE BERKELEY GUEST HOUSE, 32 BERKELEY AVE, RG1 6RE TEL: (01734) 595699**
Large, double-fronted, family-run guest house near town centre; central heating.
NO SMOKING. V, S.D. B/A.   CHILDREN WELCOME.   PETS B/A.   BEVERAGES & T.V. IN ALL ROOMS. CAR
PARKING SPACE. B. & B. FROM £18.

🚭 **TUDOR HOUSE, MAIDENHATCH, PANGBOURNE, READING, RG8 8HP TEL: (01734)
744482**
NO SMOKING.   V. STD.   CHILDREN WELCOME.   B. & B. FROM £20.

SANDY

🚭 **Highfield Farm**

TEMPSFORD RD, SANDY, BEDS, SG19 2AQ   TEL: (01767) 682332
Set well back from the road and beautifullly situated in its own grounds and arable
farm, Highfield Farm is a haven of peace and tranquillity - a rest for travellers although a
deceptive 2½ miles from the A1's junction with the A428. Accommodation is in comfortable twin, double and family rooms - with bathroom en suite; two of the rooms are on the
ground floor in the carefully converted stable block, with its original beams - lots of
character, and an ideal choice for those who find stairs difficult. Your hostess, Margaret
Codd, serves a delicious traditional English breakfast to guests (all special dietary needs
can be accommodated by arrangement) before your day's sightseeing in Cambridge or
Woburn Abbey.
OPEN ALL YEAR.   NO SMOKING.   V, S.D. B/A.   CHILDREN WELCOME.   PETS B/A.   DISABLED: 2 GROUND
FLOOR ROOMS.   EN SUITE, TV & BEVERAGES IN BEDROOMS.   B. & B. FROM £16.

🚭 **WINDSOR**

62 QUEEN'S RD, WINDSOR, BERKS, SL4 3BH   TEL/FAX: (01753) 866036
Deceptively spacious Victorian home in quiet town centre location just 10 minutes' walk
from Windsor Castle and the railway station; good restaurants nearby; private parking.
NO SMOKING.   V, FAT-FREE B/A.   GROUND FLOOR BEDROOM BUT LIMITED WHEELCHAIR ACCESS TO BATH-
ROOM.   CHILDREN WELCOME.   EN SUITE, BEVERAGES & T.V. IN ROOMS. B. & B. FROM £15.

RESTAURANTS

BEDFORD

Ⓝ *Debenhams Springles Restaurant*

48 - 54 HIGH ST, BEDS., MK40 1ST   TEL: (01234) 42581

Friendly self-service family restaurant serving snacks, hot lunches & hot and cold drinks.
OPEN STORE HOURS. NO SMOKING. V STD. DISABLED ACCESS. CHILDREN WELCOME. CREDIT CARDS.

LUTON

Ⓝ *Debenhams Pavilion Coffee Shop*

56 - 80 THE ARNDALE CENTRE, LUTON, BEDS, LU1 2SZ   TEL: (01582) 21201

A friendly self-service coffee shop serving snacks, hot lunches & hot and cold drinks.
OPEN STORE HOURS. NO SMOKING. V STD. DISABLED ACCESS. CHILDREN WELCOME. CREDIT CARDS.

NEWBURY

Ⓝ **THE CURIOUS CAT, 5 INCH'S YD, MARKET ST, NEWBURY. TEL: (01635) 35491**
NO SMOKING.   V & fresh fish a speciality.   LICENSED.   CHILDREN WELCOME (high chair, feeder mugs)

Ⓝ **WATERMILL THEATRE RESTAURANT, BAGNOR, NEWBURY. TEL: (01635) 46044**
OPEN PRE-SHOW 6 - 7.15, POST-SHOW, 9.45. NO SMOKING. V. LICENSED. CHILDREN WELCOME.

READING

CHEZ FONTANA, 3 QUEEN'S WALK, READING, BERKS. TEL: (01734) 504513
OPEN 12 - 2.30, 7 - 11.   SEPARATE AREA FOR NON-SMOKERS.   V STD.   LICENSED. CHILDREN WELCOME.

Ⓝ *Debenhams Intermission Restaurant*

125-133 BROAD ST, BERKS, RG1 2BQ   TEL: (01734) 588811

A friendly self-service family restaurant serving snacks, hot lunches & hot and cold drinks.
OPEN STORE HOURS. NO SMOKING. V STD. DISABLED ACCESS. CHILDREN WELCOME. CREDIT CARDS.

Pipers Island Restaurant

PIPERS ISLAND, READING, BERKS, RG4 8AH   TEL: (01734) 484573   FAX: (01734) 461497
OPEN 6 - 10. SEPARATE AREA FOR SMOKERS. V STD. LICENSED. CHILDREN WELCOME.

PIZZA EXPRESS, 56 ST MARY'S BUTTS, READING, BERKS.   TEL: (01734) 391920
OPEN DAILY, 12 NOON TILL 12 MIDNIGHT.   N/S 26 SEATS IN SEPARATE SECTION. V. STD.   LICENSED.

THATCHAM

Ⓝ **GARLANDS, SHOP 3, 16 HIGH ST, THATCHAM, BERKS   TEL: (01635) 61017**
OPEN MON. - SAT.   NO SMOKING.   GOOD FACILITIES FOR CHILDREN.

WINDSOR

CHAOS CAFÉ, WINDSOR ARTS CENTRE, ST LEONARDS RD, WINDSOR TEL: (01753) 859421
OPEN TUE. - SAT. 11 - 2.30, FRI. - SAT. 7.30 - 9.   50% N/S.   V STD.   CHILDREN WELCOME.

COUNTRY KITCHEN, 3 KING EDWARD COURT, WINDSOR, BERKS. TEL: (01753) 868681
50% N/S   V STD.   LICENSED.   CHILDREN WELCOME.   ACCESS, VISA.

PUBS & WINE BARS

FINCHINHAMPSTEAD

THE QUEEN'S OAK, CHURCH LN, FINCH'STEAD, NR WOKINGHAM TEL: (01734) 734855

Pub serving great pizzas and real ales, with one smoke-free bar (oldest no-smoking bar in Berkshire.).
N/S ONE ROOM.

Buckinghamshire

ACCOMMODATION

AYLESBURY

FOXHILL FARMHOUSE, KINGSEY, AYLESBURY, HP17 8LZ   TEL: (01844) 291650
Peaceful 17th C. Grade II listed oak-beamed house set in a large garden with views to the Chiltern Hills. Breakfast only. Swimming pool available.
NO SMOKING.   V B/A.   OVER 5S ONLY.   EN SUITE & TV. B. & B. AROUND £19.

POLETREES FARM, BRILL, LUDGERSHALL RD, AYLESBURY. TEL: (01844) 238276
NO SMOKING.   V B/A.   T.V. IN LOUNGE.   B. & B. AROUND £18.

BUCKINGHAM

Folly Farm
PADBURY, BUCKINGHAM, MK18 2HS   TEL: (01296) 712413
Comfortable well-appointed farmhouse on A413, 3m from the market town of Buckingham. Close to Stowe Landscape Gardens and Silverstone Circuit. 15 mins Milton Keynes.
OPEN ALL YEAR ex. Xmas.   NO SMOKING.   EN SUITE & CENTRAL HEATING ALL ROOMS.   EVENING MEALS B/A.   B. & B. FROM £17.50. SINGLE £17.50.

FARNHAM COMMON
OLDFIELDS HOTEL, BEACONSFIELD RD, FARNHAM COMMON. TEL: (01753) 643322
Beautiful detached mock tudor house which has been attractively decorated.
N/S DINING R AND MOST BEDRS.   DISABLED ACCESS . CHILDREN WELCOME.   PETS B/A.   EN SUITE SOME ROOMS.   BEVERAGES & T.V. IN ROOMS.   CREDIT CARDS.   B. & B. FROM £24.

HIGH WYCOMBE
BELMONT GUEST HOUSE, 9 PRIORY AVENUE, HIGH WYCOMBE   TEL: (01494) 27046
Splendid Victorian building in the centre of High Wycombe. Pizzas, salads and soft drinks can be ordered in the evening for serving in your room.
N/S DINING R & SOME BEDRS.   V B/A.   DISABLED ACCESS.   CHILDREN WELCOME. SOME ROOMS EN SUITE. BEVERAGES & T.V. IN BEDROOMS. CREDIT CARDS.

CHILTERN HOTEL, 181-183 WEST WYCOMBE RD, HIGH WYCOMBE. TEL: (01494) 452597.
Popular hotel with very friendly staff. Good recommendations from pr evious guests.
N/S DINING R & SOME BEDRS.   V STD, S.D. B/A.   LICENSED. DISABLED ACCESS.   CHILDREN WELCOME.   PETS B/A.   EN SUITE IN SOME ROOMS.   BEVERAGES, T.V. AND PHONE IN ROOMS.   CREDIT CARDS.   B. & B. AROUND £26.

LITTLE MARLOW

Monkton Farm
LITTLE MARLOW, BUCKS, SL7 3RF   TEL: (01494) 521082
Charming 14th C. 'cruck' farmhouse with 150 acre working dairy farm in the beautiful Chilterns. English breakfast served in the large farm kitchen.
OPEN ALL YEAR.   NO SMOKING.   V, S.D. B/A.   OVER 5s WELCOME.   BEVERAGES & T.V. IN ROOMS.   B. & B. FROM £18.

MILTON KEYNES

Chantry Farm
PINDON END, HANSLOPE, MILTON KEYNES   TEL: (01908) 510269
Farmhouse built of Northamptonshire Stone with 500 acre mixed farm. Swimming pool and trout lake.
NO SMOKING.   V STD, S.D. B/A.   DISABLED ACCESS.   CHILDREN WELCOME. PETS B/A.   BEVERAGES & T.V. IN ALL BEDROOMS.   B. & B.AROUND £15.

Richmond Lodge

MURSLEY, NR MILTON KEYNES, BUCKS, MK17 0LE   TEL: (01296) 720275

Built as a hunting lodge at the turn of the century, Richmond Lodge is set in 3 acres of gardens and an orchard which has grazing sheep and lambs. Dinner at 7 p.m. if ordered in advance.
OPEN ALL YEAR.   NO SMOKING.   OVER 6s WELCOME.   1 TWIN EN SUITE, 1 TWIN PRIVATE BATH.   BEVERAGES & T.V.   B. & B. FROM £18.

PRESTWOOD

Wildridings

3 GLEBELANDS CL, PRESTWOOD, GREAT MISSENDEN, BUCKS., HP16 0QP TEL: (012406) 3627

Traditionally-built family home in quiet situation overlooking farmland and meadows. One double en suite bedroom. Near to West Wycombe & N.T. houses. Simple suppers.
NO SMOKING.   EN SUITE, TV & BEVERAGES IN BEDROOM.   B. & B. £18, D. £7

RESTAURANTS

AMERSHAM-ON-THE-HILL

UPPER CRUST TEA RM, 103 SYCAMORE RD, AMERSHAM, HP6 5EJ TEL: (012406) 6919

Tea room above butcher's shop serving snacks and lunches.
NO SMOKING.   CHILDREN WELCOME.   CREDIT CARDS.

BEACONSFIELD

GEORGIAN COFFEE HOUSE, WYCOMBE END, BEACONSFIELD TEL: (01494) 678550
SEPARATE AREA FOR SMOKERS.   V STD.   CHILDREN WELCOME.

THE KINGS HEAD, OXFORD ROAD, HOLTSPUR, BEACONSFIELD TEL: (01494) 673337
50% N/S.   V STD.   LICENSED.   CHILDREN WELCOME.   CREDIT CARDS.

BOURNE END

THE SPADE OAK, OLDMOORHOLM LANE, WELL END, BOURNE END TEL: (016285) 20090
50% N/S.   V STD.   LICENSED.   CHILDREN WELCOME.   ACCESS, VISA.

HIGH WYCOMBE

BLACKSMITHS ARMS, OLD MARLOW ROAD, HIGH WYCOMBE TEL: (01494) 25323
NO-SMOKING.   LICENSED.   DISABLED ACCESS.   CHILDREN WELCOME.

MONI'S BISTRO, BOOKER GARDEN CENTRE, CLAY LANE, BOOKER, HIGH WYCOMBE
TEL: (01494) 462182 SEPARATE DINING ROOM FOR SMOKERS.   V STD.   DISABLED ACCESS.   CHILDREN WELCOME.   CREDIT CARDS.

MIDDLE CLAYDON

CLAYDON HOUSE, MIDDLE CLAYDON, MK18 2EY TEL: (0296) 730349
Charming tea room within stately home owned by the National Trust.
NO SMOKING.   V, S.D. B/A.   DISABLED ACCESS.   CHILDREN WELCOME.

MILTON KEYNES

FOUNTAIN HARVESTER, LONDON RD, LOUGHTON, MILTON KEYNES, TEL: (01908) 666203
50% N/S.   V STD.   LICENSED.   DISABLED ACCESS.   CHILDREN WELCOME.

Hertfordshire

ACCOMMODATION

BISHOP'S STORTFORD

THE COTTAGE, 71 BIRCHANGER LN, BIRCHANGER, CM23 5QA TEL: (01279) 812349
NO SMOKING. V. STD. LICENSED. DISABLED ACCESS. CHILDREN.

HERTFORD

HALL HOUSE, BROAD OAK END, OFF BRAMFIELD RD, SG14 2JA TEL: (01992) 582807
OPEN ALL YEAR. NO SMOKING. V. STD EN SUITE. BEVERAGES & T.V. B. &. B. FROM £30.

RICKMANSWORTH

6 Swallow Close

NIGHTINGALE ROAD, RICKMANSWORTH, HERTS, WD3 2DZ   TEL: (01923) 720069
Charming guest house in a quiet cul-de-sac just ½ hr's tube ride from central London (the
underground station is nearby). All food is home-cooked - including the bread and preserves
- and there are home-grown vegetables and home-laid eggs!
OPEN ALL YEAR.   NO SMOKING.   V B/A.   OVER 5S ONLY. B. &. B. FROM £17.

ST ALBANS

Amaryllis

25 RIDGMONT RD, ST ALBANS, HERTS, AL1 3AG   TEL: (01727) 862755 & (0850) 662371
ETB listed. A friendly, informal family home convenient for M1, M25. Frequent
trains to London (20 mins), Gatwick airport..
OPEN ALL YEAR.   NO SMOKING.   V, WH, VE, S.D. B/A.   CHILDREN.   BEVERAGES & T.V.   B. & B. Twin
£28-32, Sgl £13-20, Fmly £36-40.

The Squirrels

74 SANDRIDGE RD, ST ALBANS, HERTS, AL1 4AR   TEL: (01727) 840497
ETB Approved Listed. Edwardian terrace house; 10 mins walk to historic St Albans town
centre & 20 mins to mainline station with frequent trains to London. Imaginative breakfasts.
OPEN mid Jan.-mid Dec. NO SMOKING. V, S.D. B/A. EN SUITE, TV & BEVERAGES.   B. & B. Dblr £27.50, Sgl £17.50.

RESTAURANTS

BERKHAMSTEAD

COOKS DELIGHT, 360-364 HIGH ST, BERKHAMSTEAD, HP4 1HU TEL:(01442) 863584
NO SMOKING. V, VE, MACROB. STD. LICENSED. CHILDREN WELCOME. ACCESS, VISA.

HEMEL HEMPSTEAD

THE GALLERY, OLD TOWN HALL, HIGH ST, HP1 3AE TEL: (01442) 232416

ST ALBANS

Kingsbury Watermill Waffle House

ST MICHAELS ST, ST ALBANS, HERTS, AL3 4SJ   TEL: (01727) 853502

Kingsbury Watermill is situated in one of the loveliest
corners of St Albans on the River Ver. The building in
which it is housed is scheduled as an ancient monument
as it was used for the milling of flour until 1936 & still
has the atmosphere of a bustling workplace plus the working machinery of the original corn crushing mill. The
Millers Parlour & house is now converted into a Waffle
House where freshly baked waffles are served with tasty
toppings; many organic ingredients are used including
organically-grown, stone-ground flour, free-range
chicken & eggs, and meat from 'real meat' farms.
OPEN Tues.-Sat. 11-6, Sun. 12-6. closes 5pm winter. V STD. CHILDREN WELCOME.

Oxfordshire

ACCOMMODATION

BANBURY

 **Pond Cottage**

THE GREEN, WARMINGTON, BANBURY, OX17 1BU   TEL: (01295) 789682

Beautiful old stone-built cottage overlooking village green and duck pond.
NO SMOKING. 1 EN SUITE ROOM, ONE WITH PRIVATE BATHROOM. BEVERAGES IN BOTH BEDROOMS.   TV IN SITTING ROOM.   B. & B. AROUND £34 DOUBLE.

 Rectory Farm

SULGRAVE, BANBURY, OXON, OX17 2SG   TEL: (01295) 760261

 Rectory Farm is a 17th C. thatched farmhouse standing on the edge of Sulgrave village and opposite Sulgrave Manor, the ancestral home of George Washington. There are three double bedrooms and a family room all of which are brightly decorated and have magnificent views over the lovely Northamptonshire countryside. Children are welcome; although no longer a working farm there are usually plenty of animals for them to get to know. There is a choice of a full English breakfast or continental breakfast which includes croissants from the local bakery. A delicious three course dinner can be served by arrangement although there are several excellent pubs within a few minutes' drive. A typical evening menu at Rectory Farm would include home-made soup, stuffed shoulder of lamb with fresh vegetables followed by traditonal pudding such as apple meringue or hot baked soufflé.
OPEN ALL YEAR ex. Xmas.   NO SMOKING.   S.D. B/A.   PETS & CHILDREN WELCOME.   LICENSED.   BEVERAGES IN ROOMS.   B. & B. £16.50, D. £10 - 12

 Studleigh Farm

WALES ST, KINGS SUTTON, BANBURY, OXON, OX17 3RR   TEL: (01295) 811979

17th C. renovated and modernised farmhouse on 8 acres of pastureland in picturesque village; several good village pubs nearby and fishing rights on the Cherwell are available.
OPEN ALL YEAR.   NO SMOKING.   V, S.D. B/A.   EN SUITE & BEVERAGES IN ROOMS.   T.V. LOUNGE.   B. & B. FROM £20.

Sugarswell Farm

SHENINGTON, BANBURY, OXON, OX15 6HW   TEL: (01295) 680512

 This lovely large stone-built farmhouse looks as though it has been part of the lush Oxfordshire countryside in which it stands, for centuries. In fact it has been built relatively recently and as such boasts all the modern conveniences you could wish for - but also has a standard of cosiness and character that you would only expect with much older buildings: there are log fires in the lounge and the prettily decorated bedrooms are furnished in a cottagey style. Food is of great importance at Sugarswell combining the best of British farmhouse fare with continental dishes. Your hostess is a Cordon Bleu cook - so you can be sure of an excellent meal. There is much to see and do in the area - Warwick, Woodstock, Oxford and Stratford are all within easy reach while Banbury has much of historic interest (including its cross) to commend it.
OPEN ALL YEAR.   NO SMOKING.   EN SUITE & BEVERAGES IN ROOMS.   AMEX.   B. & B. FROM £22.

WROXTON HOUSE HOTEL, WROXTON ST MARY, NR BANBURY, OX15 6QB
TEL: (0295) 730777 N/S DINING R & PART OF BAR.   V B/A.   LICENSED.   CHILDREN WELCOME.   PETS B/A.   EN SUITE, BEVERAGES & T.V. IN ROOMS.   B. & B. FROM £49.

BICESTER

NEWBY COTTAGE, WESTON ON THE GREEN, BICESTER, OX6 8QL TEL: (01869) 50662
NO SMOKING.   V B/A.   CHILDREN WELCOME.   T.V.   B. & B. FROM £16.

CHIPPING NORTON

Southcombe Lodge Guest House
SOUTHCOMBE, CHIPPING NORTON, OXON, OX7 5JF   TEL: (01608) 643068

Southcombe Guest House is an attractive modern bungalow standing in 3 acres of grounds overlooking Chipping Norton golf course. The ground floor arrangements make it an ideal choice for disabled guests as there are no stairs to negotiate and en suite facilties are also available. An entirely smoke-free establishment, Southcombe is an ideal choice for those touring the Cotswolds, Blenheim and Stratford. Evening meals are available and guests will be pleased to hear that everything is home-cooked (using low-fat cooking methods wherever possible); the traditional British menu would typically feature soup followed by a roast dinner with fresh vegetables and a choice of home-made desserts such as apple pie.
OPEN ALL YEAR.   NO SMOKING.   V, S.D. B/A.   LICENSED.   DISABLED ACCESS.   CHILDREN WELCOME.
T.V. LOUNGE.   EN SUITE, TV & BEVERAGES IN SOME ROOMS.   B. & B. FROM £17.

FARINGDON

BOWLING GREEN FARM, STANFORD RD, SN7 8EZ TEL: (01367) 240229
Small, family-run farm 1 mile south of faringdon; packed lunches available.
OPEN ALL YEAR.   NO SMOKING.   CHILDREN.   EN SUITE, TV & TEA-MAKING IN ROOMS.   B. & B. £20.

OXFORD

Combermere House
11 POLSTEAD RD, OXFORD, OXON, OX2 6TW   TEL: (01865) 56971
Family-run guest house in quiet tree-lined road off Woodstock Road in residential N. Oxford.
OPEN ALL YEAR.   N/S DINING R.   V, S.D. B/A.   CHILDREN WELCOME.   DISABLED ACCESS: 'to ground floor
including dining room'. PETS B/A.   EN SUITE, TV & BEVERAGES IN ROOMS.   CREDIT CARDS.   B. & B. FROM £22.

COTSWOLD HOUSE, 363 BANBURY RD, OXFORD, OX2 7PL TEL: (01865) 310558
NO SMOKING. V STD, S.D. B/A (B'fast only).   CHILDREN: OVER 6S ONLY.   EN SUITE, TV & BEVERAGES
IN ALL ROOMS.   B. & B. FROM £23.

The Dial House
25 LONDON RD, HEADINGTON, OXFORD, OSON, OX3 7RE   TEL: (01865) 69944

This elegant half-timbered house, set in a beautiful garden just one and a half miles from Oxford city centre (there is a bus service with routes both to London and the centre of Oxford just outside the front door), is the perfect choice for holiday-makers in search of clean, comfortable accommodation with all the modern conveniences of a well-appointed hotel - but with the personal service and attention of a small, friendly guest house. Your hosts, Tony and Julie Lamb, will do everything possible to make your stay a happy and comfortable one - and, while breakfast is the only meal available at Dial House, it is good and hearty (with vegetarian options on request), and there are literally scores of good restaurants in Oxford.
OPEN ALL YEAR EX. XMAS.   N/S DINING R AND BEDRS.   OVER 6s ONLY.   PETS B/A.   EN SUITE/PRIVATE,
BEVERAGES & T.V. IN ALL BEDROOMS.   B. & B. FROM £22.50 (£45 FOR 2 PERSONS).

The Farmhouse Hotel & Restaurant
UNIVERSITY FARM, LEW, OXFORD, OX8 2AU   TEL: (01993) 850297/851480
This beautiful 17th C. Cotswold stone farmhouse forms part of a working farm and has a herd of black and white Friesian milking cows; it stands amidst rolling countryside just 12

miles west of Oxford in the tiny village of Lew. Beamed ceilings and rural views from the bedrooms (one ground floor room is specially designed to have wheelchair access); inglenook fireplace. Excellent food prepared from the finest of fresh ingredients.
OPEN ALL YEAR ex. Xmas.   N/S 75% DINING R.   V, S.D. B/A.   LICENSED. DISABLED ACCESS.   CHILDREN: OVER 5S.   EN SUITE, TV & BEVERAGES IN ALL ROOMS.   ACCESS, VISA. B. & B. FROM £25.

🦋*Morar Farm*
WEALD ST, BAMPTON, OXFORD, OX18 2HL TEL: (01993) 850162 FAX: (01993) 851738

Morar Farm is a spacious stone-built farm house which is pleasantly situated in the little village of Bampton which is famous for its beautiful 11th C. church and annual Spring festival of Morris dancing and wild flower garlands. Morar is the home of Janet and Terry Rouse - a lively couple who enjoy bell-ringing, barn dancing, Morris dancing and spinning! They also enjoy welcoming guests to their home, and offer a special brand of helpful hospitality which has earned them a Highly Commended status from the English Tourist Board. The food is plentiful and excellent and features lots of wholesome items such as homemade preserves and home-baked bread. There are a wealth of things to enjoy and places to visit within the area: Cheltenham, Bath, Cirencester and Oxford are all easily visited (to add to the many attractions of the latter there is now the Oxford Story: an animated recreation of Oxford's history); garden lovers would enjoy visiting nearby Waterperry Gardens, and there is a wildlife park and rare breed farm within a short drive of Morar. Blenheim Palace, Avebury Stone Circle and Didcot Steam Railway Centre are all nearby, and for those seeking to relax in situ there are lovely well-marked walks to the Thames from the farmhouse.
OPEN JAN. TO EARLY DEC.   NO SMOKING.   V, S.D. B/A.   LICENSED.   OVER 6s ONLY.   2 DOUBLE ROOMS EN SUITE, one twin room has private bathroom.   BEVERAGES IN ROOMS.   T.V. IN LOUNGE.   B. & B. FROM £20.

Mount Pleasant Hotel
76 LONDON RD, HEADINGTON, OXFORD, OXON, OX3 9AJ   TEL & FAX: (01865) 62749
The Mount Pleasant Hotel is a small family-run hotel which stands in the shopping area of Headington but is within easy reach of the main shops and colleges of Oxford. Mr and Mrs Papamichael are especially welcoming hosts and will do all they can to make you feel at home: the food is excellent - Greek, English and Continental dishes are all home-cooked from fresh ingredients - and special diets can be catered for by arrangement. Accommodation is in comfortable bedrooms - each of which has en suite facilities - and there is a safe car park for guests' use.
OPEN ALL YEAR.   N/S ex. bar.   V, S.D., B/A.   CHILDREN WELCOME.   LICENSED.   EN SUITE & BEVERAGES IN ROOMS.   CREDIT CARDS.   B. & B. FROM £35

🦋 **OLD FARMHOUSE, STATION HILL, LONG HANBORO', OX7 2JZ TEL: (01993) 882097**
16th C. house; inglenook fireplace, beamed ceilings & flag floors. 15 mins Oxford.
OPEN ALL YEAR.   NO SMOKING.   V.   OVER 12s.   EN SUITE. BEVERAGES.   T.V.   B. & B. FROM £16.

🦋 **STUDLEY FARMHOUSE, HORTON CUM STUDLEY, OXON, OX91BP   TEL: (0186735) 286**
16th C. farmhouse with flagstone floors and inglenook fireplace in peaceful rural setting 15 mins drive from Oxford and m40. 1 hr. from London &Ccotswolds.
OPEN ALL YEAR.   NO SMOKING.   V, S.D. B/A.   EN SUITE & TV IN BEDROOMS.   BEVERAGES IN GUESTS' KITCHEN.   CREDIT CARDS.   B. & B. FROM £23.

Westwood Country Hotel
HINKSEY HILL TOP, OXFORD, OXON, OX1 5BG   TEL: (01865) 735408 FAX: (01865) 736536

The Westwood Country Hotel now has a 'nature wild life' which was opened by David Bellamy and gives some indication of the fact that this charming small hotel, located just 3 miles from Oxford, boasts an exceptional abundance of wildlife in its 3 acres of grounds: woodpeckers, nightingales, badgers, foxes and, if you are lucky, deer have all been spotted in and around the 400 acres of woodland which surround the hotel grounds - which is a testament to the peace and tranquillity to be found at Westwood. The bedrooms are exceptionally comfortable & well-appointed & the food (served on lace tablecloths in a beamed dining room) is

exceedingly good; the cosy bar welcomes walkers from the footpaths that radiate from the front door. *Winner of 1991 Daily Mail Award for Tourism for All.*
OPEN ALL YEARex. Xmas.   N/S DINING R & T.V. LOUNGE. V, S.D. B/A. LICENSED.   DISABLED ACCESS. CHILDREN WELCOME.   EN SUITE, BEVERAGES & T.V. IN ROOMS.   CREDIT CARDS.   2-NIGHT COUNTRY BREAKS FROM £46, 7 NIGHTS £242.

WINDRUSH GUEST HOUSE, 11 IFFLEY RD, OXFORD TEL: (01865) 247933
Family-run guest house near Magdalen Bridge. Easy walk to shops, restaurants & places of interest. Healthy eating award. Non-smokers. Coaches to and from London airport.
OPEN ALL YEAR. N/S DINING ROOM. V B/A. CHILDREN WELCOME.   TV & BEVERAGES.   CREDIT CARDS. B. & B. FROM £16.

TOWERSEY

UPPER GREEN FARM, MANOR RD, TOWERSEY, OX9 3QR   TEL: (01844) 212496
OPEN ALL YEAR. NO SMOKING.   V S.D. B/A.   2 GROUND FLOOR BEDROOMS.

WOODSTOCK

GORSELANDS, BODDINGTON LANE, NR LONG HANBOROUGH, OX8 6PU
TEL: (01993) 881202   NO SMOKING. V. CHILDREN WELCOME.   EN SUITE.   B. & B. FROM £12.50.

Hamilton House
43 HILL RISE, OLD WOODSTOCK, OXON, OX20 1AB   TEL: (01993) 812206
OPEN ALL YEAR. NO SMOKING. PETS B/A. EN SUITE & BEVERAGES. T.V. B. & B. £15.

THE LAURELS, HENSINGTON RD, WOODSTOCK, OX7 1JL TEL: (01993) 812583
OPEN ALL YEAR. NO SMOKING. V, S.D. B/A.   CHILDREN.   B. & B. FROM £20.

RESTAURANTS

ABINGDON

POPPIES TEA ROOMS, 37 STERT ST, ABINGDON, OX14 3JF   TEL: (01235) 526660
N/S BACK ROOM.   V.   DISABLED ACCESS: 'WIDE DOORWAY & CORRIDOR FOR WHEELCHAIRS'.   CHILDREN.

THAME LANE HOUSE, 1 THAME LN, CULHAM, ABINGDON, OX14 3DS TEL: (01235) 524177
NO SMOKING. V B/A BEFORE BOOKING.   LICENSED.   CHILDREN: OVER 3s.

BURFORD

HUFFKINS, HIGH ST, BURFORD, OXON.   TEL: (01993) 822126
OPEN Apr. - Nov. daily. NO SMOKING.

CHIPPING NORTON

Nutters Healthy Lifestyle Centre
10 NEW ST, CHIPPING NORTON, OX7 5LJ   TEL: (01608) 641995
Wholefood restaurant & therapy centre. Excellent home-made food. Galettes & crêpes a speciality. Vegetarian, vegan and fish dishes.
NO SMOKING.   40 SEATS.   OPEN 9 A.M. - 10 P.M.   PRICES 'REASONABLE'.   V STD, VE, DIAB, COEL. & OTHER S.D. ON REQUEST. LICENSED.   CHILDREN WELCOME.

THE OLD BAKEHOUSE RESTAURANT & TEAROOM, 50 WEST ST, CHIPPING NORTON
TEL: (01608) 3441 NO SMOKING. ACCESS, VISA.

OXFORD

BETJEMAN'S AT BETJEMAN & BARTON LTD, 90 HIGH ST, OXFORD
TEL: (01865) 241855   NO SMOKING . V STD.   CHILDREN WELCOME.

BROWN'S, 5 - 11 WOODSTOCK RD, OXFORD, 0X2 6HA
N/S PART OF RESTAURANT.   V STD.   CHILDREN WELCOME (HIGHCHAIRS AVAILABLE).   LICENSED. WHEEL-
CHAIR ACCESS.   CREDIT CARDS.

Debenhams

MAGDALEN ST, OXFORD   TEL: (01865) 243161

Intermission, a friendly self-service restaurant serving lunches, snacks & drinks.
OPEN STORE HOURS.   NO SMOKING.   V.   DISABLED ACCESS.   CHILDREN WELCOME.   CREDIT CARDS.

Café MOMA

MUSEUM OF MODERN ART, 30 PEMBROKE ST, OXFORD, OX1 1BP   TEL: (01865) 722733

Café MOMA is a pleasant eating place which specialises in serving vegetarian food
although meat dishes are also available. It offers a wide selection of wholesome, home-
made meals and snacks, such as freshly prepared salads, mouthwatering cakes, first-rate
coffee from the Italian Cappuccino machine and a good selection of speciality teas,
including some herbal varieties. Children and nursing mothers are very welcome (although
childrens' portions are not available), and there is good access for disabled guests.
OPEN Tues. - Sat. 10 am - 5 pm, Late night opening, Thurs., Sun. 2 - 5 pm.   NO SMOKING.   80% V.   LICENSED.
DISABLED ACCESS.   CHILDREN WELCOME.

The Nosebag

6 - 8 ST MICHAEL'S ST, OXFORD, OX1 2DU
OPEN 9.30 am - 10 pm. (ex. Mon close 5.30 pm, Fri, Sat, Sun. 9 pm).   NO SMOKING.

St Aldate's Coffee House

94 ST ALDATE'S, OXFORD, OXON, OX1 1BP   TEL: (01865) 245952

St Aldate's Church Coffee House was opened in 1963 as 'a
place of Christian Hospitality and Intellectual Refreshment
for all who come within its walls' and as such - as its
brochure reminds us - forms part of the coffee house tradition of this university city where 'many famous philosop-
hers have argued their theories and dreams in such places.'
For those of us less intent on contributing to the history of
Western Civilisation and more focussed on finding tea,
cakes and a jolly good selection of coffees - St Aldate's
amply fits the bill. Here you will find delicious lunchtime
treats with loosely ecclesiastical names such as Monk's
Morsel, Parson's Plateful and Curate's Crumb; there are
baked potatoes also, and a tempting selection of home-made cakes and biscuits.
OPEN 12 - 2 for hot food, 10 - 5 for cold snacks.   NO SMOKING.   PRICES: VARIOUS.   V STD.   DISABLED ACCESS:
'yes, but toilets difficult'.   CHILDREN WELCOME.

THE WYKEHAM COFFEE SHOP, 15 HOLYWELL ST, OXFORD   TEL: (01865) 246916
NO SMOKING.   V STD.   CHILDREN WELCOME.

Annie's Tea Rooms

79 HIGH STREET, WALLINGFORD, OX10 0BX   TEL: (01491) 836308

If you are visiting the ancient and historic market town
of Wallingford, just a few miles south of Oxford, be sure
to pay a visit to these charming 17th C. tearooms. You
will receive a friendly welcome from the waitresses who
contribute to the relaxing atmosphere engendered by the
soft pink decor. Morning coffee is followed at noon by
light lunches which include soup, filled jacket potatoes
and open sandwiches together with a traditional hot dish.
Set afternoon teas include delicious scones, scrumptious
tea cakes with home-made jam accompanied by a mouth-
watering selection of cakes. Prices are exceptionally
reasonable, particularly in view of the fact that almost
everything is home-baked.
30 SEATS.   OPEN 10. TO 5. (EX. SUN. & WED).   SUN. TEAS 2.30 - 5.30. (JULY - SEPT.)   NO SMOKING.
V STD.   CHILDREN WELCOME.

THAME

THE COFFEE HOUSE, 3 BUTTERMARKET, THAME, OX9 3EW TEL: (01844) 421 2266
NO SMOKING.   V STD.   LICENSED.   DISABLED ACCESS.   CHILDREN WELCOME.

WOODSTOCK

THE 1627 COFFEE ROOM, 20 HIGH ST, WOODSTOCK   TEL: (01993) 811231

PUBS & WINE BARS

BICESTER

THE SIX BELLS, CHURCH ST, BICESTER, OXON.   TEL: (01869) 253578
NO SMOKING IN ONE ROOM.

OXFORD

KINGS ARMS, 40 HOLYWELL ST, OXFORD, OXON.   TEL: (01865) 242369/247049
NO SMOKING ONE OF THREE ROOMS.   V STD.   WHEELCHAIR ACCESS.

Central England

Gloucestershire

ACCOMMODATION

BLAKENEY

Lower Viney Country Guest House
   VINEY HILL, NR BLAKENEY, GL15 4LT   TEL: (01594) 516000
NO SMOKING.   S.D. B/A.   LICENSED.   CHILDREN WELCOME.   EN SUITE, BEVERAGES & T.V. IN ALL ROOMS.
ACCESS, VISA.   B. & B. AROUND £20.

BOURTON ON THE WATER

Coombe House
RISSINGTON RD, BOURTON-on-the-WATER, GL54 2DT TEL: (01451) 821966 FAX: (01451) 810477

Coombe House is quietly situated in pretty lawned gardens which are a delight for the enthusiast who enjoys interesting plants and shrubs. A short riverside walk leads to the heart of this beautiful village where the River Windrush gracefully wends its way through willow-draped banks on which quaint stone houses and cottages nestle. The Coombe House interior is one of informal elegance which promotes an overall feeling of comfort and relaxation. It has been awarded a Highly Commended status by the English Tourist Board and your hosts, Graham and Diana Ellis, will make you very welcome. Breakfast is the only meal available at Coombe House and it can be 'as healthy or as non-healthy as each guest wishes.' Accordingly yoghurt and Flora are available together with decaffeinated coffee & a continental alternative breakfast of a warm croissant with apricot jam.
OPEN ALL YEAR.   NO SMOKING.   V, S.D. B/A.   LICENSED.   DISABLED ACCESS: 2 ground floor rooms.   CHILDREN WELCOME.   EN SUITE, TV & BEVERAGES.   VISA, AMEX, MASTERCARD   B. & B. FROM £24.50.

Dial House Hotel

BOURTON ON THE WATER, GL54 2AN   TEL: (01451) 822244   FAX: (01451) 810126
AA Red Rosette Charming 17th C. hotel beautifully situated in the centre of one of the Cotswolds' most attractive villages in 1 acre of secluded garden. Excellent food, open fires.

OPEN ALL YEAR. N/S DINING R, SOME BEDRMS. V, S.D., BA. LICENSED. DISABLED ACCESS. EN SUITE, TV & BEVERAGES IN BEDROOMS. CREDIT CARDS. B. & B. FROM £39.50.

 FARNCOMBE, CLAPTON, BOURTON ON THE WATER, GL54 2LG   TEL: (01451) 820120
Beautifully appointed Cotswold family house standing in 2 acres of gardens some 700 ft above sea-level in the tiny hamlet of Clapton on the Hill just 2 miles from Bourton on the Water. Prettily decorated bedrooms. Full English or Continental breakfasts.
NO SMOKING. V, S.D. B/A (Breakfast only). CHILDREN WELCOME. ONE DOUBLE ROOM WITH SHOWER. BEVERAGES IN DINING ROOM. T.V. IN LOUNGE. B. & B. FROM £15.50.

WINDRUSH FARM, BOURTON ON THE WATER, GL54 3BY
TEL: (01451) 20419   NO SMOKING. V. EN SUITE, TV & BEVERAGES. B. & B. FROM £17.

BROADWAY

Cusacks Glebe

SAINTBURY, NR BROADWAY, WORCESTERSHIRE, WR12 7PX   TEL: (01386) 852210
An ancient 14th C. cruck cottage farmhouse in beautiful gardens and paddocks. Rural area of outstanding natural beauty. 2 beautiful bedrooms, antique furnishings & four-posters.
OPEN Jan.15 - Dec. 15. NO SMOKING. V, S.D. B/A. OVER 10s WELCOME. EN SUITE, TV & BEVERAGES IN ROOMS. B. & B. FROM £24.50.

CHELTENHAM

Charlton Kings Hotel

LONDON RD, CHARLTON KINGS, CHELTENHAM, GL52 6UU   TEL: (01242) 231061

Visitors to Cheltenham Spa or the Cotswolds could do no better than spend their stay at the recently refurbished Charlton Kings Hotel just 2 miles from the centre of Cheltenham. Situated in an area of Outstanding Natural Beauty in an acre of award-winning gardens, there is a footpath running from the hotel up to the famous Cotswold Way; breathtaking views to the Malverns' and beyond are available to those who take this walk. All room are en suite (the doubles and twins with bath and shower, the singles with shower). The chefs, Jan and Jason, will tempt you with an imaginative home-cooked dinner (from either the à la carte or table d'hôte selection); you may dine in either the Restaurant or Conservatory. The room information folder lists over 200 places to visit locally including 'The Romantic Road', a publication which describes a circular motor tour of the Cotswolds. A stay at the Charlton Kings Hotel is characterised by the standard of service and hospitality which only a small hotel can provide.
OPEN ALL YEAR. N/S DINING R & SOME BEDROOMS. V STD. LICENSED. DISABLED ACCESS. CHILDREN & PETS WELCOME. EN SUITE, BEVERAGES & T.V. IN ROOMS. CREDIT CARDS. B. & B. FROM £39.

Hallery House Hotel

48 SHURDINGTON RD, CHELTENHAM SPA, GL53 0JE   TEL: (01242) 578450

This lovingly-restored Victorian building is a small, family-run hotel with a welcoming atmosphere. The sixteen light, airy bedrooms are each individually furnished and there is an elegant dining room and comfortable lounge; the pleasant patio provides a suntrap in clement weather. Hallery House food is fresh, healthy and simple, prepared from the best local produce to imaginative and tasty recipes; traditional or continental breakfasts are provided and the evening meal would typically feature Chicken and Vegetable Terrine followed by Poached Salmon with Hollandaise Sauce and Milk Chocolate and Raspberry Fool.
OPEN ALL YEAR. N/S DINING R. & SOME BEDRS. V, S.D. B/A. LICENSED. CHILDREN & PETS WELCOME. EN SUITE MOST ROOMS. BEVERAGES, T.V. & SATELLITE ALL BEDROOMS. VISA, AMEX, MASTERCARD. B. & B. FROM £20.

Cleyne Hage

SOUTHAM LN, SOUTHAM, NR CHELTENHAM, GL52 3N   TEL: (01242) 518569/(0850) 285338
Cotswold stone house in quiet village in secluded garden; views to race course, Malvern Hills, Cleeve Hill; on Cotswold Way. N. of Cheltenham between B4632 & A435. Parking.
OPEN ALL YEAR.   NO SMOKING.   WELL-BEHAVED CHILDREN & PETS WELCOME.   BEVERAGES & TV. CREDIT CARDS.   B. & B. FROM £15.

KATSLYDE, CHURCH LN, TODDINGTON, CHELTENHAM.   TEL: (01242) 621509
NO SMOKING.   V, S.D. B/A.   CHILDREN WELCOME.   EN SUITE. BEVERAGES AND T.V. IN ALL BEDROOMS. B. & B. FROM £17.50.

NEW BARN FARMHOUSE, TEMPLE GUITING, CHELTENHAM, GL54 5RW TEL: (01451) 850367
N/S EX. LOUNGE. V B/A. OVER 8S ONLY. B. & B. FROM £15.

Northfield B. & B.

CIRENCESTER RD, NORTHLEACH, CHELTENHAM, GLOS, GL54 3JL   TEL: (01451) 860427

ETB 3 Crowns Commended. Northfield is a lovely detached family home set in large gardens overlooking open countryside. Although functioning principally as a bed and breakfast, packed lunches and evening meals can be taken at Northfield by arrangement and fresh, home-grown produce (including free-range eggs) are used wherever possible in cooking; in sunny weather meals may be enjoyed in the garden either on the lawn or relaxing by the pond. Northfield is conveniently situated just off the A429 a mile from the market town of Northleach, with its beautiful church and musical museum; its proximity to so many other lovely towns and villages in the Cotswolds makes it a perfect base from which to explore all the delights of this lovely part of the world.
OPEN ALL YEAR.   NO SMOKING.   V, S.D. B/A.   CHILDREN WELCOME.   EN SUITE, TV & BEVERAGES IN ROOMS.   TABLE LICENCE.   B. & B. from £18, D. £9.

OLD VINEYARDS, CHARLTON HILL, CHELTENHAM, GL53 9NE TEL: (01242) 582893
NO SMOKING.   S.D. B/A.   CHILDREN WELCOME.   BEVERAGES IN ALL ROOMS.   B. & B. FROM £19. SHORT BREAKS AT REDUCED RATES AVAILABLE ON REQUEST.

STRETTON LODGE, WESTERN RD, CHELTENHAM, GL50 3RN TEL: (0242) 528724 OR 570771
NO SMOKING, ex. SOME BEDROOMS.   V B/A.   LICENSED.   CHILDREN WELCOME.   EN SUITE, BEVERAGES & T.V. IN ALL BEDROOMS.   ACCESS, VISA.   B. & B. FROM £27.

TURRET HOUSE, ALDSWORTH, (betn Burford & Bibury), GL54 3QZ TEL: (014514) 547
NO SMOKING.   V, S.D. B/A.(B'fasts).   OVER 14SY.   BEVERAGES & T.V. IN ROOMS.   B. & B. AROUND £19

THE WYNYARDS, BUTTS LN, WOODMANCOTE, GL52 4QH TEL: (01242) 673876
NO SMOKING.   V, S.D. B/A.   CHILDREN WELCOME.   BEVERAGES AVAILABLE ALL DAY.   T.V. IN LOUNGE.   B. & B. FROM £15.

CHIPPING CAMPDEN

The Cotswold House Hotel

CHIPPING CAMPDEN, GLOS, GL55 6AN   TEL: (01386) 840330
17th C. Cotswold House is a beautiful country hotel which stands in pride of place on Chipping Campden's High Street. Originally built as the country home of a prosperous wool merchant (and with an interesting subsequent history), it has recently been painstakingly restored to its original splendour and the elegantly furnished rooms now have antiques and works of art which complement the period features. First-rate meals are served in the intimate dining room with its garden views, and the fifteen beautifully furnished bedrooms have each been individually decorated and styled. In winter open fires blaze invitingly in the lounge and sitting room, whilst in summer the willow-shaded coutryard is perfect for pre-dinner drinks or al fresco eating.
OPEN ALL YEAR Ex. Xmas.   N/S DINING R.   V, S.D. B/A.   LICENSED.   OVER 8s WELCOME.   EN SUITE & TV IN ALL ROOMS.   ROOM SERVICE.   CREDIT CARDS.   B. & B. AROUND £50.

*Wyldlands*

BROAD CAMPDEN, CHIPPING CAMPDEN, GLOS, GL55 6UR   TEL: (01386) 840478

Wyldlands is a modern house which stands in the village of Broad Campden and has lovely views of the surrounding countryside. The proprietor, Mrs Wadey, is a keen gardener and guests may enjoy her lovely, large garden. Wyldlands is a totally smoke-free house which has been comfortably furnished and appointed (it has been awarded a Commended status by the English Tourist Board), and it is an ideal base from which to explore the many attractions of the Cotswolds: Hidcote Gardens and Batsford Arboretum are within easy reach and the Cotswold Way Walk begins just 1 mile away. Mrs Wadey is unable to accommodate pets because she has a dog of her own.

OPEN ALL YEAR.   NO SMOKING.   V, B/A.   CHILDREN WELCOME.   1 EN SUITE ROOM.   TV & BEVERAGES IN ROOMS.   B. & B. FROM £18.

CIRENCESTER

WIMBORNE HOUSE, 91 VICTORIA RD, CIRENCESTER, GL7 1ES   TEL: (01285) 653890
NO SMOKING.   V, S.D. B/A.   OVER 5S.   EN SUITE, BEVERAGES & T.V. IN ROOMS.   B. & B. FROM £19.

DURSLEY

SCHOOL COTTAGE, COALEY, DURSLEY, GLOS, GL11 5ED   TEL: (01453) 890459
NO SMOKING.   CHILDREN WELCOME.   PETS: SMALL DOGS ONLY.   BEVERAGES IN ALL ROOMS.   T.V. IN 1 BEDROOM.   B. & B. FROM £14.

GLOUCESTER

Notley House and The Coach House

93 HUCCLECOTE RD, HUCCLECOTE, GLOUCESTER, GL3 3TR. TEL & FAX (01452) 611584

Notley House is a beautifully renovated cottage which dates from the early 1700s and at one time was one of Gloucester's seven private schools. Alyn and Jaki George have introduced many modern facilities - while retaining the beamed character of the original building - and guests are comfortably accommodated in attractively decorated rooms, two of which has a four-poster bed; there is also a converted two storey coach house in the grounds. The food is excellent - Jaki's cooking is imaginative and wholesome - and guests are ideally placed for visiting Gloucester (just 3 miles away) or the surrounding countryside.

OPEN ALL YEAR.   NO SMOKING.   S.D. B/A.   CHILDREN WELCOME.   CREDIT CARDS.   EN SUITE, TV & BEVERAGES IN BEDROOMS.   B. & B. FROM £15.

Old Court Hotel

CHURCH ST, NEWENT, GLOS.   TEL: (01531) 820522

ETB 3 Crown Commended. RAC 2 Star. This handsome William and Mary house stands secluded behind a high wall amidst an acre of mature gardens right in the heart of Newent. Most of the original period detail has been retained and the entrance hall is particularly fine, with its high walls and white archways. Meals are served in an elegant panelled dining room, decorated in shades of soft green and clover, and there is a comfortable drawing room with curved and fluted pillars, and detailed plasterwork on the ceiling. The bedrooms are furnished to a very high standard and are equipped with a range of helpful facilities. Newent (which, incidentally, boasts the largest falconry centre in the Northern hemisphere) is just 5 mins from the M50 and is within easy reach of the Forest of Dean, the Wye Valley, Cheltenham, Gloucester and the Malvern Hills.

OPEN ALL YEAR.   NO SMOKING.   S.D. B/A.   CHILDREN & PETS WELCOME.   EN SUITE, TV & BEVERAGES IN ROOMS.   WHEELCHAIR ACCESS.   B. & B. FROM £29, D. £13.75.

THE RED HOUSE, CRANHAM WOODS, GLOUCESTER, GL4 8HF TEL: (01452) 862616
NO SMOKING.   V, S.D. B/A.   CHILDREN WELCOME.   PETS B/A.   T.V IN ROOMS.   B. & B. FROM £14.

SEVERN BANK GUEST HOUSE, MINSTERWORTH, GLOS, GL2 8JH   TEL: (01452) 750357

Fine country house in 6 acres of grounds on the banks of the Severn. 4m Gloucester.

N/S DINING R, HALL & BEDRS.   V,'S.D. B/A.   CHILDREN WELCOME.   EN SUITE, TV & BEVERAGES IN ALL ROOMS.   B. & B. FROM £17.50.

KILCOT

 ### Orchard House

ASTON INGHAM RD, KILCOT, NR NEWENT, GLOS, GL18 1NP   TEL: (01989) 720417

 Orchard House is a beautiful Tudor-style country home which stands amidst 5 acres of peaceful grounds (including well-tended lawns, paddocks and country walks) in a tranquil country setting close to the unspoilt Wye Valley and the Forest of Dean; the oldest parts of the house date from the 18th C. and many original beams are still to be seen - in, for example, the TV lounge with its log fires. Your hosts, Anne and Basil Thompson, have done everything they can to make their home as warmly welcoming as possible: the elegant and finely furnished rooms provide a very high standard of accommodation but there is, nonetheless, a friendly relaxed feel about the place. Anne is an excellent cook and provides a wide selection of delicious and imaginative fare: only fresh produce - with local specialities - are ever used in cooking, and a typical evening menu would feature Green Pea and Mint Soup followed by Poached Salmon or Spinach Roulade with Cottage Cheese, and fresh fruit salad; coffee and mints would complete the meal. You are within easy reach of a number of interesting places including the Brecon Beacons, the Malverns, the Cotswolds and Ross-on-Wye.

OPEN ALL YEAR.   NO SMOKING.   V, S.D. B/A.   LICENSED.   OVER 12S ONLY.   EN SUITE, BEVERAGES IN ROOMS.   CREDIT CARDS.   B. & B. FROM £19.50, D. FROM £12.50.

MINCHINHAMPTON

The Owl House

MARKET SQUARE, MINCHINHAMPTON, GL6 9BW   TEL: (01453) 886378 MOBILE: (0850) 152683

The Owl House is a charming Grade II listed period stone house which stands close to the 12th C. parish church at the head of the market square in Minchinhampton; it enjoys southerly views over the unspoilt heart of this former market town. Accommodation is in comfortable rooms, each of which have been equipped with a range of helpful facilities including radio alarms, dressing gowns, colour TVs and hairdryers; there is an excellent restaurant (Michelin listed) just 20 yards away. You are surrounded bybeautiful Cotswold countryside - ideal for walking and cycling - and Minchinhampton Common itself is administered by the National Trust. Excellent touring centre.

OPEN ALL YEAR.   N/S.   S.D. B/A.   CHILDREN& WELL-BEHAVED PETS WELCOME. TV & BEVERAGES IN ROOMS. B. & B. FROM £15.

MORETON-IN-MARSH

BLUE CEDAR HOUSE, STOW RD, MORETON IN MARSH, GL56 0DW TEL: (01608) 50299

Beautiful detached residence set in attractive gardens within easy reach of the centre of the picturesque town of Moreton in Marsh. All bedrooms comfortably appointed.

N/S EX. T.V. LOUNGE.   V, S.D. B/A.   DISABLED ACCESS: 'ONE GROUND FLOOR SUITE'.   CHILDREN WELCOME. EN SUITE IN SOME ROOMS.   BEVERAGES & TV IN ALL ROOMS.   T.V. IN LOUNGE.   B. & B. FROM £15, D. FROM £7.

MR & MRS MALIN, 21 STATION RD, BLOCKLEY, GL56 9ED   TEL: (01386) 700402

NO SMOKING. V, S.D. B/A.   CHILDREN B/A.   BEVERAGES & T.V. IN ROOMS.   B. & B. FROM £16.

Newlands Farmhouse

ASTON MAGNA, MORETON IN MARSH, GLOS, GL56 9QQ   TEL: (01608) 50964

Newlands Farm is a Grade II listed Tudor farmhouse which was once a working farm; these days it has been tastefully restored and now offers bed and breakfast accommodation of a very high standard indeed. The two double and one twin-bedded rooms have each been very comfortably appointed and attractively decorated, and there is a T.V. lounge for guests' use. Breakfast is the only meal available at Newlands Farmhouse but there is a wide range of good eating places within a few minutes' drive. There is much to enjoy in the area: the

surrounding countryside is beautiful and full of lots of lovely walks, and the gardens of Hidcote, Kiftsgate and Sezincote are all within a 5 mile radius.
OPEN ALL YEAR ex. Xmas. NO SMOKING. BEVERAGES ON REQUEST. T.V LOUNGE. B. & B. FROM £15 LESS FOR 2 NIGHTS.

PAINSWICK

UPPER DOREY'S MILL, EDGE, NR PAINSWICK, GLOS, GL6 6NF TEL: (01452) 812459
NO SMOKING. V, S.D. (B'fast only). CHILDREN WELCOME. EN SUITE & BEVERAGES IN ALL ROOMS. T.V. IN LOUNGE. B. & B. FROM £17.50.

RUARDEAN

THE LAWN, RUARDEAN, GLOS, GL17 9US TEL: (01594) 543259
NO SMOKING. V, S.D. B/A. DISABLED ACCESS: 'LIMITED, GROUND FLOOR EN SUITE BEDROOM AVAILABLE.' OVER 8s ONLY. PETS B/A. EN SUITE IN SOME ROOMS. BEVERAGES IN ALL ROOMS. T.V. IN LOUNGE. B. & B. FROM £16.

ST BRIAVELS

CINDERHILL HOUSE, ST BRIAVELS, GLOS, GL15 6RH
14th C. building, complete with oak beams, inglenook fireplaces and bread oven, nestling in hillside below St Briavel's castle with breathtaking views.
N/S ex. IN SITTING ROOM. V, S.D. B/A. LICENSED. CHILDREN WELCOME. EN SUITE & BEVERAGES IN ALL ROOMS. B. & B. FROM £23.

STROUD

BURLEIGH COTTAGE, BURLEIGH, MINCHINHAMPTON, STROUD, GL5 2PW
Charming cottage with splendid views of the surrounding countryside.
TEL: (01453) 884703 OPEN ALL YEAR. NO SMOKING. CHILDREN. EN SUITE IN 2 ROOMS. BEVERAGES & T.V. IN ALL BEDROOMS.

TEWKSBURY

 LAMPITT HOUSE B. & B., LAMPITT LN., BREDON'S NORTON, GL20 7HB TEL: (01684) 72295
Large home set in 1½ acres of gardens; all food home-cooked from fresh ingredients.
NO SMOKING. V, S.D. B/A. DISABLED ACCESS: one ground floor room avail. but no wheelchair access. CHILDREN WELCOME. PETS B/A. EN SUITE, BEVERAGES & T.V. IN ROOMS. B. & B. AROUND £20.

WOTTON UNDER EDGE

 COOMBE LODGE VEG. B. & B., WOTTON under EDGE, GL12 7NB TEL: (01453) 845057
Spacious Georgian house in an acre of gardens with mature trees.
OPEN ALL YEAR ex. Xmas and New Year. NO SMOKING. V STD. OTHER MEAT-FREE S.D. B/A. OVER 3S ONLY. BEVERAGES & T.V. IN BEDROOMS. B. & B. FROM £17.

RESTAURANTS

BRIMSCOMBE

Yew Tree Tea Rooms
WALLS QUARRY, BRIMSCOMBE, STROUD, GLOS, GL5 2PA TEL & FAX: (01453) 883428
This Cotswold stone-built dwelling was once a 16th C. ale house, and access to the Tea Rooms is through what once was the barley door. Freshly brewed coffee, cakes, scones, rolls, soup and sandwiches. Fit-to-Eat Award.
NO SMOKING L. AROUND £2. S.D. CHILDREN WELCOME.

CHELTENHAM

The Baytree
REGENT ARCADE, CHELTENHAM, GLOS, GL50 1JZ TEL: (01242) 516229
Pleasantly furnished café in busy, modern Regent Arcade in the centre of Cheltenham. Vegetarian dishes always available & a wide range of beverages including speciality teas.
OPEN 8.30 - 5.30. 50% NO-SMOKING. V STD. DISABLED ACCESS. CHILDREN WELCOME.

CIRENCESTER

ROSAMOND DE MARCO, SHOP 7, SWAN YARD, WEST MARKET ST, CIRENCESTER
TEL: (01285) 659683   OPEN DAILY, 9.30 - 6 (SUMMER), 10 - 5 (WINTER).   NO SMOKING.

GLOUCESTER

The Undercroft Restaurant

CHURCH HOUSE, COLLEGE GREEN, GLOS, GL1 5ER   TEL: (01452) 307164
This lovely restaurant and coffee shop was opened in 1988. It is situated just off the cloisters
of the cathedral and above it are three historic, beamed rooms of differing sizes which are
available for private bookings. The food is first-rate and features a selection of fine coffee
and teas, lunches and afternoon teas. Everything is freshly prepared on the premises -
including the delicious cakes - and there are some good vegetarian options.
OPEN 10 - 5.   N/S 2 DINING Rs.   V STD.   LICENSED.   DISABLED ACCESS.   CHILDREN.

 Debenhams

KINGS SQUARE, GLOUCESTER   TEL; (01452) 22121
Intermission, a friendly self-service restaurant serving lunches, snacks and drinks.
OPEN STORE HOURS.   NO SMOKING.   V.   DISABLED ACCESS.   CHILDREN WELCOME.   CREDIT CARDS.

LECHLADE

KATIE'S TEAROOM & GIFT SHOP, MARLBOROUGH HOUSE, HIGH ST, LECHLADE
TEL: (01367) 52273   OPEN ALL YEAR, DAILY, 9.30 - 6 (VARIES ACCORDING TO SEASON).   NO SMOKING.

MORETON-IN-MARSH

COTSWOLD RESTAURANT &COFFEE HOUSE, HIGH ST, MORETON-IN-MARSH
OPEN APR. - DEC, DAILY EXCEPT WED. & FRI., 9.30 - 5.   NO SMOKING.

STROUD

THE RAGGED COT INN, HYDE, CHALFORD, NR STROUD, GL6 8PE TEL: (01453) 884643
16th C. 'olde worlde' inn, tastefully decorated, in the heart of the Cotswolds; friendly
personal service, good home-made food; 3 years holder of 'Fit to Eat' Award.
N/S RESTAURANT. V STD. LICENSED. WHEELCHAIR ACCESS. OVER 14S ONLY. CREDIT CARDS.

TEWKSBURY

THE ABBEY TEA ROOMS, 59 CHURCH ST, TEWKSBURY, GL20 5RZ   TEL: (01684) 292215
Pleasant 'old world' tea rooms located in 15th C. building offering range of snacks, lunches,
afternoon teas. Home-cooked foods a speciality, including excellent home-made cakes.
NO SMOKING.   V, WEIGHT WATCHERS STD.   LICENSED.   DISABLED ACCESS.   CHILDREN WELCOME.

Hereford

ACCOMMODATION

FELTON

Felton House

FELTON, HEREFORDSHIRE, HR1 3PH   TEL: (01432) 820366

Old, stone-built, former rectory in 3 acres of beautiful
grounds and gardens adjacent to the parish church in the
peaceful hamlet of Felton. Each of the centrally-heated,
guest bedrooms are decorated in original and distinctive
style; some have four posters. A wide choice of traditional
or vegetarian options are offered at breakfast, and there are
several good, local inns.

OPEN Jan. To Nov. Inc.   N/S DINING R, BEDRS, BATHRS & 1 LOUNGE.   V & STANDARD ENGLISH B'FASTS.
CHILDREN & PETS WELCOME.   BEVERAGES IN BEDROOMS.   TV IN LOUNGE.   B. & B. FROM £17.

HAY-ON-WYE

KILVERT COURT HOTEL, BULLRING, HAY-ON-WYE, HR3 5AG   TEL: (01497) 821042
NO SMOKING. V, S.D. B/A. LICENSED. DISABLED ACCESS TO RESTAURANT. CHILDREN. EN SUITE, BEVER-
AGES & T.V. IN ALL BEDROOMS. B. & B. AROUND £35.

THE HAVEN, HARDWICKE, HAY-ON-WYE, HEREFORDSHIRE, HR3 5TA TEL: (014973) 254
Early Victorian vicarage in 2 acres of mature gardens and paddocks deep in countryside
2m from Hay on Wye. Comfortable bedrooms named after the fine views they command;
both sitting & dining rooms have open log fires. Excellent: food prepared from fresh, often
home-grown, ingredients. Open air swimming pool in the garden for fine summer days.
OPEN Mar. To Nov. N/S ex. in library. V, S.D. B/A. LICENSED. DISABLED ACCESS: 1 ground floor en suite room.
CHILDREN. PETS B/A. MOST ROOMS EN SUITE. BEVERAGES & T.V. IN ROOMS. B. & B. FROM £24.

Stoneleigh Guest House
CLIFFORD, NR HAY-ON-WYE, HR3 5ER   TEL: (01497) 831361
Charming stone-built house situated on the quiet B4350 road half-way between Hay-on-
Wye & Whitney-on-Wye toll bridge. Good home-cooking. Family, twin & double rooms.
OPEN ALL YEAR. NO SMOKING. V, S.D., B/A. CHILDREN WELCOME. PETS B/A. B. & B. AROUND £15 (inc. Sgl).

York House
CUSOP, HAY ON WYE, HEREFORDSHIRE, HR3 5QX   TEL: (01497) 820705

York House is an elegant, late Victorian house which has
been sympathetically refurbished by the present owners,
Peter and Olwen Roberts, in period style to a very high
standard while retaining many of the features of the original
building. Each of the individually decorated bedrooms have
little personal touches (sewing kits, plants or dried flowers,
biscuits and tissues), as well as the usual facilities; two en
suite rooms have a single bed, a double bed and a sitting
area. The evening menu features an imaginative selection
of freshly prepared dishes such as home-made soup followed by Turkey Casserole with red
cabbage, onion and apple, and a tempting dessert such as Iced Whisky and Honey Creams.
Hay on Wye is a world famous centre for the second hand book trade; situated in a very
peaceful part of the Welsh countryside it is ideal for all year round walking on nearby Offa's
Dyke and the Wye Valley Walk. RAC Acclaimed.
OPEN ALL YEAR.   NO SMOKING.   V, DIAB., B/A.   OVER 8s ONLY.   PETS B/A.   EN SUITE MOST ROOMS.
BEVERAGES & T.V. IN ROOMS.   ACCESS, VISA, AMEX.   B. & B. FROM £17.50 - 22, D. £12.

HEREFORD

GRAFTON VILLA, GRAFTON, NR HEREFORD, HR2 8ED
TEL: (01432) 268689   NO SMOKING.   V, S.D. B/A.   CHILDREN WELCOME.   PETS B/A.   BEVERAGES & T.V. IN
ALL BEDROOMS.   B. & B. AROUND £17.

THE OLD RECTORY, BYFORD, HEREFORD, HR4 7LD
Lovely Georgian house used as a rectory from 1830 until 1960.
TEL: (098122) 218   OPEN EASTER TO NOV.   NO SMOKING. V B/A. CHILDREN WELCOME.   PETS B/A.   EN
SUITE IN 1 ROOM.   BEVERAGES.   T.V. IN ALL ROOMS.   B. & B. AROUND £15.

KINGTON

Llanarrow

HUNTINGTON, KINGTON, HEREFORDSHIRE, HR5 3QA   TEL: (01497) 831439

Llanarrow, originally two farm cottages and
a barn, lies at the end of a farm track 5 miles
from the main road overlooking the River
Arrow (which forms the Welsh border in that
part of the world). The house has retained its
traditional features, including flag floors,
beamed ceilings, stone fireplaces and bread
ovens, but has been comfortably converted
by its present owners, Jean and Tony Whiel-
don, to offer bed and breakfast (with private bath or shower), a self-catering studio and
facilities for small groups. Jean prepares delicious home-cooked food - mainly with the use
of organic and home-grown ingredients - and prices are exceptionally reasonable. Jean and
Tony have a great deal of experience in catering for the needs of small groups (they ran the
highly regarded Grimstone Manor for 11 years) and can cater for up to 10 people (either

self-catering or dining in house); the magnificent centrally heated barns form a spectacular and secluded venue for musicians, dance or drama groups, meditation or therapy.
OPEN FEB. - DEC.   NO SMOKING.   V, S.D. STD.   OVER 12s WELCOME.   PRIVATE BATH OR SHOWER IN ROOMS. WHEELCHAIR ACCESS TO 1 ROOM.   . & B. £18, D. £8.

CHURCH HOUSE, LYONSHALL, KINGTON, HERE., HR5 3HR TEL: (015448) 350
Small, Georgian country house with lovely views in all directions standing in 10 acres of gardens and paddocks; meals prepared from fresh local produce.
NO SMOKING.   V, S.D. B/A. CHILDREN WELCOME. EN SUITE IN SOME ROOMS. TEA/COFFEE-MAKING IN ALL ROOMS. T.V. IN LOUNGE. B. & B. FROM £15, SINGLE £20.

LEDBURY

Wall Hills Country Guest House
HEREFORD RD, LEDBURY, HEREFORDSHIRE, HR8 2PR   TEL: (01531) 632833
AA QQQ. ETB 3 Crown Commended. Elegant Georgian mansion in its own lovely gardens on the hill slopes overlooking Ledbury.
OPEN ALL YEAR ex. Xmas.   N/S DINING R & BEDR.   V, S.D. B/A.   LICENSED.   CHILDREN WELCOME.   EN SUITE, BEVERAGES IN ROOMS.   T.V. LOUNGE.   B. & B. from £24.

LEOMINSTER

COPPER HALL, 134 SOUTH ST, LEOMINSTER, HR6 8JN   TEL: (0568) 611622
N/S DINING R & BEDRS.   V, S.D. B/A. CHILDREN: IF WELL BEHAVED. PETS B/A. BEVERAGES & TV IN ROOMS. B. & B. FROM £15.

 GREEN HAVEN, LUCTON, LEOMINSTER, HR6 9PN TEL: (01568) 85276
*ETB Listed.*Charming country house in beautiful gardens surrounded by woods and fields.
NO SMOKING. S.D. B/A.   CHILDREN: OVER 10S ONLY.   BEVERAGES ON REQUEST. T.V.   B. & B. FROM £18.

RATEFIELD FARM, KIMBOLTON, LEOMINSTER, HR6 0JB TEL: (01568) 82507
Lovely 18th C. house in secluded position 1m Kimbolton. Home-baked bread & rolls.
N/S DINING R & BEDRS.   V, DIAB, COEL B/A.   CHILDREN WELCOME.   PETS B/A. BEVERAGES.   T.V. IN LOUNGE. AMEX.   B. & B. AROUND £17.

WITHENFIELD, SOUTH ST, LEOMINSTER, HR6 8JN   TEL: (01568) 612011
Detached Georgian house furnished with period pieces, including a four-poster bed.
N/S DINING R, LOUNGE & BEDRS.   V, S.D. B/A.   LICENSED.   CHILDREN WELCOME. EN SUITE, TV & BEVERAGES IN ROOMS.   B. & B. AROUND £28.

MORDIFORD

ORCHARD FARM, MORDIFORD, NR HEREFORD, HR1 4EJ TEL: (01432) 870253
17th C. stone farmhouse with large, natural garden and 57 acres of traditional farmland.
N/S ex. 1 sitting room.   V, S.D. B/A.   LICENSED.   CHILDREN: OVER 10S ONLY. BEVERAGES & T.V. AVAILABLE. AMEX.   B. & B. AROUND £16.

MUCH BIRCH

THE OLD SCHOOL, MUCH BIRCH, NR HEREFORD, HR2 8HJ TEL: (01981) 540006
*ETB 2 Crown Commended.*Comfortable, attractive, converted Victorian school with a lovely large garden and fantastic views. Really good home-made food. Marvellous walking country. Guest lounge with colour TV and extensive library. Central heating.
OPEN ALL YEAR.   N/S DINING R & BEDRS.   V, VE, DIAB, S.D. B/A.   CHILDREN. TRAINED PETS WELCOME. EN SUITE IN 2 ROOMS.   BEVERAGES IN ROOMS.   T.V IN LOUNGE, RADIO IN ROOMS.   B. & B. FROM £15.

ROSS ON WYE

ABERHALL FARM, ST OWEN'S CROSS, ROSS ON WYE, HR2 8LL TEL: (01989) 587256
17th C. farmhouse forming part of working mixed farm. Tastefully decorated (all bedrooms have lovely views). Meals are prepared from fresh produce by award-winning cook.
N/S PUBLIC ROOMS.   CHILDREN: OVER 10S ONLY.   EN SUITE IN SOME ROOMS. BEVERAGES IN ALL ROOMS. T.V IN LOUNGE.   B. & B. FROM £17.

THE ARCHES COUNTRY HOUSE, WALFORD RD, ROSS-ON-WYE TEL: (01989) 563348
RAC Acclaimed. AA listed. Routier Award. Small family-run guest house in ½ acre of lawns & 10 mins walk from town. All bedrooms overlook the garden. Beautiful decor.
OPEN ALL YEAR.   N/S DINING R & BEDRS.   V, S.D. B/A.   EN SUITE, TV & BEVERAGES IN BEDROOMS. CHILDREN & PETS WELCOME.   B. & B. AROUND £20.

BROOK HOUSE, LEA, NR ROSS ON WYE, HR9 7JZ   TEL: (01989) 81710
Fine Grade II listed Queen Anne building standing on the site of a mediaeval hospice.
N/S ex. in lounge.   V STD, S.D. B/A.   CHILDREN: OVER 7S ONLY.   PETS B/A.   SOME EN SUITE ROOMS.   BEVER-
AGES IN ALL ROOMS.   T.V IN LOUNGE.   B. & B. AROUND £17.

EDDE CROSS HOUSE, EDDE CROSS ST, ROSS ON WYE, HR9 7BZ TEL: (01989)5 65088
Georgian Grade II listed town house with its charming walled garden.
NO SMOKING.   V STD, A.D. B/A.   CHILDREN: OVER 10S ONLY.   EN SUITE IN SOME ROOMS.   BEVERAGES &
T.V IN ROOMS.   B. & B. FROM £21.

LAVENDER COTTAGE, BRIDSTOW, ROSS ON WYE, HR9 6QB TEL: (01989) 62836
Lavender Cottage is a delightful character property with parts dating back to the 17th
century; it enjoys a tranquil location just one mile from Ross on Wye and has fine views
of Bridstow church and May Hill; Ross church spire can be seen clearly amidst the backdrop
of the trees of Chase Woods and Goodrich Castle with the Forest of Dean beyond. The
cottage has been comfortably furnished and decorated and there is a generous breakfast.
OPEN ALL YEAR. NO SMOKING. V, S.D. B/A. SOME EN SUITE ROOMS. BEVERAGES IN ROOMS. T.V. IN LOUNGE.
B. & B. AROUND £15.

Linden House
14 CHURCH ST, ROSS ON WYE, HEREFRODSHIRE, HR9 5HN   TEL: (01989) 65373

Linden House is a comfortable, friendly, informal Georgian
town house run by the resident proprietors and standing in a
quiet street opposite St Marys church, just off the market
square. This no-smoking house provides excellent traditional
and vegetarian breakfasts (which include home-made jams
and marmalades) in a cosy, beamed dining room. The bedrooms are comfortably furnished - many have brass beds - and
each is equipped with a TV and tea and coffee making facilities; en suite rooms are available. There is a very wide
choice of excellent eating places within a two or three minute
walk of Linden House, and visitors with cars enjoy safe,
on-street parking.
OPEN ALL YEAR.   NO SMOKING.   V, S.D. B/A.   OVER 8S ONLY.   SOME
EN SUITE ROOMS.   BEVERAGES & T.V. IN ROOMS.   B. & B. FROM £20.

RUDHALL FARM, ROSS-ON-WYE, HEREFORD, HR9 7TL   TEL: (01989) 585240
Elegant country house in landscaped garden with lake & millstream in peaceful valley.
NO SMOKING.   V, S.D. B/A.   BEVERAGES & TV IN BEDROOMS.   B. & B. AROUND £20.

ST WEONARDS

THE OLD VICARAGE, ST WEONARDS, HR2 8NT   TEL: (01981) 8278
Comfortable Victorian home; 2 acre garden, in charming village; panoramic views.
NO SMOKING.   V, S.D. B/A.   CHILDREN WELCOME.   BEVERAGES & T.V. IN ROOMS.   B. & B. AROUND £20.

ULLINGSWICK

The Steppes Country House Hotel
ULLINGSWICK, HR1 3JG   TEL: (01432) 820424

The Steppes is a listed 17th C. building with a wealth
of original features (beamed ceilings, inglenook fireplaces, tiled floors) in the tiny hamlet of Ullingswick
- a community mentioned in the Domesday Book of
1082. It has been sympathetically renovated - the
ancient dairy and cider-making cellars now forming
the Cellar bar and Lounge - and the bedrooms are all
tastefully furnished and decorated. The 5-course evening meal, served by candlelight, is a gourmet treat
for the adventurous palate, and features an eclectic
variety of dishes, ranging from ancient Medieval
recipes served at Royal Banquets to revived local
delicacies and Eastern delights (a more conventional menu is available for those with

traditional tastes); all meals have been prepared from the finest fresh ingredients by the internationally renowned chef. Add to this the beauty of the unspoilt Herefordshire countryside, and you have the perfect place for a very special holiday break.
OPEN ALL YEAR.   N/S MOST PUBLIC ROOMS.   V, S.D. B/A.   LICENSED.   DISABLED ACCESS: 'NOT FOR TOTALLY WHEELCHAIR BOUND'.   CHILDREN: OVER 12S ONLY.   PETS B/A.   EN SUITE, BEVERAGES, TV, PHONE, MINI-BAR IN ROOMS.   ACCESS, BARCLAYCARD.   B. & B. AROUND £35.

RESTAURANTS

HEREFORD

'NUTTERS', CAPUCHIN YARD, OFF CHURCH ST, HEREFORD
Vegetarian restaurant.
NO SMOKING.   V STD.   LICENSED.   WHEELCHAIR ACCESS.   CHILDREN WELCOME.

Intermission Restaurant

UNIT 24, MAYLORD ORCHARDS SHOPPING CENTRE   TEL: (01432) 272500
A friendly self-service restaurant serving light lunches, snacks and hot and cold drinks.
OPEN STORE HOURS.   NO SMOKING.   V STD.   DISABLED ACCES.   CHILDREN WELCOME. CREDIT CARDS.

ROSS ON WYE

COPPERFIELDS, 29 GLOUCESTER RD, ROSS-ON-WYE   TEL: (01989) 567734
Teashop serving cakes, hot and cold snacks and a choice of teas.
NO SMOKING.

MEADER'S HUNGARIAN RESTAURANT, 1 COPSE CROSS ST, R-O-W TEL: (01989) 562803
Friendly restaurant serving delicious food, mainly Hungarian.
NO SMOKING.   V.   LICENSED.   CHILDREN WELCOME.

Shropshire

ACCOMMODATION

BRIDGNORTH

The Old Vicarage Hotel

WORFIELD, BRIDGNORTH, SHROPSHIRE, WV15 5JZ   TEL: (01746) 4497

The Old Vicarage is a magnificent Edwardian house which stands in two acres of beautifully tended grounds, overlooking fields and farmland, in the quiet Shropshire hamlet of Worfield. The proprietors, Christine and Peter Iles, have been in residence since 1979 and since that time have lovingly restored this handsome Edwardian parsonage into a country house hotel of quite exceptional quality: decorated and furnished in keeping with the period, the en suite guest rooms are nonetheless individually styled (each is named after a local village), and offer a wide range of facilities, including a direct dial phone, a mini-bar and fresh fruit; further luxury suites (including one specifically designed for disabled guests), are available in the Coach House. The candlelit dinner is exceptionally good: the menu, which is based around the availability of fresh, regional produce, changes daily and virtually everything is home-made, including the bread, ice-cream, sorbets and preserves (there are some excellent vegetarian options); the wine list is comprehensive and includes a good selection of half bottles. The Old Vicarage is a perfect venue for parties and private functions.
OPEN ALL YEAR.   N/S DINING R & SOME BEDRS.   V, S.D. B/A.   LICENSED.   RAMPS & SPECIAL SUITE FOR DISABLED.   CHILDREN WELCOME.   PETS B/A.   EN SUITE, BEVERAGES & T.V. IN ALL BEDROOMS. ACCESS, VISA, AMEX, DINERS.   B. & B. AROUND £85 FOR 2 PERSONS, D. FROM £23.

CHURCH STRETTON

Hope Bowdler Hall

CHURCH STRETTON, SHROPSHIRE, SY6 7DD   TEL: (0694) 722041
Ancient stone-built manor house with a lovely large garden at the edge of peaceful village.
OPEN April - Oct.   NO SMOKING.   B. & B. AROUND £20.

Mynd House Hotel

LITTLE STRETTON, CHURCH STRETTON, SHROPS. TEL: (01694) 722212 FAX (01694) 724180
*ETB 4 Crown Highly Commended. 3 RAC Merit Awards. AA 71%. Logis 3 Fireplaces
Award.* Award-winning small hotel in idyllic rural hamlet, where the hills sweep down all
around in superb walking country. There are two full suites available - one with a
four-poster and double spa bath - and the acclaimed restaurant offers regional cuisine along
with a superb wine selection which includes 300 bottles and 175 half bottles. Themed short
breaks are also a speciality. A brochure and information pack is available on request.
OPEN ALL YEAR.   N/S EX. IN BAR LOUNGE.   V STD, S.D. B/A.   LICENSED.   CHILDREN & PETS WELCOME.
EN SUITE, BEVERAGES & TV IN ROOMS. ACCESS, VISA, SWITCH, AMEX.   B. & B. FROM £25, D. £12.95 - £25.

CRAVEN ARMS

THE OLD RECTORY, HOPESAY, CRAVEN ARMS, SY7 8HD   TEL: (01588) 7245
NO SMOKING.   V, S.D. B/A.   NOT LICENSED, BUT BRING YOUR OWN.   OVER 12S ONLY.   EN SUITE,
BEVERAGES & T.V. IN ALL BEDROOMS.   B & B AROUND £29

ELLESMERE

THE MOUNT, ST JOHN'S HILL, ELLESMERE, SY12 OEY   TEL: (01691) 622466
OPEN ALL YEAR.   NO SMOKING.   V, S.D. B/A.   EN SUITE.   BEVERAGES. T.V. IN SITTING R. B. & B. £20.

IRONBRIDGE

The Library House

11 SEVERN BANK, IRONBRIDGE, TF8 7AN   TEL:(01952) 432299   FAX: (01952) 433697

AA QQQQ Selected, ETB 3 Crowns Highly Commended.
The Library House is a well-restored period house situated
in a World Heritage Site of The Ironbridge Gorge about 100
yards from the Ironbridge itself; the old village library,
which gives the house its name is now a comfortable guest
lounge. The house has been tastefully furnished throughout,
and the proprietors offer excellent accommodation in centrally heated en suite rooms. Breakfast is the only meal
which is usually served at the Library House, but evening
meals - in which everything has been freshly home-cooked
- can be provided by prior arrangment. You are splendidly
situated 70 yards from the Ironbridgea itself, midst wonderful countryside and just a short
distance from the Long Mynd with its famous walks. Free car park pass to all sites.
OPEN ALL YEAR.   NO SMOKING   V, S.D., B/A.   LICENSED.   CHILDREN & PETS WELCOME.   EN SUITE, TV &
BEVERAGES IN BEDROOMS.   B. & B. FROM £22.

The Severn Trow

CHURCH RD, JACKFIELD, IRONBRIDGE, SHROPS, TF8 7ND   TEL: (01952) 883551

Your hosts at the Severn Trow, Jim and Pauline Hannigan, are extending a hand of hospitality which has been
proferred by successive occupants for many centuries at
their home: travellers to the area would berth their trows
at the wharf at the end of the garden before retiring to the
Severn Trow for rest and recuperation. These days no
trow-berthing is required to appreciate the Hannigan
hospitality and the wonderful way in which they have
renovated their unique home: some things could not be
changed (the front door faces the river and its purpose
died with the river trade), but some original features still
enhance the character of the house, such as the wide
inglenook fireplace and the magnificent Jackfield mosaic tile floor in the dining room.
Accommodation is in rooms which have changed happily in both comfort and function (one

was once one of several brothel cubicles), and each has a range of helpful amenities, including the ground floor suite (a good choice for guests of limited mobility - your hosts will gladly serve breakfast therein on request).
OPEN Jan.-OCT. inc. NO SMOKING. V, S.D. B/A. WELL-BEHAVED CHILDREN WELCOME. GROUND FLOOR ROOM (but not total wheelchair access) TV IN LOUNGE. TV SOME BEDROOMS. EN SUITE & BEVERAGES IN ROOMS. B. & B. £17-21.

LINGEN

Brook Cottage

LINGEN, BUCKNELL, SHROPSHIRE, SY7 0DY   TEL: (01544) 267990
18th C. cottage in country garden with brook in idyllic village. Vegetarian food a speciality. Books, music and tranquillity to be enjoyed!
OPEN Feb.-Nov. NO SMOKING. V, S.D., GLUTEN-FREE, MILK-FREE, EGG-FREE. CHILDREN & PETS B/A. T.V. LOUNGE. B. & B. FROM £15, E.M. £9.50.

LUDLOW

Corndene

CORELEY, LUDLOW, SHROPSHIRE, SY8 3AW   TEL: (01584) 890324
*ETB 2 Crowns.*18th C. house of great charm in 2 acres of lovely gardens.
OPEN ALL YEAR ex. Xmas & New Year. NO SMOKING.   V, S.D. B/A. "TOURISM FOR ALL": category 1 disabled access.   CHILDREN WELCOME.   EN SUITE & BEVERAGES IN ROOMS. T.V. LOUNGE.   B. & B. FROM £18.50.

MINSTERLEY

Cricklewood Cottage

PLOX GREEN, MINSTERLEY, SHROPSHIRE, SY5 0HT TEL: (01743) 791229
18th C. cottage which is beautifully situated at the foot of the Stiperstones Hills
OPEN ALL YEAR. NO SMOKING. V, S.D. B/A. EN SUITE & BEVERAGES IN ROOMS.   T.V. IN LOUNGE.   B. & B FROM £17.50.

OSWESTRY

Blaen Hirnant Guest House

HIRNANT, PEN-Y-BONT-FAWR, Nr OSWESTRY, SY10 0HR   TEL: (01691) 73 330
Blaen Hirnant (its name means 'source of the long river') is a carefully renovated cruck beam farmhouse with fine views which stands amidst pleasant gardens in hills just 3 miles from Lake Vyrnwy. Accommodation is in comfortable, centrally heated en suite bedrooms and meals are served in the oak-beamed buttery; there is a pleasant lounge with inglenook and TV. There are numerous places to visit within easy reach including Pistyll Rhaeadr, Powys and Chirk Castles.
OPEN mid-Jan. - mid-Dec.   NO SMOKING.. S.D. B/A. BYO WINE. EN SUITE, TV & BEVERAGES IN ROOMS. B. & B. FROM £14, D. £9.

Bwlch y Rhiw

LLANSILIN, OSWESTRY, SHROPSHIRE, SY10 7PT   TEL: (01691) 70261
Large Victorian farmhouse perched high above the Cynllaith Valley amidst 120 acres of farmland. Carefully restored in order to retain its original character and every modern comfort is provided in the centrally heated guest bedrooms (there is a double, a twin and a family room); there is also a pleasant lounge for guests'use.
OPEN Easter - Oct. INC. N/S DINING R.   V B/A. EN SUITE, TV & BEVERAGES IN ROOMS. CHILDREN WELCOME. B. & B. FROM £16.50.

FRANKTON MANOR, WELSH FRANKTON, WHITTINGTON, OSWESTRY, SY11 4NX
Victorian country house, originally the village rectory, with superb views.
TEL: (01691) 622454 NO SMOKING. V, S.D. B/A. LICENSED.   CHILDREN WELCOME. EN SUITE, BEVERAGES & T.V. IN ROOMS. B. & B. AROUND £18.

SHREWSBURY

Anton Guest House

1 CANON ST, MONKMOOR, SHROPSHIRE, SY2 5HG   TEL: (01743) 359275
ETB 2 Crowns Commended. The Anton Guest House is an attactive corner-positioned Victorian house which stands on a main road just 5 minutes' stroll from both Shrewsbury town centre and the 10th C. abbey church. Family-owned and run, the proprietors, Tony and Anne Sandford, offer a very friendly welcome to guests and are always on hand to help you make the most of your stay. The Anton Guest House has been very tastefully decorated,

and each of the 3 bedrooms are warm and comfortable (the house is double-glazed). Breakfast is wholesome and delicious (the many repeat visits to the Anton Guest House testify to its popularity), and special diets can be accommodated by arrangement. The world-famous Brother Cadfael books, by Ellis Peters (soon to be serialised by central TV), are set in the area and visitors may be interested in retracing the intrepid monk's steps in the Brother Cadfael walks.

OPEN ALL YEAR. NO SMOKING.   CHILDREN WELCOME.   BEVERAGES & T.V. IN ROOM   B. & B. AROUND £17.

Frankbrook

YEATON LANE, BASCHURCH, SHREWSBURY, SHROPS, SY4 2HZ   TEL: (01939) 260778

Attractive, peaceful country house with interesting garden. Home-grown produce.

OPEN ALL YEAR.   NO SMOKING.   V.   CHILDREN WELCOME.   BEVERAGES IN ROOMS.   T.V. IN LOUNGE.   B. & B. FROM £13.50.

THE OLD HOUSE, RYTON, DORRINGTON, NR SHREWS., SY5 7LY   TEL: (01743) 73585

17th C. manor house in the small rural hamlet 6m south of Shrewsbury; 2 acres of superb gardens (complete with orchard & lily pond); most of the original timber frame & panelling remains including the oak-panelled dining room with antiques, pewter & fine paintings.

NO SMOKING. V, VE STD. S.D. B/A.   CHILDREN WELCOME. EN SUITE & BEVERAGES IN ROOMS.   T.V. LOUNGE. B. & B. AROUND £20.

RESTAURANTS

CHURCH STRETTON

Acorn Wholefood Restaurant Coffee House

26 SANDFORD AVE, CHURCH STRETTON, SY6 6BW   TEL: (01694) 722495 FAX: (01694) 722495

Small family run business, recommended in many food guides; all fare, except bread, made on the premises from wholefood ingredients. Excellent food; friendly, efficient service.

OPEN 9.30 - 5.30 WINTER & 10 - 6 SUMMER, SUN. & BANK HOLS, CLOSED 2 WEEKS FEB. & NOV. N/S 75% RESTAURANT (SEP. ROOM).   V, VE, S.D. STD. CHILDREN WELCOME.

CRAVEN ARMS

The Sun Inn

CORFTON, DIDDLEBURY, NR CRAVEN ARMS.   TEL & FAX: (01584) 861239

The Sun Inn is a charming old 17th C. pub which stands amidst beautiful countryside in the quiet hamlet of Corfton between Bridgnorth and Ludlow. The landlord, Norman Pearce, serves real ales - including 150 guest beers per year - and the bar menu features a number of home-made special pies, casseroles, succulent local steaks, grills, fish dishes and vegetarian meals. Teresa Pearce does the cooking and is renowned for her generous portions and 'real food' taste; there is also a good and reasonably priced menu for child-ren. Meals are served in a charming smoke-free restaurant in which the centrepiece is a well. There is a large car park and garden/play area where children can play safely.

OPEN 11 - 3 & 11 P.M. WEEKDAYS.   12 - 2.30 & 7 - 10.30 SUNDAYS.   N/S RESTAURANT.   V STD.   CHILDREN & PETS WELCOME.   DISABLED ACCESS.

MYND HOUSE HOTEL, LITTLE STRETTON, SY6 6RB TEL: (01694) 722212

For further details please see under the entry in the accommodation section.

LUDLOW

HARDWICKS RESTAURANT, 2 QUALITY SQUARE, LUDLOW. TEL: (01584) 876470

Excellent vegetarian and wholefood restaurant.

33 SEATS. N/S 65% OF RESTAURANT. V STD.   LICENSED.   CHILDREN WELCOME.

NEWPORT

ROYAL VICTORIA HOTEL, ST MARY'S ST, NEWPORT, SHROPSHIRE TEL: (01952) 820331
Buttercross Restaurant with Victorian decor.
N/S PART OF RESTAURANT.   V ON REQUEST.   LICENSED.   CHILDREN WELCOME.

SHREWSBURY

Intermission Restaurant
MEZZANINE LEVEL, PRIDE HILL CENTRE, SHREWSBURY, SY1 1BY TEL: (01743) 52393
A friendly self-service restaurant serving lunches, snacks and hot and cold drinks.
OPEN STORE HOURS.   NO SMOKING.   V STD.   DISABLED ACCESS.   CHILDREN WELCOME. CREDIT CARDS.

The Good Life
BARRACKS PASSAGE, WYLE COP, SHREWSBURY, SHROPSHIRE.   TEL: (01743) 350455
The Good Life occupies 3 rooms of a finely restored 14th C. building which is quietly
situated in one of the oldest parts of the historic and lovely county town of Shrewsbury.
There is seating for 64 (plus 2 high chairs!) at clean pine tables, and the delicious wholefood
menu makes a welcome change from 'chips with everything'. As the proprietors rightly
point out: wholefood simply means nothing added or taken away; accordingly fresh
vegetables and fruit, wholemeal flour, free-range eggs and demerara sugar are used to
prepare delicious home-cooked quiches, nut loaves, cheeses and salads as well as a variety
of tempting desserts and puddings; beverages (many caffeine-free) are chosen with the
same care and all of the menu is available to take away.
OPEN 9.30 - 3.30 (4.30 Sat.) N/S 1 ROOM.   V EXC.   LICENSED.   DISABLED ACCESS.   CHILDREN WELCOME.

TELFORD

Pavilion
DEBENHAMS, TELFORD CENTRE, SHROPSHIRE TEL: (01952) 291500
Pavilion, a friendly self-service coffee shop serving lunches, snacks and hot & cold drinks.
OPEN STORE HOURS.   NO SMOKING.   V STD.   DISABLED ACCESS.   CHILDREN WELCOME. CREDIT CARDS.

Staffordshire

ACCOMMODATION

BURTON-ON-TRENT

The Edgecote Hotel
179 ASHBY RD, BURTON ON TRENT, STAFFS, DE15 0LB   TEL: (01283) 68966
The Edgecote is an attractive family-run hotel situated on the A50 Leicester road less than
5 minutes from the centre of Burton. All 12 centrally heated bedrooms are clean and
comfortable - several have en suite facilities - and each is equipped with a range of helpful
amenities such as a radio intercom and colour TV; there is a licensed bar and a comfortable
lounge. Breakfast at the Edgecote is a real treat (the proprietors believe it to be the best in
Burton!): a selection of cereals, yoghurt, fresh fruit and fruit juice is arranged on a
self-service buffet, and to follow there is a choice of a traditional cooked breakfast or a
lighter Continental option with home-baked rolls and croissants; dinner is served in the
oak-panelled dining room and the delicious 3-course meal features imaginative vegetarian
options and excellent home-cooked puds.
OPEN ALL YEAR.   N/S DINING R & BEDR. V B/A. LICENSED.   CHILDREN WELCOME.   PETS B/A.   EN SUITE
IN SOME ROOMS.   BEVERAGES & T.V. ROOMS.   ACCESS, VISA, AMEX.

ECCLESHALL

Glenwood
CROXTON, ECCLESHALL, STAFFS, ST21 6PF
ETB 2 Crown Commended. Charming timber-framed cottage beautifully situated amidst
unspoilt countryside offering peaceful accommodation of a very high standard to guests.
OPEN ALL YEAR.   N/S DINING R & BEDRS.   V, S.D. B/A.   DISABLED ACCESS.   CHILDREN WELCOME. PETS
B/A.   EN SUITE & BEVERAGES IN ROOMS.   T.V. LOUNGE.   ACCESS, VISA.   B. & B. AROUND £16.

LEEK

PETHILLS BANK COTTAGE, BOTTOMHOUSE, NR LEEK, ST13 7PF TEL: (01538) 304277
18th C. stone farmhouse set on a hillside in landscaped gardens with beautiful views.
N/S MOST OF THE HOUSE.   V B/A.   CHILDREN: OVER 5S WELCOME. EN SUITE, BEVERAGES & T.V. IN ROOMS.
B. & B. FROM £20.

THE WHITE HOUSE, GRINDON, NR LEEK, STAFFS, ST13 7TP   TEL: (01538) 304250
South-facing house, 1,000 feet up in the Peak National Park; views of the Manifold and
Hamps Valley. Retains the stone mullions and oak beams; home-baked bread & preserves
OPEN ALL YEAR ex. Xmas & New Year.   N/S ex. in LOUNGE.   V, S.D. B/A.   CHILDREN: OVER 10S ONLY.   EN SUITE,
TV & BEVERAGES IN ROOMS.   B. & B. AROUND £20.

NEWCASTLE UNDER LYME

Durlston Guest House
KIMBERLEY RD, NEWCASTLE UNDER LYME, STAFFS, ST5 9EG   TEL: (01782) 611708
ETB 1 Crown. Friendly, family-run guest house 10 min walk from town centre. B'fast only.
OPEN ALL YEAR.   N/S DINING R & UPPER FLOOR.   V B/A.   CHILDREN WELCOME.   PETS B/A.   BEVERAGES
& T.V. IN ROOMS.   CREDIT CARDS.   B. & B. FROM £15.

STOKE-ON-TRENT

CORRIE GST HSE, 13-15 NEWTON ST, BASFORD, STOKE, ST4 6JN TEL: (01782) 614838
Fine Victorian house in a quiet cul-de-sac just off the A53 and A500 in the heart of
the Potteries. Festival Park less than a mile away. Freshly prepared breakfasts; evening
meal and snacks by arrangement. 3 single, 2 double, 2 family and 1 twin-bedded room.
OPEN ALL YEAR.   N/S ex. SMOKERS' LOUNGE.   V, S.D. B/A. CHILDREN: 'NO BABIES'.   SOME EN SUITE ROOMS.
BEVERAGES.   T.V. IN LOUNGE. B. & B. AROUND £19.

THE HOLLIES, CLAY LAKE, ENDON, STOKE-ON-TRENT, ST9 9DD TEL: (01782) 503252
Lovely Victorian house with large garden in Endon village off the B5051/A53.
NO SMOKING.   V, S.D. B/A.   CHILDREN WELCOME.   PETS B/A.   EN SUITE IN SOME ROOMS.   BEVERAGES IN
ALL ROOMS.   T.V. IN LOUNGE.   B. & B. AROUND £17.

WHITE GABLES HOTEL, TRENTHAM RD, BLURTON, STOKE TEL: (01782) 324882
Elegant, quiet, country-house-style hotel close to the M6 and with easy access to all
city centres; beautifully decorated bedrooms.
NO SMOKING. V, S.D. B/A.   LICENSED.   DISABLED ACCESS: '3 ground floor bedrooms'.   CHILDREN WELCOME.
PETS B/A.   SOME EN SUITE ROOMS.   BEVERAGES, T.V. & D.D. PHONES IN ROOMS.   B. & B. AROUND £20.

WOODSEAVES

The Old Smithy
KNIGHTLEY DALE, WOODSEAVES, STAFFS., ST20 0JS   TEL: (01785) 284278
17th C. country cottage with 3 comfortable letting rooms & large guest lounge. Heavily
beamed with log fire in huge inglenook. Centrally heated. Ideal Potteries/Ironbridge.
OPEN ALL YEAR.   NO SMOKING.   S.D. B/A.   CHILDREN & PETS WELCOME.   EN SUITE, TV & BEVERAGES IN
ROOMS.   B. & B. £14 - 22.

RESTAURANTS
BURTON-ON-TRENT

Byrkley Park Centre
RANGEMORE, BURTON-ON-TRENT, STAFFS, DE13 9RN   TEL: (01283) 716467
The Byrkley Park Centre is a garden centre with a difference; set in the beautiful countryside around Burton-on-Trent, Byrkley Park (which is named after the 13th C. Thomas
Berkley (sic.) who had a house near the site) has everything for the keen gardener including
indoor and outdoor plants, garden furniture and a garden design and landscaping service;
there is also the excellent Thomas de Byrkley Tea Room and Carvery which offers a wide
range of delicious snacks (including home-made cakes), and selections from the Carvery
and Salad Bar (there is a good selection of wines).
N/S DINING R.   V, S.D. B/A.   LICENSED.   DISABLED ACCESS: RAMPS, WHEELCHAIRS, TOILETS.   CHILDREN
WELCOME.   CREDIT CARDS.

HANLEY

Ⓥ Pavilion Coffee Shop
POTTERIES SHOPPING CENTRE, HANLEY, STAFFS.   TEL: (01782) 202495
A friendly self-service coffee shop serving lunches, snacks and hot and cold drinks.
NO SMOKING. V STD.   DISABLED ACCESS.   CHILDREN VERY WELCOME.   CREDIT CARDS.

WATERHOUSES

Ⓥ The Old School Restaurant
STAFFORDSHIRE PEAK ARTS CENTRE, CAULDON LOWE, NR WATERHOUSES, ST10 3EX
TEL: (01538) 308431
The Staffordshire Peak Arts Centre is housed in the atmospheric setting of a converted old
moorlands village school, and it displays an exceptional range of fine art, craft work and
gifts. The Old School Restaurant - housed in the same buiding - is a delightful place in
which to enjoy the wide range of home-made cakes and meals which are served throughout
the day. Wholesome ingredients have been used in cooking and there are some tasty
vegetarian options. Families are particularly welcome - there is a garden and play area
available - and on fine days you may care to walk along the Nature Trail which has been
laid out nearby on a one acre site of special scientific interest.
NO SMOKING. V, VE STD. S.D. B/A.   LICENSED.   DISABLED ACCESS.   CHILDREN WELCOME.

Warwickshire

ACCOMMODATION

HENLEY IN ARDEN

IRELANDS FARM B & B, IRELANDS FARM, IRELANDS LANE, B95 5SA TEL: (01564) 792476
OPEN ALL YEAR, ex. Xmas & New Year. N/S DINING R & BEDRS.   V B/A.   DOGS B/A.   EN SUITE SOME ROOMS.
BEVERAGES & T.V. IN ALL ROOMS.   B. & B. AROUND £20.

ROYAL LEAMINGTON SPA

Ⓥ **AGAPE, 26 ST MARY RD, ROYAL LEAMINGTON SPA   TEL: (01926) 882896**
Pleasant guest house situated on southern edge of town & within easy walking distance of
its many attractions. Warm, friendly atmosphere. BTA member. Home-made jams.
OPEN ALL YEAR.   NO SMOKING.   V, S.D. B/A.   OVER 5S WELCOME.   EN SUITE, TV & BEVERAGES IN
BEDROOMS. B. & B. FROM £18.50.

Ⓥ Northton
77 TELFORD AVENUE, ROYAL LEAMINGTON SPA, CV32 7HQ   TEL: (01926) 425609

ETB 2 Crowns Commended. Northton is a private
family home situated just off the A445 offering first
class accommodation in a quiet and peaceful residential area on the northern outskirts of Leamington
Spa; very comfortably furnished (both guest rooms
face south and overlook extensive gardens) and a full
English breakfast is served with national daily
papers!). Northton is ideally situated for visitors to
the city of Coventry (just 20 minutes drive away), its
Management Training Centre and National Agricul-
tural Centre (just 2 miles away); taxis can be arranged to and from these two centres and Northton.
OPEN Feb. - Oct.   NO SMOKING.   V, S.D. B/A.   CHILDREN WELCOME.   EN SUITE, BEVERAGES AND T.V. IN ALL
ROOMS.   B. & B. AROUND £20.

Ⓥ **THE WILLIS, 11 EASTNOR GR., LEAMINGTON SPA, CV31 1LD   TEL: (01926) 425820**
Spacious Victorian town house with peaceful garden in a quiet residential cul-de-sac.
OPEN ALL YEAR.   NO SMOKING.   V, S.D. B/A.   CHILDREN WELCOME.   PETS B/A.   EN SUITE IN TWIN-
BEDDED ROOM.   BEVERAGES IN ROOMS.   T.V.   B. & B. AROUND £19.

RUGBY

Manor Farm
WILLEY, NR RUGBY, WARWICKSHIRE, CV23 0SH   TEL: (01455) 553143

Manor Farm is a 93 acre stock farm which stands on the edge of the small village of Willey, surrounded by a pretty cottage garden and overlooking open farmland. Although its rural situation is quiet and peaceful, the farm is just 5 miles from the A14 and the Midlands motorway network, and thus easily accessible. Each of the centrally heated bedrooms overlook the garden and farmland, and there is a pleasant lounge for guests' use. Guests have a choice of a full English breakfast or a lighter option, and there is a delightful village pub where you can enjoy an evening meal.
NO SMOKING.   OPEN ALL YEAR (ex. Xmas & New Year).   BEVERAGES IN ROOMS.   EN SUITE & TV IN 1 ROOM. B. & B. FROM £17.

SHIPSTON-ON-STOUR

LONGDON MANOR, SHIPSTON-ON-STOUR, CV36 4PW   TEL: (01608) 82235
14th C. manor house with history and records dating from 10th C.
OPEN Mar. - Nov.   NO SMOKING.   V, S.D. B/A.   CHILDREN WELCOME.   EN SUITE & TV IN ALL ROOMS. BEVERAGES IN ROOMS ON REQUEST.   CREDIT CARDS.   B. & B. FROM £35.

STRATFORD UPON AVON

Abberley
12 ALBANY RD, STRATFORD UPON AVON, WARWICKS, CV37 6PG   TEL: (01789) 295934

Abberley is a comfortable family home, centrally situated in a quiet residential part of Stratford upon Avon within easy walking distance of the three Royal Shakespeare Company theatres and the River Avon. It is an exclusively smoke-free establishment and, while breakfast is the only meal available, it is a healthy treat (home-made Seville marmalade; vegetarian breakfast options) and there are plenty of good restaurants in the town. Abberley provides the perfect base from which to visit the Shakespearean properties and explore the Cotswolds, Warwick Castle and the many nearby National Trust properties. Car parking
OPEN ALL YEAR.   NO SMOKING.   S.D. B/A.   EN SUITE. BEVERAGES & T.V.   B. & B. FROM £19.

ASHBURTON HOUSE, 27 EVESHAM PLACE, STRATFORD UPON AVON, CV37 6HT
Small, friendly guest house close to the town centre and specialising in Japanese breakfasts and pre-theatre dinners; traditional English breakfast is also available.
TEL: (01789) 292444   FAX: (01789) 415658   N/S PUBLIC ROOMS.   V, S.D. B/A.   CHILDREN WELCOME. BEVERAGES & T.V IN ROOMS.   AMEX.   B. & B. AROUND £19.

AVON CROFT, OLD TOWN, STRATFORD UPON AVON, CV37 6BG   TEL: (01789) 292600
16th C. listed house close to town centre, theatres and Holy Trinity Church.
OPEN Mar. - Nov.   NO SMOKING.   S.D. B/A.   CHILDREN WELCOME. EN SUITE & BEVERAGES IN ALL ROOMS. B. & B. AROUND £20.

Bishopton Hill Nursery
BIRMINGHAM RD, STRATFORD-UPON-AVON, CV37 0RN   TEL: (01789) 267829

Formerly a nursery, this attractive modern bungalow stands in 4 acres of grounds 1½ miles north of Stratford-upon-Avon on the A3400 Henley-in-Arden road. It is a spacious family home, beautifully situated in an elevated position with wonderful views over Stratford-upon-Avon towards the Cotswold Hills. It is run by Muriel Hardwicke who offers a full English breakfast to guests: lacto-vegetarian and other diets can be catered for by arrangement and there are plenty of restaurants in Stratford-upon-Avon. Accommodation is in comfortable rooms and there is a ground floor room.
OPEN ALL YEAR.   NO SMOKING.   V, S.D. B/A.   OVER 8S WELCOME.   EN SUITE, TV & BEVERAGES IN BEDROOMS.   B. & B. AROUND £20..

BROOK LODGE, 192 ALCESTER RD, STRATFORD-U-AVON, CV37 9DR TEL: (01789) 295988
OPEN ALL YEAR ex. Xmas & New Year.   N/S PUBLIC ROOMS.   CHILDREN WELCOME.   PETS B/A.   EN SUITE IN MOST ROOMS. BEVERAGES & T.V IN ROOMS. B. & B. AROUND £20.

Clomendy Guest House
157 EVESHAM RD, STRATFORD, CV37 9BP   TEL: (01789) 266957

ETB 2 Crowns. Clomendy Guest House is a small, detached, family-run guest house which is built in the mock tudor style and stands on the main Stratford to Evesham road; there is a very pleasant garden which recently won a 'Stratford in Bloom' commendation. Breakfast

is the only meal to be served at Clomendy, but you are within easy reach of Stratford town centre in which there are numerous good restaurants. Guests choosing to arrive by coach or rail can be collected free of charge from the stations, and you will find the guest house is within easy each of the theatres and Anne Hathaway's cottage, as well as within driving distance of the Cotswolds.
OPEN ALL YEAR.   NO SMOKING.   CHILDREN WELCOME.   BEVERAGES & T.V.   B. & B. AROUND £19.

GREEN GABLES, 47 BANBURY RD, STRATFORD, CV37 7HW TEL: (01789) 20557
OPEN ALL YEAR.   NO SMOKING.   CHILDREN.   EN SUITE & T.V . B. & B. AROUND £17.

Moonraker House
ALCESTER RD, STRATFORD-UPON-AVON, WARWICKS, CV37 9DB   TEL: (01789) 299346/267115   FAX: (01789) 295504

Moonraker House is situated in Stratford-upon-Avon, the perfect centre for exploring the Cotswolds, and is personally run by the owners, Mike and Mauveen Spencer. All the rooms have been individually designed and decorated to a very high standard of comfort and cosiness by Mauveen and her daughter, and there is a collection of Edwardian furniture in the main lounge/dining room. For an extra touch of luxury there is also a four-poster bedroom (with garden patio) a 2-room suite and a half-testa bedroom. Moonraker House is a home-from-home down to the home-made jams & marmalade which are part of the delicious, freshly cooked English breakfast.
OPEN ALL YEAR ex. Xmas & Boxing Day.   NO SMOKING.   V, S.D., B/A.   SOME GROUND FLOOR ROOMS.
CHILDREN WELCOME.   PETS B/A.   EN SUITE, COLOUR TV, CLOCK RADIO, HAIRDRYER & BEVERAGES IN
ROOMS.   CREDIT CARDS.   B. & B. £19.50 - 29.50.

MOSS COTTAGE, 61 EVESHAM RD, STRATFORD, CV37 9BA TEL: (01789) 294770
Detached cottage offering spacious en suite accommodation with TV & tea tray. Traditional b'fast; free range eggs. Close to Shakespeare properties & theatres.
NO SMOKING.   EN SUITE, TV & BEVERAGES IN BEDROOMS.   B. & B. AROUND £20

Parkfield
3 BROAD WALK, STRATFORD-UPON-AVON, WARWICKS, CV37 6HS   TEL: (01789) 293313
Parkfield is an elegant Victorian house which is quietly situated in the peaceful 'old town' part of Stratford. Bedrooms are all warm, comfortable and centrally heated, and have been equipped with a range of helpful amenities including TV, hot-drink facilities and an easy chair. Your hosts offer a delicious breakfast which includes pancakes and vegetarian sausages in addition to the more traditional English breakfast fare: everything is free-range, home-made and organic wherever possible and unrefined sugar, wholemeal bread and low-fat milk are all available. Travellers by car will be glad to know that they can leave their car safely at Parkfield without having to worry about parking in town: it is just a few minutes' pleasant walk along the river from Parkfield to the Royal Shakespeare Theatre or to the centre of Stratford-upon-Avon.
OPEN ALL YEAR.   V, VE, S.D. STD.   NO SMOKING.   CHILDREN WELCOME.   EN SUITE, TV & BEVERAGES IN
ROOMS.   CREDIT CARDS.   B. & B. £17-22.

Penshurst Guest House
34 EVESHAM PL., STRATFORD, CV37 6HT   TEL: (01789) 205259 FAX: (01789) 295322
Penshurst is a prettily refurbished, totally non-smoking Victorian town house which stands just 5 minutes' walk from the town centre. A delicious full English or appetising Continental breakfast is served from 7 a.m. till 10.30 a.m., and a home-cooked evening meal is available by arrangement. There are eight attractively furnished bedrooms, one of which is on the ground floor, and two of which have en suite facilities; all bedrooms have a TV and beverage-making equipment, and hot bed-time drinks are provided free of charge.
OPEN ALL YEAR.   NO SMOKING.   V, S.D. B/A.   CHILDREN WELCOME.   WHEELCHAIR ACCESS.   2 EN
SUITE ROOMS.   TV & BEVERAGES.   B. & B. FROM £13.50.

Pond Cottage
THE GREEN, WARMINGTON, BANBURY, OX17 1BU   TEL: (0129589) 682
Old, stone-built cottage with honeysuckle climbing up the wall in a lovely, peaceful Conservation Area just 6 miles from the M40 midway betn J11 & J12.
OPEN April - Oct. inc.   NO SMOKING.   DOUBLE ROOM: SHOWER W. BASIN EN SUITE; SINGLE: BATHROOM NEXT
DOOR.   BEVERAGES IN BOTH BEDROOMS.   TV IN SITTING ROOM.   B. & B. AROUND £17.

TWELFTH NIGHT, EVESHAM PL., STRATFORD, CV37 6HT TEL: (01789) 414595
Elegantly refurbished Victorian house. Superb pre-theatre meals available.
OPEN ALL YEAR. NO SMOKING. V, S.D. B/A. B'fast B/A. OVER 5S ONLY. MOST EN SUITE ROOMS. BEVER-
AGES & T.V IN ROOMS. B. & B. FROM £18.

WARWICK

The Croft
HASELEY KNOB, WARWICK, CV35 7NL (0926) 484 447
ETB 2 Crowns Commended. Family house and small holding in picturesque village.
Friendly family atmosphere. Generous food featuring home-produce like fresh farm eggs,
vegetables & home-made jam & marmalade. Convenient for Birmingham airport & NEC.
OPEN ALL YEAR. NO SMOKING. V, S.D. B/A. DISABLED ACCESS: 'GROUND FLOOR BEDROOM BUT NOT
SUITABLE FOR WHEELCHAIRS'. CHILDREN WELCOME. PETS B/A. SOME EN SUITE ROOMS. BEVERAGES &
T.V IN ALL BEDROOMS. B. & B. AROUND £20.

The Garden Suite
44 HIGH ST, WARWICK, CV34 4AX   TEL: (01926) 401512

Its owners tell me that while the origins of their lovely old home
have been lost in the mists of time, it nevertheless has the
dubious distinction of having been one of the first houses to have
been burned in the fire of 1694; an event unlikely to be repeated
as No. 44 is now a completely smoke-free establishment! It has
much else to commend it: overlooking (as its name suggests) a
tranquil private garden, it provides a haven of peace for visitors
to this historically interesting, active old town. Accommodation
is in one of two superbly appointed suites, equipped to the very
highest standards, with hairdryer, fridge, a large hot drinks selection, and books and magazines - a home from home! Supper trays
and evening meals are available only by prior arrangement.
OPEN ALL YEAR. NO SMOKING. 1 GROUND FLOOR SUITE OF ROOMS SUIT-
ABLE FOR FAMILIES. CHILDREN WELCOME. PETS B/A. EN SUITE, TV &
BEVERAGES IN ROOMS. B. & B. AROUND £21.

Northleigh House
FIVE WAYS RD, HATTON, NR WARWICK, WARWICKS., CV35 7HZ   TEL: (01926) 484203

ETB 3 Crowns Highly Commended. This small,
country house, set in the quiet of rural Warwickshire,
is really rather a special place: from its beautiful
furnishings (all rooms have been individually designed with colour coordinating linen and uphol-
stery) to its glorious setting amidst private gardens
and open fields (several rooms have views), Northleigh House is, as its proprietor endeavours to make
it, an exceptionally nice small hotel. Service is an
important feature of a stay at Northleigh, where
nothing seems to be too much trouble to your hostess
(a laundry service, an extra hot water bottle, shoe-cleaning equipment...just ask and it's
there). The food is first-rate - breakfasts are freshly prepared to suit individual requirements
and evening meals or supper trays are available on request (although guests might want to
sample the many fine restaurants in the area).
OPEN ALL YEAR ex. Xmas & Jan. NO SMOKING. V, S.D. B/A. CHILDREN WELCOME. PETS B/A. EN SUITE,
TV & BEVERAGES IN ROOMS. CREDIT CARDS. Singles from £28, Double from: £40.

Redlands Farm
BANBURY RD, LIGHTHORNE, NR WARWICK, CV35 0AH   TEL: (01926) 651241
A lovely 17th C. stone farmhouse in 2 acres of gardens complete with swimming pool and
beautiful views across open countryside. Comfortably furnished throughout (there is also
central heating), but the basic character of the house remains unchanged, and there are still
open fires and beamed ceilings; bedrooms are very attractively decorated - one has a
Victorian brass bed - and there are en suite facilities. Redlands Farm is an excellent base
from which to explore the Warwickshire countryside: Stratford and the Cotswolds are all
within easy touring distance, and Warwick is just 10 minutes' drive away.
OPEN April - Oct. N/S DINING R & BEDRS. V, S.D. B/A. CHILDREN WELCOME. EN SUITE & TV AVAILABLE.
B. & B. AROUND £17.

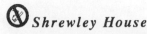

Shrewley House

SHREWLEY, NR WARWICK, WARWICKS, CV35 7AT   TEL: (01926) 842549   FAX: (01926) 842216
AA 5Qs Premier Selected. RAC Highly Acclaimed. ETB Highly Receommended.

Shrewley House is a Grade II listed Georgian farmhouse which stands amidst 1½ acres of garden by the peaceful village of Shrewley, the whole surrounded by beautiful Warwickshire countryside. Accommodation is in elegantly furnished en suite bedrooms, each of which has a range of helpful amenities (hair dryers, direct dial phones, clock radios, etc); there are also several de luxe rooms, perfect for a honeymoon or special weekend break, which have the added luxury of king-sized four poster beds. Meals are served in an elegant dining room which opens out onto the lawned gardens. Shrewley House is an ideal venue for a small meeting or conference: in addition to the aforementioned accommodation, there are two superbly equipped self-catering cottages; guests staying therein are welcome to take breakfast in the main house if they so wish.
OPEN ALL YEAR.   NO SMOKING.   V, S.D. B/A.   CHILDREN & PETS WELCOME.   EN SUITE, BEVERAGES & TV IN ROOMS.   B. & B. £37.60 - 72.85.

WILLOWBROOK HSE B. & B., LIGHTHORNE RD, KINETON, NR WARWICK, CV35 0JL
Comfortable house & smallholding with sheep, chickens, gardens & paddocks in lovely countryside. Nr Warwick, Stratford, Cotswolds. Furnished with antiques.
TEL: (0926) 640475 FAX: (0926) 641747   OPEN ALL YEAR ex. Xmsa.   NO SMOKING.   V, S.D. B/A.   PETS B/A. EN SUITE, TV & TEA/COFFEE-MAKING IN BEDROOMS. B. & B. FROM £14. 3 MILES J12 M40.

RESTAURANTS

ROYAL LEAMINGTON SPA

The Pavilion Coffee Shop

UPPER MALL, ROYAL PRIORS SHOPPING CENTRE   TEL: (01926) 450133
OPEN STORE HOURS.   NO SMOKING.   V STD.   DISABLED ACCESS.   CHILDREN WELCOME. CREDIT CARDS.

STRATFORD UPON AVON

CAFÉ NATURAL, GREENHILL ST, STRATFORD-U-AVON, CV37 6LF TEL: (01789) 415741
Wholefood and vegetarian restaurant serving good range of meat-free snacks and meals.
OPEN Mon. To Sat. 9 - 5 P.M.   NO SMOKING.   V EXC, VE ON REQUEST. DISABLED ACCESS.   CHILDREN.

HATHAWAY'S RESTAURANT & TEA-ROOM, HIGH ST, STRATFORD UPON AVON.
NO SMOKING IN SEPARATE ROOM.

WARWICK

CHARLOTTE'S TEAROOMS, 6 JURY ST, WARWICK.
NO SMOKING.

West Midlands

ACCOMMODATION

BIRMINGHAM

NORTON PLACE HOTEL, 180 LIFFORD LN, KINGS NORTON, B30 3NT TEL: (0121) 433 5656
Country-house hotel within walled gardens of Patrick Collection; excellent food.
OPEN ALL YEAR.   N/S DINING R & SOME BEDRS.   V STD.   LICENSED.   DISABLED ACCESS.   CHILDREN WELCOME.   ROOM SERVICE.   EN SUITE & T.V.   B. & B. AROUND £50.

COVENTRY

BROOKLANDS GRANGE HOTEL, HOLYHEAD ROAD, CV5 8HX TEL: (01203) 601601
OPEN ALL YEAR.   N/S RESTAURANT & SOME BEDRS.   V.   LICENSED.   DISABLED ACCESS.

Westwood Cottage

WESTWOOD HEATH ROAD, WESTWOOD HEATH, W. MIDLANDS, CV4 8GN　TEL & FAX: (01203) 471084

One of 4 sandstone cottages built in 1834 and set in rural surroundings; pleasingly renovated and retaining many period features. Late access.

OPEN ALL YEAR ex. Xmas. N/S. DINING R, BEDRS & LOUNGE.　V, B/A.　DISABLED ACCESS.　CHILDREN WELCOME. EN SUITE ALL ROOMS.　BEVERAGES.　T.V. LOUNGE.　B. & B. FROM £18.

FILLONGLEY (Nr COVENTRY)

MILL FARMHOUSE, MILL LN, FILLONGLEY, NR COVENTRY.　TEL: (01676) 41898

Peace and tranquillity in country residence in idyllic countryside. Super home-cooking. Private gardens and car park. Exceptionally comfortable bedrooms. Near NEC B'ham.

OPEN ALL YEAR.　NO SMOKING.　V, S.D. B/A.　EN SUITE, TV & BEVERAGES IN BEDROOMS. B. & B. apartment (double) £40; One Person £30; Single Room £15 (shared Facilities).

SUTTON COLDFIELD

NEW HALL, WALMLEY ROAD, SUTTON COLDFIELD, B76 8QX　TEL: (0121) 378 2442

OPEN ALL YEAR.　N/S DINING R.　V.　LICENSED.　DISABLED ACCESS.　OVER 7S ONLY.

WALSALL

Abberley Hotel

BESCOT ROAD, WALSALL, W. MIDLANDS, WS2 9AD　　TEL: (01922) 27413

ETB 4 Crowns. Well-established hotel, tastefully furnished with designer fabrics to complement the craftsmanship and skill of the original Victorian building. AA, RAC 2 star.

OPEN ALL YEAR.　N/S RESTAURANT & SOME BEDRS.　V, B/A.　LICENSED.　DISABLED ACCESS.　CHILDREN WELCOME.　PETS B/A.　EN SUITE, TV & TEA MAKING IN ROOMS.　ACCESS, VISA, AMEX.

RESTAURANTS & PUBS

BIRMINGHAM

WILD OATS, 5 RADDLEBARN ROAD, SELLY OAK　TEL: (0121) 471 2459

OPEN 12 - 2, 6 - 9.　NO SMOKING.　V, VE EXC.　DISABLED ACCESS.　CHILDREN.

COVENTRY

DEBENHAMS, WEST ORCHARD SHOPPING CENTRE, SMITHFORD WAY, COVENTRY

Pavilion, a friendly self-service coffee shop serving lunches, snacks, hot & cold drinks.

OPEN STORE HOURS.　NO SMOKING.　V.　DISABLED ACCESS.　CHILDREN.　CREDIT CARDS.

THE OLD CLARENCE, EARLSON AVE., COVENTRY

Three room pub with totally separate smoke-free lounge.

35 SEATS.　NO SMOKING IN LOUNGE BAR.　DISABLED ACCESS.

DUDLEY

DEBENHAMS, THE MERRY HILL CENTRE, PEDMORE RD, BRIERLEY HILL, DY5 1SY TEL: (01384) 480440

Intermission, self-service coffee shop serving lunches, snacks, hot & cold drinks.

OPEN STORE HOURS.　NO SMOKING.　V.　DISABLED ACCESS.　CHILDREN WELCOME.　CREDIT CARDS.

RYTON ON DUNSMORE

Ryton Organic Gardens and Restaurant

RYTON ON DUNSMORE, COVENTRY, CV8 3LG　TEL: (01203) 303517　FAX: (01203) 639229

There are 10 acres of beautiful gardens at Ryton Organic Gardens and it is a wonderful day out for all the family (there is an excellent children's area). The commitment to organic growing extends to the restaurant in which almost all of the home-cooked food is organically grown - much of it on site - and the delicious menu features at least six vegetarian and one vegan dish each day. The shop sells a wide range of organic food and wine, books, gifts and garden products.

OPEN ALL YEAR ex. Xmas.　NO SMOKING.　V, WH, ORG, VE, S.D. STD.　CHILDREN WELCOME.　WHEELCHAIR ACCESS.　　GUIDE DOGS WELCOME (shade & water provided for others).

Worcestershire

ACCOMMODATION

BEWDLEY

ALTON GUEST HOUSE & TEA ROOMS, LONG BANK, BEWDLEY TEL: (01299) 266733

Ⓝ Pleasing guest house cum tea room serving home-made snacks, lunches and teas.
OPEN ALL YEAR.   N/S ex. Smoker's Lounge. V, S.D. B/A.   CHILDREN WELCOME.   EN SUITE IN SOME ROOMS.
BEVERAGES & T.V. IN ROOMS.   ACCESS, VISA.   B. & B. AROUND £18.

BROADWAY

CUSACKS GLEBE, SAINTBURY, NR BROADWAY, WORCS, WR12 7PX   TEL: (01386) 852210
For full details please see entry under *Gloucestershire.*

Eastbank

STATION DRIVE, BROADWAY, WORCS., WR12 7DF.   TEL: (01386) 852659
Friendly 'home-from-home' in very quiet location, 12 mins walk to village. Ideal touring.
OPEN ALL YEAR.   N/S EX. LOUNGE.   S.D. B/A.   CHILDREN & PETS WELCOME.   EN SUITE, TV & BEVERAGES
IN BEDROOMS.   B. & B. £15 - 25.

Ⓝ*Orchard Grove*

Ⓝ STATION RD, BROADWAY, WORCS, WR12 7DE   TEL: (01386) 853834

ETB 2 Crown Highly Commended. Orchard Grove is an attractive modern detached stone house which is pleasantly situated just a few minutes' walk from the centre of the charming Cotswold village of Broadway. Orchard Grove is privately owned and run and offers an exceptionally high standard of accommodation and comfort to guests; your host, Angela McSweeney, does everything she can to make you feel welcome and at home, and will gladly give help and advice to help you plan your stay. Breakfast is the only meal to be served at Orchard Grove but there are numerous restaurants and pubs in the area and your hosts will gladly make table reservations for you in advance of your stay. You are ideally placed for touring all the many beautiful little towns and villages in the Cotswolds, and you will also find yourself within easy touring distance of Oxford, Cheltenham, Stratford & Warwick.
OPEN ALL YEAR.   NO SMOKING.   V, S.D. B/A (B'fast only).   CHILDREN WELCOME.   EN SUITE IN SOME ROOMS.
BEVERAGES & T.V. IN ROOMS.   B. & B. FROM £17-£19.

Ⓝ PYE CORNER FARM, BROADWAY, WORCS., WR12 7JP TEL: (01386) 853740
OPEN May - Oct NO SMOKING. V B/A. CHILDREN WELCOME. B. & B. AROUND £15.

The Old Rectory

CHURCH ST, WILLERSEY, NR BROADWAY, WORCS, WR12 7PN   TEL: (01386) 853729

Standing in a beautiful, flower-filled walled garden, this splendid 17th C. rectory, built of mellow Cotswold stone, has been lovingly restored by its owners who have been careful to retain all the original period features of the building such as the oak beams and quaint stone-built fireplaces. It has been charmingly decorated and furnished: the bedrooms, with charming four-poster beds, have an individual style and are very romantic (honeymooners are very welcome!); some rooms have views of Bredon and the Welsh hills. Breakfast is the only meal to be served at the Old Rectory, but it is a generous feast and vegetarian or continental options are available for meat-free or lighter appetites. The Old Rectory stands opposite the ancient church (first built in the 11th C.). Willersey, with its picturesque duck pond and quaint cottages, is typical of all that is best in the Cotswolds, and is an ideal centre for touring this lovely area. The Old Rectory was the RAC Guest House of the Year winner in 1991.
OPEN ALL YEAR.   N/S ex. Smoking Lounge.   V B'fasts B/A.   CHILDREN: OVER 8S ONLY.   EN SUITE, BEVERAGES
& SATELLITE T.V. IN ROOMS.   ACCESS, VISA.   B. & B. AROUND £30 PP

BROMSGROVE

VICTORIA GUEST HOUSE, 31 VICTORIA RD, BROMSGROVE, B61 0DW   TEL: (01527) 75777
OPEN ALL YEAR ex. Xmas.   N/S ALL PUBLIC ROOMS.   V, S.D. B/A.   CHILDREN WELCOME.   BEVERAGES & T.V.
IN ROOMS.   B. & B. AROUND £16.

MALVERN

Holdfast Cottage Hotel
WELLAND, NR MALVERN, WORCS, WR13 6NA   TEL: (01684) 310288
17th C. cottage with Victorian extensions; oak-beamed hall, log fire & Victorian-style bar.
OPEN ALL YEAR.   N/S DINING R & BEDRS.   V STD, S.D. B/A.   LICENSED.   CHILDREN WELCOME.   PETS B/A.
EN SUITE, BEVERAGES & T.V. IN ROOMS.   B. & B. AROUND £36.

THE LAURELS, 108 GRAHAM RD, MALVERN, WR14 2HX   TEL: (01684) 575996
Victorian stone-built house close to town centre with its Winter Gardens, park, priory,
museum & shops. Good centre for touring Wales, Cotswolds, Shrops. & Gloucestershire.
OPEN ALL YEAR. N/S DINING R, BEDRS & LOUNGE.   CHILDREN.   TV & BEVERAGES IN ROOMS. B. & B. £15.

THE NUPEND, CRADLEY, NR MALVERN, WR13 5NP   TEL: (01886) 880881
Former farmhouse in 2 acres of grounds just 10 mins drive from the Malvern Hills.
OPEN ALL YEAR.   NO SMOKING.   V B/A.   EN SUITE, TV & BEVERAGES.   B. & B. AROUND £20.

Oakwood
BLACKHEATH WAY, MALVERN, WORCS, WR14 4DR   TEL: (01684) 575508
ETB 3 Crown Highly Commended. Beautiful, detached Victorian residence in 4 acres of
grounds with terrace on S.W. slopes of Malvern Hills looking towards Wales. Furnished
with antiques; prettily decorated bedrooms. Cordon Bleu cuisines (with simpler options).
OPEN ALL YEAR.   NO SMOKING.   V, S.D. B/A.   LICENSED.   CHILDREN WELCOME.   EN SUITE MOST ROOMS.
BEVERAGES & T.V IN ALL ROOMS.   B. & B. AROUND £18.

ONE EIGHT FOUR, 184 WEST MALVERN RD, MALVERN, WR14 4AZ TEL: (01684) 566544
Beautiful 5-storey Victorian house high on the W. side of Malvern hills; beautifully
decorated (lots of stripped pine) and west-facing rooms have views to the Welsh mountains.
OPEN ALL YEAR.   N/S ex 1 lounge.   V B'fast B/A.   LICENSED.   EN SUITE, TV & BEVERAGES.   B. & B. FROM £18.

THE RED GATE, 32 AVENUE RD, GREAT MALVERN, WR14 3BJ   TEL: (01684) 565013
Family-run hotel near station & town centre yet with the atmosphere of a country home.
OPEN ALL YEAR.   N/S DINING R & BEDRS.   V, S.D. B/A.   LICENSED.   OVER 6S ONLY.   EN SUITE MOST ROOMS.
BEVERAGES & T.V. IN ROOMS.   B. & B. AROUND £24.

St Just
WORCESTER RD, MALVERN, WORCS, WR14 1EU   TEL: (01684) 562023
ETB 2 Crowns. St Just is a splendid Victorian residence standing in a lovely garden
overlooking a large expanse of open countryside yet is close to most amenities. It has been
sympathetically restored by its present owners and beautifully decorated to provide bed
and breakfast accommodation of a particularly high standard (indeed it comes to me with
several high recommendations). Bedrooms are cosy and comfortable - and all very well-
appointed - and the elegant dining room has lovely garden views. Breakfast is the only
meal served at St Just but there are several good restaurants in and around Malvern. St Just
has a 2 Crown status.
OPEN ALL YEAR ex. Xmas & New Year.   NO SMOKING.   V, S.D. B/A.   CHILDREN: OVER 5S ONLY.   PETS B/A.   SOME
EN SUITE ROOMS.   BEVERAGES & TV IN ROOMS.   B. & B. AROUND £16.

MALVERN WELLS

The Cottage in the Wood Hotel
HOLYWELL RD, MALVERN WELLS, WORCS., WR14 4LG   TEL: (01684) 573487
Twice voted the hotel with the best view in England, this charming country hotel is in fact
three separate white-painted buildings perched high in the Malvern Hills in 7 acres of
woodland.
OPEN ALL YEAR. N/S DINING R.   V STD.   LICENSED.   CHILDREN & PETS WELCOME.   CREDIT CARDS.   EN SUITE,
BEVERAGES & T.V. IN ALL BEDROOMS.   B. & B. FROM £48.50.

CYPRUS HOUSE, 210 WELLS RD, MALVERN WELLS, WR14 4HD   TEL: (01684) 563824
Pleasant, early Victorian house situated in the centre of the village.
OPEN EASTER TO SEPT.   NO SMOKING.   V, S.D. B/A.   CHILDREN WELCOME.   PETS B/A.   BEVERAGES IN
ALL ROOMS.   T.V. IN LOUNGE.   B. & B. AROUND £16.

PERSHORE

SAMARES, 11 CHERRY ORCHARD, CHARLTON, WR10 3LD   TEL: (01386) 860461
Comfortably furnished dormer bungalow, peacefully situated in a cul-de-sac in pretty village in the Vale of Evesham; excellent food prepared from fresh ingredients.
OPEN ALL YEAR.   NO SMOKING.   V, S.D. B/A.   2 GROUND FLOOR BEDROOMS.   OVER 10S ONLY.   BEVER-
AGES.   T.V. IN LOUNGE.   B. & B.AROUND £16, D. AROUND £10.

TENBURY WELLS

COURT FARM, HANLEY CHILDE, TENBURY WELLS, WR15 8QY   TEL: (01885) 410265
Charming 15th C. farmhouse, with adjoining listed buildings on 200 acre mixed farm, quietly situated near the church in pretty village of Hanley Childe. Good home-cooking.
OPEN Apr. - Oct.   NO SMOKING.   V, S.D. B/A.   CHILDREN.   BEVERAGES IN ROOMS.   T.V. LOUNGE.

WORCESTER

Ivy Cottage

SINTON GREEN, HALLOW, WORCESTER, WR2 6NP   TEL: (01905) 641123
Attractive house and garden in small village only 4m from Worcester. Very peaceful, surrounded by unspoilt countryside.
OPEN ALL YEAR.   NO SMOKING.   S.D. B/A.   CHILDREN & PETS.   EN SUITE, TV & BEVERAGES IN ROOMS.   B.
& B. £17.50.

RESTAURANTS

BEWDLEY

ALTON GUEST HOUSE AND TEA ROOMS, ALTON HOUSE, LONG BANK, DY12 2UL
40 SEATS.   OPEN 9 - 6.   L. AROUND £7.50.   N/S TEA ROOM.
For further details please see under the entry in the accommodation section.

MALVERN WELLS

CROQUE-EN-BOUCHE, 221 WELLS RD, MALVERN WELLS, WORCESTER, WR14 4HF
Excellent restaurant serving exceptional cuisine (6-course table d'hote dinner).
TEL: (01684) 565612 24 SEATS.   N/S DINING ROOM.   V, S.D. B/A.   LICENSED.   DISABLED ACCESS: 'ONE FOUR
INCH STEP'.   CHILDREN WELCOME.   ACCESS, VISA.

WORCESTER

Hodson's Coffee House

100 HIGH ST, WORCESTER, WORCS.   TEL: (01905) 21036
Clean Food Award, National Heartbeat Award. Excellent Coffee House and Patisserie, with lovely *al fresco* dining area. Interesting selection of dishes, including 'platters', which are exceedingly generous platefuls of hearty fare.
OPEN 9.30 - 5; CLOSED SUNDAYS.   80% N/S.   LICENSED.   DISABLED ACCESS.   CHILDREN WELCOME.

East Anglia

Cambridgeshire

ACCOMMODATION
CAMBRIDGE

Arundel House Hotel
53 CHESTERTON RD, CAMBRIDGE, CB4 3AN   TEL: (01223) 67701

Health-award-winning hotel converted from fine Victorian terrace near centre of Cambridge.

OPEN ALL YEAR EX. Xmas. N/S MOST OF DINING R. & 50% BEDRS. V STD, S.D. B/A. LICENSED. CHILDREN WELCOME.   EN SUITE MOST ROOMS.   BEVERAGE, TV, DD PHONE, RADIO, HAIRDRYER ALL BEDROOMS. CREDIT CARDS. B. & B. FROM £28.50.

Bon Accord House
20 ST MARGARET'S SQ., OFF CHERRY HINTON RD, CAMBRIDGE TEL; (01223) 411188/246568

Guest house situated down a quiet cul-de-sac on a good bus route to the city centre. Breakfast only with a wide variety of options. Cycle hire if you wish.

OPEN ALL YEAR ex. Xmas.   NO SMOKING. V, S.D. B/A.   CHILDREN WELCOME.   1 ROOM EN SUITE. BEVERAGES & T.V. IN ROOMS.   VISA, MASTERCARD. B. & B. AROUND £20.

EL SHADDAI, 41 WARKWORTH ST, CAMBRIDGE, CB1 1EG TEL; (01223) 327978
OPEN July - Sept. inc.   NO SMOKING. S.D. B/A.   CHILDREN. BEVERAGES & T.V. B. & B. AROUND £16.

KINGS TITHE, 13A COMBERTON RD, BARTON, CAMBRIDGE. TEL: (01223) 263610
Quiet family home in pleasant village just over 3 miles south west of Cambridge.
OPEN ALL YEAR ex. Xmas & New Year.   NO SMOKING. V, S.D. B/A. OVER 8S ONLY. BEVERAGES & T.V. IN ROOMS.   B. & B. AROUND £18.

PURLINS, 12 HIGH ST, LITTLE SHELFORD, CAMBRIDGE. TEL: (01223) 842643
Relatively new house in 2 acres of maturing woodland & lawned gardens.
OPEN Feb. - Dec. 18th.   NO SMOKING. V, S.D. B/A.   DISABLED ACCESS. OVER 8S ONLY.   EN SUITE & T.V. IN ROOMS.   BEVERAGES ON REQUEST.   B. & B. AROUND £21.

ST. MARK'S VICARAGE, BARTON ROAD, CAMBRIDGE, CB3 9JZ
Victorian vicarage with garden; short walk from central Cambridge.
OPEN ALL YEAR.   NO SMOKING. V, S.D. B/A.   CHILDREN.   BEVERAGES & T.V. B. & B. AROUND £18.

The Willows
102 HIGH STREET, LANDBEACH, CAMBRIDGE, CB4 4DT   TEL: (01223) 860332

Centrally heated farmhouse in village 3m N. of Cambridge. Family, double & twin rooms.
OPEN ALL YEAR ex Xmas. NO SMOKING.   V, B/A.   CHILDREN WELCOME.   1 GROUND FLOOR ROOM.   PETS B/A. BEVERAGES & TV IN ROOMS. B. & B. FROM £15.

ELY

Springfields
ELY ROAD, LITTLE THETFORD, ELY, CB6 3HJ   TEL: (01353) 663637   FAX: (01353) 663130

English Tourist Board De Luxe Award. Springfields is a lovely large home set in an acre of beautiful landscaped gardens and orchard in which guests are invited to wander and sit awhile to enjoy the tranquillity of the setting and (in summer) to smell the roses! The guest accommodation is housed in a separate wing and consists of three double rooms which have each been tastefully furnished and appointed with many delightful touches and everything you could wish to make your stay a happy and memorable one; all rooms have wash

hand basins. Breakfast is served in a pleasant dining room in which guests sit around a large table to enjoy together the delicious, freshly prepared food. Springfields is set in a very quiet location yet is only two miles from historic Ely with its famous cathedral, Oliver Cromwell's house (he lived here from 1637 to 1644) and many other buildings of great architectural and historic interest, and of course it is a perfect base from which to explore the changeless beauty of the Fens!
OPEN ALL YEAR. ex. Dec.   NO SMOKING .   V B/A.   EN SUITE ROOMS AVAILABLE.   BEVERAGES & T.V. IN ALL ROOMS.   B. & B. FROM £20.

WARDEN'S HOUSE, LODE LANE, WICKEN, ELY CB7 5XP   TEL: (01353) 624165
OPEN ALL YEAR ex. Xmas.   NO SMOKING.   V b'fast.   DOGS, B/A.   BEVERAGES.   B. & B. AROUND £15.

PETERBOROUGH
Swallow Hotel
PETERBOROUGH BUSINESS PARK, LYNCH WOOD, PETERBOROUGH, PE2 6GB TEL: (01733) 371111 FAX: (01733) 236725
Luxuriously appointed 163-bedroom business class hotel conveniently situated just 2 minutes from the A1 and within easy reach of Peterborough city centre.
OPEN ALL YEAR.   N/S 50% DINING R/PUB/BAR AREA; 55% OF BEDRS. V, VE, DIAB, STD; S.D. B/A.   LICENSED. DISABLED ACCESS.   CHILDREN WELCOME.   DOGS ALLOWED IN BEDROOMS.   EN SUITE, BEVERAGES & T.V. IN ROOMS.   CREDIT CARDS.   B. & B. AROUND £50.

RESTAURANTS
CAMBRIDGE
BROWNS RESTAURANT, 23 TRUMPINGTON STREET, CAMBRIDGE TEL: (01223) 461655
N/S 45% OF RESTAURANT.   V.   LICENSED.   DISABLED ACCESS.   CHILDREN.

Debenhams
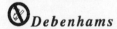
36-40 THE GRAFTON CENTRE, CAMBRIDGE   TEL: (01223) 353525
Springles, a friendly self-service restaurant serving lunches, snacks, hot and cold drinks.
OPEN STORE HOURS.   NO SMOKING.   V STD.   DISABLED ACCESS.   CHILDREN WELCOME. CREDIT CARDS.

Hobbs Pavilion Restaurant
PARK TERRACE, CAMBRIDGE, CB1 1JH   TEL: (01223) 67480

As its name suggests, Hobbs Pavilion Restaurant is located in the pavilion of a cricket ground whose substantial history is recorded on the back of the restaurant's menu; it is too lengthy to even précis here but it make interesting reading and is just one of several reasons for choosing the Hobbs Pavilion as a Cambridge eatery. The best reason of all is, of course, the food. Stephen and Susan Hill have been offering first-class fare at the Pavilion since 1978 (in which dim and distant days they were regarded as being avant garde for having a smoke-free area and serving vegetarian options). These days what was once deemed precocious is just sound culinary - and business - sense: feed people good food and they will return and return and return: accordingly everything served at the Hobbs Pavilion has been made on the premises from fresh ingredients and the imaginative menu caters for everyone from babies (highchairs at the ready), through students (try the Cyclists'pancake) to Cambridge Revisited (sic.) folk (excellent 3-course meal for just £7.95).
SEPARATE ROOM FOR SMOKERS.   3-course meal £7.95 (£12.25 inc. side salad, coffee & .25 L plonk).   OPEN 12 - 2.15, 7 - 9.45.   V, VE, STD.   S.D. B/A.   LICENSED.   CHILDREN.

HENRY' S TEASHOP, 5A PEMBROKE ST, CAMBRIDGE   TEL: (01223) 61206
OPEN MON. - SAT., 9 - 5.15, ALL YEAR.   NO SMOKING..

Kings Pantry
9A KINGS PARADE, CAMBRIDGE, CB2 1SJ   TEL: (01223) 321551
First-rate vegetarian restaurant located in the heart of Cambridge.
OPEN 8 - 5.30. 7 DAYS & TUE. - SAT. 6.30 - 9.30.   NO SMOKING.   V, VE EXC.   LICENSED.   CHILDREN WELCOME.   CREDIT CARDS.

PETERBOROUGH

PETERBOROUGH CATHEDRAL SHOP, 24 MINSTER PRECINCTS, PETERBOROUGH
Pleasant café situated above gift shop.
TEL: (01733) 555098   OPEN 10 - 4.   NO SMOKING.   V. STD.   CHILDREN WELCOME (HIGH CHAIR AVAIL.)

The Queensgate Centre
PETERBOROUGH, PE1 1NH   TEL: (01733) 311666 SHOP MOBILITY: (01733) 313133
One hundred stores plus specialist coffee shops in a spacious, light and air-conditioned
shopping centre. Ten restaurants offering almost 1,500 seats mostly in non-smoking zones.
Half of the public seating areas designated non-smoking. Late shopping until 8 p.m.
Thursdays plus Fridays in December. Free wheelchair loan for the disabled. Half-term
entertainment for children.

SIX MILE BOTTOM

SWYNFORD PADDOCKS, SIX MILE BOTTOM, CAMBRIDGESHIRE   TEL: (01638) 70234
NO SMOKING.   V STD.   DISABLED ACCESS.   CHILDREN WELCOME.   CREDIT CARDS.

PUBS & WINE BARS

CAMBRIDGE

The Cambridge Blue
85/87 GWYDIR ST, CAMBRIDGE, CB1 2LG   TEL: (01223) 61382
19th C. terrace pub in side street off Mill Road. Real ale (Nethergate).
NO SMOKING IN 1 BAR.   V STD.   WHEELCHAIR ACCESS.   CHILDREN WELCOME IN CONSERVATORY &
GARDEN ONLY (MODEL RAILWAY IN LATTER).

Free Press

PROSPECT ROW, CAMBRIDGE, CB1 1DU   TEL: (01223) 68337
Busy pub serving good food and real ales.
NO SMOKING.   V STD.   CHILDREN WELCOME.

HOLYWELL

OLDE FERRY BOAT, HOLYWELL (OFF A1123 IN NEEDINGWORTH)
OPEN PUB HOURS.   N/S 2 ROOMS.   V STD.   CHILDREN WELCOME.

WHITTLESFORD

The Tickell Arms
NORTH RD, WHITTLESFORD, CAMBRIDGE, CB2 4NZ   TEL: (01223) 833128
The Tickell Arms is a fine 17th C. building which has been attractively furnished and
decorated. It is a great rarity - a pub with two large smoke-free dining and drinking areas
- and not only that, it serves exceptionally good food: menus feature dishes which are
imaginative and tasty and vegetarians are very well catered for. There is a Winter Garden
in which smoking is permitted, and during the warmer months a large terrace, which
overlooks the lovely water garden, is also used for dining.
NO SMOKING IN 2 ROOMS.   LICENSED.   WELL-BEHAVED CHILDREN WELCOME.

Essex

ACCOMMODATION

ARDLEIGH

Dundas Place

COLCHESTER ROAD, ARDLEIGH, COLCHESTER, ESSEX, CO7 7NP TEL: (01206) 230625

Dundas Place is a lovely 17th C. cottage in the centre of Ardleigh. There are one double and one twin-bedded room with wash basins and one twin-bedded room with en suite facilities; all have colour TV and tea and coffee-making facilities. Centrally heated throughout and with double glazing, a log fire adds to the cosiness in cooler weather. There is a lounge cum library for guests' use. You are just 12 miles from Harwich and 20 miles from Felixstowe, and also within easy reach of Constable Country and the pretty villages of Suffolk .

OPEN ALL YEARex Xmas & New Year. NO SMOKING. V, S.D. B/A. OVER 12s ONLY. PETS B/A. T.V., WASH-BASINS & BEVERAGES IN ROOMS. 1 EN SUITE ROOM. B. & B FROM £17.

BRAINTREE

THE OLD HOUSE, 11 BRADFORD ST, BRAINTREE, ESSEX, CM7 6AS TEL: (01376) 550457

Spacious 16th C. family house of great historical interest standing in an acre of gardens.

OPEN ALL YEAR. N/S EX. IN BAR. V B/A. LICENSED. DISABLED ACCESS. CHILDREN WELCOME. EN SUITE, BEVERAGES & T.V. IN ALL ROOMS. B. & B. AROUND £18.

CASTLE HEDINGHAM

THE POTTERY, ST JAMES ST, CASTLE HEDINGHAM, CO9 3EW TEL: (01787) 460036

Comfortable Georgian house 5 mins from castle in mediaeval village, Castle Hedingham.

OPEN ALL YEAR ex Xmas. NO SMOKING. V, S.D. B/A. OVER 12S ONLY. BEVERAGES IN ROOMS. B & B FROM £17.50.

CHELMSFORD

Boswell House Hotel

118 SPRINGFIELD ROAD, CHELMSFORD, ESSEX, CM2 6LF TEL: (01245) 287587

The Boswell House is a 19th C. town house which was beautifully renovated and converted into a charming small hotel in 1980. It has been very tastefully furnished throughout with stripped pine furniture and each of the thirteen en suite bedrooms have excellent facilities including direct dial phones. The food is very good indeed: everything has been home-prepared on the premises from fresh ingredients and the menu offers a wide selection of traditional dishes; wedding receptions, private lunch or dinner parties may be booked for up to 25 people. Chelmsford is the county town of Essex and amongst its many features are the cathedral, Essex County Cricket Ground and shopping facilities.

OPEN ALL YEAR ex Xmas. N/S DINING R, SITTING R & 9 BEDRS. V, S.D. B/A. LICENSED. CHILDREN WELCOME (COTS, HIGH CHAIRS, BABY LISTENING SERVICE . DISABLED ACCESS: GROUND FLOOR BEDROOMS & 1 STEP AT HOTEL ENTRANCE. EN SUITE, BEVERAGES & TV IN ROOMS. CREDIT CARDS. B & B FROM £28.

MEADOWVIEW, 101 KEENE WY, GALLEYWOOD, CHELMSFORD TEL: (01245) 259273
OPEN ALL YEAR. NO SMOKING. V B/A. CHILDREN & PETS WELCOME. BEVERAGES IN ROOMS. T.V. IN ONE BEDROOM. B & B AROUND £14.

CLACTON-ON-SEA

CHELSEA HOUSE, COLLINGWOOD RD, MARINE PARADE WEST. TEL: (01255) 424018
OPEN ALL YEAR. NO SMOKING. V, S.D. B/A. CHILDREN WELCOME. EN SUITE IN 17 ROOMS.

Ⓝ **CROCKLEFORD GRANGE, BROMLEY RD, COLCHESTER, CO7 7SE TEL: (01206) 864405**
Attractive converted Grade II Listed barn; oak beams & thatched roof. Crystal chandeliers
in bedrooms. Easy reach of Dedham & Flatford. 20 mins Harwich, 5 mins Essex University.
NO SMOKING.   CHILDREN WELCOME.   EN SUITE, TV & BEVERAGES IN ROOMS.   B. & B. AROUND £20,
HONEYMOON SUITE AROUND £50.

COLCHESTER

Ⓝ **GILL NICHOLSON, 14 ROMAN ROAD, COLCHESTER, CO1 1UR TEL: (01206) 577905**
Spacious Victorian town house in quiet square near the centre of town with easy access to
both the bus and railway station; all the places of interest are within easy walking distance.
The full, home-cooked English breakfast features a number of home-made items, including
the bread, jam and lemon curd.
OPEN ALL YEAR ex. Xmas Week.   NO SMOKING. V, S.D. B/A. CHILDREN B/A. 1 EN SUITE ROOM. BEVERAGES
& T.V. IN ROOMS.   B. & B. AROUND £32.

Ⓝ **KINGS VINEYARD, FOSSETTS LN, FORDHAM, COLCHESTER. TEL: (01206) 240377**
Lovely detached house on southfacing slope in gentle rolling countryside. Beautiful views.
OPEN ALL YEAR.   NO SMOKING.   V STD.   CHILDREN WELCOME.   PRIVATE BATHROOM AVAIL.   BEVER-
AGES & T.V. FACILITIES.   AMEX.   B. & B. AROUND £19.

DUNMOW

The Four Seasons Hotel
WALDEN RD, THAXTED, NR DUNMOW, CM6 2RE TEL: (01371) 830129 FAX: (01371) 830835

The Four Seasons Hotel is a lovely, quiet country
hotel set in approximately 2 acres of carefully maintained grounds with lawned gardens and natural
pond on the outskirts of the beautful mediaeval town
of Thaxted. Whilst many of the original features of
the building have been retained, the house has been
sympathetically modernised to a very high standard
and offers comfortable accommodation in each of
the centrally heated, en suite guest bedrooms. Meals
served in the dining room have been prepared with care from fresh, local produce and the
à la carte menu features such dishes as Seafood Crêpes, Breast of Duck in Châtelaine Sauce
and a selection of desserts. The hotel is an ideal choice for the business traveller.
OPEN ALL YEAR. N/S DINING R, BEDRS & RES. LOUNGE. BAR 50% N/S. LICENSED. OVER 12S ONLY. EN SUITE,
TV, DD PHONES & BEVERAGES IN ROOMS. CREDIT CARDS. B. & B. AROUND £35.

EPPING

Ⓝ *Uplands*
181aLINDSEY ST, EPPING, ESSEX, CM16 6RF   TEL: (01992) 573733
Uplands is a comfortable, centrally heated private house with rural views over the Essex
countryside. Accommodation is in single, twin or family rooms (with cots if required), and
a continental breakfast is served to guests. With its proximity to the M11, M25, Stanstead
Airport and the central line tube for London, Uplands is an excellent base for non-smoking
travellers who wish to break their journey before an overseas flight. Children up to 12 years
of age can be accommodated at half price, and babies can stay free. Safe, off-street parking.
OPEN ALL YEAR.   NO SMOKING.   CHILDREN WELCOME.   BEVERAGES & TV IN ROOMS.   B. & B. FROM £16.

FRINTON-ON-SEA

UPLANDS, 41 HADLEIGH RD, FRINTON-ON-SEA, CO13 9HQ TEL: (01255) 674889
OPEN ALL YEAR ex. Xmas. N/S DINING R & BEDRS. LICENSED. OVER 6S ONLY. 4 EN SUITE ROOMS. BEVER-
AGES IN ROOMS. T.V. LOUNGE. AMPLE CAR PARKING. B. & B. AROUND £20.

GREAT DUNMOW

Ⓝ **'GREYS', ONGAR ROAD, MARGARET RODING, NR GREAT DUNMOW, CM6 1QR**
Beamed house pleasantly situated on the family arable and sheep farm, with dining
and sitting rooms and a large garden. Just off the A1060 by the telephone box in the village
and is 8 miles from Great Dunmow (it's advisable to check the map before travelling).
TEL: (01245) 31509 OPEN MOST OF YEAR.   NO SMOKING.   V B/A.   OVER 10S ONLY.   TEA/COFFEE ALWAYS
AVAILABLE.   T.V. DOWNSTAIRS. B & B AROUND £18.

MANNINGTREE

Dimbols Farm

WRABNESS, MANNINGTREE, ESSEX, CO11 2TH   TEL: (01255) 880328
N/S DINING R & BEDRS.   V, B/A.   CHILDREN WELCOME.   BEVERAGES IN ROOMS.   T.V. IN SITTING R.   B & B
FROM £14.

SOUTHEND-ON-SEA

Strand Guest House

165 EASTERN ESPLANADE, SOUTHEND-ON-SEA, ESSEX, SS1 2YB   TEL: (01702) 586611
OPEN April - Nov.   N/S DINING R & 1 BEDROOM.   V B/A.   CHILDREN WELCOME.   MOST ROOMS EN SUITE.
BEVERAGES & T.V. IN ROOMS.   B. & B. FROM £16.

TIPTREE

Linden

8 CLARKESMEAD, MALDON RD, TIPTREE, COLCHESTER, ESSEX, CO5 0BX   TEL: (01621)
819737   FAX: (01621) 818033
ETB Listed. Modern architect-designed house in quiet cul-de-sac 10 mins from A12.
OPEN ALL YEAR.   NO SMOKING.   S.D.   CHILDREN WELCOME.   WHEELCHAIR ACCESS.   GUIDE DOGS
ONLY.   EN SUITE, TV & BEVERAGES IN BEDROOMS.   B. & B. FROM £18.

The Swallow Hotel

OLD SHIRE LN., WALTHAM ABBEY, ESSEX, EN9 3LX TEL: (01992) 717170 FAX: (01992) 711841

The Swallow Hotel at Waltham Abbey is a spacious modern 4-star hotel which stands near J26 of the M25. All 165 en suite bedrooms are equipped with D.D. phone, mini-bar, hairdryer and trouser press, and 55 rooms are designated non-smoking. There is a Coffee Shop, Cocktail Bar and two restaurants to choose from: the Glade Restaurant offers a range of à la carte and table d'hôte dishes while the Brooks Brasserie has a more informal atmosphere, the menu featuring a lunchtime carvery and a choice of continental meals. The Swallow Leisure Club has a pool, steam room, mini-gym and solarium - an ideal place to relax after an intense business meeting - and the conference and meeting rooms have facilities for up to 250 delegates.
OPEN ALL YEAR.   N/S PART DINING R, SOME BEDROOMS & LEISURE CLUB.   V, S.D. B/A.   CHILDREN WELCOME.
WHEELCHAIR ACCESS.   EN SUITE, TV &BEVERAGES IN ROOMS.

RESTAURANTS

CASTLE HEDINGHAM

RUMBLES CASTLE RESTAURANT, ST JAMES ST, CASTLE HEDINGHAM, CO9 3EJ
TEL: (01787) 61490   OPEN ALL YEAR.   N/S DINING R, ALLOWED IN COFFEE LOUNGE & BAR AREA.   V STD.
LICENSED.   DISABLED ACCESS.   CHILDREN WELCOME.

CHELMSFORD

Debenhams

27 HIGH ST, CHELMSFORD, ESSEX.   TEL: (01245) 355511
Springles, a friendly self-service restaurant serving lunches, snacks & hot and cold drinks.
OPEN STORE HOURS.   NO SMOKING.   V.   DISABLED ACCESS.   CHILDREN WELCOME.   CREDIT/DEBIT
CARDS.

Scott's

THE STREET, HATFIELD PEVEREL, CHELMSFORD, ESSEX, CM3 2DR   TEL: (01245) 380161
OPEN Mon.-Sat., 7 until late by booking.   NO SMOKING.   V.   LICENSED.   DISABLED ACCESS.

Farmhouse Feast

THE STREET, ROXWELL, CHELMSFORD, ESSEX, CM1 4PB   TEL & FAX: (01245) 248 583

Farmhouse Feast is a charming restaurant housed in a late 15th C. building in the centre of Roxwell village. The food is first-rate - everything has been home-cooked on the premises from fresh ingredients - and there are some excellent vegetarian options; indeed Farmhouse Feast has hosted some exclusively vegetarian events such as a Good Friday meat-free meal featuring Vegetable Kebabs in curried batter with yoghurt dip followed by Red Cabbage and Apple Soup, Lentil Terrine with Cream and Mushroom Sauce and Ricotta Stuffed Pears in Apricot dressing. As well as catering for individuals, Farmhouse Feast is especially adept at hosting small parties and will also undertake outside catering: their menus are imaginative and their prices very keen - and, more pertinently for our purposes, a whole floor is smoke-free.

OPEN ALL YEAR, including Xmas Day. GOURMET EVENINGS LAST FRI. IN MONTH.   75% N/S (ON SEPARATE FLOOR).   ORG, WH, V, VE S.D. B/A.   LICENSED.   DISABLED ACCESS.   CHILDREN WELCOME.

COLCHESTER

DEBENHAMS, 34 CULVER ST WEST, COLCHESTER, ESSEX. TEL: (01206) 763434

Intermission, a friendly self-service coffee shop serving popular light lunches, snacks and a wide range of hot and cold drinks.

OPEN STORE HOURS.   NO SMOKING.   V.   DISABLED ACCESS.   CHILDREN WELCOME.   CREDIT CARDS.

DUNMOW

RUMBLES COTTAGE RESTAURANT, BRAINTREE ROAD, FELSTED, DUNMOW, CM6 3DJ
TEL: (01371) 820996   OPEN ALL YEAR.   GUINEA PIG MENU £12.50, À LA CARTE £16.50-£19.50.   SEPARATE DINING RS FOR NON-SMOKERS B/A.   V STD.   LICENSED.   DISABLED ACCESS.   CHILDREN WELCOME.

ROMFORD

DEBENHAMS, MARKET PLACE, ROMFORD, ESSEX. TEL: (01708) 766066

Intermission, a friendly self-service restaurant serving popular light lunches, snacks and a wide range of hot and cold drinks.

OPEN STORE HOURS.   NO SMOKING.   V.   DISABLED ACCESS.   CHILDREN WELCOME.   CREDIT CARDS.

SOUTHEND-ON-SEA

DEBENHAMS, THE ROYALS, HIGH ST, SOUTHEND-ON-SEA TEL: (01702) 460237

Pavilion, a friendly self-service coffee shop serving popular light lunches, snacks and a wide range of hot and cold drinks.

OPEN STORE HOURS.   NO SMOKING.   V.   DISABLED ACCESS.   CHILDREN WELCOME.   CREDIT CARDS.

THURROCK

DEBENHAMS, LAKESIDE SHOPPING CENTRE, THURROCK, ESSEX. TEL: (01708) 860066

Intermission, a friendly self-service restaurant serving popular light lunches, snacks and a wide range of hot and cold drinks.

OPEN STORE HOURS.   NO SMOKING.   V.   DISABLED ACCESS.   CHILDREN WELCOME.   CREDIT CARDS.

PUBS & WINE BARS

CHELMSFORD

SEABRIGHTS BARN, GALLEYWOOD RD, GT BADDOW, NR CHELMSFODR TEL: (01245) 478033
OPEN MON. TO SAT. 12 - 2, 6 - 11, SUN. 12 - 10.   N/S CONSERVATORY FAMILY ROOM.   V STD. S.D. B/A. WHEELCHAIR ACCESS.   GOOD FACILITIES FOR CHILDREN.   ACCESS, VISA.

Norfolk

ACCOMMODATION
AYLSHAM

⊗ *The Old Pump House*

HOLMAN RD, AYLSHAM, NORFOLK, NR11 6BY   TEL: (01263) 733789

The Old Pump House is a Georgian family home by the thatched pump one minute's walk from historic Aylsham's church and market square. The house has been extended four times between the 1750s and the 1890s, and there are steps up and down throughout the house. Accommodation is in comfortable, centrally heated rooms, and traditional English breakfasts (with free range eggs and local bacon) are served in the pine-shuttered Red Sitting Room overlooking the peaceful garden. Friendly Aylsham is an ideal centre for visiting Norwich, the North Norfolk coast, the Broads and National Trust houses. The unspoilt surrounding countryside is perfect for walking, bird-watching and cycling (bikes can be hired locally). Aylsham has a weekly livestock, household and produce auction, with regular sales of antiques, paintings and books. A steam railway runs from the town to Wroxham (9 miles away) and there are several other steam railways within easy reach. Norfolk has some excellent pub restaurants, and one of the best is a short drive from Aylsham. The Old Pump House offers weekly terms, evening meals by prior arrangement and Half Board Awaybreaks between October and June.

OPEN ALL YEAR.   NO SMOKING.   V B/A.   WELL-BEHAVED CHILDREN WELCOME.   PETS B/A.   3 EN SUITE ROOMS; BEVERAGES & TV IN ROOMS.   B. & B. FROM £19.75.

BLAKENEY

⊗ *Flintstones Guest House*

WIVETON, BLAKENEY, NORFOLK, NR25 7TL   TEL: (01263) 740337

Flintstones Guest House is a charming single storey residence set in picturesque surroundings near to the village green in the quiet village of Wiveton one mile from the sea at Cley and Blakeney. It has been beautifully furnished throughout - the bedrooms have each been very comfortably appointed - and a friendly and relaxed atmosphere prevails. Food is of the good old-fashioned British variety and is served in good old-fashioned quantities, too: a typical evening meal would feature fresh grapefruit followed by Roast Chicken with all the trimmings and a home-made dessert such as Sherry Trifle; tea and coffee would complete the meal. The area is perfect for walkers and birdwatchers: the heathland at Salthouse and Kelling have stunning scenery, and the North Norfolk Coastal Path passes nearby.

OPEN ALL YEAR.   NO SMOKING.   V, S.D. B/A.   LICENSED.   CHILDREN WELCOME.   PETS B/A.   EN SUITE, BEVERAGES & T.V. IN ROOMS.   B. & B. FROM £16.

CASTLE ACRE

THE OLD RED LION, BAILEY STREET, CASTLE ACRE, PE32 2AG   TEL: (01760) 755557
OPEN ALL YEAR.   NO SMOKING. V B/A.   CHILDREN WELCOME.

CROMER

⊗ *Beverley Holiday Flats*

17 ALFRED RD, CROMER, NORFOLK, NR27 9AN   TEL: (01394) 450343
Maureen and Barry Marshall, the proprietors of Beverley Holiday Flats, are proud to be able to say that they are the five times winner of the Norfolk Tourism Award for Excellence. And deservedly so, I might add: their beautiful self-catering apartments are situated just a

stone's throw from the seafront in a very pleasant part of Cromer and have been furnished with just about everything that you could wish for including microwaves, coffee percolators and, on the beds, excellent orthopaedic mattresses. Cromer is an excellent base for visiting the many attractions in the area which include historic houses, nature reserves and the North Norfolk Steam Railway.
OPEN MAY TO SEPT.   NO SMOKING.

 *Birch House*

34 CABBELL RD, CROMER, NORFOLK, NR27 9HX   TEL: (01263) 512521
Friendly guest house, close to all the amenities of Cromer; tastefully furnished & scrupulously clean . B'fast menu includes oak-smoked kippers and haddock.
OPEN ALL YEAR.   NO SMOKING.   V, S.D. B/A.   CHILDREN WELCOME.   PETS B/A.   SOME EN SUITE. BEVERAGES & T.V. IN ALL ROOMS. B. & B. AROUND £18

Corner Cottage

WATER LANE, WEST RUNTON, CROMER, NORFOLK, NR27 9QP   TEL: (01263) 758180
Ssmall, friendly guest house on the North Norfolk coast near train & bus stops; just 3 mins' walk from excellent beach. Very comfortable, centrally heated accommodation.
OPEN ALL YEAR.   NO SMOKING.   CAR PARKING.   OVER 5S WELCOME.   BEVERAGES IN ALL ROOMS.   T.V. IN LOUNGE.   B. & B. AROUND £16.

DISS

The Old Rectory

GISSING, DISS, NORFOLK, IP22 3XB   TEL: (01379) 677575 FAX: (01379) 674427

ETB 2 Crown Highly Commended. The Old Rectory is a large, spacious Victorian house standing amidst 3 acres of garden and woodland in the peaceful hamlet of Gissing; the village has an abundance of mature trees from the time when it formed part of a private estate and the church has an unusual round tower and double hammer beam roof. The guest bedrooms at the Old Rectory are large and beautifully appointed: each has en suite or private facilities and fresh flowers, hairdryers and notepaper in addition to the usual amenities; the elegant drawing and dining room each have welcoming open fires. A delicious 4-course evening meal, or lighter option, is available by prior arrangement, and packed lunches can be prepared on request; breakfast offers an extensive menu choice. There is much to enjoy - guests may play croquet on the lawns, swim in the indoor heated pool, or relax on the terrace - while those venturing a little further afield will find much to enjoy nearby including the part-Tudor town of Diss, Bressingham Gardens, Thetford Forest and the unspoilt coast-line at Southwold and Walberswick.
OPEN ALL YEAR.   N/S DINING R, BEDROOMS & MOST PUBLIC AREAS.   V B/A   OVER 8s WELCOME.   EN SUITE, TV & BEVERAGES IN ALL ROOMS.   B. & B. FROM £24, D. FROM £19.50.

Ingleneuk Lodge

HOPTON RD, GARBOLDISHAM, DISS, NORFOLK, IP22 2RQ   TEL: (01953) 81541

Ingleneuk Lodge is a lovely modern single storey home standing in 11 acres of grounds and woodlands; its quiet rural situation makes it a haven for wildlife, and guests in search of peace, tranquillity and a comfortable and homely atmosphere need look no further. Food is first-rate: (witness the numerous visitors who return annually) and there is a sunny south-facing patio overlooking the garden and pond on which guests can relax and enjoy a pre-dinner drink. Cooking is imaginative and a typical evening meal would feature Celery and Leek Soup followed by Stuffed Pork Chops with Cider and a delicious home-made dessert, such as Chocolate Rum Truffle; cheese and biscuits with tea or coffee complete the meal. Special breaks all year (ex Bank Hols).
OPEN ALL YEAR.   N/S DINING R & SOME BEDR.   V B/A.   LICENSED.   DISABLED ACCESS.   CHILDREN WELCOME.   PETS B/A.   EN SUITE IN MOST ROOMS.   BEVERAGES, COLOUR T.V., PHONE AND ELECTRIC BLANKETS IN ALL ROOMS.   B. & B. FROM £18-£24.50 Sharing. SINGLES WELCOME. D. £14.

Strenneth

AIRFIELD RD, FERSFIELD, DISS, NORFOLK, IP22 2BP   TEL: (0379) 688182   FAX: (0379) 688260

This family-run 17th C. former farmhouse stands in a lovely lawned garden close to the market town of Diss; it has been renovated to a very high standard indeed while retaining the period features of the building (oak beams, casement windows, open fires, window seats) and the bed-rooms are decorated and furnished with taste and style and have en suite facilities and colour TVs (most of them are on the ground floor); one of the Executive rooms has a magnificent four poster bed and 'Pharaoh' bath. There is an especially attractive lounge which has been furnished with period furniture to harmonise with the heavily beamed ceilings and walls. The food is of a very high standard: special diets can be catered for and local produce is used extensively by the chef-owner. Diss is a charming town and is central to most of East Anglia's tourist attractions.

OPEN ALL YEAR.   N/S PART OF DINING R & 1 LOUNGE.   V, S.D. (NOT VE) B/A.   LICENSED.   PETS WELCOME. EN SUITE, BEVERAGES & TV IN ROOMS.   CREDIT CARDS.   B. & B. FROM £22. D. £13.

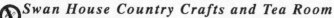

Swan House Country Crafts and Tea Room

SWAN HOUSE, HOPTON RD, GARBOLDISHAM, NR DISS, NORFOLK, IP22 2RQ TEL: (01953) 688221

ETB Approved and Listed. Attractive 17th C. former coaching inn offering a warm welcome and home-baking. Three comfortable and characterful guest rooms, some with exposed beams.

OPEN ALL YEAR ex. Xmas & Jan.   NO SMOKING.   V B/A.   WHEELCHAIR ACCESS TO TEASHOP.   CHILDREN WELCOME IN TEA SHOP ONLY.   T.V. IN BEDROOMS.   DINERS CARD.   B. & B. FROM £16.

FAKENHAM

Manor Farmhouse

STIBBARD RD, FULMODESTONE, NORFOLK, NR21 0LX   TEL & FAX: (01328) 829353

ETB 1 Crown Commended. Lovely white-painted Georgian farmhouse with beautiful lawned gardens; lots of home-prepared food from fresh or home-produce.

OPEN ALL YEAR.   NO SMOKING.   ACCESS, VISA, DINERS CLUB.   B. & B. FROM £17.50, D. B/A. £10.

GREAT YARMOUTH

Carina Guest House

18 WELLESLEY RD, GREAT YARMOUTH, NR30 2AR   TEL:(01493) 844041

Small 6-roomed guest house just 2 mins walk from beach and shopping centre.

OPEN BANK HOLS, JULY - LATE SEPT.   NO SMOKING.   S.D. B/A.   CHILDREN WELCOME.   WHEELCHAIR ACCESS.   BEVERAGES ON REQUEST.   TV IN GUEST LOUNGE.   B. & B. FROM £12.

THE DRIFTWOOD, 82-84 WALPOLE RD, GT YARMOUTH, NR30 4NE TEL: (01493) 857878
OPEN April - Oct.   N/S DINING R, SITTING R & SOME BEDRS.   CHILDREN WELCOME. BEVERAGES & T.V. IN ROOMS.   B. & B. AROUND £16.

SIESTA LODGE, 53/54 YORK RD, GT YARMOUTH, NR30 2NE   TEL: (01493) 843207
Tastefully decorated guest house with a friendly, welcoming atmosphere.
OPEN ALL YEAR.   N/S DINING R & BEDRS.   S.D. B/A.   LICENSED.   CHILDREN WELCOME.   BEVERAGES. T.V. IN LOUNGE.   B. & B. AROUND £15.

HUNSTANTON

Claremont Guest House

35 GREEVEGATE, HUNSTANTON, NORFOLK, PE36 6AF   TEL: (01485) 533171

Large Victorian guest house offering luxurious accommodation with sea views. Central location with car parking. Special breaks available.

OPEN ALL YEAR.   NO SMOKING.   S.D. B/A.   OVER 5s WELCOME.   EN SUITE, TV & BEVERAGES IN ALL BEDROOMS.   B. & B. £18 - 22.

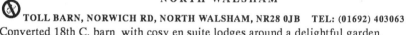 Salacia Lodge

56 GREEVEGATE, HUNSTANTON, PE36 6AE   TEL: (01485) 533702
Salacia Lodge is a warm, friendly well-established guest house which offers superb, well-appointed accommodation and an excellent breakfast. You are conveniently situated close to several sports and recreational facilities, and additionally you are just a few minutes'walk from the town centre, theatre and sea front; there are a number of good eating places in the town. Hunstanton is a perfect centre for walkers and birdwatchers.
NO SMOKING.   V, S.D. B/A.   EN SUITE IN ALL ROOMS.   B. & B. FROM £16.

NEATISHEAD

Regency Guest House

NEATISHEAD, NR NORWICH, NR12 8AD   TEL: (01692) 630233
Lovely 18th C. house in the unspoilt village of Neatishead; beautifully furnished rooms (Laura Ashley). Exceptionally generous breakfasts; good vegetarian options.
OPEN ALL YEAR.   N/S DINING R & PUBLIC AREAS.   V, S.D. B/A.   CHILDREN WELCOME.   PETS B/A.   EN SUITE.
BEVERAGES & T.V. IN ROOMS.   B. & B. FROM £16.

NORTH WALSHAM

TOLL BARN, NORWICH RD, NORTH WALSHAM, NR28 0JB   TEL: (01692) 403063
Converted 18th C. barn with cosy en suite lodges around a delightful garden.
OPEN ALL YEAR.   NO SMOKING.   V B/A.   WHEELCHAIR ACCESS 'POSSIBLE'. CHILDREN & PETS WELCOME.
EN SUITE, BEVERAGES & T.V. IN ROOMS.   B. & B. FROM £18.

NORWICH

GABLES FARM, HEMBLINGTON HALL RD, HEMBLINGTON. TEL: (01605) 49548
Beautiful period thatched farmhouse in the centre of Broadland between Norwich and Great Yarmouth. Family room available for up to 4 people.
OPEN ALL YEAR.   NO SMOKING.   EN SUITE, BEVERAGES & T.V. IN ROOMS. B. & B. FROM £20.

FUCHSIAS GUEST HOUSE, 139 EARLHAM RD, NORWICH, NR2 3RG   TEL: (01603) 51410
Friendly, family-run Victorian guest house convenient for city, UEA & countryside.
OPEN ALL YEAR.   N/S DINING R, SOME BEDRS & PUBLIC AREAS.   V, S.D. B/A.   EN SUITE. TV & BEVERAGES.
CHILDREN WELCOME.   B. & B. AROUND £19.

The Georgian House Hotel

32 - 34 UNTHANK RD, NORWICH, NR2 2RB   TEL: (01603) 615655   FAX: (01603) 765689

The Georgian House Hotel is two Victorian buildings which have been beautifully linked together to form a charming small hotel. Family-owned and run, The Georgian House Hotel offers the sort of comfort and personal service that only a smaller hotel can provide. There are 27 well-furnished en suite bedrooms, each of which has been equipped with TV, radio alarm, hairdryer, hospitality tray and complimentary shower pack; some have four-poster beds. Both à la carte and table d'hôte menus are available and all food is prepared from fresh local produce; there is a fully licensed bar and a comfortable lounge with Satellite TV. The hotel's facilities for car parking in the grounds, together with its city centre location, makes it an excellent choice for business visitor and tourist alike,
OPEN 7 Jan - 18 Dec. inc.   N/S DINING R & SOME BEDR.   V, STD. S.D. B/A.   CHILDREN & PETS. LICENSED.   EN
SUITE, TV & BEVERAGES IN ROOMS. CREDIT CARDS.   B. & B. FROM £35.

GREY GABLES COUNTRY HOUSE HOTEL AND RESTAURANT, NORWICH RD, CAWSTON, NORWICH, NR10 4EY
Formerly Brandiston Rectory, this beautiful house offers very comfortable accommodation and fine food prepared from fresh ingredients served by candlelight. 200 item wine list.
TEL: (01603) 871259 OPEN ALL YEAR.   N/S DINING R.   V STD, S.D. B/A.   LICENSED.   SOME DISABLED ACCESS.
OVER 5S ONLY.   MOST ROOMS EN SUITE.   BEVERAGES, T.V. & PHONE IN ALL ROOMS.   ACCESS, VISA.   B. & B.
AROUND £25.

KINGSLEY LODGE, 3 KINGSLEY RD, NORWICH, NR1 3RB   TEL: (01603) 615819
Friendly, Edwardian house in the city centre close to the bus station & just a few mins'
walk from the Market Place and shops. Well-equipped en suite guest rooms. A full English
breakfast or a vegetarian option. Street parking with permits outside the house.
OPEN ALL YEAR.   NO SMOKING.   V, S.D. B/A.   EN SUITE, TV & BEVERAGES IN ROOMS. B. & B. AROUND £25.

PINE TREES, HOLLY LANE, BLOFIELD, NORWICH, NR13 4BV   TEL: (01603) 713778
Large, modern house in quiet rural area 1m Blofield & by-pass. Ground floor suite for 2-6
people; private bath & entrance. Range of healthy b'fasts. Close Norwich, Broads, coast.
OPEN ALL YEAR Ex. Xmas.   NO SMOKING.   V, VE STD.   S.D. B/A.   SOME DISABLED ACCESS.   CHILDREN
WELCOME.   BEVERAGES.   T.V. IN LOUNGE.

Welbeck House
BROOKE, NORWICH, NORFOLK, NR15 1AT   TEL: (01508) 550292
Quiet Georgian farmhouse 7m S. of Norwich offering comfortable B. & B.for non-smokers.
OPEN ALL YEAR.   NO SMOKING.   V, S.D. B/A.   OVER 12S & PETS.   BEVERAGES IN ROOMS.   B. &B. £16 - 20.

SHERINGHAM
Beeston Hills Lodge
CLIFF RD, SHERINGHAM, NORFOLK, NR26 8BJ   TEL: (01263) 825936
Edwardian Lodge next to cliff path and hills. All bedrooms have superb sea views.
OPEN Feb. - Dec.   NO SMOKING (& NO SMOKERS)   S.D. B/A.   CHILDREN & PETS B/A.   EN SUITE, TV &
BEVERAGES IN ROOMS.B. & B. FROM £16.50.

ACHIMOTA, 31 NORTH ST, SHERINGHAM, NR26 8LW   TEL:(01263) 822379
ETB 2 Crowns Commended. Comfortable guest house quietly situated a few mins'
stroll from the sea. Home-cooked food.
OPEN ALL YEAR.   NO SMOKING. V, S.D. B/A.   WELL-BEHAVED CHILDREN & PETS WELCOME.   BEVERAGES IN
ROOMS.   T.V. IN LOUNGE AND BEDROOMS ON REQUEST. B. & B. FROM £15.

SLOLEY
Cubitt Cottage
LOW ST, SLOLEY, NR NORWICH, NORFOLK, NR12 8HD   TEL: (01692) 538295
18th C. cottage in an acre of pretty gardens with 100 varieties of old-fashioned rose.
OPEN ALL YEAR.   NO SMOKING.   V, VE, DIAB, S.D. B/A.   CHILDREN WELCOME.   BEVERAGES IN ROOMS.
T.V. IN LOUNGE.   B. & B. FROM £18.50. D. £10.

SWAFFHAM
CORFIELD HOUSE, SPORLE, NR SWAFFHAM, PE32 2EA   TEL: (01760) 723636
ETB 3 Crowns Highly Commended. Beautiful brick-built country house in lawned gardens
in the peaceful village. Bedrooms have country views. Excellent food.
OPEN Easter - Dec.   NO SMOKING.   V, DIAB B/A.   LICENSED.   GROUND FLOOR ROOM. S. CHILDREN WELCOME.
PETS B/A. 5 EN SUITE ROOMS.   T.V. IN ROOMS.   B. & B. FROM £18.50.

Strattons Hotel
ASH CLOSE, SWAFFHAM, NORFOLK, PE37 7RS   TEL: (01760) 723845   FAX: (01760) 720458

Formerly known as the villa, Strattons is essentially an 18th C. Palladian house which has been restored to its former splendour by its present owners, Les and Vanessa Scott. The Palladian ideal of the villa being a place where 'the mind fatigued by the agitations of the city be restored and comforted'is alive and well at Strattons: the bedrooms are furnished in abundant style, with glorious drapes and sumptuous bedding, and the Drawing Room, with its open fire, books, magazines, pictures and amply cushioned sofas, invite guests to relax, unwind, and perhaps enjoy an afternoon tea.
The food is fabulous: a lazy breakfast of freshly squeezed orange juice, creamy porridge,

locally smoked bacon and free-range eggs sets you up for the day, and the evening meal is prepared fromfresh, home-grown produce. Those who can tear themselves away from the creature comforts of Strattons will find themselves in an ideal part of the world for exploring rural Norfolk with its unspoilt villages and bustling market towns.
OPEN ALL YEAR ex Xmas. N/S ex. in lounge.   V, S.D. B/A.   CHILDREN & PETS.   EN SUITE, TV & BEVERAGES IN ROOMS.   B. & B. FROM £35, D. £22.50.

WALSINGHAM

THE OLD RECTORY, WATERDEN, WALSINGHAM, NR22 6AT TEL: (01328) 823298
Beautiful Victorian rectory on the Holkham Estate in peaceful rural surroundings; beautifully furnished with antiques.
OPEN ALL YEAR.   N/S ex. 1 Bedroom. V, S.D. B/A.   DISABLED ACCESS.   CHILDREN WELCOME.   PETS B/A. EN SUITE & BEVERAGES IN ROOMS. T.V. IN 1 ROOM. B. & B. AROUND £18

WALTON HIGHWAY

STRATTON FARM, WEST DROVE NTH., WALTON HIGHWAY, PE14 7DP TEL: (01945) 880162
OPEN ALL YEAR.   NO SMOKING. V, DIAB B/A.   GOOD ACCESS FOR WHEELCHAIR USERS. OVER 5S ONLY.   EN SUITE ROOMS. BEVERAGES & TV IN ROOMS.   B. & B. AROUND £20.

WENDLING

Greenbanks Country Hotel & Restaurant
SWAFFHAM RD, WENDLING, NORFOLK, NR19 2AR   TEL: (01362) 687742
ETB 3 Crowns., Highly Commended. Greenbanks is a charming 18th C. family-run hotel which stands amidst 9 acres of lakes and meadows in the heart of Norfolk's delightful countryside. It has been sympathetically restored and retains its original character in the elegant dining room and en suite bedrooms.All the food is home-prepared from fresh local produce wherever possible, and most recipes, including many vegetarian specialities, are created by the Chef proprietor. You are just 5 miles from the quaint Market towns of Dereham and Swaffham, and just 20 mins drive from Norwich. Golf, fishing and walking are all available in the area.
OPEN ALL YEAR.   N/S DINING R.   V, S.D. B/A.   CHILDREN WELCOME.   PETS B/A.   LICENSED.   EN SUITE, TV & BEVERAGES IN ROOMS.   B. & B. FROM £21.

WELLS NEXT THE SEA

Eastdene Guest House
NORTHFIELD LAN, WELLS-NEXT-THE-SEA, NORFOLK, NR23 1LH   TEL: (01328) 710381
Eastdene is a homely guest house which stands close to the marshes in Wells-next-the-Sea. Your hostess, Jean Court, offers a warm welcome and accommodation is in comfortable, centrally heated rooms. Breakfast is served to guests and an evening meal, traditionally prepared using fresh garden produc, is availble on request. You are in an ideal place for visiting Cley and Titchwell bird reserves, and of course the coastal walks are lovely.
OPEN ALL YEAR. NO SMOKING. V, S.D. B/A. PETS WELCOME. EN SUITE, TV & BEVERAGES. B. & B. £14 -16.

WORSTEAD

Geoffrey The Dyer House
CHURCH PLAIN, WORSTEAD, NORTH WALSHAM, NR28 9AL TEL: (01692) 536562
Across the village square from Worstead's famous church. The beams and stays that hold up the house's lofty ceilings once supported the looms that made the famous Worstead cloth; careful restoration of this 17th C. listed building has preserved its unique character while creating a comfortable home of great charm with an inglenook fireplace.
OPEN ALL YEAR.   NO SMOKING. V, S.D. B/A.   CHILDREN WELCOME.   PETS B/A.   EN SUITE, BEVERAGES & T.V. IN ROOMS.   B. & B. AROUND £19.

RESTAURANTS

CASTLE ACRE

THE OLD RED LION, BAILEY ST, CASTLE ACRE, PE32 2AG
For further details please see under entry in the accommodation section.

DISS

THE WAFFLE HOUSE, MARKET PLACE, DISS   TEL; (01379) 650709
Family restaurant offering good food at reasonable prices. Menu includes dishes prepared from organic meat and produce, as well as a choice of vegetarian and vegan dishes; delicious home-made cakes and scones are baked on the premises daily.
70% N/S (separate area). V STD.   WHEELCHAIR ACCESS.   PARTY BOOKINGS.

GREAT YARMOUTH

LANES BISTRO, NO. 3, ROW 75, HOWARD ST STH, GT YARMOUTH   TEL: (01493) 330622
NO SMOKING.   V STD.

KINGS LYNN

Debenhams

19 - 16 HIGH ST, KINGS LYNN, NORFOLK.   TEL: (01553) 772668
Pavilion, a friendly self-service coffee shop serving lunches, snacks & hot & cold drinks.
OPEN STORE HOURS.   NO SMOKING.   V STD.   DISABLED ACCESS.   CHILDREN.   CREDIT CARDS.

NORWICH

THE ALMOND TREE, 441 DEREHAM RD, COSTESSEY, NR5 0SG TEL: (01603) 748798/749114
NO SMOKING.   LICENSED.   DISABLED ACCESS.   CHILDREN WELCOME. VISA, AMEX, MASTERCARD, DINERS.

THE ASSEMBLY HOUSE, 12 THEATRE ST, NORWICH, NR2 1RQ TEL: (01603) 626402
NO SMOKING.   V STD.   LICENSED.   DISABLED ACCESS.   CHILDREN WELCOME.

Debenhams

OXFORD PLACE, NORWICH, NORFOLK   TEL: (01603) 626181
Springles, a self-service restaurant serving lunches, snacks & hot & cold drinks.
OPEN STORE HOURS.   NO SMOKING.   V STD.   DISABLED ACCESS.   CHILDREN.   CREDIT CARDS.

LLOYD'S OF LONDON ST RESTAURANT, 66 LONDON ST, NORWICH. TEL: (01603) 624978
50% N/S   V STD.   CHILDREN WELCOME, 'BUT NOT THE VERY YOUNG'.

PIZZA EXPRESS, 15 ST BENEDICTS ST, NORWICH, NORFOLK TEL: (01603) 622157
N/S PART OF RESTAURANT.   V STD.   LICENSED.   DISABLED ACCESS.   CHILDREN WELCOME.

Pizza One Pancakes Too!

24 TOMBLAND, NORWICH, NORFOLK, NR3 1RF   TEL; (01603) 621583

Exceptionally popular pizza restaurant in the centre of Norwich. Situated alongside the ancient cathedral walls with cobblestones along the front and the famous spire of Norwich cathedral as a backdrop, it has long been one of Norwich's favourite eating places. The tempting menu includes pizzas, pancakes, excellent pasta dishes and delectable puddings (crepes with maple syrup, roasted almonds, peaches and cream - you name it, and you can have it!). The proprietors are nothing if not accommodating to guests: you can order pancakes without fillings and fillings without pancakes - for dessert you can choose a bowl of toppings. There is also a welcome sense of humour: there is a monthly competition for the best poem, comment or doodle and the winner has the honour of having his/her contribution displayed on the giant doodleboard as well as winning a meal for two.
OPEN 12 - 11.   N/S 60% RESTAURANT.   L. AROUND £5.85.   V STD.   LICENSED.
DISABLED ACCESS.   CHILDREN WELCOME.   CREDIT CARDS.

LA TIENDA, 10 ST GREGORY'S ALLEY, NORWICH, NR2 1ER TEL: (01603) 629122
NO SMOKING.   V, VE, DIAB & GLUTEN-FREE AVAIL.   LICENSED.   CHILDREN.

The Treehouse Restaurant
14 DOVE ST, NORWICH, NORFOLK   TEL: (01603) 763258

The Treehouse Restaurant is situated above Rainbow Wholefoods in the centre of Norwich close to the city's famous historic market. The restaurant interior is warm and bright with extensive window seating providing a lively view of the city. A co-operatively owned establishment, the Treehouse is renowned for its warm welcome and some of the best vegetarian cooking in the land. Vegan, gluten-free and sugar-free meals are always available on the daily-changing menu with prices ranging from £2.20 for soup up to £5 for larger main courses. A good selection of organic wines and beverages are also available. Opening hours are from 10 a.m. to 5 p.m. Mondays to Wednesdays and 10 a.m. to 9 p.m. Thursdays to Saturdays. The restaurant is closed on Sundays and most Bank Holidays. Hours sometimes vary so please phone ahead.

48 SEATS. OPEN 10 a.m. - 5 p.m. plus some evenings. NO SMOKING. L. under £5, D. £5 - £10. V, VE, SUGAR-FREE AND GLUTEN-FREE STD. CHILDREN WELCOME (HIGH CHAIRS AVAILABLE).

THE WAFFLE HOUSE, 39 ST GILES ST, NORWICH, NR2 1JN
N/S FIRST FLOOR OF RESTAURANT AND IN 60% OF DOWNSTAIRS SEATING AREA.

SHERINGHAM
THE JOLLY TAR, 55 STATION RD, SHERINGHAM, NR26 8RG   TEL: (01263) 822475
50% N/S (2 SEPARATE ROOMS). LICENSED. DISABLED ACCESS.

WELLS-NEXT-THE-SEA

The Moorings Restaurant
6 FREEMAN ST, WELLS-NEXT-THE-SEA, NORFOLK, NR23 1BA   TEL: (01328) 710949

Bernard and Carla Phillips

The Moorings Restaurant is, as its name suggests, situated in a charming old building a short walk from the beach at Wells-next-the-Sea. Unsurprisingly, much of the delicious home-cooked food has a marine flavour: home-smoked mussels, spicy fish soup or a half dozen locally raised oysters feature as appetisers on the extensive menu (even the Taramasalata is made from locally caught cods' roe), followed by Monkfish Fillet with Cumin and Coriander or Filo Parcel of Sea Bass as a main course. There are several good non-fish selections, too, such as Wild Mushroom Soup followed by Gratin of Pasta and Aubergine. Puddings are scrumptious (Butterscotch Pie with Walnut Crust or Special Trifle with Marsala, Amaretto & Almonds), and coffee with home-made chocolates completes the meal.

NO SMOKING   V STD.   LICENSED.   DISABLED ACCESS.   CHILDREN

PUBS & WINE BARS

BLAKENEY

The Kings Arms
WESTGATE ST, BLAKENEY, HOLT, NORFOLK, NR25 7NQ   TEL; (01263) 740341

Unspoilt and original well-established pub serving good reasonably priced bar food home-prepared using much local produce; lovely large garden and children's play area. Accommodation in delightful fully-equipped self-contained flatlets. B'fast if required.
N/S 1 ROOM.   V STD & S.D. B/A.   CHILDREN WELCOME.   WHEELCHAIR ACCESS.

Suffolk

ACCOMMODATION

BURY ST EDMUNDS

THE ANGEL HOTEL, BURY ST EDMUNDS, SUFFOLK TEL: (01284) 753926
The hotel has 2 restaurants, one in the 12th C. undercroft, the other overlooking the square and Abbey gateway. Recommended by Mr Pickwick!
OPEN ALL YEAR. N/S DINING R & SOME BEDRS. V, S.D. B/A. LICENSED. CHILDREN WELCOME. PETS B/A. EN SUITE ALL ROOMS. CREDIT CARDS. B. & B. AROUND £56.

Goldmartin

HIGH ST, RATTLESDEN, BURY ST EDMUNDS, SUFFOLK, IP30 0RA   TEL: (01449) 736410
Goldmartin is a 15th C. Grade II listed timber framed hall-house which has been beautifully preserved and maintained, and has oak beams and fine antique furniture. It stands in the conservation village of Rattlesden amidst the tranquillity of rural East Anglia. Accommodation is in spacious rooms with oak beams and diamond-paned windows, and in addition to traditional furnishings there are welcome modern conveniences such as central heating, wash basins and beverage-making facilities; the double and twin rooms overlook a meadow. Delicious meals are served in the charming dining room with its 17th C. fireplace. An excellent touring centre.
OPEN ALL YEAR. NO SMOKING. CHILDREN & PETS WELCOME. BEVERAGES & TV IN BEDROOMS. B. & B. FROM £16.50 (discount for 3 or more nights).

HAMILTON HOUSE, 4 NELSON RD, BURY ST EDMUNDS, IP33 3AG   TEL: (01284) 702201
Elegant Edwardian villa in quiet cul-de-sac 3 mins from town; easy access to A45.
OPEN ALL YEAR. NO SMOKING. V, S.D. B/A. CHILDREN WELCOME. EN SUITE IN 2 ROOMS. BEVERAGES & T.V. IN ROOMS. CREDIT CARDS. B. & B. AROUND £20.

EYE

BARLEY GREEN FARM, LAXFIELD RD, STRADBROKE, EYE. TEL: (01379) 384281
Tudor farmhouse in 8 acres, surrounded by attractive garden & ponds, near village.
OPEN Mar. - Oct. NO SMOKING. EN SUITE 1 ROOM. BEVERAGES IN ROOMS. B. & B. AROUND £18.

Oldcott

LAXFIELD RD, FRESSINGFIELD, NR EYE, SUFFOLK, IP21 5PU   TEL: (01379) 868186
*ETB 2 Crowns Highly Commended.*16th C. oak-beamed house standing well back from the road in a large garden, at the centre of the village. Comfortable accommodation and sitting room for guests'use. Welcoming afternoon tea on arrival. B'fast features home-made wheaten scones. Evening meals 5 minutes'walk.
OPEN ALL YEAR. NO SMOKING. V, S.D. B/A. SMALL BABIES WELCOME. EN SUITE, BEVERAGES & TV IN ROOMS. B. & B. FROM £17.50.

FELIXSTOWE

DORINCOURT G. H., 16 GARFIELD RD, FELIXSTOWE, IP11 7PU   TEL: (01394) 270447
OPEN ALL YEAR. NO SMOKING. V, S.D. B/A. CHILDREN WELCOME. BEERAGES & T.V. IN ROOMS. B. & B.AROUND £18.

FRAMLINGHAM

Shimmens Pightle

DENNINGTON RD, FRAMLINGHAM, SUFFOLK, IP13 9JT   TEL: (01728) 724036
ETB Listed Commended. B. & B. in landscaped garden. Ground floor rooms with wash basins. Home-made preserves & locally cured bacon. Convenient for countryside & coast.
OPEN ALL YEAR ex. Xmas Day. NO SMOKING. V, S.D. B/A. DISABLED ACCESS. OVER 5s ONLY. BEVERAGES. T.V. LOUNGE. B. & B. FROM £16.50.

HADLEIGH

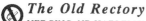

The Old Rectory
NEDGING, NR HADLEIGH, SUFFOLK.   TEL: (01449) 740745

Set in 2 acres of beautiful gardens, the Old Rectory has been carefully restored: each of the comfortable bedrooms is individually decorated and has an en suite bathroom. English breakfast includes eggs from our own free-range hens and an excellent 4-course dinner is also available. Nedging is a rural hamlet of only a few houses 4 miles north of Hadleigh and 6 miles east of Lavenham. It is surrounded by some of Suffolk's most picturesque rolling countryside and is within easy reach of the Stour Valley made famous by John Constable. Visitors will also find that there are numerous galleries and museums including Gainsborough's House in Sudbury. The peaceful location ensures a restful visit.

OPEN ALL YEAR.   NO SMOKING.   OVER 12s WELCOME.   EN SUITE & BEVERAGES IN BEDROOMS.   B. & B. FROM £27.50.

IPSWICH

Otley House
HELMINGHAM RD, OTLEY, IPSWICH, SUFFOLK, IP6 9NR   TEL: (01473) 890253 FAX: (01473) 890009

ETB 2 Crowns Highly Commended. Otley House has origins in the 17th C. but subsequent modernisations have created a building of great charm and it now boasts a Georgian facade and a fine listed Georgian staircase; it has been beautifully decorated and appropriately furnished (it has a lovely relaxed atmosphere) and it stands in its own spacious grounds, complete with small lake, surrounded by mature trees. Your hostess, Colette Hoepli, is Swiss and the excellent breakfast and evening menus feature a number of Continental dishes as well as more traditional English fare. Otley House is within easy reach of a number of local attractions including the Concert Hall at Snape Maltings, Minsmere Bird Sanctuary and the coast at Aldeburgh.

OPEN Mar. - Oct. inc.   NO SMOKING ex. billiard room.   LICENSED.   OVER 12S ONLY.   EN SUITE ALL ROOMS. T.V. 3 BEDROOMS.   B. & B. FROM £24, Sgl £34, D. £15.50.

Pipps Ford
NORWICH RD, NEEDHAM MARKET, IPSWICH   TEL: (01449) 760208 FAX: (01449) 760561

16th C. farmhouse; delightful old-fashioned garden on beautiful stretch of River Gipping.

OPEN Mid Jan. - mid Dec.   N/S DINING R & BEDRS.   V, S.D. B/A.   LICENSED.   DISABLED ACCESS. OVER 5S ONLY.   EN SUITE & BEVERAGES IN ROOMS.   T.V. IN 2 LOUNGES.   B. & B. £25 - 33.

Redhouse
LEVINGTON, IPSWICH, OP10 OLZ   TEL: (01473) 659670

Redhouse is a substantial Victorian farmhouse which stands in 3 acres of gardens & paddocks surrounded by farmland. It is situated on the edge of the tiny village of Levington in an area of Outstanding Natural Beauty with magnificent views over the Orwell Estuary; the proprietors, Mr and Mrs Matthews, are organic gardeners and keep horses and small livestock. Although Redhouse is primarily a bed and breakfast establishment, an evening meal can be obtained by prior arrangement and there are restaurants and pubs within easy reach. You will find Redhouse an ideal base for exploring the Suffolk countryside, including its Heritage Coast and mediaeval wool villages, and additionally there is an equestrian centre nearby and lots of lovely walks.

OPEN Mar. - Nov.   N/S PART DINING R & BEDRS.   V, S.D. B/A.   CHILDREN WELCOME.   BEVERAGES IN ROOMS.   T.V. IN LOUNGE.   B. & B. AROUND £15.

are prepared from fresh, local produce (some home-grown).
OPEN ALL YEAR.   NO SMOKING.   V, S.D. B/A.   CHILDREN WELCOME.   1 EN SUITE ROOM.   BEVER-
AGES IN ROOMS.   T.V. IN LOUNGE.   B. & B. AROUND £18.

LAVENHAM

THE SWAN HOTEL, HIGH ST, LAVENHAM, SUFFOLK.   TEL: (01787) 247477
OPEN ALL YEAR.   N/S DINING R & SOME BEDRS.   V STD, S.D. B/A.   LICENSED.   DISABLED ACCESS.
CHILDREN WELCOME.   EN SUITE, TV & BEVERAGES IN ROOMS.

LOWESTOFT

FAIR HAVENS CHRISTIAN GUEST HSE, 8 WELLINGTON ESP., NR33 OQQ
TEL: (01502) 574927 OPEN ALL YEAR ex Xmas.   NO SMOKING.   V, S.D. B/A.   CHILDREN WELCOME.
BEVERAGES IN ROOMS.   T.V. LOUNGE.   B. & B. FROM £14.50.

SAXMUNDHAM

Sans Souci
MAIN RD, YOXFORD, NR SAXMUNDHAM, SUFFOLK, IP17 3EX   TEL: (01728) 668268

Sans Souci is a spacious Georgian residence of considerable character and charm, which stands in its own 2
acres of mature timbered grounds just off the A12 in
the attractive village of Yoxford. The house is centrally
heated throughout and there are three spacious and
well-furnished bedrooms. A generous breakfast is
served to guests (featuring orange juice, a choice of
cereals, a cooked breakfast, toast and the beverage of
your choice), and there are restaurants and pubs where
you may enjoy an evening meal, just a few minutes'
walk from the house. Popular with tourists and bird watchers alike, the surrounding
countryside is a haven of tranquillity and the RSPB Reserve at Mismere is within easy
reach. Additionally, you are just 5 miles from the Suffolk Heritage coast, with its quaint
sea side towns, picturesque villages and unspoilt beaches.
OPEN ALL YEAR.   NO SMOKING.   V, S.D. B/A.   CHILDREN & PETS WELCOME.   TV & BEVERAGES IN ROOMS.
B. & B. FROM £17.

SUDBURY

BORLEY PLACE, BORLEY, SUDBURY (NEXT TO PARISH CHURCH) TEL: (01787) 71120
18th C. farmhouse set amidst rolling countryside in Constable country.
OPEN ALL YEAR.   N/S DINING R, BEDRS & SITTING R.   CHILDREN WELCOME.   EN SUITE.   BEVERAGES
ON REQUEST.   T.V. LOUNGE.   B. & B. AROUND £18.

BULMER TYE HOUSE, NR SUDBURY, SUFFOLK, CO10 7ED   TEL: (01787) 269315
Historic & characterful house with friendly atmosphere in a beautiful garden.
OPEN ALL YEAR.   NO SMOKING.   V, B/A.   CHILDREN WELCOME.   B. & B. AROUND £18.

WOODBRIDGE

Bantry
CHAPEL RD, SAXTEAD, NR FRAMLINGHAM, WOODBRIDGE, SUFFOLK, IP13 9RB   TEL:
(01728) 685578
Bantry is situated in the attractive village of Saxtead with its windmill overlooking the
village green. It offers 3 purpose-built en suite apartments, two of which are on the ground
floor (providing accommodation to suit the less mobile). Patio doors lead onto the half acre
of garden and orchard. Each of the apartments has its own lounge cum dining room with
colour TV and drink-making facilities. Breakfast and evening meals are served to each
apartment.
OPEN ALL YEAR.   NO SMOKING.   S.D. B/A.   CHILDREN WELCOME.   EN SUITE, TV & BEVERAGES IN ROOMS.
B. & B. FROM £18, D. £9.50.

OLD SCHOOL, SAXTEAD, WOODBRIDGE, IP13 9QP   TEL: (01728) 723887
Exclusively vegetarian & vegan accommodation in converted school.
OPEN ALL YEAR.   NO SMOKING.   V EXC, VE STD.   S.D. B/A.   CHILDREN WELCOME. PETS B/A.   2 EN SUITE
ROOMS.   BEVERAGES.   B. & B. AROUND £12.

PRIORY COTTAGE, LOW CORNER, BUTLEY, NR WOODBRIDGE, IP12 3QD
TEL: (01394) 450382   OPEN ALL YEAR Ex. Xmas/Boxing Day.   NO SMOKING.   V, S.D. B/A.
CHILDREN: OVER 5S ONLY.   PETS B/A.   T.V. LOUNGE.   B. & B. AROUND £17.

WRENTHAM

Albion Rose Proprerties
94 SOUTHWOLD RD, WRENTHAM, NR34 7JF TEL: (01502) 675757 FAX: (01502) 675462
ETB registered agency for self-catering accommodation in Norwich, Norfolk and Suffolk.
OPEN ALL YEAR.   SOME PLACES SMOKE-FREE.   SOME PROPERTIES CHILDREN/PETS.

RESTAURANTS

BRANDON

COPPER KETTLE, 31 HIGH ST, BRANDON, SUFFOLK   TEL: (01842) 814185

BURY ST EDMUNDS

THE ANGEL HOTEL, BURY ST EDMUNDS, SUFFOLK   TEL: (01284) 753926

LOWESTOFT

Bistro East
10 BEVAN ST, EAST LOWESTOFT, SUFFOLK, NR32 2AA   TEL: (01502) 539400
Coffee shop & restaurant with blackboard menu. From a 'bottomless'cup of coffee, Danish,
carrot cake, thro'snacks, salads, pastas, all food is cooked to order. Excellent wine list.
OPEN Oct - Jun, Tues - Sat, 10 am - 10pm.   NO SMOKING.   V STD.   LICENSED.   WHEEL CHAIRS.   CHILDREN.

East Midlands

Derbyshire

ACCOMMODATION

ALKMONTON
DAIRY HOUSE FARM, ALKMONTON, DERBY, DE6 3DG TEL: (01335) 330359
ETB 3 Crowns Commended. NO SMOKING.   V, S.D. B/A.   LICENSED.   OVER 5S.   EN SUITE 3 ROOMS.
BEVERAGES IN ROOMS.   T.V. LOUNGE.   B. & B. AROUND £16.

ASHBOURNE

Lichfield Guest House
BRIDGE VIEW, MAYFIELD, ASHBOURNE, DE6 2HN   TEL: (01335) 344422

ETB 2 Crowns Highly Commended. AA QQQQ. Lichfield Guest House is a beautiful Georgian house standing in 2 acres of land-scaped gardens and grounds and enjoying magnificent views over the River Dove and valleys beyond. It is conveniently situated on the edge of the village of Mayfield, just 1¼ miles from Ashbourne on the Staffordshire / Derbyshire border. Accommodation is in comfortable, centrally heated rooms which include a family room and double room with en suite facilities and there is also a pleasant lounge for guests' use. There is also a self-catering cottage, which stands in the grounds of Lichfield House and sleeps up to 3 people. Lichfield Guest House is ideally situated for those wishing to visit Alton Towers, Chatsworth House and the Peak District; Ashbourne is also well worth a visit.

OPEN ALL YEAR (ex. Xmas & Boxing Day).   NO SMOKING.   V B'FAST.   CHILDREN WELCOME.   SOME EN SUITE
ROOMS.   BEVERAGES & TV IN BEDRS.   B. & B. £15-17.50. Sgle. £16-18. Under-12s: £5-8.50.

THE MANSE VEGETARIAN & VEGAN GUEST HOUSE, WETTON, DE6 2AF
TEL: (01335) 27259   NO SMOKING. V EXC, MAINLY VE.   CHILDREN WELCOME.   PETS B/A.   EN SUITE
1 ROOM.   BEVERAGES.   T.V. IN SITTING R.   B. & B. FROM £12.50.

THE OLD CHAPEL, WETTON, NR ASHBOURNE, DE6 2AE   TEL: (01335) 27378
Charmingly converted 19th C. chapel. Excellent home-cooked food.
OPEN Feb. - Nov.   N/S IN DINING R & BEDRS.   V, S.D. B/A.   OVER 7S ONLY.   PETS B/A.   EN SUITE &
BEVERAGES IN BEDRS.   T.V. AVAILABLE.   B. & B. AROUND £30.

Holly Cottage
ROWLAND, NR BAKEWELL, DE45 1NR   TEL: (01629) 640624
Beautiful 18th C. Farmhouse in peaceful rural setting. Attractive panelled hall & sitting
room with log fires for guests'use.
OPEN Jan. - OcT.   NO SMOKING.   V B/A.   CHILDREN WELCOME.   BEVERAGES IN BEDRS. B. & B. FROM £17.

RIVERSIDE COUNTRY HOUSE HOTEL, ASHFORD IN THE WATER, DE4 1QF
Exceptionally beautiful Georgian house in mature gardens overlooking River Wye.
TEL: (01629) 814275   NO SMOKING.   V STD.   LICENSED.   DISABLED ACCESS to restaurant.
CHILDREN WELCOME.   DOGS B/A.   EN SUITE, TV & BEVERAGES IN ROOMS.   B. & B. AROUND £46.

Sheldon House
CHAPEL STREET, MONYASH, NR. BAKEWELL, DE45 1JJ   TEL: (01629) 813067
ETB 2 Crown Highly Commended. Beautiful 18th century listed building in the pic-
turesque village of Monyash in the heart of the Peak District National Park, recently
renovated to a very high standard. Healthy b'fasts and a warm wlcome. Guest sitting room.
OPEN ALL YEAR ex Xmas & New Year.   NO SMOKING.   V, S.D. B/A.   OVER 7S ONLY.   EN SUITE, BEVERAGES
IN RS.   T.V. AVAILABLE.   B. & B. FROM £18.

BELPER

Dannah Farm Country Guest House
DANNAH FARM, BOWMANS LANE, SHOTTLE, NR BELPER, DE56 2DR TEL: (0773) 550 273 OR
630 FAX: (0773) 550590

*AA 4Q Selected, RAC Highly Acclaimed. Fi-
nalists In 1992 Alternative Farmer Of The
Year.* Dannah Farm is an attractive Georgian
building serving a 128 acre mixed farm on the
beautiful Chatsworth Estate. The accommodation is very comfortable, and there is a superb
4-poster suite available. Joan Slack is very
interested in (and knowledgeable about)
healthy food and uses wholefood ingredients
where possible in cooking. Muesli, yoghurt
and fruit are always available at breakfast and
the imaginative evening menu might feature
Spinach and Cottage Cheese Filo, followed by
Earl Grey Sorbet, Seafood Pie and a delicious
dessert such as Stuffed Apple Pancakes with Cream. Joan recently opened her highly
acclaimed non-residential restaurant, The Mixing Place, on the Dannah Farm site, offering
the same superlative food; the excellence of her achievements have been recognised by the
English Tourist Board (Dannah Farm is 3 Crown Highly Commended) and she has won the
National Award for Farm Catering. Lots to see and do in the area which is, incidentally,
excellent for walking.
OPEN ALL YEAR EX. XMAS.   N/S BEDRS & DINING R.   V, S.D. B/A.   LICENSED.   CHILDREN WELCOME.
ALL ROOMS PRIVATE FACILITIES, BEVERAGES & COLOUR T.V.   CREDIT CARDS.   B. & B. FROM £24.

BUXTON

ALPINE G. H., HARDWICK MOUNT, BUXTON, SK17 6PS   TEL: (01298) 26155
Traditional Victorian Guest House in the beautiful market town of Buxton. Nourishing and wholesome food; both traditional and vegetarian menus are available.

NO SMOKING.   V STD, S.D. B/A.   CHILDREN WELCOME.   BEVERAGES & T.V. IN BEDRS.   B. & B. AROUND £16.

Coningsby Guest House
6 MACCLESFIELD ROAD, BUXTON, DERBYS, SK17 9AH   TEL: (01298) 26735
ETB 3 Crowns Highly Commended. Elegant Victorian house within walking distance of centre of town. Fresh produce used in cooking.
NO SMOKING. V, S.D. B/A.   EN SUITE SHOWER, BEVERAGES & T.V. IN ROOMS.   B. & B. AROUND £20.

IVY HOUSE, NEWHAVEN, BIGGIN BY HARTINGTON, BUXTON, DERBYS, SK17 0DT
19th C. former Grade II listed coaching inn renovated with many original features. Flag stone floors. Log fires. Ideal walking, touring. Ground floor apartment.
TEL: **(01298) 84709** NO SMOKING. V, S.D. B/A. GROUND FLOOR APARTMENT. CHILDREN & PETS WELCOME. EN SUITE, TV & BEVERAGES IN ROOMS.   B. & B. AROUND £25.

Lynstone Guest House
3 GRANGE RD, BUXTON, DERBYS, SK17 6NH   TEL: (01298) 77043
Small family-run guest house in a quiet location 5 mins walk from the Opera House, Pavilion Gardens, Pooles Cavern, railway station and shopping centre of Buxton.
NO SMOKING. V, S.D. B/A. TV & BEVERAGES IN ROOMS. CHILDREN.   B. & B. AROUND £16.

MILNE HOUSE, MILLERS DALE, BUXTON, DE4 1JJ   TEL: (01298) 872315
Charming converted watermill situated near wooded hills in the heart of Derbyshire.
OPEN ALL YEAR. N/S ex lounge. V, S.D. B/A. LICENSED. CHILDREN WELCOME. BEVERAGES. T.V. AVAILABLE.   B. & B. FROM £11.

Oldfield Guest House
8 MACCLESFIELD RD, BUXTON, DERBYSHIRE, SK17 9AH   TEL: (01298) 24371
Large detached Victorian property, recently restored and now run as a friendly family guest house. The Oldfields also have a self-catering cottage - further details below.
OPEN ALL YEAR.   NO SMOKING.   V B/A.   EN SUITE, TV & BEVERAGES IN ROOMS.   CHILDREN WELCOME.   B. & B. AROUND £18.

S/Catering, 1 SILVERLANDS COTTAGE, TRINITY PASS. BUXTON TEL: (01298) 24371
This lovely stone cottage has a small garden is in a tranquil cul de sac. There is a kitchen/dining room, a sitting room, two bedrooms & a bathroom; Teletext TV & video and an automatic washing machine. Within easy walking distance of the town centre.
OPEN ALL YEAR.   NO SMOKING.   CHILDREN WELCOME.   AROUND £150 - 250 per week.

CHESTERFIELD
SHEEPLEA COTTAGE FARM, BASLOW ROAD, EASTMOOR, CHESTERFIELD
TEL: **(01246) 566785**   OPEN Mar. - Oct. Inc.   NO SMOKING. V STD, S.D. B/A. OVER 12S ONLY. PETS B/A. BEVERAGES IN ROOMS.   T.V. IN LOUNGE.   B. & B. AROUND £14.

MATLOCK BATH
Cliffeside Bed & Breakfast
BRUNSWOOD RD, MATLOCK BATH, DERBYS, DE4 3PA TEL: (01629) 56981
Friendly, family-run B. & B. with a lovely garden in the heart of the Derbyshire Dales with spectacular country views. Comfortable rooms including double en suite bedroom with adjacent room with bunks ideal for families (cot, highchair, baby-sitting available).
OPEN ALL YEAR. NO SMOKING. VEGETARIAN & OTHER DIETS B/A. CHILDREN & PETS WELCOME. 1 DOUBLE/FAMILY EN SUITE; 1 DOUBLE. TV & TEA/COFFEE-MAKING IN BOTH RS. B. & B. FROM £13.

MATLOCK
DERWENT HOUSE, KNOWLESTON PLACE, MATLOCK, DERBYS, DE4 3BU
Charming 17th C. Grade II listed building in secluded backwater 50 yds from Hall Leys Park. 5 comfortably furnished guest rooms. Family owned; children very welcome.
TEL: (01629) 584681 OPEN ALL YEAR Ex. Xmas & New Year. NO SMOKING. V STD. CHILDREN WELCOME. PETS B/A. EN SUITE IN 1 BEDR.   BEVERAGES & T.V. IN ROOMS.   B. & B. AROUND £18.

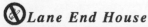

Lane End House
GREEN LANE, TANSLEY, DERBYS, DE4 5FJ   TEL: (01629) 583981

Small Georgian farmhouse behind Tansley village green near to the church and with open fields and green hills to the rear. Beautifully decorated. All food is home-made, including the soups and pâtés.

OPEN ALL YEAR.   NO SMOKING.   V, S.D. B/A.   LICENSED.   DISABLED ACCESS: 2 STEPS AT FRONT DOOR.   CHILDREN WELCOME.   PETS B/A.   EACH BEDR HAS A PRIVATE BATHR.   BEVERAGES & T.V. IN ALL ROOMS.   ACCESS, VISA, MASTERCARD.   B. & B. AROUND £25.

SUNNYBANK GUEST HOUSE, 37 CLIFTON RD, MATLOCK BATH, MATLOCK, DE4 3PW

Spacious, comfortable Victorian residence; excellent accommodation in peaceful surroundings; lovely views of the Derwent Valley. Ideal centre for touring & walking.

TEL: (01629) 584621   OPEN ALL YEAR.   NO SMOKING.   V, S.D. B/A.   OVER 10S ONLY.   EN SUITE IN 3 ROOMS.   TV IN LOUNGE & 3 RS.   BEVERAGES IN ROOMS.   CREDIT CARDS.   B. & B. AROUND £19.

Woodside
STANTON LEES, MATLOCK, DERBYSHIRE.   TEL: (01629) 734320

Woodside is a comfortable family home which stands amidst landscaped gardens in the Peak District National Park; surrounded by ancient moors and woodland which are teeming with wildlife, there are panoramic country views from many of the rooms. Accommodation is in either a double or a twin-bedded room, both with private facilities, and there is a comfortable lounge with a TV.. Guests are treated to a full English breakfast and an evening meal is available by arrangement. The visitor's book testifies to the warmth of the welcome, the deliciousness of the food and the beauty of the location - many entries represent repeat visits.

OPEN Easter - Oct. inc.   NO SMOKING.   S.D. B/A.   CHILDREN WELCOME.   EN SUITE, TV & BEVERAGES IN RS.   B. & B. £16.

SPINKHILL

Park Hall Hotel & Uplands Manor Restaurant
SPINKHILL, SHEFFIELD, S31 9YD   TEL: (01246) 434897   FAX: (01246) 436282

Park Hall has existed since the 14th C. although the main part of the house was completed in the 17th C. It stands amidst extensive grounds (the wisteria hung terrace is a blaze of colour in summer), yet is just a few minutes' drive from J30 on the M1. The house has been considerably renovated in recent years: the modernisation programme has managed to retain the most interesting architectural features of the building yet provided for every creature comfort, including central heating; each of the nine guest bedrooms have beeen furnished and decorated to a very high standard. Guests may enjoy a drink in the oak-panelled Armoury Bar, with its open grated fire, before dining on a superb selection of home-cooked food (prepared from fresh produce) in the candle-lit restaurant. There are also two oak-panelled conference rooms: audio-visual and other equipment is available on request.

OPEN ALL YEAR.   N/S DINING R. & 4 BEDRS.   V, S.D. B/A.   LICENSED.   OVER 12s WELCOME.   WHEELCHAIR ACCESS.   EN SUITE, TV & BEVERAGES IN ROOMS.   B. & B. FROM £37.50, L. FROM £7.50, D. FROM £15.95.

WIRKSWORTH

Avondale Farm
GRANGEMILL, NR WIRKSWORTH, DERBYS, DE4 4HT   TEL: (01629) 650820

Peaceful and private B. & B. in tastefully converted barn on non-working farm in Peak District National Park. Totally self-contained & centrally heated accommodation of exceptionally high standard. Spacious dining/sitting area with cosy log burner, twin bedroom and a private bathroom. The breakfast is excellent with lots of healthy treats.

OPEN ALL YEAR.   NO SMOKING.   V, S.D. B/A.   CHILDREN & PETS B/A.   PRIVATE BATHROOM.   BEVERAGES, T.V., RADIO & HAIRDRYER IN R.   B. & B. AROUND £22.

RESTAURANTS & PUBS

BAKEWELL

GREEN APPLE, DIAMOND COURT, WATER STREET, DE4 1EW   TEL: (01629) 814404
Charming little restaurant converted from five old cottages & retaining beamed ceilings and the exposed stone walls. Home-prepared food
NO SMOKING.   V. STD.   LICENSED.   DISABLED ACCESS.   CHILDREN.

BELPER

THE MIXING PLACE, DANNAH FARM COUNTRY GUEST HOUSE, DANNAH FARM, BOWMANS LANE, SHOTTLE, NR BELPER, DE5 2DR
For further details please see under the entry in the accommodation section.

CHESTERFIELD

THE HOUSE OF YORK, 26 THE GREEN, HASLAND, NR CHESTERFIELD TEL: (01246) 211241
N/S SEPARATE DINING R.   V STD.   LICENSED.   CHILDREN WELCOME.

ROYAL OAK INN, HIGH STREET, BARLBOROUGH, CHESTERFIELD   TEL: (01246) 810425
N/S SEPARATE SECTION.   V STD.   LICENSED.   CHILDREN ALLOWED.

DERBY

THE BRUNSWICK PUB, 1 RAILWAY TERRACE, DERBY   TEL: (01332) 290677
N/S ONE ROOM.

Debenhams
17 - 24 VICTORIAN ST, DERBY, DERBYS.   TEL: (01332) 44252
Springles, a friendly self-service restaurant serving lunches, snacks and drinks.
OPEN STORE HOURS.   NO SMOKING.   V STD.   DISABLED ACCESS.   CHILDREN.   CREDIT CARDS.

ORCHARD RESTAURANT, 21 FRIARGATE, DERBY, DERBYS. TEL: (01332) 40307
N/S MOST OF RESTAURANT.   MAINLY V.   LICENSED.   CHILDREN WELCOME.

QUATTIES RESTAURANT, 109 NORMANTON ROAD, DERBY, DERBYS. TEL: (01332) 368701
NO SMOKING.   V STD.   LICENSED.   WELL-BEHAVED CHILDREN WELCOME.

MELBOURNE

JOHN THOMPSON INN, INGLEBY, MELBOURNE, DE7 1HW   TEL: (01332) 862469
A 16th C. country pub with brewery and extensive gardens and picture gallery. 4 miles from Calke Abbey, 2 miles from Melbourne Hall and 5 miles from E. Midlands airport.
N/S SEPARATE LOUNGE.   WHEELCHAIR ACCESS TO N/S LOUNGE. CHILDREN'S ROOM AVAIL. EVES.

TICKNALL

Daisy's Tearoom
THE OLD COACH HOUSE, HAYES FARM, TICKNALL, DE7 1JZ   TEL: (01332) 862696
Situated in the coach house of a lovely large Georgian farmhouse in lovely informal gardens with antiques showroom to the rear of the tea room. Lace tablecloths, fresh flowers, gentle background music all create a peaceful ambience. Excellent food.
OPEN 10.30 - 5.30.   NO SMOKING.   V STD. S.D. B/A. CHILDREN WELCOME.

Leicestershire

ACCOMMODATION

BROUGHTON ASTLEY

Ⓝ THE OLD FARMHOUSE, OLD MILL RD, BROUGHTON ASTLEY, LE9 6PQ TEL: (01455) 282254
NO SMOKING. V, S.D. B/A. CHILDREN WELCOME. BEVERAGES IN ROOMS.

LEICESTER

Leicestershire Moat House

WIGSTON RD (B582), OADBY, LEICESTER, LE2 5QE   (0116) 271 9441
Excellent, business-class hotel, once a gentleman's residence dating back to 1898. Offering excellent facilities including in-house movies. Conveniently situated in the village-like residential area of Oadby yet has easy access to Leicester city centre and the M1.
OPEN ALL YEAR. N/S RESTAURANT & SOME BEDRS. V STD. LICENSED. DISABLED ACCESS. CHILDREN WELCOME. PETS B/A.   EN SUITE, TV & BEVERAGES IN ROOMS.

Ⓝ*Richard's Backpacker's Hostel*

157 WANLIP LN., BIRSTALL, LEICS, LE4 4GL   TEL: (0116) 267 3107
Independent hostel for cyclists, backpackers & young tourists. Bus from Stand B at the city bus station to hostel's nearest stop at Windmill Avenue, Birstall. Home-made bread.
NO SMOKING. V, VE STD, S.D. B/A.   NOT LICENSED, BUT BYO.   OVER 5S ONLY.   B. & B. FROM £8.

LUTTERWORTH

Ⓝ*Highcross House*

HIGHCROSS, LUTTERWORTH, LEICS, LE17 5AT   TEL: (01455) 220840
16th C. Grade II listed building at the historic crossing of Fossways and Watling Street; flowers & refreshments to greet you! Picnic basket on request.Tasteful rooms. Fresh, home-made food.
OPEN ALL YEAR.   NO SMOKING.   V, S.D. B/A.   LICENSED.   DISABLED ACCESS.   CHILDREN WELCOME. PETS B/A.   EN SUITE. BEVERAGES, T.V. IN ALL ROOMS. B. & B. FROM £20.

WHEATHILL FARM, CHURCH LN, SHEARSBY, LUTTERW'TH, LE17 6PG TEL: (0116) 247 8663
OPEN ALL YEAR.   N/S DINING R, LOUNGE & BEDRS.   V B/A.   CHILDREN WELCOME. DISABLED FACILITIES.
EN SUITE. BEVERAGES IN ROOMS.   T.V. IN LOUNGE.   B. & B. FROM £15.

MELTON MOWBRAY

Ⓝ*Church Cottage*

MAIN ST, HOLWELL, MELTON MOWBRAY, LEICS, L14 4SZ   TEL: (01664) 444255
A charming 18th C. listed cottage next to village green, 4m from Melton Mowbray. Landscaped gardens & use of summer house. Own sitting room & parking area.
OPEN ALL YEAR.   NO SMOKING.   S.D. B/A.   CHILDREN & PETS.   1 EN SUITE.   TV & BEVERAGES IN ROOMS.
B. & B.FROM £16.

STAPLEFORD PARK COUNTRY HOUSE HOTEL, STAPLEFORD PARK, LE14 2EF
16th C. stately home converted to use as a hotel of grandeur and eclectic of style
TEL: (01572) 84522 OPEN ALL YEAR. N/S DINING R. V, S.D. B/A.   LICENSED. DISABLED ACCESS. PETS
B/A.   EN SUITE IN ALL ROOMS.   T.V. FACILITIES.   CREDIT CARDS.   B. & B. AROUND £140.

OAKHAM

Ⓝ*Barnsdale Lodge Hotel*

THE AVENUE, RUTLAND WATER, OAKHAM, LE15 8AH   TEL: (01572) 724678 FAX: (01572) 724961
17th C. converted country farmhouse. Edwardian decor throughout. Function & conference facilities. Traditional home-cooked food.
OPEN ALL YEAR.   N/S DINING R.   S.D. B/A.   CHILDREN & PETS.   WHEELCHAIR ACCESS.   EN SUITE, TV &
BEVERAGES IN ROOMS.   LICENSED.   B. & B. FROM £35.

UPPINGHAM

Rutland House

61 HIGH ST EAST, UPPINGHAM, RUTLAND, LEICS.   TEL: (01572) 822497
OPEN ALL YEAR.   N/S DINING R & SOME BERS.   DISABLED ACCESS.   CHILDREN WELCOME.   PETS B/A.
EN SUITE, TV & BEVERAGES IN ROOMS.   B. & B. FROM £18.50.

RESTAURANTS & PUBS

ASHBY-DE-LA-ZOUCH

Staunton Stables Tea Room

THE FERRERS CENT., STAUNTON HAROLD, NR ASHBY-de-la-ZOUCH, LE6 5RU TEL: (01332) 864617

 Staunton Stables is situated in a converted stable block, surrounding a magnificent Georgian courtyard behind Staunton Harold Hall in the beautiful Vale of Staunton Harold near Calke Abbey. Home-made cakes, pastries and lunches are served therein on lovely Rose Chintz pottery, and the indoor seating is supplemented by more tables and chairs in the courtyard for sunny al fresco dining. The extended Staunton lunch menu consists of daily hot 'specials', such as Casserole or Fruit Lamb, traditional oven-baked potatoes with various fillings, soup, toasted sandwiches and hot puddings. Cream teas and Hovis teas are served every afternoon. Home-made cakes, home-made preserves and Twinings Speciality Teas are available for sale, and The Stables also houses a number of craft workshops, a gift shop and the Ferrers Gallery.
OPEN 10.30 - 5.   NO SMOKING.   V STD.   DISABLED ACCESS.   CHILDREN WELCOME.

EMPINGHAM

WHITE HORSE PUB, 2 MAIN ST (A606), EMPINGHAM
NO SMOKING IN PART OF LOUNGE BAR.

LEICESTER

Debenhams

THE SHIRES CENTRE, ST PETERS LANE, LEICESTER   TEL: (0116) 251 5300
Intermission, a friendly self-service restaurant serving lunches, snacks drinks.
OPEN STORE HOURS.   NO SMOKING.   V STD.   DISABLED ACCESS.   CHILDREN.   CREDIT CARDS.

PARSONS GALLERY, 399 RATBY LN., KIRBY MUXLOE, LEICESTER, LE9 9AQ
TEL: (0116) 239 3534   NO SMOKING.   ONLY WELL-BEHAVED CHILDREN WELCOME.

THE GOOD EARTH, 19 FREE LANE, LEICESTER, LE1 1JX
TEL: (0116) 262 6260   N/S 50% OF RESTAURANT (SEPARATE FLOOR).   V, VE STD.   LICENSED.

LOUGHBOROUGH

The Greenhouse

27/29 BIGGIN ST (FIRST FLOOR), LOUGHBOROUGH, LE11 1UA   TEL: (01509) 262018
NO SMOKING.   V EXC.   LICENSED.   CHILDREN WELCOME.

OAKHAM

MUFFINS TEA ROOMS, 9 MILL ST, OAKHAM, LE15 6EA TEL: (01572) 723501
NO SMOKING.   WHEELCHAIR ACCESS.   CHILDREN WELCOME.

UPPINGHAM

BAINES TEA ROOM, HIGH ST WEST, UPPINGHAM TEL: (01572) 823317
OPEN MON. TO SAT., 9 - 5., (CLOSED MON. & THURS. P.M. IN WINTER). NO SMOKING.

Lincolnshire

ACCOMMODATION

ALFORD

Halton House

50 EAST ST, ALFORD, LINCS., LN13 9EH TEL: (01507) 462058

Situated on the edge of the Lincolnshire Wolds in the small market town of Alford. Craft market during summer. Local pottery and a working mill within walking distance.
OPEN ALL YEAR. NO SMOKING. OVER 5S WELCOME. TV & BEVERAGES. B. & B. FROM £15.

BOSTON

Barn Croft

MAIN ST, MAREHAM LE FEN, BOSTON, LINCS, PE22 7QJ TEL; (01507) 568264

Barn Croft is a charming bed and breakfast which is situated in the rural village o f Mareham le Fen. Although breakfast is the only meal to be served at Barn Croft, evening meals are available at the local 16th C. pub, which is just 5 minutes' walk from the house. Accommodation is in comfortable en suite rooms, and there is a TV lounge for guests' use. Barn Croft is an excellent base from which to visit Lincoln, Boston, the coast and the wolds.
OPEN ALL YEAR. NO SMOKING. S.D. B/A. TV LOUNGE. EN SUITE & BEVERAGES IN ROOMS. B. & B. FROM £15.

POUNDSWORTH, MAIN ST, MAREHAM-LE-FEN, BOSTON, PE22 7QJ TEL: (01507) 568444
NO SMOKING. V B/A. CHILDREN WELCOME. B. & B. AROUND £17.

CASTLE BYTHAM

Bank House

CASTLE BYTHAM, NR GRANTHAM, LINCS, NG33 4SQ TEL: (01780) 410523

ETB De Luxe. B. & B. of the Year (Mid. Eng. Best of Tourism Awards). Located just 3 miles east of the A1 between Stamford and Grantham. Superbly appointed and comfortable private home, set in well-maintained secluded grounds and overlooking countryside
OPEN ALL YEAR. NO SMOKING. V, S.D. B/A. EN SUITE, TV & BEVERAGES. B. & B. AROUND £23.

EAST BARKWITH

THE GRANGE, TORRINGTON LNE, EAST BARKWITH, LN3 5RY TEL: (01673) 858249
*ETB 2 Crowns De Luxe.*Welcoming Georgian farmhouse quietly situated amidst extensive grounds with lawn tennis court; spacious bedrooms with views of farm & gardens.
OPEN ALL YEAR. N/S BEDRS & MOST PUBLIC AREAS. V, DIAB, S.D. B/A. CHILDREN WELCOME. ALL ROOMS EN SUITE. B. & B. AROUND £21.

GRANTHAM

The Lanchester Guest House

84 HARROWBY RD, GRANTHAM, LINCS, NG31 9DS TEL: (01476) 74169
OPEN ALL YEAR. N/S DINING R, BEDRS & MOST PUBLIC AREAS. V, B/A. CHILDREN. EN SUITE IN SOME ROOMS.
BEVERAGES & TV IN ROOMS. B. & B. FROM £15.

Sycamore Farm

BASSINGTHORPE, GRANTHAM, LINCS. NG33 4ED TEL: (01476) 85274

Working family farm with a spacious Victorian farmhouse in peaceful countryside. Comfortably furnished throughout: each of the spacious guest bedrooms have views.
OPEN Mar. - Oct. NO SMOKING. EN SUITE 1 ROOM. TV & BEVERAGES IN ROOMS. OVER 6S WELCOME. B. & B. AROUND £17.

HAINTON

THE OLD VICARAGE, SCHOOL LANE, HAINTON, LINCS, LN3 6LW TEL: (01507) 313660
NO SMOKING. OVER 12S PRIVATE BATHROOM. BEVERAGES & T.V. B. & B. AROUND £16.

LINCOLN

*ABC Charisma Guest House*

126 YARBOROUGH RD, LINCOLN, LN1 1HP   TEL: (01522) 543560

The ABC Guest House is a large, detached red brick built house overlooking the Trent Valley by the side of the old Lincoln race course and just 10 minutes walk from the cathedral and city centre. All bedrooms have been comfortably furnished and have pleasant views of the common and the Carholme golf course; some of the rear bedrooms have balconies. Your hosts, Wendy and Terry Cain, offer just breakfast to guests but it is a generous meal and there are lots of good pubs and restaurants just a short walk away in the cathedral area of the city. With its lovely green views, yet convenient proximity to the city centre, the ABC is a perfect choice for business travellers to Lincoln, or those seeking a short break in this historically interesting city.

OPEN ALL YEAR.   NO SMOKING.   WH, V, S.D.   DISABLED ACCESS.   SOME EN SUITE ROOMS.   BEVERAGES & T.V. IN ROOMS.   B. & B. FROM £16.

The Carline Guest House

1 - 3 CARLINE RD, LINCOLN, LINCS, LN1 1HL   TEL: (01522) 530422

Set in the heart of historic Lincoln, the Carline Guest House is a charming double fronted Edwardian house which offers first-class accommodation to guests. It has been tastefully furnished throughout, in classical style, and each of the 12 luxuriously appointed en suite bedrooms has been equipped with a hospitality tray, hair dryer, and other helpful amenities; there are two sitting rooms well-stocked with tourist literature to help you make the most of your stay. A generous full English breakfast is served to guests, and there are numerous eating places within the city where you may enjoy an evening meal. The prices, based on room occupancy with discounts for singles, are exceptionally reasonable.

OPEN ALL YEAR ex Xmas.   NO SMOKING.   S.D. B/A.   CHILDREN WELCOME.   EN SUITE, TV & BEVERAGES IN ROOMS.   B. & B. £16 - 19.

*Mayfield Guest House*

213 YARBOROUGH RD, LINCOLN, LINCS, LN1 3NQ   TEL: (01522) 533732

The Mayfield Guest House is a small, homely Victorian building situated in the old part of Lincoln just a short level walk from the Cathedral and the Castle; it has panoramic views of the Trent Valley. Breakfast is the only meal available at the Mayfield Guest House but there are a number of very good restaurants and pubs serving food locally and your hosts will gladly help you make a choice; the bedrooms are very comfortably furnished and all have excellent facilities. Lincoln is a unique city: its Cathedral is perched high on a hillside and a steep street (with many intriguing little shops and a hand-rail to help your descent) takes you to the main shopping area which has some interesting buildings.

OPEN ALL YEAR.   NO SMOKING.   V STD.   CHILDREN WELCOME.   EN SUITE, BEVERAGES & T.V. IN ROOMS. B. & B. FROM £15.

LOUTH

WICKHAM HOUSE, CHURCH LANE, CONISHOLME, NR LOUTH, LN11 7LX

ETB 3 Crown Commended. Attractive 18th C. cottage in pleasant gardens near Conisholme church. Attractively furnished bedrooms; guest sitting room and library.

TEL: (01507) 358465   OPEN ALL YEAR.   NO SMOKING.   BRING YOUR OWN WINE.   OVER 8S ONLY.   EN SUITE, BEVERAGES & COLOUR T.V. IN ROOMS.   B. & B. FROM £17.50.

MARKET RASON

The Waveney Guest House
WILLINGHAM RD, MARKET RASON, LN8 3DN   TEL: (01673) 843236
ETB 2 Crowns Commended. Tudor-style cottage converted from old stable standing amidst traditional gardens. Meals are home-cooked from fresh, local produce.
OPEN ALL YEAR.   NO SMOKING.   V, S.D. B/A.   CHILDREN & PETS WELCOME.   EN SUITE, TV & BEVERAGES IN ROOMS.   B. & B. FROM £15, D. B. & B. FROM £21. FAMILY RATE FROM £40.

NORTH THORESBY

The Hen House
HAWERBY HALL, NORTH THORESBY, LINCS, DN36 5QL   TEL: (01472) 840278
Handsome Georgian manor house surrounded by gardens, fields and woods which has now been established for several years as a unique venue for women to come 'for reunions, celebrations, holidays, short breaks...or just to unwind'. Wonderful food & numerous walks.
OPEN ALL YEAR.   N/S ALMOST THROUGHOUT.   V, S.D. B/A.   LICENSED.   GOOD DISABLED ACCESS.
CHILDREN WELCOME.   EN SUITE SOME ROOMS.   T.V. IN LOUNGE.   D., B.& B. AROUND £36.

SPALDING

Guy Wells Farm
WHAPLODE, SPALDING, PE12 6TZ   TEL: (01406) 422239
Guy Wells is a lovely Queen Anne family home on a flower farm. Your hosts, Anne and Richard Thompson offer a warm welcome to guests; choice of dinner or light supper.
OPEN ALL YEAR.   NO SMOKING.   V., S.D. B/A.   1 ROOM EN SUITE, WASH BASINS IN ALL ROOMS.   BEVERAGES IN ROOMS.   T.V. IN LOUNGE.   B. & B. FROM £17.

STAMFORD

Birch House
4 LONSDALE RD, STAMFORD, LINCS, PE9 2RW   TEL: (01780) 54876
Family-run house in a quiet location less than 1m from Stamford.
OPEN ALL YEAR.   NO SMOKING.   CHILDREN WELCOME.   BEVERAGES & T.V. IN ROOMS.   B. & B. FROM £14.

CASTERTON TAVERNER MOTOR INN, CASTERTON HILL, STAMFORD, PE9 4DE TEL: (01780) 52441
N/S DINING R. V, S.D. B/A.   CHILDREN WELCOME.   PETS B/A.   EN SUITE, BEVERAGES & T.V. IN ROOMS.

HILLCROFT HOUSE, 25 HIGH ST, EASTON-ON-THE-HILL, NR STAMFORD, LINCS, PE9 3LN TEL: (01780) 55598
NO SMOKING. V, S.D. B/A.   OVER 12s. DOGD B/A.   EN SUITE.   BEVERAGES.   T.V.   B. & B. FROM £14-£18.

The Priory
KETTON, STAMFORD, LINCS.   TEL: (01780) 720215
ETB 3 Crown Highly Commended. Large 16th C. house, meticulously restored in recent years and is now a charming family. The house faces south towards the River Chater and large gardens which are a year-round delight
OPEN ALL YEAR.   N/S Ex. In Guest Lounge.   V, S.D. B/A.   EN SUITE, TV, DD PHONES & BEVERAGES INROOMS.   CHILDREN WELCOME.   WHEELCHAIR ACCESS.   B. & B. AROUND £20.

WASHINGBOROUGH

Washingborough Hall Hotel
CHURCH HILL, WASHINGBOROUGH, LINCS, LN4 1BE   TEL: (01522) 790340
Beautiful country house quietly situated amidst 3 acres of lawns and woodland on the edge of Washingborough village; very good food.
OPEN ALL YEAR. N/S DINING R & SOME BEDRS. V, S.D. B/A.   LICENSED.   CHILDREN WELCOME.   PETS B/A.   EN SUITE, TV & BEVERAGES IN ROOMS.   B. & B. AROUND £45.

RESTAURANTS

GRANTHAM

CLAIRE'S CONCOCTIONS, 15A BRIDGE ST, GRANTHAM, NG31 9AE　TEL: (01476) 76981
Vegetarian restaurant serving 'imaginative and healthy cuisine'.
N/S IN 2 OF 3 ROOMS. S.D. STD or B/A.　LICENSED. DISABLED ACCESS.　CHILDREN.

LOUTH

Mr Chips Fish Restaurant

17-21 ASWELL ST, LOUTH, LINCS, LN11 9BA　TEL: (01507) 603756
Licensed self-service fish & chip restaurant with modern decor & lighting; fully air-conditioned; good amenities for the physically disabled; mother and baby room available.
N/S 40% OF RESTAURANT.　V STD.　LICENSED. DISABLED ACCESS.　CHILDREN WELCOME.

CRUSTYS, PAWN SHOP PASSAGE, LOUTH, LINCS.
OPEN TUES. & WED., FRI. & SAT., 10 - 4.　NO SMOKING.

SLEAFORD

BUMBLES BISTRO, 7 HANDLEY CT MEWS, SOUTHGATE, SLEAFORD　TEL: (01529) 413996
NO SMOKING.　V STD.　LICENSED.　DISABLED ACCESS.　CHILDREN WELCOME.

STAMFORD

CASTERTON TAVERNER MOTOR INN, CASTERTON HILL, STAMFORD, PE9 4DE
Restaurant in two Pullman dining cars which once ran as part of the Yorkshire Pullman.
TEL: (01780) 52441　OPEN ALL DAY.　N/S RESTAURANT.　S.D. B/A.　LICENSED.　CHILDREN WELCOME.

Northamptonshire

ACCOMMODATION

NORTHAMPTON

FORTE POST HOUSE HOTEL NORTHAMPTON, CRICK, NN6 7XR　TEL: (01788) 822101
OPEN ALL YEAR.　50% N/S DINING R & ALL BEDRS.　V STD.　LICENSED.　SOME DISABLED ACCESS.
CHILDREN WELCOME.　PETS B/A.　EN SUITE, TV & BEVERAGES IN ROOMS.

WOLD FARM, OLD, NORTHAMPTON, NORTHANTS, NN6 9RJ　TEL: (01604) 781258
OPEN ALL YEAR.　N/S DINING R & BEDRS.　V, S.D. B/A.　CHILDREN WELCOME. PETS B/A.　EN SUITE.
BEVERAGES.　T.V. IN LOUNGE.　B. &. B.AROUND £20.

WINWICK MANOR, WINWICK, NORTHAMPTON, NN6 7PD
OPEN ALL YEAR.　NO SMOKING.　V B/A.　CHILDREN.　EN SUITE.　B. & B. AROUND £25.

RUSHDEAN

The Old Rectory

45 RUSHDEAN RD, WYMINGTON, NR RUSHDEAN, NORTHANTS　TEL: (01933) 314486

The Old Rectory is a charming red brick Victorian house which stands in private grounds one mile from Rushdean. It has been very comfortably furnished and appointed and there is a lounge with a TV for guests' use. Meals are home-cooked from fresh produce, and special diets can be accommodated by arrangement. You are in a beautiful part of the world at Wymington: there is easy access to Peterborough, Bedford and Northampton, and there is a swimming pool and leisure centre at Rushdean.
OPEN ALL YEAR.　NO SMOKING.　S.D. B/A.　CHILDREN WELCOME.　WHEELCHAIR ACCESS.　TV & BEVERAGES IN ROOMS.　B. & B. £13.50.

WELLINGBOROUGH

High View Hotel

156 MIDLAND RD, WELLINGBOROUGH, NORTHANTS TEL: (01933) 278733 FAX: (01933) 225948
Situated in a quiet tree-lined area between station & town centre. Pleasant bar.
OPEN ALL YEAR.   N/S DINING R.   V B/A.   CHILDREN & PETS WELCOME.   EN SUITE, TV & BEVERAGES IN
ROOMS. LICENSED. B. & B. FROM £20 (reduced w/e rates).

YARDLEY GOBION

OLD WHARF FARM, YARDLEY GOBION, NR TOWCESTER, NN12 7UE   TEL: (01908) 542454
OPEN ALL YEAR.   N/S DINING R, BEDRS & MOST PUBLIC AREAS.   V B/A.   CHILDREN WELCOME.   PETS
B/A.   BEVERAGES.   B. & B. AROUND £20.

RESTAURANTS & PUBS

BRIGSTOCK

HILL FARM HERBS, PARK WLK, BRIGSTOCK, NORTHANTS, NN14 3HH TEL: (01536) 373694
NO SMOKING.   WHEELCHAIR ACCESS.   CHILDREN WELCOME.

NORTHAMPTON

Debenhams

THE DRAPERY, NORTHAMPTON, NORTHANTS, NN1 2EZ   TEL: (01604) 34391
Pavilion, a friendly self-service coffee shop serving lunches, snacks & hot & cold drinks.
OPEN STORE HOURS.   NO SMOKING. V STD.   CHILDREN WELCOME.   CREDIT/DEBIT CARDS.

THE MANNA HOUSE, ST GILES ST, NORTHAMPTON   TEL: (01604) 22666
NO SMOKING.   SOME DISABLED ACCESS.   CHILDREN WELCOME.

THURNING

THE TITHE BARN AT THURNING, HOME FARM, THURNING, NR OUNDLE, PE8 5RF
NO SMOKING.   V STD.   WHEELCHAIR ACCESS.   CHILDREN PLAY AREA.   CREDIT CARDS

TWYWELL

THE OLD FRIAR, TWYWELL, NR KETTERING, NN14 3AH   TEL: (01832) 2625
N/S 1 DINING AREA.   V STD. LICENSED. WHEELCHAIR ACCESS.   CHILDREN.

Nottinghamshire

ACCOMMODATION

NEWARK

THE APPLETON HOTEL, 73 APPLETONGATE, NEWARK, NG24 1LN (0636) 71616
OPEN ALL YEAR. NO SMOKING. V STD.   LICENSED.   CHILDREN WELCOME.   EN SUITE, BEVER-
AGES, T.V. & DIRECT DIAL PHONES IN ROOMS.   CREDIT CARDS.   B. & B. FROM £25.

NOTTINGHAM

Laurel Farm

BROWNS LANE, STANTON-on-thE-WOLDS, NOTTINGHAM, NG12 5BL TEL: (0115) 937 3488
Laurel Farm is a lovely old farmhouse which stands in 4 acres of paddock and garden in
Stanton-on-the-Wolds near Nottingham. Only fresh local produce and home-laid free-range
eggs are used in cooking, and an evening meal is available by prior arrangement. The
proprietress, Mrs Moffat, has lots of friendly pets of her own, so visiting animals are housed
in the stables. Families are very welcome and your hostess will gladly babysit.
OPEN ALL YEAR.   NO SMOKING.   V, B/A.   CHILDREN WELCOME.   2 EN SUITE ROOMs.   BEVERAGES &
COLOUR TV IN ROOMS.   B. & B. FROM £13.

THE LUCIEVILLE HOTEL, 349 DERBY RD, NOTTINGHAM, NG7 2DZ   TEL: (0115) 9787389 FAX: (0115) 979 0346
Executive-class hotel 1m from city centre & a short drive from exit 25 of the M1
OPEN ALL YEAR.   NO SMOKING.   V STD.   LICENSED.   DISABLED ACCESS.   EN SUITE, BEVERAGES, T.V. , PHONE & HAIRDRIER IN ROOMS.   VISA, ACCESS.

Nottingham Moat House

MANSFIELD RD, NOTTINGHAM, NOTTS, NG5 2BT   TEL: (0115) 960 2621
The Nottingham Moat House is a modern, business-class 172-bedroomed hotel which is conveniently situated less than a mile from the city centre and has free parking for 300 cars. Each of the comfortably furnished en suite bedrooms has been tastefully decorated and equipped with a range of amenities including colour TV, in-house movie channel, radios, trouser-presses and beverage-making facilities; 50% of the rooms are non-smoking. A wide range of delicious meals are served in the restaurants, one of which is a completely smoke-free a la carte dining room and two of which have smoke-free areas.
OPEN ALL YEAR.   N/S 1 RESTAURANT, PARTS OF 2 OTHER RESTAURANTS & 50% OF BEDROOMS.   V STD, S.D. B/A.   DISABLED ACCESS.   CHILDREN WELCOME.   EN SUITE, BEVERAGES & T.V. IN ROOMS. ACCESS, VISA, AMEX, DINERS.   B. & B. AROUND £70.

SOUTHWELL

Old National School Hotel

NOTTINGHAM RD, SOUTHWELL, NG25 0LG TEL: (01636) 814360
Former Victorian school which has been tastefully converted into a charming guest house; some of the beamed bedrooms have four-posters.
OPEN ALL YEAR. N/S DINING R & LOUNGE.   V, S.D. B/A.   DISABLED ACCESS.   CHILDREN WELCOME. EN SUITE & T.V. IN ROOMS.   B. & B. AROUND £24.

TROWELL

Church Farm Guest House

1 NOTTINGHAM RD, TROWELL, NOTTS, NG9 3PA   TEL: (0115) 930 1637
300 year old former farmhouse amidst pleasant, mature gardens in a prominent position on the the A609 overlooking Trowell village. Private parties & functions also accommodated. The food is excellent recent winners of the Salon Culinaire Bronze Medal).
OPEN ALL YEAR.   NO SMOKING. V, S.D. B/A.   CHILDREN WELCOME.   T.V.   B. & B. AROUND £20.

WORKSOP

Duncan Wood Lodge Guest House

CARBURTON, NR WORKSOP, S80 3BP TEL: (01909) 483614
Former estate lodge in the heart of Sherwood Forest in an acre of secluded gardens. Tastefully modernised offering comfortable accommodation in well-equipped rooms.
OPEN ALL YEAR. N/S DINING R & SOME BEDRS.   V, S.D. B/A.   CHILDREN & PETS.   B. & B. around £19.

RESTAURANTS

CALVERTON

Painters Paradise Restaurant

PATCHINGS FARM ART Centre, OXTON RD, CALVERTON, NG14 6NU TEL: (0115) 965 3479
Unique enterprise on a 38 acre rural site consisting of a conversion of farm buildings with two galleries; art, pottery and textiles studios; a gift shop, and a restaurant.
OPEN 9 A.M. TO 10 P.M. (GARDENS CLOSE AT 6 P.M.).   NO SMOKING.   V, DIAB & ADDITIVE-FREE DIETS B/A.   LICENSED.   DISABLED ACCESS.   CREDIT CARDS.

MANSFIELD

Debenhams

40 FOUR SEASONS CENTE, MANSFIELD, NOTTS. TEL: (01623) 35311
Pavilion, a friendly self-service coffee shop serving lunches, snacks and drinks.
OPEN STORE HOURS.   NO SMOKING.   V STD.   DISABLED ACCESS.   CHILDREN.   CREDIT CARDS.

NEWARK

Gannets Café/Bistrot

35 CASTLEGATE, NEWARK, NOTTS, NG24 1AZ   TEL: (01636) 702066

Gannets was established in 1979 by Hilary and David Bower in an attractive Grade II listed Georgian building overlooking the castle on the main road through Newark. Over 16 years later they are still going strong and a second generation of Nottinghamshire diners can enjoy morning coffee, lunches and afternoon teas in the downstairs café throughout the week (a garden room extension is planned for completion by March '95) with a choice of wonderful home-made cakes and 'adventurous' salads (made from more than 25 ingredients); *al fresco* dining is available, weather permitting. Upstairs in the bistrot, lunchtime and evening diners can enjoy a wider choice of dishes. Prepared by Colin White, who used to be head chef at the Sharrow Bay Hotel, a typical menu selection might feature green herb soup with Parmesan croutons, followed by Jacob Mutton Chops with pot barley risotto and apricots, and a choice of desserts wuch as caramel cream pot with pecan biscuits. Everything on the menu has been home-made from fresh (always) and additive-free (wherever possible) ingredients.
CAFÉ OPEN 9.30 - 4.30 DAILY. BISTROT OPEN TUES. TO SAT., 12 NOON - 2.30 & 6.30 - 9.30 NO SMOKING. V STD. LICENSED. CHILDREN WELCOME.

NOTTINGHAM

Debenhams

LONG ROW, NOTTINGHAM, NOTTS. TEL: (0115) 947 5577

Springles, a friendly self-service restaurant serving popular light lunches, snacks and a wide range of hot and cold drinks.
OPEN STORE HOURS. NO SMOKING. V STD. DISABLED ACCESS. CHILDREN WELCOME.   CREDIT/ DEBIT CARDS.

Debenham's Intermission Coffee Shop

FLYING HORSE WALK, NOTTINGHAM

Intermission, a friendly self-service coffee shop serving popular light lunches, snacks and a wide range of hot and cold drinks.
OPEN STORE HOURS. NO SMOKING. V STD. DISABLED ACCESS. CHILDREN WELCOME.   CREDIT/ DEBIT CARDS.

Maxine's Salad Table

56-58 UPPER PARLIAMENT ST, NOTTINGHAM, NOTTS. TEL: (0115) 947 3622

Vegetarian restaurant serving home-made food; good vegan options.
75 SEATS. OPEN 9A.M. - 5P.M. 75% N/S (SEP. ROOM).   V, VE STD. LICENSED. CHILDREN WELCOME.

PUBS & WINE BARS

SCAFTWORTH

KING WILLIAM, SCAFTWORTH (OFF A361), NOTTS. TEL: (10302) 710292
N/S IN ONE ROOM.

Cumbria & the North West

Cumbria

ACCOMMODATION

ALSTON

Loaning Head Wholefood Vegetarian Guesthouse
GARRIGILL, ALSTON, CUMBRIA   TEL: (01434) 381013
17th C. stone barn; woodburning stove in the lounge with its exposed beams and splendid views; well-stocked bar (including organic & vegan wines). Home-baked bread.
OPEN ALL YEAR.   NO SMOKING.   V EXC.   OVER 2S WELCOME.   LICENSED.   GROUND FLOOR BATH & BEDROOM.   BEVERAGES IN BEDR.   B. & B. FROM £27.50

SHIELD HILL HOUSE, GARRIGILL, ALSTON, CA9 3EX   TEL: (01434) 381238
ETB 2 Crowns. Stone-built former farmhouse with views in the North Pennines.
OPEN ALL YEAR Ex. Xmas.   NO SMOKING.   CHILDREN WELCOME.   EN SUITE & BEVERAGES IN ROOMS.   TV LOUNGE.   CREDIT CARDS.   B. & B. AROUND £19.

AMBLESIDE

Borrans Park Hotel
BORRANS ROAD, AMBLESIDE, CUMBRIA, LA22 0EN   TEL: (015394) 33454
Exceptionally comfortable and well-appointed hotel in grounds. Superbly furnished bedrooms; *de-luxe* rooms have a four-poster bed and a bubbling spa bath! Excellent food.
OPEN ALL YEAR.   N/S BEDRS & DINING R.   V, S.D. B/A.   LICENSED.   DISABLED ACCESS.   CHILDREN.   EN SUITE, BEVERAGES & TV IN ROOMS.   CREDIT CARDS.   B. & B. AROUND £30.

Borwick Lodge
OUTGATE, HAWKSHEAD, AMBLESIDE, CUMBRIA, LA22 0PU   TEL: (015394) 36332

ETB 2 Crown Highly Commended. Twice winners of the "Award for Accommodation of the Highest Standards". A leafy driveway entices you to what must be one of the most enchantingly situated houses in the Lake District, a very special 17th C. country residence in an elevated position with magnificent panoramic lake and mountain views, quietly secluded in beautiful gardens. Ideally placed in the heart of the Lakes and close to the pretty village of Hawkshead with its good choice of restaurants and inns, the surrounding fells and countryside provide excellent opportunities for enjoyable walking. The beautiful en suite bedrooms include 'Special Occasions' and 'Romantic Breaks', two king-size four-poster rooms. Prize-winning home-made breads. Linda and Alan Bleasdale welcome you to their haven of peace and tranquillity in this most beautiful corner of England.
OPEN ALL YEAR.   NO SMOKING.   S.D. ON REQUEST.   OVER 8s ONLY.   EN SUITE, TV & BEVERAGES IN BEDROOMS.   B. & B. FROM £18.

COMPSTON HOUSE HOTEL, COMPSTON RD, AMBLESIDE, CUMBRIA TEL: (015394) 32305
Family-run hotel with superb views of park & fells. Recommended by major guides.
OPEN ALL YEAR.   N/S DINING R & 2 BEDRS.   V, S.D. B/A.   LICENSED.   CHILDREN: OVER 5S ONLY.   EN SUITE, BEVERAGES & TV IN ROOMS.   B. & B. AROUND £20.

Cross Parrock
5 WATERHEAD TERRACE, AMBLESIDE, CUMBRIA, LA22 0HA   TEL: (015394) 32372
Lakeland stone guest house 1 min walk from the shores of Lake Windermere. Comfortably furnished, and with prettily decorated bedrooms. Imaginative home-cooked meals.
OPEN ALL YEAR.   NO SMOKING.   V B/A.   CHILDREN WELCOME.   BEVERAGES IN ROOMS.   T.V. IN LOUNGE.   B. & B. AROUND £16.

GREY FRIAR LODGE, CLAPPERSGATE, AMBLESIDE, CUMBRIA TEL: (015394) 33158
N/S DINING R & BEDRS.   LICENSED.   OVER 12'S ONLY.   EN SUITE, BEVERAGES & TV.   B. & B. AROUND £40..

Horseshoe Hotel

ROTHAY RD, AMBLESIDE, CUMBRIA, LA22 0EE   TEL: (015394) 32000
Pleasant 2 star hotel close to the centre of Ambleside. Magnificent mountain views. Comfortable and tastefully decorated bedrooms. Excellent home-cooked food.
OPEN ALL YEAR.   N/S DINING R, SOME BEDRS & OTHER PUBLIC AREAS.   V STD, S.D. B/A.   LICENSED.
CHILDREN   PETS B/A.   MOST ROOMS EN SUITE.   BEVERAGES & T.V. IN ROOMS.

Riverside Lodge Country House

NEAR ROTHAY BRIDGE, AMBLESIDE, CUMBRIA, LA22 0EH   TEL: (015394) 34208
Beautiful ivy-clad building in a splendid riverside setting; self-catering also available.
OPEN ALL YEAR.   N/S ALL PUBLIC AREAS.   V B/A.   LICENSED.   CHILDREN WELCOME.   PETS IN
COTTAGES.   EN SUITE, TV & BEVERAGES IN ROOMS.   CREDIT CARDS.   B. & B. AROUND £27.

ROTHAY GARTH HOTEL, ROTHAY RD, AMBLESIDE, CUMBRIA, LA22 0EE   TEL: (015394) 32217
Fine hotel, beautifully constructed of Lakeland stone and set in attractive gardens.
OPEN ALL YEAR.   N/S ex. In Bar.   V STD.   LICENSED.   DISABLED ACCESS.   CHILDREN WELCOME.
PETS B/A.   EN SUITE, TV & BEVERAGES IN ROOMS.   B. & B. AROUND £35.

Rothay Manor Hotel

ROTHAY BRIDGE, AMBLESIDE, CUMBRIA, LA22 0EH   TEL: (015394) 33605
Hotel offering, in addition to tourist accommodation, a number of winter courses and special weekends (e.g. 'Music in Imperial Russia'), and free use of local leisure centre.
N/S DINING R & 1 LOUNGE.   V B/A.   LICENSED.   CHILDREN.   DISABLED ACCESS.   EN SUITE, TV &
BEVERAGES IN ALL BEDROOMS.   CREDIT CARDS.   B. & B. FROM £54

 Rowanfield Country House

KIRKSTONE RD, AMBLESIDE, CUMBRIA, LA22 9ET   TEL: (015394) 33686

Rowanfield is a beautiful period country home which stands in its own gardens amidst peaceful countryside with panoramic views of Lake Windermere and the surrounding mountains. The house has been carefully restored by its current owners who have complemented the original features of the house - such as its window seats, flagged floors and pine doors - with lots of Laura Ashley and Liberty fabrics. Bedrooms are comfortable and well-appointed with power showers, excellent beds and heated towel rails; there is a cosy guest lounge with a woodburning stove. The food is outstandingly good (your host, Philip Butcher, is renowned in the area for his culinary skills); everything is prepared from the finest of fresh, local produce. Evening meals are served by candlelight with gentle background classical music. Another superb meal is served in the morning with all the little extras that are so typical of Philip and Jane's standards; freshly squeezed orange juice, home-made bread rolls and home-made marmalade.Rowanfield is an excellent base from which to explore the Lake District, and additionally many good walks begin from the front door.
OPEN Feb. - Dec.   NO SMOKING.   V, S.D. B/A.   OVER 5S ONLY.   PETS WELCOME.   WHEELCHAIR ACCESS.   EN
SUITE, TV & BEVERAGES IN ROOMS.   CREDIT CARDS.   B. & B. FROM £23, D., B. & B. FROM £35.

RYDAL HOLME, RYDAL, AMBLESIDE, CUMBRIA.   TEL: (015394) 33110
NO SMOKING.   V B/A.   EN SUITE.   BEVERAGES IN T.V. LOUNGE.   B. & B. FROM £20.

SUMMER HILL, HAWKSHEAD HILL, AMBLESIDE, LA22 0PP TEL: (019666) 311
OPEN Mar. - Dec.   NO SMOKING.   V B/A.   OVER 10S.   EN SUITE, BEVERAGES & T.V.   B. & B. FROM £19.

Swingletrees Guest House

LAKE RD, AMBLESIDE, CUMBRIA, LA22 0DF   TEL: (015394) 34097
Swingletrees is a small family-run guest house in the popular village of Ambleside. Accommodation is in comfortable en suite rooms, each of which enjoys lovely views of the village and countryside beyond, and there is a residents' lounge with an open fire in chilly weather. There is a choice of English or Continental breakfasts, and packed lunches are also available; at 9.30 p.m. guests are welcome sample Mrs Bradley's delicious home-made confectionery, served with tea or coffee. Ambleside is an excellent base from which to enjoy your Lakeland holiday.
NO SMOKING.   OPEN Mar. - Nov.   S.D. B/A.   CHILDREN WELCOME.   DOGS B/A.   EN SUITE, TV & BEVERAGES
IN ROOMS.   B. & B. £16 - 18. Reduced rates for children.

Yewfield Guest House

HAWKSHEAD HILL, HAWKSHEAD, AMBLESIDE, LA22 0PR   TEL: (015394) 36765

ETB 2 Crown Commended. Situated in 25 acres of its own grounds, this impressive house with its Gothic architecture was formerly an award-winning hotel; it stands in an elevated position with panoramic views over the Vale of Esthwaite. Although now a private residence, it is a peaceful retreat in the heart of the Lakes and there are a few letting rooms for bed and breakfast on a vegetarian basis. The double and twin rooms are appointed to a very high standard, and each has an en suite bath and shower, colour TV, radio and beverage-making facility; there is a lounge and library area for guests' use. Breakfast is a wholefood continental buffet and includes fresh fruits, mueslis, cereals, home-baked breads, toast, preserves, coffee and teas. Although Yewfield does not serve an evening meal, there are two vegetarian restauants within a few miles of the house.

OPEN ALL YEAR.   NO SMOKING.   V EXC, VE, S.D, ORG, WH STD.   OVER 10s WELCOME.   EN SUITE, TV & BEVERAGES IN ROOMS.   B. & B. FROM £22.50.

APPLEBY

Appleby Manor Hotel

ROMAN RD, APPLEBY-IN-WESTMORLAND, CA16 6JB   TEL: (07683) 51571

Comfortable hotel set in private wooded grounds; swimming pool, sauna and solarium avail. All food prepared from fresh ingredients.

OPEN ALL YEAR.   N/S DINING R. V STD; DIAB., S.D. B/A.   LICENSED.   DISABLED ACCESS GOOD: SOME GROUND FLOOR BEDROOMS AVAIL.   CHILDREN WELCOME.   EN SUITE, BEVERAGES & TV IN BEDROOMS.

 THE FRIARY, BATTLEBARROW, APPLEBY, CA16 6XT   TEL: (017683) 52702
OPEN ALL YEAR.   NO SMOKING.   CORDON VERT V, DEMI-V, DIAB, VE, ARTHRITIC, GLUTEN-FREE & S.D. B/A.   LICENSED.   OVER 6s   EN SUITE & BEVERAGES.   T.V. IN LOUNGE.   B. & B. AROUND £20.

ARNSIDE

 STONEGATE G.H., THE PROMENADE, ARNSIDE, LA5 DAA TEL: (01524) 761171
OPEN Feb. - Dec.   NO SMOKING. V, VE, STD. CHILDREN. BEVERAGES.   T.V.   B. & B.AROUND £17.

BASSENTHWAITE LAKE

The Pheasant Inn

BASSENTHWAITE LAKE, NR COCKERMOUTH, CUMBRIA, CA13 9YE   TEL: (017687) 76234

The Pheasant Inn was a farm in the 18th C. but has been a hotel since 1826. A listed building, it has retained all its period character including the original old bar with its mellow brown walls, and oak beamed dining room; the proprietors have decided to further eschew 20th C. discomforts by deciding not to have television or piped music and smoking has never been allowed in the dining room - thus ensuring that the timeless atmosphere of the inn and the peacefulness of its tranquil surroundings in the countryside between Bassenthwaite Lake and Thornthwaite Forest, are unmarred. The hotel has been furnished in an elegant, but unobstrusive style: each of the 20 en suite bedrooms is comfortable and pleasingly decorated, and a log fire blazes in the lounge inglenook in cooler weather; the food is excellent, and packed lunches and afternoon teas are also available. Bassenthwaite has been designated a "Quiet Lake" by the National Park Authority and as such is an important wild life centre; those in search of sailing, boating, fishing, walking and other outdoor activities will find numerous opportunities to pursue them, while those seeking nothing more than peace, quiet, an armchair by the fire and the prospect of a delicious dinner in the evening will also find that they have picked the right destination.

OPEN ALL YEARex Xmas.   N/S DINING R & 1 RESIDENT'S LOUNGE.   V STD.   LICENSED.   DISABLED ACCESS. PETS B/A.   EN SUITE ALL ROOMS.   B. & B. FROM £52.

BORROWDALE

 **Youdale Knot**

MANESTY, KESWICK, CUMBRIA, CA12 5UG.   TEL: (017687) 77216   FAX: (017687) 77384
Country house offering B. & B. or room only in en suite smoke-free rooms. Heart of the
Lake District. Beautiful views.
OPEN ALL YEAR.   NO SMOKING.   CHILDREN WELCOME.   EN SUITE, BEVERAGES & TV IN ROOMS.   B. &
Continental B. £17.50.

BRAMPTON

CRACROP FARM, CRACROP, KIRKCAMBECK TEL: (016978) 245
OPEN ALL YEAR   NO SMOKING.   CHILDREN.   EN SUITE , BEVERAGES & T.V. B. & B. AROUND £20..

Hullerbank

TALKIN, BRAMPTON, CUMBRIA, CA8 1LB   TEL: (016977) 46668

Hullerbank is a 17th C. Georgian farmhouse set well
back from the road and standing in its own grounds
complete with orchard and gardens; adjoining the house
is 14 acres of pastureland on which your hosts, Sheila
and Brian, keep a small flock of commercial sheep. "A
peaceful retreat" is how one guest recently described
Hullerbank - an apt description given its situation in
unspoilt countryside, notwithstanding its proximity to
such places of interest as Hadrian's Wall, Talkin Tarn
Country Park and the Lake District (just one hour's drive away). The house itself has been
comfortably furnished and tastefully decorated: an open fire supplements the central
heating in chilly weather and each of the three bedrooms has en suite or private bath
facilities, together with a range of other helpful amenities including an electric under-blan-
ket. Good home-cooking prepared from fresh, home-grown ingredients is served in the
dining room - the speciality being home-produced lamb - and packed lunches are also
available.
OPEN ALL YEAR Ex. Xmas & New Year.   NO SMOKING. V, S.D. B/A.   OVER 10S ONLY.   EN SUITE/PRIVATE
BATH & BEVERAGES IN ROOMS.   TV LOUNGE.   B. & B. £17-17.50.

BUTTERMERE VALLEY

Pickett Howe

BRACKENTHWAITE, BUTTERMERE VALLEY, CUMBRIA, CA13 9UY TEL: (01900) 85444

ETB De Luxe Grading. After a successful first two years
at Pickett Howe, a '17th C. Lakeland statesman's long
house' David and Dani Edwards, (ex of the highly acclaimed Low Hall) are looking forward to welcoming a
third season of guests to their lovely home in the beautiful
Buttermere Valley. With characteristic flair and meticu-
lous attention to detail the Edwards have clearly taken
great pleasure in decorating and furnishing their lovely
home: bedrooms are individually styled and Laura Ashley
fabrics, lace bedspreads, and elegant furniture (the bed-
steads are restored Victorian) recreate the 17th & 18th centuries while power showers and
whirlpool baths wash away the cares of the 20th; the original features, such as mullioned
windows, flagged floors and oak beams have been retained and add to Pickett Howe's
already considerable charm. Dani's culinary skills are as exceptional as ever; and the
5-course evening menu includes such delights as Spiced Apple Soup, Fennel, Lemon and
Walnut in a Gougere Pastry Ring and Juniper Pudding. Crystal, candlelight and chamber
music all combine to provide the all important sense of occasion which is the hallmark of
dining in the Edwards' home.
OPEN MARCH TO NOV.   NO SMOKING. V STD, S.D. B/A.   LICENSED.   OVER 10S WELCOME.   EN SUITE
& BEVERAGES IN ROOMS.   T.V. AVAILABLE ON REQUEST.

CALDBECK

High Greenrigg House

NR CALDBECK, CUMBRIA, CA7 8HD   TEL: (016998) 430

Carefully restored stone-built 17th C. farmhouse at the foot of the Caldbeck Fells. Ideal centre for fell-walkers. Original features include flagged floor and exposed beams; open fires. Excellent food prepared from fresh local produce.

N/S MOST OF HOUSE. S.D. B/A. LICENSED. DISABLED ACCESS. CHILDREN WELCOME. PETS B/A. EN SUITE IN ROOMS. BEVERAGES IN T.V. LOUNGE. B. & B. AROUND £20.

CARLISLE

BANK END FARM, BEWCASTLE, ROADHEAD, CA6 6NU TEL: (016977) 48644

Luxurious, private suite for two with twin-bedded room in warm, peaceful farmhouse. Delicious home-cooking including bread, cakes, soups.

NO SMOKING. B.Y.O. WINE. EN SUITE, BEVERAGES & TV IN SITTING ROOM.   B. & B. AROUND £23.

COCKERMOUTH

Graythwaite

LOWESWATER, COCKERMOUTH, CUMBRIA, CA13 0SU   TEL: (01946) 861555

12 acre small holding ½ mile from road, with beautiful fell views. Self-catering also avail.

OPEN Mar. - Nov. NO SMOKING. S.D. CHILDREN WELCOME. 1 dble EN SUITE, BEVERAGES. B. & B. FROM £13.

The Rook

CASTLEGATE, COCKERMOUTH, CUMBRIA, CA13 9EEN TEL: (01900) 822441

Excellent totally smoke-free accommodation in Cockermouth.

OPEN MOST OF THE YEAR. NO SMOKING. V, S.D. B/A. BEVERAGES. TV.

CONISTON

Arrowfield Country Guest House

LITTLE ARROW, TORVER, CONISTON, CUMBRIA, LA21 8AU   TEL: (015394) 41741

Attractive Victorian house amidst lovely gardens with beautiful country views; spacious lounge and cosy dining room with open fires. A hearty British breakfast or Continental with hot croissants and patisseries, home-made bread, jams, marmalades and honey from own hives. Lovely walks.

OPEN Mar. - Nov. inc. N/S DINING R & BEDRS. V, S.D. B/A. LICENSED. OVER 3S ONLY. EN SUITE IN 2 BEDROOMS. TV & BEVERAGES IN BEDROOMS. B. & B. £16-22.

Beech Tree

YEWDALE ROAD, CONISTON, CUMBRIA, LA21 8DX   TEL: (015394) 41717
OPEN ALL YEAR. NO SMOKING. V STD, VE, S.D. B/A. WH. OVER 6 yrs ONLY. PETS B/A. SOME EN SUITEROOMS. BEVERAGES. T.V. IN LOUNGE. B. & B. FROM £16.50.

BLACK BECK COTTAGE, EAST SIDE OF THE LAKE, CONISTON   TEL: (015394) 41607
OPEN Apr. - Oct. NO SMOKING. V B/A. DISABLED ACCESS. CHILDREN WELCOME. BEVERAGES & TV IN ROOMS. B. & B. FROM £14.

Coniston Lodge Hotel

CONISTON, CUMBRIA, LA21 8HH   TEL: (015394) 41201

RAC Highly Acclaimed, ETB Highly Commended. AA 'Premier select' Status. Coniston Lodge Hotel is managed by Anthony and Elizabeth Robinson - who are the 3rd generation of hoteliers to have been looking after visitors since 1911! It offers a high standard of accommodation and comfort - bedrooms are all attractively decorated and furnished, one with a four-poster - and the dining room and lounge are very much of the country-cottage school of interior design, with lots of antique accessories and bits and pieces to

add to their charm. Food is of especial importance at Coniston Lodge where traditional English and local dishes are presented with originality and flair (dine on freshly caught Consiton Char, for instance - a fish peculiar to Coniston and 3 other lakes, or set yourself up for the day with a stupendous breakfast in which local Cumberland sausage, and wholemeal toast and croissants are just some of the attractions). Coniston is just far enough away from the bustle of the centre of Lakeland to provide a base for a truly relaxing holiday. It is a haven for ramblers - and your hosts, who are experienced fell-walkers, will happily give you guidance and advice. **RAC Small Hotel of the year 1992 (Northern Region).**
OPEN ALL YEAR ex. Xmas.   NO SMOKING.   V, DIAB, B/A.   LICENSED.   UNDER 10S B/A.
EN SUITE, BEVERAGES & T.V. IN ROOMS.   CREDIT CARDS.   B. & B. FROM £26.

OAKLANDS B. & B., YEWDALE ROAD, CONISTON, LA21 8DX TEL: (015394) 41245
OPEN ALL YEAR.   NO SMOKING.   BEVERAGES & T.V. IN ROOMS.   B. & B. AROUND £16

THWAITE COTTAGE, WATERHEAD, CONISTON, LA21 8AJ   TEL: (015394) 41367
17th C. Lakeland farmhouse; 2 acres of gardens ½m E Coniston village.
OPEN Feb. - Nov.   NO SMOKING.   V, S.D. B/A.   CHILDREN WELCOME.   BEVERAGES & T.V. IN SITTING ROOM.   B. & B. AROUND £18.

DENT

Stone Close Tea Shop & Guest House
MAIN ST, DENT, NR SEDBERGH, CUMBRIA.   TEL: (015396) 25231
Stone Close is a 17th C. listed building which was once two farm cottages and still retains much of its original character with exposed beams, flagged floors and two cast-iron ranges. The tea shop is open for most of the year and provides delicious home-made meals, cakes and pastries which have been prepared from fresh and wholesome ingredients. B. & B. is also available in three comfortable cottage-style rooms which have each been equipped with wash hand basins and beverages. Dent is situated within the National Park - so Stone Close is an ideal base from which to enjoy a walking or touring holiday within the beautiful Yorkshire Dales.
OPEN Mar. - Dec. inc.   NO SMOKING.   V, WH.   CHILDREN & PETS WELCOME.   LICENSED.   BEVERAGES.   B. & B. FROM £14.50.

GLENRIDDING

Moss Crag Guest House
GLENRIDDING, CUMBRIA, CA11 0PA   TEL: (017684) 82500

Moss Crag, a family-run guest house, is a charming stone-built house situated opposite Glenridding Beck in the heart of the Lake District hills and fells. Just 300 yards away is the hauntingly beautiful Lake Ullswater and, although you can fish, sail, canoe or windsurf thereon, it is best enjoyed (I feel) by just looking at it - perhaps the fishermen have got it right. Freshly prepared food is a feature of a stay at Moss Crag where a typical evening menu would feature Parton Bree (Crab Soup) followed by Beef and Noodle Bake or Spinach and Leek Pancakes and a delicious home-made dessert such as Citrus Condé or Coffee Fudge Pudding. Morning coffee, light lunch and afternoon tea are also served.
OPEN Feb. - Nov. Inc.   NO SMOKING.   V, S.D. DIAB B/A.   LICENSED.   CHILDREN WELCOME.   EN SUITE IN SOME ROOMS.   BEVERAGES & T.V. IN ROOMS.   B. & B. FROM £15.50 - 19.50.   D., B. & B. FROM £28 - 32. ALL INCLUSIVE   D., B. & B. BREAKS AVAILABLE FROM NOV. TO MARCH INCL., EX DEC., JAN. 10% REDUCTION ON B. & B. ONLY FOR WEEKLY STAY IN SUMMER.

GRANGE-OVER-SANDS

Mayfields
3 MAYFIELD TERR., KENTS BANK RD, GRANGE-over-SANDS, LA11 7DW TEL: (015395) 34730
Small, charming, well-appointed guest house, recommended for good, home-cooking and hospitality. Non-residents welcome for lunch and dinner.
OPEN ALL YEAR (EX. XMAS).   NO SMOKING.   S.D. *'where possible'*   CHILDREN WELCOME.   TV & BEVERAGES IN ROOMS.   B. & B. £16.50, D. £7.50 - 10.95.

ABBOT HALL, KENTS BANK, CUMBRIA, LA11 7BG   TEL: (015395) 32896
OPEN ALL YEAR.   NO SMOKING. V, S.D. B/A.   DISABLED ACCESS.   CHILDREN WELCOME.   EN SUITE
& BEVERAGES IN ROOMS. T.V. IN LOUNGES. B. & B. AROUND £22.

GRASMERE

Lancrigg Vegetarian Country House Hotel

EASEDALE, GRASMERE, CUMBRIA, LA22 9QN   TEL: (015394) 35317
Beautiful house in 27 acres of gardens overlooking Easedale; charmingly decorated.
First-rate vegetarian cuisine.
OPEN ALL YEAR.   N/S LOUNGE AND DINING R.   V EXC, VE, S.D. B/A.   LICENSED.   DISABLED ACCESS.
CHILDREN.   PETS B/A.   MOST ROOMS EN SUITE.   BEVERAGES & T.V. D., B. & B. AROUND £40.

Woodland Crag Guest House

HOW HEAD LANE, GRASMERE, CUMBRIA.   TEL: (015394) 35351

Woodland Crag is a Lakeland country house which
stands in beautful, landscaped gardens enjoying panoramic views over Grasmere Lake. It has been carefully
renovated and, while retaining much of its Victorian
charm now offers every modern facility to ensure guests'
comfort: all the bedrooms have been attractively furnished and have lake or fell views, and most have en
suite facilities. Your hosts, John and Ann Taylor, offer a
full Enlglish breakfast to guests, and packed lunchesare
available on request. You are just a short stroll from
Dove Cottage, and numerous beautiful walks radiate
from the house.

OPEN Feb. - Nov.   NO SMOKING.   S.D. B/A.   OVER 12s WELCOME.   EN SUITE, TV & BEVERAGES IN ROOMS.
B. & B. FROM £24.

HAWKSHE AD

 FOXGLOVES, HAWKSHEAD, CUMBRIA, LA22 ONR   TEL: (015394) 36352
Private house with beautiful views on the edge of picturesque Hawkshead.
OPEN ALL YEAR.   NO SMOKING.   V STD.   CHILDREN: OVER 12S ONLY.   1 EN SUITE ROOM.   BEVERAGES IN
ROOMS.   T.V. IN LOUNGE.   B. & B. AROUND £16.

Silverholme

GRAYTHWAITE, HAWKSHEAD, CUMBRIA, LA12 8AZ   TEL: (015395) 31332

Set in an elevated position on the West side
of Lake Windermere, this unique Georgian
mansion house, stands in its own lovely
grounds and is approached by a long azalea
and rhododendron lined drive. Retaining
most of its original features, the beautifully
proportioned rooms have been furnished in
traditional style and the atmosphere is par-
ticularly welcoming and relaxing. Each of the large, comfortable, centrally heated bedrooms have mahogany beds, en suite facilities and enjoy spectacular views of the lake.
Meals are served in a charming dining room overlooking the colourful gardens and lake,
and there is also an elegant lounge with a log fire. Close to the picturesque village of
Hawkshead, Silverholme is an ideal base from which to explore the Lake District.
OPEN ALL YEAR.   NO SMOKING   V STD.   BYO WINE.   EN SUITE & BEVERAGES IN ROOMS.   B. & B. FROM
£19.50, D. £9.50.

IREBY

Woodlands Country Guest House

IREBY, CUMBRIA, CA5 1EX   TEL: (016973) 71791   FAX: (016973) 71482
Woodlands is a charming former Victorian vicarage which stands in the unpoilt Cumbrian
village of Ireby, some 4 miles north of Bassenthwaite; situated in its own grounds at the
edge of the village, it enjoys magnificent open views over the tranquil northern fells. Each
of the eight en suite bedrooms is centrally heated and has a range of helpful facilities; there
is also a residents'bar and a lounge with blazing log fires in cooler weather. Evening meals
are also available. Your hosts, Pauline and John Bibby, are keen outdoor enthusiasts and
make every effort to cater for walkers, fishermen and country lovers: they provide packed

lunches, a drying room and emergency laundry services - and are, of course, happy to give
any advice you may require. The 3 ground floor bedrooms are ideally suited to wheelchair
users and have direct access to the car park and reception rooms.
OPEN ALL YEAR. N/S. V, S.D. B/A. PETS & OVER 5Ss WELCOME. WHEELCHAIR ACCESS. LICENSED. EN SUITE,
TV & BEVERAGES. VISA, MASTERCARD, EUROCARD, SWITCH. B. & B. £20-25;D. B. & B. £30-35

KENDAL

7 THORNY HILLS, KENDAL, CUMBRIA.   TEL: (01539) 720207
OPEN Jan. - Nov.   NO SMOKING.   V B/A.   CHILDREN WELCOME.   1 EN SUITE ROOM.   BEVERAGES & TV
IN ROOMS.   B. & B. AROUND £15.

BIRSLACK GRANGE, LEVENS, NR KENDAL, CUMBRIA.   TEL: (015395) 60989
OPEN ALL YEAR.   NO SMOKING.   S.D. B/A.   DISABLED ACCESS.   CHILDREN WELCOME.   PETS B/A.   3
EN SUITE ROOMS.   BEVERAGES & T.V. IN ROOMS.   B. & B. AROUND £17.

FAIRWAYS, 102 WINDERMERE RD, KENDAL, CUMBRIA, LA9 5EZ   TEL: (01539) 725564
Victorian guest house with lovely views. 4-poster bedroom. Private parking.
OPEN ALL YEAR.   NO SMOKING.   V, S.D. B/A.   CHILDREN WELCOME.   EN SUITE, BEVERAGES & TV IN ROOMS.
B. & B. AROUND £19.

GARDEN HOUSE HOTEL, FOWL-ING LN, KENDAL.   TEL: (01539) 731131 FAX: (01539) 740064
Beautiful 19th C. house in 2 acres of wooded grounds; excellent food and service.
N/S RESTAURANT & MOST BEDRS.   V B/A.   EN SUITE, TV & BEVERAGES IN ROOMS.   GROUND FLOOR
ROOM.   CHILDREN & PETS.   LICENSED. B. & B. AROUND £26..

Holmfield
41 KENDAL GREEN, KENDAL, CUMBRIA, LA9 5PP   TEL: (01539) 720790
ETB De Luxe. Elegant Edwardian house; 1acre garden, with pool and panoramic views.
OPEN ALL YEAR.   NO SMOKING.   V, S.D. B/A.   OVER 12s.   BEVERAGES, TV & RADIO. B. & B. FROM £17.

PUNCHBOWL HOUSE, GRAYRIGG, NR KENDAL, LA8 9BU   TEL: (0153984) 345
Large, Victorian stone-built farmhouse in Grayrigg village, just outside Kendal. Fully
modernised, spacious rooms & log fires. B. & B./self-catering. Walkers welcome.
OPEN ALL YEAR.   NO SMOKING.   V, S.D. B/A.   OVER 5S WELCOME.   1 EN SUITE ROOM.   BEVERAGES
& TV IN ROOMS.   B. & B. AROUND £20.

KESWICK
Anworth House
27 ESKIN STREET, KESWICK, CUMBRIA, CA12 4DQ   TEL: (017687) 72923
Small, friendly guest house near the centre of Keswick. Tasty, home-cooked food. Comfortable en suite bedrooms. Packed lunches are available on request.
OPEN ALL YEAR.   NO SMOKING.   S.D. B/A.   CHILDREN.   EN SUITE, TV & BEVERAGES.   B. & B. AROUND £19.

Avondale
20 SOUTHEY ST, KESWICK, CUMBRIA, CA12 4EF   TEL: (017687) 72735
Avondale is a small, family-run guest house which offers a friendly welcome to all
non-smokers. Conveniently situated just 5 minutes level walk from the town centre and
parks (Derwentwater is a mere 10 minute stroll), Avondale is a comfortable base from which
to explore Keswick and the Northern lakes. Meals are served in an attractive dining room:
there is a hearty traditional English breakfast and a 4-course, home-cooked Table d'hôte
evening meal. Keswick is a well-known centre for outdoor pursuits and the area abounds
with nature trails, country rambles, forest or fell walks.
OPEN ALL YEAR.   NO SMOKING.   S.D. ON REQUEST.   OVER 12S WELCOME.   EN SUITE, TV & BEVERAGES IN
ROOMS.   B. & B. FROM £17.

Beckside Guest House
5 WORDSWORTH ST, KESWICK, CUMBRIA, CA12 4HU   TEL: (017687) 73093
ETB 2 Crowns Commended. AA 3Qs. RAC Highly Acclaimed. Small, very comfort-
able guest house. Good food, convenient location.
OPEN ALL YEAR.   NO SMOKING.   S.D. B/A.   OVER 8s ONLY.   EN SUITE, TV & BEVERAGES IN ROOMS.   B. & B.
FROM £17, D £10.

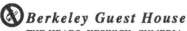 Berkeley Guest House

THE HEADS, KESWICK, CUMBRIA.   TEL: (017687) 74222

Relaxed friendly guest house. Comfortable rooms with magnificent mountain views. Close to town and lake.

OPEN Feb. - Nov.   NO SMOKING.   CHILDREN WELCOME.   SOME EN SUITE.   TV & BEVERAGES IN ROOMS.

BRIENZ GUEST HOUSE, 3 GRETA ST, KESWICK, CA12 4HS   TEL: (017687) 71049

ETB Commended. Friendly guest house; easy walking distance town centre, lakes, parks. High standards of comfort. Imaginative home-cooked food & menu choice.

OPEN ALL YEAR ex. Xmas & New Year.   NO SMOKING.   V, S.D. B/A.   LICENSED.   WHEELCHAIR ACCESS.
OVER 6s.   EN SUITE, BEVERAGES & TV IN ROOMS.   B. & B. AROUND £15.

Clarence House

14 ESKIN STREET, KESWICK, CUMBRIA, CA12 4DQ   TEL: (017687) 73186

Well-established quality B. & B. Ground floor and four-poster rooms.

OPEN ALL YEAR ex. Xmas.   NO SMOKING.   V B/A.   LICENSED.   CHILDREN WELCOME.   EN SUITE,
BEVERAGES & T.V. IN ROOMS.   B. & B. FROM £18.

Cottage in the Wood Hotel

WHINLATTER PASS, BRAITHWAITE, KESWICK   TEL: (017687) 78 409

The Cottage in the Wood is a charming 17th C. former coaching house which is beautifully situated atop Whinlatter Pass in the heart of the pine forest with superb views of the Skiddaw mountain range. It offers peaceful and pleasant seclusion to guests yet is just 10 minutes drive from the centre of Keswick. The Cottage in the Wood has been very comfortably furnished: log fires in the welcoming lounge greet guests on colder days and each of the seven bedrooms has been tastefully decorated and well-appointed with private facilities; there are two Honeymoon Suites with four-poster beds. The food is excellent: meals are served in an elegant dining room and all dishes have been home-prepared from fresh ingredients; the 5-course evening meal has been thoughtfully planned to include some traditional Lakeland dishes and vegetarian and other special diets can be accommodated by arrangement; morning coffee and afternoon teas are also available.

OPEN MAR. - NOV.   NO SMOKING.   V, S.D., B/A.   LICENSED.   CHILDREN.   PETS B/A.   EN SUITE & BEVERAGES
IN ROOMS.   B. & B. FROM £27, D £11 (£15 - 17 non-res.)

CROFT HOUSE, APPLETHWAITE, NR KESWICK, CA12 4PN TEL: (017687) 73693
OPEN Feb. - Nov.   NO SMOKING.   V, S.D. B/A.   LICENSED.   CHILDREN WELCOME. PETS B/A.   ALL ROOMS
EN SUITE.   BEVERAGES.   T.V. IN LOUNGE.   B. & B. AROUND £16.

Dalegarth House Country Hotel

PORTINSCALE, KESWICK, CUMBRIA, CA12 5RQ   TEL: (017687) 72817

Spacious, Edwardian property in sunny elevated position in an acre of gardens. Wholesome, delicious, home-cooked food. Superb views of the beautiful northern fells.

OPEN ALL YEAR.   NO SMOKING .   V B/A.   LICENSED.   CHILDREN: OVER 5S ONLY. E N SUITE, TV &
BEVERAGES IN ROOMS.   ACCESS, VISA.   B. & B. AROUND £27.

Derwent Cottage

PORTINSCALE, KESWICK, CA12 5RF   TEL: (017687) 74838

ETB 3 Crowns Highly Commended Derwent Cottage is no mere cottage say the proprietors, Mike and Sue Newman, for the original 18th C. dwelling was greatly extended in Victorian times in the picturesque but rather grand style favoured by those who built estates in the Lake District in those days. The result is generously proportioned rooms with high ceilings oriented to the full advantage of the site. The house is set well back from the road through the quiet village of Portinscale in well-established grounds of nearly an acre with terraced lawns and stately conifers. The accommodation, which has full central heating, includes 5 spacious en suite

rooms with elegant furnishings, a bar and lounge. A candle-lit 4-course table d'hôte meal of fresh home-cooked food, plus coffee, is served at 7 p.m. in an attractive dining room with crisp linen, silver and sparkling crystalware; background classical music accompanies the meal. Derwent Cottage is 1 mile from Keswick and close to the shores of Derwentwater, and is an ideal location for fell-walking and touring throughout the National Park.
OPEN Mar. - Nov.   NO SMOKING.   V, S.D., B/A.   OVER 12S.   LICENSED.   EN SUITE, TV & BEVERAGES IN ROOMS.   CREDIT CARDS.   B. & B. FROM £24, D. £12.

Derwent House

GRANGE-IN-BORROWDALE, KESWICK, CA12 5UY TEL: (017687) 77658 FAX: (017687) 77217
Set amidst beautiful country and with a spacious garden leading down to the river, Derwent House was traditionally built of local stone more than 100 year ago. The breakfast room retains much of its original character, including a stone floor and log-burning grate, and there is a separate dining room for the optional evening meal. The house enjoys lovely views of the surrounding fells from all its windows and, except for Christmas and Janury, is open all year, giving you a good starting base for walking in all seasons. There are 10 comfortable bedroooms, most of which have private facilities, and a hair dryer, iron and shoe cleaning materials are available on request. The food is excellent: fresh local produce is used wherever possible, and a typical evening menu would feature smoked trout fillet followed by boned chicken breast in wine and mushroom sauce with new potatoes and buttered carrots.
OPEN Feb. - Dec.   N/S DINING R & BEDRS.   V B/A.   LICENSED.   CHILDREN.   EN SUITE, TV & BEVERAGES IN ROOMS.   B. & B. FROM £19.

⊘Glencoe Guest House

21 HELVELLYN ST, KESWICK, CUMBRIA, CA12 4EN   TEL: (017687) 71016
Attractive guest house offering comfortable accommodation near the centre of Keswick. Your hosts are also both qualified caterers and offer excellent home-cooked meals.
OPEN ALL YEAR ex. Jan.   NO SMOKING.   V, S.D. B/A.   CHILDREN WELCOME (FAMILY ROOMS AVAIL.). BEVERAGES & TV IN ROOMS.   B. & B. FROM £11.

⊘ HEATHERLEA, 26 BLENCATHRA STREET, KESWICK, CA12 4HP TEL: (017687) 72430
Traditional Lakeland stone house quietly situated near Keswick town centre; freshly cooked breakfast served in dining room with views of Skiddaw fells.
NO SMOKING.   OVER 5S ONLY.   PETS B/A.   EN SUITE, TV & BEVERAGES.   B. & B. AROUND £18.

⊘ JENKIN HILL COTTAGE, THORNTHWAITE, CUMBRIA. TEL: (01596) 82443
OPEN ALL YEAR.   NO SMOKING.   V, S.D. B/A.   OVER 12S ONLY.   EN SUITE, BEVERAGES & TV IN ROOMS.   B. & B. AROUND £20.

⊘ KENDOON, BRAITHWAITE, KESWICK, CA12 5RY TEL: (017687) 78430
"A warm welcome for wet walkers!" Panoramic views from sitting room.
OPEN Feb. - Nov.   NO SMOKING.   V, VE, S.D. B/A.   PETS B/A.   BEVERAGES.   B. & B. FROM £12.

⊘Lynwood

12 AMBLESIDE RD, KESWICK, CA12 4DL   TEL: (017687) 72081 FAX: (017687) 75021
Large Victorian house in a quiet residential area near Keswick. The proprietorscater exclusively for non-smokers. Excellent, home-cooked food.
OPEN ALL YEAR.   NO SMOKING.   V, S.D. B/A.   LICENSED.   CHILDREN WELCOME (COT & HIGHCHAIR AVAILABLE).   EN SUITE, BEVERAGES & TV IN ROOMS.   B. & B. AROUND £20.

⊘ ORCHARD HOUSE, BORROWDALE RD, KESWICK, CA12 5DE TEL: (017687) 72830
Exclusively vegetarian guest house offering superb, freshly-cooked 4 course dinners prepared from locally grown organic fruit and vegetables; attractively decorated.
OPEN mid Feb. - mid Nov. Plus Xmas.   NO SMOKING.   V, VE EXC.   S.D. B/A.   LICENSED.   CHILDREN WELCOME.   DOGS B/A.   SOME EN SUITE ROOMS.   BEVERAGES IN ROOMS.   T.V. IN SEPARATE LOUNGE. D., B. & B. FROM £29.50. OPEN TO NON-RESIDENTS FOR DINNER.

⊘ SKIDDAW GROVE, VICARAGE HILL, KESWICK, CA12 5QB TEL: (017687) 73324
Georgian mansion on a quiet lane atop small hill 10 mins' walk from Keswick.
OPEN ALL YEAR ex. Xmas.   N/S ex. In Bar.   V B/A.   LICENSED.   CHILDREN WELCOME.   EN SUITE & BEVERAGES IN ROOMS.   T.V. IN ROOMS ON REQUEST.   B. & B. AROUND £21.

SQUIRREL LODGE, 43 ESKIN STREET, KESWICK, CUMBRIA. TEL: (017687) 73091
Attractive guest house in the centre of Keswick; emphasis on home-cooking.
OPEN ALL YEAR.　NO SMOKING.　V B/A.　LICENSED.　CHILDREN WELCOME.　BEVERAGES & T.V. IN ROOMS.　CREDIT CARDS.　B. & B. AROUND £17.

Thornleigh Guest House

23 BANK ST, KESWICK, CUMBRIA, CA12 5JZ　TEL: (017687) 72863
Completely refurbished guest house with magnificent views. Delicious breakfasts. Warm welcome.
OPEN Feb. - Nov.　N/S DINING R.　EN SUITE, TV & BEVERAGES IN ROOMS.

Thwaite Howe Hotel

THORNTHWAITE, NR KESWICK, CUMBRIA, CA12 5SA　TEL: (017687) 78281
Victorian stone-built country house in lovely gardens overlooking Derwent valley and mountains. Excellent home-cooked food, comfortable rooms and log fires.
OPEN Mar. - Oct. inc.　N/S DINING R & LOUNGE.　V, S.D. B/A.　LICENSED.　OVER 12S ONLY.　PETS WELCOME.　EN SUITE, TV & BEVERAGES IN ROOMS.　B. & B. AROUND £28.

Winchester Guest House

58 BLENCATHRA ST, KESWICK, CUMBRIA, CA12 4HT　TEL: (017687) 73664
ETB 1 Crown Commended. Winchester Guest House is a spacious, end-of-terrace Victorian town house which stands just a few minutes' walk from the centre of the attractive market town of Keswick. Entirely smoke-free, the Winchester guest house has a clean, pleasant atmosphere and each of the centrally heated bedrooms has been attractively furnished (some have views of Skiddaw, Blencathra and Latrig); there is a comfortable lounge for guests'use. Home-cooked breakfasts are served in a pleasant dining room - and traditional evening meals may be enjoyed during winter months. Keswick is the northern centre of the Lake District National Park and as such has easy road access to all the places of interest within Cumbria; there are numerous walks to be enjoyed - many of which begin from the Winchester front door - or, for the less nimble, a lazy stroll along the nearby riverbank.
OPEN ALL YEAR.　NON-SMOKERS ONLY.　V B/A.　OVER 3S WELCOME.　BEVERAGES & TV IN ROOMS.　B. & B. FROM £14, D. £7.

KIRKBY LONSDALE

Lupton Tower Vegetarian Country House Hotel

KIRKBY LONSDALE, CUMBRIA, LA6 2PR　TEL: (015395) 67400
Imaginative vegetarian cuisine. *Vegetarian Restaurant of the Year. 1992.*
OPEN ALL YEAR.　NO SMOKING. V EXC.　LICENSED.　CHILDREN WELCOME.　PETS B/A.　MOST ROOMS EN SUITE. BEVERAGES IN ROOMS.　B. & B. AROUND £26.

KIRKBY STEPHEN

ANNEDD GWYON, 46 HIGH ST, KIRKBY STEPHEN, CA17 4SH TEL: (017683) 72302
This late Victorian home is run along 'green'lines, with home-cooked wholefoods & a relaxing, healthy environment. Meditation room & guest lounge.
OPEN JAN. 7 - DEC. 22.　NO SMOKING.　V STD. BEVERAGES.　TV ON REQUEST. CHILDREN & PETS WELCOME.　B. & B. AROUND £17.

Fat Lamb Hotel

RAVENSTONEDALE, KIRKBY STEPHEN, CUMBRIA, CA17 4LL　TEL: (015396) 23242

The Fat Lamb Country Inn stands in the magnificent open countryside between the Lake District and the Yorkshire Dales National Park. Originally a 17th C. farmhouse its solid stone walls and welcoming open fires convey something of its original purpose and under the management of the present owners it has been sympathetically refurbished: each of the centrally heated bedrooms has a private bathroom and several are situated on the ground floor with good wheelchair access. The food is excellent: all dishes are prepared from fresh, local ingredients and there are two residents' lounges for pre- and post-prandial chats and drinks. The Fat Lamb Hotel is an excellent base for fell-walking (the aerial photograph shows the Fat Lamb to be a literal oasis of hospitality amidst the splendid Cumbrian fells). OPEN ALL YEAR.   N/S DINING R. & BEDROOMS.   S.D. B/A.   WHEELCHAIR ACCESS.   CHILDREN & PETS WEL-COME.   LICENSED.   EN SUITE & BEVERAGES IN ROOMS.   B. & B. FROM £25, D. B. & B. FROM £37.

KIRKOSWALD

 HOWSCALES HOLIDAY. COTTAGES FOR NON-SMOKERS, HOWSCALES, KIRKO-SWALD, CA10 1JG
TEL: (01768) 898666 FAX:(01768) 898710   OPEN ALL YEAR.   NO SMOKING.   OVER 12S ONLY.

MILLOM

 Whicham Hall Farm

SILECROFT, MILLOM, CUMBRIA, LA18 5LT   TEL: (01229) 772637
OPEN ALL YEAR.   NO SMOKING.   V B/A.   DISABLED ACCESS.   CHILDREN WELCOME.   PETS B/A.   EN SUITE 1 ROOM.   BEVERAGES & T.V.   B. & B. FROM £10.

MOSEDALE

 MOSEDALE HOUSE, MOSEDALE, CUMBRIA.   TEL: (017687) 79371
An emphasis on home-made and home-grown provision: vegetables, fruit, produce (such as eggs and lamb), home-baked bread and rolls. Vegetarians very welcome.
NO SMOKING . S.D. B/A.   DISABLED ACCESS.   CHILDREN WELCOME.   PETS B/A.   4 EN SUITE ROOMS. BEVERAGES IN ROOMS. T.V. MOST BEDROOMS.   B. & B. AROUND £22.

NEWBY BRIDGE

Swan Hotel

NEWBY BRIDGE, NR ULVERSTON, LA12 8NB TEL: (015395) 31681 FAX: (015395) 31917

 The Swan Hotel enjoys what is undoubtedly one of the most picturesque settings in the whole of the lakes: situated by the 17th C. arched bridge over the slow-flowing Leven at the Southern edge of Lake Winder-mere, the Swan has much to offer the visitor in search of comfortable accommodation, good food and specta-cular surroundings. Each of the 36 bedrooms has been furnished to a very high standard and thoughtfully equipped with a range of amenities including radio, hairdryer, telephone and trouser press. The food and service are similarly excellent: the smoke-free Tithe Barn restaurant offering a choice of traditional meals, including vegetarian dishes, and an extensive choice of wines. The Swan Hotel is the perfect choice for a very special holiday; in addition, however, the proprietors offer facilities for the smaller conference (including ample parking and a heli-pad).
OPEN ALL YEAR.   N/S RESTAURANT.   S.D.   CHILDREN WELCOME.   LICENSED.   EN SUITE, TV & BEVERAGES IN ROOMS.   CREDIT CARDS.   B. & B. FROM £44, D. FROM £18.50

PENRITH

 'Fair Place' Wholefood and Vegetarian Guest House

FAIR PLACE, WATERMILLOCK, NR PENRITH, CA11 0LR TEL: (017684) 86235 FAX: (017684) 86066

 This handsome rag-stone building, set in se-cluded grounds 200 yards past Watermillock Church, used to be the village school. Its proprie-tors, whose family home it has been, converted it over 30 years ago, and it has been beautifully renovated and modernised. Now a charming small guest house (though retaining many of the original features), it is an exclusively vegetarian and vegan B. & B., serving only the best and freshest of free-range and 'whole'breakfasts. The bedrooms are all en suite (and have very comfortable beds), and, if you like music, there is an especially good room for listening (bring your own CDs). Drive if you must- but there

is ample countryside within walking distance of 'Fair Place'; Aira Force, a spectacular waterfall is just over 3 miles away; and Ullswater is an especially lovely Lakeland haunt.
OPEN Feb. - Nov.   NO SMOKING.   V, VE, b'fast. S.D. B/A.   CHILDREN WELCOME.   PETS B/A.   EN SUITE, BEVERAGES & T.V. IN ALL ROOMS.   B. & B. FROM £17.50.

Low Beckside Farm
MUNGRISDALE, PENRITH, CUMBRIA, CA11 0XR   TEL: (017687) 79246
Working hill farm. Excellent walking area. Golf, sailing, para-gliding & all outdoor pursuits available locally. All food freshly prepared to a very high standard.
OPEN 6 Jan - 7 Dec.   NO SMOKING.   S.D. B/A.   CHILDREN & PETS.   1 EN SUITE.   BEVERAGES IN ROOMS.   TV LOUNGE.B. & B. £12.50 - 14.50.

Low Garth Guest House
PENRUDDOCK, PENRITH, CUMBRIA, CA11 0QU   TEL: (017684) 83492
ETB 3 Crown Approved. Tastefully converted 18th C. barn in peaceful surroundings with magnificent views. Fresh, home-cooked food.
OPEN ALL YEAR.   NO SMOKING.   V, S.D. B/A.   CHILDREN & PETS.   EN SUITE, TV & BEVERAGES IN ROOMS.
B. & B. £17, D. £10.

NETHERDENE GUEST HOUSE, TROUTBECK, NR PENRITH, CA11 0SJ   TEL: (017684) 83475
Small, country guest house in its own quiet grounds with extensive mountain views 9 miles from Penrith on the A5091 to Ullswater (just off the A66). Four comfortable bedrooms. Cosy lounge with log fire. Pony-trekking, golf, fell-walking, boating, all nearby.
OPEN Feb. - Nov. N/S DINING R & SOME BEDRS.   S.D. B/A.   CHILDREN: OVER 7S ONLY.   EN SUITE, TV & BEVERAGES IN ROOMS.   B. & B. AROUND £17.

Waterside House
WATERMILLOCK, PENRITH, CUMBRIA, CA11 0JH   TEL: (017684) 86038
Beautiful 18th C. statesman's house, surrounded by gardens, meadows & by Ullswater. Comfortable and peaceful: an idyllic location, popular with honey-mooners.
OPEN ALL YEAR.   NO SMOKING.   S.D. B/A.   CHILDREN WELCOME, DOGS B/A.   WHEELCHAIR ACCESS. LICENSED.   EN SUITE & BEVERAGES IN ROOMS. CREDIT CARDS.   B. & B. £20 - 35.

THE WHITE HOUSE, CLIFTON, NR PENRITH, CUMBRIA   TEL: (01768) 65115
Beautiful 18th C. farmhouse in the village of Clifton. Exclusively for non-smokers.
OPEN Jan. - nov.   NO SMOKING.   V, DIAB, GLUTEN-FREE B/A.   LICENSED.   CHILDREN WELCOME.   2 EN SUITE ROOMS.   BEVERAGES IN ROOMS.   B. & B. AROUND £18.

Woodland House Hotel
WORDSWORTH STREET, PENRITH, CA11 7QY   TEL: (01768) 864177 FAX: (01768) 890152

An elegant and spacious licensed private hotel with a large car park, just five minutes walk from the centre of the town. All rooms are en suite and all have tea/coffee making facilities and a colour T.V. The meals are delicious and have been prepared from the best of fresh and local produce and, with notice, special dietary requirements can be catered for. There is a large library of maps and books for walkers, nature-lovers and sightseers and the proprietors will gladly help you plan your stay. Woodland House Hotel is an ideal centre for exploring the Lake District, Northern Pennines, Borders, Eden Valley, and is a perfect spot for an overnight stop on journeys to and from Scotland.
OPEN ALL YEAR.   NO SMOKING.   V, S.D. B/A.   RESIDENTIAL LICENCE.   CHILDREN WELCOME. EN SUITE, BEVERAGES & T.V. IN ALL BEDROOMS.   B. & B. FROM £20.

SEDBERGH

ASH-HINING FARM, HOWGILL, SEDBERGH, CUMBRIA, LA10 5HU   TEL: (015396) 20957
OPEN Mar. - Oct.   NO SMOKING.   V, S.D. B/A.   OVER 5S ONLY.   PETS B/A.   T.V. IN LOUNGE.   CREDIT CARDS.   B. & B. AROUND £20.

Cross Keys Hotel
CAUTLEY, SEDBERGH, CUMBRIA, LA10 5NE   TEL: (015396) 20284

The Cross Keys is a tiny 400 year-old inn magnificently situated at a dramatic corner of the Howgill Fells in the Yorkshire Dales National Park; the view of Cautley Spout, one of the country's highest waterfalls, can be enjoyed from the dining room. Owned by the National Trust, most of the original features of the building have been retained, including the very low-beamed ceilings, flag stone floors, mullioned windows and open fireplaces. Even the atmosphere is special: 'homely, traditional, informal and relaxing', and the delicious food, which includes home-made bread, biscuits, preserves and icecreams, definitely predates the convenience food era. You will be very warmly welcomed - there are maps and guide books to help you plan your stay - and, as Cross Keys is unlicensed, you are asked to bring your own wine to enjoy with your meal.
OPEN Easter - New Year. NO SMOKING.   V, S.D. B/A.   CHILDREN WELCOME.   EN SUITE 1 ROOM.   BEVERAGES IN ROOMS. B. & B. FROM £24-29.

Oakdene Country Hotel
GARSDALE RD, SEDBERGH, CUMBRIA, LA10 5JN   TEL: (015396) 20280   FAX: (015396) 21501

Oakdene is a splendid Victorian house which retains many of its original features such as the fine pitch pine staircase, stained glass windows, gas light fittings, marble fireplaces and a wood-panelled bath in one of the bedrooms. Centrally heated and pleasantly furnished throughout in traditional style, there is a comfortable sitting room and bar (both with open fires), and each of the six guest bedrooms has views of the fells. The service is professional and friendly, the food simple, healthy and freshly prepared, a typical evening menu featuring a choice of Watercress Soup or Smoked Turkey Breast with a Lime Dressing, followed by Haddock baked with Tomato and Coriander or Penne Pasta with Spicy Aubergine Sauce; desserts are home-made and there are always vegetarian options on the menu. Sedbergh is a relatively undiscovered part of Cumbria and offers holiday-makers in search of peace, tranquillity and good walks some of the finest scenery in the country in both the Lake District and the Yorkshire Dales National Parks; outdoor pursuits available locally include horse-riding, fishing, cycling and golf. For guests arriving by car there is ample (inconspicuous) parking and for those arriving by train there is free collection from the station.
OPEN Feb. - Dec. inc. N/S DINING R., HALL, SITTING R. & 4 BEDRS. V STD, S.D. B/A. CHILDREN WELCOME. EN SUITE, TV & BEVERAGES IN BEDROOMS. LICENSED. ACCESS, DINERS, VISA, AMEX. B. & B. £25-30, D. £12.50.

ULVERSTON

APPLETREE HOLME FARM, BLAWITH VIA ULVERSTON, LA12 8EL TEL: (0122985) 618
OPEN ALL YEAR. N/S ex SITTING R.   V, S.D. B/A.   LICENSED.   EN SUITE, BEVERAGES & T.V. IN ROOMS.
VISA, AMEX.   D., B. & B. FROM £49.

WINDERMERE

Aaron Slack
48 ELLERTHWAITE RD, WINDERMERE, CUMBRIA, LA23 2BS   TEL: (105394) 44649

Aaron Slack is a small guest house in a quiet part of Windermere about ½ mile from the railway station, 1 mile from the main access to the lake at Bowness Bay and within walking distance of shops and restaurants. The proprietor, Stephanie Townsend, is a keen painter, fell-walker and naturalist, and has an in-depth knowledge about this beautiful part of the world which she is happy to share with guests to help them make the most of their stay. There are two double and one twin-bedded rooms for guests: each has a colour TV and tea/coffee-making facilities, and there is a cosy sitting room. Breakfast is the only meal to be served at Aaron Slack, but visitors can look forward to a hearty meal of locally produced sausages and free-range eggs to set them up for the day; there are many restaurants and pubs serving food in Windermere village. Windermere is an ideal holiday choice for

Lakeland visitors who want easy access to the unspoilt parts of the National Park but who enjoy the hustle and bustle - and leisure amenities - of staying in a popular holiday village.
OPEN ALL YEAR.   NO SMOKING.   V, S.D. B/A.   CHILDREN B/A.   EN SUITE 2 ROOMS.   TV & BEVERAGES IN ROOMS.   CREDIT CARDS.   B. & B. FROM £14.

Ashleigh Guest House

11 COLLEGE ROAD, WINDERMERE, CUMBRIA.   TEL: (015394) 42292

Delightful Victorian guest house in Windermere village; comfortably furnished & tastefully decorated (fresh flowers in the bedrooms), many rooms have mountain views.
OPEN ALL YEAR.   NO SMOKING.   V B/A.   CHILDREN: OVER 12S WELCOME.   EN SUITE AVAILABLE.
BEVERAGES & TV IN ROOMS.   B. & B. AROUND £17.

The Archway

13 COLLEGE ROAD, WINDERMERE, CUMBRIA   TEL: (015394) 45613

This guest house was the one about which I received the most readers' recommendations when I was compiling the second edition of the Healthy Holiday Guide. A small, 'impeccable' Victorian guest house furnished tastefully throughout with antiques, paintings and fresh flowers allows its reputation, nevertheless, to rest (and rest soundly) on the high standard of its cuisine: the best of fresh local ingredients are brought together in imaginative and nutritionally thoughtful menus (the breakfast fare offers everything from freshly squeezed fruit or vegetable juice to home-made spicy apple griddle cakes; bread, of course, is wholemeal and home-baked), while the 3-course evening menu includes a wine recommendation and home-made lemonade!
OPEN ALL YEAR.   NO SMOKING.   V, VE, DIAB STD.   LICENSED.   OVER 12s ONLY.   EN SUITE IN 5 ROOMS. BEVERAGES & T.V. IN ROOMS.   CREDIT CARDS.   B. & B. FROM £22 - 25.

Boston House

4 THE TERRACE, WINDERMERE, CUMBRIA, LA23 1AJ   TEL: (015394) 43654

Delightful Victorian Gothic building in elevated position on edge of the village with panoramic views of the lake . Tastefully furnished bedrooms. Delicious home-cooked food.
OPEN ALL YEAR.   NO SMOKING.   V, S.D. B/A.   LICENSED.   CHILDREN WELCOME.   3 EN SUITE ROOMS.
BEVERAGES & TV IN ROOMS.   B. & B. AROUND £18.

Braemount House Hotel

SUNNY BANK RD, WINDERMERE, CUMBRIA, LA23 2EN   TEL: (015394) 45967

Braemount House is a small, family-run hotel which was built traditionally of Lakeland stone in 1879 and still retains much of its original, Victorian character and charm; it nestles quietly midway between Bowness and Windermere within easy walking distance of the lake. Accommodation is in six prettily decorated en suite guest rooms, each of which have been well-equipped with a range of helpful amenities including a radio-alarm and direct-dial phone; there is also a comfortable lounge for guests' use. The food is excellent: everything has been home-prepared from fresh, local ingredients (including garden herbs), and a typical 5 course evening menu would consist of Parfait of Lunesdale Duckling followed by Apple and Mint Sorbet, Lamb with Leek and Thyme Sauce, and a mouthwatering dessert such as Warm Nectarine in Nut Caramel with Fromage Blanc; there is a good selection of wines to accompany the meal, and cheese, coffee and sweetmeats to complete it. Windermere is an excellent touring centre and affords easy access to all the other parts of Lakeland; there is much to do within the vicinity of the village however, including golf, water sports, riding and, of course, fell-walking.
OPEN ALL YEAR.   NO SMOKING.   V, S.D. B/A.   LICENSED.   CHILDREN WELCOME.   EN SUITE, TV & BEVERAGES IN ROOMS.   VISA, MASTERCARD.   B. & B. FROM £30, D. B. & B. FROM £42.50.

DENEHURST, 40 QUEENS DRIVE, WINDERMERE, CUMBRIA. TEL: (015394) 44710
19th C. Lakeland stone guest house. B'fast only, but an imaginative, varied menu.
N/S DINING R & BEDRS.   V, S.D. B/A.   CHILDREN WELCOME.   EN SUITE, BEVERAGES & TV IN ROOMS.
B. & B. AROUND £19.

HAZEL BANK, HAZEL STREET, WINDERMERE, CUMBRIA TEL: (015394) 45486
OPEN Mar. - Nov inc.   NO SMOKING.   V B/A.   NOT LICENSED, BUT B.Y.O.   EN SUITE &BEVERAGES IN ROOMS.
T.V. IN LOUNGE.   B. & B. AROUND £20.

Hilton House Hotel
NEW RD, WINDERMERE, CUMBRIA, LA23 2EE   TEL: (015394) 43934

ETB 2 Crowns. Hilton House Hotel is one of the most ornate buildings in Windermere. Built in the Edwardian times by the finest of Lakeland craftsmen, the quality of stonework, hand-carved woodwork and stained glass is quite exceptional. Modernised and extended by the owners, Patricia and Andrew Barnicott, all six bedrooms have comfortable new double beds, en suite showers, toilets and washbasins, TVs, chairs and beverage-making facilities. The family room also has bunk-beds and a cot; a full bathroom is also available. The new non-smoking ground floor rooms have insulation plus an extra toilet and wash basin. The dining room overlooks the front garden and woodland beyond, and 14 guests can be seated at oaken tables; there is a small, well-stocked bar in the corner. A wide archway leads from the dining room to the elegant TV lounge with its magnificent carved fireplace with beautiful stained glass set into the alcoves; there are cosy arm chairs and a log fire in the grate. The hotel is centrally heated, has a full fire certificate and a large car and boat park at the rear.
OPEN ALL YEAR ex Xmas & New Year. N/S ex. 1 bedrooms.   V STD.   CHILDREN & PETS.   EN SUITE, TV & BEVERAGES.
LICENSED.   CREDIT CARDS.   B. & B. £16 - 22.50.

Kirkwood Guest House
PRINCE'S ROAD, WINDERMERE, CUMBRIA, LA23 2DD   TEL: (015394) 43907
Attractive stone-built guest house in a quiet area of Windermere . Individually furnished bedrooms. First-rate b'fast with a range of options, including vegetarian.
OPEN ALL YEAR.   N/S DINING R.   V, S.D. B/A.   CHILDREN WELCOME.   PETS B/A.   4 EN SUITE ROOMS.
BEVERAGES & TV IN ROOMS.   CREDIT CARDS.   B. & B. AROUND £17.

LAURIESTON, 40 OAK ST, WINDERMERE, CUMBRIA, LA23 1EN TEL: (015394) 44253
OPEN ALL YEAR . NO SMOKING.   V B/A.   LICENSED.   DOUBLE GROUND FLOOR ROOM AVAIL.   CHILD-REN WELCOME.   SOME EN SUITE ROOMS.   BEVERAGES & TV IN ROOMS.

Orrest Close Guest House
3 THE TERRACE, WINDERMERE, LA23 1AJ   TEL: (015394) 43325

Orrest Close is an elegant Victorian residence dating from 1847, and still retaining many original features. It is peacefully situated in a private tree-scaped drive - witha mple parking - yet is just 300 yards from the centre of Windermere. The comfortable bedrooms - some with views of the lakeland hills - are warm and tastefully furnished; the majority have en suite facilities, and one has a fourposter bed. Orrest Close is ideally situated for both walking and touring the Lake District, and your hosts, Mr and Mrs Curme, will help you plan your stay. Dinner and packed lunches are also available by arrangement.
OPEN ALL YEAR.   NO SMOKING.   S.D. B/A.   CHILDREN.   PETS.   EN SUITE, TV & BEVERAGES IN ROOMS.   B. & B. FROM £17.50

Rockside
AMBLESIDE ROAD, WINDERMERE, CUMBRIA, LA23 1AQ   TEL: (019662) 5343
19th C. traditional Lakeland house. Centrally heated. Excellent breakfast menu.
OPEN ALL YEAR.   N/S DINING R & 1 BEDR.   V, VE STD. S.D. B/A.   GROUND FLOOR ROOM. CHILDREN WELCOME.   MOST ROOMS EN SUITE.   BEVERAGES & TV IN ROOMS.   CREDIT CARDS.   B. & B. AROUND £20.

Rosemount

LAKE ROAD, WINDERMERE, CUMBRIA, LA22 2EQ   TEL: (015394) 43739
Charmingly hospitable guest house; healthy breakfasts. Packed lunches on request.
OPEN ALL YEAR.   NO SMOKING. V, S.D.B/A.   CHILDREN WELCOME.   EN SUITE, TV & BEVERAGES IN
ROOMS.   ACCESS, VISA, MASTERCARD.   B. & B. AROUND £22.

RESTAURANTS

AMBLESIDE

HARVEST VEG. RESTAURANT, COMPSTON RD, AMBLESIDE. TEL: **(015394) 33151**
   Freshly prepared vegetarian food. Exhibitions of Lakeland Landscapes.
NO SMOKING.   V, VE, GLUTEN-FREE STD. LICENSED. DISABLED ACCESS.

SHEILA'S COTTAGE, THE SLACK, AMBLESIDE, CUMBRIA. TEL: **(015394) 33079**
   NO SMOKING.   V.   LICENSED. DISABLED ACCESS.   CHILDREN WELCOME.

WILF'S CAFE, 5 LAKE RD, AMBLESIDE, CUMBRIA, LA22 0AB TEL: **(015394) 34749**
   Wholefood café with vegetarian & vegan choices. Situated above White Mountain.
NO SMOKING.   LICENSED. DISABLED ACCESS. CHILDREN WELCOME.

CARLISLE

FANTAILS, THE GREEN, WEATHERHALL, CARLISLE, CUMBRIA.   TEL: **(01228) 60239**
N/S 1 SECTION.   V STD.   LICENSED. CHILDREN WELCOME.

HUDSON'S, TREASURY COURT, FISHER ST, CARLISLE . TEL: **(01228) 47733**
   Centrally located café serving wide range of home-made meals and snacks.
   NO SMOKING. V STD. LICENSED.   DISABLED ACCESS.   CHILDREN WELCOME.

COCKERMOUTH

QUINCE & MEDLAR, 13 CASTLEGATE, COCKERMOUTH, CA13 9EU TEL: **(01900)**
   823579
VSUK Best Vegetarian Restaurant '89. Vegetarian Living Best Veg. Restaurant '91.
NO SMOKING.   V STD.   LICENSED. CHILDREN: OVER 5S ONLY

DENT

The Hop Bine Restaurant

   DENT CRAFTS CENTRE, HELMSIDE, DENT, CUMBRIA.   TEL: (015875) 400
Situated in a beautiful converted farm building (which also houses the Dent Crafts Centre)
serving a wide range of delicious home-prepared food including home-made cakes, pastries
and teas. Evening menu by prior arrangement.
NO SMOKING.   LICENSED. DISABLED ACCESS.   CHILDREN WELCOME.

HAWKSHEAD

THE MINSTRELS GALLERY, THE SQUARE, HAWKSHEAD. TEL: **(019666) 423**
   NO SMOKING.   DISABLED ACCESS. CHILDREN WELCOME.

KENDAL

Waterside Wholefoods

   KENT VIEW, KENDAL, CUMBRIA.   TEL: (01539) 729743
   Day-time restaurant & shop serving fresh food; organic ingredients where possible.
OPEN 9 - 4. L. AROUND £3.50.   NO SMOKING.   V, VE EXC. S.D. B/A. DISABLED ACCESS: 'EXCELLENT'.
CHILDREN WELCOME.

Grange Bridge Cottage Tea Shop

GRANGE IN BORROWDALE, NR KESWICK, CUMBRIA, CA12 5OQ   TEL: (017687) 77201

An 18th C. beamed cottage by the bridge over the River Derwent at Grange in the beautiful Borrowdale Valley. Delicious food - much of it home-prepared.

OPEN April - Oct. 11.30 am - 7 pm   NO SMOKING.   L. UP TO £5 (INCLUDING V).   V STD.   DISABLED ACCESS. CHILDREN WELCOME.

THE WILD STRAWBERRY, 54 MAIN ST, KESWICK, CUMBRIA. TEL: (017687) 74399

Friendly, cosy tea room with green slate floors & wooden beams; excellent range of delicious home-made snacks & meals; speciality coffees & teas; vegetarian options.

NO SMOKING. V, S.D.STD.   WHEELCHAIR ACCESS, BUT NO TOILET FACILITIES.

KIRKBY LONSDALE

LUPTON TOWER VEG. GUEST HOUSE & RESTAURANT, LUPTON, NR KIRKBY LONSDALE
For full details please see under entry in accommodation section.

MEWS COFFEE HOUSE, MAIN STREET, KIRBY LONSDALE, CUMBRIA TEL: (01468) 71007
N/S 1 SEPARATE DINING R. V STD.   LICENSED. DISABLED ACCESS. CHILDREN.

KIRKBY STEPHEN

OLD FORGE BISTRO, 39 NORTH RD, KIRBY STEPHEN, CA17 4RE TEL: (017683) 71832

Converted 17th C. smithy specialising in vegetarian/wholefood and traditional fare.

NO SMOKING. V, WH STD.   LICENSED.   DISABLED ACCESS.   CHILDREN WELCOME.

THE LORTON VALE

THE BARN, NEW HOUSE FARM, LORTON, COCKERMOUTH, CA13 9UU TEL: (01900) 85404

The Barn is situated on the B5289 between Lorton and Loweswater in the beautiful Lorton Vale. It offers a wide range of delicious lunches and teas are served therein.

NO SMOKING.

MELMERBY

THE VILLAGE BAKERY, MELMERBY, CUMBRIA, CA10 1HE   TEL: (0176 881) 515

Converted 18th C. barn serving home-baked wholefood bread, cakes and pastries.

NO SMOKING. V STD. LICENSED. DISABLED ACCESS. CHILDREN WELCOME.

PENRITH

PASSEPARTOUT, 51 CASTLEGATE, PENRITH, CUMBRIA, CA11 7HY TEL: (01768) 65852
NO SMOKING. V, S.D. B/A.   LICENSED.   DISABLED ACCESS. CHILDREN WELCOME.

ULVERSTON

BAY HORSE INN & BISTRO, CANAL FOOT, ULVERSTON, CUMBRIA. TEL: (01229) 53972
N/S RESTAURANT. S.D. B/A. LICENSED. DISABLED ACCESS. OVER 12S ONLY.

WORKINGTON

IMPRESSIONS RESTAURANT, 173 VULCANS LN, WORKINGTON. TEL: (01900) 605446
NO SMOKING.   V STD.   LICENSED. DISABLED ACCESS. CHILDREN WELCOME.

PUBS & WINE BARs

DENT

THE SUN INN, MAIN ST, DENT, SEDBERGH, CUMBRIA. TEL: (015875) 208
NO SMOKING IN 1 ROOM. V STD.   WHEELCHAIR ACCESS. CHILDREN WELCOME.

Cheshire

ACCOMMODATION

CHESTER

⊘ *Broughton House*
THREAPWOOD, MALPAS, CHESHIRE.   TEL & FAX: (01948) 770610

Broughton House has been converted from the elegant Georgian stables which were built for a former 17th C. mansion; they stand amidst 5 acres of lawned grounds, paddocks, garden and orchard. Although the house has been refurbished to the highest standards of comfort, many of the original features have been retained, such as the cobbled courtyards, dovecot and forge. The bedrooms are all on the ground floor and are easily accessible, even for the wheeelchair-bound; they are tastefully decorated, centrally heated and furnished in a period style. Each bedroom has been well-equipped and your hosts are pleased to lend you other items, such as a hairdryer or iron. In summer guests are served breakfast in a conservatory overlooking parkland with views to the Welsh Hills. Broughton House lies in the historic borderland between England and Wales (the old stone Cheshire cheese presses in the paddock mark the frontier!); the area is renowned for its rolling countryside divided into farms and estates. From A41 Chester to Whitchurch Rd go into Malpas & take B5069 towards Wrexham. After 3 miles pass small filling station in Threapwood *carry straight on* & turn left just before Clwyd border sign.
OPEN ALL YEAR. NO SMOKING. V, S.D. B/A. OVER 10s WELCOME. WHEELCHAIR ACCESS. EN SUITE, TV & BEVERAGES IN ROOMS. B. & B. FROM £22.

STONE VILLA, 3 STONE PLACE, HOOLE ROAD, CHESTER, CH2 3NR TEL: (01244) 345014
OPEN ALL YEAR. N/S IN BEDRS & DINING R.   CHILDREN WELCOME.   EN SUITE, TV & BEVERAGES IN ROOMS. B. & B. AROUND £21.

CREWE

THE OLD HALL, MADELEY, NR CREWE, CW3 9DX   TEL: (01782) 750209
OPEN ALL YEAR ex. Xmas. N/S DINING R, LOUNGE & SOME BEDRS. 1 ROOM EN SUITE.   BEVERAGES & T.V. IN ROOMS.

KNUTSFORD

⊘ PICKMERE G.H., PARK LN, PICKMERE, KNUTSFORD, WA16 0JX TEL; (01565) 733433
Listed Georgian house; extensive views over Cheshire countryside; 2m W J19 M6.
OPEN ALL YEAR.   NO SMOKING. V, S.D.B /A. CHILDREN WELCOME. PETS B/A.   MOST ROOM EN SUITE. BEVERAGES & T.V. IN ROOMS.   B. & B. AROUND £20.

⊘ TATTON DALE FARM, ASHLEY ROAD, KNUTSFORD, WA16 6QJ TEL: (01565) 654692
NO SMOKING. V, S.D. B/A. DISABLED ACCESS.   CHILDREN WELCOME.   1 EN SUITE ROOM. BEVERAGES IN ROOMS.   T.V. AVAILABLE. B. & B. AROUND £17.

⊘ TOFT HOTEL, TOFT ROAD, KNUTSFORD, WA16 9EH   TEL: (01565) 3470
NO SMOKING. V STD. LICENSED. OVER 10s ONLY. 6 EN SUITE ROOMS. BEVERAGES IN ROOMS. T.V. IN 6 BEDROOMS. CREDIT CARDS. B. & B. AROUND £18.

MACCLESFIELD

CHADWICK HOUSE, 55 BEECH LANE, MACCLESFIELD, SK10 2DS   TEL: (01625) 615558
N/S ex TV room. LICENSED. CHILDREN WELCOME.   8 EN SUITE ROOMS. BEVERAGES & T.V. IN ROOMS. SAUNA, SOLARIUM & EXERCISE ROOM. B. & B. AROUND £26.

GOOSE GREEN FARM, OAK ROAD, MOTTRAM ST ANDREW, MACCLESFIELD, SK10 4RA TEL: (01625) 828814
N/S DINING R & BEDRS. V, S.D. B/A. CHILDREN WELCOME.   1 EN SUITE ROOM. BEVERAGES & TV IN ROOMS. B. & B. AROUND £19.

MOBBERLEY

LABURNUM COTTAGE, KNUTSFORD RD, MOBBERLEY, NR KNUTSFORD, WA16 7PU
TEL: (01565) 872464   NO SMOKING.   V, S.D. B/A.   CHILDREN: OVER 5S ONLY.   SOME EN SUITE ROOMS.
BEVERAGES & T.V. IN ROOMS.   B. & B. AROUND £24.

NANTWICH

ROOKERY HALL, WORLESTON, NR NANTWICH, CHESHIRE, CW5 6DQ   TEL: (01270) 610016
N/S DINING R & SOME BEDRS.   V, S.D. B/A.   LICENSED.   DISABLED ACCESS.   CHILDREN WELCOME.   EN SUITE
& SATELLITE TV IN ROOMS.   ROOM SERVICE.   CREDIT CARDS.

NORTHWICH

BEECHWOOD HOUSE, 206 WALLERSCOTE RD, WEAVERHAM, NORTHWICH, CW8 3LZ
TEL: (01606) 852123   NO SMOKING.   V, S.D. B/A.   BEVERAGES & T.V.   B. & B. AROUND £16.

SALE

Brooklands Luxury Lodge

208 MARSLAND RD, SALE, CHESHIRE, M33 3NE   TEL; (0161) 973 3283
Built in 1851 in a more elegant age, this attractive Lodge of Austrian design offers a very
high standard of accommodation to guests. Each of the cosy, centrally heated studio
bedrooms have easy chairs, remote control TVs and mini-fridges; one has a four-poster
bed. Breakfast can be either Continental style or a traditional cooked breakfast, and evening
meals are available if booked in advance. All meals are served in your room. There is also
a whirlpool bath to enjoy. You are conveniently close to the train service and the M63.
OPEN ALL YEAR.   50% N/S   V, S.D. B/A.   CHILDREN WELCOME.   EN SUITE, TV, BEVERAGES & MINI-FRIDGE IN
ROOM.   B. & B. FROM £24.

STOCKPORT

MRS KENNINGTON, 35 CORBAR ROAD, STOCKPORT, SK2 6EP   TEL: (0161) 483 4000
NO SMOKING.   V, S.D. B/A.   BEVERAGES.   T.V. LOUNGE.   B. & B. FROM £15.

RESTAURANTS

ALTRINCHAM

Debenhams

ALTRINCHAM, CHESHIRE.
Pavilion, a friendly self-service coffee shop serving lunches, snacks and drinks.
OPEN STORE HOURS.   NO SMOKING.   V STD.   DISABLED ACCESS.   CHILDREN.   CREDIT CARDS.

CHESTER

ABBEY GREEN, 2 ABBEY GREEN, NORTHGATE STREET, CHESTER, CH1 2JH
TEL: (01244) 313251   NO SMOKING.   V EXC.   LICENSED.   DISABLED ACCESS.   CHILDREN WELCOME.

Browns of Chester

34-40 EASTGATE ROW, CHESTER, CH1 3SB   TEL: (01244) 350001
The Crypt, waitress service of light lunches & snacks in original 13th C. crypt.
OPEN STORE HOURS.   NO SMOKING.   V.   LICENSED.   CHILDREN WELCOME.   CREDIT CARDS.

Springles, a friendly self-service restaurant serving lunches, snacks & hot & cold
drinks.
OPEN STORE HOURS.   NO SMOKING.   V.   LICENSED.   CHILDREN WELCOME.   CREDIT CARDS.

The Blue Bell Restauran

65 NORTHGATE STREET, CHESTER, CHESHIRE.   TEL: (01244) 317758
Chester's only surviving mediaeval inn. Relaxing and unpretentious atmosphere. High
standard of service and excellent food.
N/S ONE ROOM (13-15 SEATS).   V, S.D. STD.   LICENSED.   CHILDREN WELCOME.   CREDIT CARDS.

CREWE

ROCKEFELLA'S REST., 11 HIGHTOWN, CREWE, CW1 3BP   TEL: (01270) 215668
Family restaurant specialising in steaks, hamburgers, etc. Self-serve salads.
NO SMOKING.   V STD.   LICENSED.   DISABLED ACCESS.   CHILDREN WELCOME.

MACCLESFIELD

DUKES COFFEE HOUSE, DUKES COURT, MACCLESFIELD   TEL: (01625) 511453
N/S IN PART OF CAFÉ.

NANTWICH

STAPELEY WATER GARDENS & PALMS TROPICAL OASIS, LONDON RD, STAPELEY, NANTWICH TEL: (01270) 628628
Three separate restaurants in attractive garden settings.
N/S 1 RESTAURANT & 40+% BAN IN OTHER 2.   V, DIAB, B/A.   LICENSED.   DISABLED: ENTIRE SITE DESIGNED FOR DISABLED.   CHILDREN.   ACCESS, VISA.

RUNCORN

GIOVANNI'S PIZZA & PASTA, 23 NANTWICH ROAD, CW2 6AF TEL: (01270) 500276
NO SMOKING.   V STD.   LICENSED.   DISABLED ACCESS ex upstairs toilet.

STOCKPORT

DEBENHAMS, PRINCES ST, STOCKPORT, CHESHIRE   TEL: (0161) 477 4550
Pavilion, a friendly self-service coffee shop serving lunches, snacks and drinks.
OPEN STORE HOURS.   NO SMOKING.   V.   DISABLED ACCESS.   CHILDREN.   CREDIT CARDS.

PUBS & WINE BARS

NANTWICH

THE JOLLY TAR INN, WARDLE, NANTWICH, CHESHIRE, CW5 6BE
Pleasant canal side pub with large beer garden.
TEL: (01270) 73283 N/S 50% RESTAURANT & 50% OF PUB.   V STD. DISABLED ACCESS.   CHILDREN.

Greater Manchester

ACCOMMODATION & RESTAURANTS

BURY

The Ramsbottom Victuallers Company Ltd
16-18 MARKET PLACE, RAMSBOTTOM, BURY   TEL: (01706) 825070
The award-winning Village Restaurant has been established for 8 years and is renowned for its 6-course celebration dinners (no choice, but no disappointment either!), while "The Ramsbottom Victuallers Supper Room" provides simple 3-course evening meals.
NO SMOKING.   V, S.D. B/A.   LICENSED.   SOPHISTICATED CHILDREN WELCOME.   ACCESS, VISA.

MANCHESTER

DEBENHAMS, MARKET ST, MANCHESTER   TEL: (0161) 832 8666
A friendly self-service restaurant serving lunches, snacks and drinks.
OPEN STORE HOURS.   NO SMOKING.   V STD.   DISABLED ACCESS.   CHILDREN. CREDIT CARDS.

THE GALLERY BISTRO, WHITWORTH ART GALLERY, OXFORD RD, MANCHESTER
TEL: (0161) 273 5651   NO SMOKING.   V STD. LICENSED.   DISABLED ACCESS.   CHILDREN WELCOME.

On the Eighth Day
109 OXFORD ROAD, MANCHESTER, M1 7DU   TEL: (0161) 273 1850

On The Eighth Day celebrated 24 years as a non-smoking wholefood café in 1994. Manchester's oldest cooperative continues to offer a daily changing menu of both vegan and vegetarian food. Only 10 minutes from the city centre, it well deserves its reputation for friendly service and the finest vegetarian cooking. The attached wholefood shop also offers a wide selection of tasty take-away food and produce.   Outside catering service available.
OPEN MON-FRI 10 A.M. - 7 P.M. SAT 10 A.M. - 4.30 P.M.   NO SMOKING.   V, S.D. STD.   CHILDREN AND GUIDE DOGS WELCOME.   LICENSED.

THE GREENHOUSE VEGETARIAN RESTAURANT, 331 GT WESTERN ST, RUSHOLME
NO SMOKING.   V, VE STD.   WHEELCHAIR ACCESSS.   CHILDREN 'IF FULLY SUPERVISED'.

SADDLEWORTH

Woody's Vegetarian Restaurant
5 KING ST, DELPH, SADDLEWORTH, G.M.C.   TEL: (01457) 871197

Vegetarian restaurant with a charming and elegant atmosphere. Excellent meat-free fare. Woody's has been a 'Vegetarian Restaurant of the Year' finalist in 1989, 1990 and 1991.
NO SMOKING.   V, VE EXC.   LICENSED.   DISABLED ACCESS.   ACCESS, VISA.

Lancashire

ACCOMMODATION
BLACKPOOL

The Birchley Hotel
64 HOLMFIELD RD, BLACKPOOL NORTH SHORE, LANCS, FY2 9RT   TEL: (01253) 54174

Small, comfortable, licensed hotel privately owned and manged for 15 seasons by the resident proprietorsx. Excellent home-cooking and a choice of menu is offered.
OPEN MOST OF THE YEAR.   NO SMOKING.   LICENSED.   CHILDREN: OVER 5S ONLY.   EN SUITE. BEVERAGES & T.V. IN ROOMS.   CREDIT CARDS.   B. & B. AROUND £19.

CHADWICK'S, 20A CLIFF PLACE, BISPHAM, BLACKPOOL, FY2 9JT TEL: (01253) 54188
N/S DINING R & BEDRS.   V, S.D. B/A.   CHILDREN WELCOME.   EN SUITE, TV & BEVERAGES IN ROOMS.   B. & B. AROUND £17.

IMPERIAL HOTEL (THF), NORTH PROMENADE, BLACKPOOL, FY1 2HB TEL: (01253) 23971
70% N/S DINING R & BEDRS.   V, S.D. B/A.   LICENSED.   DISABLED ACCESS.   CHILDREN WELCOME.   PETS B/A. EN SUITE, TV & BEVERAGES IN ROOMS.

The Old Coach House
50 DEAN ST, BLACKPOOL, LANCS, FY4 1BP   TEL: (01253) 344330

ETB 3 Crowns. AA Listed QQQ. RAC Highly Acclaimed. This historic Tudor style detached house was built in 1851 and is surrounded by its own award-winning gardens. It offers a superb range of facilities including en suite shower/toilet, phone, colour TV, trouser press and hair dryer in each bedroom, and there isa licensed restaurant with a smoke-free dining room; family rooms are also available. With full central heating, a sun lounge and car park, The Old Coach House is an ideal choice for visitors to Blackpool.
OPEN ALL YEAR.   N/S DINING R.   CHILDREN WELCOME.   LICENSED.   EN SUITE, TV & BEVERAGES IN ROOMS. B. & B. FROM £20.

CARNFORTH

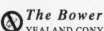

The Bower
YEALAND CONYERS, CARNFORTH, LANCS, LA5 9SF   TEL: (01524) 734585

The Bower is a small Georgian country house set at the northernmost tip of Lancashire in the Arnside and Silverdale Area of Outstanding Natural Beauty; it stands in the picturesque

and peaceful village of Yealand Conyers, and has extensive views of Ingleborough and the surrounding hills. It is a private house which has recently been modernised (sympathetically - it retains many original features), and accommodation is in two comfortable guest rooms, each of which has been equipped with a hairdryer and electric blankets. The food is wholesome and delicious (prepared from local or home-grown vegetables wherever possible) and, while the proprietors cater for too small a number to offer a choice, they always consult with guests about likes and dislikes; meals are served in a delightful dining room with French windows opening out onto the garden, and a typical evening meal would feature Stilton Soufflé followed by Chicken Chasseur and a tempting dessert, such as Gooseberry Fool with Amaretti Biscuits. Many beautiful walks may be enjoyed within the vicinity of The Bower - which is also conveniently placed for visiting Leighton Moss RSPB reserve and Morecambe Bay - and entertainment *in situ* may be provided for guests who play bridge (your hosts are keen players) or who sing (they also play the harpsichord and piano)!
OPEN ALL YEAR.   NO SMOKING.   S.D. B/A.   CHILDREN: OVER 12S ONLY.   PETS B/A.   EN SUITE, TV & BEVERAGES IN ROOMS.   B. & B. FROM £28.

 ## Capernwray Country House
CAPERNWRAY, CARNFORTH, LANCS, LA6 1AE   TEL: (01524) 732363
Splendid country house in 5½ acres of grounds, in the midst of unspoilt countryside. Beautifully furnished throughout. Centrally heated bedrooms have views.
OPEN ALL YEAR.   NO SMOKING.   S.D. B/A.   CHILDREN WELCOME.   EN SUITE, TV & BEVERAGES IN ROOMS.   B. & B. AROUND £22.

Thie-ne-shee
MOOR CLOSE LN, OVER KELLET, CARNFORTH, LANCS, LA6 1DF   TEL: (01524) 735882
Hillside bungalow with superb views across to the Lake District and Morecambe Bay. Close to Leighton Moss R.S.P.B. Reserve and Carnforth Steam town. Healthy breakfasts.
OPEN ALL YEAR ex. Xmas & New Year.   NO SMOKING. V, S.D. B/A.   CHILDREN WELCOME.   BEVERAGES: PERSONAL SERVICE.   T.V IN LOUNGE.   B. & B. AROUND £14.

Willowfield Hotel
THE PROMENADE, ARNSIDE, via CARNFORTH, LANCS, LA5 0AD   TEL: (01524) 761354
Willowfield Hotel is a small, family-run hotel, which is beautifully situated immediately overlooking the Estuary towards the Lakeland hills. All bedrooms are well furnished and have wash basins, central heating, electric blankets and shaver points (most have en suite showers), and the comfortable lounge and spacious dining room both overlook the estuary, as do most of the bedrooms. Willowfield Hotel is an ideal base for exploring South Cumbria and North Lancashire.
OPEN ALL YEAR.   NO SMOKING.   S.D. B/A.   CHILDREN WELCOME.   PETS B/A.   TABLE LICENCE.   SOME EN SUITE ROOMS.   TV & BEVERAGES IN ROOMS.   B. & B. FROM £18.

 ### COLNE
148 KEIGHLEY RD, COLNE, LANCS., BB8 0PJ   TEL: (01282) 862002
*ETB Listed and Highly Commended.*Edwardian town house with many original features, including stained glass, panelled doors & cornices. Comfortable bedrooms.
OPEN ALL YEAR Ex. Xmas.   NO SMOKING.   V, S.D. B/A.   TV & BEVERAGES IN ROOMS. B. & B. FROM £14.

KIRKBY LONSDALE

Killington Hall
KILLINGTON, KIRKBY LONSDALE, VIA CARNFORTH, LA6 2HA   TEL: (01539) 620542
16th C. house. Very comfortably appointed.
NO SMOKING.   S.D. B/A.   CHILDREN WELCOME.   BEVERAGES IN ROOMS.   B. & B.AROUND £16.

LANCASTER

The Old Mill House

WAGGON RD, LOWER DOLPHINHOLME, NR LANCASTER, LA2 9AX   TEL: (01524) 791855
ETB 3 Crown Standard. Listed in the Domesday Book as the site of a Yeoman Farm, the Old Mill House dates from the 17th C. and stands in the village of Lower Dolphinholme amidst 3 a cres of beautiful woodland and garden on the River Wyre. It is a haven of peace and traquillity yet is just 5 minutes drive from J33 on the M6 and is within easy reach of the Fylde Coast, the Lune Valley and the Forest of Bowland. Accommodation consists of 11 twin and 1 double room which share a bathroom, and one De Luxe room with a four-poster bed and en suite facilities; full central heating and double glazing ensure maximum comfort. There is a spacious Oval Lounge with an open log fire, and quality cuisine is served in the dining room.
OPEN ALL YEAR.   NO SMOKING.   CHILDREN WELCOME.   LICENSED.   1 EN SUITE ROOM.   BEVERAGES IN ROOMS.   TV IN LOUNGE.   B. & B. AROUND £19 - 35.

ELSINORE HOUSE, 76 SCOTFORTH RD, LANCASTER   TEL: (01524) 65088
NO SMOKING ex lounge.   V, S.D. B/A.   EN SUITE, BEVERAGES & TV IN ROOMS.   B. & B. AROUND £18.

OLDHAM

HANSON HOUSE, GRAINS RD, DELPH, NR OLDHAM TEL: (01457) 873419
Beautiful Grade II listed building 30 mins from Manchester city centre.
OPEN ALL YEAR ex. Xmas.   NO SMOKING.   V STD. CHILDREN: OVER 5S. ONLY. T.V. B. & B. FROM £14.

RAMSBOTTOM

EDWARDIA, 416 BOLTON RD WEST, RAMSBOTTOM, LANCS. TEL: (01204) 888061
Beautifully refurbished Edwardian town house on a semi-rural main road.
OPEN ALL YEAR.   NO SMOKING.   OVER 5S ONLY.   BEVERAGES & T.V.   B. & B. AROUND £20.

SILVERDALE

Lindeth House

LINDETH RD, SILVERDALE, CARNFORTH, LANCS, LA5 0TX   TEL: (01524) 701238
Country residence in a area of Outstanding Natural Beauty, surrounded by woodland walks, just a few mins' walk from the sea. Attractively decorated & appointed with individually furnished bedrooms. Excellent home-cooked food prepared from fresh produce.
OPEN Feb. - Dec.   N/S DINING R BY REQUEST & IN 1 LOUNGE & BEDRS.   V, B/A.   OVER 12S WELCOME.
LICENSED.   DISABLED ACCESS.   EN SUITE, BEVERAGES & TV IN ROOMS.   B. & B. FROM £20.

SOUTHPORT

Ambassador Private Hotel

13 BATH ST, SOUTHPORT, LANCS, PR9 0DP   TEL: (01704) 543998

ETB 3 Crown Commended. The Ambassador Hotel occupies one of the most central positions in Southport adjacent to beautiful Lord Street, with its covered boulevard, elegant shops and the promenade. The en suite bedrooms are comfortably furnished and well-equipped with a range of amenities including a TV, radio alarm, hair dryer, a hospitality tray, (with various drinks and snacks), a shoe cleaner and a mending kit. Your host, Margaret Bennett, is a qualified chef and prepares tasty meals from fresh, seasonal produce: the breakfast menu is tremendous offering a wide variety of options including, in addition to the traditional English bacon, eggs & sausage, cheese on toast, kippers, smoked haddock or omelettes. There are many interesting places to visit including Martin Mere Wildfowl Sanctuary, Formby Red Squirrel Colony & Liverpool's Albert Dock & Maritime Museum. For the more energetic there is golf to be enjoyed at one of Southport's

six courses, or the facilities of a leisure centre. There is a comfortable bar (not open to non-residents)where you will be entertained by the organist.
OPEN ALL YEAR Ex. Xmas.   N/S DINING R & BEDRS.   V, S.D. B/A.   LICENSED.   OVER 5S ONLY.   PETS WELCOME.   EN SUITE, BEVERAGES & T.V IN ROOMS.   CREDIT CARDS.   B. & B. FROM £23.

LYNWOOD HOTEL, 11A LEICESTER ST, SOUTHPORT, PR9 0ER   TEL: (01704) 540794
OPEN ALL YEAR Ex. Nov.   NO SMOKING.   V B/A.   LICENSED.   CHILDREN WELCOME.   PETS B/A.   SOME EN SUITE ROOMS.   BEVERAGES & T.V IN ROOMS.   CREDIT CARDS.   B. & B. AROUND £16.

RESTAURANTS & PUBS

BLACKBURN

DEBENHAMS, NORTHGATE, BLACKBURN, LANCS.   TEL: (01254) 63543
Springles, a friendly self-service restaurant serving lunches, snacks and drinks.
OPEN STORE HOURS.   NO SMOKING.   V STD.   DISABLED ACCESS.   CHILDREN.   CREDIT CARDS.

BOLTON

DEBENHAMS, THE MARKET PLACE, BOLTON, LANCS.   TEL: (01204) 381511
Intermission, a friendly self-service coffee shop serving lunches, snacks & drinks.
OPEN STORE HOURS. NO SMOKING.   V STD.   DISABLED ACCESS.   CHILDREN. CREDIT CARDS.

LANCASTER

LIBRA WHOLEFOOD RESTAURANT, 19 BROCK ST, LANCASTER TEL: (01524) 61551
NO SMOKING.   V, WH EXC.   LICENSED.   DISABLED ACCESS.   CHILDREN WELCOME.

LYTHAM ST ANNES

SERENDIPITY, BEDFORD HOTEL, 307-311 CLIFTON DRIVE STH, LYTHAM ST ANNES.
TEL: (01253) 724636   NO SMOKING.

MAWDESLEY

ROBERTS & CO., CEDAR FARM, MAWDESLEY, LANCS.
NO SMOKING THROUGHOUT.   V STD.   CHILDREN WELCOME.

PRESTON

EAT FIT, 20 FRIARGATE, PRESTON, LANCS.   TEL: (01772) 555855
30% N/S.   V STD.   LICENSED.   DISABLED: 'THREE SHALLOW STEPS, WHICH DO NOT PROHIBIT WHEELCHAIRS'.

SOUTHPORT

 *Debenhams*
535-563 LORD ST, SOUTHPORT, LANCS. TEL: (01704) 36060
Pavilion, a friendly self-service coffee shop serving lunches, snacks and drinks.
OPEN STORE HOURS.   NO SMOKING.   V STD.   DISABLED ACCESS.   CHILDREN WELCOME. CREDIT CARDS.

WIGAN

Debenhams
17 - 25 STANDISH ST, WIGAN, LANCS. TEL: (01942) 46231
A friendly self-service coffee shop serving lunches, snacks and hot and cold drinks.
OPEN STORE HOURS.   NO SMOKING.   V STD.   DISABLED ACCESS.   CHILDREN WELCOME.   CREDIT CARDS.

Merseyside

ACCOMMODATION

LIVERPOOL

The Grange Hotel

HOLMEFIELD ROAD, LIVERPOOL, L19 3PG   TEL: (0151) 4272950

Charming 19th C. building standing amidst beautiful well-maintained gardens in a quiet residential area just 3 miles from the centre of Liverpool and 3 miles from the airport. Comfortably furnished en suite bedrooms. Excellent food served in elegant dining room overlooking gardens. Conference and function facilities available.

OPEN ALL YEAR.   N/S DINING R & SOME BEDR.   V, S.D. B/A.   LICENSED.   CHILDREN WELCOME. EN SUITE, BEVERAGES & T.V. IN ROOMS.   CREDIT CARDS.

NEWTON-LE-WILLOWS

Haydock Post House Hotel

LODGE LANE, NEWTON-LE-WILLOWS, WA12 0JG

Large hotel close to the junction of the M6 and A580 Liverpool to Manchester road.

OPEN ALL YEAR.   N/S PART OF DINING R & N/S BEDRS.   V, S.D. B/A.   LICENSED.   DISABLED ACCESS. CHILDREN WELCOME.   PETS B/A.   EN SUITE, BEVERAGES & TV IN ROOMS.   CREDIT CARDS.

WIRRAL

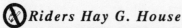Riders Hay G. House

198 GREASBY RD, GREASBY, WIRRAL, L49 2PE TEL: (0151) 6770682

Small, friendly, family-run guest house in the rural village of Greasby; just 10 minutes from Hilbre Bird Sanctuary and the Wirral Country Park. Lovely garden.

OPEN ALL YEAR.   NO SMOKING.   V, S.D. B/A.   DISABLED ACCESS.   CHILDREN WELCOME.   BEVER-AGES. T.V. IN LOUNGE.   B. & B. FROM £15.

RESTAURANTS

LIVERPOOL

Everyman Bistro

EVERYMAN THEATRE, HOPE ST, LIVERPOOL   TEL: (0151) 708 9545

A very busy, but friendly, buffet style restaurant in the University/Poly area close to the 2 cathedrals. All food freshly cooked on the premises from fresh produce. Cask beers.

NO SMOKING IN 1 OF 3 ROOMS BEFORE 8 P.M.   V, VE, S.D. STd.   LICENSED.

PUBS & WINE BARS

LIVERPOOL

Everyman Bistro

EVERYMAN THEATRE, HOPE ST, LIVERPOOL   TEL: (0151) 708 9545
ONE DINING/DRINKING AREA SMOKE-FREE BEFORE 8P.M.

For further details please see under the entry in the restaurant section.

Yorkshire and Humberside

North Yorkshire

ACCOMMODATION

ARKENGARTHDALE

The White House

ARKLE TOWN, ARKENGARTHDALE, N. YORKS, DL11 6RB   TEL: (01748) 84203
18th C. former farmhouse in the tiny hamlet of Arkle. Extensively renovated but still retaining old world charm. 3 centrally heated bedrooms; visitor's lounge with open fire and dale views. Hearty breakfasts, packed lunches and freshly home-cooked dinners.
OPEN Jan. - Nov.   NO SMOKING.   V, S.D. B/A.   OVER 10S WELCOME.   EN SUITE AVAIL.   BEVERAGES IN ROOMS.   TV LOUNGE.   B. & B. AROUND £17.

BEDALE

Hyperion House

88 SOUTH END, BEDALE, N. YORKS, DL8 2DS   TEL: (01677) 422334
Attractive well-appointed Victorian house in the charming market town of Bedale. Comfortably furnished throughout. 3 double and one twin-bedded rooms.
OPEN ALL YEAR Ex. Xmas & New Year.   NO SMOKING.   V, S.D. B/A.   B. & B. AROUND £17.

THE OLD RECTORY, PATRICK BROMPTON, BEDALE, DL8 1JN   TEL: (01677) 50343
OPEN Feb. - Nov.   NO SMOKING.   V, B/A.   LICENSED.   PETS B/A.   EN SUITE, TV & BEVERAGES IN ROOMS.   B. & B. FROM £18. D. £12

'SOUTHFIELD', 96 SOUTHEND, BEDALE, N. YORKS, DL8 2DS   TEL: (01677) 423510
Well established 3 bedroomed bed and breakfast establishment.
OPEN ALL YEAR Ex. Xmas & New Year.   N/S DINING R & UPPER FLOOR.   V, S.D. B/A.   CHILDREN WELCOME.
BEVERAGES.   B. &. B. AROUND £17.

COXWOLD

WAKENDALE HOUSE, OLDSTEAD GRANGE, COXWOLD, YO6 4BJ TEL: (013476) 351
ETB 2 Crown Commended. Well-appointed farmhouse; peacefulwith views.
NO SMOKING. V, S.D. B/A.   CHILDREN WELCOME.   T.V. LOUNGE.   B. & B. AROUND £18.

CROPTON

The New Inn & New Inn Restaurant

CROPTON, NR PICKERING, N. YORKS, YO18 8HH   TEL: (01751) 417330

In spite of its name, the New Inn at Cropton is an old established inn which is peacefully situated close to Cropton Forest and the beautiful unspoilt wilderness of the North York Moors. In addition to offering comfortable accommodation to residential guests (bedrooms are beautifully furnished and have en suite facilities - two specially rated family rooms are available), there is an excellent Victorian restaurant (in which smoking is completely banned), and a first-rate pub (with a smoke-free conservatory); guests preferring a more secluded break can take refuge in the self-catering cottage in the grounds. Guests can dine in the bar/conservatory (on dishes such as home-made Steak and Kidney Pie or Lentil Lasagne) or can choose from an excellent à la carte menu in the elegant restaurant; a typical evening meal would feature Black Pudding or Smoked Salmon

followed by Rabbit Pie or Fillet Steak au Poivre; speciality hand-made desserts or tradi-
tional "puds" would complete the meal.
OPEN 11 - 3, 5.30 - 11 (Winter 12 - 2.30, 7 - 11), RESTAURANT OPEN 7-9.30.   N/S RESTAURANT & CONSERVATORY.
L. AROUND £5, CARVERY £4.95; BAR MEALS £3-7, D. £12-£15.   V, VE, LOW-FAT AVAILABLE.   CREDIT CARDS.
WHEELCHAIR ACCESS.   CHILDREN WELCOME.

FILEY

Abbott's Leigh Hotel
7 RUTLAND ST, FILEY, N. YORKS, YO14 9JA   TEL: (01723) 513334
Abbot's Leigh is a pleasant Victorian terrace house which is situated in a peaceful
residential location close to the beach, gardens and town centre of Filey. The guest
bedrooms are all comfortably furnished and have en suite facilities, and one room is on the
ground floor. The food is wholesome and nourishing and the 5-course evening meal features
a variety of dishes including some good vegetarian options. The proprietors offer reduced
terms for weekly bookings and some attractive Spring and Autumn bargain breaks are also
available. Filey has 7 miles of golden sands and is ideal for sailing, windsurfing and
swimming; additionally you will find that you are ideally placed for touring the Yorkshire
Wolds and the North York Moors National Park.
OPEN ALL YEAR.   N/S DINING R & BEDRS.   V, DIAB, STD.   LICENSED.   OVER 3S ONLY. EN SUITE &
BEVERAGES IN ROOMS.   T.V.   ACCESS, VISA.   B. & B. FROM £18, D. £8.

GRASSINGTON

ASHFIELD HOUSE HOTEL, GRASSINGTON, NR SKIPTON, BD23 5AE TEL: (01756) 752584
Secluded 17th century hotel, superbly situated in quiet backwater near village square.
Family-owned and run; individually styled bedrooms and log fires. Home-cooked food,
OPEN Mid-jan. - Early Nov. N/S ex. entrance lounge. V, S.D. B/A.   LICENSED. OVER 5S ONLY. 6 EN SUITE
ROOMS.   BEVERAGES & TV IN ROOMS.   B. & B. AROUND £32.

HARROGATE

The Alexander
88 FRANKLIN RD, HARROGATE, N. YORKS, HG1 5EN   TEL: (01423) 503348
ETB 2 Crown Highly Commended. Friendly family-run guest house in tree-lined street
close to conference centre & town centre. Beautiful decor, central heating & double glazing.
Excellent centre for touring the Dales.
OPEN ALL YEAR.   NO SMOKING.   CHILDREN WELCOME.   SOME EN SUITE AVAILABLE.   TV & BEVERAGES IN
ROOMS.   B. & B. FROM £19.

Amadeus Vegetarian Hotel
115 FRANKLIN RD, HARROGATE, N. YORKS, HG1 5EN TEL: (01423) 505151
Elegant Victorian house with luxurious en suite rooms. Superb vegetarian cuisine.
OPEN ALL YEAR Ex Xmas.   NO SMOKING.   EXC V, VE, S.D. B/A.   LICENSED.   CHILDREN WELCOME.   PETS
B/A.   4 EN SUITE ROOMS.   EN SUITE, TV & BEVERAGES IN ROOMS.   B. & B. FROM £22. D. £12.50.

The Duchy Hotel
51 VALLEY DRIVE, HARROGATE, HG2 0JH   TEL: (01423) 565818

The Duchy Hotel is a small hotel of quality which
overlooks the famous Valley Gardens with its glorious year round floral display. It is owned and managed by Alan Drake and Marilyn Bateson who
recently won the regional award for her full English
breakfasts. There are nine centrally heated, su-
premely comfortable en suite rooms, all with direct
dial phones, hair dryers, toiletries and easy chairs,
and additionally there is a comfortable sunny
lounge, overlooking the gardens, with a well-
stocked bar. Delicious home-cooked meals are
served in a cosy dining room and special diets can
be accommodated with notice. Harrogate is a town
of unique elegance and charm: there are excellent restaurants and theatres, and within a
short drive are all the treasures of the North York Moors and the Dales.
OPEN Jan 9 - Dec 20.   N/S DINING R.   S.D. B/A.   CHILDREN WELCOME.   LICENSED.   EN SUITE, TV & BEVER-
AGES IN ROOMS.   B. & B. FROM £25, d. £10.50.

Number Twenty-Six

26 HARLOW MOOR DRIVE, HARROGATE, N. YORKS, HG2 0JY.   TEL & FAX: (01423) 524729
ETB 3 Crown Highly Commended.Number Twenty-Six is a family-run establishment in a
lovely Victorian town house overlooking the Valley Gardens; it is an ideal base for visiting
Harrogate as it is just a short walk from the town centre and has parks and woodlands on
the doorstep. The house is beautifully decorated throughout, with many original features,
and the atmosphere is warm and welcoming. Breakfast and dinner are provided at times to
suit guests and special diets can be accommodated with notice. Three well-appointed guest
rooms are available - all on the first floor - and each is equipped with a range of amenities
including clock radio/alarm, hairdryer, toiletries and towels.
OPEN ALL YEAR. NO SMOKING. V, S.D. B/A. CHILDREN WELCOME. EN SUITE, TV & BEVERAGES IN ROOMS.
B. & B. FROM £20.

Parnas Hotel

98 FRANKLIN RD, HARROGATE, N. YORKS, HG1 5EN   TEL: (01423) 564493
Elegant 10-bedroom private hotel. Emphasis on good food: full Danish breakfast & trolley
meals served informally in the lounge. Very comfortable bedrooms. Off-street parking.
OPEN ALL YEAR. NO SMOKING. S.D. B/A. LICENSED. CHIDREN WELCOME. 5 EN SUITE ROOMS. TV &
BEVERAGES IN ROOMS. B. & B. £19.50 - 25.

'Rose Garth'

44 RIPON RD, KILLINGHALL, HARROGATE, N. YORKS, HG3 2DF   TEL: (01423) 506469
Rose Garth is a very pleasant smoke-free B. & B. which stands in a lovely garden just 2
miles from Harrogate & Bettys Café and 1¼ miles from Ripley Castle. Central for touring
the Lake District, York, Knaresborough, 'Emmerdale and Herriot Country'. 2 mins. walk
to the 2 village pubs providing excellent food at reasonable prices. Radio, hair dryer in
rooms. Parking for 11 cars.
OPEN ALL YEAR. NO SMOKING. V, S.D. B/A. CHILDREN WELCOME. EN SUITE. PETS B/A. TV WITH
SKY & BEVERAGES IN ROOMS. B. & B. FROM £17.50.

Shannon Court Hotel

65 DRAGON AVE, HARROGATE, HG1 5DS   TEL: (01423) 509858 FAX: (01423) 530606
RAC Highly Acclaimed. A Victorian town house of charm & character overlooking the
famous Harrogate 'Stray'. It is personally run by the resident owners, and there is a warm
and friendly atmosphere. A few minutes walk from town centre & conference facilities with
easy access to all main roads. Off road parking. Bargain breaks throughout year.
OPEN ALL YEAR ex. Xmas. NO SMOKING S.D. B/A. CHILDREN WELCOME. LICENSED. EN SUITE, TV &
BEVERAGES IN ROOMS. B. &B. FROM £18.

Spring Lodge Guest House

22 SPRING MOUNT, HARROGATE, N. YORKS, HG1 2HX   TEL: (01423) 506036
Edwardian town house in a quiet cul-de-sac close to town & conference centre. Full
central heating. 6 very comfortable bedrooms. 2 or 3-course dinner on request. W/E breaks.
OPEN ALL YEAR. NO SMOKING. LICENSED. CHILDREN WELCOME. SOME EN SUITE ROOMS. SOME ROOMS
WITH TV. BEVERAGES IN ROOMS. B. & B. FROM £18.

HAWES

Brandymires Guest House

MUKER RD, HAWES, N. YORKS, DL8 3PR TEL: (01969) 667482
Brandymires is a lovely 19th C. 3-storey house which
stands at the head of Wensleydale just outside the market
town of Hawes; it has, as you might imagine, wonderful
views from all sides. The house is exceptionally comfortable and welcoming - a necessary requisite for those
holidaying in such beautiful but bracing countryside - an
open fire blazes in the lounge, and two of the bedrooms
have four-poster beds (each room, of course, has lovely
views). The food is excellent: everything is home-cooked
with imagination and care, and fresh produce is used
whenever possible; there is no formal bar but you can
enjoy a pre-dinner drink, order a bottle of wine and enjoy

a liqueur or a leisurely drink in the lounge - much more civilised. There is much to enjoy within the vicinity of Brandymires: there are several dramatic waterfalls nearby and a number of castles and museums; perhaps the main attraction of the area is the wonderful opportunity for fell-walking (bring gumboots and warm, dry clothes!).
OPEN Feb. - mid Oct. NO SMOKING. LICENSED. OVER 8s ONLY. PETS WELCOME. NO TV. BEVERAGES. B. & B. £17.50.

HELMSLEY

The Pheasant Hotel
HAROME, HELMSLEY, N. YORKS, YO6 5JG   TEL: (01439) 771241/770416
Delightful hotel created from existing village dwellings with a large garden and paddock, overlooking the village pond. Heated indoor swimming pool.
OPEN Mar. - Nov. N/S DINING R. V, S.D. B/A. LICENSED. DISABLED ACCESS. OVER 12S ONLY. EN SUITE, TV & BEVERAGES IN ALL ROOMS. D., B. & B. £49.95 - 60.

HUNMANBY

WRANGHAM HOUSE, STONEGATE, HUNMANBY, YO14 ONS TEL: (01723) 891333
OPEN ALL YEAR. NO SMOKING. V, B/A. LICENSED. DISABLED ACCESS. EN SUITE, TV & BEVERAGES IN ROOMS. ACCESS, AMEX, DINERS, VISA. B. & B. AROUND £35..

INGLETON

STORRS DALE, HAWES RD, INGLETON, N. YORKS, LA6 3AN   TEL: (01468) 41843
Small guest house specialising in wholesome home cooking.
OPEN ALL YEAR. NO SMOKING. V B/A. LICENSED. CHILDREN WELCOME. BEVERAGES IN ROOMS. T.V. ON REQUEST. B. & B. AROUND £17.

KIRKBYMOORSIDE

The George & Dragon
17 MARKET PLACE, KIRKBYMOORSIDE, N. YORKS.   TEL: (01751) 431637
Award-winning inn. Excellent home-cooked food; extensive bar menu and restaurant meals. Carefully chosen wines. Restful atmosphere, log fires. Very comfortable bedrooms.
OPEN ALL YEAR. N/S DINING R. CHILDREN WELCOME. EN SUITE, TV & BEVERAGES IN ROOMS.

SINNINGTON COMMON FARM, KIRKBYMOORSIDE, YORK, YO6 6NX TEL: (01751) 31719
ETB 2 Crowns Commended N/S DINING R & BEDRS. V, B/A. WHEELCHAIR ACCESS. CHILDREN WELCOME. PETS B/A. EN SUITE, BEVERAGES & T.V. IN ROOMS. B. & B. FROM £15.

LEYBURN

COUNTERSETT HALL, COUNTERSETT, ASKRIGG, LEYBURN. TEL: (01969) 50373
OPEN Feb. - Oct. NO SMOKING. V B/A. LICENSED. OVER 8S ONLY. PETS B/A. BEVERAGS IN ROOMS. T.V. LOUNGE. B. & B. AROUND £20..

THE HOLLY TREE, EAST WITTON, LEYBURN   TEL: (01969) 22383
OPEN Easter - Oct. inc. N/S DINING R, BEDRS, LOUNGE, T.V. R & B'FAST R. V B/A. LICENSED. EN SUITE. BEVERAGES ON REQUEST. T.V. LOUNGE. D., B. & B. AROUND £32..

Ivy Dene Country House
WEST WITTON, LEYBURN, WENSLEYDALE, N. YORKS, DL8 4LP TEL: (01969) 22785
ETB 2 Crown Commended. Charming 17th C. listed Dales house in the National Park 3m from Aysgarth Falls on the A684. Attractive bedrooms with views and Four-poster available. Period lounge with oak beams and log fire. Superb home cooking prepared from fresh local produce. Also self-catering cottage available.
OPEN ALL YEAR. NO SMOKING. LICENSED. OVER 5S WELCOME. EN SUITE, TV & BEVERAGES. B. & B. FROM £18, D. £12, REDUCTIONS FOR CHILDREN.

Wensley House
GROVE SQ., LEYBURN, NORTH YORKS, DL8 5AG   TEL: (01969) 23792
Wensley House is part of a Georgian terrace flanking Grove Square, the original market place of Leyburn - an ideal centre from which to see the Dales.
OPEN ALL YEAR.   NO SMOKING.   S.D. (b'fast only).   CHILDREN & PETS B/A. EN SUITE SHOWERS, BEVERAGES & TV IN BEDROOMS.   B. & B. £13 - 15.

MALTON

LEONARD HOUSE, 45 OLD MALTONGATE, MALTON, YO17 0EH   TEL: (01653) 697242
Georgian house in attractive market town. Warm welcome. Ideal for touring Ryedale.
OPEN ALL YEAR ex. Xmas.   NO SMOKING.   V, S.D. B/A.   CHILDREN: OVER 4S ONLY.   BEVERAGES IN ROOMS.   B. & B. AROUND £16.

NEWSTEAD GRANGE, NORTON, MALTON, N. YORKS, YO17 9PJ   TEL: (01653) 692502
*ETB Commended.*Elegant Georgian country house. Log fire.s Home-cooked food.
OPEN mid-Feb - Dec.   NO SMOKING.   V B/A.   LICENSED.   OVER 12S ONLY.   EN SUITE, BEVERAGES & TV IN ROOMS.   B. & B. AROUND £28.

OSMOTHERLEY

Quintana House
BACK LANE, OSMOTHERLEY, NORTHALLERTON, N. YORKS, DL6 3BJ TEL: (01609) 883258
Modern house constructed on traditional 19th lines of weathered York stone. Wonderful moorland views. Hearty b'fast and generous packed lunches. Dinner by arrangement.
OPEN ALL YEAR Ex. XmaS. NO SMOKING. V B/A.   CHILDREN WELCOME.   BEVERAGES & TV IN ROOMS.
B. & B. AROUND £16.

PATELEY BRIDGE

MOORHOUSE COTTAGE, PATELEY BRIDGE, N. YORKS, HG3 5JF   TEL: (01423) 711123
OPEN Easter - end Oct.   NO SMOKING.   V B/A.   CHILDREN.   BEVERAGES & T.V.   B. & B. FROM £17.

PICKERING

BRAMWOOD GUEST HOUSE, 19 HALLGARTH, PICKERING, N. YORKS, YO18 7AW
18th C. Grade II listed house centrally situated in the historic town of Pickering.
TEL: (01751) 74066   OPEN ALL YEAR.   NO SMOKING.   V B/A.   CHILDREN: OVER 3S ONLY.   SOME EN SUITE ROOMS.   BEVERAGES IN ROOMS.   T.V. IN LOUNGE.   ACCESS, VISA.   B. & B. AROUND £19.

GRINDALE HOUSE, 123 EASTGATE, PICKERING, N. YORKS.   TEL: (01751) 76636
18th C. building on tree-lined street. Beautifully refurbished and with antiques (they have a small shop next door); handsome beamed lounge with welcoming fire.
NO SMOKING.   PETS B/A.   SOME EN SUITE ROOMS.   BEVERAGES & T.V.   B. & B. AROUND £21.

Heathcote Guest House
100 EASTGATE, PICKERING, N. YORKS, YO18 7DW   TEL: (01751) 476991
Heathcote Guest House is a lovely Victorian house retaining a number of original features including a magnificent mahogany staircase, a galleried landing and arched fireplaces (though there is central heating too). Situated in the charming town of Pickering on the edge of the North York Moors National Park, it is a perfect placefrom which to explore the Moors, Coast and Wolds. Bedrooms are comfortably furnished and have en suite or private facilities. Dinner is first-rate: a typical home-cooked evening menu featuring Stuffed Mushrooms, followed by Pork Chops in Barbecue Sauce (with a selection of vegetables) and a dessert, such as Plum Pie with Ice Cream; freshly brewed coffee and mints would complete the meal.
OPEN JAN. - DEC. Ex Xmas.   NO SMOKING.   V A SPECIALITY. S.D. B/A.   CREDIT CARDS.
EN SUITE 3 ROOMS, BEVERAGES & TV IN ALL ROOMS.   B. & B. FROM £18-21, D. £10.

RICHMOND

The Kings Head Hotel
MARKET PLACE, RICHMOND, N. YORKS, DL10 4HS   TEL: (01748) 850220 FAX: (01748) 850635
OPEN ALL YEAR. N/S DINING R, LOUNGE, SOME BEDRS. V, VE STD. S.D. B/A. LICENSED. DISABLED ACCESS.
CHILDREN WELCOME.   PETS B/A. EN SUITE, BEVERAGES & T.V. IN ROOMS. CREDIT CARDS. B. & B. FROM £41.

PEAT GATE HEAD, LOW ROW IN SWALEDALE, RICHMOND, N. YORKS, DL11 6PP
TEL: (01748) 86388.   OPEN ALL YEAR.   N/S DINING R, 1 SITTING R & BEDRS.   V STD. S.D. B/A.   LICENSED.
GROUND FLOOR BEDROOM. OVER 5S ONLY. 3 EN SUITE ROOMS. BEVERAGES IN ROOMS. T.V. IN 1 SITTING R.
D., B. & B. AROUND £40

The Restaurant on the Green

5 - 7 BRIDGE ST, RICHMOND, N. YORKS, DL10 4RW TEL: (01748) 826229
Situated beneath the castle ramparts and near to the rushing River Swale. Established in July 1989 by the chef/owners. Good food, fine wines, efficient service, and overnight accommodation if required, in bedrooms with views.
OPEN ALL YEAR Ex. Xmas.   NO SMOKING. V, S.D. B/A.   LICENSED. CHILDREN WELCOME. EN SUITE, TV & BEVERAGES IN ROOMS. CREDIT CARDS. B. & B. AROUND £20, D. AROUND £15.

Ridgeway Guest House

47 DARLINGTON RD, RICHMOND, N. YORKS, DL10 7BG   TEL: (01748) 823801
1920's detached York stone house in an acre of lovely gardens. 4-poster bed available. Locally grown produce is used where possible in cooking.
OPEN ALL YEAR.   NO SMOKING. V, S.D. B/A.   TABLE LICENCE. CHILDREN & PETS B/A.   EN SUITE & BEVERAGES IN ROOMS.   T.V. IN SITTING R.   B. & B. AROUND £20.

ROBIN HOODS BAY

FALCONHURST WHOLEFOOD G.H., MOUNT PLEASANT S., ROBIN HOODS BAY, YO22 4RQ
TEL: (01947) 880582 OPEN Easter - Sept.   NO SMOKING.   V, WH STD.   CHILDREN & PETS B/A. BEVERAGES IN ROOMS. TV IN LOUNGE. B. & B. AROUND £20.

MEADOWFIELD B. & B., MOUNT PLEASANT N., ROBIN HOOD'S BAY, YO22 4RE
Victorian house; clean and comfortable with plenty of good food. Centrally heated.
TEL: (01947) 880564 OPEN ALL YEAR.   N/S DINING R & ALL PUBLIC AREAS.   V, VE STD.   CHILDREN WELCOME. 1 EN SUITE ROOM. BEVERAGES.   T.V. AVAILABLE.   B. & B. AROUND £16.

SCARBOROUGH

Ainsley Hotel

4 RUTLAND TERRACE, QUEENS PARADE, SCARBOROUGH, N. YORKS.   TEL: (01723) 364832
Th Ainsley is a comfortable family-run hotel which stands on Scarborough's famous North Cliff enjoying panoramic views of the North Bay, Castle and Headland. Accommodation is in comfortable centrally heated rooms and there is a quiet sea view lounge for guests' use. Traditional home-cooked meals are served in a cosy dining room and there is a well-stocked bar in which meals are also available between 9 and 10 p.m.
OPEN Feb - OCt. inc.   N/S DINING R.   S.D. B/A.   CHILDREN WELCOME, PETS B/A.   LICENSED.   50% EN SUITE. TV & BEVERAGES IN ROOMS.   B. & B. FROM £16.

Amber Lodge

17 TRINITY RD, SCARBOROUGH, N. YORKS, YO11 2TD   TEL: (01723) 369088
Edwardian house of great charm and character, peacefully situated in a conservation area 10 mins walk from South Bay & the town centre. Centrally heated. Fresh ingredients used in cooking.
OPEN Mar. - Oct. NO SMOKING.   V STD, S.D. B/A.   CHILDREN WELCOME.   EN SUITE 5 ROOMS. BEVERAGES & T.V. IN ROOMS.   CREDIT CARDS B. & B. FROM £17. D. £7.

Excelsior Private Hotel

1 MARLBOROUGH ST, SCARBOROUGH, N. YORKS, YO12 7HG   TEL: (01723) 360716

ETB 2 Crowns Approved. Roy Castle Good Air Award. The Excelsior is a small, unlicensed private hotel beautifully situated on a corner of the North Bay sea front; both the North and South bays can be seen from the hotel; there is a comfortable sea view lounge. There are five double, one family and two single rooms available. Much of the food is home made from fresh ingredients - including the bread, preserves, cakes, soups and sweets. You are well placed at the Excelsior for enjoying cliff and coastal walks, the beaches and parks and many attractions of Scarborough and your hosts, Raymond and Irene Brown, will do everything they can to ensure your stay is a happy and memorable one. Weekly terms and short breaks available. **Discounts for senior citizens over 60.**
OPEN Easter - Oct.   NO SMOKING.   V, S.D. B/A.   OVER 4s WELCOME.   MOST ROOMS EN SUITE.   BEVERAGES & TV IN ROOMS.   B. & B. FROM £17.50, D. B. & B. FROM £22.50.

Flower in Hand Guest House

BURR BANK, SCARBOROUGH, N. YORKS, YO11 1PN   TEL: (01723) 371471

The Flower in Hand, nestling beneath the castle walls and overlooking the harbour and South Bay, has for 150 years been a much-loved feature of Scarborough's Old Town.
OPEN ALL YEAR Ex. Xmas/New Year.   N/S DINING R.   V, S.D. STD.   OVER 2S ONLY.   EN SUITE IN 3 ROOMS.
BEVERAGES & T.V. IN ALL ROOMS.   CREDIT CARDS.   B. & B. FROM £17.50.

FOXCLIFFE TEAROOM, STATION SQ., RAVENSCAR, SCARBOROUGH, N. YORKS
19th C. building superbly situated overlooking the countryside. All items freshly prepared including lunches & teas. Four spacious letting rooms have sea views.
TEL: (01723) 871028   OPEN Easter - Sept.   NO SMOKING.   V B/A.   TV & BEVERAGES.   CHILDREN WELCOME. B. & B. £13, E.M. £7.

Glenderry Guest House

26 THE DENE, PEASHOLM, SCARBOROUGH, YO12 7NJ   TEL: (01723) 362546

ETB 2 Crowns. 5-bedroom guest house in quiet residential area close to town centre & North Bay attractions. Convenient touring centre Yorkshire coast, moors, Heartbeat country & York.
OPEN ALL YEAR.   NO SMOKING.   V, S.D. B/A.   OVER 2s & PETS WELCOME.   2 ENSUITE ROOMS.   BEVERAGES IN ROOMS.   CREDIT CARDS.   B. & B.F ROM £12.50, EN SUITE £15, E.M. £4.50.

'THE GYPSY', VEGETARIAN GUESTHOUSE, CHURCH RD, RAVENSCAR, N. YORKS.
TEL: (01723) 870366   OPEN ALL YEAR.   NO SMOKING.   V/WH STD, S.D. B/A.   CHILDREN WELCOME.

The Highbank Non-smoking Private Hotel

5 GIVENDALE RD, SCARBOROUGH, N. YORKS, YO12 6LE   TEL; (01723) 365265

ETB Commended. The Highbank is a modern family-run hotel set in a quiet tree-lined area within walking distance of North Bay. Centrally heated and double glazed throughout, it is an ideal choice for a winter break. There are nine comfortable bedrooms, each equipped with a range of amenities including TV with video link-up and radio alarms; there is also a comfortable lounge for reading and relaxing. Wholesome home-cooked English food is served in the pleasant dining room, and vegetarian meals and packed lunches can be provided on request.
OPEN ALL YEAR.   N/S DINING R, PUBLIC AREAS & FIRST FLOOR BEDROOMS.   CHILDREN WELCOME.   EN SUITE & TV IN ROOMS.   24 HR DRINKS MACHINE.   B. & B. FROM £14.50.

NORTHCOTE HOTEL, 114 COLUMBUS RAVINE, SCARBORO', YO12 7QZ
TEL: (01723) 367758 OPEN May - Oct.   NO SMOKING.   OVER 3s .   EN SUITE, BEVERAGES & T.V.

Villa Marina

59 NORTHSTEAD MANOR DRIVE, SCARBOROUGH, N. YORKS, YO12 6AF   TEL: (01723) 361088

ETB 3 Crowns.T he Villa Marina is a superbly appointed detached hotel overlooking Peasholm Park and the Lake, near to the beach and well situated for many of Scarborough's attractions including Kinderland, an indoor pool, Splash World and the Sea-life Centre. The welcome is warm and friendly; bedrooms are light and pleasantly decorated and are equipped with colour T.V. and en suite facilities. Meals are plentiful and varied and are served in the spacious dining room. For the comfort of guests, the Villa Marina is completely smoke-free. Special offers for senior citizens.
OPEN April - Oct.   NO SMOKING.   OVER 3s ONLY.   EN SUITE, BEVERAGES & T.V. IN ROOMS.   ACCESS, VISA.
B. & B. FROM £18. D., B. & B. FROM £24.

WHITESTONE FARM, DOWNDALE RD, STAINTONDALE, SCARBOROUGH, YO13 OE2
TEL: (01723) 870612   OPEN Mar. - Oct.   NO SMOKING.   V B/A.   CHILDREN WELCOME.   PETS B/A.
BEVERAGES IN ROOMS.   T.V. IN ONE LOUNGE.   B. & B. AROUND £16.

WREA HEAD HOUSE, WREA HEAD FARM, BARMOOR LN, SCALBY, SCARBORO', YO13 0PB
TEL: (01723) 375844 OPEN ALL YEAR. NO SMOKING.   V B/A.   OVER 8S ONLY.   EN SUITE, BEVERAGES & TV IN ROOMS.   CREDIT CARDS.   B. & B. AROUND £24.

SELBY

HAZELDENE GUEST HOUSE, 32-34 BROOK ST, DONCASTER RD, SELBY, YO8 0AR
Family-run guest house close to town centre. Private parking. AA listed.
TEL: (01757) 704809 OPEN ALL YEAR, Ex. Xmas And New Year.   NO SMOKING.   S.D.B /A.   CHILDREN
WELCOME.   BEVERAGES & T.V. IN ROOMS.   B. & B. AROUND £19.

SETTLE

Burnside
HORTON-IN-RIBBLESDALE, SETTLE, NORTH YORKS, BD24 0EX   TEL: (01729) 860223
Family home offering bed and breakfast in the Three Peaks area of the Yorkshire Dales
on the Pennine and Ribble Ways.
OPEN Mid Feb. - End Oct.   NO SMOKING.   S.D. B/A.   1 EN SUITE & TV IN ROOM.   BEVERAGES IN ROOMS.   B. & B.
£15.50 - 18.

"HALSTEADS" B. & B., 3 HALSTEADS TERRACE, DUKE ST, SETTLE, BD24 9AP
Victorian terraced house. Ideal base for touring Dales, Lakes & Settle-Carlisle
Railway. Variety of pubs & restaurants for evening meal.
TEL: (01729) 822823   OPEN Mar. - Nov.   NO SMOKING.   V B/A.   CHILDREN WELCOME.   SOME EN SUITE
ROOMS.   TV & BEVERAGES IN ROOMS.   B. & B. AROUND £21.

Liverpool House
CHAPEL SQUARE, SETTLE, N. YORKS, BD24 9HR   (0729) 822247
18th C. house in quiet, but central, part of Settle. Comfortable bedrooms. Home-cooked
food prepared from fresh ingredients; two cosy lounges for guests' use.
OPEN Feb. 1st To Dec. 22nd Incl.   NO SMOKING.   V, S.D. B/A.   LICENSED.   OVER 12S ONLY.   BEVERAGES
IN ROOMS.   T.V. IN LOUNGE.   VISA, MASTERCARD, EUROCARD.   B. & B. AROUND £21.

SKIPTON

Bridge End Farm
GRASSINGTON, THRESHFIELD, SKIPTON, N. YORKS, BD23 5NH   TEL: (01756) 752463
A charming Dales cottage with beams, window seats; welcoming log fires; its large gardens
run down to the river. Private fishing & parking. Music room.
OPEN ALL YEAR.   NO SMOKING.   V B/A.   CHILDREN WELCOME.   NO PETS IN HOUSE: KENNEL PROVIDED.
T.V. IN ROOMS.   B. & B. FROM £18. D. £12.

Devonshire Arms Country House Hotel
BOLTON ABBEY, SKIPTON, N. YORKS, BD23 6AJ   TEL: (01756) 710 441

The Devonshire Arms is an historic hotel (hospitality has
been offered on this site since the 17th C.) which stands
in the heart of the Yorkshire Dales, midway between the
east and west coasts. It has been carefully restored and
extended, under the personal supervision of the Duchess
of Devonshire, to create an hotel of great elegance,
character and charm: a stone-flagged reception hall with
an open log fire leads into handsome lounges furnished
with antiques and family portraits from Chatsworth, and
the recenty refurbished Burlington restaurant extends
into the new, Georgian-style conservatory with its fine
views over the lawned gardens to the hills and moors
beyond. The food served therein is first-rate: a range of
English and Continental dishes are prepared with im-
agination and flair, and a typical à la carte selection might feature Mille Feuilles of Smoked
Duck and Red Cabbage on a Raspberry Dressing followed by King Prawns Deep Fried in
a Cinnamon Batter and Pan Fried Loin of Venison served with a Confit of Cabbage, Bacon
and Thyme Spatzle; the desserts are irresistible. The extensive grounds include croquet
lawns, a 9-hole putting green and fly-fishing. The Devonshire Club, open to non-residents
of the hotel, has an indoor heated pool, floodlit tennis court and the latest in health, beauty
and fitness facilities.
OPEN ALL YEAR.   N/S DINING R & BEDRS.   V, B/A.   LICENSED.   DISABLED ACCESS.
CHILDREN WELCOME.   PETS B/A.   EN SUITE, BEVERAGES & TV IN ROOMS.   ACCESS, VISA, AMEX,
DINERS.   B. & B. FROM £85.

Low Skibeden Farm House

SKIBEDEN RD, SKIPTON, N. YORKS, BD23 6AB   TEL: (01756) 793849   MOBILE: (0831) 126473

ETB 2 Crowns. Low Skibeden is a traditional farm house, with a two-bedroomed holiday cottage nearby, which stands in its own grounds on a livestock smallholding; it has been comfortably furnished throughout and there is a pleasant T.V. lounge for guests' use. Your hosts, Mr and Mrs Simpson, offer tea, coffee and cakes to welcome newly arriving guests and a traditional farmhouse breakfast is served each morning; light refreshments are available each evening at 9.30 p.m. Plenty of safe, private parking.
OPEN ALL YEAR.   NO SMOKING.   OVER 12s WELCOME.   EN SUITE IN 2 ROOMS.   BEVERAGES IN ROOMS. T.V. IN LOUNGE.   B. & B. FROM £16 - 18.

Sparth House Hotel

MALHAM, NR SKIPTON, NN. YORKS, BD23 4DA   TEL; (01729) 830315

Small country house hotel with great individuality and charm, in the heart of the Yorkshire Dales National Park. Imaginative home cooking, well-stocked bar. Ideal base for walking.
OPEN ALL YEAR.   N/S DINING R.   S.D. B/A.   CHILDREN WELCOME.   WHEELCHAIR ACCESS.   LICENSED. EN SUITE, TV & BEVERAGES IN ROOMS.   B. & B. FROM £18.50, D. £13.50.

WHITBY

 Cote Bank Farm

EGTON RD, AISLABY, WHITBY, N. YORKS.   TEL: (01947) 85314

Substantial, stone-built 18th C. farmhouse with mullioned windows, log fires and period furniture; wonderful country views. Wholesome and delicious food prepared from fresh produce wherever possible. Evening meal on request.
OPEN ALL YEAR ex. Xmas.   NO SMOKING.   V, S.D. B/A.   CHILDREN WELCOME.   H & C, SHAVER POINTS & BEVERAGES IN ROOMS.   T.V. IN LOUNGE.   AMEX.   B. & B. AROUND £20.

 Falcon Guest House

29 FALCON TERRACE, WHITBY, N. YORKS, YO21 1EH   TEL: (01947) 603507

Guest house in quiet location 7 mins walk from town centre and harbour. Lounge with TV. Sunny breakfast room.
OPEN ALL YEAR.   NO SMOKING.   V, VE STD.   S.D. B/A.   CHILDREN WELCOME.   BEVERAGES IN BEDROOMS. B. & B. FROM £13.

Larpool Hall Country House Hotel

LARPOOL LANE, WHITBY, N. YORKS.   TEL: (01947) 602737

Larpool Hall is an elegant Georgian Mansion steeped in a rich local history; it stands in its own landscaped gardens, overlooking the beautiful Esk Valley with its stupendous views. The hotel is owned by Keith and Electra Robinson who have worked hard to create a hotel with a very special ambience for guests: from its beautiful entrance hall with its original mahogany balustered starcase to the tastfully decorated bedrooms (there is a bridal suite on the top floor), Larpool Hall endeavours to offer something out of the ordinary - unsurprisingly it is a very popular venue for weddings and other special occasions. Meals are served in a charming dinng room, with bay window, sea views and a 17th C. fireplace, and the food served therein reflects Electra's wide interest in - and knowledge of - culinary matters from traditonal, regional dishes to more exotic fare.
OPEN ALL YEAR.   N/S DINING R.   S.D.   CHILDREN.   WHEELCHAIR ACCESS. LICENSED.   EN SUITE, TV & BEVERAGES IN ROOMS.   B. & B. FROM £35, D. FROM £15.95.

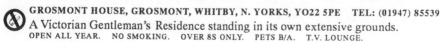

'THE LOW HOUSE', BAYSDALE, KILDALE, NR WHITBY, YO21 2SF TEL: (01642) 722880
Small 18th C. guest house surrounded by moorland with river nearby; superb views.
OPEN Easter - Sept.   NO SMOKING.   V EXC.   OVER 5S ONLY.   B. & B., Plcnic Lunch & D. AROUND £26.

GROSMONT HOUSE, GROSMONT, WHITBY, N. YORKS, YO22 5PE   TEL: (01947) 85539
A Victorian Gentleman's Residence standing in its own extensive grounds.
OPEN ALL YEAR.   NO SMOKING.   OVER 8S ONLY.   PETS B/A.   T.V. LOUNGE.

1 WELL CLOSE TERRACE, WHITBY, N. YORKS, YO21 3AR TEL: (01947) 600173
OPEN MOST OF YEAR.   NO SMOKING.   V STD.   B. & B. AROUND £15.

 ## Wentworth House

27 HUDSON ST, WEST CLIFF, WHITBY, N. YORKS, YO21 3EP   TEL: (01947) 602433

 Wentworth House is a beautiful 4-storey Victorian house which is conveniently situated just 5 minutes' walk from the harbour, beach and town centre of Whitby. The house is spacious and offers very comfortable centrally heated accommodation in its attractive guest bedrooms, some of which have en suite facilities. The food is wholesome and delicious: everything is freshly prepared (from organic ingredients wherever possible - including free-range eggs) and the proprietors specialise in wholefood vegetarian meals, although non-vegetarian dishes are also available; vegan and other special diets can be accommodated by arrangement and there is a good selection of reasonably priced organic wines. Whitby is a picturesque fishing town with a maze of cobbled streets and houses which huddle on the steep hillsides which sweep down to the harbour; it has much of historical interest to commend it, too, in its ancient abbey, the church of St Mary's & the places which commemorate one of its most famous sons, Cpt. James Cook.

OPEN ALL YEAR.   NO SMOKING.   V/WH A SPECIALITY. S.D. VE, B/A.   LICENSED.   CHILDREN WELCOME. GROUND FLOOR EN SUITE ROOM with suitable fittings in shower room for less able-bodied people. 3 EN SUITE ROOMS. BEVERAGES IN ROOMS.   T.V. LOUNGE.   CREDIT CARDS.   B. & B. FROM £15. D. £8.

 ## York House Private Hotel

HIGH HAWSKER, NR WHITBY, N. YORKS, YO22 4LW   TEL: (01947) 880314

 ***ETB 3 Crowns. RAC Highly Acclaimed. Roy Castle Clean Air Award Winner.*** York House is a detached house standing in its own pleasant grounds close to the coast and surrounded by the moorland and farmland of North York Moors National Park, less than 3 miles fom Robin Hood's Bay and Whitby. The en suite bedrooms are tastefully furnished, and each is equipped with a range of helpful amenities including a hairdryer, courtesy tray and colour T.V. The proprietors offer a full English breakfast in the elegant dining room: everything has been home-cooked & an evening meal is available; there is a pleasant lounge and bar for guests' use.

OPEN Mar.- Oct. inc.   NO SMOKING.   S.D. B/A.   LICENSED.   EN SUITE, BEVERAGES & T.V. IN ROOMS.   B. & B. FROM £20. D. £10.

YORK

 ## 4 South Parade

4 SOUTH PARADE, YORK, N. YORKS, YO2 2BA   TEL & FAX: (01904) 628229

 Number 4 South Parade is one of 20 Grade II listed houses which form an elegant Georgian terrace in a private cobbled street just outside York's city walls. It has been lovingly and carefully restored by Robin and Anne McClure who have furnished the house in keeping with the period, ensuring that the ambience of a private home has been retained. Each of the 3 lovely guest bedrooms has an individual character: there are Edwardian fireplace, with working cast iron hob grate, and the welcoming touches include the provision of fresh flowers, a bowl of pot pourri and fruit. Rooms are also equipped with direct dial phones and teletext remote control TVs with video channels.Robin and Anne have given a great deal of thought to the pampering aspect required by - but rarely found - by holiday-makers: a newspaper is served with your early morning tea, a tray of freshly made

tea and coffee is bought at any time of day, lifts to - and from - the station can be provided. Nothing seems too much trouble, and candle-lit suppers are available on request (bring your own wine).
OPEN ALL YEAR.   NO SMOKING.   S.D.   NOT LICENSED BUT BYO WINE.   EN SUITE & TV IN ROOMS.   B. & B. £34 p.p. sharing double. Sgl from £60

BOWEN HOUSE, 4 GLADSTONE ST, HUNTINGTON RD, YO3 7RFTEL: (01904) 636881

Late Victorian town house, carefully decorated and furnished with antiques. Private car park and close to city centre. English and vegetarian breakfasts. Reduced winter rates.
OPEN ALL YEAR.   NO SMOKING. V STD.   CHILDREN WELCOME.   PETS B/A.   2 EN SUITE ROOMS. BEVERAGES & T.V. IN ROOMS.   CREDIT CARDS. B. &. B. AROUND £18.

Byron House Hotel
THE MOUNT, YORK, YO2 2DD   TEL: (01904) 632525   FAX: (01904) 639424

Byron House Hotel Is an elegant Georgian house which is beautifully situated on the Mount in York. The hotel is owned and run by Mr and Mrs Tyson whose aim is to provide a friendly atmosphere and personal service in relaxing surroundings: certainly the elegant proportions of the house help them to achieve a relaxing, gracious ambience - an effect which they have enhanced by their judicious use of furnishings and wallcoverings. The food is also excellent: meals are served in a charming dining room, and packed lunches can be provided on request. The hotel is licensed and the lounge bar is a particuarly pleasant place to enjoy a pre-dinner - or post-dinner - drink. The hotel is about 10 minutes' walk from the city walls, the railway station and the race course and, as guests can enjoy private parking, you can forget about your car while you enjoy the charms of this historic city - a privelege which few visiting drivers can hope for!
OPEN ALL YEAR (ex. Xmas)   N/S DINING R. & SOME BEDROOMS.   V STD, VE, S.D., ORG, WH B/A.   CHILDREN & SOME PETS.   LICENSED.   CREDIT CARDS.   EN SUITE, TV & BEVERAGES IN ROOMS.

City Guest House
68 MONKGATE, YORK, N. YORKS, YO3 7PF   TEL: (01904) 622483
ETB 2 Crowns. Lovely Victorian terraced house just a few minutes' walk from the ancient city walls. Comfy, cosy, and a haven for non-smokers.
OPEN ALL YEAR. NO SMOKING. V STD, S.D. B/A.   CHILDREN WELCOME.   MOST ROOMS EN SUITE. BEVERAGES & T.V. IN ROOMS.   CREDIT CARDS.   B. & B. AROUND £18.

Claremont Guest House
18 CLAREMONT TERRACE, GILLYGATE, YORK, N. YORKS, YO3 7EJ   TEL: (01904) 625158
ETB Commended Listed. Small personally-run city centre establishment in a quiet cul-de-sac of late Victorian terraced houses close to York Minster.
OPEN ALL YEAR.   NO SMOKING. V, S.D. B/A.   1 EN SUITE ROOM.   TV & BEVERAGES IN ROOMS.   CHILDREN; OVER 12S ONLY.   CREDIT CARDS.   B. & B. AROUND £20.

Dairy Wholefood Guesthouse
3 SCARCROFT RD, YORK, N. YORKS, YO2 1ND   TEL: (01904) 639367
Tasteful in many ways! Traditional and wholefood guest house.
OPEN Feb. - Dec.   N/S DINING R & SITTING R.   V / WH A SPECIALITY. S.D. B/A.   CHILDREN WELCOME. EN SUITE IN 2 ROOMS.   BEVERAGES & TV IN ROOMS.   B. & B. FROM £15.

Eastons

90 BISHOPTHORPE RD, YORK, YO2 1JS   TEL: (01904) 626646
Built in 1878 and originally a city wine merchant's residence, Easton's has been sympathetically restored in keeping with its period character; open fires blaze in the original fireplaces in cooler weather, and the William Morris decor and period furnishings have helped create a guest house with a very special ambience - at affordable prices. Accommodation is in individually designed bedrooms - each centrally heated and with every possible amenity - and the Victorian Sideboard breakfast menu offers an excellent choice of both traditional and vegetarian dishes. There is

private parking at Eastons so you can explore York without worrying about car parks and traffic. The mediaeval city walls are just 250 yards away, while the Jorvik Centre, Clifford's Tower and the Castle Museum are all within strolling distance.

OPEN ALL YEAR (ex. Xmas).   NO SMOKING.   S.D. V.   OVER 4s WELCOME.   EN SUITE, TV & BEVERAGES IN BEDROOMS.   CREDIT CARDS.   B. & B. FROM £17.50.

The Hazelwood

24-25 PORTLAND ST, GILLYGATE, YORK, N. YORKS, YO3 7EH   TEL: (01904) 626548
FAX: (01904) 628032

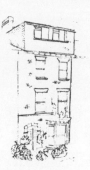

ETB 2 Crown Commended. The Hazelwood is an elegant Victorian town house which was built in 1862 and stands in a conservation area close to the city walls. Although only 400 yards from the Minster and within easy walking distance of the city centre's shops, restaurants and tourist attractions, the house is in an extremely quiet location and has its own car park. The comfortable tastefully decorated rooms, most of which are en suite and two of which have four poster beds, have a range of facilities including hospitality trays, hair dryers, and complimentary toiletries. There is a secluded walled garden in which guests may relax on sunny days, and a residents' lounge, well-stocked with travel books and visitor information, in which tea and coffee are always available. Breakfasts are generous, of a high quality and there is a choice of dishes to suit all tastes. Your hosts will gladly help you plan your stay, and can even show you menus of good local restaurants.

OPEN ALL YEAR.   NO SMOKING.   V, S.D. B/A.   CHILDREN WELCOME.   PETS B/A.   EN SUITE, TV & BEVERAGES IN ROOMS.   VISA, MASTERCARD.   B. & B. from £16, WINTER RATES.

Hobbits Hotel

9 ST PETER'S GROVE, YORK, N. YORKS, YO3 6AQ   TEL: (01904) 624538
Comfortable Victorian house with parking in quiet cul-de-sac 10 mins' walk from York centre. Off-street parking.

OPEN ALL YEAR ex. Xmas.   N/S DINING ROOM & BEDRS.   V, B/A.   LICENSED.   CHILDREN WELCOME.   PETS B/A.   EN SUITE, TV & BEVERAGES IN ROOMS.   CREDIT CARDS.   B & B FROM £25.

Holmlea Guest House

6/7 SOUTHLANDS RD, YORK, N. YORKS, YO2 1NP   TEL: (01904) 621010

ETB 3 Crown Commended. Warm and friendly family-run guest house in a quiet position off the main road. Comfortable guests' lounge. 15 min walk from the centre of York.

OPEN Feb. - OCt. inc.   NO SMOKING. V B/A.   LICENSED. CHILDREN WELCOME.   PETS B/A.   4 EN SUITE ROOMS.   BEVERAGES & T.V. IN ROOMS.   B. & B. FROM £14.

Holmwood House

114 HOLGATE RD, YORK, N. YORKS, YO2 4BB   TEL: (01904) 626183   FAX: (01904) 670899

Built as two private houses in the middle of the 19th C. and backing onto one of the prettiest squares in York, these two listed buildings have been lovingly restored to create a charming guest house with the ambience of a much-loved private home. Each of the peaceful, elegant bedrooms is different in decoration and character, and the many extra little touches include direct dial phone, radio alarm and hair dryer; there are three rooms on the ground floor and one at garden level. Breakfast is an abundant feast catering for every taste including vegetarian (there is a special muesli) and the lighter appetite (croissants, coffee and toast). There is a large, private car park to the rear of the hotel - a real asset in York where parking is at a premium - and you are just 10 minutes' walk from the centre of York with its many tourist attractions.

OPEN ALL YEAR.   N/S DINING R & SOME BEDRS.   V STD, S.D. B/A.   OVER 8s WELCOME.   SMALL DOGS B/A. EN SUITE, TV & BEVERAGES IN ROOMS.   B. & B. FROM £27.50 - 32.50(jacuzzi) Sgl £42 - 45.

The Lodge

EARSWICK GRANGE, EARSWICK, YORK, N. YORKS, YO3 9SW   TEL: (01904) 761387

ETB 1 Crown. The Lodge is a modern family home which stands amidst large, well-kept gardens, complete with paddock, free-range hens and apiary (fresh eggs and plenty of honey for breakfast!) in a lovely rural setting near the historic city of York. The house has been very comfortably furnished throughout - there are two spacious bedrooms - and a welcoming open fire burns in the grate on cooler days. You are perfectly situated for visiting both the city of York and for touring the North York Moors & Dales; additionally you are near to Ryedale Sports Stadium & York golf club.

OPEN ALL YEAR.   NO SMOKING.   V, S.D. B/A.   CHILDREN WELCOME.   BEVERAGES.   T.V. IN LOUNGE. B. &. B. FROM £13.

LUND HOUSE, MAIN STREET, HELPERBY, NR YORK, YO6 2NT TEL: (01423) 360392
OPEN ALL YEAR.   NO SMOKING.   V B/A.   CHILDREN WELCOME.   EN SUITE. BEVERAGES IN ROOM. T.V. IN ROOM.   B. & B. AROUND £16.

MAY COTTAGE, 44 MAIN ST, BISHOPTHORPE, YORK, YO4 4TP TEL: (01759) 318846
ETB 4 Keys Commended. S/C 2-bed. cottage beautifully furnished with antiques.
OPEN ALL YEAR   NO SMOKING.   CHILDREN & PETS WELCOME.   COLOUR T.V.   £145-£295 P.W.

Mulberry Guest House

124 EAST PARADE, HEWORTH, YORK, N. YORKS, YO3 7YG   TEL: (01904) 423468

Beautifully restored Victorian town house in a residential area of York just a short walk from the city centre. Retaining many original features. Traditonal or Continental b'fasts.

OPEN ALL YEAR.   N/S DINING R.   V, S.D. B/A.   CHILDREN WELCOME.   EN SUITE, TV & BEVERAGES IN ROOMS.   B. & B. AROUND £20.

Newton Guest House

NEVILLE ST, HAXBY RD, YORK, N. YORKS, YO3 7NP   TEL: (01904) 635627

The Newton Guest House is a small, family-run establishment which is situated in a pleasant residential area just 10 minutes' walk from the city centre. It is run by John and Diana Tindall, a friendly and welcoming couple, who will do all that they can to ensure that your stay is a happy and memorable one. Accommodation is in comforatable en suite rooms, with full central heating, and a generous breakfast is served to guests. York is one of England's most beautiful and interesting historic cities: in addition to its many attractions - the city walls, the museums and the Minster - you are within easy reach of the North York Moors, the East Coast and the York-shire Dales. Fire certificate. private parking.

OPEN ALL YEAR.   NO SMOKING.   CHILDREN WELCOME.   EN SUITE, TV & BEVERAGES IN ROOMS.

Nunmill House

85 BISHOPTHORPE RD, YORK, N. YORKS, YO2 1NX   TEL: (01904) 634047

Nunmill House is an elegant Victorian residence which has been lovingly restored by its present owners and now offers accommodation of an exceptionally high standard to guests: each of the bedrooms has been furnished and decorated in traditional style - two rooms have four-posters - and there is a range of helpful amenities such as tea-making trays and colour TVs (do send for a colour brochure). Traditional or Continental breakfasts are served in the elegant dining room, and there are numerous restaurants nearby where you may enjoy an evening meal. Your hosts, Mr and Mrs Whit-bourn-Hammond, really do everything they can to make your stay happy and memorable: they are very knowledgeable about the city and are happy to advise you about its numerous historic attractions - which are within easy walking distance (there is parking available at the house). Having lived in York

for 12 years we are biased about its charms, but share the view that York is a city for everyone: the Minster (Europe's largest medieval cathedral), the Castle Museum, the city walls appeal historically, aesthetically, architecturally and in every other pleasing way. A city to enjoy - and to share.
OPEN Feb. - Nov.   NO SMOKING.   V, S.D. B/A.   CHILDREN WELCOME.   EN SUITE, TV & BEVERAGES IN ROOMS.   B. & B. FROM £18 - 22.

Papillon

43 GILLYGATE, YORK, N. YORKS, YO3 7EA   TEL: (01904) 636505
City centre guest house just 300 yards from York Minster. Private parking. High standards.
OPEN ALL YEAR Ex Xmas & New year.   N/S.   V B/A.   CHILDREN WELCOME.   EN SUITE MOST ROOMS.
BEVERAGES & T.V. IN ALL ROOMS.   B. & B. FROM £17.50.

POND COTTAGE, BRANDSBY RD, STILLINGTON, NR YORK, YO6 1NY
OPEN Feb. - Nov. inc.   NO SMOKING.   V, B/A.   CHILDREN WELCOME.   BEVERAGES IN ROOMS.   T.V. LOUNGE.   B. & B. AROUND £16.

Regency House

7 SOUTH PARADE, BLOSSOM ST, YORK, N. YORKS, YO2 2BA TEL: (01904) 633053
Regency House is a Grade II listed building which dates from 1824 and stands in a private cobbled road within strolling distance of the centre of the city of York, and just 6 minutes' walk from the railway station. Each of the centrally heated bedrooms has been furnished to a very high standard and some have en suite facilities; helpful guide books and brochures have been left in each bedroom to help you plan your stay. The dining room features an old Yorkshire range and a low beamed ceiling and your hostess, Mrs. Podmore, cooks an excellent breakfast therein (her Visitors Book bears testament to its popularity); there are numerous good restaurants within easy walking distance at which you may enjoy an evening meal. There is so much to see and do in the city of York itself, but visitors are further attracted by the range of other beautiful places within easy touring distance, such as Whitby, Harrogate, Ripon and the splendours of the North York Moors National Park. Parking and garageing available.
OPEN JAN. TO MID-DEC.   NO SMOKING.   V, DIAB. STD.   OVER 8S ONLY.   BEVERAGES & T.V. IN ALL BEDROOMS.   B. & B. FROM £15.50.

Saxon House Hotel

FISHERGATE, 71-73 FULFORD RD, YORK, YO1 4BD   TEL: (01904) 622106   FAX: (01904) 633764
Friendly family-run hotel a short distance fromthe city centre attractions. Non-smoking bar lounge. Car park.
OPEN ALL YEAR ex. Xmas.   N/S DINING R. & BAR LOUNGE.   V, S.D. B/A.   CHILDREN & PETS WELCOME.   EN SUITE, TV & BEVERAGES IN ROOMS.   B. & B. FROM £20.

Swallow Hotel

TADCASTER RD, DRINGHOUSES, YORK, N. YORKS, YO2 2QQ   TEL: (01904) 701000
 A member of the Swallow Group, this luxurious and comfortable hotel is surrounded by gardens and overlooks York's scenic Racecourse and the Knavesmire parkland. The Atrium restaurant with its high glass roof and hanging flowers provides a light airy atmosphere and offers first-class cuisine. The Leisure Club has a wide range of free facilities including a fitness section, a relaxation area (with spa bath and sauna), and an indoor heated swimming pool with a separate pool for young children. You are just 5 minutes' drive from the centre of York.
OPEN ALL YEAR.   N/S DINING R & PART OF COFFEE SHOP.   V STD.   LICENSED.   GOOD DISABLED ACCESS: 2 ESPECIALLY DESIGNED BEDROOMS.   CHILDREN WELCOME.   PETS B/A.   EN SUITE, TV & BEVERAGES IN ROOMS.   ACCESS, VISA, AMEX.   B. & B. FROM £47.50. D. £17.95.

RESTAURANTS

CROPTON

THE NEW INN & NEW INN RESTAURANT, CROPTON, NR PICKERING, YO18 8HH
For further details please see under the entry in the Accommodation section.

GRASSINGTON

DALES KITCHEN TEAROOMS, 51 MAIN STREET, GRASSINGTON, BD23 5AA
TEL: (01756) 753077   N/S RESTAURANT.   LICENSED.   VERY GOOD DISABLED ACCESS.

HARROGATE

BETTY'S CAFÉ TEAROOMS, 1 PARLIAMENT ST, HARROGATE, HG1 2QU
TEL: (01423) 502746   80% N/S   V STD.   LICENSED.   CHILDREN VERY WELCOME.   ACCESS, VISA.

 *Debenhams*

22-30 PARLIAMENT ST, HARROGATE, N. YORKS.   TEL: (01423) 68234
Springles, a friendly self-service restaurant serving lunches, snacks and drinks.
OPEN STORE HOURS.   NO SMOKING .   V STD.   DISABLED ACCESS.   CHILDREN WELCOME.
CREDIT/DEBIT CARDS.

GREEN PARK HOTEL, VALLEY DRIVE, HARROGATE, N. YORKS, HG2 OJT
TEL: (01423) 504681 FAX (01423) 530811 N/S RESTAURANT.   V B/A.   LICENSED.   CHILDREN WELCOME.

LOW HALL HOTEL & COACHHOUSE REST., RIPON RD, KILLINGHALL, HARROGATE.
TEL: (01423) 508598 N/S RESTAURANT.   V, VE STD. S.D. B/A.   LICENSED.   DISABLED ACCESS.

ILKLEY

BETTY'S CAFÉ & TEA ROOMS, 32 - 34 THE GROVE, ILKLEY, N. YORKS.
TEL: (01943) 608029   80% N/S. LICENSED.   DISABLED ACCESS to restaurant but not toilets.   CHILDREN.

KNARESBOROUGH

BLENKHORN'S CAFÉ, 2 WATERSIDE, KNARESBOROUGH, N. YORKS, HG5 9AZ
Waterside café and snack bar in the picturesque town of Knaresborough.

 4 PARK PLACE RESTAURANT, 4 PARK PLACE, KNARESBORO', N. YORKS, HE5 OGR
TEL: (01423) 868002   NO SMOKING.   LICENSED.   V B/A.   CHILDREN WELCOME.   VISA.

 POLLYANNA'S TEA ROOM, JOCKEY LANE, HIGH ST, KNARESBOROUGH, N. YORKS.
TEL: (01423) 869208   NO SMOKING.   LICENSED.   V STD.   DISABLED ACCESS.   CHILDREN WELCOME.

NORTHALLERTON

BETTYS CAFÉ TEAROOMS, 188 HIGH ST, NORTHALLERTON, DL7 8LF
TEL: (01609) 775154   70% N/S.   V STD.   LICENSED.   DISABLED ACCESS BUT NOT TO TOILETS.   CHILDREN.

PICKERING

THE BLACKSMITH'S ARMS AND RESTAURANT, AISLABY, PICKERING, YO18 8PE
TEL: (01751) 472182 N/S RESTAURANT.   V, VE STD.   LICENSED.   DISABLED ACCESS.   CHILDREN WELCOME.

RICHMOND

THE KING'S HEAD HOTEL, RICHMOND, N. YORKS, DL10 4HS
For further details please see under entry in accommodation section.

RIPON

THE OLD DEANERY RESTAURANT, MINSTER RD, RIPON, HG4 1QS
NO SMOKING.   LICENSED.   V, DIAB STD.   DISABLED ACCESS.   CHILDREN WELCOME.

SCARBOROUGH

BONNET & SON, 38 HUNTRISS ROW, SCARBOROUGH, N. YORKS.
TEL: (01723) 361033   NO SMOKING.   V STD.   CHILDREN WELCOME.

DEBENHAMS, BRUNSWICK PAVILION, VERNON RD, SCARBORO' TEL: (01723) 368181
OPEN STORE HOURS.   NO SMOKING.   V STD.   DISABLED ACCESS.   CHILDREN.   CREDIT CARDS.

FOXCLIFFE TEAROOM, STATION SQ., RAVENSCAR, SCARBOROUGH, N. YORKS.
TEL: (01723) 871028   NO SMOKING.   V B/A.   CHILDREN WELCOME.   WHEELCHAIR ACCESS.

SETTLE

CAR AND KITCHEN, SETTLE, N. YORKS, BD24 9EF
Family run business; snacks & lunches from the finest fresh ingredients.
TEL: (01729) 823638   NO SMOKING.   V STD.   CHILDREN WELCOME.   CREDIT CARDS.

PEN-Y-GHENT CAFÉ, HORTON-IN-RIBBLESDALE, NR SETTLE, BD24 OHE
NO SMOKING.   V, S.D. B/A.   CHILDREN WELCOME.

SKIPTON

DALES TEAPOT, ROPEWALK, ALBION SQUARE, SKIPTON, N. YORKS.
TEL: (01756) 793416   NO SMOKING.   V STD.   LICENSED.   GOOD DISABLED ACCESS.

DEVONSHIRE ARMS COUNTRY HOUSE HOTEL, BOLTON ABBEY, SKIPTON, BD23 6AJ
For further details please see under the entry in the accommodation section.

'HERBS', HEALTHY LIFE NATURAL FOOD CENTRE, 10 HIGH ST, SKIPTON, N.
YORKS.
TEL: (01756) 790619   NO SMOKING.   V EXC, S.D. B/A.   CHILDREN'S PORTIONS.

WHITBY

Magpie Café
14 PIER RD, WHITBY, N. YORKS.   TEL: (01947) 602058

The Magpie Café building dates from the 1750s when it was owned by a whaler. Subsequently it became a shipping office and then, in the 1930's, a café which is now in the third generation of the McKenzie family. All the food is fresh -notably the fish (including crab, lobster, and salmon) which is landed at the quayside opposite - and the menu offers a choice of over 30 home made desserts as well as cakes, jam and chutney. Children will love the food on their own menu with shortbread elephants, chocolate fish ice cream and jelly baby jelly! Something for everyone - including those on special diets.
98 SEATS. OPEN FEB - EARLY JAN. 11.30 - 6.30 SUN - THURS. 11.30 - 9 FRI & SAT. L. FROM AROUND £6. 80%
NO-SMOKING. V, WEIGHT WATCHERS, DIAB. AND GLUTEN-FREE STD. LICENSED.   EXCELLENT FACILITIES
FOR CHILDREN, INCLUDING CHILDREN'S MENU.   VISA, MASTERCARD.

YORK

BETTYS CAFÉ TEAROOMS, ST HELENS SQUARE, YORK, N. YORKS.
TEL: (01904) 659142   70% N/S.   LICENSED.   V STD.   DISABLED ACCESS but not to toilets. CHILDREN.

THE BLAKE HEAD VEGETARIAN CAFÉ, 104 MICKLEGATE, YORK, N. YORKS, YO1 1JX
TEL: (01904) 623767   N/S RESTAURANT.   DISABLED ACCESS.   CHILDREN'S PORTIONS.

Debenhams
5 CONEY ST, YORK, N. YORKS.   TEL: (01904) 656644
Chinwags, a friendly self-service coffee shop serving lunches, snacks and drinks.
OPEN STORE HOURS.   NO SMOKING.   V STD.   DISABLED ACCESS.   CHILDREN VERY WELCOME.
CREDIT/DEBIT CARDS.

Four Seasons Restaurant
45 GOODRAMGATE, YORK   TEL: (01904) 633787
15th C. half timbered restaurant - a culinary and architectural treat!
50% NO-SMOKING. V STD. LICENSED. CHILDREN WELCOME. CREDIT CARDS.

Gillygate Wholefood Bakery

MILLERS YARD, YORK, N. YORKS, YO3 7EB   TEL: (01904) 610676
Wholefood vegetarian bakery, shop and café. Vegan food always available. Outside seating.
NO SMOKING.   V. EXC.   DISABLED ACCESS.   CHILDREN WELCOME.

THE GREEN HOUSE CAFÉ, 12A CHURCH ST, YORK, N. YORKS, YO1 2BB
TEL: (01904) 629615   NO SMOKING. V STD.   LICENSED.   DISABLED ACCESS.   CHILDREN WELCOME.

THE RUBICON, 5 LITTLE STONEGATE, YORK, N. YORKS.
TEL: (01904) 676076   NO SMOKING. V EXC. BYO WINE. CHILDREN WELCOME.

TAYLORS IN STONEGATE, 46 STONEGATE, YORK, N. YORKS, YO1 2AS
Family run Tea Rooms and Coffee shop founded in 1886. Outstanding variety of teas
and coffees offered together with many Yorkshire and Continental specialities.
TEL: (01904) 622865   70% N/S.   CHILDREN'S PORTIONS.   ACCESS, VISA.

TREASURER'S HOUSE TEA ROOMS, MINSTER YARD, YORK, N. YORKS.
Tastefully furnished tea room in 17th C. Treasurer's House behind York Minster.
TEL: (01904) 624247/646757   OPEN   DAILY APRIL - DEC.   NO SMOKING.

THE YORK ARMS, HIGH PETERGATE, YORK, N. YORKS.
TEL: (01904) 624508   N/S UPSTAIRS DINING R (LUNCHTIME).   V STD.

PUBS & WINE BARS

CROPTON

THE NEW INN & NEW INN RESTAURANT, CROPTON, NR PICKERING
NO SMOKING IN CONSERVATORY WHICH IS FOR DRINKING AND DINING.

YORK

WILDE'S WINE BAR AND BRASSERIE, GRAPE LANE, YORK
Small, intimate wine bar/bistro with one smoke-free room; imaginative dishes prepared
from fresh local produce. Comprehensive wine list. Live jazz on Saturday nights.
SEPARATE N/S ROOM.   V STD.   WHEELCHAIR ACCESS.   CHILDREN WELCOME.   ACCESS, VISA, AMEX.

South Yorkshire

ACCOMMODATION

DONCASTER

CANDA, HAMPOLE BALK LANE, SKELLOW, DONCASTER   TEL: (0302) 724028
OPEN ALL YEAR.   NO SMOKING.   GOOD DISABLED ACCESS: 6 ROOMS ON GROUND FLOOR.
OVER 9S ONLY.   6 EN SUITE ROOMS. BEVERAGES.   T.V.   CREDIT CARDS.   B. & B. AROUND £20.

SHEFFIELD

PARKFIELD HOUSE, 97 NORFOLK RD, SHEFFIELD (0742) 720404
OPEN ALL YEAR.   NO SMOKING.   V STD, S.D. B/A.   BEVERAGES & TV IN ROOMS. B. & B.
AROUND £19.

RESTAURANTS & PUBS

DONCASTER

WOOLWORTHS, ST SEPULCHRE'S GATE, DONCASTER, DN1 1JY TEL: (01302) 368486
142 SEATS. OPEN MON - THURS 9 - 5, FRI, SAT 8.30 - 5. L. 11.30 - 2.30. NO SMOKING.   V, LOW-FAT
STD.   DISABLED ACCESS. CHILDREN WELCOME. CREDIT CARDS.

SHEFFIELD

CRUCIBLE COFFEE SHOP, CRUCIBLE THEATRE, NORFOLK ST, SHEFFIELD, S1 1DA TEL; TEL: (01742) 760621
Theatre coffee shop. Snacks, baked potatoes, cakes.
N/S 75% OF COFFEE SHOP & FOYER AREAS. V STD. DISABLED ACCESS. CHILDREN WELCOME.

THE FAT CAT PUB, 23 ALMA ST., SHEFFIELD   TEL: (01742) 728195
Award-winning hostelry with exceptionally wide variety of beverages including draught cider, Old Organic Wines and 10 draught beers (including their own brew!).
N/S 1 BAR (separated from smoking bar by corridor). V, VE STD. DISABLED ACCESS. PETS WELCOME.

FROG & PARROT, DIVISION ST, SHEFFIELD   TEL: (01742) 721280
SMOKING BANNED IN 2 AREAS OF PUB.

West Yorkshire

ACCOMMODATION

BINGLEY

Ashley End
22 ASHLEY RD, BINGLEY, W. YORKS, BD16 1DZ   TEL: (01274) 569679
Private house appreciated by guests for friendly, welcoming atmosphere. Situated off Bradford Road with easy access to public transport.
OPEN ALL YEAR. NO SMOKING. V STD. BEVERAGES IN ROOMS. B. & B. £15.

DEWSBURY

Ayton Guest House
11 PARK RD, WESTBOROUGH, DEWSBURY, W. YORKS, WF13 4LQ   TEL: (01924) 469480
OPEN ALL YEAR.   NO SMOKING.   V B/A.   CHILDREN WELCOME.   EN SUITE IN 2 ROOMS.   BEVERAGES ON REQUEST.   T.V. LOUNGE.   B. & B. FROM £15.

HALIFAX

Glenmore Guest House
19 SAVILE PARK, HALIFAX, W. YORKS, HX1 3EA   TEL: (01422) 341500
ETB Highly Commended. Surrounded by beautiful countryside, Glenmore faces directly onto a tree-lined park and has a welcoming serenity and charm, Spacious en suite bedrooms. Continental/English b'fast. Excellent public transport at door. Trains can be met.
OPEN Feb. - Dec. NO SMOKING. V, S.D. B/A. CHILDREN WELCOME.   EN SUITE, BEVERAGES & T.V. (INCLUDING SATELLITE) IN ROOMS.   B. & B. AROUND £22.

WOOD END, LIGHTHAZELS RD, RIPPONDEN, SOWERBY BRIDGE, HX6 4NP
TEL: (01422) 824397 OPEN ALL YEAR. NO SMOKING. V, B/A. CHILDREN WELCOME. PETS B/A. EN SUITE IN 1 ROOM. BEVERAGES IN ROOMS. T.V. LOUNGE. B. & B. AROUND £20.

HEBDEN BRIDGE

Prospect End
8 PROSPECT TERR., SAVILE RD, HEBDEN BRIDGE, W. YORKS. HX7 6NA   TEL: (01422) 843586
Stone-built Victorian house. Comfortable well-appointed accommodation with own entrance. Convenient for public transport. Ideal base for walking and touring South Pennines.
OPEN ALL YEAR.   N/S DINING & BEDRS.   S.D. B/A.   EN SUITE, TV & BEVERAGES.   B. & B. FROM £15.50.

Redacre Mill
MYTHOLMROYD, HEBDEN BRIDGE, HX7 5DQ   TEL: (01422) 885563
ETB 3 Crown Highly Commended. Small, Victorian cotton mill in peaceful countryside by the Rochdale Canal. Luxuriously furnished to high standards. Home-cooked meals.
OPEN Feb. - Nov.   NO SMOKING. V, S.D. B/A.   LICENSED.   CHILDREN WELCOME. EN SUITE, BEVERAGES & T.V. IN ROOMS.   ACCESS, VISA.   B. & B. AROUND £28.

HOLMFIRTH

Holme Castle Country Hotel

HOLME VILLAGE, HOLMFIRTH, W. YORKS, HD7 1QG TEL: (01484) 686764 FAX: (01484) 687775

Unusual Victorian house with panoramic views. Conservation village within Peak District National park. Special offers October - April. BBC Environment award.

OPEN ALL YEAR. NO SMOKING. V B/A. LICENSED. CHILDREN WELCOME. EN SUITE 5 ROOMS.   T.V., RADIO ALARM, HAIRDRYER IN ROOMS. ACCESS, VISA, AMEX. B. & B. from £25 (reduced Fri. & Sun.) D. £19 & £10.

HUDDERSFIELD

Elm Crest Guest Hotel

2 QUEENS RD, EDGERTON, HUDDERSFIELD, W. YORKS, HD2 2AG   TEL: (01484) 530990 FAX: (01484) 516227

*AA 3 "Q" Award. Les Routier. ETB 3 Crown Commended.*Elm Crest Guest Hotel is a large detached 8-bedroomed Victorian house which stands amidst its own attractive gardens in a peaceful tree-lined residential street just a few minutes' drive from both the town centre and junction 24 of the M62. It has been very comfortably furnished and appointed (it has 3 Crowns from the English Tourist Board and the Good Room Award), and the proprietors extend a very warm and friendly welcome to guests. With its proximity to the town centre - and its easy access via the M62 to so many of the attractions of both West and North Yorkshire - the Elm Crest is the perfect choice for both the business traveller and tourists enjoying a short break.

OPEN JAN. TO DEC.   NO SMOKING.   LICENSED.   OVER 5S ONLY.   EN SUITE IN 5 ROOMS. T.V. IN ALL ROOMS.   ACCESS, VISA, AMEX.   B. & B. FROM £22.

ILKLEY

BEECH HOUSE, 5 ST JAMES RD, ILKLEY, W. YORKS, LS29 9PY   TEL: (01943) 601995
Spacious Victorian house, close to the town centre and public transport. Quiet location within easy walking distance of riverside and moor.

OPEN ALL YEAR.   NO SMOKING.   V, S.D. B/A.   CHILDREN WELCOME.   PETS B/A.   BEVERAGES IN ROOMS.   T.V. IN MOST ROOMS.   B. & B. AROUND £16.

LEEDS

Beegee's Guest House

18 MOOR ALLERTON DRIVE, OFF STREET LN, MOORTOWN, LEEDS, LS17 6RZ   TEL: (01532) 666221   FAX: (01532) 753300

Guest house with full central heating, personally run by Betty and Bernard Gibbs.

OPEN JAN. TO DEC.   NO SMOKING.   V. B/A.   GROUND FLOOR FAMILY ROOM. CHILDREN WELCOME. SOME ROOMS EN SUITE,   BEVERAGES & T.V. IN ROOMS. SINGLE £20-24, DOUBLE £30-34, FAMILY ON REQUEST.

B. & B. Leeds

118 GROVEHALL DRIVE, LEEDS, W. YORKS, LS11 7ET TEL: (01532) 704445
OPEN ALL YEAR. NO SMOKING. CHILDREN WELCOME.   T.V. AVAILABLE.   B. & B. AROUND £16.

The White House

157 MIDDLETON PARK RD, LEEDS, W. YORKS, LS10 4LZ   TEL; (01532) 711231
Smoke-free guest house in South Leeds suburb. Safe parking. *Non-smokers only.*

NON-SMOKERS ONLY.   V B/A.   TV & BEVERAGES.   B. & B. AROUND £19.

OSSETT

Dimple Well Lodge Hotel

THE GREEN, OSSETT, W. YORKS, WF5 8JX   TEL: (01924) 264352   FAX: (01924) 274024

ETB 3 Crowns Highly Commended. Roy Castle Award. Civic Society Award winner. The Dimple Well Lodge is a family-run Georgian House Hotel which dates from 1812 and stands in an acre of beautiful grounds on the site of the Old Nell Pond. The present owners have extensively restored and refurbished the building to provide every modern amenity that today's hotel guest requires, without sacrificing the original character of the house: indeed each of the bedrooms has the original fireplace in addition to en suite facilities and a hospitality tray. The food is of a very high standard: meals are prepared from fresh, local produce and served in the Morning Room overlooking the lawned gardens and old cherry tree; an à la carte menu is now available. The tranquil elegance of Dimple Well Lodge renders it perfectly suited to weddings and other celebratory parties; it is also very accessible - just minutes away from J40 on the M1. OPEN ALL YEAR.   N/S DINING R. & SOME BEDRS.   S.D. B/A.   LICENSED.   EN SUITE, TV & BEVERAGES IN BEDROOMS.   CREDIT CARDS.   B. & B. FROM £33.

WETHERBY

Glendales

MUDDY LANE, LINTON, NR WETHERBY, W. YORKS, LS22 4HW   TEL: (01937) 585915

Large detached house overlooking village green in Linton near Wetherby; country setting yet 10 mins from the A1 and at half way point bet'n London & Edinburgh. NO SMOKING.   V, S.D. B/A.   CHILDREN: OVER 12S ONLY.   PETS WELCOME.   EN SUITE IN 1 ROOM. BEVERAGES.   T.V.   B. & B. FROM £15.

50 WESTGATE, WETHERBY, W. YORKS, LS22 4NJ   TEL: (01937) 63106 N/S RESTAURANT & MOST PUBLIC AREAS.   V B/A.   CHILDREN WELCOME.   BEVERAGES IN ROOMS.   T.V IN LOUNGE.   B. & B. AROUND £16.

WOOD HALL, LINTON, NR WETHERBY, W. YORKS, LS22 4JA   TEL: (01937) 67271 N/S DINING R & BEDRS.   V STD.   LICENSED.   DISABLED ACCESS.   CHILDREN WELCOME.   PETS B/A.   EN SUITE & T.V. IN ROOMS.   CREDIT CARDS.   B. & B. AROUND £60.

RESTAURANTS

BRIGHOUSE

BROOK'S RESTAURANT, 6 BRADFORD RD, BRIGHOUSE, HD6 1RW TEL: (01484) 715284 N/S DINING R.   V STD.   LICENSED.   CHILDREN WELCOME (NO HIGH CHAIRS).

HUDDERSFIELD

The Blue Rooms

9 BYRAM ARCADE, WESTGATE, HUDDERSFIELD, W. YORKS.   TEL: (01484) 512373

The Blue Rooms are situated in a beautiful, refurbished Victorian arcade in the heart of bustling Huddersfield. The proprietor has worked hard to create just the right kind of ambience - classical music, pleasing decor, an informal, friendly atmosphere - and as a consequence the café is exceedingly popular with a wide cross-section of Huddersfield folk, 'from lawyers to students to shoppers...'Pleasing ambience notwithstanding, the repeat visits are clearly a direct result of the dependably excellent food: everything is home-prepared daily from fresh, additive-free ingredients (including free-range eggs), and the mouth-watering menu features a wide range of tasty options including, in addition to tasty sandwiches, snacks and full meals, some wonderful hot French bread sandwiches, baked potatoes, pancakes and, to follow, delicious wholemeal cakes and puddings; vegan, gluten-free and vegetarian

dishes are clearly denoted so on the menu. The Blue Rooms now has a high quality outside catering service for small parties to weddings, etc.
OPEN 10 - 5, Mon.- Sat.   N/S 80% RESTAURANT.   L. AROUND £3.   V, WH., STD; VE, GLUTEN-FREE AVAIL. LICENSED.   CHILDREN WELCOME.

ILKLEY

BETTYS CAFÉ TEA ROOMS, 32/34 THE GROVE, ILKLEY, LS29 9EE TEL: (01943) 608029
75% N/S.   LICENSED.   DISABLED ACCESS to restaurant but not toilets. CHILDREN WELCOME.   ACCESS, VISA.

CHRISTCHURCH CAFÉ, THE GROVE, ILKLEY, LS29 8LW TEL: (01943) 603209
NO SMOKING.   DISABLED ACCESS: RAMP.   CHILDREN WELCOME.

MUFFINS, RAILWAY ROAD, ILKLEY, W. YORKS. TEL: (01943) 817505
NO SMOKING.   V STD.   WHEELCHAIR ACCESS.   CHILDREN WELCOME.

ROMAN PERGOLA, 7 LEEDS RD, ILKLEY, LS29 8DH TEL: (01943) 608639
NO SMOKING.   LICENSED.   CHILDREN WELCOME.

SWEET INDULGENCE TEAROOMS, 8 THE GROVE, ILKLEY.   TEL: (01943) 816927
NO SMOKING.   CHILDREN WELCOME.   CREDIT CARDS.

LEEDS

Debenham's

121 BRIGGATE, LEEDS, W. YORKS, LS1 6LX   TEL: (01532) 435333
Pavilion, a friendly self-service coffee shop serving lunches, snacks and drinks.
OPEN STORE HOURS.   NO SMOKING.   V STD.   DISABLED ACCESS.   CHILDREN.   CREDIT CARDS.

LEWIS'S LTD, THE HEADROW, LEEDS, W. YORKS, LS1 TEL: (01532) 413131 EXT 17
3 smoke-free restaurants within department store at Lewis's.
OPEN 9 - 5.30.   N/S IN ALL RESTAURANTS.   CHILDREN WELCOME.   WHEELCHAIR ACCESS TO ALL RESTAURANTS.

Strawberry Fields Bistro & Wine Bar

159 WOODHOUSE LANE, LEEDS 2, W. YORKS.   TEL: (01532) 431515
Intimate friendly family-run bistro serving a wide variety of home-made vegetarian and meat dishes. Wine Bar upstairs.
40 SEATS.   OPEN Mon. - Fri., 11.45 - 2.00, Mon. - Sat. 5.30 - 10.30 (last orders).   MAIN COURSE £4 - £10. N/S 75% OF RESTAURANT.   V, VE STD., S.D. B/A. (phone first)   DISABLED ACCESS, BUT NOT TO TOILETS. CHILDREN WELCOME. CREDIT CARDS, LV.

WETHERBY

THE PENGUIN HOTEL, LEEDS RD, WETHERBY, W. YORKS, LS22 SHE TEL: (01937) 63881
V STD. S.D. B/A.   N/S 50% OF RESTAURANT.   DISABLED ACCESS.   LICENSED.   CHILDREN.   CREDIT CARDS.

WOOD HALL HOTEL, LINTON, NR WETHERBY, W. YORKS, LS22 4JA TEL; (01937) 67271
Delightful Georgian house in its own parkland, sumptuously furnished and with views.
N/S RESTAURANT.   V B/A.   DISABLED ACCESS.   LICENSED.   CHILDREN WELCOME.   CREDIT CARDS.

PUBS & WINE BARS

BRADFORD

HALFWAY HOUSE, 45 OTLEY RD, BAILDON, BRADFORD. TEL: (01274) 584610
N/S AREA.

GUISELEY

THE STATION, 70 OTLEY RD, GUISELEY (0943) 872061
NO SMOKING IN ONE AREA UNTIL 6PM.

LEEDS

FOX AND HOUNDS, TINSHILL RD, COOKRIDGE, LEEDS.   TEL: (01532) 678415
N/S AREA.

OLD GRIFFIN HEAD INN, BRANCH END, GILDERSOME, LEEDS. TEL: (01532) 533159S
N/S 1 ROOM. WHEELCHAIR ACCESS.

NAGS HEAD, 20 TOWN ST, CHAPEL ALLERTON, LEEDS. TEL: (01532) 624938
N/S ONE ROOM.

PUNCH CLOCK, LOW RD, HUNSLET, LEEDS, W. YORKS, LS10   TEL: (01532) 774165
N/S AREA.

TRAVELLERS, SELNY RD, HALTON, LEEDS, W. YORKS, LS15   TEL: (01532) 645340
N/S AREA.

WELLINGTON INN, WETHERBY RD, LEEDS, W. YORKS, LS17   TEL: (01532) 651991
N/S AREA.

WRENS HOTEL, 61 NEW BRIGGATE, LEEDS, W. YORKS   TEL: (01532) 458888
N/S ONE ROOM.

SOWERBY BRIDGE

THE MOORINGS, CANAL BASIN, SOWERBY BRIDGE, W. YORKS.   TEL: (01422) 833940
Converted 1790 canal side warehouse, serving food, imported bottled beers and real ales.
N/S FAMILY ROOM. V STD.   CHILDREN WELCOME IN FAMILY ROOM UNTIL 8.30.   WHEELCHAIR ACCESS.

Humberside

ACCOMMODATION

BRIDLINGTON

The Tennyson

19 TENNYSON AVE., BRIDLINGTON, YO15 2EU   TEL: (10262) 604382
A family run hotel with luxurious lounge and comfortable bedrooms close to the beach,
leisure world indoor pool and entertainment.
OPEN ALL YEAR.   N/S DINING R & BEDRS.   V STD, S.D. B/A.   LICENSED.   EN SUITE, BEVERAGES & T.V.
B. & B. FROM £15. D. FROM £8.

DRIFFIELD

MIDDLETON WOLD COTTAGES, MIDDLETON-on-the-WOLD, DRIFFIELD TEL: (0137781) 635
Stone cottage in secluded grounds. Beautifully furnished south facing bedrooms.
OPEN ALL YEAR.   NO SMOKING. V VE B/A.   CHILDREN.   BEVERAGES.   T.V. IN ROOMS.

HORNSEA

Sea View Guest House

6 VICTORIA AVE, HORNSEA, EAST YORKS.   TEL: (01964) 536133
Elegant, family run Victorian home overlooking sea. 3 bedrooms. Entirely non-smoking.
OPEN ALL YEAR.   NO SMOKING.   V, S.D. B/A.   CHILDREN & PETS WELCOME.   BEVERAGES IN ALL BED-
ROOMS.   TV IN SOME BEDROOMS.   B. & B. £13, E.M. £5.

RESTAURANTS

DRIFFIELD

THE BELL HOTEL, MARKET PLACE, DRIFFIELD, YO25 7AP
N/S IN RESTAURANT AREA.   V STD.   DISABLED ACCESS.   PETS B/A.

HULL

DEBENHAMS, PROSPECT ST, HULL   TEL: (01482) 25151
Chinwags, a friendly self-service coffee shop serving lunches, snacks and drinks.
OPEN STORE HOURS.   NO SMOKING.   V STD.   DISABLED ACCESS.   CHILDREN.   CREDIT CARDS.

STAMFORD BRIDGE

THREE CUPS, STAMFORD BRIDGE   TEL: (01759) 71396
OPEN PUB HOURS. N/S RESTAURANT. CHILDREN IN DINING AREAS UNTIL 9PM.

The North East

Cleveland

ACCOMMODATION

MIDDLESBOROUGH

THE HIGHFIELD HOTEL, MARTON ROAD, MIDDLESBOROUGH, CLEVELAND, TS4 2PA
TEL: (01642) 817638
Highfield is set in pleasant grounds overlooking the A172 but reasonably secluded.
OPEN ALL YEAR.   N/S 50% OF DINING R & IN PUBLIC BAR.   V B/A.   LICENSED.   DISABLED ACCESS.
CHILDREN WELCOME.   EN SUITE, TV & BEVERAGES IN ROOMS. CREDIT CARDS.

STOCKTON-ON-TEES

Swallow Hotel

JOHN WALKER SQUARE, STOCKTON-ON-TEES, TS18 1AQ   TEL: (01642) 679721

The Swallow Hotel at Stockton on Tees is a modern 4 star hotel right in the heart of the town centre. 50 of the 124 en suite bedrooms are totally smoke-free and each is equipped with a Satellite TV, direct dial phone, hairdryer, iron and trouser press. There are two restaurants: in the Portcullis both table d'hote and a la carte menus are available and, with a less formal atmosphere, the Matchmaker Brasserie (named after John Walker, the Stockton man who first came up with the bright idea of the match!), offers a range of meals and snacks. The Swallow Leisure club has an Egyptian theme and includes a heated pool, jacuzzi, sauna and steam room in addition to a minigym, climbing and cycling machines, rower and sunbeach area.
There are conference and banqueting facilities for up to 300 delegates - each conference receives free use of overhead projector, flip charts and notepads - and the professional team can provide any additional equipment that you require. Free covered parking.
OPEN ALL YEAR.   N/S BOTH RESTAURANTS & IN SOME BEDROOMS.   V, S.D. B/A.   LICENSED.   DISABLED
ACCESS.   CHILDREN WELCOME.   PETS B/A.   EN SUITE, BEVERAGES & TV IN ROOMS.   CREDIT CARDS.   B.
& B. FROM £47.50.

RESTAURANTS

MIDDLESBROUGH

Barneys

19 ST BARNABAS RD, LINTHORPE, MIDDLESBORO', TS5 6JR   TEL: (01642) 826385
Heartbeat Award. Retail shop & café staffed by volunteers from St Barnabas Parish Church; all food cooked fresh on the premises; home-made soup, quiches & savoury dishes such as lasagne, Moussaka, vegetarian loaf, filled potatoes & salads. Sweets include gateaux, cheesecakes, fruit pies, fruit salad. Shop sells range of gifts, books & greeting cards.
20 SEATS.   OPEN 11.30 - 4. L. FROM £1.   NO SMOKING. V STD.   DISABLED ACCESS.   CHILDREN
ESPECIALLY WELCOME (PLAYING AREA PROVIDED).

DEBENHAMS, THE CORNER, 1 NEWPORT RD, MIDDLESBORO'. TEL: (01642) 245201
Springles, a friendly self-service restaurant serving lunches, snacks and drinks.
OPEN STORE HOURS.   NO SMOKING.   V STD.   DISABLED ACCESS.   CHILDREN.   CREDIT CARDS.

STOCKTON-ON-TEES

DEBENHAMS, 149 HIGH ST, STOCKTON-ON-TEES, CLEVELAND. TEL: (01642) 607881
A friendly self-service coffee shop serving lunches, snacks and hot and cold drinks.
OPEN STORE HOURS.   NO SMOKING.   V STD.   DISABLED ACCESS.   CHILDREN.   CREDIT CARDS.

Co Durham & Tyne & Wear

ACCOMMODATION

BARNARD CASTLE

Low Startforth Hall
BARNARD CASTLE, CO. DURHAM, DL12 9AR TEL: (01833) 637957
ETB 2 Crowns. A 17th C. manor house, situated in glorious Teesdale, within walking distance of Barnard Castle and Bowes Museum. Three twin-bedded rooms all with en suite facilties, tea/coffee making, TV, radio & fridge.
OPEN Easter - Oct. inc. NO SMOKING. V, S.D. B/A. CHILDREN WELCOME. EN SUITE, TV & BEVERAGES IN ROOMS.
B. & B. AROUND £20.

BISHOP AUCKLAND

GROVE HOUSE, HAMSTERLEY FOREST, BISHOP AUCKLAND, CO. DURHAM, DL13 1NL TEL: (01388) 88203
OPEN Jan. - Nov.   NO SMOKING.   V, S.D. B/A   CHILDREN: OVER 8S ONLY.   BEVERAGES IN ROOMS.   T.V. IN LOUNGE.   B. &. B. AROUND £22.

CONSETT

Bee Cottage Farm
CASTLESIDE, CONSETT, DH8 9HW   TEL: (01207) 508224

Bee Cottage Farm is a working farm set in peaceful and picturesque surroundings close to the Northumberland/Durham border. It is a very friendly place: visitors are welcome to see the animals - mainly young stock - and children especially are encouraged to participate in the easier (and nicer!) bits of farming life (bottle-feeding baby lambs, perhaps even milking the goat!). The farmhouse itself has been very comfortably decorated - there is a welcoming lounge with an open fire - and smoking is restricted to the two external bungalow-type accommodation areas. Guests may stay as self-caterers or take breakfast if they wish, but most visitors will be tempted by the Tea Room which is open from Easter to September and serves delicious cream teas!
OPEN ALL YEAR. N/S MAIN FARMHOUSE BUILDING. V, S.D. B/A. SOME DISABLED ACCESS. SOME EN SUITE.
BEVERAGES. T.V. IN GUESTS' LOUNGE. B. & B. AROUND £18.

DURHAM

ACORN GUEST HOUSE, 5 MOWBRAY ST, DURHAM, DH1 4BH TEL: (0191) 386 3108
Pleasantly appointed Victorian town house 5 min stations; close to park, woods and city.
N/S DINING R & DISCOURAGED THROUGHOUT. V, DIAB, STD. CHILDREN WELCOME. BEVERAGES IN ROOMS.
T.V. IN GUEST LOUNGE.

BEES COTTAGE GUEST HOUSE, BRIDGE ST, DURHAM, DH1 4RT TEL: (0191) 384 5775
Durham's oldest cottage in a central location close to cathedral and castle. Museums, university, river walks and shops all nearby. Private parking.
OPEN ALL YEAR. N/S DINING R & BEDRS.   V, S.D. B/A.   CHILDREN WELCOME.   EN SUITE, TV &
BEVERAGES IN ROOMS.   B. & B. FROM £20, Sgl £29.

COLEBRICK, 21 CROSSGATE, DURHAM, DH1 4PS   TEL: (0191) 384 9585
NO SMOKING. V B/A. DISABLED ACCESS: 'GOOD'.   CHILDREN: OVER 4S ONLY. BEVERAGES & TV IN ROOMS.   B. &. B. AROUND £22.

Ramside Hall Hotel
CARRVILLE, DURHAM, DH1 1TD TEL: (0191) 386 5282
Ramside Hall is a splendid castellated building set in large grounds just off the A1(M)/A690 motor interchange. Formerly the home of the Pemberton family, it was opened as a hotel in 1964 by two businessmen whose families still own it. It has been very luxuriously

appointed - there is a pleasing blend of the traditional and the contemporary in the furnishings - and bedrooms are not only individually decorated and styled but are equipped with every modern convenience (free in-house movies, fresh fruit, trouser-presses, the lot); two presidential suites are available offering the ultimate in luxury. Dining is in one of three elegant restaurants - each of them serving a selection of excellent home-made dishes - and a typical evening meal would feature Tuna and Pasta Salad in Raspberrry Vinaigrette, followed by Poached Salmon with Fresh Spinach and Hollandaise Sauce, and a selection of sweets and cheeses; conference and business facilities are first-rate.

OPEN ALL YEAR.   N/S at breakfast, in part of buffet carvery and in some bedrooms.   V, S.D. ON REQUEST. LICENSED.   DISABLED ACCESS.   CHILDREN WELCOME.   PETS B/A.   EN SUITE, BEVERAGES & T.V. IN ROOMS.   ACCESS, VISA, AMEX, DINERS.   B. & B. AROUND £80.

Royal County Hotel

OLD ELVET, DURHAM, DH1 3JN TEL: (0191) 386 6821
The Royal County Hotel is a first-class 150-bedroomed hotel, which has been stylishly appointed and beautifully furnished. The hotel is in the luxury business-class category and therefore has a superb range of leisure amenities including an indoor swimming pool, a spa pool, sauna, steam room, solarium and mini-gym. The bedrooms are very comfortable and have excellent facilities, and a large percentage of smoke-free rooms are available. A wide choice of menu is served in the hotel's restaurants and these, too, have good smoke-free areas.

OPEN ALL YEAR. N/S PART OF BOTH RESTAURANTS & IN SOME BEDROOMS. V STD. VE, DIAB & S.D. ON REQUEST. LICENSED. DISABLED ACCESS. CHILDREN WELCOME. PETS B/A. EN SUITE, BEVERAGES & TV IN ROOMS. CREDIT CARDS. B. & B. AROUND £90. special w/e & summer breaks available.

NEWCASTLE-ON-TYNE

'BYWELL', 54 HOLLY AVENUE, JESMOND, NEWCASTLE-ON-TYNE, NE2 2QA
TEL: (0191) 281 7615   NO SMOKING.   V STD.   CHILDREN WELCOME.   B.& B. AROUND £20.

ROWLANDS GILL

CHOPWELLWOOD HOUSE B. & B., CHOPWELL WOOD, CO. DURHAM, NE39 1LT
Charming detached house in Derwent Valley 1m into a 600 acre Forestry Commission wood & 10 mins A1; Newcastle, Durham, Hexham. Excellent walks nearby.
TEL: (01207) 542765 NO SMOKING. CHILDREN WELCOME. BEVERAGES/TV IN ROOMS. B. & B. AROUND £20.

WESTGATE-IN-WEARDALE

BRECKON HILL COUNTRY GUEST HOUSE, WESTGATE-IN-WEARDALE, CO DURHAM.
Comfortable, newly restored Dale's house in large, south-facing walled garden commanding breathtaking views of Weardale.Open fires. Home-cooked food.
TEL: (01388) 517228 OPEN ALL YEAR. NO SMOKING. V, S.D. B/A. CHILDREN WELCOME.   EN SUITE, BEVERAGES & T.V. IN ROOMS. B. & B. AROUND £22.

WHITLEY BAY

LINDISFARNE HOTEL, 11 HOLLY AVENUE, WHITLEY BAY, CO. DURHAM, NE26 1EB
TEL: (0191) 251 3954 OPEN ALL YEAR.   N/S DINING R & SOME BEDRS.   V B/A.   LICENSED.   CHILDREN WELCOME.   SOME EN SUITE ROOMS.   BEVERAGES & TV IN ROOMS.   B. & B.AROUND £19.

WHITE SURF GUEST HOUSE, 8 SOUTH PARADE, WHITLEY BAY, CO. DURHAM, NE26 2RG
TEL: (0191) 253 0103 OPEN ALL YEAR. N/S DINING R, BEDRS & MOST PUBLIC AREAS.   V B/A. CHILDREN: OVER 2S ONLY.   SOME EN SUITE ROOMS.   T.V. IN ALL ROOMS.   B. & B. AROUND £18.

WOLSINGHAM

FRIARSIDE FARM, WOLSINGHAM, WEARDALE, CO. DURHAM, DL13 3BH
TEL: (01388) 527361   N/S DINING R & BEDRS.   V, DIAB B/A. LOW-FAT STD.   CHILDREN: OVER 5S ONLY.   PETS B/A.   T.V. IN LOUNGE.   B. & B. FROM £14. D. £8.

RESTAURANTS & PUBS

BARNARD CASTLE

🚭 *'Priors'*

7 THE BANK, BARNARD CASTLE, CO. DURHAM, DL12 8PH   TEL: (01833) 638141
Excellent wholefood, vegetarian restaurant with organic wine list; craft shop & gallery.
OPEN Mon.-Fri. 10-5, Sat. 10-5.30, Sun: 12-5.   NO SMOKING.   V, VE, S.D. STD.   LICENSED.   CHILDREN
WELCOME.   CREDIT CARDS.

EAST HOWDEN

DUKE OF WELLINGTON, NORTHUMBERLAND DOCK RD, EAST HOWDEN, CO. DURHAM.
TEL: (0191) 262 3079   N/S IN PART OF PUB.

NEWCASTLE-ON-TYNE

RUPALI RESTAURANT, 6 BIGG MARKET, NEWCASTLE-ON-TYNE TEL: (0191) 232 8629
Excellent restaurant specialising in Indian, Vegetarian, Tandoori & English cuisine.
N/S 50% V STD. LICENSED. CHILDREN WELCOME. CREDIT CARDS.

LEGENDARY YORKSHIRE HEROES, ARCHBOLD TERR., JESMOND. TEL: (0191) 281 3010
N/S IN PART OF PUB.

WILLINGTON

Stile Restaurant

97 HIGH ST, WILLINGTON, NR CROOK, DL15 0PE.   TEL: (01388) 746615
Originally a mine-owner's country cottage and now with two beautiful conservatories overlooking an attractive garden. Excellent home-prepared food from fresh, local ingredients.
N/S DINING R (28 SEATS), ALLOWED IN CONSERVATORY BAR AREA ONLY. V STD, S.D. B/A. LICENSED.   SOME
DISABLED ACCESS: 'TWO STEPS.' CHILDREN WELCOME. ACCESS, VISA.

Northumberland

ACCOMMODATION

ALNMOUTH

🚭 *The Grange*

NORTHUMBERLAND ST, ALNMOUTH, NORTHUMB., NE66 2RJ TEL: (01665) 830401

ETB 2 Crown Highly Commended. 200 year-old stone-built house formerly used as a granary; now totally refurbished & retains many period features. Large landscaped gardens overlooking the River Aln 2 min from the beautiful sandy beach. Excellent breakfasts.
OPEN Mar. - Nov. NO SMOKING. V B/A. CHILDREN: OVER 5S ONLY. SOME EN SUITE ROOMS. BEVER-
AGES & T.V. IN ROOMS.   B. & B. AROUND £22.

🚭 *High Buston Hall*

HIGH BUSTON, ALNMOUTH, NORTHUMBERLAND, NE66 3QH   TEL: (01665) 830341

High Buston Hall is a Grade II listed Georgian house which stands amidst 5 acres of landscaped gardens and paddocks in a commanding position overlooking the Heritage coastline of Northumberland midway between the historic villages of Alnmouth and Warkworth. Traditionally furnished, the house has an atmosphere of elegant informality: there is the welcome opportunity to relax and feel at home, yet the surroundings are gracious enough to make you feel special. The food is excellent: fresh ingredients - some home-grown - are

home-cooked and special diets can be accommodated by arrangement. Northumberland abounds with historic houses and castles: the dramatic coastal fortress of Dunstanburgh Castle, home of John of Gaunt, stands 10 miles to the North and can be reached from the tiny fishing port of Craster, famous for its oak-smoked kippers (which are served for breakfast at High Buston Hall).
OPEN ALL YEAR. NO SMOKING. V., S.D., B/A. LICENSED. NO PETS. CHILDREN WELCOME. EN SUITE, TV & BEVERAGES IN ROOMS. B & B. FROM £30, SINGLE £37.50, d. £20.

ALNWICK

Norfolk
     41 BLAKELAW RD, ALNWICK, NORTHUMBERLAND. TEL: (01665) 602892
Norfolk is a pleasant detached house, tastefully furnished and offering a high standard of accommodaiton. It is quietly situated in this historic town. There is a friendly and relaxed atmosphere and traditional home cooking prepared from fresh produce, often home-grown. The house has full central heating and there is a guest lounge and attractive garden. Light refreshments are served at 9 p.m. There is a separate guest sitting room with a TV.
OPEN MAY - OCT. NO SMOKING. OVER 8s WELCOME. EN SUITE & BEVERAGES IN ROOMS. SEPARATE TV LOUNGE. B. & B. AROUND £19.

TOWNFOOT FARM, TOWNFOOT, LESBURY, ALNWICK, NE66 3AZ TEL: (01665) 830755
OPEN Mar. - Oct. N/S DINING R & UPSTAIRS. V B/A. CHILDREN WELCOME. PETS B/A. BEVERAGES IN ROOMS. T.V. IN LOUNGE. B. & B. AROUND £19.

BAMBURGH

WAREN HOUSE HOTEL, WAREN MILL, NR BAMBURGH, NORTHUMBERLAND, NE70 7EE
*ETB 4 Crown Highly Commended.*Exceptionally good hotel in 6 acres of grounds situated on the edge of Budle Bay overlooking Holy Island, 2 miles from Bamburgh Castle. Beautifully furnished with antiques. Excellent meals prepared from fresh ingredients.
TEL: (016684) 581 OPEN ALL YEAR. N/S ex. library. V B/A. LICENSED. EN SUITE, BEVERAGES & TV IN ROOMS. VISA, AMEX, MASTERCARD, DINERS. D., B. & B. AROUND £74.

BARDON MILL

ELDOCHAN HALL, WILLIMOTESWYKE, BARDON MILL, NE47 7DB TEL: (01434) 344465
     NO SMOKING. V,S.D. B/A. CHILDREN WELCOME. PETS B/A. EN SUITE & BEVERAGES IN ROOMS. T.V. IN LOUNGE. B. & B. AROUND £17.

BEADNELL

Low Dover
     HARBOUR RD, BEADNELL, NORTHUMBERLAND, NE67 5BH TEL: (01665) 720291 FAX: (02860) 370866
ETB 1 Crown Highly Commended. Low Dover is a large residence in a superb location overlooking Beadnell Bay. It offers quiet comfortable luxurious accommodation. All rooms are en suite and have a private patio door entrance, and it is just a 20 yard walk to the golden sandy beach and 18th C. harbour. You are just 3 miles from the Farne Islands. There is also at the same location a luxury apartment and residential caravan.
TEL: (01665) 720291 NO SMOKING. DISABLED ACCESS. OVER 5S ONLY. SOME EN SUITE ROOMS. BEVER-AGES & TV IN ROOMS. B. & B. AROUND £19.

BELLINGHAM

EALS LODGE, TARSET, BELLINGHAM, NORTHUMBERLAND, NE48 1LF TEL: (01434) 240269
OPEN ALL YEAR. N/S DINING R & BEDRS. V, DIAB STD. LICENSED. EN SUITE, BEVERAGES & T.V. IN ROOMS. B. & B. FROM £21.

IVY COTTAGE, LANEHEAD, BELLINGHAM, NR HEXHAM, NE48 1NT TEL: (01434) 240337
N/S DINING R & BEDRS. V, VE STD. S.D. B/A. CHILDREN WELCOME. PETS B/A. EN SUITE. BEVERAGES & T.V. IN ROOMS. B. & B.AROUND £17.

BERWICK-UPON-TWEED

'TREE TOPS', VILLAGE GREEN, EAST ORD, BERWICK-UPON-TWEED, TD15 2NS
     TEL: (01289) 330679 OPEN Mar. - Oct. NO SMOKING. V STD. DISABLED ACCESS: 'yes, with helper: single storey accomm. & wide doors'. EN SUITE ALL ROOMS. BEVERAGES. T.V. B. & B. AROUND £25.

THE ESTATE HOUSE, FORD, BERWICK-UPON-TWEED, TD15 2QG   TEL: (0189 082) 297
Beautiful Edwardian country house in large, well-maintained lawned gardens. Comfortably
furnished bedrooms; open fires in public rooms. Wholesome, home-cooked food.
N/S DINING R.   V, GLUTEN-FREE, S.D. B/A.   CHILDREN: OVER 5S ONLY.   BEVERAGES IN ROOMS.   T.V.
LOUNGE.   B. & B. AROUND £18.

Mrs Sandra Thornton
4 NORTH RD, BERWICK-ON-TWEED, NORTHUMBERLAND, TD15 1PL   TEL: (01289) 306146
ETB 1 Crown. Spacious stone-built Edwardian house, tastefully decorated. Warm wel-
come. Comfortable stay assured.
OPEN ALL YEAR.   NO SMOKING.   S.D. B/A.   OVER 5s WELCOME.   BEVERAGES & TV IN ROOMS.   B. & B.
FROM £15.

CORNHILL-ON-TWEED
THE COACH HOUSE, CROOKHAM, CORNHILL-ON-TWEED, TD12 4TD   TEL: (0189 082) 293
Oldest cottage in north Northumberland; for disabled guests all doors are wheelchair-wide.
OPEN Mar. - Nov.   N/S DINING R & LOUNGE.   V STD.   LICENSED.   EXCELLENT DISABLED ACCESS.
DOGS WELCOME.   MOST ROOMS EN SUITE.   BEVERAGES IN ROOMS. B. & B. AROUND £25.

FENWICK
THE MANOR HOUSE, FENWICK, NR BERWICK-upon-TWEED, TD15 2PQ   TEL: (01289) 81381
OPEN ALL YEAR.   N/S DINING R, LOUNGE & BEDRS.   V STD.   LICENSED.   CHILDREN WELCOME.   PETS B/A.
BEVERAGES & T.V. IN ROOMS.   B. & B. AROUND £18.

GREENHEAD-IN-NORTHUMBERLAND

Holmhead Farm Licensed Guest House & Holiday Flat
HADRIAN'S WALL, GREENHEAD IN NORTHUMBERLAND, VIA CARLISLE CA6 7HY   TEL:
(016977 47402)

ETB 3 Crown Commended 3 Keys Commended.
AA QQQ. Holmhead Farm is a charming old
house, which stands amidst pretty gardens (complete with stream) surrounded by the unspoilt and
rugged beauty of the Northumberland countryside; it literally stands on Hadrian's Wall and is
built from its stones. Understandably the views
are quite spectacular. Accommodation is in four
cosy and comfortable en suite bedrooms - each
with lovely rural views - and there is a separate
self-catering cottage for non-smokers in which the range of excellent amenities includes
first-class facilities for disabled guests. Perhaps the best thing about a stay at Holmhead is
the food: the proprietors boast correctly that their breakfast menu is the longest in the world:
I have no reason to doubt them and wish I could do justice to the range of dishes on offer;
suffice to say that if you are in Northumberland and wish to dine at 8 a.m. on a choice of
English or Scottish porridge followed by Devilled Kidneys, waffles and Raspberry tea -
Holmhead Farm would be your best bet. The evening meal lacks choice (most guests
doubtless welcome a break from menu-reading) but does not lack quality: fresh, local
ingredients are included in the imaginative and tasty 3-course meal, and guests dine
together by candlelight at a large, oak table in the cosy beamed dining room. *Winner of
Heartbeat Award & Disabled Category 2 by Holiday Care Service.*
OPEN JAN 6TH - DEC. 20TH.   NO SMOKING. V, S.D. B/A.   LICENSED.   DISABLED ACCESS TO HOLIDAY
FLAT & GROUND FLOOR B. & B. (Nov. - Mar. the latter).   CHILDREN WELCOME.   ALL ROOMS EN SUITE.
BEVERAGES & TV IN LOUNGE.   ACCESS, VISA.   B. & B. FROM £21. D. £17

HALTWHISTLE
Alde White Craig Farm
SHIELD HILL, HALTWHISTLE, NORTHUMBERLAND, NE49 9NW   TEL: (01434) 320565
Heartbeat Award. 17th C. croft-style farmhouse. Sympathetically modernised &
sitting room has open fireplace & timber ceiling beams; B. & B. plus self-catering cottages
OPEN ALL YEAR.   NO SMOKING.   V, S.D. B/A.   DISABLED ACCESS.   OVER 10S ONLY.   EN SUITE,
TV & BEVERAGES IN ROOMS.   B. & B. AROUND £20.

ASHCROFT GUEST HOUSE, HALTWHISTLE, NE49 0DA   TEL: (01434) 320213
Heartbeat Award. Victorian vicarage in its own private grounds in quiet market town.
Comfortably furnished bedrooms 1 with 4-poster. Excellent b'fast with lighter option.
OPEN ALL YEAR.   NO SMOKING.   V B/A.   CHILDREN.   T.V. IN LOUNGE. B. & B. FROM £14.

HEXHAM

CROWBERRY HALL, ALLENDALE, HEXHAM, NE47 9SR   TEL: (01434) 683392
Crowberry Hall in Allendale offers a warm welcome to walkers & fabulous food!
OPEN ALL YEAR.   NO SMOKING.   V STD, S.D. B/A.   CHILDREN: OVER 5S ONLY.   PETS B/A.   SOME EN
SUITE ROOMS.   T.V. IN LOUNGE.   B. & B. AROUND £17.

DUKESLEA, 33 DUKES RD, HEXHAM, NORTHUMBERLAND.   TEL: (01434) 602947
ETB Registered Listed. Tastefully refurbished family home with open country views.
OPEN ALL YEAR.   NO SMOKING.   V B/A.   CHILDREN WELCOME.   EN-SUITE SHOWER, RADIO ALARM,
BEVERAGES & T.V. IN ROOM.   B. & B. AROUND £17.

GEESWOOD HOUSE, WHITTIS RD, HAYDON BRIDGE, HEXHAM.   TEL: (01434) 684220
OPEN ALL YEAR.   NO SMOKING.   V, LOW-FAT, GLUTEN-FREE, DIAB., S.D. B/A.   CHILDREN: OVER 10S
ONLY.   PETS B/A.   T.V. IN LOUNGE.   B. & B. AROUND £17.

Middlemarch

HENCOTES, HEXHAM, NORTHUMBERLAND, NE46 2EB   TEL: (01434) 605003
Beautiful listed Georgian house overlooking the Sele and the Abbey in the centre of
Hexham. Comfortable and spacious centrally heated rooms one of which has en suite
facilities and a four poster bed; the breakfast is excellent and accommodation is available
throughout the year. You are just a short walk from all the attractions and amenities of this
charming little border town, and Hadrian's Wall is 10 mins drive away; for those venturing
a little further afield, within an hour's drive it is possible to reach the Northumberland Coast,
the Lakes or Scotland.
OPEN ALL YEAR.   N/S DINING ROOM & BEDRS.   V, S.D. B/A.   CHILDREN: OVER 10S ONLY.   PETS B/A.
EN SUITE SOME ROOMS.   TEA/COFFEE-MAKING & T.V. IN ROOMS. B. & B. £16-£22.

KIELDER WATER

The Pheasant Inn

STANNERSBURN, FALSTONE, BY KIELDER WATER, NE48 1DD   TEL: (01434) 240382

The Pheasant is a 360 year-old country inn with stone
walls, low beamed ceilings and open fires; it stands
in a small hamlet of 12 houses one mile from the
Kielder Water Reservoir in the Northumberland National Park. Accommodation is in beautifully refurbished en suite bedrooms and meals are served in a
dining room which has been furnished in mellow
pine giving it a welcoming feeling of warmth; the
food is traditional and freshly prepared (the inn has
an excellent reputation for its deliciously cooked
vegetables) and meals can also be enjoyed in the two bars; some particular menu favourites
are Smoked Trout with Creamed Horseradish followed by Noisette of Lamb with Apricot
and Ginger Sauce and home-made Sticky Toffee Pudding. The Pheasant Inn is very central
for visiting all the places of interest in Northumberland: the coast between Alnmouth and
the Scottish borders is particularly beautiful and Hadrian's Wall is just to the South of the
inn. Water sports may be enjoyed on the reservoir and bikes may be hired. Hexham is the
nearest market town, with its abbey and historic buildings, and there are castles to visit.
OPEN ALL YEAR ex. Xmas.   N/S DINING R & BEDRS.   V B/A.   CHILDREN WELCOME.   WHEELCHAIR
ACCESS.   EN SUITE, TV & BEVERAGES IN ROOMS.   B. & B. FROM £19, SINGLE FROM £21.

KIRKWHELPINGTON

THE OLD VICARAGE, KIRKWHELPINGTON, NE19 2RT   TEL: (01830) 40319
OPEN Apr. - Oct.   N/S DINING ROOM & LOUNGE.   V, S.D. B/A.   CHILDREN WELCOME.   PETS B/A.   SOME EN
SUITE ROOMS.   BEVERAGES IN ROOMS.   T.V. LOUNGE.   B. & B. FROM £12.50-16.

MORPETH

Ⓝ THE BAKERS CHEST, HARTBURN, MORPETH, NE61 4JB   TEL: (01670) 72214
Beautiful stone-built house in delightful countryside in the charming village of Hartburn;
comfortable accommodation & excellent food; beautiful walks through tranquil woods.
OPEN Easter - Oct.   NO SMOKING. V, S.D. B/A. CHILDREN WELCOME. BEVERAGES.   T.V. IN LOUNGE.
B. & B. AROUND £18.

ROTHBURY

Ⓝ THROPTON DEMESNE FARMHOUSE, THROPTON, ROTHBURY.   TEL: (01669) 20196
    Victorian stone-built farmhouse in walled garden; excellent home-cooked food.
OPEN ALL YEAR. NO SMOKING. V, S.D. B/A. CHILDREN WELCOME.   EN SUITE, TV & BEVERAGES IN
ROOMS. B. & B. AROUND £18.

SLALEY

RYE HILL FARM, SLALEY, NR HEXHAM, NE47 0AH   TEL: (01434) 673259
300-year-old stone farmhouse in its own 30 acres of working farm in rural Tynedale;
self-catering and B. & B. (dinner B/A) available; log fires; good home-cooking.
OPEN ALL YEAR. N/S DINING R & BEDRS. V , S.D. B/A. LICENSED. CHILDREN WELCOME.   PETS B/A.
EN SUITE, TV & BEVERAGES IN ROOMS.   B. & B. AROUND £24.

WARKWORTH

Ⓝ AULDEN, 9 WATERSHAUGH RD, WARKWORTH, NE65 0TT   TEL: (01665) 711583
    ETB 1 Crown Commended. Warm, comfortable, friendly guest house in historic
village; 1m from sandy deserted beaches; beautiful riverside walk to hermitage & castle.
OPEN Mar. - Oct.   NO SMOKING. BEVERAGES IN ROOMS.   T.V. IN LOUNGE.   B. & B. AROUND £16.

Ⓝ North Cottage

BIRLING, WARKWORTH, MORPETH, NORTHUMBERLAND, NE65 0XS   TEL: (01665) 711263
            ETB Highly Commended 2 Crowns. AA Listed
            QQQ. 300 year-old North Cottage stands in a lovely,
            large garden just a short stroll from the river and
            sandy beach on the outskirts of the pretty village of
            Warkworth, with its historic castle, hermitage and
            church. Your hosts, Mr and Mrs Howliston, are a
            particularly welcoming couple - and theirs is a par-
            ticularly comfortable and welcoming home: after-
            noon tea is served (free) on arrival, and home-baked
            cakes and biscuits are served with bedtime cuppas.
            Bedrooms have been pleasantly furnished and well-
equipped with a range of helpful amenities (radios, electric blankets, etc), and there is a
large sitting room with colour TV. North Cottage was a recent runner-up in the Northumbria
in Bloom competition - and you do not need to travel much further afield to find other
delights: Alnwick, Alnmouth and Rothbury are all within easy visiting distance, as are
numerous other castles, historic houses and towns.
OPEN ALL YEAR. NO SMOKING. V, S.D. B/A. EN SUITE, TV & BEVERAGES IN ROOMS. B. & B. FROM £16.

Ⓝ Roxbro House

5 CASTLE TERRACE, WARKWORTH, NORTHUMBERLAND, NE65 0UP TEL: (01665) 711416
Roxbro House enjoys a splendid situation directly opposite Warkworth Castle. It offers
comfortable bed and breakfast accommodation in twin, double or family rooms, each of
which has hot and cold water and private showers. There is a pleasant lounge for guests'
use, and tea or coffee is available.
OPEN JAN - DEC. NO SMOKING. CHILDREN WELCOME. EN SUITE ROOMS. B. & B. AROUND £16.

WOOLER

BELMONT, 15 GLENDALE RD, WOOLER, NE71 6DN   TEL: (01668) 81625
Small family home in centre of country town at the base of the Cheviots.
OPEN Mar. - Oct.   N/S DINING R & BEDRS. V, S.D. B/A. CHILDREN WELCOME. BEVERAGES IN ROOMS.
T.V. IN LOUNGE.   B. & B. AROUND £17.

RESTAURANTS

ALNWICK

BEAMISH COUNTRY HOUSE HOTEL, POWBURN, ALNWICK, NORTHUMBERLAND, NE66 4LL TEL: (0166578) 266/544
N/S RESTAURANT. V STD. LICENSED. OVER 12S ONLY.

BAMBURGH

 ## The Copper Kettle Tearooms
21 FRONT ST, BAMBURGH, NORTHUMBERLAND, NE69 7BW   TEL: (01668) 214315

The Copper Kettle Tearooms is one of a row of 18th C. cottages in the picturesque and historically significant village of Bamburgh with its magnificent castle overlooking the sea. The tearooms are full of character and interest: there is a unique set of oak panelling on which are carved various scenes depicting local life, and the original beams are festooned with assorted copperware; the walls are hung with original paintings (most of which are for sale) and there is a fine range of food-orientated products - including preserves, tea, biscuits and pickles - also for sale. With the exception of the bread and teacakes which are provided by a local baker, the owners, Rosemary Christie and David Bates, bake ε nd prepare all the items on their extensive menu using their own recipes and choosing only the finest ingredients: there is a very wide choice of beverages (including eleven speciality teas and twenty-five herbal infusions), and the delicious home-made cakes feature such tempting delights as Walnut and Caramel Fudge with Cream or Ginger Bread and Cherry Madeira.
28 SEATS PLUS 20 IN GARDEN.   OPEN MARCH TO OCT., 7 DAYS, USUALLY 10.30 - 5.30.   NO SMOKING INDOORS.   V OFTEN AVAIL. TABLE LICENCE. WELL-BEHAVED CHILDREN WELCOME.

MORPETH

CHANTRY TEAROOM, 9 CHANTRY PLACE, MORPETH, NE61 1PJ   TEL: (01670) 514414
Pretty country-style tearoom with views of old chantry building; all home-baking.
NO SMOKING. V STD. LICENSED. SOME DISABLED ACCESS. CHILDREN WELCOME.

ROTHBURY

THE VALE MILK BAR, HIGH STREET, ROTHBURY, MORPETH. TEL: (01669) 20461
Café serving morning coffee, light lunches and afternoon tea.
NO SMOKING. V STD, S.D. B/A. DISABLED ACCESS: GOOD. CHILDREN WELCOME.

Channel Islands

ACCOMMODATION

ALDERNEY

FARM COURT GUEST HOUSE, LE PETIT VAL, ALDERNEY TEL: (01481) 822075
OPEN Mar. - Oct.   NO SMOKING.   LICENSED.   SOME DISABLED ACCESS.   CHILDREN WELCOME.   EN SUITE,
TV & BEVERAGES IN ROOMS.   B. & B. AROUND £25.

GUERNSEY

Hotel Hougue du Pommier

CASTEL, GUERNSEY TEL: (01481) 56531 FAX: (01481) 56260
18th C. farmhouse beautifully converted into an elegant hotelamidst 10 acres of grounds.
Very peaceful. Excellent food. Licensed bar with inglenook fireplace and beamed ceilings.
Leisure amenities include heated pool, sauna, solarium and games room; 10 mins beach.
OPEN ALL YEAR.   N/S 50% DINING R & SOME BEDRS.   V, S.D. B/A.   CHILDREN WELCOME. LICENSED.
WHEELCHAIR ACCESS TO GROUND FLOOR ROOMS.   CREDIT CARDS.   D., B. & B. AROUND £45.

La Favorita Hotel

FERMAIN BAY, GUERNSEY TEL: (01481) 35666

La Favorita is an attractive hotel set amidst pleasant gardens in the beautiful wooded valley which leads down to Fermain Bay. It was once a privately owned country house and, although it has been considerably extended and modernised, it retains the character (and of course magnificent sea views!) of its former life. From the elegant drawing room with its open fire to the intimate dining room with its lovely garden views, everywhere there is an atmosphere of peaceful tranquility and guests are encouraged to relax, unwind and enjoy. The food is excellent: the menu, which changes daily, is based around traditional English cooking (with some imaginative Continental culinary excursions). A typical evening meal could feature Baked Blue Brie with Mushroom Sauce, followed by Cream of Chicken Soup, Baked Sea Bream with Tomato, and a delicious home-made dessert; there is a good vegetarian option on each evening menu. A recent successful addition to La Favorita is its pleasant Coffee Shop, overlooking the garden, in which light meals are served during the day, & an indoor heated pool, spa & sauna.
OPEN Mar. - Nov.   N/S DINING R.   V STD, S.D. B/A.   LICENSED.   DISABLED ACCESS: 1 BEDROOM
PURPOSE-EQUIPPED FOR DISABLED GUESTS.   CHILDREN WELCOME (nappy-changing room).   EN SUITE, TV
& BEVERAGES IN ROOMS.   VISA, AMEX, MASTERCARD.   B. & B. AROUND £36.

SUNNYDALE GUEST HOUSE, BRAYE RD, VALE, GUERNSEY TEL: (01481) 47916
OPEN ALL YEAR.   NO SMOKING.   V B/A.   EN SUITE, TV & BEVERAGES IN ROOMS.

JERSEY

HINCHCLIFFE GUEST HOUSE, VICTORIA AVE, FIRST TOWER, ST HELIER, JERSEY
TEL: (01534) 21574 OPEN Mar. - Oct.   NO SMOKING.   DIETS B/A.   BEVERAGES.   T.V. LOUNGE.

La Bonne Vie Guest House

ROSEVILLE ST, ST HELIER, JERSEY TEL: (01534) 35955   FAX: (01534) 33357
La Bonne Vie Guest House is a beautiful Victorian house which retains many original period features; it has been tastefully furnished throughout - some bedrooms have antique brass beds or hand-made French four-posters - and there is an inviting open fire in the lounge and dining room in winter; there is even a library for guests' use, and games - such as Trivial Pursuit and backgammon - are available for your enjoyment. La Bonne Vie is very conveniently situated just a minute's walk from the beach and five minutes' walk from the town centre.

OPEN Mar - Nov. inc. ex. Xmas & New Year.   N/S DINING R & DISCOURAGED IN BEDRS.   S.D. B/A.   OVER 8S ONLY.
EN SUITE, BEVERAGES & T.V. IN ROOMS.   CREDIT CARDS.   B. & B. FROM £17.

SARK
Beauvoir Guest House and Tea Shop
SARK (0481) 832352   TEL: (01481) 832046 FAX: (01481) 832551
Charming granite-built house. Exceptionally comfortable accommodation with a charming tea garden and tea shop specialing in home-baking prepared from organically home-grown produce. Sark is the smallest Channel Island: there are no street lights and as the sandy beaches are reached by steep paths it is unsuitable for the disabled.
OPEN ALL YEAR.   NO SMOKING.   V, VE, LOW-CAL., GLUTEN-FREE & S.D. B/A.   LICENSED.   DISABLED ACCESS; GROUND-FLOOR ROOMS WITH RAMPED ACCESS.   OVER 10S ONLY.   EN SUITE, BEVERAGES, CENTRAL HEATING & T.V. IN ROOMS.   CREDIT CARDS.   B. & B. AROUND £25.

HOTEL PETIT CHAMP, SARK   TEL: (01481) 832046
Charming hotel in unrivalled position on the west coast of the unique island of Sark. Restaurant renowned for good cuisine. Solar-heated swimming pool.
OPEN Apr. - Oct.   N/S DINING R & 1 LOUNGE/LIBRARY.   V STD, S.D. B/A.   LICENSED. CHILDREN: OVER 7S ONLY.
EN SUITE IN ROOMS.   CREDIT CARDS.   HALF BOARD FROM £40.

RESTAURANTS
GUERNSEY
ROCQUAINE BISTRO, ROCQUAINE BAY, WEST SIDE OF THE ISLAND TEL: (01481) 63149
OPEN DAILY Apr - Oct.   N/S PART OF RESTAURANT.

BEAUVOIR GUEST HOUSE AND TEA SHOP, SARK TEL: (01481) 832352
For further details please see under entry in accommodation section.

Northern Ireland
ACCOMMODATION & RESTAURANTS
CO ANTRIM
AHIMSA, 243 WHITEPARK RD, BUSHMILLS   TEL: (0126 57) 31383
OPEN ALL YEAR.   NO SMOKING.   V EXC. CHILDREN & PETS.   BEVERAGES.   B. & B. AROUND £13.

BELFAST
THE MORTAR BOARD, 3 FITZWILLIAM STREET, BELFAST TEL: (01232) 332277
Coffee house very near the university & museum area; home-cooked snacks.
NO SMOKING.   V STD.   CHILDREN WELCOME.

CO FERMANAGH
BRINDLEY, TULLY, KILLADEAS, ENNISKILLEN, CO FERMANAGH (013656) 28065
Standing in an extensive garden with views of Lower Lough Erne & islands.
OPEN ALL YEAR.   NO SMOKING.   V, S.D. B/A.   DISABLED ACCESS.   CHILDREN WELCOME.   EN SUITE IN MOST ROOMS.   BEVERAGES.   TV B. & B. FROM £15.

GLEN HOUSE, 212 CRAWFORDSBURN RD, CRAWFORDSBURN, BT19 1HY (01247) 852229
OPEN ALL YEAR.   N/S DINING R, MOST BEDRS & LOUNGE.   V B/A.   EN SUITE, TV & BEVERAGES IN ROOMS.   CHILDREN WELCOME.   CREDIT CARDS.   B. & B. FROM £20.

CO DOWN
PAT'S RESTAURANT, 88 CASTLEWELLAN RD, LENISH, RATHERILAND.
NO SMOKING.   V ON REQUEST.   LICENSED.   DISABLED ACCESS.

THE RED FOX COFFEE SHOP, 6 MAIN ST, HILLSBOROUGH, CO DOWN (01846) 682586
NO SMOKING.   V STD, S.D. ON REQUEST. DISABLED ACCESS.

CO FERMANAGH
FLORENCE COURT, ENNISKILLEN, CO FERMANAGH (0136 582) 249

Borders

ACCOMMODATION

DENHOLM

BARNHILLS FARM, nr DENHOLM, ROXBUR'SHIRE, TD9 8SH TEL: (0145 087) 577
Beautiful ex-farmhouse set in a wild garden with orchard and vegetables.
OPEN ALL YEAR. NO SMOKING. V, WH EXC. CHILDREN. BEVERAGES. B. & B. AROUND £17.

GALASHIELS

Ettrickvale

33 ABBOTSFORD RD, GALASHIELS, ETTRICK-LAUDERDALE, BORDERS, TD1 3HW TEL: (01896) 755224
STB Commended. Family-run home in quiet part of town. Short distance to all local amenities.
OPEN ALL YEAR. ex Xmas. N/S DINING R. S.D. B/A. CHILDREN & PETS WELCOME. WHEELCHAIR ACCESS. TV & BEVERAGES IN ROOMS. B. & B. £13.

HAWICK

Whitchester Christian Guest House & Retreat Centre

BORTHAUGH, HAWICK, ROXBURGHSHIRE, TD9 7LN TEL: (01450) 77477
Mid 19th C. manor standing in 3 acres of lawned grounds and offering 'a place of rest, rehabilitation and peace'within a Christian context; beautifully furnished throughout.
N/S ex. TV Lounge. V STD, S.D. B/A. DISABLED ACCESS. CHILDREN WELCOME. PETS B/A. 5 EN SUITE ROOMS. BEVERAGES IN ROOMS. T.V. IN LOUNGE. B. & B. AROUND £15

JEDBURGH

Froylehurst

FRIARS, JEDBURGH, ROXBURGHSHIRE, BORDERS, TD8 6BN TEL: (01835) 862477
STB Highly Commended. AA QQQQ. Detached late Victorian house with lovely garden offering comfortable accommodation in tastefully decorated rooms; full Scottish breakfast.
OPEN Mar - Nov. N/S DINING R. V. OVER 5S ONLY. BEVERAGES & T.V. IN ROOMS. B. & B. FROM £16.

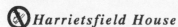
Harrietsfield House

ANCRUM, BY JEDBURGH, ROXBURGHSHIRE, BORDERS, TD8 6TZ TEL: (01835) 830327

Harrietsfield House is a spacious and comfortable ex-farmhouse with a lovely garden set in beautiful countryside just 5 miles from Jedburgh. Breakfast is the only meal which is usually available at Harrietsfield, but all food is prepared from wholefoods and, when possible, organically home-grown produce. Accommodation is in warm, comfortable rooms and there is an inviting lounge with a log fire in the evening as well as a cup of tea and home-baking. You are centrally situated in this part of the world for visiting all the Border towns and are just 44 miles from Edinburgh; golf, riding and fishing may all be enjoyed locally.
OPEN Easter/April - Oct. NO SMOKING. WH STD, S.D. B/A. 2 TWIN BEDRS, 1 DOWNSTAIRS, 1 DOUBLE WITH W.H.B. CHILDREN WELCOME (at full tariff). PETS B/A. BEVERAGES & TV IN LOUNGE. B. & B. FROM £16.

KELSO

DUNCAN HOUSE, CHALKHEUGH TERR., KELSO, BORDERS, TD5 7DX TEL: (01573) 25682
Lovely listed Georgian house in beautiful elevated position overlooking River Tweed.
N/S ex. some bedrooms. V B/A. DISABLED ACCESS. CHILDREN WELCOME. PETS B/A. EN SUITE. BEVERAGES & T.V. IN ROOMS. B. & B. AROUND £15.

MELROSE

PRIORY VIEW, 15 PRIORS WALK, MELROSE, BORDERS. TEL: (01896) 822087
NO SMOKING. V, DIAB, B/A. CHILDREN WELCOME. BEVERAGES & T.V. B. & B. AROUND £16.

PEEBLES

Kingsmuir Hotel

SPRINGHILL RD, PEEBLES, BORDERS, EH45 9EP   TEL: (01721) 720151   FAX: (01721) 721795

Kingsmuir is a charming century old country house which stands amidst leafy grounds on the quiet, South side of Peebles looking across parkland to the River Tweed; indeed it is just 5 mins'walk through the park to the High Street. It is a family-run hotel and as such offers friendly, efficient service; the bedrooms are exceptionally comfortable and there is a stylish new lounge for guests'use. The modern refurbishments and additions have been sympathe-tically undertaken, but the original character of the building is still clearly in evidence in the other comfortable lounge and in the dining room. The food is excellent: everything is prepared from fresh, local produce, and in addition to the imaginative à la carte menu, there are some good choices for children and vegetarians on separate menus; the Kingsmuir Hotel is "Taste of Scotland Recommended", incidentally. Peebles is a Royal and Ancient Borough just 40 minutes'drive South of Edinburgh; there are many fine shops in the city and in addition you are close to many stately homes and castles of great historic interest. OPEN ALL YEAR Ex. Xmas Day.   N/S DINING R & LOUNGE.   V STD.   LICENSED.   CHILDREN & DOGS WELCOME.   EN SUITE, TV & BEVERAGES IN ROOMS.   CREDIT CARDS.   B. & B. AROUND £32.

10 GALLOW HILL, PEEBLES, BORDERS, EH45 9BG TEL: (01721) 20372
OPEN ALL YEAR.   NO SMOKING.   V, S.D.B/A.   CHILDREN.   PETS B/A.   BEVERAGES.   B. & B. AROUND £15.

RESTAURANTS, PUBS & WINE BARS

SELKIRK

TIBBIE SHIELS INN, ST MARY'S LOCH, SELKIRK TD7 5NE   TEL: (01750) 42231
ONE N/S ROOM.   V STD.   CHILDREN WELCOME.   DISABLED ACCESS.

SWINTON

THE WHEATSHEAF HOTEL, MAIN ST, SWINTON, BORDERS.
NO SMOKING IN CONSERVATORY.

Dumfries and Galloway

ACCOMMODATION

CASTLE DOUGLAS

Airieland House

GELSTON, CASTLE DOUGLAS, DUMFRIES & GALLOWAY, DG7 1SS   TEL: (01556) 68375
STB Highly Commended. Listed Victorian mansion in 3 acre woodland garden. Beautifully refurbished and retaining original features; panoramic views. Luxurious bedrooms. Central heating & open fire. Delicious home-cooked food. Close Glasgow & Edinburgh.
OPEN Mar. - Sept. inc.   NO SMOKING.   OVER 12S WELCOME.   EN SUITE/PRIVATE BATH & BEVERAGES IN ROOMS.   TV IN LOUNGE.   B. & B. AROUND £35.

BLAIRINNIE FARM, BLAIRINNIE, PARTON, CASTLE DOUGLAS, KIRKCUDBRIGHT, D & G. TEL: (01556) 67268
OPEN May. - Sept.   NO SMOKING.   V, S.D. B/A.   CHILDREN.   BEVERAGES   T.V. IB & B AROUND £15.

CAIRNRAWS, NEW GALLOWAY, CASTLE DOUGLAS, KIRKCUDBRIGHTSHIRE DG7 3SB   TEL: (016442) 293
1m New Galloway with panoramic views over Loch Ken. Idealbirdwatchers, walkers.
NO SMOKING.   V, S.D. B/A.   OVER 12S ONLY.   BVERAGES.   B. & B. AROUND £17.

CRAWFORD

"Field End" Guest House

CRAWFORD, LANARKSHIRE, DUMF. & GALL, ML12 6TN   TEL: (018642) 276
STB 2 Crowns, RAC & AA Acclaimed. Attractive stone-built villa on quiet, private road
opposite church. Ideal halfway house & touring centre. Private parking.
OPEN ALL YEAR Ex. Xmas & New Year Days.   NO SMOKING.   V B/A.   NO PETS.   CHILDREN WELCOME.
2 EN SUITE ROOMS. BEVERAGES & TV IN ROOMS. B. & B. FROM £14. red. children & senior citizens.

DALBEATTIE

TORBAY FARMHOUSE, ROCKCLIFFE, BY DALBEATTIE, KIRKCUDBRIGHTSHIRE,
DG5 4QE   TEL: (01556) 63403
NO SMOKING.   V B/A.   DISABLED ACCESS.   CHILDREN WELCOME.   PETS B/A.   EN SUITE & BEVER-
AGES IN ROOMS.   T.V. IN LOUNGE.   B & B FROM £14.

DUMFRIES

LOCHENLEE, 32 ARDWALL RD, DUMFRIES, DG1 3AQ   TEL: (01387) 65153
Large semi-detached sandstone family home in quiet residential street 10 mins' walk
from centre of Dumfries, 5 mins' walk from station. Forest walks, bowling, swimming, golf.
OPEN ALL YEAR.   NO SMOKING.   V, DIAB B/A.   CHILDREN WELCOME.   BEVERAGES & T.V. IN ROOMS.
B. & B. AROUND £15.

GRETNA

The Beeches

LOANWATH ROAD, GRETNA, VIA CARLISLE, CA6 5EP   TEL: (01461) 37448
STB 2 Crown Commended & QQQ AA Listed. The Beeches is an attractive 19th C.
former farmhouse which is peacefully situated in a quiet area half a mile from the A74 at
Gretna. A very high standard of accommodation is offered to guests - indeed the proprietors
have been awarded a 2 Crown Commended status by the Scottish Tourist Board. There are
two charming bedrooms, each of which have panoramic views of the Solway Firth and
Lakeland Hills, and there is a comfortable lounge with a colour T.V. for guests' use.
Breakfast is the only meal to be served at The Beeches, but there is a good choice of
restaurants nearby.
OPEN Jan. To Nov.   NO SMOKING.   V B/A.   CHILDREN: OVER 12S ONLY.   EN SUITE & BEVERAGES IN ROOMS.
TV ON REQUEST.   B & B AROUND £17.

KIRKCUDBRIGHT

Millburn House

MILLBURN ST, KIRKCUDBRIGHT, DUMF. & GALL, DG6 4ED   TEL: (01557) 330926

Millburn House is an old traditional Galloway
building which stands in a quiet residential area
close to Kirkcudbright town centre. Accommodation is in comfortable rooms, some of which have
private facilities, and a speciality of the house is
the delicious home-baking, prepared to welcome
you back after a day's sightseeing. A full Scottish
breakfast is served in the charming conservatory
breakfast room and there are several places nearby
where you may enjoy an evening meal. The busy
fishing and market town of Kirkcudbright, nestling on the Solway at the estuary of the River Dee,
gives visitors a marvellous central axis from which
to explore the Galloway region. The area is steeped
in history but is also highly creative: there is a large group of craftsmen and artists living
and working in Kirkcudbright, and their work is much in evidence in the local shops.
OPEN ALL YEAR.   NO SMOKING.   V, S.D. B/A.   CHILDREN WELCOME AT FULL TARIFF.   EN SUITE &
BEVERAGES IN ROOMS.   T.V. IN LOUNGE.   B & B FROM £20.

LOCKERBIE

 Lochaber Cottage

EAGLESFIELD, LOCKERBIE, DUMFRIES & GALLOWAY.   TEL: (01461) 500546

Small & friendly 1850s cottage in grounds in quiet area. Open fire in winter. Parking.
NO SMOKING.   OPEN ALL YEAR.   S.D. B/A.   CHILDREN WELCOME.   WHEELCHAIR ACCESS.   BEVERAGES &
TV IN ROOMS.   B. & B. £13.

SANQUHAR

NITHSDALE GUEST HOUSE, GLASGOW RD, SANQUHAR, D. & G. TEL: (01659) 50288

Charming stone-built house; lovely gardens overlooking picnic area, loch & golf course.
OPEN ALL YEAR.   N/S DINING R & BEDRS.   V, S.D. B/A.   CHILDREN WELCOME.   BEVERAGES IN ROOMS.
T.V. IN LOUNGE.   B & B AROUND £16.

STRANRAER

 Fernlea Guest House

LEWIS ST, STRANRAER, WIGTOWNSHIRE, D. & G., DG9 7AQ   TEL: (01776) 3037

Lovely large detached Victorian villa in a private garden close to town centre. Pleasantly
furnished throughout. Traditional home-cooking.
OPEN ALL YEAR.   NO SMOKING.   V, S.D. B/A.   CHILDREN B/A.   EN SUITE IN 2 ROOMS.   TEA/COFFEE
MAKING & T.V. IN ROOMS.   B & B AROUND £17.

RESTAURANTS

GATEHOUSE OF FLEET

 BOBBIN COFFEE SHOP, 36 HIGH ST, GATEHOUSE OF FLEET, D. & G. TEL: (015574) 229
NO SMOKING

MOFFAT

 WELL VIEW, BALLPLAY RD, MOFFAT, DUM'SHIRE, DG10 9JU TEL: (01683) 20184
NO SMOKING. V, S.D. B/A.   LICENSED. CHILDREN WELCOME. ACCESS, VISA.

NEW ABBEY

 Abbey Cottage Coffees & Crafts

26 MAIN STREET, NEW ABBEY, DUMFRIES, DG2 8BY   TEL: (01387) 85377

Country restaurant in a charming setting next to Sweetheart Abbey, serving home-made
meals; good vegetarian selection.
OPEN 10 - 5.30.   L. AROUND £4.   NO SMOKING.   V STD, S.D. B/A.   LICENSED.   CHILDREN WELCOME.
DISABLED ACCESS: 'WIDE DOORS, RAMP, DISABLED LOO'.

Edinburgh

ACCOMMODATION

Adam Guest House

2 HARTINGTON GARDENS, EDINBURGH, EH10 4LD TEL: (0131) 229 8664 FAX: (0131) 228 5807

Adam House is a family-run guest house which is situated in a quiet cul-de-sac (free from
parking restrictions), just fifteen minutes' walk from the city centre and close to bus routes,
shops, theatres and restaurants; Bruntsfield Links and The Meadows public parks are just
a short walk away. The house has recently been completely refurbished by the present
owners and all the rooms are now bright, comfortable and well-equipped with a T.V., hot
drink facilities and wash hand basin; some have en suite facilities. The proprietors and staff
offer warm hospitality and a very friendly service, and families and children are particularly
welcome with reduced rates being available throughout the year.
OPEN ALL YEAR.   NO SMOKING (ex in proprietor's wing).   V, S.D. B/A.   CHILDREN WELCOME.   PETS B/A.
SOME ROOMS EN SUITE.   BEVERAGES & T.V. IN ROOMS.   B. & B. FROM £17 PER PERSON.

Airlie Guest House
29 MINTO ST, EDINBURGH, EH9 1SB   TEL: (031) 667 3562   FAX: (0131) 662 1399
STB 2 Crowns Commended. Comfortably appointed guest house. Easy access city centre.
OPEN ALL YEAR.   NO SMOKING.   CHILDREN WELCOME.   SOME EN SUITE.   TV & BEVERAGES IN ROOMS.
B. & B. £15 - 25

Allan Lodge Guest House
37 QUEEN'S CRESC., EDINBURGH.   TEL: (0131) 668 2947
Totally smoke-free guest house with 6 letting rooms. 2 en suite. Children are very welcome.
OPEN ALL YEAR (ex. Xmas)   NO SMOKING.   CHILDREN WELCOME.   2 EN SUITE ROOMS.   BEVERAGES IN
ROOMS.   B. & B. FROM £16.

Ashdene House
23 FOUNTAINHALL RD, EDINBURGH, EH9 2LN   TEL: (0131) 667 6026
Comfortable Edwardian villa in quiet leafy suburb; 10 mins city centre. Breaks Nov. -
Easter.
OPEN ALL YEAR.   NO SMOKING.   S.D. B/A.   CHILDREN WELCOME.   EN SUITE, TV & BEVERAGES IN ROOMS.
B. & B. £19 - 26.

Brunswick Hotel
7 BRUNSWICK ST, EDINBURGH, EH7 5JB   TEL: (0131) 556 1238   FAX: (0131) 556 1238
Georgian listed town house refurbished to high standard. Two four-poster bedrooms.
Central for rail and bus stations, shops, theatres and restaurants.
OPEN ALL YEAR.   NO SMOKING.   S.D. B/A.   OVER 5S WELCOME.   EN SUITE, TV & BEVERAGES IN ROOMS.
B. & B. £25 - 45.

Camore Guest House
7 LINKS GARDENS, EDINBURGH, EH6 7JH   TEL: (0131) 554 7897
Georgian listed house with panoramic views over Leith Links. 10-15 mins from city centre
on main bus route. 5 mins walk from local restaurants and Leith's new Waterworld.
OPEN ALL YEAR.   N/S DINING R.   V B/A.   LICENSED.   CHILDREN WELCOME.   PETS B/A.   T.V. WITH
SATELLITE CHANNELS & BEVERAGES IN ROOMS.   B. & B. AROUND £17.

Classic Guest House
50 MAYFIELD RD, EDINBURGH, EH9 2HH   TEL: (0131) 667 5847 FAX: (0131) 662 1016
AA QQQQ. STB Highly Commended. The family-run Classic Guest House is a traditional
Edinburgh town house which stands just a few minutes' walk from Princes Street, the
university and the other tourist attractions of Edinburgh. Centrally heated throughout,
accommodation is in comfortable rooms, each of which has been equipped with a hair dryer
and hospitality tray. A full Scottish breakfast is served in a charming dining room overlooking the garden and there are many places nearby where you may enjoy an evening
meal.
OPEN ALL YEAR.   NO SMOKING.   S.D. B/A.   CHILDREN WELCOME.   EN SUITE, TV & BEVERAGES IN ROOMS.
B. & B. FROM £18.

Hopetoun Guest House
15 MAYFIELD ROAD, EDINBURGH, EH9 2NG   TEL: (0131) 667 7691

Hopetoun is a small, friendly, family-run guest house which
is conveniently situated close to the university and just
2½ kilometres to the south of Princes Street. A pleasant
25-minute walk will take you to the Castle and Royal Mile
in the historic heart of Edinburgh's Old Town. The establishment offers very comfortable centrally heated accommodation in a completely smoke-free environment and this is
complemented by a friendly, informal atmosphere. Hopetoun is rated as One Crown Commended by the Scottish
Tourist Board, and is also a member of Edinburgh Tourist
Board and the Edinburgh Hotel and Guest House Associ-
ation, the two city organisations which promote high standards in the accommodation industry. There is also off street-
parking.
OPEN ALL YEAR.   NO SMOKING.   V, S.D. B/A.   CHILDREN WELCOME.
BEVERAGES & TV IN ROOMS.   B. & B. FROM £16.

Mrs C A King

103 WILLOWBRAE AVENUE, EDINBURGH   TEL: (0131) 661 2852
OPEN Apr. - Oct, Easter & Xmas. NO SMOKING.   V B/A.   CHILDREN WELCOME.   BEVERAGES & T.V. IN ROOMS.
B & B FROM £12.

Highfield Guest House

83 MAYFIELD ROAD, EDINBURGH, EH9 3AE   TEL: (0131) 667 8717

STB Commended. Highfield is a small, friendly, guest house within ten minutes drive from the city centre. The rooms are spacious, comfortable, centrally heated and equipped with wash basins. Tuck into the full cooked breakfast and help yourself to cereals, oatcakes, yoghurt, toast, etc. Home-made porridge is also available. Children are very welcome and a cot, high chair and toys are provided. The house is well situated for all the main tourist attractions, the university and King's Buildings, and is also within walking distance of Arthur's Seat and Blackford Hill.
OPEN ALL YEAR.   NO SMOKING.   V, S.D. B/A.   CHILDREN WELCOME.   PETS B/A.   BEVERAGES IN BEDROOMS.
T.V. IN LOUNGE.   B. & B. FROM £14.

Sandeman

33 COLINTON RD, EDINBURGH, EH10 5DR   TEL: (0131) 447 8080

STB 2 Crowns Commended. 33 Colinton Road is a Victorian family home which is conveniently situated within easy walking distance of the city centre. Your hosts take just 6 guests at any one time. The healthy breakfast menu features a full Scottish breakfast and oat-cakes and home-made preserves (organic in the case of raspberry & strawberry) and a good choice of teas; organically home-grown fruits are also available in season.
OPEN Mar - Oct. (other times by arrangement).   NO SMOKING.   V, S.D. B/A.   CHILDREN WELCOME.   PETS B/A
EN SUITE, TV & TEA/COFFEE IN ROOMS.   B. & B. FROM £20.

Sandilands House

25 QUEENSFERRY RD, EDINBURGH   TEL: (0131) 332 2057

B. & B. superbly situated 1m from city centre. Some en suite. Well-furnished, attractive rooms.
OPEN ALL YEAR.   NO SMOKING.   S.D. B/A.   CHILDREN WELCOME.   SOME EN SUITE; TV & BEVERAGES IN
ROOMS.

Sibbet House

26 NORTHUMBERLAND ST, EDINBURGH, EH3 6LS   TEL: (0131) 556 1078   FAX: (0131) 556 9445

STB 3 Crowns De Luxe. Sibbet House is a lovely stone-built Georgian town house which is situated within a few minutes' walk of Princes Street. Elegantly decorated and well-appointed, Sibbet House offers a particularly high standard of accommodation: antiques all add to the atmosphere (as does the bag-pipe loving owner!). A self-contained de luxe apartment (with 4 bedrooms and 2 bathrooms) is also available.
OPEN ALL YEAR.   NO SMOKING.   S.D. B/A.   CHILDREN.   EN SUITE, TV, BEVERAGES IN ROOMS.   B. & B. £25-35.

Six Mary's Place Guest House

RAEBURN PLACE, STOCKBRIDGE, EDINBURGH, EH4 1JH   TEL & FAX: (0131) 332 8965

STB 2 Crown Commended. Elegant Georgian guest house in fashionable Stockbridge district. Beautifully furnished & with landscaped gardens. Hearty, mainly vegetarian meals.
OPEN 4 Jan - 24 Dec.   NO SMOKING.   V STD, S.D. B/A.   CHILDREN WELCOME.   1 ROOM EN SUITE.
BEVERAGES IN ROOMS.   B. & B. £25, FULL BOARD £33.

STUDIO BED & BREAKFAST, 173 BRUNTSFIELD PLACE, EDINBURGH, EH10 4DG
TEL: (0131 229) 2746   NO SMOKING.   V, S.D. B/A.   CHILDREN. BEVERAGES.   B. & B. AROUND £18.

Teviotdale House

53 GRANGE LOAN, EDINBURGH, EH9 2ER   TEL: (0131) 667 4376

Elegant, stone-built Victorian town house in a beautiful tree-lined street; very comfortably furnished and appointed; *fabulous* food!
OPEN ALL YEAR.   NO SMOKING.   V, S.D. B/A.   CHILDREN WELCOME.   EN SUITE, BEVERAGES & T.V. IN
ROOMS.   CREDIT CARDS (surcharge).   B. & B. AROUND £25

THE TOWN HOUSE GUEST HOUSE, 65 GILMORE PLACE, EDINBURGH, EH3 9NU
Charming 3-storey Victorian town house,beautifully renovated. Breakfast only.
TEL: (0131) 229 1985 OPEN ALL YEAR. NO SMOKING. V B/A. CHILDREN WELCOME. SOME EN
SUITE ROOMS. BEVERAGES & T.V. IN ROOMS. B. & B. AROUND £18.

10A DEAN TERRACE, EDINBURGH, EH4 1ND   TEL: (0131) 332 0403
Garden flat of Georgian building overlooking Water of Leith; B. & B./self-catering.
NO SMOKING. V B/A. CHILDREN WELCOME. T.V.   B. & B. AROUND £18.

RESTAURANTS

Alp-Horn Restaurant
167 ROSE STREET, OFF CHARLOTTE SQUARE, EDINBURGH, EH2 4LS   TEL: (0131) 225 4787
The Alp-horn is a chalet-style restaurant, owned by the Denzlers, which stands just 2
minutes from Princes Street in the heart of Edinburgh. It specialises in serving delicious
Swiss cuisine - but with a French basis - and diners may feast on such house specialities
as Bündnerfleisch (air-dried beef and ham from the Swiss mountains), Veal Zürichoise and
Rösti, Venison and Spätzli and Apfel Strudel, and those feeling less adventurous may dine
on a freshly prepared soup followed by Rump Steak Toreador (garnished with diced
mushrooms and peppers on tomato sauce). The extensive wine list includes Swiss Fendant
and Dôle, and there are some tempting desserts.
OPEN 12 - 2, 6.30 - 10.   L. AROUND £10, D. AROUND £17.   NO SMOKING 1 DINING ROOM.   V B/A. LICENSED.
CHILDREN WELCOME.   ACCESS, VISA, AMEX, DINERS.

CHAPTER ONE, 57 GEORGE STREET, EDINBURGH, EH2 2JQ   TEL: (0131) 225 4495
Café located in general bookshop/newsagents in the centre of the city.
75% N/S. V STD.   CHILDREN WELCOME.

CORNERSTONE CAFÉ, ST JOHN'S CHURCH, PRINCES ST. TEL: (0131) 229 0212
Vegetarian/vegan/wholefood cafe serving hot food, salads, snacks, cakes, etc.
NO SMOKING. DISABLED ACCESS difficult, but there is a ramp; toilet has wheelchair access'.

CRAWFORDS COUNTRY KITCHENS, 26/27 ST JAMES CENTRE. TEL: (0131) 556 3098
N/S UPPER FLOOR. V, S.D. STD. DISABLED ACCESS. CHILDREN WELCOME.

Debenhams
109 PRINCES ST, EDINBURGH   TEL: (0131) 225 1320
Self-service restaurant serving popular light lunches, snacks range of hot and cold drinks.
OPEN STORE HOURS. NO SMOKING. V STD. DISABLED ACCESS. CHILDREN. CREDIT CARDS.

HELIOS FOUNTAIN, 7 GRASSMARKET, EDINBURGH, EH1 2HY TEL: (0131) 229 7884
Excellent vegetarian/wholefood cafe at the rear of book shop.
NO SMOKING. V, VE, SUGAR-FREE STD. DISABLED ACCESS. CHILDREN WELCOME.

The Indian Cavalry Club
3 ATHOLL PLACE, EDINBURGH, EH3 8HP   TEL: (0131) 228 3282

The Indian Cavalry Club is not a club, of course, but a wonderful
restaurant which won itself so many friends that it soon began to
feel like a real club. It serves the kind of modern Indian cuisine
favoured by the most exclusive circles of Delhi and Bombay and
especially at the banquets for which the officers' mess of the
Cavalry Regiment is famous (hence their name). These dishes are
lighter and less fiery than traditional fare and rely on the finest,
freshest ingredients. The main courses range from exquisitely
prepared meat and poultry to seafood and vegetarian delicacies.
However you don't have to be a maharajah, tycoon or field
marshal to eat here! The à la carte selection is very reasonably
priced and there are some splendid set banquets which are most
economical, particularly for families or parties.
60 SEATS. OPEN 12 - 2.30, 5.30 - 11.30. L. AROUND £10.   N/S 25%. V, S.D. ON
REQUEST. LICENSED. DISABLED ACCESS. CHILDREN WELCOME. CREDIT
CARDS.

The Kalpna Restaurant

2-3 ST PATRICK SQUARE, EDINBURGH, EH8 9EZ   TEL: (0131) 667 9890

Widely recommended, award-winning Indian vegetarian restaurant specialising in Indian vegetarian wholefood cuisine from the Gujarat region. The name Kalpna denotes a combination of 'imagination' and 'creation' and the logo is the elephant, which reminds diners that you do not have to eat meat to be big, strong and intelligent.
OPEN 12 - 2, 5.30 - 11. NO SMOKING. CHILDREN WELCOME. WHEELCHAIR ACCESS.

Parrots

3-5 VIEWFORTH, EDINBURGH, EH10 4JD   TEL: (0131) 229 3252

Very popular restaurant - parrots abound - serving a wide range of dishes ranging from good vegetarian options to wonderful meat pies; excellent cooking; booking essential.
OPEN Fri. & Sat. 5 - 11.30 P.M. (last orders), Sun. - Thurs. 6 - 11.30 P.M. D. AROUND £12. NO SMOKING. LICENSED.
DISABLED ACCESS.   CHILDREN WELCOME from 5 - 7 pm & at lunchtime functions.

PIZZA HUT (UK) LTD, 34-36 HANOVER ST, EDINBURGH, EH2 2DR TEL: (0131) 226 3652
66% N/S. V, VE STD. LICENSED. DISABLED ACCESS, 'not to toilet'. CHILDREN.

THE POTTING SHED, BRUNTSFIELD HOTEL, 69 BRUNTSFIELD PL. TEL: (0131) 229 1393
N/S CONSERVATORY. V STD. LICENSED. DISABLED ACCESS. CHILDREN WELCOME.

THE QUEEN'S HALL, CLERK STREET, EDINBURGH   TEL: (031 668) 3456
Excellent wholefood restaurant.
75% N/S V/WH STD. LICENSED. DISABLED ACCESS: 'ramp/toilets etc.' CHILDREN.

"REEDS" RESTAURANT & COFFEE SHOP, 124 PRINCES ST.   TEL: (0131) 225 6703
50% N/S V STD. LICENSED. DISABLED ACCESS. CHILDREN WELCOME.

Seeds Wholefood Café

53 WEST NICOLSON ST, EDINBURGH, EH8 9DB   TEL: (0131) 667 8729
NO SMOKING. CHILDREN WELCOME.

"THE STEDDING", 118 BIGGAR ROAD, EDINBURGH, EH10 7DH TEL: (0131) 445 1128
50% N/S V STD. LICENSED. DISABLED ACCESS. CHILDREN 'LIMITED'.

Fife

ACCOMMODATION

ABERDOUR

HAWKCRAIG HOUSE, HAWKCRAIG POINT, ABERDOUR, FIFE, KY3 0TZ TEL: (01383) 860335

STB 2 Crown Highly Commended. Beautiful white-painted house by the sea.
NO SMOKING. V B/A. BYO WINE. OVER 8S. EN SUITE & TV. BEVERAGES. B. & B. AROUND £20.

The Woodside Hotel

HIGH ST, ABERDOUR, FIFE, KY3 0SW   TEL: (01383) 860920   FAX: (01383) 860920

Listed building in picturesque village, convenient for Edinburgh by train or car.
OPEN ALL YEAR. N/S PART OF DINING R. V, S.D. B/A. WHEELCHAIR ACCESS. CHILDREN & PETS. LICENSED.
EN SUITE, TV & BEVERAGES. CREDIT CARDS. B. & B. FROM £24, D., B. & B. FROM £39.50.

ANSTRUTHER

CORNCERES FARM, ANSTRUTHER, FIFE   TEL: (01333) 310337
NO SMOKING. V B/A. CHILDREN WELCOME. BEVERAGES & TV IN LOUNGE. B. & B. AROUND £15.

CULROSS

WOODHEAD FARM, CULROSS, FIFE, KY12 8ET TEL: (01383) 880270
NO SMOKING. V, S.D. B/A. CHILDREN WELCOME. BEVERAGES & TV IN ROOMS. B. & B. AROUND £20.

CUPAR

GREIGSTON FARMHOUSE, PEAT INN, CUPAR, FIFE, KY15 5LF   TEL: (01334) 84284
16th/17th C. Scottish Laird's house with light, airy, spacious south-facing rooms.
NO SMOKING. V B/A. DISABLED ACCESS. CHILDREN WELCOME. PETS B/A. EN SUITE & BEVERAGES
IN ROOMS. T.V. IN LOUNGE. B. & B. AROUND £17.

FREUCHIE

Lomond Hills Hotel
LOMOND ROAD, FREUCHIE, FIFE, KY7 7EY   TEL: (01337) 57329
White-painted 25-bedroom hotel in picturesque village of Freuchie.
OPEN ALL YEAR. N/S REST, 24 BEDROOMS, CONSERVATORY & LEISURE CENTRE. V STD. LICENSED. DIS-
ABLED: "RESTAURANT & 1 BEDROOM ON GROUND FLOOR". CHILDREN WELCOME. EN SUITE, BEVERAGES &
T.V. IN ROOMS. B. & B. FROM £36.

PITTENWEEM

VICTORIA COTTAGE, 11 VIEWFORTH PL., PITTENWEEM, FIFE, KY10 2PZ   TEL: (01333) 311998
Charming cottage in a small, active fishing village within the East Neuk of Fife.
NO SMOKING. V, S.D. B/A. CHILDREN WELCOME. PETS B/A. BEVERAGES & T.V. IN ROOMS. B. & B.
AROUND £16.

ST ANDREWS

Edenside House
EDENSIDE, ST ANDREWS, FIFE, KY16 9SQ   TEL: (01334) 838108   FAX: (01334) 838493

STB 2 Crown Commended. Edenside House enjoys a superb waterfront setting with fine views of the estuary bird sanctuary /nature reserve yet it is within 2½ miles of historic St Andrews (5 minutes by car on A91). A listed former Scottish farmhouse predating 1775, now tastefully modernised, Edenside House offers a high standard of comfort to discerning guests and is non-smoking throughout. All nine double/twin rooms are furnished to 3 Crown Commended standard and have en suite facilities, colour TV and beverage tray (some are on the ground floor). Edenside House provides guaranteed parking within private grounds. The traditional and extensive breakfast menu includes fish dishes. Edenside Riding Stable is nearby. As well as the world-renowned Old Course and additional five St Andrews courses, other fine tests of golf, including Carnoustie, abound locally and we are happy to discuss your golf requirements at time of booking. Contact Dr and Mrs Jim Mansell for brochure and booking procedure.
OPEN ALL YEAR. NO SMOKING. V, VE STD, SOME WH. SOME S.D. B/A. OVER 12s WELCOME. PETS B/A.
DISABLED ACCESS: SOME GROUND FLOOR ROOMS. EN SUITE, BEVERAGES & TV IN ROOMS. ACCESS, VISA.
B. & B. FROM £20.

Rufflets Country House
STRATHKINNESS LOW RD, ST ANDREWS, KY16 9TX TEL: (01334) 72594 FAX: (01334) 78703

Designed by Dundee architect Donald Mills and built in 1924, this outstanding country house stands in 10 acres of award-winning gardens and has been privately owned and personally managed by the same family since 1952. Over the years the house has been extended and refurbished, but all additions have been in keeping with the original building, and an overall atmosphere of gracious calm prevails: each of the spacious public rooms overlooks the magnificent gardens, and the 21 en suite bedrooms have been furnished to a very high standard and are equipped with a range of useful amenities including a direct dial phone; a cottage in the grounds has equally splendid accommodation

for 3 further sets of guests. The food is excellent: everything is prepared from fresh, seasonal and local produce; indeed many of the vegetables, fruits and herbs come from the hotel's kitchen garden. This idyllic retreat offers the best of both worlds: a sense of rural tranquillity, yet the proximity to the world famous "Home of Golf", St Andrews.
OPEN JAN. TO DEC. N/S DINING R, PART OF BAR, SOME BEDR. V STD. DIAB. B/A. LICENSED. CHILDREN WELCOME. EN SUITE, TV & BEVERAGES IN ROOMS. CREDIT CARDS.

St Andrews Golf Hotel
40 THE SCORES, ST ANDREWS, FIFE, KY16 9AS   TEL: (01334) 72611

Situated on the cliffs overlooking St Andrews Bay and links, and 200 metres from the 'old course', St Andrews Hotel is a tastefully modernised, listed Victorian building with comfortable bedrooms and elegant public rooms (including a charming oak-panelled restaurant). The food is excellent: everything is prepared from fresh, local seafood, game and meats, and is complemented by a first-rate choice of wines; meals are served by candlelight in the aforementioned dining room or, if you prefer a more informal atmosphere, you could dine in Ma Bells basement bar and restaurant with its vast array of foreign and local beers. The hotel is owned and run by the Hughes family and specialises in providing golfing holidays for individuals and small groups.
OPEN ALL YEAR.   N/S RESTAURANT.   V, S.D. B/A.   LICENSED. CHILDREN WELCOME.   PETS B/A.   EN SUITE, BEVERAGES & T.V. IN ROOMS.   CREDIT CARDS.

West Park House
5 ST MARY'S PLACE, ST ANDREWS, FIFE. TEL: (01334) 475933
Beautiful Georgian house in centre of historic town near university, beach and golf courses.
OPEN Mar - Nov.   NO SMOKING.   V, S.D. B/A.   CHILDREN WELCOME.   EN SUITE IN MOST ROOMS. BEVERAGES & T.V. IN ROOMS.   B. & B. FROM £18.50.

RESTAURANTS

FREUCHIE

LOMOND HILLS HOTEL, LOMOND ROAD, FREUCHIE, FIFE, KY7 7EY   TEL: (01337) 57329
For further details please see under the entry in the accommodation section.

Glasgow & Central

ACCOMMODATION

DOLLAR

STRATHDEVON HOUSE, HARVIESTOUN RD, DOLLAR, GLAS. & CENT., FK14 7PT   TEL: (01259) 42320   NO SMOKING. V, S.D. B/A. CHILDREN WELCOME.   ALL ROOMS EN SUITE. BEVERAGES ON REQUEST.   T.V. IN LOUNGE.   CREDIT CARDS.   B & B AROUND £15.

GLASGOW

THE COPTHORN E GLASGOW, GEORGE SQUARE, GLASGOW, G2 1DS TEL: (0141) 332 6711
OPEN ALL YEAR. N/S SOME BEDRS & 50% RESTAURANT.   V B/A.   LICENSED.   CHILDREN WELCOME (under 16s free).   EN SUITE, BEVERAGES & T.V. IN ROOMS.   B. & B. ARUND £55.

ALISON COUSTON, 13 CARMENT DR, SHAWLANDS, GLASGOW, G41 3PP   TEL: (0141) 632 019
Victorian house in quiet street close to shops and restaurants; friendly atmosphere.
NO SMOKING. V B/A.   CHILDREN.   PETS B/A.   BEVERAGES.   B. & B. AROUND £16.

Mrs J Freebairn-Smith

14 PROSPECT AVENUE, CAMBUSLANG, GLASGOW, G72 8BW   TEL: (0141) 641 5055
STB Listed Approved. Large Victorian villa standing in half an acre of lovely gardens.
OPEN ALL YEAR.   NO SMOKING IN PUBLIC ROOMS & SOME BEDROOMS.   V B/A.   CHILDREN WELCOME.
PETS B/A.   BEVERAGES & T.V. IN ROOMS.   B & B FROM £13.

Regent Guest House

44 REGENT PARK SQ., STRATHBUNGO, GLASGOW, G41 2AG   TEL: (0141) 422 1199
Charming 'B' listed Victorian terraced house 2m Glasgow 1m Burrell. Exceptionally
well-appointed. First-rate breakfasts. Evening meals available & many local restaurants.
OPEN ALL YEAR.   N/S ex. 3 bedrooms.   V, S.D. B/A.   CHILDREN WELCOME.   PETS B/A.   BEVERAGES & T.V. IN
ROOMS.   CREDIT CARDS.   B. & B. AROUND £25.

STIRLING

MRS THELMA HARPER, 67 BURNHEAD ROAD, LARBERT, STIRLING, FK5 4BD
TEL: (01324) 553168   NO SMOKING.   V, S.D. B/A.   CHILDREN.   BEVERAGES.   B. & B. AROUND £18

MR AND MRS D MCLAREN, "ALLANDALE", 98 CAUSEWAYHEAD RD, STIRLING
TEL: (01786) 465643   NO SMOKING.   V B/A.   CHILDREN.   BEVERAGES.   T.V.   B & B AROUND £12.

MRS J COLVILLE, 12 ARGYLL AVENUE, RIVERSIDE, STIRLING, FK8 1UL
TEL: (01786) 62632   NO SMOKING.   CHILDREN. BEVERAGES.   T.V. IN LOUNGE.   B & B AROUND £14.

RESTAURANTS

DRYMEN

DRYMEN POTTERY TEAROOM, THE SQUARE, DRYMEN   TEL: (01360) 60458
OPEN DAILY 9.30 - 5.30.   NO SMOKING.

GLASGOW

BURNBANK HOTEL, 67/85 WEST PRINCES ST, GLASGOW TEL: (0141) 332 4400
NO SMOKING. V, S.D. STD. LICENSED. DISABLED ACCESS. CHILDREN WELCOME.

CAFÉ JJ, 180 DUMBARTON ROAD, GLASGOW, G11 6XE   TEL: (0141) 357 1881
Small, family-run café offering a selection of reasonably priced home-made food.
NO SMOKING. V, S.D. STD. LICENSED. CHILDREN WELCOME.

THE COACH HOUSE, BALMORE, TORRANCE, GLASGOW, G64 4AE TEL: (01360) 20742
Charitable enterprise offering home-baked snacks & cakes. Craft/gift shop.
NO SMOKING. V STD. CHILDREN WELCOME.

THE COPTHORNE GLASGOW, GEORGE SQUARE, GLASGOW, G2 1DS   TEL: (0141) 332 6711
For further details please see under entry in accommodation section.

DEBENHAMS, GLASGOW
Two self-service restaurants and a coffee shop serve this premium store in Glasgow.
Somewhere to suit everyone with a family restaurant at the top of the shop.
OPEN STORE HOURS.   NO SMOKING.   V STD.   CHILDREN WELCOME. CREDIT CARDS.

SHISH MAHAL RESTAURANT, 45-47 GIBSON STREET, GLASGOW TEL: (0141) 334 7899
Excellent restaurant serving Western and Indian food.
N/S PART OF RESTAURANT.   V STD.   LICENSED.   DISABLED ACCESS.   CHILDREN.

STIRLING

BROUGHTON'S REST., BLAIR DRUMMOND, STIRLING, FK9 4XE   TEl: (01786) 841897
N/S RESTAURANT.   V STD.   LICENSED.   DISABLED ACCESS.   CHILDREN LUNCHTIME.

Grampian

ACCOMMODATION

ABERDEEN

Brentwood Hotel

101 CROWN ST, ABERDEEN, GRAMPIAN.   TEL: (01224) 595440   FAX: (01224) 571593
The Brentwood Hotel is a warm, friendly town house hotel which is conveniently situated
in the city centre. There are 64 beautifully appointed bedrooms, including 2 executive
suites, each with an en suite bathroom, direct dial phone, TV and beverages. Meals can be
enjoyed in the Carriages Brasserie and Bar which serves excellent food from a varied and
adventurous menu: everything has been prepared from fresh ingredients and special diets
are catered for. There is also a well-stocked bar which boasts an extensive choice of
traditional cask-conditioned ales and Scottish malt whiskies.
OPEN ALL YEAR.   50% N/S DINING R.   S.D. ON REQUEST.   CHILDREN WELCOME.   LICENSED.   CREDIT CARDS.
EN SUITE, TV & BEVERAGES IN BEDROOMS.   B. & B. FROM £30 (W/E RATE)

ST ELMO, 64 HILTON DRIVE, ABERDEEN,GRAMPIAN, AB2 2NP   TEL: (01224) 483065
NO SMOKING.   CHILDREN.   BEVERAGES & T.V. IN ROOMS.   B. & B. AROUND £17.

BALLATER

CRAIGENDARROCH G. H., 36 BRAEMAR RD, BALLATER, AB35 5RQ TEL: (013397) 55369
N/S ex. in 1 bedroom.   V B/A.   DISABLED ACCESS: "GROUND FLOOR.".   CHILDREN WELCOME.   PETS B/A.   EN
SUITE, TV &BEVERAGES IN ROOMS.   B. & B. AROUND £18.

Creag Meggan

BRIDGE OF GAIRN, BALLATER, ROYAL DEESIDE, GRAMP., AB35 5UD TEL: (013397) 55767
Large detached granite-built house 1m Ballater & 5m Balmoral. Beautiful countryside -
bedrooms have lovely views. Excellent home-cooked food prepared from fresh produce.
OPEN May - Sept.   NO SMOKING.   OVER 12S ONLY.   TV & BEVERAGES IN ROOMS.   B. & B.AROUND £18

The Green Inn

9 VICTORIA ROAD, BALLATER, GRAMPIAN, AB3 5QQ   TEL: (013397) 55701
Granite-built former temperance hotel overlooking Ballater village green. Excellent food
prepared from local, fresh produce. Traditional Scottish specialities. Good wine list.
OPEN ALL YEAR.   N/S DINING R.   V STD, S.D. B/A.   LICENSED.   DISABLED ACCESS.   CHILDREN WEL-
COME.   PETS B/A.   EN SUITE, TV & BEVERAGES IN ROOMS.   ACCESS, VISA.   B. & B. AROUND £24

ELGIN

Non Smokers Haven

37 DUFF AVE, ELGIN, MORAY, GRAMPIAN, IV30 1QS TEL: (01343) 541993
STB Commended. Bungalow with walled garden in quiet central residential area; 4 mins
walk from railway station; private parking; ideal for golfers, ornithologists, ramblers.
OPEN ALL YEAR.   NO SMOKING.   WASHBASINS, BEVERAGES & T.V. IN ROOMS.   B. & B. FROM £14.

MORAY

SEAVIEW B & B, 82 GRANARY ST, BURGHEAD, MORAY, IV30 2UA TEL: (01343) 830034
Commended guest house on harbour front of the small fishing village of Burghead.
NO SMOKING.   V B/A.   '1 GROUND FLOOR BEDROOM'.   CHILDREN WELCOME.   PETS B/A.   BEVER-
AGES & T.V. IN ROOMS.   B. & B. AROUND £15.

MUIR OF ORD

The Dower House

MUIR OF ORD, ROSS-SHIRE, GRAMPIAN, IV6 7XN   TEL & FAX: (01463) 870090
3 Crowns Highly Commended. The Dower House offers exceptionally comfortable accommodation and award-winning food.
OPEN ALL YEAR.   N/S DINING ROOM & SOME BEDROOMS.   V B/A.   LICENSED.   DISABLED ACCESS.
CHILDREN WELCOME.   DOGS B/A.   EN SUITE & T.V. IN ROOMS.   CREDIT CARDS.   B. & B. FROM £45.

FORRES

 PARKMOUNT HOUSE HOTEL, ST LEONARD'S RD, FORRES, GRAMPIAN, IV36 0DW
TEL: (01309) 73312 NO SMOKING. V B/A. LICENSED. CHILDREN WELCOME. PETS B/A. EN SUITE, TV
& BEVERAGES IN ROOMS. ACCESS, MASTERCARD. B. & B. AROUND £35.

GLENLIVET

MINMORE HOUSE HOTEL, GLENLIVET, BALLANDALLOCH, GRAMPIAN, AB3 9DB
TEL: (018073) 378 N/S ex. in bar & some bedrooms. V B/A. LICENSED. CHILDREN WELCOME. PETS B/A. EN
SUITE & BEVERAGES IN ROOMS. B. & B. AROUND £30.

HUNTLY

FAICH-HILL FARMHOUSE HOLIDAYS, GARTLY, HUNTLY, GRAMPIAN, AB54 4RR
TEL: (0146688) 240 N/S EX. sun lounge. V B/A. OVER 4S ONLY. 1 EN SUITE BEDROOM. BEVERAGES. T.V.
LOUNGE. B. & B. AROUND £17. *Twice Scottish 'farmhouse Of The Year' Winner.*

KEITH

THE HAUGHS FARM GUEST HOUSE, KEITH, GRAMPIAN. TEL: (015422) 2238
Comfortable farmhouse with lovely large southfacing dining room overlooking garden
N/S DINING R & BEDRS.   V, DIAB, B/A.   DISABLED ACCESS. CHILDREN WELCOME. 3 EN SUITE
ROOMS. BEVERAGES & T.V. IN ROOMS. B. & B. FROM £12.50.

STONEHAVEN

Car-Lyn-Vale
RICKARTON BY STONEHAVEN, KINCARDINESHIRE, GRAMPIAN.   TEL: (01569) 762406
STB Highly Commended. B. & B. in lovely countryside on A957.
OPEN ALL YEAR. NO SMOKING. S.D. B/A. EN SUITE, TV & BEVERAGES IN ROOMS. B. & B. FROM £17.50.

RESTAURANTS

ABERDEEN

 Charles Michie Chemists

391 UNION STREET, ABERDEEN, GRAMPIAN.   TEL: (01224) 585312
Beautiful store with fresh and pretty coffee shop. Delicious home-prepared food. Open for
morning coffee, lunches and afternoon tea.
OPEN SHOP HOURS. NO SMOKING. V, DIAB STD. DISABLED: 'STAFF HELP WITH WHEELCHAIRS'.

 DEBENHAMS, TRINITY CENTRE, ABERDEEN, GRAMPIAN TEL: (01224) 573111
Springles, a friendly self-service restaurant serving lunches, snacks and drinks.
OPEN STORE HOURS. NO SMOKING. V STD. DISABLED ACCESS. CHILDREN. CREDIT CARDS.

BALLATER

MONALTRIE HOTEL, 5 BRIDGE SQUARE, BALLATER, GRAMPIAN. TEL: (013397) 55417
N/S RESTAURANT.   V, S.D. B/A. LICENSED. DISABLED ACCESS. CHILDREN WELCOME.

FOCHABERS

 THE GALLERY, 85 HIGH ST, FOCHABERS, GRAMPIAN.   TEL: (01343) 820981
NO SMOKING.

FORRES

PARKMOUNT HOUSE HOTEL, ST. LEONARD'S ROAD, FORRES, GRAMPIAN, IV36 0DW
TEL: (01309) 73312 N/S RESTAURANT.   V STD. S.D. B/A. LICENSED. DISABLED ACCESS TO DINING R. CHILD-
REN WELCOME. VISA, MASTERCARD.

FRASERBURGH

 **RITCHIES COFFEE SHOP, 30 CROSSS ST, FRASERBURGH, GRAMPIAN. TEL: (01346)
2774**
NO SMOKING.

Highlands

ACCOMMODATION

AULTBEA

CARTMEL G.H, BIRCHBURN RD, AULTBEA, ACHNASHEEN, W. ROSS, HIGHL. TEL:
(01445) 731375
NO SMOKING.   V B/A.   'GOOD' DISABLED ACCESS.   CHILDREN WELCOME.   PETS B/A.   1 EN SUITE
ROOM.   BEVERAGES.   T.V. LOUNGE.   D. B. & B. AROUND £26.

Oran Na Mara

DRUMCHORK, **AULTBEA**, ROSS-SHIRE, HIGHLAND, IV22 2HU   TEL: (01445) 731394
Spacious, comfortable hill side guest house with stunning views from all rooms. Two *STB*
Highly Commended self-catering apartments.
OPEN Easter - Oct. inc.   NO SMOKING.   V, VE STD.   DISABLED: 'ALL ON GROUND FLOOR'.   OVER 8s
WELCOME.   PETS B/A.   WASH-BASIN, BEVERAGES & TV IN ROOMS.   B. & B. FROM £14.

"Sandale"

5 PIER RD, AULTBEA, ROSS-SHIRE, HIGHLANDS, IV22 2JQ   TEL: (01445) 731336
Modern house in colourful gardens in croft and fishing village of Aultbea. Spectacular
views of Loch Ewe. Evening meals prepared from fresh, local produce. Home-baking.
OPEN Mar. - Oct.   NO SMOKING.   V, S.D. B/A.   CHILDREN WELCOME.   BEVERAGES IN ROOMS.   T.V. IN
LOUNGE.   B. & B. AROUND £16.

AVIEMORE

Aviemore Self Catering

17 CRAIG-NA-GOWER AVE, AVIEMORE, INVERNESS-SHIRE, PH22 1RW TEL: (01479) 810031
STB 2 & 4 Crown Commended. Comfortable family home with open views to the hill; peat
fire. Safe off-road parking and self catering accommodation.
OPEN ALL YEAR.   NO SMOKING.   V B/A.   CHILDREN WELCOME.   ALL ROOMS EN SUITE.   BEVERAGES
ON REQUEST.   T.V. IN LOUNGE.   B. & B. AROUND £16.

BOAT OF GARTEN

Avingormack Guest House

BOAT OF GARTEN, INVERNESSSHIRE, HIGHLANDS, PH24 3BT.   TEL: (01479) 83614
Converted croft in a beautiful rural location with magnificent, uninterrupted views of the
Cairngorm mountains. 4m Aviemore. Central heating. Delicious Scottish and vegetarian
cuisine prepared from organic/homegrown where possible. Home-baked bread.
OPEN ALL YEAR.   NO SMOKING.   V STD. S.D. B/A.   CHILDREN WELCOME.   SOME EN SUITE ROOMS.
BEVERAGES & T.V. IN ROOMS.   B. & B. AROUND £17.

Heathbank - The Victorian House.

BOAT OF GARTEN, INVERNESS-SHIRE, HIGHLAND, PH24 3BD   TEL: (01479) 831234
Cooking with imagination, style and flavour prepared from local game, salmon, lamb and
beef etc and served in a stunning conservatory dining room. The chef proprietor was
previously an owner of a successful restaurant and has been awarded "Taste of Scotland
1995". Enchantingly beautiful Victoriana-filled bedrooms. Two have four-posters, one a
sunken bathroom.
OPEN Dec. - Oct; NO SMOKING; V, S.D. B/A; LICENSED; CHILDREN ACCEPTED; SOME EN SUITE ROOMS;
BEVERAGES IN ROOMS; T.V. IN LOUNGE; B. & B. FROM £20 - 30, D. £15.

BRORA

Ard Beag

BADNELLAN, BRORA, SUTHERLAND, HIGHLANDS, KW9 6NQ TEL: (01408) 621398
Small, comfortable former croft house in a pleasant south-facing garden with fine views.
OPEN May - Sept.   N/S DINING R & BEDRS.   V B/A.   CHILDREN.   BEVERAGES.   B. & B. AROUND £16.

CARROL GUEST HOUSE, GOLF ROAD, BRORA, SUTHERLAND, HIGHL, KW9 6QS
TEL: (01408) 21065 OPEN May - Sept. NO SMOKING. V B/A. CHILDREN WELCOME. 2 EN SUITE ROOMS.
BEVERAGES & TV IN ROOMS.   B. & B. AROUND £22.

SUMUNDAR VILLA, HARBOUR RD, BRORA, SUTHERLAND, HIGHLANDS, KW9 6QF
TEL: (01408) 21717 OPEN Feb. - Nov.   NO SMOKING. V, DIAB STD. DISABLED ACCESS.   CHILDREN
WELCOME. BEVERAGES & TV IN ROOMS.   B. & B. AROUND £17.

Tigh Fada (Non-smokers Haven)
GOLF ROAD, BRORA, HIGHLANDS, KW9 6QS   TEL: (01408) 621332
OPEN ALL YEAR. NO SMOKING. V B/A. CHILDREN WELCOME, 'NOT TODDLERS'. PETS B/A.   BEVER-
AGES IN ROOMS. B. & B. AROUND £16 with reduced price for 2+ nights.

CARRBRIDGE

KINCHYLE G. H., CARRBRIDGE, INVERNESS-SHIRE, HIGHLANDS, PH23 3AA
TEL: (01479) 84243 OPEN ALL YEAR. NO SMOKING. V, LOW-FAT B/A. CHILDREN WELCOME.   BEVER-
AGES IN ROOMS. T.V. IN LOUNGE. B. & B. AROUND £18.

DRUMBEG

Drumbeg House
DRUMBEG, NR LOCHINVER, SUTHERLAND, IV27 4NW   TEL: (015713) 209
Charming Victorian house standing amidst 3 acres of garden beside water lily loch. Good
home-cooking, delicious desserts; coal fire. Centrally heated throughout.
OPEN ALL YEAR. NO SMOKING. V, S.D. B/A. CHILDREN: OVER 10S ONLY. EN SUITE & BEVERAGES IN
ROOMS. T.V. IN LOUNGE. B. & B. AROUND £25.

DULNAIN BRIDGE

Auchendean Lodge Hotel
DULNAIN BRIDGE, INVERNESS-SHIRE, HIGHLAND, PH26 3LU TEL & FAX: (01479) 851347

Visitors to Auchendean Lodge Hotel will feel that they have stepped
back into another era. Beautifully appointed throughout with period
antiques, furnishings and paintings which have been chosen to complement the building's many original Edwardian features, Auchendean
Lodge has outstanding views across the River Spey and over the Aber-
nethy Forest to the Cairngorm Mountains. Its owners, Eric Hart and Ian
Kirk, have created an ambience of comfort, style and good service,
which prevails in an atmosphere of informality and great friendliness.
Both owners share the cooking and specialize in an imaginative cuisine
(and some traditional Scottish dishes), which have been prepared not
only from local and home-grown produce but from ingredients culled from the moors and
woods (such as the wild mushrooms which Eric picks in late summer and autumn). Staying
at Auchendean Lodge is an enjoyable and unique experience, and whether your strongest
memories will be of the house, the food or the surroundings will be for you to decide.
OPEN ALL YEAR. N/S DINING & SITTING R. V, VE, S.D. B/A. LICENSED. DISABLED ACCESS.   CHILDREN
WELCOME. PETS B/A. MOST BEDROOMS EN SUITE. BEVERAGES & T.V. ALL ROOMS. B. & B. FROM £21.

DURNESS

Port-na-Con House
PORT-NA-CON, LOCH ERIBOLL, BY ALTNAHARRA, DURNESS, LAIRG, SUTHERLAND,
HIGHLAND, IV27 4UN. TEL: (01971) 511367

Port-na-Con stands on the west side of Loch
Eriboll, 6 miles east of Durness, and was built
200 years ago as a Custom House and harbour
store. Completely renovated in 1984, it is now a
comfortable, centrally heated guest house in
which all bedrooms overlook the loch: the first
floor lounge and balcony have particularly impressive views and here guests can enjoy not
only the scenery, but also the varied wild life,
including seals, otters and birds. The food is the

very best of Scottish fare, and the restaurant is open to non-residents by arrangement: all dishes are home-cooked from fresh, local ingredients and the à la carte menu might feature Salmon and Crab Terrine with home-made bread, followed by Roast Beef with fresh vegetables, and a delicious dessert, such as Chocolate & Orange Cheesecake.

OPEN mid Mar. - Oct. inc. Restaurant open to non-residents by prior arrangement.   NO SMOKING.   V, S.D. B/A.
LICENSED.   CHILDREN & WELL-BEHAVED DOGS WELCOME.   BEVERAGES IN ROOMS.   ACCESS & VISA.
D., B. & B. £27, SINGLE £33 (May - Sept inc. out of ain season single at standard rate.

FORT WILLIAM

Ashburn House

17 ACHINTORE RD, FORT WILLIAM, HIGHLAND, PH33 6RQ   TEL & FAX: (01397) 706000

RAC Highly Acclaimed. AA QQQQQ. STB de Luxe. Nestling deep in the heart of Highland Jacobite country at the foot of Ben Nevis is the old garrison town of Fort William. Ashburn House is just 5 minutes walk from the centre of town, and sits on the shore of romantic Loch Linnhe. It is a modernised and centrally heated Victorian house which has been furnished to a very comfortable standard; each of the guest bedrooms has been tastefully appointed and some have loch views. Breakfast is served in a corniced dining room, and there is a charming conservatory lounge which enjoys stunning views of the Ardgour Hills across Loch Linnhe.

OPEN ALL YEAR.   NO SMOKING.   S.D. B/A.   CHILDREN WELCOME.   EN SUITE, TV & BEVERAGES IN ROOMS.
CREDIT CARDS.   B. & B. £20 - 30.

NEVIS VIEW, 14 FARROW DR, CORPACH, F. WILLIAM, INVERN'SHIRE, PH33 7JW2
TEL: (01397) 772447   FAX: (01397) 772800   OPEN ALL YEAR. NO SMOKING. V STD, VE B/A.   CHILDREN
WELCOME.   PETS B/A.   BEVERAGES & TV IN ROOMS.   B. & B. AROUND £15.

Taransay

SEAFIELD GARDENS, FORT WILLIAM, INVERN'SHIRE, PH33 6RJ   TEL: (01397) 703303

STB 2 Crowns Commended. Comfortable, modern family home in quiet residential area just off the A82. Panoramic views over Loch Linnhe and the Ardgour Hills. Families welcome. Delicious breakfasts and packed lunches on request.

OPEN Jan. - Oct.   NO SMOKING.   V STD, S.D. B/A.   CHILDREN WELCOME.   EN SUITE.   BEVERAGES IN
ROOMS.   T.V. LOUNGE.   B. & B. AROUND £16.

GLENFINNAN

The Stage House

GLENFINNAN, INVERNESS-SHIRE, HIGHLAND, PH37 4LT   TEL: (01397) 83246

Beautiful 17th C. coaching inn in picturesque glen at head of Loch Shiel. Excellent food prepared from fresh, local produce. Fishing rights & boats and mountain bikes for hire.

OPEN Mar. - Jan.   N/S ex. 2 bars.   V STD, DIAB B/A.   LICENSED.   CHILDREN: OVER 5S ONLY.   PETS B/A.
EN SUITE, TV & BEVERAGES IN ROOMS.   ACCESS, VISA.   B. & B. AROUND £30.

GRANTOWN-ON-SPEY

Ardconnel House

WOODLANDS TERR., GRANTOWN-ON-SPEY, HIGHL, PH26 3JU   TEL & FAX: (01479) 872104

STB 3 Crown De Luxe. AA QQQQQ Premier Selected. A Taste of Scotland Selected House. Built in 1890, Ardconnel House stands in its own spacious grounds of mature gardens in a quiet residential area of Grantown-on-Spey, overlooking a glorious pine forest, lochan and the Cromdale hills; the town centre and the River Spey are just a short walk away. The house has been beautifully furnished throughout: there is a spacious sitting room, with a log fire for cooler evenings and comfortably furnished bedrooms which have been equipped with a range of facilities including a hairdryer and remote control TV. Meals are prepared from the finest local produce and candle-lit dinners are served in the elegant chandeliered dining room; a selection of moderstly priced wines complement the evening meal, and there is also a good choice of Speyside malt whiskies.

OPEN ALL YEAR. NO SMOKING. S.D., B/A. OVER 10s WELOME. LICENSED. EN SUITE, BEVERAGES & TV IN ROOMS. ACCESS, VISA. B. & B. FROM £23, D. £12.50.

Kinross House
WOODSIDE AVENUE, GRANTOWN-ON-SPEY, MORAYSHIRE, HIGHLAND, PH26 3JR
TEL: (01479) 872042   FAX: (01479) 873504

This charming guest house sits on a quiet avenue, an easy stroll from the river and pinewoods, and from the centre of this delightful country town. Grantown is set in the splendour of the Central Highlands - an ideal starting point for a wide choice of holiday delights. Bedrooms are very comfortable, warm and spacious, and the atmosphere is relaxed and peaceful. Our delicious traditional dinner is freshly prepared with quality ingredients and served by David dressed in his McIntosh tartan kilt. We take a pride in giving our guests highland hospitality and comfort at its very best. Brochure available on request.

OPEN Apr. - Oct. NO SMOKING.   V, S.D. B/A.   RESIDENTIAL LICENCE.   OVER 7S ONLY. DISABLED ACCESS. EN SUITE ROOMS.   BEVERAGES & T.V. IN ROOMS.   B. & B. £18 - 23, D. £11.

STONEFIELD COTTAGE, 28 THE SQUARE, GRANTOWN-ON-SPEY, HIGHL, PH26 3HF
TEL: (01479) 873000   NO SMOKING. V, S.D. B/A. CHILDREN. BEVERAGES. B. & B. AROUND £16.

INVERNESS

Ardmuir House Hotel
16 NESS BANK, INVERNESS, HIGHLAND, IV2 4SF   TEL: (01463) 231151
Charming stone-built Georgian house on the east bank of the River Ness near to the town centre and the Ness Islands. Delicious home-cooked food prepared from fresh ingredients.
OPEN ALL YEAR. N/S DINING R. V, S.D. B/A. LICENSED. DISABLED ACCESS. CHILDREN WELCOME. PETS B/A.   EN SUITE & HAIRDRYERS IN ROOMS. BEVERAGES. T.V.

Borlum Farmhouse B. & B.
DRUMNADROCHIT, INVERNESS, HIGHLAND, IV3 6XN   TEL & FAX: (01456) 62358
18th C. farmhouse overlooking Loch Ness. Comfortably furnished with antiques. Centrally heated & wood-stove in cooler months. BHS approved Riding Centre. 20 mins Inverness.
OPEN ALL YEAR. NO SMOKING. CHILDREN & PETS WELCOME. SOME EN SUITE ROOMS. TV IN SITTING ROOM. CREDIT CARDS. B. & B. AROUND £20.

'CLACH MHUILINN', 7 HARRIS RD, INVERNESS, HIGHLAND, IV2 3LS
STB 2 Crown Highly Commended Spacious modern detached house in lovely garden in quiet residential area 1m. S. of city. Bar meals nearby. Excellent touring base. B.& B.
TEL: (01463) 237059   OPEN Mar. - Nov. NO SMOKING. S.D. B/A. CHILDREN: OVER 10S WELCOME. BEVERAGES IN ROOMS. T.V. IN LOUNGE. B. & B. AROUND £20.

DARNAWAY HOUSE, 5 DARNAWAY ROAD, INVERNESS, HIGHLAND, IV2 3LF
TEL: (01463) 234002   OPEN Mar. - Oct. NO SMOKING. BEVERAGES IN ROOMS.   B. & B. AROUND £20.

GLENCAIRN GUEST HOUSE, 19 ARDROSS ST, INVERNESS, HIGHLAND, IV3 5NS
TEL: (01463) 232965   OPEN ALL YEAR.   NO SMOKING. V, S.D. B/A.   CHILDREN WELCOME. 2 EN SUITE ROOMS. BEVERAGES IN HALL. T.V. IN LOUNGE. B. & B. AROUND £22.

Glendruidh House Hotel
BY CASTLE HEATHER, OLD EDINBURGH RD SOUTH, GLEN DRUIDH, INVERNESS, IV1 2AA

TEL: (01463) 226499   FAX: (10463) 710745
Glendruidh House is a charming and unusual building standing in its own pleasant grounds overlooking Inverness, the Moray Firth and the Black Isle. Its design is extraordinary: with its interesting tower over the entrance hall, the many dormer windows and an amazing circular drawing room which has beautiful garden views; its rare peace and tranquillity bely the fact that it is just 2 miles from the centre of Inverness.

The cuisine reflects a largely traditional menu and offers home-cooked dishes which have been superbly prepared from fresh local produce. A typical table d'hote dinner selection might be Cream of Potato and Chives Soup or Chicken Liver Paté with cranberries, followed by Poached Fresh Wild Salmon with Parsley and Lemon Butter or Roast Leg of Chicken Stuffed with Raisins and Nuts (and fresh vegetable accompaniments); dessert might be Toffee Apple Sponge or Poached Victoria Plums in Port. Whilst many small hotels are totally smoke-free, Glendruidh House is unusual in that it has a small luxurious bar open to the public which is also smoke-free. The Glendruidh House brochure rightly eulogises the Highlands as a place for all seasons: spring is the time of endless days (blue skies at midnight!) and autumn is the time when heather purples the mountains; winter is not just when the skiers repair to Aviemore, but is the season when the cognoscenti come to appreciate Scotland's beautiful frozen lochs and to see waterfalls hanging like crystal from the mountains.

OPEN ALL YEAR.   NO SMOKING.   V, S.D. B/A.   LICENSED.   DISABLED ACCESS: 'With Assistance; ground floor Rooms & Wide Doors'.   CHILDREN WELCOME.   EN SUITE , BEVERAGES & T.V. IN ROOMS.   CREDIT CARDS B. & B. £29 - 39.

Hebrides

120A GLENURQUHART RD, INVERNESS, IV3 5TD   TEL: (01463) 220062
Attractive family-run B. & B.1m town on A82. Adjacent leisure centre & Caledonian Canal.
OPEN ALL YEAR.   NO SMOKING.   S.D. B/A.   CHILDREN WELCOME.   EN SUITE, TV & BEVERAGES IN ROOMS. B. & B. £18 - 22.

Ness Bank Guest House

7 NESS BANK, INVERNESS, HIGHLAND, IV2 4SF   TEL: (01463) 232939
Comfortable Victorian guest house in superb location on banks of the River Ness overlooking cathedral & few mins walk from town. Many scenic walks.
OPEN ALL YEAR.   NO SMOKING.   V, S.D. B/A.   BEVERAGES & TV IN ROOMS.   B. & B. AROUND £20

ROSE LODGE, 6 KENNETH STREET, INVERNESS, HIGHLAND, IV2 5NR
TEL: (01463) 233434 NO SMOKING. 2 EN SUITE ROOMS. BEVERAGES. T.V. B. & B. FROM £10.

SKY HOUSE, UPPER CULLERNIE, BALLOCH, INVERNESS, IV1 2HU
Spacious, modern home in beautiful countryside 5 mins drive from the highland capital & airport. Magnificent views across the Moray Firth. Wholesome and healthy b'fast.
TEL: (01463) 792582 OPEN ALL YEAR. NO SMOKING. V B/A. PETS B/A. SOME EN SUITE ROOMS. BEVERAGES & T.V. IN ROOMS. ACCESS, VISA. B. & B. AROUND £20.

The Tilt

OLD PERTH RD, INVERNESS, HIGHLAND.   TEL: (01463) 225352
Friendly, family-run B. & B. within easy access of A9. 1m town centre. 10m Loch Ness.
OPEN ALL YEAR. N/S. S.D. B/A. CHILDREN WELCOME. TV & BEVERAGES IN ROOMS. B. & B. FROM £13.

KINGUSSIE

CORNERWAYS, NEWTONMORE ROAD, KINGUSSIE, HIGHLAND, PH21 1HE
Modern detached house in attractive flower-filled gardens in Kingussie. B'fast only.
TEL: (01540) 661446 OPEN Mar. - OCt. NO SMOKING. V B/A. CHILDREN: OVER 6S ONLY. 1 EN SUITE ROOM. BEVERAGES IN ROOMS. T.V. IN LOUNGE. B. & B. AROUND £16.

HOMEWOOD LODGE, NEWTONMORE ROAD, KINGUSSIE, HIGHLAND, PH21 1HD
Charming country house; log fires; home-made bread, scones, icecreams.
TEL: (01540) 661507 NO SMOKING. V STD. LICENSED. CHILDREN WELCOME. PETS B/A. EN SUITE & BEVERAGES IN ROOMS. T.V. IN LOUNGE. B. & B. AROUND £23.0

The Royal Hotel

29 HIGH STREET, KINGUSSIE, INVERNESS-SHIRE, HIGHLAND, PH21 1HX   TEL: (01540) 661898
FAX: (01540) 661061
Family-owned & run hotel in the quiet village of Kingussie; excellent cuisine prepared from fresh, local produce.
OPEN ALL YEAR. N/S DINING R, Part of bar & reception. V, S.D. B/A. LICENSED. DISABLED ACCESS. CHILDREN WELCOME. PETS B/A. EN SUITE, TV & BEVERAGES IN ROOMS. CREDIT CARDS. B. & B. from £26 D. £12.

KYLE OF LOCHALSH

 CULAG, CARR BRAE, DORNIE, KYLE, ROSS-SHIRE, HIGHLAND, IV40 8HA
TEL: (01599) 555341 OPEN Mar. - Nov.   NO SMOKING. V, VE EXC. CHILDREN WELCOME. BEVERAGES
IN ROOMS. B. & B. AROUND £15.

Conchra House Hotel
NR ARDELVE, KYLE OF LOCHALSH, ROSS-SHIRE, HIGHLAND, IV40 8DZ   TEL & FAX:
(01599) 555233

Conchra House dates from the 1760s and has had a prestigious history: first as the home of the Government constable, 'planted' to keept the peace after the Jacobean uprising, and subsequently as the ancestral home of the Macraes of Conchra.More recently it has been sympathetically restored and refurbished by the present proprietors and is now a comfortable and distinctive country house hotel. It is a substantial Georgian 12 bedroomed mansion with separate east and west wings; guests have their own entrance hall, a large inviting lounge (with open fire) and eight comfortably furnished bedrooms; the twin 2nd floor attic rooms make excellent family suites and there is also self-catering accommodation in the adjacent farm cottages. The appetising food is home-prepared from fresh and locally produced ingredients. The proprietors are both committed Christians and extend a particularly warm hospitality to guests: during quieter periods the house is well suited to hosting retreat weeks and similarly orinentated activities.
OPEN ALL YEAR.   NO SMOKING.   S.D. B/A.   CHILDREN WELCOME.   WHEELCHAIR ACCESS. EN SUITE &
BEVERAGES IN ROOMS.   B. & B. £18 - £32

 THE RETREAT, MAIN STREET, KYLE, ROSS-SHIRE, HIGHLAND, IV40 8BY
TEL: (01599) 4308 OPEN ALL YEAR.   NO SMOKING. V, S.D. B/A.   RESTRICTED LICENCE. CHILDREN:
OVER 14S ONLY. BEVERAGES IN ROOMS.   T.V. IN LOUNGE.   B. & B. AROUND £17.

 ### *Tigh Tasgaidh*
DORNIE, KYLE OF LOCHALSH, ROSS-SHIRE, HIGHLAND.   TEL: (01599) 555242
OPEN Mar. - Nov.   NO SMOKING. EN SUITE & BEVERAGES. T.V. LOUNGE.   B. & B. FROM £16.

KYLESKU

 ### *Linne Mhuirich*

UNAPOOL CROFT RD, KYLESKU, VIA LAIRG, SUTHERLAND, IV27 4HW TEL: (01971) 502227
STB 2 Crowns Commended. Modern croft house superbly situated on hillside leading down to the shore of Loch Glencoul; its quiet, peaceful, accessible. 'Taste of Scotland' recommended. All food home-made from fresh, local ingredients; fish & seafood a speciality.
OPEN May - Oct.   NO SMOKING. V, LOW-FAT, HIGH-FIBRE B/A. BYO WINE. CHILDREN WELCOME.   PETS B/A.
ONE ROOM WITH PRIVATE BATHROOM. BEVERAGES IN ROOMS.   B. & B. AROUND £19.

 ### LAIRG
GNEISS HOUSE, INVERSHIN, BY LAIRG, SUTHERLAND, IV17 4ET TEL: (01549) 421282
Attractive bungalow in pretty garden amidst the glorious unspoilt Sutherland countryside.
OPEN ALL YEAR. NO SMOKING. V, S.D. B/A. PETS B/A. EN SUITE & BEVERAGES IN ROOMS.   T.V. IN LOUNGE.
B. & B. AROUND £17.

LOCHCARRON

 LADYTREK SCOTLAND, 'FOXGLOVES', LEACANASHIE, LOCHCARRON, W. ROSS
TEL: (01520) 722238 OPEN Easter - Oct.   NO SMOKING. V B/A. BEVERAGES incl. walking hol. price.

LOCHINVER

'POLCRAIG', LOCHINVER, SUTHERLAND, IV27 4LD TEL: (01571) 844429
OPEN Apr. - Sept.   NO SMOKING. BEVERAGES IN ROOMS. T.V. LOUNGE.   B. & B. AROUND £16.

LOCHNESS-SIDE

THE FOYERS HOTEL, LOCHNESS-SIDE, INVERNESS, IV1 2XT TEL: (01456) 486216
OPEN ALL YEAR.   NO SMOKING.   V STD. VE, S.D. B/A.   LICENSED.   CHILDREN WELCOME.
SOME EN SUITE ROOMS.   T.V. LOUNGE.   CREDIT CARDS.   B. & B. AROUND £31.

NETHYBRIDGE

TALISKER, DELL RD, NETHYBRIDGE, INVERNESS-SHIRE, HIGHLAND, PH25 3DG
TEL: (01479) 821624   OPEN ALL YEAR.   NO SMOKING. DIAB B/A.   CHILDREN: OVER 8S ONLY.   PETS BY
ARRANGEMENT. TEA/COFFEE MAKING FACILITIES. T.V. IN LOUNGE. B. & B. FROM £11.50.

NEWTONMORE

Craigellachie House

MAIN ST, NEWTONMORE, INVERNESS-SHIRE, HIGHLAND. TEL: (01540) 673360
Comfortable family home built in the 1800s and thought to be the oldest house in
Newtonmore. Excellent breakfast with lots of options. Evening meals by arrangement.
OPEN ALL YEAR ex Xmas.   NO SMOKING.   V, VE STD. S.D. B/A. CHILDREN WELCOME.   PETS B/A.
BEVERAGES IN ROOMS.   T.V. IN LOUNGE.   B. & B. AROUND £18.

The Pines Hotel

STATION ROAD, NEWTONMORE, INVERNESS-SHIRE, HIGHLAND.   TEL: (01540) 673271
Country house set in secluded pine wooded gardens; log fire in the lounge; excellent
food. Ideal for touring and birdwatching.
OPEN April - Oct.   NO SMOKING.   S.D. B/A.   LICENSED.   EN SUITE ALL ROOMS. BEVERAGES.   T.V. IN
LOUNGE.   B. & B. FROM £23.

REAY

ASKIVAL, REAY, CAITHNESS, HIGHLAND, KW14 7RE   TEL: (0184 781) 470
Angling holidays run from angling school & resource centre in attractive village.
OPEN Mar. - Nov. NO SMOKING V B/A.   CHILDREN WELCOME. T.V. IN LOUNGE.

SPEAN BRIDGE

Invergloy Halt

BY SPEAN BRIDGE, INVERNESS-SHIRE, HIGHLAND, PH34 4DY TEL: (01397) 712621
Modern single-storey house peacefully situated on the site of a former railway halt.
OPEN Mar. - Oct.; other times by arrangement. NO SMOKING. V STD. DISABLED ACCESS. CHILDREN: OVER
14S ONLY.   PETS B/A.   BEVERAGES IN ROOMS.   T.V. LOUNGE.

Old Pines

GAIRLOCHY ROAD, SPEAN BRIDGE, INVERNESS-SHIRE, PH34 4EG   (01397) 712324
**STB 3 Crowns Highly Commended. The Taste of Scotland Member. Best Small Hotel in
Britain Winner.** Family home in 30 acres with views of Aonach Mor and Ben Nevis.
OPEN ALL YEAR. NO SMOKING INDOORS. V, S.D. B/A. BYO WINE. DISABLED ACCESS: 'COMPLETELY
ACCESSIBLE; 3 SPECIALLY ADAPTED GROUND FLOOR BEDROOMS.' CHILDREN WELCOME. PETS B/A.
MOST ROOMS EN SUITE. BEVERAGES ON REQUEST. T.V. IN LOUNGE.   D., B. & B. FROM £45.

STRATHPEFFER

Gardenside Guest House

STRATHPEFFER, ROSS AND CROMARTY, HIGHLAND, IV14 9BJ   TEL: (01997) 421242
Charming 19th C. house in a splendid situation surrounded by woodland and fields.
OPEN 1 Mar. - 4 Jan. NO SMOKING. V B/A. LICENSED. GROUND FLOOR ROOMS AVAIL. CHILDREN
WELCOME.   EN SUITE. BEVERAGES IN ROOMS. T.V. LOUNGE. B. & B. AROUND £17.

TONGUE

Ben Loyal Hotel

TONGUE, SUTHERLAND, HIGHLAND, IV27 4XE (0847 55) 216
White-painted building in a splendid location overlooking mountains and the Kyle of
Tongue. Views from almost every room. Excellent food prepared from fresh produce.

OPEN ALL YEAR.   N/S DINING R.   V, S.D. B/A.   LICENSED.   DISABLED ACCESS: 'PARTIAL, WITH ASSISTANCE'.   CHILDREN WELCOME.   PETS B/A.   MOST ROOMS EN SUITE.   BEVERAGES IN ROOMS. T.V. ON REQUEST.   ACCESS, VISA.   D., B. & B. AROUND £47. (discounts for stays of 3 or more nights).

ULLAPOOL

Altnaharrie Inn
ULLAPOOL, HIGHLAND, IV26 2SS   TEL: (01854) 633230
Beautiful old house standing on the south shores of Loch Broom; can only be reached by launch (6 trips daily)! & has an atmosphere of great tranquillity;outstanding cuisine.
OPEN Easter - late Oct.   NO SMOKING.   V, S.D. B/A.   LICENSED.   OVER 8S ONLY.   PETS B/A.
EN SUITE IN ALL ROOMS.   BEVERAGES AVAIL.   D., B & B FROM £125 - 145.

THE OLD MANSE, CLACHAN, LOCHBROOM, BY ULLAPOOL, ROSS-SHIRE, HIGHL.
TEL: (01854) 85264   NO SMOKING.   V STD.   CHILDREN. BEVERAGES   B. & B. AROUND £15.

Tigh-Na-Mara (House by the Sea)
THE SHORE, ARDINDREAN, NR ULLAPOOL, LOCH BROOM, WESTER-ROSS, IV23 2SE
TEL & FAX: (01854) 655282
Highly Acclaimed base from which to discover the beautiful countryside around Inverness to Sutherland. Gourmet Scottish Vegetarian cooking.
OPEN FEB - NOV.   NO SMOKING.   V & other meat-free diets STD.   CHILDREN WELCOME.   BEVERAGES IN BEDROOMS.   D., B. & B. FROM £28.50.

RESTAURANTS

DORNOCH

DORNOCH CASTLE HOTEL, CASTLE STREET, DORNOCH, SUTHERLAND, IV25 3SD
TEL: (01862) 810216   N/S RESTAURANT.   V STD.   LICENSED.   DISABLED ACCESS.   CHILDREN WELCOME.

KINGUSSIE

THE CROSS, 25/27 HIGH STREET, KINGUSSIE, HIGHLAND, PH21 1HX
TEL: (01540) 661166   NO SMOKING.   V B/A.   LICENSED.   ACCESS, VISA.

KYLE OF LOCHALSH

WHOLEFOOD CAFÉ, HIGHLAND DESIGN WORKS, PLOCKTON RD, KYLE OF LO-
CHALSH   TEL: (01599) 534388/534702
NO SMOKING.   V, VE, DIAB & GLUTEN-FREE STD.   LICENSED.   DISABLED ACCESS.   CHILDREN.

LOCHINVER

ACHINS BOOKSHOP AND COFFEE SHOP, INVERKIRKAIG, LOCHINVER, HIGHL.
Small coffee shop attached to book shop; open seasonally.
TEL: (01571) 844262   NO SMOKING.   V STD.   DISABLED ACCESS.   CHILDREN WELCOME.

NAIRN

CAWDOR CASTLE RESTAURANT, CAWDOR CASTLE, NAIRN, HIGHLAND, IV12 5RP
Café/restaurant serving wide range of snacks & teas prepared in the castle kitchens.
TEL: (01667) 404615   NO SMOKING.   V, S.D. B/A.   LICENSED.   DISABLED ACCESS.   CHILDREN WELCOME.

NETHYBRIDGE

POLLYANNA'S, NETHYBRIDGE, INVERNESS-SHIRE, HIGHLAND, PH25 3DA
NO SMOKING.   V, S.D. B/A.   DISABLED ACCESS.   CHILDREN WELCOME.   ACCESS, VISA.

NEWTONMORE

THE TEA COSY, MAIN ST, NEWTONMORE, HIGHLAND.   TEL: (01540) 673315
NO SMOKING.

CEILIDH PLACE, WEST ARGYLE ST, ULLAPOOL, HIGHLAND. TEL: (01854) 612103
Pleasant café-bar, serving good range of vegetarian options.
N/S RESTAURANT. V STD. CHILDREN WELCOME IN DINING AREAS ONLY.

PUBS & WINE BARS

INVERNESS

GLENDRUIDH HOUSE, OLD EDINBURGH RD, INVERNESS, HIGHL TEL: (01463) 226499
For full details please seeunder entry in accommodation section.

Lothian

ACCOMMODATION & RESTAURANTS

DALKEITH

Belmont
47 ESKBANK ROAD, DALKEITH, MIDLOTHIAN, EH22 3BH   TEL: (0131) 663 8676
Large Victorian house with many original period features; conservatory and garden.
OPEN ALL YEAR. NO SMOKING. S.D. B/A. CHILDREN & PETS. 1 EN SUITE 1 ROOM. B. & B. FROM £15.

DUNBAR

St Helen's Guest House
QUEEN'S ROAD, DUNBAR, E. LOTHIAN, EH42 1LN   TEL: (01368) 863716
Victorian house in quiet residential area. Just a few minutes'walk from golf course & beach.
OPEN Mar. - Oct. NO SMOKING. V B/A. CHILDREN & PETS WELCOME. EN SUITE IN 1 ROOM. BEVERAGES
IN 2 ROOMS. T.V. IN LOUNGE. B. & B. FROM £15.

HADDINGTON

PETER POTTER GALLERY, 10 THE SANDS, OFF CHURCH ST, HADDINGTON
NO SMOKING.

Orkney

ACCOMMODATION & RESTAURANTS

N. BERWICK

HARDING'S RESTAURANT, 2 STATION ROAD, NORTH BERWICK, EH39 4AU
TEL: (01620) 894737 NO SMOKING. V, S.D. B/A. LICENSED. DISABLED ACCESS: 'RAMPED
ENTRY; WIDE ENTRY WC'. CHILDREN WELCOME.

KIRKWALL

BRIAR LEA, 10 DUNDAS CRESCENT, KIRKWALL, ORKNEY TEL: (01856) 872747
N/S DINING R & BEDR. V, VE STD. S.D. B/A. CHILDREN. BEVERAGES IN ROOMS. T.V. IN LOUNGE.

2 DUNDAS CRESCENT, KIRKWALL, ORKNEY, KW15 1JQ   TEL: (01856) 872465
OPEN ALL YEAR. NO SMOKING. V B/A. CHILDREN. BEVERAGES & T.V. B. & B. AROUND £12.

PAPA STOUR

NORTH HOUSE, PAPA STOUR, SHETLAND, ZE2 9PW TEL: (01595) 873238
Stone-built house. Working croft on small island on West of Shetland. Own boat.
OPEN Apr. - Sept. NO SMOKING. V B/A. DISABLED:'GROUND FLOOR BEDROOM'. CHILDREN WELCOME.
PETS B/A. 1 EN SUITE. BEVERAGES. T.V. IN LOUNGE. B. & B. AROUND £13.

LERWICK

PUFFINS, PUFFIN HOUSE, MOUNTHOOLY STREET, LERWICK. TEL: (01595) 695065
OPEN ALL DAY. NO SMOKING. CHILDREN WELCOME.

Strathclyde

ACCOMMODATION

AYR

Strathcoyle

HILLHEAD, COYLTON, AYR, STRATHCLYDE, KA6 6JR TEL: (01292) 570366
Detached bungalow with ground floor rooms. Private parking. on A70 4m east of Ayr.
OPEN Feb. - Nov. NO S MOKING. S.D. B/A. CHILDREN WELCOME. BEVERAGES IN ROOMS. TV LOUNGE.
B. & B. £14 - 15, Single £16 - 18.

THE TWEEDS, 6 MONTGOMERIE TERR., AYR, STRATH., KA7 1JL TEL: (01292) 264556
OPEN ALL YEAR. NO SMOKING. V B/A. CHILDREN WELCOME. PETS B/A. BEVERAGES & T.V. IN
ROOMS. B. & B. AROUND £15.

BIGGAR

CANDYBANK FARM, BIGGAR, STRATHCLYDE, ML12 6QY TEL: (01899) 20422
OPEN Apr. - Oct. NO SMOKING. V B/A. DISABLED ACCESS 'TO GROUND FLOOR BEDROOM'. CHILD-
REN WELCOME. PETS B/A. BEVERAGES & T.V. IN ROOMS. B. & B. AROUND £15.

CRAWFORD

Field End Guest House

CRAWFORD, LANARKSHIRE, STRATHCLYDE, ML12 6TN (OFF A74/M74) TEL: (018642) 276
*ETB & STB 2 Crowns. AA QQ RAC Acclaimed. Attr*active stone-built villa on quiet,
private road up the hill opposite Crawford church. Ideal halfway house & touring centre.
World-wide commendations. Parking. J14 off M74.
OPEN ALL YEAR Ex. Xmas & New Years Day. NO SMOKING. V, S.D., TO ORDER. NO PETS. CHILDREN WEL-
COME. 3 EN SUITE ROOMS. BEVERAGES & TV. CREDIT CARDS. B. & B. FROM £14. (red. children & sen. cits.)

DUNOON

The Anchorage

SHORE RD, ARDNEDAM, SANDBANK,DUNOON, ARGYLL, PA23 8QG TEL: (01369) 5108

*STB 3 Crowns Highly Commended. RAC Highly Ac-
claimed. AA Selected QQQQ.* The Anchorage was built
in the late 19th C. by a Victorian craftsman and stands
along the coastal road, some 3 miles north of the town
of Dunoon, on the banks of the Holy Loch. Your hosts,
Dee and Tony Hancock offer an exceptionally friendly
welcome to their beautiful home, and pride themselves
on offering quality accommodation at a reasonable price.
The bedrooms have been designed with comfort in mind:
each has en suite facilities and a range of helpful
amenities. All the delicious meals are prepared from
fresh, local produce, and breakfast, lunch and dinner are served in a stylish dining room
with a large panoramic window overlooking the loch; a typical evening meal would feature
a choice of dishes such as Carrot and Lemon Soup followed by Scottish Salmon with fresh
vegetables, and a home-made dessert; cheese, biscuits, coffee and mints would complete
the meal. There is also a small bar area and conservatory rstaurant. Although the beach is
less than a stone's throw from the front door, there is a tranquil garden for you to enjoy. In
Dunoon there are modern leisure facilities, and you are in an excellent place for exploring
Argyll and the west coast of Scotland.
OPEN ALL YEAR. NO SMOKING. S.D. B/A. CHILDREN WELCOME. EN SUITE, TV & BEVERAGES IN ROOMS.
B. & B. FROM £17.50 - 23.50.

GALSTON

Auchencloigh Farm

GALSTON, AYRSHIRE, STRATHCLYDE, KA4 8NP TEL: (01563) 820567
Family-run farm dating from the 18th C. in large shrubbed gardens in 240 acres of

Ayrshire country. Traditionally furnished; open fires. Home-cooked food. Family room.
OPEN EASTER - OCT.   NO SMOKING. S.D. B/A.   CHILDREN WELCOME.   TV & BEVERAGES IN ROOMS. B. & B. FROM £14.

HAMILTON

RoadChef Hamilton Motorway Service Area, M74 Northbound

HAMILTON, LANARKSHIRE, ML3 6JW   (0698) 282176
Hamilton is the site of RoadChef's first 36 bedroom Lodge in Scotland. Each of the bedrooms have been comfortably furnished and well-appointed with a trouser press, hairdryer and tea and coffee making facilities in addition to other amenities. The self-service Orchards restaurants have good smoke-free areas (50 of the 140 seats are smoke-free), and serve a wide selection of popular meals. There is always a vegetarian option on the menu and baby foods are also available (there is a changing room). Other facilities include a tourist information centre, a fully equipped conference room, totally refurbished shopping and forecourt facilities.
OPEN ALL YEAR Ex. Xmas Day. N/S PART OF RESTAURANT & SOME BEDRS.   V STD.   WHEELCHAIR ACCESS. CHILDREN WELCOME.   EN SUITE, TV & BEVERAGES.   CREDIT CARDS.   B. & B. FROM £36.

HELENSBURGH

Longleat
39 EAST ARGYLE ST, HELENSBURGH, G84 7EN   TEL: (01436) 672465
Comfortable family house with large garden in quiet, residential area overlooking Clyde Estuary. 5 mins town centre.
OPEN ALL YEAR. N/S.   CHILDREN WELCOME.   BEVERAGES IN BEDROOMS.   B. & B. £16-17.

Thorndean
64 COLQUHOUN ST., HELENSBURGH, DUMBARTONSHIRE, STRATHCLYDE, G84 9JP. TEL: (01436) 674922
Friendly Scottish welcome in spacious 19th C. house standing in extensive gardens; Private parking. Handy for Loch Lomond and Glasgow airport.
OPEN ALL YEAR.   NO SMOKING.   V, S.D. B/A.   CHILDREN WELCOME.   MOST ROOMS EN SUITE. BEVERAGES IN ROOMS.   B. & B. FROM £16.

South Whittlieburn Farm
BRISBANE GLEN, LARGS, STRATH., KA30 8SN   TEL: (01475) 675881
STB 2 Crown Commended. Attractive farmhouse on working sheep farm 2m NE Largs. Golf, horse-riding, sailing, fishing & hill-walking. Near ferry to Arran, Cumbrae & Bute.
OPEN ALL YEAR. N/S DINING R & SOME BEDRS.   V, S.D. B/A.   CHILDREN WELCOME.   1 EN SUITE ROOM. TV & BEVERAGES IN ROOMS.   B. & B. AROUND £18.

LOCH LOMOND

Tarbet House

TARBET BY ARROCHAR, LOCH LOMOND, DUNBARTONSHIRE, G83 7DE   TEL: (01301) 702349
Set in extensive wooded grounds, Tarbet House offers tranquil accommodation of a very high standard. Its south-facing guest rooms overlook Loch Lomond, and its many amenities include a sun terrace, library, hard tennis court and private launching facility. Although principally geared towards providing activity holidays (your hosts are experienced sailors and mountaineers and offer a variety of organised outdoor pursuits for the reasonably fit), Tarbet House also welcomes visitors who wish to arrange their own holiday programme in this beautiful part of the world. Whether guests have spent the day touring the Highlands by car or sailing around Loch Lomond on Compass Rose, the Tarbet House boat, palates will be tempted in the evening by the home-cooked dinner (by arrangement some evenings), which will have been prepared from local produce (including salmon and venison).
OPEN Jan - Oct.   NO SMOKING.   V B/A.   CHILDREN & PETS B/A.   B.Y.O. WINE.   1 EN SUITE.   BEVERAGES IN ROOMS. TV IN LOUNGE. B. & B FROM £15.

OBAN

ARDLONAN, DRUMMORE ROAD, OBAN, ARGYLL, STRATHCLYDE, PA34 4JL
TEL: (01631) 62529 OPEN Mar. - Oct. NO SMOKING. V B/A. DISABLED ACCESS: 'GROUND FLOOR ROOMS'.
EN SUITE, TV & BEVERAGES IN ROOMS.   B. & B. AROUND £18.

Asknish Cottage

ARDUAINE, BY OBAN, ARGYLL, STRATHCLYDE, PA34 4XQ   TEL: (01852) 200247

Asknish Cottage is a small, modern detached house which stands on a hillside with
wonderful views across the sea to the nearby islands of Jura, Scarba, Shuna and Luing;
swimming and fishing may both be enjoyed just 100 yards away at the small sandy beach
with its pier. Bedrooms are comfortable - each has a wash hand basin and can take an extra
bed or cot for a child at a reduced rate - and, although breakfast is the only meal to be served
at Asknish, there are a several restaurants locally which offer a variety of good, freshly-
prepared meals. Guests at Asknish Cottage are made to feel very much at home and to come
and go as they please; your hostess, Elspeth Campbell, is very knowledgeable about the
area however, and will gladly help you plan your itinerary if you wish. You are midway
between Lochgilphead and Oban, and horseriding, boating, birdwatching and hillwalking
can all be enjoyed locally.
OPEN ALL YEAR.   NO SMOKING.   V, S.D. B/A.   CHILDREN & PETS WELCOME.   BEVERAGES IN ROOMS.
T.V. IN LOUNGE. B. & B. FROM £14.

Hawthornbank Guest House

DALRIACH RD, OBAN, ARGYLL, STRATHCLYDE, PA34 5JE   TEL: (01631) 562041

Hawthornbank Guest House is a delightful Victorian villa which is quietly situated overlooking the bay at Oban, just 5 minutes' walk from the town centre. All bedrooms have
central heating and are comfortably appointed to a very high standard (one has an antique
four-poster bed and furnishings), and there are single, double, twin and family rooms
available. Dinner can be taken as an option (special diets are catered for by arrangement)
and there is safe, private parking. Guests may wish to make use of the tennis courts,
swimming pool and bowling green which are situated just opposite the guest house;
additionally Oban is an excellent touring base for the West Highlands, with regular ferries
and boat trips to the islands of the Inner Hebrides.
OPEN APR. - OCT.   NO SMOKING.   S.D. B/A.   CHILDREN WELCOME.   EN SUITE, TV & BEVERAGES IN ROOMS.   B.
& B. £15 - 22, D. FROM £7.

PAISLEY

Myfarrclan Guest House

146 CORSEBAR RD, PAISLEY, RENFREWSHIRE, SCOTLAND, PA2 9NA. TEL: (0141) 884 8285

PROPRIETORS: KEITH & BRENDA FARR STB Graded 2 CROWNS DE LUXE. Guest
house in quiet residential area, convenient for Glasgow airport, Loch Lomond, Ayrshire &
Glasgow city centre. Quiet, safe garden with childrens' play area. Luxury sun & guest
lounges.
OPEN ALL YEAR.   NO SMOKING (PERMITTED IN GARDEN IF YOU MUST!).   V & LOW-FAT DIETS B/A.   CHILDREN
WELCOME.   EN SUITE/PRIVATE, BEVERAGES,   TROUSER PRESSES, T.V., VIDEO, SATELLITE IN ALL BEDROOMS.
B. & B. FROM £22.50.

SEAMILL

Spottiswoode Guest House

SANDY RD, SEAMILL, W. KILBRIDE, AYRSHIRE, STRATH., KA23 9NN TEL: (01294) 823131

Built in 1896, Spottiswoode is a spacious Victorian
home which has been tastefully decorated and traditionally appointed by its present owners who have taken
care to retain the house's original charm and character.
It stands just feet away from the Firth of Clyde - the
beautiful sea and island views can be appreciated from
the dining room and bedrooms - and the surrounding
countryside is both rich in natural wildlife and also an
ideal base from which to explore Ayrshire and the nearby islands (Glasgow is just 45 minutes away by train or
car). Your hosts at Spottiswoode, Christine and Jim Ondersma, are thoroughly committed
to quality and guest satisfaction: each of the guest bedrooms have been decorated to a very
high standard and are equipped with fluffy towels, reading materials, well-lit mirrors and

prepared (24 hours notice, please). There is much to enjoy *in situ* - a soak in the deep Victorian bath, afternoon tea on the lawn, games and music at the fireside . . . There is no reason at all to move from base except, perhaps, to enjoy a ramble in the magnificent surrounding countryside or the lovely walks along the shore coast; golf can also be arranged.
OPEN ALL YEAR.   NON-SMOKERS ONLY.   V A SPECIALITY, S.D. B/A.   CHILDREN: OVER 10S ONLY.   EN SUITE, TV, BEVERAGES & HAIRDRYER IN ROOMS.   CREDIT CARDS.

ARNISH COTTAGE LOCHSIDE G. H, POLL BAY, ST CATHERINE'S, ARGYLL, PA25 8BA
Lovely house in conservation area midway betn St Catherine's & Strachur. A truly idyllic spot on a private road 20 ft from the loch. A wealth of wildlife; walks from doorstep.
TEL: (01499) 302405 OPEN ALL YEAR. NO SMOKING. V, S.D. B/A.   EN SUITE & BEVERAGES IN ROOMS.   TV IN LOUNGE.   B. & B. AROUND £20.

RESTAURANTS

BRIDGE OF ORCHY HOTEL, BRIDGE OF ORCHY, ARGYLL, STRATHCLYDE, PA36 4AD
TEL: (01838) 400208   N/S RESTAURANT.   V, DIAB, VE STD.   LICENSED.   CHILDREN WELCOME.

THE SMIDDY, SMITHY LN, LOCHGILPHEAD, ARGYLL, STRATHCLYDE, PA31 8TE
Vegetarian and seafood restaurant.
TEL: (01546) 603606   NO SMOKING.   V EXC.   CHILDREN WELCOME.   ACCESS, VISA.

PAISLEY ARTS CENTRE, NEW ST, PAISLEY, STRATH., PA1 1EZ TEL: (0141) 887 1010
N/S AREA.   V STD.   LICENSED.   DISABLED ACCESS.   CHILDREN WELCOME.

TAYNUILT

SHORE COTTAGE TEAROOM, BESIDE LOCH ETIVE, TAYNUILT, STRATHCLYDE
TEL: (018662) 654   OPEN Easter - Oct.   NO SMOKING.   GOOD DISABLED ACCESS.

Tayside

ACCOMMODATION

BLAIRGOWRIE

Dryfesands Guest House
BURNHEAD ROAD, BLAIRGOWRIE, TAYSIDE, PH10 6SY TEL: (01250) 873414
Spacious white-painted bungalow in pretty gardens on a hillside overlooking Blairgowrie.
NO SMOKING.   OVER 10S.   EN SUITE & BEVERAGES.   T.V.   B & B AROUND £20

BRECHIN

BLIBBERHILL FARMHOUSE, BRECHIN, ANGUS, TAYS., DD9 6TH   TEL: (01307) 830225
NO SMOKING.   V B/A.   EN SUITE & BEVERAGES.   B & B AROUND £18.

BROUGHTY FERRY

Invermark Hotel

23 MONIFIETH ROAD, BROUGHTY FERRY, DUNDEE, TAYSIDE, DD5 2RN   TEL: (01382) 739430
The Invermark is a small privately run hotel conveniently situated in the Dundee suburb of Broughty Ferry; the furnishings are modern and attractive - there are two large public rooms which can comfortably host small functions, such as weddings or birthday parties - and all bedrooms have been tastefully furnished and appointed. The food is exceptionally good: only fresh produce is used in the cooking and, while breakfast is the only meal which is usually available at Invermark,

evening meals may be taken on request. Originally a fishing village, Broughty Ferry is now a bustling, residential city suburb; it still has lots of character, though: the seafront is guarded by a 15th C. castle, and the high street is full of interesting craft shops.
OPEN ALL YEAR.   NO SMOKING.   V, S.D. B/A.   RESTRICTED LICENCE.   CHILDREN WELCOME.
SOME EN SUITE ROOMS.   BEVERAGES & TV IN ROOMS.   B & B FROM £20.

CALLANDER

BROOK LINN COUNTRY HOUSE, LENY FEUS, CALLANDER, TAYSIDE, FK17 8AU
TEL: (01877) 330103 OPEN Easter -Oct.   NO SMOKING.   V B/A.   LICENSED.   CHILDREN WELCOME.
PETS B/A. EN SUITE, TV & BEVERAGES IN ROOMS. B & B FROM £18.

Arran Lodge

LENY RD, CALLANDER, PERTHSHIRE, TAYSIDE, FK17 8AJ   TEL: (01877) 330976
STB 3 Crown De Luxe, AA Selected QQQQ and RAC Highly Acclaimed. Delightful period riverside bungalow, luxuriously appointed, near Callander. Tranquil riverside garden. Excellent home-cooked food.
OPEN Mar. - Nov.   NO SMOKING.   V B/A.   EN SUITE, TV & BEVERAGES.   BYO WINE.   B. & B. AROUND £28. D. £13.

THE LUBNAIG HOTEL, LENY FEUS, CALLANDER, TAYSIDE, FK17 8AS
TEL: (01877) 330376 OPEN Mar. - Nov.   N/S ex. in bar.   V B/A.   LICENSED.   CHILDREN: OVER 7S ONLY. PETS B/A.
EN SUITE, TV & BEVERAGES IN ROOMS.   D., B & B AROUND £40..

ORCHARDLEA HOUSE, MAIN STREET, CALLANDER, TAYSIDE, FK17 8BG
TEL: (01877) 330798   OPEN May. - Oct.   NO SMOKING.   V B/A.   GROUND FLOOR BEDROOMS.   MOST ROOMS EN SUITE.   BEVERAGES ON REQUEST.   T.V. IN ROOMS.   B & B AROUND £20.

ROSLIN COTTAGE GUEST HOUSE, LAGRANNOCH, CALLANDER, PERTHSHIRE, FK17 8LE
TEL: (01877) 330638   OPEN ALL YEAR. N/S ex. lounge.   V B/A.   CHILDREN & PETS WELCOME.   BEVERAGES IN ROOMS.   T.V. IN LOUNGE.   B & B AROUND £16.

CRIANLARICH

Allt-Chaorain Country House Hotel

CRIANLARICH, PERTHSHIRE, TAYSIDE, FK20 8RU   TEL: (10838) 300283   FAX: (01838) 300283

Magnificently situated looking towards Ben More, Allt-Chaorain House is a small 8 bedroomed hotel, with 4 ground floor bedrooms, whose proprietor, Roger MacDonald, has endeavoured to make a true home from home for visitors to the Highlands. Everything about the Allt-Chaorain beckons guests to relax: log fires blaze in the lounge grate throughout the year (there is a Trust Bar for guests' use), and meals are served in an elegant, wood-panelled dining room. All the delicious food has been home-cooked from fresh ingredients (the MacDonalds are members of the Taste of Scotland scheme), and menu requirements are discussed with guests. Allt-Chaorain is the ideal base for those who enjoy the outdoor life: keen ramblers can tackle the West Highland Way which passes close by the house, and more intrepid climbers will doubtless be lured to the cluster of nearby Munroes: there are numerous lochs for fishermen and boats are for hire nearby.
OPEN Mar. - Nov. inc. N/S EXCEPT ONE ROOM. S.D. B/A. LICENSED. OVER 8S & PETS WELCOME. WHEELCHAIR ACCESS. EN SUITE, TV & BEVERAGES IN ROOMS. B. & B. £27 - 33, D. B. & B. £42 - 48.

Portnellan Lodge Hotel

BY CRIANLARICH, TAYSIDE, FK20 8QS   TEL: (01838) 300284 FAX: (01838) 300332
19th C. house in wooded grounds of a private estate overlooking Glen Dochart; spacious, warm and comfortable accommodation, retaining original Victorian character. Central heating and wood-burning stove. Delicious home-cooked food made from fresh, local produce.
OPEN ALL YEAR.   N/S BEDRS, DINING R & DRAWING R.   V, S.D. B/A.   LICENSED.   ALL ROOMS EN SUITE.
BEVERAGES, T.V., VIDEO & HAIRDRYER INROOMS.   B. & B. AROUND £25.

*Glenardran Guest House*

CRIANLARICH, PERTHSHIRE, TAYSIDE, FK20 8QS
TEL: (01838) 300236

STB Commended. AA & RAC Listed. Glenardran is a late Victorian house which stands in a scenic mountainous area of the Western Highlands. Overlooked by Ben More, Stob Binnein, Ben Challum and Cruach Ardrain, it is a comfortable family-run guest house which provides an excellent base for walking, touring and climbing, or a restful base for the traveller, making a more extensive tour of Scotland. Crianlarich is conveniently situated at the cross-roads between Glasgow and Loch Lomond to the South, Glencoe and Fort William to the North and Stirling, Perth and Pitlochry to the East. Linda and John Champion will be pleased to welcome you to their home to share the pleasures of good food and wine. All meals are prepared to order from fresh produce.

OPEN ALL YEAR. NO SMOKING. S.D. B/A. CHILDREN & PETS WELCOME. 1 EN SUITE ROOM. TV & BEVERAGES IN ROOMS. B. & B. £17, D. B. & B. £26.

CRIEFF

CAIRNLEITH, NORTH FORR, CRIEFF, TAYSIDE, PH7 3RT TEL: (01764) 652080
OPEN ALL YEAR. NO SMOKING. V B/A. CHILDREN WELCOME. PETS B/A.

DALCHONZIE, 28 BURRELL ST, CRIEFF, PERTHSHIRE, TAYSIDE, PH7 4DT TEL: (01764) 653423
OPEN Apr. - Oct. NO SMOKING. V STD. CHILDREN WELCOME. BEVERAGES & T.V. IN LOUNGE.

ST NINIAN'S CENTRE, COMRIE ROAD, CRIEFF, TAYSIDE, PH7 4BG TEL: (01764) 653766
OPEN ALL YEAR. N/S ex. lounge. V B/A. CHILDREN WELCOME. BEVERAGES & T.V.

DUNKELD

Heatherbank

1 GUTHRIE VILLAS, ST MARYS RD, BIRNAM, DUNKELD, TAYSIDE. TEL: (01350) 727413

Attractive 3-storey Victorian house offering very comfortable accommodation and retaining the interesting features of the original building. Imaginative and wholesome food.

OPEN April - Dec. NO SMOKING. V B/A. CHILDREN. PETS B/A. BEVERAGES. B. & B. AROUND £16.

Oronsay House

OAK ROAD, BIRNAM, DUNKELD, TAYSIDE, PH8 0BL TEL: (01350) 727294

Elegant Victorian villa in an attractive garden close to the River Tay. Beautifully furnished and appointed; 3 bedrooms have hill views of the hills. Generous breakfast of home-made preserves, oakcakes, wholemeal bread, porridge, trout or bacon, sausage and tomato.

OPEN Apr. - Oct. NO SMOKING. V S.D. B/A. EN SUITE & BEVERAGES IN ROOMS. B & B AROUND £22

KILLIECRANKIE

DRUIMUAN HOUSE, KILLIECRANKIE, TAYSIDE, PH16 5LG TEL: (01796) 473214
OPEN Apr. - Oct. NO SMOKING. V STD. CHILDREN WELCOME. EN SUITE, BEVERAGES & TV IN ROOMS. B & B AROUND £22.

KINLOCH RANNOCH

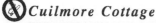*Cuilmore Cottage*

KINLOCH RANNOCH, TAYSIDE, PH16 5QB TEL: (01882) 632218

18th C. stone croft nestling under wooded hills on the edge of the village. Log fires, home-cooking fromorganically home-produced vegetables & home-baked bread.

OPEN Feb. - Nov. NO SMOKING. V, S.D., B/A. PETS B/A. BEVERAGES IN ROOMS. D. B. & B. AROUND £45

KIRRIEMUIR

Purgavie Farm
LINTRATHEN, KIRRIEMUIR, TAYSIDE.   TEL & FAX: (01575) 560213
Beautful old stone-built farmhouse at the foot of Glen Islaall; food is home-prepared.
OPEN ALL YEAR. N/S DINING R & BEDRS.   V B/A.   CHILDREN WELCOME.   PETS B/A.   2 EN SUITE ROOM.
BEVERAGES IN ROOMS.   T.V.   B & B FROM £14.

LOCHEARNHEAD

Stronvar Country House Hotel
BALQUHIDDER, LOCHEARNHEAD, TAYSIDE, FK19 8PB   TEL: (01877) 384688
Elegant 19th C. mansion on the shores of Loch Voil overlooking the Braes O'Balquhidder.
Completely renovated and restored to its former glory, it offers first-class accommodation
to guests: many bedrooms have brass beds or fourposters - and all have spectacular views.
OPEN Mar. - Oct.   N/S DINING R & BEDRS.   V, DIAB B/A.   LICENSED.   CHILDREN WELCOME.   EN SUITE,
BEVERAGES & TV IN ROOMS.   ACCESS, VISA.   B. & B. AROUND £33.

PERTH

Almond Villa
51 DUNKELD RD, PERTH, TAYSIDE, PH1 5RP   TEL: (01738) 629356

Almond Villa is a small, family-run guest house which has been commended by the Scottish Tourist Board for its high standard of accommodation and friendly, efficient service. It is a Victorian villa - centrally heated and double-glazed throughout - which is situated just a few minutes'walk from the banks of the River Tay and just 10 minutes' walk from the centre of Perth. A traditional cooked breakfast is served between 7.30 and 8.30 a.m. and a 3-course evening meal is available with advance booking. Perth lies at the very heart of Scotland and here, at the nation's cross-roads, has evolved an attractive, prosperous and compact city with some excellent leisure facilities, including an ice rink, leisure pool and an indoor bowling centre. The
surrounding area boasts some of Scotland's most magnificent mountains and there are countless places of interest to be visited including castles, distilleries, craft workshops, museums and gardens.
OPEN ALL YEAR.   NO SMOKING.   V, S.D. B/A.   CHILDREN & WELL-BEHAVED PETS WELCOME.   3 ROOM EN
SUITE.   TV & BEVERAGES IN ROOMS.   ACCESS, VISA.   B. & B. £16-18, D. FROM £9.

ST LEONARD'S MANSE, 112 DUNDEE RD, PERTH, TAYS, PH2 7BB TEL: (01738) 627975
B. & B. with 1 twin, 1 double & 1 family room. Adjoins National Trust gardens.
Lovely views. Residents' lounge. Private parking. 15 mins walk town centre.
OPEN ALL YEAR.   NO SMOKING.   V S.D. B/A.   CHILDREN.   PETS B/A.   BEVERAGES.   TV.   B. & B.
AROUND £16.

BURNSIDE APARTMENTS, 19 WEST MOULIN RD, PITLOCHRY, TAYSIDE, PH16 5EA
Converted Victorian building with award-winning serviced apartments. Coffee shop.
TEL: (01796) 472203   N/S COFFEE SHOP & SOME APARTMENTS.   V STD.   LICENSED.   DISABLED ACCESS.
CHILDREN WELCOME.   PETS B/A.   EN SUITE BATHROOMS, GALLEY KITCHENS & T.V. IN ALL BEDROOMS.

PITLOCHRY

Kinnaird House
KIRKMICHAEL RD, PITLOCHRY, TAYSIDE, PH16 5JL   TEL: (01796) 472843
STB 2 Crowns Highly Commended. Situated on the hillside above Pitlochry with wonderful scenery yet within easy reach of all local attractions. Commended for warm welcome.
Food & accommodation of the highest quality.
OPEN ALL YEAR.   NO SMOKING.   V, S.D. B/A.   TV & BEVERAGES IN ROOMS.   OVER 12s ONLY.
B. & B. FROM £18.

SILVERHOWE, PERTH ROAD, PITLOCHRY, TAYSIDE, PH16 5LY TEL: (01796) 472181
OPEN ALL YEAR. NO SMOKING. V B/A. PETS B/A. SOME EN SUITE. BEVERAGES & TV.   B & B AROUND
£16.

Knockendarroch House

HIGHER OAKFIELD, PITLOCHRY, TAYSIDE, PH16 5HT TEL: (01796) 473473 FAX: (01796) 474068

Knockendarroch is a quality hotel which offers accommodation at a reasonable price. It is a splendid Victorian mansion which stands on a hill within the small town of Pitlochry where it provides fine views over the Tummel Valley and the surrounding hills. The house is warm, friendly and stylish. All 12 bedrooms are en suite and have colour TV, tea and coffee-making facilities, and so on. The menus concentrate on providing food which is completely fresh; the cooking draws on classical and traditional Scottish sources and the standard is such that the AA has awarded Knockendarroch a Red Rosette for its food. Guests can enjoy performances at the Pitlochry Festival Theatre; there is salmon and trout fishing, pony trekking and golf locally; the surrounding hills and glens offer walks to suit all abilities.

OPEN 1 MAR - 30 NOV. NO SMOKING. V, S.D. B/A. CHILDREN & PETS WELCOME. LICENSED. EN SUITE, TV & BEVERAGES IN ROOMS. B. & B. £25.50 - £35. D. & B. £37 - 50.

Tigh-Na-Cloich Hotel

LARCHWOOD ROAD, **PITLOCHRY**, TAYSIDE, PH16 5AS   TEL: (0796) 472216

Scottish Tourist Board 3 Crowns Commended. Tigh-Na-Cloich (Gaelic for 'house on the sentinel stone') is a beautiful stone-built Victorian villa, southfacing and peacefully situated in its own lovely gardens just a short walk from the centre of Pitlochry. The house has been completely refurbished in recent years with the emphasis on creating a home atmosphere for guests. The food is exceptionally good: everything is homemade from the best, fresh local produce, and a typical evening menu would feature Baked Brie in Filo Pastry followed by Medallions of Venison with Wild Mushroom Sauce or Fillet of Salmon steamed with Aromates and a delicious dessert suh as Hazelnut Parfait with Plum Sauce. The proprietors are not only very helpful to those with special dietary needs, but will even offer to cook a favourite dish for you on request! Pitlochry is Scotland's premier inland tourist resort and as such offers something to every visitor, from sailing on rivers and lochs or walking amidst the beautiful hill scenery to visiting the many woollen mills, distilleries or craft centres in the region.

OPEN MAR. - OCT. NO SMOKING. V, S.D. B/A. LICENSED. CHILDREN WELCOME. EN SUITE IN ALL TWIN/DBLE ROOMS. BEVERAGES & T.V. IN ROOMS. B & B FROM £22.

"TOM-NA-MONACHAN" VEGETARIAN B. & B., CUILC BRAE, PITLOCHRY, TAYSIDE. Large family house quietly situated in 1 acre wooded garden. 10 mins' walk to town.

TEL: **(01796) 473744** OPEN ALL YEAR. NO SMOKING. V, VE, WH EXC. S.D. B/A. 1 GROUND FLOOR BEDR & BATHR; RAMP. CHILDREN WELCOME. PETS B/A. BEVERAGES IN ROOMS. B & B AROUND £20.

SCONE

SANDABEL HOUSE, NETHERLEA, SCONE, PERTHSHIRE, TAYSIDE, PH2 6QA Highly acclaimed guest house near Scone.

TEL: **(01738) 551062** OPEN ALL YEAR. NO SMOKING. V, S.D. B/A. DISABLED ACCESS. CHILDREN WELCOME. EN SUITE, TV & BEVERAGES IN ROOMS. B & B AROUND £20.

STRATHYRE

Creagan House Restaurant with Accommodation

STRATHYRE, PERTHSHIRE, FK18 8ND   TEL: (01877) 384638   FAX: (01877) 384638

17th C. farmhouse which has been sympathetically restored and renovated to provide excellent accommodation; the baronial style dining hall with its grand fireplace is a perfect setting for celebratory occasions; excellent cuisine made from fresh local produce.

OPEN Mar.-Jan. N/S BEDRS & DINING R. V, S.D. B/A. LICENSED. DISABLED ACCESS. CHILDREN & PETS WELCOME. 3 EN SUITE ROOMS. BEVERAGES IN ROOMS. VISA, MASTERCARD. B. & B. FROM £24.50.

GLENTURRET DISTILLERY LTD, THE HOSH, CRIEFF, TAYS, PH7 4HA TEL: (01764) 652424
NO SMOKING ex. in bar & 50 seats in restaurant.   V STD   LICENSED.   DISABLED ACCESS.   CHILDREN

DUNDEE

DEBENHAMS, 15 WHITEHALL CRESCENT, DUNDEE, TAYSIDE.   TEL: (01382) 21212
Freebodys Coffee Shop, waitress-service of popular food & drinks.
OPEN STORE HOURS.   NO SMOKING.   V STD.   CHILDREN VERY WELCOME.   CREDIT/DEBIT CARDS.

CREAGAN HOUSE, RESTAURANT WITH ACCOMMODATION, STRATHYRE, FK18 8ND
For full details please see under entry in accommodation section.

Western Isles

ACCOMMODATION

ISLE OF ARRAN

Grange House Hotel

WHITING BAY, ISLE OF ARRAN, KA27 8QH   TEL: (01770) 700263

3 Crown Highly Commended. Grange House Hotel was built in 1896 and stands amidst delightful gardens overlooking the sea with views to the Ayrshire coast and out towards Holy Island. Recently refurbished to a very high standard, and in a style in keeping with the period features of the house, Grange House Hotel has every modern convenience including (for those who wish to pamper themselves a little!) a sauna and spa bath suite; on cooler evenings a log fire welcomes you in the lounge. The cooking is first rate: your hosts, Janet and Clive Hughes, base the evening's menu selection around the availability of good, fresh local produce: accordingly, while dishes are often Victorian or Scottish in flavour (Steak Kidney and Oyster Pie followed by Bread and Butter Pudding with whisky cream), everything has been expertly prepared on the premises from fresh produce; the proprietors also have a sound awareness of healthy nutritional principles: wholefoods are used wherever possible, and cream and animal fats are only used in moderation. Arran is popularly known as 'Scotland in miniature'- ont the island you will find no less than 7 golf courses, 4 pony-trekking centres, and numerous opportunities for mountaineering and fishing.
OPEN Mar.-Oct. inc.   NO SMOKING.   V, S.D. AVAILABLE.   LICENSED.   DISABLED FACILITIES INCLUDING
CONVERTED DOWNSTAIRS BEDROOM.   CHILDREN WELCOME.   BEVERAGES & T.V. IN ROOMS.   ACCESS,
VISA.   B. & B. FROM £25. D. £15.

ISLE OF HARRIS

SCARISTA HOUSE, ISLE OF HARRIS, PA85 3HX   TEL: (01859) 550238 FAX: (01859) 550277
OPEN Easter - mid Oct.   N/S ex 2 sitting rooms.   V, S.D. B/A.   LICENSED.   DISABLED ACCESS: '4 BEDRS,
DINING R & LIBRARY.   OVER 8S ONLY.   PETS B/A.   EN SUITE & BEVERAGES.   B. & B. AROUND £48.

ISLE OF IONA

Argyll Hotel

ISLE OF IONA, PA76 6SJ   TEL & FAX: (01681) 700334

This beautiful sea-facing hotel (the front lawn runs down to the shore and jetty) is one of the hotels about which I invariably receive a large number of recommendations throughout the year; guests comment on the peace and tranquility which seems to pervade the place - a sense doubtless partly attributable to the fact that the beautiful louges (with their open fires), spacious dining room and plant-filled sun lounge all look out over the Sound of Iona to the hills of Mull; external beauty recreating inner peace. I am sure that the excellence of the food is also an inexorable part of the lure of the place, too: wholefood and organically home-grown vegetables and produce are used in the preparation of excellent meals which would typically feature local smoked trout followed by Chicken Paprika, Lemon and Blackberry Sponge and a cheeseboard; the vegetarian options are excellent.

OPEN EASTER TO MID OCT. N/S DINING R. & LOUNGE. V, S.D. B/A. LICENSED. CHILDREN WELCOME. PETS B/A. EN SUITE 10 ROOMS. BEVERAGES IN ROOMS. ACCESS, VISA. B. & B. FROM £28, D. £17.

ISLE OF ISLAY

CEOL-NA-MARA, BRUICHLADDICH, ISLE OF ISLAY, PA49 7UN TEL: (01496) 850419
OPEN ALL YEAR. NO SMOKING. V VE, S.D. B/A. CHILDREN. PETS B/A. T.V. B & B AROUND £25.

ISLE OF LEWIS

BAILE-NA-CILLE, TIMSGARRY, ISLE OF LEWIS, PA86 9JD TEL: (01851) 672241
Beautifully remote converted manse and stables on the shore at Timsgarry; great food.
OPEN Mid-Mar. - Mid-Oct. N/SDINING R, 2 SITTING RS & BEDRS. V B/A. LICENSED. CHILDREN & PETS WELCOME. EN SUITE. BEVERAGES. T.V. LOUNGE. B. & B. AROUND £30.

ESHCOL GUEST HOUSE, BREASCLETE, ISLE OF LEWIS, PA86 9ED TEL: (01851) 672357
OPEN Mar. - Oct. NO SMOKING. V B/A. CHILDREN WELCOME. PETS B/A. EN SUITE IN MOST ROOMS. BEVERAGES & T.V. IN ROOMS. B. & B. AROUND £20.

ISLE OF MULL

DRUIMARD COUNTRY HOUSE, DERVAIG, PA75 6QW TEL: (01688) 400345
STB Highly Commended, AA Red Rosette, 1992 Catering & Care Award. Country house hotel/restaurant. 1st-class cuisine made from fresh, local produce.
NO SMOKING. V STD. S.D. B/A. LICENSED. DISABLED ACCESS. CHILDREN.

DRUIMNACROISH, DERVAIG, PA75 6QW TEL: (01688) 400274 FAX: (01688) 400311
OPEN Mid-apr. - Mid-oct. N/S ex. Smoking Lounge. V B/A. LICENSED. DISABLED ACCESS. OVER 12S ONLY. PETS B/A. EN SUITE, BEVERAGES & T.V. IN ROOMS.

KEEPER'S COTTAGE, TORLOISK, ULVA FERRY, PA74 6NH TEL: (01688) 500265
NO SMOKING. V B/A. CHILDREN WELCOME. T.V. B. & B. AROUND £19.

Tigh an Allt

DERVAIG, ISLE OF MULL, PA75 6QR TEL: (01688) 400247
STB 1 Crown Commended. Modern bungalow in secluded setting in grassy, wooded area. Wholefood ingredients used where possible in cooking. Wide choice of breakfasts and 3-course evening meal. Central heating.
OPEN ALL YEAR (ex Xmas). NO SMOKING. S.D. B/A. WH STD. CHILDREN & PETS B/A. WHEELCHAIR ACCESS: 'reasonable'. BEVERAGES IN ROOMS. B. & B. £16, D. £9.

ISLE OF RAASAY

ISLE OF RAASAY HOTEL, RAASAY, BY KYLE OF LOCHALSH, ROSS-SHIRE, IV40 8PB (01478) 660222/660226
OPEN Apr. - Oct. N/S DINING R & T.V. LOUNGE. V B/A. LICENSED. DISABLED ACCESS. CHILDREN WELCOME. PETS B/A. EN SUITE, TV & BEVERAGES IN ROOMS. B. & B. AROUND £32.

ISLE OF SKYE

Atholl House

DUNVEGAN, ISLE OF SKYE, IV55 8WA TEL: (01470) 521 219 FAX: (01470) 521 481
Centrally situated in Dunvegan village, the Atholl commands panoramic views of Macleods Tables & Loch Dunvegan. Comfortably furnished. Excellent food & wines; lounge with log fire.
OPEN Mar. - Dec. N/S DINING R. S.D. B/A. LICENSED. CHILDREN & PETS WELCOME. EN SUITE, TV & BEVERAGES IN ROOMS. B. & B. £18 - 22.

LANGDALE G.H., WATERLOO, BREAKISH, ISLE OF SKYE, IV42 8QE TEL: (01471) 822376
OPEN ALL YEAR. N/S ex. lounge. V B/A. LICENSED. CHILDREN WELCOME. PETS B/A. BEVERAGES IN ROOMS. T.V. IN LOUNGE. B. & B. AROUND £20.

THE TABLES HOTEL & RESTAURANT, DUNVEGAN, ISLE OF SKYE, IV55 8WA
Traditional 19th C. merchant's house overlooking Loch Dunvegan & MacLeod's Tables Mountains. Homely & welcoming with good food, wines & malt whiskies. Peat fires.
TEL: (01470) 521404 OPEN ALL YEAR. N/S DINING R & BEDRS. V STD, S.D. B/A. RESTRICTED LICENCE. CHILDREN WELCOME. PETS B/A. 1 EN SUITE ROOM. CREDIT CARDS. B. & B. AROUND £25.

Wales

Clwyd

ACCOMMODATION

BRYNEGLWYS

CAE CRWN FARM, BRYNEGLWYS, CLWYD, LL21 9NF TEL: (01490) 450243
Lovely old detached farmhouse overlooking the village of Bryneglwys.
OPEN ALL YEAR. NO SMOKING. V STD. CHILDREN WELCOME. PETS B/A. BEVERAGES IN ROOMS.
T.V. IN LOUNGE. B. & B. AROUND £15.

COLWYN BAY

THE HAVEN G.H., 14 CANNING RD, COLWYN BAY, CLWYD. TEL: (01492) 531779
OPEN ALL YEAR. NO SMOKING. V B/A. CHILDREN WELCOME. ROOM SERVICE.

Westwood Hotel

COED GORLLEWIN, 51 PRINCES DRIVE, COLWYN BAY, CLWYD, LL29 8PL TEL: (01492) 532078
WTB 3 Crowns. "Taste of Wales". Comfortable, family-run guest house. Good food.
OPEN ALL YEAR. N/S DINING R. V, S.D. STD. CHILDREN & PETS WELCOME. LICENSED. CREDIT CARDS.
EN SUITE, TV & BEVERAGES IN ROOMS. B. & B. FROM £14, D. £6.

HANMER

Buck Farm

HANMER, CLWYD, SY14 7LX TEL: (01948) 74339
Beautiful half-timbered 16th C. farmhouse. 8 acres woodland & paddocks. Fabulous food.
OPEN ALL YEAR. NO SMOKING. V B/A. CHILDREN WELCOME. BEVERAGES AVAILABLE ON REQUEST.
T.V. IN LOUNGE. B. & B. AROUND £16.

LLANGOLLEN

Hillcrest

HILL STREET, LLANGOLLEN, CLWYD, LL20 8EU TEL: (01978) 860208
W.T.B 3 Crowns Commended. Lovely Victorian house in an acre of pretty gardens 3 mins
walk from the centre of Llangollen & the River Dee. Evening meals on request.
OPEN ALL YEAR. NO SMOKING. V, S.D. B/A. 1 DOWNSTAIRS DOUBLE ROOM. CHILDREN WELCOME.
LICENSED. EN SUITE & BEVERAGES IN ROOMS. T.V. LOUNGE. B. & B. AROUND £20.

MOLD

The Old Mill

MELIN-Y-WERN, DENBIGH RD, NANNERCH, MOLD, CLWYD, CH7 5RH   TEL: (01352) 741542
Beautifully converted complex of rural water-mill buildings in a conservation area adjacent
to an area of Outstanding Natural Beauty. Very comfortable en suite bedrooms with central
heating and double glazing. Excellent home-cooked food.
OPEN ALL YEAR ex. Xmas. NO SMOKING. S.D. B/A. LICENSED. CHILDREN WELCOME. PETS B/A. EN
SUITE, TV & BEVERAGES IN ROOMS. CREDIT CARDS. B. & B. AROUND £25.

RHOS-ON-SEA

The Cedar Tree

27 WHITEHALL RD, RHOS-ON-SEA, COLWYN BAY, CLWYD, LL28 4HW TEL: (01492) 545867
WTB 2 Crown Commended. Friendly, family-run, guest house. Parking. 300 yds promenade.
OPEN Jan 15 - Dec. 15.   N/S. S.D. B/A. CHILDREN WELCOME. EN SUITE & BEVERAGES IN ROOMS. B. & B.
£15 - 16. CHILDREN WELCOME.

Sunnydowns Hotel

66 ABBEY RD, RHOS-ON-SEA, CLWYD, LL28 4NU　　TEL: (01492) 544256　FAX; (01492) 543223
Hotel just 2 mins walk to the beach & shops, & just 5 mins drive to the towns of Llandudno
& Colwyn Bay. Car park, bar, restaurant, games room, sauna. All rooms en suite.
OPEN ALL YEAR.　N/S DINING R, SOME BEDRS & GAMES R.　S.D. B/A.　CHILDREN & PETS WELCOME.
EN SUITE, TV & BEVERAGES IN ROOMS.　CREDITS CARDS.　D., B. & B. £32.

RESTAURANTS

COLWYN BAY

GOOD TASTE BISTRO, 18 SEAVIEW RD, COLWYN BAY, CLWYD. TEL: (01492) 534786
Charming bistro, faithfully decked out in 30s style, with craft and gift gallery. Imaginative,
freshly prepared food (the bistro is a longstanding winner of the Heartbeat Wales Award).
N/S 80% OF RESTAURANT; TOTALLY SMOKE-FREE 12 - 2PM.　V STD.　LICENSED.　DISABLED ACCESS.　CHILDREN
WELCOME.

HANMER

BUCK FARM, HANMER, CLWYD, SY14 7LX　　TEL: (0194 874) 339
Non - resident diners are accommodated with 24 hrs notice.
For further details please see under the entry in the accommodation section.

LLANGOLLEN

GOOD TASTE, MARKET STREET, LLANGOLLEN, CLWYD, LL20 8PT　　TEL: (01978) 861425
For further details please see under entry in accommodation section.

Dyfed

ACCOMMODATION

ABERAERON

Moldavia

7 & 8 BELLEVUE TERRACE, ABERAERON, DYFED, SA46 0BB　　TEL: (01545) 570107
A warm welcome at this award-winning guest house overlooking Aberaeron Harbour. Town
& beach just 2 mins walk away. Relax in a flower-filled conservatory! Send for brochure.
OPEN ALL YEAR.　N/S DINING R & 1 BEDR.　WHEELCHAIR ACCESS.　V B/A.　EN SUITE 2 BEDROOMS.　TV &
BEVERAGES IN ROOMS.　B. & B. £19 - 21.

ABERYSTWYTH

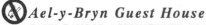

Ael-y-Bryn Guest House

CAPEL BANGOR, ABERYSTWYTH, DYFED, SY23 3LR　TEL: (01970) 84681

Ael-y-Bryn is a small family-run guest house
which is situated 100 yards off the A44, 5
miles from Aberystwyth. It has lovely views
overlooking the Rheidol Valley and isan ideal
base from which to explore the beautiful
beaches of Dyfed and its many other places
of interest. An evening meal is provided at
6.15 each weekday, and a generous breakfast
is served each morning. Each of the centrally
heated bedrooms has a wash basin and tea-
making facilities, and some have valley
views. There is safe parking within the
grounds of Ael-y-Bryn.

NO SMOKING.　OPEN ALL YEAR.　CHILDREN WELCOME.　BEVERAGES & TV IN ROOMS.　B. & B. FROM £15.

Glyn-Garth Guest House
SOUTH ROAD, ABERYSTWYTH, DYFED, SY23 1JS   TEL: (01970) 615050

A pleasantly appointed family-run guest house situated close to the South Promenade of Aberystwyth; bedrooms have been comfortably furnished and tastefully decorated and many enjoy sea views. Your hosts, Mr & Mrs Evans, offer wholesome food in the pleasant dining room, and the comfortable lounge, with its colour television, has drinks available at most times; the service is excellent and Glyn-Garth has received the Highly Commended status by the Mid Wales Tourism Council together with several other high acclamations.
OPEN ALL YEAR ex Xmas. N/S DINING R, LOUNGE , PUBLIC AREAS & MOST BEDRS.   V, S.D. B/A.   CHILDREN. MOST ROOMS EN SUITE. BEVERAGES & T.V. IN ROOMS.   B. & B. FROM £16, EN SUITE FROM £19.

Sinclair Guest House
43 PORTLAND ST, ABERYSTWYTH, DYFED, SY23 2DX   TEL & FAX: (01970) 615158
Quality guest house with 3 spacious en suite rooms in peacful tree-lined street.
OPEN ALL YEAR. NO SMOKING. EN SUITE, TV & BEVERAGES IN ROOMS. B. & B. £20.

Yr Hafod
1 SOUTH MARINE TERRACE, ABERYSTWYTH, DYFED, SY23 1JX   TEL: (01970) 617579
Guest house situated on the promenade; most rooms have panoramic sea views.
OPEN ALL YEAR. N/S ALL PUBLIC AREAS & SOME BEDRS.   V B/A. CHILDREN WELCOME.   SOME EN SUITE ROOMS. BEVERAGES & T.V. IN ROOMS.   B. & B. AROUND £19.

BONCATH
Gwelfor Country Guest House
BLAENFFOS, BONCATH, PEMBROKESHIRE, SA37 0HZ TEL: (01239) 831599

WTB 2 Crowns. Small guest house amidst beautiful Preseli Hills. Wholesome, imaginative traditional & vegetarian dishes made from home-grown, local or organic produce.
OPEN ALL YEAR. NO SMOKING. V, VE STD. S.D. B/A.   CHILDREN WELCOME. PETS B/A.   SOME EN SUITE ROOMS. BEVERAGES IN ROOMS. T.V. LOUNGE. B. & B. AROUND £18.

CARDIGAN
Trellacca Guest House
TREMAIN, CARDIGAN, DYFED, SA43 1SJ   TEL: (01239) 810730
Superbly converted from two slate & stone cottages; beautifully furnished with handcrafted pine furniture and fittings; lovely rural setting. Studio flat for self-caterers £140 pw.
OPEN ALL YEAR Ex. Xmas. N/S BEDRS & DINING R. CHILDREN WELCOME. BEVERAGES IN ROOMS. T.V. IN LOUNGE & BEDR ON REQUEST. B. & B. AROUND £18.

CAREW
Old Stables Cottage
CAREW, DYFED, SA70 8SL TEL: (01646) 651889
Grade II listed stone cottage, originally a stable and carthouse for Carew Castle, overlooking River Carew. Low beams and inglenook in lounge. Aga-cooked meals prepared from fresh produce; home-baked bread.
OPEN 10 Mar. - 30 Nov. NO SMOKING. V, S.D. B/A. OVER 5s WELCOME. EN SUITE, TV & BEVERAGES IN ROOMS. B. & B. AROUND £25.

CARMARTHEN
Troedyrhiw
LLANFYNYDD, CARMARTHEN, DYFED, SA32 7TQ   TEL: (01558) 668792
Troedyrhiw is a delightful 18th C. farmhouse which stands amidst 8 acres of wooded grounds in a peaceful and sheltered valley. The house has been exceptionally well appointed: each of the three centrally heated guest rooms (named after woodland plants) has

a range of amenities, including tissues, magazines and fresh flowers, and cosy woodburning stoves warm the dining room and lounge (the latter has a large collection of books and tourist information). A delicious 4-course evening meal is available on request (home-cooked on the Aga from home-grown or locally supplied produce), and a glass of wine is included (you are welcome to bring your own). There is also a superbly equipped self-catering cottage for holiday let.

OPEN ALL YEAR. NO SMOKING. V B/A. B.Y.O. WINE. EN SUITE & BEVERAGES IN ROOMS. TV IN LOUNGE. B. & B. £21 - 23.

CRYMYCH

Felin Tygwyn

CRYMYCH, DYFED, SA41 3RX   TEL: (01239) 79603

Traditional earth & slate farmhouse at foor of Preseli mountains 9m Cardigan & Newport beach. Beamed ceilings, open fires. Organic smallholding. Fresh produce in cooking.

OPEN ALL YEAR. NO SMOKING. V, S.D. B/A. LICENSED. CHILDREN. PETS B/A. B. & B. AROUND £18.

FISHGUARD

Coach House Cottage

GLENDOWER SQUARE, GOODWICK, FISHGUARD, PEMBROKESHIRE, SA64 0DH   TEL: (01348) 873660

Traditional Pembrokeshire stone cottage in secluded location next to mountain stream; vegetarian, vegan and wholefood fare a speciality; organic produce wherever possible.

OPEN ALL YEAR. NO SMOKING. V STD. S.D. B/A. BYO WINE. CHILDREN WELCOME. PETS B/A. BEVERAGES IN ROOMS. T.V. IN LOUNGE. B. & B. FROM £12. D. £8.50 & £6.

Gilfach Goch Farmhouse

GARN GELLI HILL, FISHGUARD, PEMBROKESHIRE, SA65 9SR TEL & FAX: (01348) 873871

WTB Award. Gilfach Goch is a 10 acre smallholding which stands in the Pembrokeshire National Park enjoying magnificent views across rolling countryside to the sea. The house itself is an 18th C. stone built farmhouse which has been carefully renovated and retains much of its original character: central heating and log fires warm guests in winter, and in sunnier months there is a lovely flowered garden, with seating areas, to enjoy. Accommodation is in comfortable rooms and meals are served in a sunny dining room with views. Much of the food is home-produced and wholesome, imaginative country cooking is the order of the day. You are within easy reach of the Preseli Hills, the coastal path and numerous beaches and coves.

NO SMOKING. OPEN EASTER - Nov. CHILDREN WELCOME. EN SUITE, BEVERAGES & TV IN ROOMS. B. & B. £17 - 22, D. FROM £10.

Tregynon Country Farmhouse Hotel

GWAUN VALLEY, NR FISHGUARD, SA65 9TU   TEL: (01239) 820531 FAX: (01239) 820808

It is over a decade since Peter Heard decided to abandon the stress-filled London rat race for a more peaceful way of life in a Welsh farmhouse. A tremendous amount of renovation work had to be done on Tregynon but, with a lot of hard work and enthusiasm, the run-down farmhouse soon became a thriving Country Farmhouse Hotel which has won several awards and received much national acclaim. Much of the recognition is due not just to the wonderfully comfortable surroundings (in winter evenings, log fires in the inglenook fireplace in the oakbeamed lounge, beautiful bedrooms) but to the superlative quality of Jane's cuisine. Jane, co-author of 'Dining with Angels'(an anthology of food and verse), uses fresh produce - much of it local - wherever possible in the preparation of all meals. Free-range eggs, organic and unpasteurised cheeses, home-smoked bacon and gammon for non-vegetarians, are all part of the Tregynon gastronomic experience - as are the range of speciality additive-free breads and rolls. But

Tregynon's surroundings provide the enduring lure for guests who return year after year...situated on the edge of the Gwaun Valley with its ancient oak forest, this beautiful part of the world is a haven for wildlife - badgers, buzzards and herons are regularly seen, whilst red kites and peregrine falcons are also spotted from time to time.

OPEN ALL YEAR.   N/S RESTAURANT & BEDRS; DISCOURAGED ELSEWHERE.   V STD, S.D. ON REQUEST. LICENSED. DISABLED ACCESS.   CHILDREN WELCOME.   EN SUITE, BEVERAGES & T.V. IN ROOMS.   B. & B. FROM £23.

Glanmoy Country House Hotel

GOODWICK, FISHGUARD, PEMROKESHIRE, DYFED.   TEL: (01348) 872844

Luxurious Edwardian country house with large en suite rooms standing in 8 acres in a peaceful area. Chef-owner offers multi-choice menu with vegetaraian options. Library, classical music.

OPEN ALL YEAR.   N/S DINING R.   V STD, S.D. B/A.   OVER 8s WELCOME.   DOGS IN 2 ANNEXE ROOMS.   LICENSED. EN SUITE, TV & BEVERAGES IN ROOMS.   CREDIT CARDS.   B. & B. £21 - 25.

HAVERFORDWEST

Wolfscastle Country Hotel

WOLF'S CASTLE, HAVERFORDWEST, SA62 5LS   TEL: (01437) 741225 FAX: (01437) 741383

Comfortable, friendly hotel known for excellent food (British & International cuisine).

OPEN ALL YEAR.   N/S DINING R.   S.D. B/A.   CHILDREN WELCOME.   PETS B/A. EN SUITE, TV & BEVER- AGES IN ROOMS.   CREDIT CARDS.   B. & B FROM £32.50.

NEW QUAY

Ty Hen Farm Country Hotel & Cottages

LLWYNDAFYDD, NEW QUAY, DYFED, SA44 6BZ   TEL: (01545) 560346

This charming stone-built farmhouse (Ty Hen means simply 'Old House') offers a very high standard of accommodation to guests and stands in spacious gardens in a peaceful location just 2 miles from the rocky cliffs and sandy beaches of the Cardiganshire coast. Health is a priority at Ty Hen where the generous breakfast features a number of very laudable items such as yoghurt, muesli and fresh fruit as well as a huge platter of bacon, eggs, mushrooms and anything else breakfasty you care to name. The restaurant offers a 4-course evening menu and specialises in fish and vegetarian options. The leisure centre at Ty Hen has an indoor heated pool where private lessons, particularly for adults, are available, and also contains a gymnasium, sauna, sunbed and skittles alley; further leisure facilities are planned. Stone-built self-catering cottages are also available.

OPEN ALL YEAR.   NO SMOKING.   V STD. S.D. B/A.   LICENSED.   DISABLED ACCESS.   PETS B/A. CHILDREN WELCOME.   EN SUITE, BEVERAGES & T.V. PLUS VIDEO CHANNEL IN ROOMS.   VISA, MASTERCARD. B. & B. FROM £20.

TENBY

The Ark

ST FLORENCE, TENBY, DYFED.   TEL: (01834) 871654

ETB 2 Crowns Highly Comended. The Ark is a 17th C. Pembrokeshire cottage which has been totally refurbished and now provides accommodation of a very high standard for six guests. The lounge/dining room is part of the original building and retains its warmth and character (exposed stone work and beams); log fires burn in the open grate in early and late season. Situated just 4 miles inland from Tenby, this picturesque village has received numerous floral awards.

OPEN ALL YEAR.   NO SMOKING.   S.D. B/A.   OVER 10S.   EN SUITE, TV & BEVERAGES IN ROOMS.   B. & B. £15.

Clarence House Hotel

ESPLANADE, TENBY, SA70 7DU   TEL: (01834) 844371   FAX: (01834) 844372

The Clarence House Hotel stands on the South sea-front at Tenby. It has a lovely flower-filled garden and has retained much of its original Victorian character, but has been considerably refurbished and now offers every modern comfort to visiting guests. There is an excellent choice of dishes on the table d'hôte menu, and the hotel's lift and good wheel-chair access make it a favourable choice for semi-disabled guests able to walk to use the toilet and showers.

OPEN APRIL - OCT. INC. N/S DINING R. & SOME BEDROOMS.   S.D. STD. LICENSED.   PETS & CHILDREN WELCOME.   WHEELCHAIR ACCESS.   EN SUITE, TV & BEVERAGES IN BEDROOMS.   B. & B. £15 - £30.

Accommodation   Dyfed   *Wales* 227

🚭 *Fairway*

THE GOLF LINKS, SOUTH BEACH, TENBY, DYFED, SA70 7EL   TEL: (01834) 842141
Attractive detached house 200 yds from Tenby's South Beach & 5 mins walk from town.
Central heating. Comfortable beds. Large lounge with picture window overlooking dunes.
OPEN Easter - Sept. inc.   NO SMOKING. BYO WINE. EN SUITE & TEA/COFFEE-MAKING IN BEDROOMS.
REGRET NO CHILDREN OR PETS. TV IN LOUNGE. B. & B. FROM £17, D. £7.

🚭 *Kingsbridge House Hotel*

WARREN ST, TENBY, DYFED.   TEL: (01834) 844148
WTA 3 Crown Commended. Family-run hotel.
OPEN ALL YEAR. NO SMOKING. V B/A. CHILDREN WELCOME. LICENSED. EN SUITE, TV & BEVERAGES.

🚭

MYRTLE HOUSE HOTEL, ST MARY'S ST, TENBY, SA70 7HW   TEL: (01834) 842508
OPEN Mar. - Nov. NO SMOKING. V, S.D. B/A. LICENSED. CHILDREN WELCOME. MOST ROOMS EN SUITE.
BEVERAGES & T.V. IN ROOMS. ACCESS, VISA. B. & B. AROUND £20.

TREGARON

🚭 *The Edelweiss Country Guest House*

PENUWCH. TREGARON, DYFED, SY25 6QZ   TEL: (01974) 821601

The Edelweiss is a charming oak-beamed house set in 1½ acres of grounds in the beautiful Ceridigion countryside; the proprietors find that the stunning scenery with which their home is surrounded makes it a natural magnet for artists, walkers, ornithologists, flower arrangers, botanists and naturalists as well as holiday-makers in search of peace, tranquillity and good food. On the latter point it is worth noting that all meals served at The Edelweiss have been home-prepared (including the soups) and the traditional English/Welsh menu is also available to non-residential guests. Morning coffee and afternoon cream teas are available either in the house or garden. The Edelweiss is 6 miles from both the coastal road and Tregaron, the pony-trekking centre of Mid-Wales. A beautiful self-contained caravan for up to 6 people is also available, with all amenities provided plus meals in the guest house if required; additionally there is an en suite, ground floor studio, fully self-contained, which sleeps 2 adults and one child.
OPEN ALL YEAR. NO SMOKING. V, S.D. B/A. BYO WINE.   CHILDREN WELCOME. BEVERAGES SERVED 7 - 11.   T.V. IN ROOMS. B. & B. FROM £13-£16, WEEKLY £73 - £78. B., B. & D. £17-£20, £111 - £116 WEEKLY. 3-DAYS SPECIAL SEPT. - JUNE. £55. STUDIO & CARAVAN £95 - 120.

YSTRAD MEURIG

🚭 *Hillscape Walking Holidays*

BLAEN-Y-DDÔL, PONTRHYDYGROES, YSTRAD MEURIG, SY25 6DS   TEL: (0974) 282640
Blaen-y-Ddôl is an idyllic rural guest house: beautifully isolated and surrounded by peaceful countryside with footpaths leading from the front door. Thus it is the perfect base for Hillscape Walking Holidays with its choice of 40 exclusive self-guided routes ranging from 5 - 20 miles and graded to suit all levels of fitness. The food is excellent, too: home-grown vegetables, herbs and fruits are used in the preparation of substantial and tasty vegetarian meals, and the delicious bread is also home-made. Cyclists and bird-watchers will also appreciate a stay at Blaen-y-Ddôl.
OPEN Mar. - Nov. NO SMOKING. V, VE, S.D. B/A. ACCOMPANIED OVER 11S WELCOME. EN SUITE & BEVERAGES IN ROOMS. D., B. & B. £29.50.

RESTAURANTS

LLANWRDA

🚭 *Felin Newydd - the Mill at Crugybar*

LLANWRDA, DYFED, SA19 8UE   TEL: (015585) 375
One of the last working watermills in Wales with converted milking parlour as tea shop
NO SMOKING INCLUDING MILL & CRAFT WORKSHOP. DISABLED ACCESS. CHILDREN WELCOME.

Glamorgan

ACCOMMODATION

CARDIFF

Annedd Lon Guest House

3 DYFRIG ST, PONTCANNA, CARDIFF, SOUTH GLAM., CF1 9LR   TEL: (01222) 223349

Annedd Lon Guest house is a lovely Victorian town house which is situated in a quiet residential close off Cathedral Road just a short walk from a frequent bus route, and a few minutes' stroll from Cardiff's shopping centre, castle, the National Sports Centre and Arms Park. Although furnished and decorated in keeping with its original period, Annedd Lon has every modern comfort including colour T.V., tea-making facilities and central heating in the bedrooms. The breakfasts are delicious (witness the repeated commendations in the visitors' book), and from Annedd Lon you will find yourself within easy reach of the Wye Valley, Bath, Bristol & the Forest of Dean.
OPEN ALL YEAR.   NO SMOKING.   V, S.D. B/A.   CHILDREN WELCOME.   SOME EN SUITE ROOMS. BEVERAGES & T.V. IN ROOMS.   B. & B. FROM £18.

HOLIDAY INN, MILL LN, CARDIFF, GLAM., CF1 1EZ TEL: (01222) 399944
Well-appointed business-class hotel with excellent leisure amenities.
OPEN ALL YEAR.   N/S PART OF DINING R & SOME BEDRS.   V STD, S.D. B/A.   LICENSED.   DISABLED ACCESS.   CHILDREN WELCOME.   EN SUITE, BEVERAGES & T.V. IN ROOMS.   B. & B. AROUND £50.

RHOOSE

LOWER HOUSE FARM G.H., RHOOSE RD, RHOOSE, GLAMORGAN. TEL: (01446) 710010
OPEN ALL YEAR.   NO SMOKING.   V STD.   CHILDREN WELCOME.   B. & B. AROUND £20.

SWANSEA

THE BAYS GUEST HOUSE, 97 MUMBLES ROAD, MUMBLES, SWANSEA, GLAMORGAN.
TEL: (01792) 404775   NO SMOKING.   V STD.   OVER 10S.   EN SUITE.   B. & B. AROUND £20.

RESTAURANTS & PUBS

CARDIFF

Debenhams

46 - 50 ST DAVID'S WAY, CARDIFF, GLAMORGAN.   TEL: (01222) 399789

Intermission, a friendly self-service restaurant serving lunches, snacks and drinks.
OPEN STORE HOURS.   NO SMOKING.   V STD.   DISABLED ACCESS.   CHILDREN WELCOME. CREDIT/DEBIT CARDS.

NEATH

PENSCYNOR WILDLIFE PARK, CILFREW, NR NEATH, WEST GLAMORGAN, SA10 8LF
TEL: (01639) 642189   NO SMOKING INSIDE.   DISABLED ACCESS.   CHILDREN WELCOME.

LLANTRISANT

TALBOT GRILL, J. LOBB & SONS LTD, 41-45 TALBOT RD, TALBOT GREEN, LLANTRISANT
50% N/S.   BYO WINE.   WHEELCHAIR ACCESS.   CHILDREN WELCOME.   ACCESS, VISA.

SWANSEA

Debenhams

22 THE QUADRANT, SWANSEA, GLAMORGAN.   TEL: (10792) 462500

Springles, a friendly self-service restaurant serving lunches, snacks and hot & cold drinks.
OPEN STORE HOURS.   NO SMOKING.   V STD.   DISABLED ACCESS.   CHILDREN. CREDIT CARDS

TREORCHY

RED COW, HIGH ST, TREORCHY, MID GLAMORGAN. TEL: (01443) 773032
N/S LOUNGE BAR.

Gwent

ACCOMMODATION

ABERGAVENNY

Pentre House

LLANWENARTH, ABERGAVENNY, GWENT, NP7 7EW   TEL: (01873) 853435

WTB Highly Commended. Small, pretty country house set in lovely award-winning gardens; comfortably furnished & offering generous breakfasts with a variety of options. OPEN ALL YEAR.   N/S DINING R & BEDRS.   V, S.D. B/A.   CHILDREN & PETS B/A.   BEVERAGES IN ROOMS. T.V. IN SITTING ROOM.   B. & B. FROM £15.

CHEPSTOW

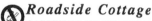

Roadside Cottage

CAERWENT, NR CHEPSTOW, GWENT, NP6 4AZ   TEL: (01291) 420184

WTB Highly Commended Roadside Cottage was built some 250 years ago and stands in the ancient village of Caerwent which was founded around 75 A.D. as the Roman town of Venta Silurium (the cottage stands alongside one of the completed archaeological excavations). The cottage has lots of character, including exposed stone walls and an open log burner - and the two pretty guest rooms have all the comforts of home. Your host, June Goulding, provides a hearty Welsh breakfast and excellent evening meals may be enjoyed at one of the local pubs (just 2 minutes' walk away) or restaurant (just a short drive away). OPEN Apr.-Sept. inc.   NO SMOKING.   S.D. B/A.   CHILDREN WELCOME.   BEVERAGES & TV IN ROOMS.   B. & B. FROM £20.

CWMBRAN

GLEBE FARM, CROESYCEILIOG, CWMBRAN, NP44 2DE

100 acre family farm with a modern bungalow in a lovely parkland. OPEN ALL YEAR ex. Xmas and New Year.   NO SMOKING.   DISABLED ACCESS.   CHILDREN WELCOME. BEVERAGES.   T.V. AVAILABLE. B. & B. FROM £13.

THE PARKWAY HOTEL, CWMBRAN DR, CWMBRAN, GWENT. TEL: (01633) 871199 OPEN ALL YEAR.   N/S DINING R & SOME BEDRS.   V B/A.   LICENSED.   DISABLED ACCESS.   CHILDREN WELCOME.   PETS B/A.   EN SUITE, TV & BEVERAGES IN ROOMS.   CREDIT CARDS.

NEWPORT

ANDERLEY LODGE HOTEL, 216 STOW HILL, NP9 4HA   TEL & FAX: (01633) 266781 Award-winning family-run 19th C. hotel offering spacious, elegant accommodation. OPEN ALL YEAR.   NO SMOKING.   CHILDREN.   EN SUITE, BEVERAGES & T.V. B. & B. FROM £15.

CHAPEL G.H., CHURCH RD, ST BRIDES, WENTLOOG, NR NEWPORT, NP1 9SN Converted chapel in small country village; breakfast only. 3m. from M4 junction 28. TEL: (01633) 681018 OPEN ALL YEAR.   NO SMOKING.   V,S.D. B/A.   CHILDREN WELCOME.   PETS B/A. TWO EN SUITE ROOMS.   BEVERAGES & T.V. IN ROOMS.   B. & B. FROM £14.

The West Usk Lighthouse

ST BRIDES, WENTLOOGE, NR NEWPORT, GWENT, NP1 9SF   TEL: (01633) 810126/815860

Light house with magnificent views of Bristol Channel. Evening meal by arrangement. High standards all round. Flotation tank. OPEN ALL YEAR.   NO SMOKING.   V, VE.   CHILDREN.   EN SUITE, BEVERAGES & T.V.   B. & B. FROM £20.

Widecombe

OLD CHEPSTOW RD, LANGSTONE, NEWPORT, GWENT, NP6 2ND   TEL: (01633) 413311

WTB 2 Crowns Commended. Family home with large garden. Central for Usk and Wye valleys.

OPEN ALL YEAR.   N/S DINING R. & BEDRS.   S.D. B/A.   BEVERAGES IN ROOMS.   WELL-BEHAVED PETS &
CHILDREN WELCOME.   B. & B. FROM £16.

TINTERN

The Old Rectory
TINTERN, GWENT, NP6 6SG   TEL: (01291) 689519
Lovely old house, once used as a rectory for the Church of St Mary's (now in ruins on the
hillside opposite the Abbey); architectural extensions & additions over the years have added
to its charm; fresh natural spring water for most of the year; own produce used in cooking.
OPEN ALL YEAR.   N/S ex. sitting room.   V, S.D. B/A.   CHILDREN.   PETS B/A.   B. & B. FROM £13, D. £8.

Valley House
RAGLAN ROAD, TINTERN, GWENT, NP6 6TH   TEL: (01291) 689652
Charming Georgian house opposite picturesque woods within a mile of Tintern Abbey;
numerous places to eat nearby. Beautiful forest walks begin from the Valley House
doorstep.
OPEN ALL YEAR.   N/S DINING R & BEDROOMS.   V, B/A.   PETS B/A.   EN SUITE, TV & BEVERAGES IN
ROOMS.   B. & B. FROM £15, D. £12.50.

USK

Ty-Gwyn Farm
GWEHELOG, USK, GWENT, NP5 1RT   TEL: (01291) 672878

WTB 3 Crowns Highly Commended. Ty-Gwyn is a charming award-winning farmhouse which stands in an elevated
position between the Wye Valley and the beautiful valley of
the River Usk enjoying extensive views over fields and
mountains. The inglenoook fireplace lends a cosy ambience
to the spacious rooms, and on sunny days you can relax in
the pleasant conservatory overlooking the secluded lawns.
Good, farmhouse cuisine is served each evening (prepared
with fresh vegetables and fruit), and home-made preserves
and free-range eggs guarantee a hearty breakfast; vegetarians
are welcome. The beautiful surrounding countryside has a
rich historical culture: there are Roman ruins at Caerlon,
medieaval castles and a mining museum at Blaenavon. You
are within easy reach of the Brecon Beacons National Park, and the many leisure pursuits
include gliding, grass skiing & golf; there are daily or weekly river permits on the Usk.
OPEN ALL YEAR.   NO SMOKING.   S.D. B/A.   CHILDREN WELCOME.   EN SUITE, TV & BEVERAGES IN ROOMS.
B. & B. FROM £14 - 17. Special Xmas & New Year Breaks available.

Gwynedd

ACCOMMODATION
ABERDOVEY

The Harbour Hotel
ABERDOVEY, GWYNEDD, LL35 0EB   TEL: (01654) 767250

The Harbour Hotel is a lovely, award-winning, Victorian hotel
which stands on the seafront in the heart of the picturesque
village of Aberdovey overlooking miles of golden sandy
beaches. Owned and run by the resident proprietors, the Harbour Hotel has been beautifully restored and its furnishing and
decor are of an exceptionally high standard; bedrooms are very
comfortable and family suites are available (with separate children's and parents' bedrooms). Excellent, home-cooked food
may be enjoyed in the Alacarte (sic.) Restaurant, and there is a
family restaurant, 'Rumbles', which has good children's options; there is also a basement wine bar.
OPEN ALL YEAR.   N/S DINING R, SITTING R & SOME BEDRS.   V STD, S.D. B/A.
LICENSED.   PETS B/A.   CHILDREN WELCOME.   EN SUITE, BEVERAGES & TV IN ROOMS.   CREDIT CARDS.
B. & B. FROM £29.75.

One Trefeddian Bank

ABERDOVEY, GWYNEDD, LL35 0RU   TEL: (01654) 767487

Lovely house in quiet, elevated position with stunning views over the Dovey Estuary.
OPEN Mar. - Oct. inc.   NO SMOKING.   V, S.D. B/A.   CHILDREN WELCOME.   TV & BEVERAGES IN ROOMS.
T.V. IN LOUNGE.   B. & B. FROM £13, D. £8.50.

BANGOR

RAINBOW COURT, PENTIR, NR BANGOR, GWYNEDD, LL57 4UY TEL; (01248) 353099
Excellent restaurant nr Bangor on B4366 at Caerhun turnoff; with accommodation.
OPEN ALL YEAR.   NO SMOKING.   V B/A.   BYO WINE.   CHILDREN B/A.   MOST ROOMS EN SUITE.
BEVERAGES & T.V. IN ROOMS.   CREDIT CARDS.   B. & B. FROM £12.50.

PEN PARC G.H., PARK RD, BARMOUTH, GWYNEDD, LL42 1PH   TEL: (01341) 280150
Small guest house in quiet location overlooking bowling & putting green.
OPEN ALL YEAR.   NO SMOKING.   V STD. S.D. B/A.   BYO DRINKS.   OLDER CHILDREN B/A.   BEVERAGES.
T.V. IN LOUNGE.   B. & B. AROUND £18.

BETWS-Y-COED

The Ferns Guest House

HOLYHEAD RD, BETWS-Y-COED, GWYNEDD, LL24 0AN   TEL: (01690) 710587

The Ferns Guest House is situated in in the popular village of Betws-y-Coed and is owned and run by Keith and Teresa Roobottom. They have worked hard to create a high standard of accommodation for guests: bedrooms have each been attractively furnished (there are double, twin and family rooms, and several have en suite facilities), and there is a beautifully appointed lounge with garden views. Home-cooked breakfasts are served in a pleasant dining room and packed lunches are also available. Betws-y-Coed is an ideal base for touring in North Wales: there are numerous places of interest within easy reach - including Llanwrst, Conwy, Caernarfon and Llanberis (the base for the Snowdon Mountain Railway) - and many outdoor activities, such as walking, climbing, birdwatching and fishing, may be enjoyed locally.
OPEN ALL YEAR.   NO SMOKING.   V, S.D. B/A.   OVER 4S WELCOME.   EN SUITE ROOMS.   BEVERAGES
& TV IN ROOMS.   B. & B. FROM £17.

Henllys Hotel (The Old Court House)

OLD CHURCH RD, BETWS-Y-COED, GWYNEDD, LL24 0AL   TEL: (01690) 710534

In Victorian times Henllys Hotel was the magistrates' court and police station at Betws-y-Coed, well known to the ruffians and ne'er-do-wells of the region. Times have now changed and this beautifully converted building, peacefully situated on the banks of the River Conwy, plays host to a very different clientèle, its guests, who dine on excellent home-cooked cuisine in the galleried dining room (once the court) or enjoy a drink in the cosy fire-side bar which was once the police station. The en suite bedrooms are stylishly decorated (they were once the judge's chambers, magistates' room and convicted felon's cell!) and are equipped with a range of helpful amenities. The breathtaking views and superb nearby scenic walks combine to make Henllys a perfect destination for a break in the heart of Snowdonia.
OPEN Feb. - Nov. NO SMOKING. V, S.D. B/A. LICENSED. CHILDREN WELCOME. WHEELCHAIR ACCESS. EN
SUITE, TV & BEVERAGES IN ROOMS. B. & B. FROM £21.50.

SWN-Y-DWR, PENTREFELIN, BETWS-Y-COED, GWYN, LL24 0BB TEL: (01690) 710648
Traditional Welsh stone house centrally situated on the banks of the River Llugwy at the famous Pont y Pair Bridge; lovely views of river and hills.
OPEN ALL YEAR.   NO SMOKING.   BEVERAGES & TV IN ROOMS.   B. & B. FROM £14.

Tan-y-Foel Country House

CAPEL GARMAN, NR BETWS-Y-COED, GWYNEDD, LL26 0RE   TEL: (01690) 710507 FAX: (01690) 710681

A recent and highly deserving winner of the WTB Best Small Hotel Award, Tan-y-Foel (whose name means The House under the Hillside) is is set in 8 acres of grounds and stands high above the beautiful Conwy Valley enjoying fabulous views of both the valley and the high peaks of Snowdonia. Its owners, Peter and Janet Pitman, have worked hard to create an interior in harmony with the tranquil beauty surrounding the house: bedrooms are beautifully furnished, there are crisp linen sheets on firm beds, fresh flowers and lovely views; lots of lovely little extras have been provided to make you feel special - bath robes, toiletries, even chocolates - and winter guests may curl up in the cosy lounge in front of a log fire (summer visitors have use of the heated pool from June to September). The food is fabulous - fresh fish straight from the sea, local Welsh lamb and home-made bread all feature on the menu: there is a bumper breakfast to set you up for the day, and a delicious selection of dishes on the evening menu such as Fresh Asparagus with Chive Hollandaise followed by Poached Assorted Sea Fish in Creamy Wine Sauce; a tempting dessert - perhaps Almond Biscuit Basket filled with fresh strawberries and cream - together with local cheeses, biscuits, tea or coffee would complete the meal.

OPEN ALL YEAR.   NO SMOKING.   V, S.D. B/A.   LICENSED.   EN SUITE & BEVERAGES IN ALL BEDROOMS. OVER 9S WELCOME.   CREDIT CARDS.   D., B. & B. FROM £57.50 PER PERSON.

Ty'n-y-Celyn House

LLANRWST RD, BETWS-Y-COED, SNOWDONIA NATIONAL PARK, N. WALES, LL24 0HD

TEL: (01690) 710202 FAX: (01690) 710800

Ty'n-y-Celyn is a large Victorian house which nestles in a quiet elevated position overlooking the picturesque village of Betws-y-Coed. It has been very comfortably furnished: there are 8 bedrooms - 3 of which are family rooms - and each has been tastefully refurbished with new beds and fitted furniture, together with a range of helpful amenities including TV, hairdryer, radio-cassette and tea-making facilities; most bedrooms have magnificent views of the Llugwy Valley, surrounding mountains or the Conwy River. Your hosts, Ann and Clive Muskus, will do all they can to make your stay a happy and comfortable one - including picking you up from the station if you are arriving by rail. Betws-y-Coed is a perfect touring base: it is in the heart of the Snowdonia National Park, yet is also within easy reach of the fine coastlines; in addition to walking and climbing, it is an excellent centre for other outdoor pursuits such as fishing (which can be arranged in the nearby streams, rivers and reservoirs) and horse riding.

OPEN ALL YEAR.   N/S DINING R.   V, S.D. B/A.   LICENSED.   CHILDREN & PETS WELCOME. EN SUITE, TV & BEVERAGES IN ROOMS.   B. & B. £20 - 22.

CAERNARFON

 # Pengwern

SARON, LLANWNDA, CAERNARFON, GWYNEDD, LL54 5UH   TEL: (01286) 830717

Pengwern is a charming, spacious farmhouse which stands amidst 130 acres of land between the mountains and sea near the Snowdonia National Park; the house has been charmingly furnished throughout, and each of the en suite bedrooms has a range of helpful facilities (one has a jacuzzi). Your hostess, Jane Rowlands, has a cookery diploma and provides excellent meals which have been prepared from fresh farm produce including home-reared beef and lamb. You are just 3 miles from both Caernarfon and Dinas Dinlle beach at Pengwern; additionally the lovely beaches of Anglesey and the Lleyn Peninsula are within easy reach.

OPEN Feb. - Nov. NO SMOKING. S.D. B/A. CHILDREN WELCOME. EN SUITE, TV & BEVERAGES IN ROOMS. B. & B. £19, D. £9.50.

TY MAWR FARMHOUSE, SARON, LLANWNDA, CAERNARFON, GWYNEDD, LL54 5UH
Charming farmhouse: country antiques & modern comforts. Coastal /mountain views.
TEL: (01286) 830091 OPEN Jan. - Oct. NO SMOKING. V, S.D. B/A. CHILDREN: OVER 3S ONLY. PETS B/A. EN SUITE, TV & BEVERAGES IN ROOMS. B. & B. £14-17

TY'N RHOS, SEION, LLANDDEINIOLEN, CAERNARFON, GWYNEDD, LL55 3AE
Modern farmhouse, traditional furnishings; home-produced eggs, milk, yoghurt, cheese.
TEL: (01248) 670489 OPEN ALL YEAR. N/S DINING R. V, VE & S.D. B/A. LICENSED. DISABLED ACCESS. OVER 6s ONLY. PETS B/A. EN SUITE, BEVERAGES & T.V. IN ROOMS. B. & B. from £18.

CONWY

Castle Bank Hotel
MOUNT PLEASANT, CONWY, GWYNEDD, LL32 8NY TEL: (01492) 593888
Castle Bank Hotel is an impressive stone-built Victorian house which stands in its own grounds close to Conwy town walls overlooking the estuary of the river and the surrounding countryside. It has been comfortably furnished: each of the en suite bedrooms has a range of helpful amenities and there is an attractive well-stocked bar in which to enjoy a pre-dinner drink; all meals are prepared from fresh local produce wherever possible. Conwy is considered to be one of the best preserved mediaeval walled towns in Europe: it is possible to walk round most of the walls (3 of the original gates remain), and there are a number of interesting historic buldings to be visited.
OPEN Mid Feb. - Mid Dec. N/S. V, S.D. B/A. LICENSED. CHILDREN WELCOME. EN SUITE, TV & BEVERAGES IN ROOMS. CREDIT CARDS. B. & B. £26.50

CASTLE HOTEL, HIGH STREET, CONWY, GWYNEDD, LL32 8DB TEL: (01492) 592324
OPEN ALL YEAR. N/S DINING R. V STD. S.D. B/A. LICENSED. CHILDREN WELCOME. PETS B/A. EN SUITE, TV & BEVERAGES IN ROOMS. CREDIT CARDS. B. & B. FROM £35.

The Old Rectory
LLANSANFFRAID GLAN CONWY, NR CONWY, GWYN., LL28 5LF TEL: (01492) 580611

There has been a rectory on this beautiful site on the Conwy Estuary with its spectacular views from Conwy Castle to Snowdonia, for the last 5 centuries. Sadly, in 1740, the Tudor House was burnt down, but the elegant Georgian replacement is a splendid house - skilfully restored by the Vaughan family and now functioning as a comfortable and charming small country house: sympathetically decorated and furnished with antiques (the collection of Victorian watercolours is a delight) and all the individually styled bedrooms have excellent facilities (including bathrobes, ironing centres & hairdryers). The cuisine is exceptionally good: the finest local produce is used in imaginative dishes, and a typical evening menu would feature Mediterranean Vegetable & Herb in Strudel Pastry with Tomato Sauce followed by Spinach & Salmon Terrine, Lamb with Leek Garnish & a delicious dessert, such as Chocolate Roulade, and a selection of Welsh Cheeses.
OPEN Feb. - Dec. NO SMOKING. V, S.D. B/A. LICENSED. CHILDREN: OVER 10S ONLY. EN SUITE & TV IN ALL ROOMS. ROOM SERVICE. CREDIT CARDS. B. & B. FROM £56.

The Whins
WHINACRES, CONWY, GWYNEDD, LL32 8ET TEL: (01492) 593373
Charming house with lots of character. Good home-cooking. Close to Conwy.
OPEN Mar. - Oct. NO SMOKING . V, S.D. B/A. WELL-BEHAVED CHILDREN WELCOME. PETS B/A. 2 EN SUITE ROOMS. BEVERAGES IN ROOMS. T.V. LOUNGE. B. & B. FROM £16. D. £9.50.

CRICIETH

MURIAU, CRICIETH, GWYNEDD, LL52 0RS TEL: (01766) 522337
OPEN ALL YEAR. NO SMOKING. V, S.D. B/A. CHILDREN WELCOME. SOME EN SUITE ROOMS. BEVERAGES IN ROOMS. T.V. IN DRAWING ROOM. B. & B. AROUND £20

DOLGELLAU

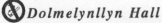

Dolmelynllyn Hall

GANLLWYD, DOLGELLAU, GWYNEDD, LL40 2HP   TEL & FAX: (01341) 440273

Dolmelynllyn Hall dates from the 16th C. although several spates of subsequent rebuilding have made for an eclectic building whose style reflects that of three different architectural periods. It stands amidst 3 acres of formal terraced gardens the whole surrounded by 1200 acres of National Trust owned mountains, forest and river: you can walk for miles without crossing a road or encountering a car - bliss! Your hosts, father and daughter Jon Barkwith and Jo Reddicliffe, have refurbished their home in splendid style: each of the en suite bedrooms has a different decorative theme, and the conservatory bar and elegant lounge with wonderful valley views are relaxing venues for pre-prandial drinks (or post-prandial chats). Meals are served in a charming dining room: Jo is responsible for the cooking (traditional British, with imagination), and the comprehensive wine list has over a hundred items.
NO SMOKING   OPEN Feb. - Nov.   S.D. B/A.   OVER 10s & PETS B/A.   LICENSED.   EN SUITE, BEVERAGES & TV IN ROOMS.   B. & B. £40 - 50; Sgle £45 - 52.50; D. £22.50; Special Breaks avail.

Penmaenuchaf Hall

PENMAENPOOL, DOLGELLAU, GWYNEDD, LL40 1YB   TEL & FAX: (01341) 422129
It would be difficult to imagine a more beautiful and idyllic situation than the one enjoyed by this lovely country manor hotel which nestles in the foothills of Cader Idris overlooking the famous Mawddach Estuary. Upon entering the hall you are instantly transported back to an age of gracious living: the oak panelling, exquisite furnishings, fresh flowers and blazing log fires encourage a feeling of relaxation and well-being. Lulled thus into a condition of happy anaesthesia with respect to 20th C. concerns, the most stressful decision you are likely to have to make is whether your choice of afternoon tea will spoil your appetite for the superb evening meal: the food is fabulous and not to be missed, an evening menu choice perhaps featuring Tomato Consommé with Coriander, Madeira and Herb Dumplings followed by Pan-fried Pork with Apple and Rosemary and some outstandingly irresistible desserts (Apricot Soufflé and Orange Caramel Sauce, Mille Feuilles of Chocolate on a Compote of Cherries).
OPEN ALL YEAR.   N/S DINING R, 2 LOUNGES & BEDROOM.   V STD. S.D. STD.   LICENSED.   CHILDREN.   EN SUITE, TV & BEVERAGES IN ROOMS.   CREDIT CARDS.   B. & B. FROM £47.50.

HARLECH

ARIS GUEST HOUSE, PEN-Y-BRYN, HARLECH, GWYN., LL46 2SL TEL: (01766) 780409
OPEN ALL YEAR.   NO SMOKING.   V, VE, S.D. B/A.   CHILDREN WELCOME.   PETS B/A.   BEVERAGES & T.V. IN ROOMS.   B. & B. AROUND £16.

MAES-Y-NEUADD, TALSARNAU, NR HARLECH, GWYN, LL47 6YA TEL: (01766) 780200
Ancient Welsh manor on a wooded mountainside in 8 acres of landscaped grounds.
OPEN ALL YEAR ex. 2 weeks mid Dec.   N/S DINING R.   V B/A.   LICENSED.   DISABLED ACCESS.   CHILDREN & PETS B/A.   ALL ROOMS EN SUITE.   T.V.   CREDIT CARDS.   B. & B. AROUND £50.

TREMEIFION VEGETARIAN HOTEL, TALSARNAU, NEAR HARLECH, GWYN.
Charming house, with beautiful views of Portmeirion, the estuary & Snowdonia.
TEL: (01766) 770491   OPEN ALL YEAR.   NO SMOKING.   V, VE, EXC. S.D. B/A.   LICENSED.   CHILDREN.   PETS B/A.   SOME EN SUITE ROOMS.   BEVERAGES.   T.V. LOUNGE.   D., B. & B. AROUND £31.

LLANBERIS

Maesteg

HIGH ST, LLANBERIS, CAERNARFON, GWYNEDD, LL5 4HB   TEL: (01286) 871187
Privately owned house with a very friendly atmosphere at the foot of Mount Snowdon in Llanberis village. Packed lunches on request. Private guided car and walking tours.
OPEN ALL YEAR.   NO SMOKING.   V, S.D. B/A.   DISABLED ACCESS.   CHILDREN: OVER 12S ONLY.   BEVERAGES IN ROOMS.   T.V. IN SOME ROOMS.   B. & B. AROUND £16.

LLANDUDNO

BODNANT G.H., 39 ST MARY'S ROAD, LLANDUDNO, LL30 2UE (0492) 876936
Small, elegant Edwardian guest house in a pleasant residential area of Llandudno.
OPEN Jan. - Nov. inc. NO SMOKING. LICENSED. CHILDREN: OVER 12S ONLY. EN SUITE, BEVERAGES &
T.V. IN ROOMS. B. & B. AROUND £20.

BRIN-Y-BIA LODGE HOTEL, CRAIGSIDE, LLANDUDNO, GWYNEDD, LL30 3AS
Charming 18th C. hotel in walled grounds on the Little Orme overlooking the town & sea.
TEL: (01492) 549644 OPEN ALL YEAR ex. Xmas & New Year. N/S DINING R. V B/A. LICENSED. CHILD-
REN WELCOME. PETS B/A. EN SUITE, TV & BEVERAGES IN ROOMS. B. & B. AROUND £30.

 The Cliffbury Hotel

34 ST DAVID'S RD, LLANDUDNO, GWYNEDD, LL30 2UH   TEL: (01492) 877224
Small, non-smoking, family-run hotel 5 mins walk from the attractions of Llandudno.
OPEN ALL YEAR. NO SMOKING. V, S.D. B/A. LICENSED. CHILDREN & PETS WELCOME. EN SUITE,
TV & BEVERAGES IN ROOMS. B. & B. AROUND £14.

 Cranberry House

12 ABBEY RD, LLANDUDNO, GWYNEDD, LL30 2EA   TEL: (01492) 879760
WTB Commended. AA QQQ Small, elegant Victorian house a few mins' walk from the
pier & promenade of Llandudno. Home-cooked meals prepared from fresh ingredients.
OPEN Mid Mar. - Mid Oct. NO SMOKING. V, S.D. B/A. EN SUITE, TV & BEVERAGES IN ROOMS. CREDIT
CARDS. B. & B. AROUND £20.

THE GRAFTON HOTEL, PROMENADE, CRAIG-Y-DON, LLANDUDNO, GWYNEDD, LL30 1BG
TEL: (01492) 876814 OPEN Feb. - Nov. N/S DINING R & SOME BEDRS. V B/A. LICENSED. DISABLED ACCESS.
CHILDREN WELCOME. EN SUITE, TV & BEVERAGES IN ROOMS. B. & B. AROUND £20.

 Hafod-y-Mor Hotel

HILL TERRACE, LLANDUDNO, GWYNEDD, LL30 2LS   TEL: (01492) 876925
Hotel with original Victorian exterior & sympathetically modernised interior. Fantastic
views of Snowdonia and Llandudno Bay from all rooms.
OPEN Easter - Oct. NO SMOKING. V, S.D. B/A. EN SUITE, TV & BEVERAGES IN ROOMS. LICENSED. B. & B.
£20 - 30.

Headlands Hotel

HILL TERRACE, LLANDUDNO, GWYNEDD.   TEL: (01492) 877485
The Headlands is a highly recommended hotel which stands at the foot of the Great Orme
enjoying some of the best views of Llandudno's magnificent bay. Your hosts, Brenda and
George Woods, have worked hard to create a hotel of character and charm: each of the
centrally heated, en suite bedrooms has either sea or country views, and some have four
poster beds. Meals are served in an elegant dining room, again with wonderful headland
views, and both the classical dishes and the traditional Welsh recipes are prepared from
fresh produce. There is a welcoming cocktail bar and a relaxing area on the first floor
surrounded by Victorian stained glass.
OPEN MAR. - DEC. N/S DINING & LOUNGE. S.D. B/A. LICENSED. OVER 5S & PETS WELCOME. EN SUITE
& TV IN ROOMS. B. & B. FROM £26, D £10.

 Hollybank

9 ST DAVID'S PLACE, LLANDUDNO, GWYNEDD, LL30 2UG TEL: (01492) 878521
WTB 3 Crowns Highly Commended. Small central Edwardian hotel. Sunny, spacious
rooms.
OPEN EASTER - NOV. NO SMOKING. S.D. B/A. CHILDREN & PETS. WHEELCHAIR ACCESS. LICENSED. EN
SUITE, TV & BEVERAGES IN ALL ROOMS. B. & B. £17 - 21.

OAKWOOD HOTEL, 21 ST DAVIDS ROAD, LLANDUDNO, GWYNEDD, LL30 2UH
Family hotel situated in the beautiful garden area of Llandudno within walking distance of
the promenade and all amenities; attractive gardens in which tea may be served.
TEL: (01492) 879208 OPEN ALL YEAR. N/S DINING R. V, S.D. B/A. LICENSED. CHILDREN WELCOME. PETS
B/A. 2 EN SUITE ROOMS. BEVERAGES & T.V. IN ROOMS. B. & B. AROUND £15.

PLAS MADOC PRIVATE HOTEL, 60 CHURCH WALKS, LLANDUDNO, GWYNEDD, LL30 2HL
TEL: (01492) 876514 OPEN ALL YEAR. N/S DINING R, BEDRS. V, S.D. B/A. LICENSED. CHILDREN WELCOME.
EN SUITE, BEVERAGES & T.V. IN BEDROOMS. B. & B. AROUND £20.

⊗*Summer Hill Luxury Apartments*

C/O 10 CRESCENT COURT, LLANDUDNO, GWYNEDD, LL30 1AT   TEL: (01492) 879300

Summer Hill accommodation is spotlessly clean and has been awarded the Wales Tourist Board's top grade 5 for the sixth consecutive year.

OPEN Jan. - Dec.   NO SMOKING.   OVER 8S ONLY.   SOME PETS B/A.   1 BEDR. APARTMENT, fully self-contained, with separate lounge, kitchen, bathroom and toilet.   T.V.   TARIFF £99 TO £259 PER WEEK.

LLANFAIRFECHAN

RHIWIAU RIDING CENTRE, LLANFAIRFECHAN, GWYN., LL33 0EH TEL: (01248) 680094

Family owned & run riding centre with friendly, relaxed atmosphere; good home-cooking.

OPEN ALL YEAR.   NO SMOKING.   V, S.D. B/A. LICENSED. CHILDREN. BEVERAGES.   T.V.

LLWYNGWRIL

⊗*Bryn-y-Mor Guest House*

FAIRBOURNE, LLWYNGWRIL, GWYNEDD, LL37 2JQ   TEL: (01341) 250043

Large, red-brick Victorian house with large, colourful garden & sea views and, to the rear, wooded hillsides. Comfortable bedrooms.

OPEN Mar. - Nov.   NO SMOKING.   V, S.D. B/A.   CHILDREN & PETS.   EN SUITE & BEVERAGES.   T.V.

⊗*Pentre Bach*

LLWYNGWRIL, GWYNEDD, LL37 2JU   TEL: (01341) 250294   FAX: (01341) 250885

Former manor house, splendidly situated with views of the sea and the mountains. Free-range eggs, organic fruit, vegetables & preserves, are all produced on the premises.

OPEN ALL YEAR Ex. Xmas.   NO SMOKING.   V & Trad. B'fast STD, S.D. B/A.   CHILDREN WELCOME.   EN SUITE, TV & BEVERAGES IN ROOMS.   B. & B. FROM £18.

NEFYN

⊗ CRAIG Y MOR, FFORDD DEWI SANT, NEFYN, GWYN, LL53 6EA TEL: (01758) 721412

OPEN ALL YEAR.   NO SMOKING.   V, B/A.   BYO WINE.   CHILDREN WELCOME.   PETS B/A.   BEVERAGES IN ROOMS.   T.V. IN LOUNGE.   B. & B. FROM £15. D. FROM £7.50.

TALSARNAU

⊗ TEGFAN, LLANDECWYN, TALSARNAU, GWYN, LL47 6YG   TEL: (01766) 771354

Lovely old detached house in an elevated position & surrounded by panoramic views.

OPEN ALL YEAR ex. Xmas.   NO SMOKING.   BEVERAGES.   B. & B. FROM £12.

TREFRIW

⊗ CRAFNANT G.H., MAIN ST, TREFRIW, GWYN, LL27 0JH   TEL: (01492) 640809

OPEN ALL YEAR.   NO SMOKING.   V a speciality, S.D. B/A.   CHILDREN & GROUPS WELCOME.   PETS B/A.   EN SUITE. BEVERAGES & T.V. IN ROOMS.

Old Mill Farmhouse

FRON OLEU FARM, TRAWSFYNYDD, SNOWDONIA NAT. PARK, LL41 4UN   (01766) 540397

Traditional built 18th C. Welsh farmhouse with inglenooks; fresh home-cooked food a speciality; own produce; free-range eggs, used in cooking. *Holiday Care Award Nov. '93*.

OPEN ALL YEAR.   N/S IN ALL PUBLIC AREAS.   V, S.D. B/A.   BYO WINE.   DISABLED ACCESS.   CHILDREN WELCOME.   PETS B/A.   EN SUITE, TV & BEVERAGES IN ROOMS.   B. & B. FROM £17.50.

⊗*Glenydd Guest House*

OFF PIER RD, TYWYN, GWYNEDD, LL36 0AN   TEL: (01654) 711373

Glenydd guest house is a charming modernised Edwardian house which stands in a private road just 200m from the beach and station, and 300m from the Talyllyn Steam Railway. Accommodation is in comfortably furnished, centrally heated rooms, and the delicious home-cooking is prepared from fresh, organic produce, much of it home-grown. Glenydd is an excellent base for touring: there are several good, sandy beaches nearby, and of course climbing in Snowdonia.

OPEN ALL YEAR.   NO SMOKING.   V STD, S.D. B/A.   CHILDREN WELCOME.   PETS B/A.   BEVERAGES IN ROOMS. B. & B. £12.50, d. £8.

RESTAURANTS

ANGLESEY

BODEILIO CRAFT CENTRE, BODEILIO, TALWRN, NR LLANGEFNI, ANGLESEY, GWYNEDD.
TEL: (01248) 722535   NO SMOKING. V STD.   LICENSED.   CHILDREN WELCOME.   CREDIT CARDS.

BALA

Y RADELL, 81 HIGH ST, BALA, GWYNEDD TEL: (01678) 520203
NO SMOKING.   ACCESS, VISA.

BANGOR

RAINBOW COURT, PENTIR, NR BANGOR, GWYNEDD, LL57 4UY TEL: (01248) 353099

BARMOUTH

THE OLD TEA ROOMS, 'WALSALL HOUSE', CHURCH ST, BARMOUTH, LL42 1EG
TEL: (01341) 280194   NO SMOKING.

LLANBERIS

Y BISTRO, 43-45 HIGH ST, LLANBERIS, GWYNEDD, LL55 4EU

LLANGEFNI

THE WHOLE THING, 5 FIELD ST, LLANGEFNI, GWYNEDD.   TEL: (01248) 724832

PORTHMADOG

Blossoms Restaurant

BORTH Y GEST, PORTHMADOG, GWYNEDD, LL49 9TP   TEL: (01766) 513500
NO SMOKING IN UPSTAIRS DINING R.   V STD.   LICENSED.   CHILDREN WELCOME.   ACCESS, VISA.

TREFRIW

Chandler's Brasserie

TREFRIW, GWYNEDD, LL27 0JH   TEL: (01492) 640991
NO SMOKING.   V STD.   LICENSED.   CHILDREN WELCOME.   ACCESS, VISA.

Powys

ACCOMMODATION

BRECON

BEACONS GUEST HOUSE, 16 BRIDGE ST, POWYS, LD3 8AH   TEL: (01874) 623339
Friendly Georgian guest house close to town centre & River Usk. 4-poster bed.
OPEN ALL YEAR.   N/S DINING R.   V, S.D. B/A.   CHIDREN & PETS WELCOME.   LICENSED.   EN SUITE, TV &
BEVERAGES IN ROOMS.   CREDIT CARDS.   B. & B. AROUND £17.

The Coach Guest House

ORCHARD ST, BRECON, POWYS, LD3 8AN   TEL: (01874) 623803
The Coach Guest House is a totally smoke-free town house in Brecon. The standard of
accommodation is very high indeed (Highly Commended, 4 Crown & Dragon Award by
the WTB and has a RAC Highly Acclaimed and QQQQ status from the AA), and each of
the six en suite bedrooms has been equipped with clock radio, telephone, hairdryer, TV &

beverage-making in addition to the usual amenities. Excellent accommodation & an ideal centre for touring the Brecon Beacons National Park.
OPEN ALL YEAR. NO SMOKING. V, S.D. B/A. EN SUITE, BEVERAGES & TV IN ROOMS. B. & B. FROM £18.

FORGE FARM HOUSE, HAY ROAD, BRECON, POWYS, LD3 7SS   TEL: (01874) 611793
Beautiful 17th C. house of historical interest in a quiet, secluded position in the valley of the River Honddu; good home-cooking including bread and jams.
OPEN ALL YEAR ex. Xmas. NO SMOKING. V, S.D. B/A. CHILDREN. BEVERAGES & TV. B. & B. AROUND £15

Llanddetty Hall Farm
TALYBONT-ON-USK, BRECON, POWYS, LD3 7YR TEL & FAX: (01874) 676415
Llanddetty Hall Farm is still a working sheep farm and forms part of a 17th C. Grade II listed building which has recently undergone a complete (though sympathetic) refurbishment. It stands in the National Park, with direct accesss onto bridleways and footpaths, and enjoys magnificent views over the Usk valley. Accommodation is in comfortable rooms and there is a pleasant TV lounge for guests'use; there is also stabling if guests wish to bring their own horses. Evening meals are available on request, but there are numerous excellent bars and restaurants nearby.
OPEN ALL YEAR. NO SMOKING. S.D. B/A.   CHILDREN & PETS WELCOME. EN SUITE & BEVERAGES IN ROOMS. B. & B. £16, D. £8.

Lodge Farm
TALGARTH, BRECON, POWYS. TEL; (01874) 711244
WTB 3 Crown Commended. Lodge Farm is a family-run traditional Welsh sheep farm which stands in the eastern section of the Brecon Beacons National Park just 1½ miles from Talgarth off the A479. The farmstead is a typical 18th C. Welsh stone farmhouse which is surrounded by walks and enjoys a southerly aspect with views of the Brecon Beacons. Centrally heated, the establishment offers family, double and twin-bedded rooms, and there is a cosy sitting room with a log fire on chilly evenings. All meals are freshly prepared from locally produced meat, vegetables and fruit (there are tasty vegetarian options), and guests dine in an oak-beamed room with flagstone floor and inglenook.
OPEN ALL YEAR. NO SMOKING. V, S.D. B/A. CHILDREN WELCOME. EN SUITE & BEVERAGES IN ALL ROOMS. B. & B. £16 - 18.

BUILTH WELLS

COURT FARM, ABEREDW, NR BUILTH WELLS, POWYS, LD2 3UP TEL: (01982) 560277
Spacious farmhouse in peaceful, picturesque valley. Home-produce used in cooking including meat, poultry, eggs, honey and organically home-grown vegetables and fruit. Farm, riverside and hill walking, with 3 golf courses nearby.
NO SMOKING. V B/A. OVER 12S ONLY. BEVERAGES & T.V. B. & B. AROUND £15.

NANT-Y-DERW FARM, BUILTH WELLS, POWYS, LD2 3RU   TEL: (01982) 553675
Working sheep farm 4m N. of Builth Wells on a south-facing slope amidst 45 acres of farmland. Home from home in which to relax & unwind. One-level accommodation.
OPEN May - Dec. ex. Xmas. NO SMOKING. V B/A. DISABLED ACCESS. OVER 7s ONLY. PETS B/A. BEVERAGES IN ROOMS. T.V. LOUNGE. B. & B. FROM £14. D. FROM £5.

HAY-ON-WYE
YORK HOUSE, CUSOP, HAY ON WYE, HEREFORD   TEL: (01497) 820705
For further details please see the entry in the Herefordshire section.

LLANDRINDOD WELLS
CORVEN HALL, HOWEY, LLANDRINDOD WELLS, POWYS, LD1 5RE TEL: (01597) 823368
Large Victorian house in 4 acres of peaceful gardens, in open country. Disabled suite.
OPEN Feb. - Nov. N/S DINING R & LOUNGE.   V B/A. LICENSED. DISABLED ACCESS.   CHILDREN WELCOME. PETS B/A. EN SUITE. BEVERAGES. T.V. LOUNGE. B. & B. AROUND £18.

LLANGAMMARCH WELLS
THE LAKE COUNTRY HOUSE HOTEL, LLANGAMMARCH WELLS, POWYS, LD4 4BS
TEL: (015912) 202 OPEN Mid Jan. - Dec. inc. N/S DINING R & SOME BEDRS.   V B/A. LICENSED.   DISABLED ACCESS. CHILDREN WELCOME. PETS B/A. EN SUITE & T.V. IN ROOMS.

MACHYNLLETH

GWALIA, CEMMAES, MACHYNLLETH, POWYS, SY20 9PU   TEL: (01650) 511377
Exclusively vegetarian, family-run 10 acre smallholding; lovely house with beautiful views outside Snowdonia National Park; virtually all food home-grown/produced.
OPEN ALL YEAR.   NO SMOKING. V, VE STD.   CHILDREN WELCOME.   PETS B/A.   BEVERAGES ON REQUEST. B. & B. FROM £14. D. £8

TY BACH, CWM EINION, ARTISTS VALLEY, FURNACE, MACHYNLLETH, SY20 8PG
W.T.B. 5 Dragon Grade. Ty Bach (Little House) offers fully equipped S/C.
TEL: (01654) 781298 OPEN ALL YEAR ex. Xmas. NO SMOKING . SLEEPS 2/3.   AROUND £170 PER WEEK.

The Wynnstay Arms Hotel
MACHYNLLETH, POWYS, SY20 8AE   TEL: (01654) 702941 FAX: (01654) 703884
OPEN ALL YEAR.   N/S PART OF DINING R, 2 LOUNGES & SOME BEDROOMS.   V STD.   LICENSED.   CHILDREN WELCOME.   EN SUITE, BEVERAGES & T.V. IN ALL ROOMS.   CREDIT CARDS.   B. & B. FROM £26.25

NEWTON

Dyffryn Farm Holidays
ABERHAFESP, NEWTOWN, POWYS, SY16 3JD TEL: (01686) 688817 & (0585) 206412 FAX: (01686) 688324

WTB 3 Crowns. De Luxe Grade. Dyffryn Farm is a lovely 17th C. converted barn which stands on the banks of a stream in the heart of a 200 acre working sheep and beef farm. Your hosts, Dave and Sue Jones, offer accommodation of an exceptionally high standard in pretty en suite bedrooms which have full central heating and colour TVs. A generous breakfast is served to guests and there are scrumptious evening meals featuring both traditional and vegetarian dishes. Dyffryn Farm is a wonderful place to spend a holiday for those interested in the countryside: there is a badger sett in the woodland and the banks of the stream teem with wild life. There are numerous lovely walks and a Nature Reserve just 3 miles away. Golf, pony-trekking and fishing are all available locally.
OPEN ALL YEAR.   NO SMOKING.   S.D. B/A.   EN SUITE, TV & BEVERAGES.   B. & B. FROM £19, d. FROM £10.

RHAYADER

TRE GARREG, ST HARMON, NR RHAYADER, POWYS, LD6 5LU TEL: (01597) 88604
OPEN Easter - Oct.   NO SMOKING.   EN SUITE.   BEVERAGES & T.V.   B. & B. FROM £15. D. £10.

RESTAURANTS

MACHYNLLETH

Old Mill Tea Shop, Felin Crewi
PENEGOES, MACHYNLLETH, POWYS, SY20 8NH   TEL: (01654) 703113
NO SMOKING. V, VE & LOW-FAT STD.   DISABLED ACCESS.   CHILDREN WELCOME.

THE OLD STATION COFFEE SHOP, DINAS MAWDDWY, MACHYNLLETH, SY20 9LS
TEL; (016504) 338 NO SMOKING. V STD. LICENSED. DISABLED. WELL-BEHAVED CHILDREN.

THE QUARRY SHOP, WHOLEFOOD CAFÉ, 13 MAENGWYN ST, MACHYNLLETH
Part of the Centre for Alternative Technology at Machynlleth.
NO SMOKING.   V, VE, WH STD.

MIDDLETON, WELSHPOOL
BORDER RESTAURANT, MIDDLETOWN, WELSHPOOL, SY21 8EN (01938) 570201
OPEN ALL YEAR. NO SMOKING. V STD. WHEELCHAIR ACCESS. CHILDREN. LICENSED.

RHAYADER
CAROLE'S CAKE SHOP AND TEA ROOM, SOUTH ST, RHAYADER, POWYS, LD6 5BH
TEL: (01597) 811060   NO SMOKING. V STD. CHILDREN WELCOME.